1995

University of St. Francis
GEN 920 C634
Cleugh, James
T
W9-DEI-676
3 0301 0000000

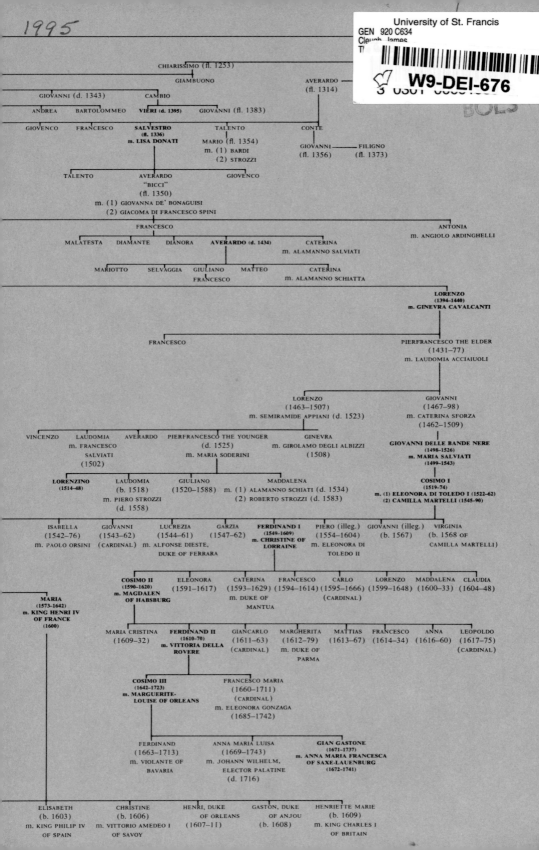

.755   75

ci

THE MEDICI

A Tale of Fifteen Generations

THE
MEDICI

A Tale of
Fifteen Generations

JAMES CLEUGH

DOUBLEDAY & COMPANY, INC.
GARDEN CITY, NEW YORK
1975

LIBRARY
College of St. Francis
JOLIET, ILLINOIS

BUR OAK LIBRARY SYSTEM

Library of Congress Cataloging in Publication Data

Cleugh, James.
    The Medici: a tale of fifteen generations.
    Bibliography: p. 379
    Includes index.

    1. Medici, House of. 2.   Florence—History—1421–1737. I. Title.
DG737.42.C55   929.7′5′51
ISBN 0-385-08293-2
Library of Congress Catalog Card Number 68–22521

Copyright © 1975 by Maria Nora Cleugh
ALL RIGHTS RESERVED
PRINTED IN THE UNITED STATES OF AMERICA
FIRST EDITION

920
C 634

CONTENTS

I FLORENCE AND THE EARLY MEDICI (*1291–1429*) *1*

II COSIMO THE ELDER (*1429–64*) *42*

III LORENZO THE MAGNIFICENT (*1464–92*) *99*

IV THE LOSING BATTLE (*1492–1530*) *194*

 1. Piero di Lorenzo de' Medici and Fra Girolamo Savonarola *194*

 2. The Return of the Medici *223*

 3. Pope Clement VII *250*

 4. The End of the Republic *262*

V THE DECADENCE (*1530–1743*) *274*

 1. Alessandro de' Medici *274*

 2. Cosimo I *281*

 3. Catherine de' Medici *292*

 4. A Century of Masks: *308*

  FRANCESCO DE' MEDICI *308*

  MARIA DE' MEDICI *314*

  FERDINAND I, COSIMO II, AND FERDINAND II *330*

 5. Cosimo III *347*

 6. Gian Gastone *370*

EPILOGUE *377*

BIBLIOGRAPHY *379*

INDEX *383*

154,627

452
G.434

THE MEDICI
A Tale of Fifteen Generations

I

FLORENCE AND
THE EARLY MEDICI
(*1291–1429*)

There are names that carry within themselves something of an evocative charm. One need only speak the word "Florence," and the splendor of Italy in its prime, the magnificence of the Renaissance, flash in the mind with the brilliance of the noonday sun. It is a bizarre effect, for Florence, even in her most glorious days in the fifteenth and sixteenth centuries, was never the first city of Italy, and she possessed no extraordinary advantages, natural or otherwise. To the contrary, of the six major political divisions of Italy at the end of the Middle Ages, she seemed the least endowed. The kingdoms of Sicily and Naples enjoyed a far richer cultural and intellectual heritage. Rome, fortified by an imperial tradition and sustained by a series of ambitious and powerful popes, had long claimed, and sometimes realised, the hegemony not only of Italy but of all of Europe. Venice and Milan both possessed greater political and military power. Yet it was in Florence, rather than in any of her more obviously blessed sisters, that the glory of the Renaissance was to germinate and come to fruition. All the panorama of Italian history, the almost indecipherable kaleidoscope of interrelated events, during those two centuries, seem colorless and insignificant when compared to the tremendous revolution that was wrought in that city. It was by virtue of that revolution, that Renaissance, that the city of the Medici was raised above the rest of Italy and placed alongside the Athens of Pericles as a historical paradigm of human attainment.

Yet, Florence, superficially illuminated as she may appear in the light of history, has always been something of an enigma. That no one has ever completely grasped her temperament, her paradoxical devotion to both genius and gold, to freedom and violence, to stability and change, is a commonplace of history. The veil of mystery obscures even such comparatively mundane considerations as the origins of the city, so that the early history of Florence recedes into the mists of fable and legend. One Florentine tradition maintains that the city originally was a colony of the ancient Etruscan city of Fiesole. Another, equally ancient—and equally respectable, having been adduced by Machiavelli, among others—has it that Florence was founded by a Roman general, Sulla, in the first century before Christ. The variety of opinions almost equals the number of respected authorities on the subject, and all of these experts have buttressed their opinions with sound arguments and irrefutable data. In the face of these conflicting explanations, the student of history may be left to choose from among them according to his own preference. The most plausible explanation of Florence's origin seems to be that the city originally sprang from Fiesole. Villani, a fourteenth-century historian of the city, tells us that "the people of Fiesole held their market there once a week . . . and it was always, from the very first, the market of the Fiesolines; and such was it called before the city of Florence ever existed." According to this theory, the settlement eventually prospered sufficiently to rise to the rank of a Roman city and of a provincial capital. While the Empire flourished, therefore, Florence would have been a miniature of Rome, with its Field of Mars, its Capitol, its Forum, its aqueducts, baths, theatres, and amphitheatre—all erected, as was the custom, in reverential imitation of the Eternal City. And, in fact, traces of such buildings and monuments still exist, either in name or in substance, in modern Florence.

The significance of the name "Florence" is equally a matter for speculation and legend rather than of certifiable fact. If certain Florentine historians are correct in stating that a Roman praetor, "Florinus, with a Roman army, encamped beyond the Arno towards Fiesole and established two small villages there," then we may believe that Florentia (as the city was known in Roman times) took its name from that otherwise obscure praetor. Yet a flood of contrary and contradictory traditions persist, rendering the name of Florence as nebulous as the origins of the city, and a thousand opinions have claimed the attention of historians and vexed the minds of their readers without much enlightening either of them. The most insistent legend, and perhaps the most appealing, states that the city derived its name from the immense profusion of flowers (*flores*) growing on the meads between the rivers Arno and Mugnone, and that Florentia means simply "the flowering place." It would seem that at least the early Florentines themselves inclined to this opinion, for they named their cathedral Santa Maria del Fiore (St. Mary of the Flower) and adopted the *giagiolo,* or iris, in a stylized lily form, as their official emblem.

Whatever the origins of the city and its name, it is certain that Florence existed in the first century before Christ, and that it already showed evidence of that talent for turning a decent profit that was to distinguish it later on, for both Cicero and Sallust speak of the great "wealth of the Florentines." Similarly, the people of the city developed early that spirit of fierce independence that was to make of them, a thousand years later, alternately the hope and despair of Italy. Tacitus relates, for example, that during the reign of the Emperor Tiberius—a despot who did not gladly suffer contradiction in any form—a Florentine embassy came to Rome to protest a plan by which the waters of the Chiana were to be diverted into the Arno. The project, as the ambassadors declared with no little passion, would bring destruction upon their city. So persuasively and so eloquently did they plead that the Senate was moved to cancel the planned diversion, while the dread Tiberius looked on in silence.

Florence prospered until the Western Empire disintegrated during the fifth century. Then, along with the rest of the province of Tuscany, she fell under the rule of the Goths. One of the most treasured stories of the Florentines relates that the city was attacked in 405 by a horde of these barbarians, under a chief named Radagasius, but that the Goths were thrown back through the intervention of St. Reparata. The saint was thereupon adopted as the city's patron, and her feast day was celebrated in memory of the battle during which she is said to have appeared "bearing a red banner in her hand, on which was emblazoned the lily, the emblem of the Virgin." Be that as it may, the fact is that Florence eventually passed into a succession of barbarian hands, and her fortunes waxed or waned, along with those of the rest of Italy, according to the whim of the barbarians who repeatedly swept over the peninsula during the early Middle Ages. With the extension of Charlemagne's power into Italy in the ninth century, however, the city once again set her feet solidly upon prosperity's path. By the year 1000, she had so grown that her boundaries touched those of Fiesole, and the daughter, as it were, ended up by swallowing the mother. The two cities united, becoming one people and combining their armorial bearings—a white lily on a red field being the arms of Florence, and an azure moon on a white field those of Fiesole—into a common standard of red and white. The story that Florence forcibly annexed Fiesole to herself is, like much of the liveliest parts of Italian history, an invention of the weavers of legends.

During the Middle Ages, the dominant fact of political life in Italy was the perennial and violent struggle between the papacy and the Holy Roman Empire for supremacy. Florence, more to preserve herself from the exactions of a series of cloddish German emperors than from any pious motives, devoted herself ardently to the papal cause and more than once had occasion to shelter popes fleeing the imperial wrath. That

Florence was resolutely Guelf (as the papal partisans were called) rather than Ghibelline (the name given to supporters of the imperial party) is easy to understand. A strong imperial power in Italy meant, among other things, that the autonomous city-states of the peninsula, Florence included, would be subjected to policies formulated and taxes levied from beyond the Alps, and that the rulers of Italy would be the nobles of the Empire (who were usually of Teutonic blood) rather than themselves. The popes, on the other hand, despite their enormous prestige and even more enormous pretensions, generally were content to leave to their own devices the cities outside the papal domains. And the popes, even when their means matched their sometimes unbridled ambitions, at least were mostly men of Italy and could therefore be reasoned with, whereas the Germanic emperors, according to the accepted Italian view, were beyond the reach of human sensibilities.

This preoccupation with civic independence and individual liberty amounted, in Florence, to an unquenchable passion. And it was perhaps to that passion more than to any other single factor that the city owed the greatness that was to be hers. True, Florence was as fickle, changeable, capricious, wayward, ungrateful, and deceitful as any other Italian republic of the era. Nonetheless, the free constitution of the city, despite all the abuses connected with its history and its exercise, gave ample scope to individual commercial enterprise and rendered possible the exploitation of the resources of the citizens both individually and collectively. In the Florentine view, a man should exercise civic power not because he bore a distinguished name, or because he enjoyed great wealth, or even because he knew how to please his fellow citizens, but only because he contained in himself that force of authority and judgement that were essential to good government. A man was given authority in Florence, in other words, solely because he was worthy of it. Such was the ideal; but the reality was something quite different. The Florentines would have been the first to admit that they occasionally treated even their most distinguished rulers unjustly, driving them from office, and even from the city, for reasons no more noble than jealousy, or envy, or boredom. But even in such cases—the reasoning went—the republic had profited by the services and example of the deposed ruler while proving itself unworthy of them.

In the pursuit of this ideal, in the passion for independence, and in the exercise of their native restlessness, the Florentines were constantly casting about for new forms of government. From ancient times, Florence, like the other cities of Italy, had been governed in the Roman style, by two consuls. About the year 100, at the time of the union with Fiesole, Florence added to these consuls a Senate of one hundred men chosen "from among the most worthy citizens." Thereafter, the consuls varied in number, and at times there were as many as twelve serving simultaneously. Regardless of their number, however, the consuls were traditionally chosen from among the nobility of the city. Their office was the most constant element in the government of Florence so long as the city remained independent and free. The consuls came to be called Consuls of the *arti* (the trades), *anziani* (ancients), *buon'uomini* (good men), and, more generally, *priori* (priors), but the character of the office remained the same throughout such permutations.

Amid all these changes in the form, if not in the substance, of government, the German emperor, by virtue of his title to the throne of the Holy Roman Empire (which, in theory, included Italy), was regarded as the suzerain of the city. Most of the time, however, the emperor exercised no actual power in Florence, and Florentine policy from time immemorial had been designed to keep him from doing so. Indeed, after the cities of northern Italy had defeated Emperor Frederick Barbarossa, the latter conceded to them, by the Peace of Constance (1183), the autonomy that they had always claimed and most often exercised, retaining for himself only nominal rights of sovereignty over the cities. The citizens were left free to elect their municipal officers and, with comparatively unimportant exceptions, to administer justice and manage their own affairs. Each city agreed, in return, to accept as its nominal governor an imperial appointee known as a *podestà,* who was to act as the emperor's representative. Barbarossa no doubt had originally intended to retain some control over Italian affairs through these governors, but the imperial prerogative of appointment fell into disuse, and soon the citizens of Florence were electing their own *podestà,* as were the other Italian cities. This official supplanted the consuls in their more important functions, becoming the head of both the civil and military services. He was always a nobleman, and always chosen, in the hope of avoiding local partisanship, from another Italian city. The Florentines, of course, always chose a Guelf, while Ghibelline Genoa just as logically always chose a Ghibelline. When the *podestà's* term of office began, he came to the city bringing with him his own staff—two knights, several judges, councillors, notaries, and various attendants both personal and official—so as to be spared the pressures of local prejudice from his own family. Upon his entry into the city, he took an oath of office in the *piazza,* swearing to observe the laws of the place, to do justice to all men, and to wrong no one. His duties, and even his movements, were peculiarly circumscribed. Sometimes he was not allowed to enter any house other than the one officially assigned to him, so as to prevent his being influenced by private relationships with the local citizenry. Even the dress of the *podestà* was carefully regulated, perhaps to facilitate the surveillance of his movements, and he usually wore a floor-length robe of yellow, white, or cloth-of-gold, and a cap of red velvet. The *podestà,* during the course of his term—which was usually no more than six months or a year—could reasonably expect to be spared harassment or accusations from his subjects, even from those he had wronged. At the expiration of that term, however, he was required to remain in the city for a certain period of time, so that anyone with a legitimate complaint might obtain relief. In an unofficial variation upon that theme, it happened occasionally that a peccant *podestà* never lived to quit the city that he had ruled so briefly.

By the middle of the thirteenth century, the citizens of Florence had tired of this rather exotic form of government. They met together and divided themselves into a number of groups—either thirty-six or fifty of them, depending on the reliability of various contemporary observers —with each group electing its own leader. These leaders composed the governing council of the city, which, in place of the now unfashionable *podestà,* elected a captain of the people. In a short time, however, while retaining the latter office, the citizens reinstituted that of the *podestà* and assigned to the captain and to the *podestà* separate tribunals so that they might act as a check one upon the other. At the same time, the city was divided into six parts or wards, with each ward (*sesto,* or *sestiere,* a "sixth") being supervised by two *anziani,* or ancients. The twelve ancients were elected for a term of only two months, during which they were required to live, eat, and sleep in the public palace. They could not wander alone about the city, or even about their own wards, but were required to leave the palace only in a group. Collectively, these ancients were called the Signoria, or Signory.

At this time the government of Florence assumed the general form that it was to retain during the ascendency of the Medici family and throughout the Renaissance, although various experiments were tried as time passed and either adopted for their proved value or abandoned for their inefficiency. In this manner, various councils or committees were added to the government with the passage of time, by whom all laws enacted by the Signory had to be approved before they were promulgated. The tendency throughout this evolution of governmental organs was towards more and more democratic forms. But the Florentines loathed consistency as much as they loved freedom, and from time to time they tired of the turbulence of popular government and fell into the security of despotism—only, in a short time, to throw off that self-imposed yoke. On the whole, however, progress was made, and the trend was indisputably towards government by the enfranchised citizens of the republic. It should be noted, certainly, that Florentine democracy was a limited thing, for only a small percentage of the citizens had the franchise—even in Florence's heyday, not more than three thousand souls out of a population of some ninety-one thousand.

In order to belong to that favoured class, it was required not only that one's family have been resident in the city for several generations, but also that the candidate for enfranchisement be a man of substantial property. The reasoning behind this arrangement seems to have been that only a man of tried loyalty and considerable wealth could be counted upon, in the exercise of government, to act consistently in the best interests of the city. The remainder of the citizens, however, were not wholly excluded from a voice in the conduct of public affairs. At regular intervals, a Parlamento, or formal assembly of all citizens, was convoked in the public *piazza,* and the people were invited to express their approval or disapproval, *viva voce,* of such proposals as the government put to them.

It was democracy of a sort, one particularly adapted to the ideals and the practical requirements of the time. And it was a democracy that was founded and flourished—indeed, one that could only flourish —in an atmosphere of material well-being. Perhaps the task of self-government requires that the citizens be sufficiently free from material want to view civic problems dispassionately; or perhaps a functional democracy requires not only an interest in civic affairs on the part of the citizens, but also sufficient leisure to indulge that interest. Whatever the cause, from the standpoint of prosperity, Florence seemed an ideal place for the seeds of democratic government to take root. This prosperity, upon which the political power of Florence was founded, came from trade; and it was the tradesmen and the crafts that controlled the government. There were seven "greater guilds"—judges and notaries, wool merchants, refiners and dyers of foreign wool, silk merchants, money-changers, physicians and apothecaries, and furriers—and fourteen "lesser guilds," the latter comprising butchers, shoemakers, carpenters, smiths, etc. Every freeman not of the nobility was required to belong to one of the guilds, for membership conferred not only an aura of respectability but also served to assure the city as a whole that so-and-so was a productive citizen who would not become a public charge for lack of means to earn a livelihood. Even some of the Florentine nobility had been known to desert their caste and seek membership in the guilds, sometimes under an assumed name, for in time noble rank constituted an absolute bar to public office in Florence.

Some of the merchant guilds carried on a very extensive business. That of the wool-refiners and dyers, for example, were particularly successful, and the members owed their prosperity to a happy combination of enterprise, ingenuity, and chance. The wool of Tuscany, they had long since discovered, was of such hopelessly inferior quality that it was impossible to weave good cloth of it. The merchants therefore imported raw wool from Tunis, Barbary, Spain, Flanders, and England, and wove it into a cloth so fine, and so inexpensive, that foreigners could not compete with them. Soon this "Florentine wool" was being sold back, at a considerable profit, to the very countries from which the raw material had come. Trade with Europe, however, was generally less important than trade with the East. Merchandise was carried over the seas more easily and less expensively than over the Alps, and in many respects the products of the Orient were more desirable as items of trade than those of trans-Alpine Europe. The Florentines, therefore, along with the rest of the Italian cities of the north, loaded the galleys of the maritime cities—Genoa, Venice, and Pisa—with silken and woollen stuffs, oil, wine, pitch, tar, and metal, and shipped them out into the Mediterranean. In due time, if neither tempests nor pirates had intervened, the galleys would return from the ports of Alexandria, Constantinople, Asia Minor, and Syria, laden with pearls, gold, spices, sugar, oriental silks, cotton, goat-skins, dyes—and, not infrequently, oriental slaves. All these were items that the less venturesome, but equally luxury-loving, inhabitants of Europe were happy to buy from the merchants of Florence and the other cities.

This widespread network of international commerce soon outstripped the limited capacity of medieval Europe for barter and cash, and it became necessary to establish a system of banking, with its credits and bills of exchange, to sustain this industry and commerce and to invest the money being made. The quick-witted Florentines excelled at this, and the eighty banking-houses of Florence—of which the most important were the Bardi, the Medici, the Peruzzi, the Pitti, and the Strozzi—had, by the end of the thirteenth century, established a complete system of commercial banking. They cashed checks, exchanged merchandise as well as credit, supplied letters of credit, and even prospered to the point where kings, popes, and emperors applied to them for loans. A combine of Florentines once lent over one million florins—approximately thirty million dollars—to the English King, Edward III; but their pride turned to horror when that unhappy prince defaulted (1345), and they were virtually ruined.

As the wealth, and therefore the power, of the merchants and bankers waxed and that of the ancient nobility waned, there inevitably began to flourish in Florence a new order of nobility—or, more properly, a new aristocracy. It was an aristocracy founded not upon birth or upon nobiliary pretensions, but upon wealth and upon the qualities necessary for the accumulation of wealth. Among the families of this new aristocracy that drew their power from the trades and the professions, there was one particularly destined for greatness: the Medici.

* * *

The earliest public figure to bear this name* was Chiarissimo de'

---

* The word *medici* means "physicians," but there is no evidence to support the assumption that the practice of medicine was ever popular in the family, or that

Medici, who is listed as a member of the Communal Council of Florence in 1201, and about whom hardly more is known than the fact of his existence and his participation in government. Thereupon, the Medici disappear from view—at least from the view of history—for several generations. It was not until the end of the thirteenth century that they reappeared, in the person of one Ardingho de' Medici who, in 1291, was a member of the Signory and the first of his family to hold the office of prior. The time of Ardingho's priorship, and that immediately before and after, saw the consolidation of political power by the Florentine traders to the detriment of the nobility. In 1289, the priors had abolished serfdom, for reasons humanitarian enough and for motives political enough: to weaken the power of the noble landowners by compelling them to pay for the work done by the peasants on their estates. In the same year, the priors added five of the lesser guilds to the number of the greater guilds, thereby, as it was intended, increasing the influence of the *popolo minuto,* or common people. In 1291, the year in which Ardingho is inscribed on the roster of the Signory, heavy penalties were decreed by that body for any nobleman who dared plead exemption from the authority of the municipal courts on the basis of any papal, royal, or imperial—i.e., foreign—dispensation. At the same time, the civic rights of the *grandi,* or nobles, were greatly circumscribed by the requirement to the effect that, for election to the Signory, a man must actively be engaged in the exercise of a respectable trade. Too many of the *grandi,* apparently, had been evading the earlier requirement that a candidate must merely belong to a guild.

One may conclude for all this that Ardingho de' Medici was, at the time, actively engaged in industry and, moreover, that he was a man of his class in every sense, sharing the prejudices, fears, and ambitions of the other rising merchants of Florence. Indeed, those characteristics affected the rights and privileges of classes other than the nobility. Between 1289 and 1293, for instance, priests were prohibited from carrying weapons of any kind, merchants were forbidden to establish or to seek to establish commercial monopolies, the *podestà* was limited to a necessarily ineffectual six-month term of office, and the priors themselves were declared ineligible for re-election during the three years following a term in office. Such changes were symptomatic of an ideological evolution that affected the political and social views of all Europe at the end of the thirteenth century. In this advance, Italy had led the way, and Florence led Italy. Precocious commercial growth had come gradually to favor a flexibly economic, rather than a rigidly theocentric, guide to success in a community. Man had discovered that

---

the famous balls on the Medici coat of arms are, in reality, pills. It is likely that the early Medici joined the guild of physicians, according to custom, simply for the political and economic leverage that such membership offered.

a knowledge of markets and human nature were indispensable auxiliaries to prayer. Yet, in spite of the increasingly democratic character of
the Florentine government, feudalism was a long time a-dying. For
centuries, all over Europe, aristocratic birth had been the most important factor in political advancement. The *grandi* continued to control, to a very large extent, the administration of the Guelf party in
Florence. They were often employed as ambassadors, and always as
commanders in war. In the privacy of their palaces they regularly took
the law into their own hands. Compagni records: "The Bostichi family
continually did many evil deeds. In their houses adjoining the New
Market, in the very center of the city, they tied up and tortured men
in broad daylight." Such practices, which the perpetrators hardly
troubled to conceal, were the subject of common gossip in Florence.

In these circumstances it would have been difficult to foresee, during
the thirteenth century, the future eminence of the city in art and literature. Generally speaking, the Pisans and the Sienese were more interested in these fields than the almost wholly commercial, politically
minded, litigious, and warlike Florentines. It is significant that the first
notable painter born in Florence, Giovanni Cimabue, (1240–c. 1303),
was reported by the art historian Giorgio Vasari (1511–74) to have
been "so arrogant and proud of his unique professional skill that if
anyone, or he himself, noticed a fault in his work, he would instantly
destroy it utterly, however valuable it might be in other respects."†

The spirit of the times, and the temper of the Florentines, were
further manifested in 1298 by the enactment of the famous Ordinamenti
della Giustizia, or Statutes of Justice. This legislation was due largely
to the efforts of one Giano della Bella, something of a renegade
sprig of the nobility who, for reasons of his own, had thrown in his
lot with the commoners. Its chief purpose was, through a series of
restrictions, to reduce the still inordinate power of the old aristocracy,
a class represented and epitomized at the time by Corso Donati, one of
Florence's military heroes. Della Bella himself had repudiated his class
in order to engage in trade and consequently was not affected by the
new decrees, for he had become a partner in the banking firm of the
Pazzi family. But he had, like Corso Donati, also distinguished himself at the battle of Campaldino. He now stood forth as Donati's
opponent, as the recognised leader of the populace. Although he seems
to have been perfectly sincere in his devotion to republican ideals
and prepared to defend them in the face of all comers, his character
was described by his contemporaries as somewhat overbearing and

† It was Cimabue, according to tradition, who found Giotto, then a shepherd
lad of ten, in a meadow, drawing a lamb with a piece of coal on a slate. The
stern perfectionist apparently carried the boy off to Florence, where he taught
and supported him until his own death, after which Giotto inherited his master's
studio.

imprudent. Nor was he believed to be above using official power for private ends in the old feudal style. But this failing applied to most Florentine citizens, whatever their origin, who came to authority in those days.

In addition to excluding nobles from the government, the Ordinamenti increased penalties for offences by the *grandi* against the masses of the people and strengthened the influence of the guilds. The post of *gonfalonier,* or standard-bearer, of justice was instituted for the purpose of inflicting punishment for violations of the Ordinamenti. This officer soon became the most important figure in the state, disposing of troops that eventually reached the strength of four thousand. He could execute nobles found guilty of murdering a *popolano* and confiscate the murderer's property. But it was the *podestà* who had to investigate such crimes and arrest the perpetrator. In the case of less serious offences, failure to pay the fine imposed could result in the offender's right hand being severed.

In fact, the Statutes of Justice gave evidence of certain features that suggested vengeance rather than *giustizia.* It was decreed, for instance, that secret accusations against the nobility could be deposited in boxes outside the office buildings of the *gonfalonier* and the captain of the people. Obviously such a practice could encourage indiscriminate persecution of the aristocracy. There were other glaring examples of that vindictive party spirit that had embittered internal Florentine politics for a hundred years.

In these circumstances it could not be expected that the *grandi* would meekly accept lawful violence as a means of suppressing their own outbreaks of lawlessness. One of the lords who fell foul of the Ordinamenti demanded with furious sarcasm whether his house would be destroyed if his horse swished its tail into the face of a *popolano* or accidentally jostled pedestrians in a crowd. Others called impatiently for instant retaliation, by force of arms, on the insolent masses. But wiser aristocrats decided on a plot to evict Giano della Bella, now a prior, both from office and from the city. Della Bella, for his part, was persuaded to take drastic steps against his allegedly corrupt and disorderly followers and actually to propose the abolition of the Guelf party, though he was himself a member of it, on the ground that many other members, men of his former social standing, were using the powerful party organisation for private schemes.

At this juncture, in 1295—when another Medici, Bernardino, not otherwise recorded, was serving as a prior—an affray broke out between the followers of one Simone Galastroni and those of the formidable Corso Donati, who was still a hero to many patriotic Florentines. Some of the Galastroni were killed, but the *podestà,* on false evidence, acquitted the guilty Donati and convicted Galastroni, who had only defended himself. The *popolani* knew the truth better than the *podestà*. They rushed his palace in a murderous onslaught, while he and his wife, and Donati, who was with him at the time, just managed to save their lives by scrambling over the roofs of adjoining buildings. Della Bella was blamed for this disturbance, though he had actually done his best to stop it. When his friends took up arms to protect him, he left Florence, hoping that while he remained away matters would be settled peaceably. They were not. The citizens continued to riot, and no attempt was made to recall the absent statesman.

It was during this confused and alarming situation, which lasted into 1296, that Ardingho de' Medici, prior in 1291, was elected *gonfalonier*. It was the first time that the highest post in the Republic had been held by a member of his family, although they were already prominent in public affairs, as Bernardino's appointment shows. During his term of office, Ardingho was subjected to peculiar intractable pressures owing to the aristocratic aggression that followed the expulsion of della Bella and the fierce popular reaction to the consequent loss of power by less privileged citizens. How much influence Ardingho could exercise in his legally limited two months of office is not clear. But it is probable that, however broadminded (like most of the Medici) he might be, he perceived the practical impossibility, for the time being, of full democracy in Florence. His native realism and his connection by marriage with the powerful Bardi family (his wife was Gemma de' Bardi, a noblewoman) would incline him to listen sympathetically to the complaints of the *grandi,* backed though they may have been by threats of violence from their numerous military representatives. At any rate, later in the year some of the more vindictive paragraphs in the *Ordinamenti* were modified in detail. The most important revision was the repeal of the regulation rendering the actual exercise of a trade an essential qualification for a seat on the board of the Signory. The priors responsible for this excision were stoned in the streets by the people, but to no avail. Never again, except for one brief interval in 1377, when a Medici took the popular side, were the commoners of Florence to achieve such political ascendancy as della Bella had secured for them.

Despite such domestic turbulence, the thirteenth century closed, for the Florentines, in a blaze of outward glory. The rest of the peninsula, and even of the continent, were struck by the rising commercial, political, and intellectual significance of the city that was by then the most important in Tuscany, with a population of perhaps eighty thousand. In 1300 Pope Boniface VIII, a very active and cultivated Pontiff, if also of a decidedly hectoring disposition, remarked with astonishment that no fewer than twelve of the ambassadors representing European countries at the Jubilee Year celebrations were from Florence. They were acting for King Edward I of England, King Philip the Fair of France, and the sovereigns of Bohemia, Russia, Tartary, Naples, and Sicily, as well as for such Italian towns as Verona and Pisa. "The men of Florence form a fifth element," the Holy Father observed. He meant, no doubt, that they were as much to be reckoned with as earth, air, fire, and water.

Parties in Florence, as the fourteenth century dawned, were still known as Guelf and Ghibelline, although at this date the city was essentially Guelf. But names capable of arousing even more bitter animosities began to be current. They were first heard in Pistoia, a town some thirty miles north-west of Florence and just as turbulent, though far less powerful. The chief Pistoian family, the Cancellieri, was witnessing a feud between two of its branches, one descended from a certain Biance and therefore called Bianchi (Whites), and the other called the Neri, or Blacks—a designation adopted simply to emphasize the supposedly irreconcilable nature of the differences between the latter and the former. The encounters between these warring cousins became so frequent, so bloody, and so violent that the municipal authorities of Pistoia appealed to Florence for aid. The Florentine Signory thought to settle the dispute by removing the leaders of the factions from their native city to Florence, where, hopefully, the Signory's watchful eye might be able to forestall any further outbreaks. The necessary orders were issued, and the culprits came, reluctantly, to Florence, where they were well received, given the freedom of the city, and received as the honored guests of various noble houses. The Pistoian infection, however, rather than being contained by its transference to Florence, soon spread. The Cerchi family, who were quartering the Bianchi, and the Frescobaldi clan, whose guests the Neri chiefs were, soon fell out publicly; other noble houses and their retainers chose sides according to family ties, friendship, and whim, and soon the Blacks and Whites of Florence were battling in the streets with a vigor that made their Pistoian models seem like amateurs at the game. Before long the entire city seemed to be divided. About half of the nobles and all of the *popolo minuto* were Bianchi, while the Neri claimed the other half of the nobility and most of the great mercantile families.

Nearly all the combatants, both Whites and Blacks, were Guelfs by tradition. The factor that separated them ideologically was that the Blacks in general wished to abolish the controversial Ordinamenti, while the Whites accepted them. For this reason, the common people sided with the Whites and despised the (richer) Blacks. The conflict therefore took on something of the character of a clash between capital and labor. The "capitalist" party was led during this period by an able but headstrong soldier named Corso Donati, while the "labor" faction was headed by Vieri de' Cerchi, the head of a wool concern.

Vieri had made a reputation for himself at the Battle of Campaldino, but he had nothing of the presence, charm, and dash of Corso, and seems to have been considered, on the whole, a somewhat uncouth sort, a businessman of very ordinary parts. Donati was a typical feudalist of the old school, proud, rather poor, handsome, and relatively well educated, but given to outbursts of merciless fury. He both despised and envied the wealthy but vulgar Cerchi men, who "came from the gutter."

Dante, who hated cruelty more than bad manners, joined the Bianchi, being perhaps aware that democratic principles were the key to the future of civilisation. The Pope, however, was of a different opinion. After swords had been drawn on May Day 1300, on the Piazza di Santa Trinità at Florence, and many on both sides had been wounded, Boniface VIII sent a cardinal legate to the city. The legate announced that he came to arbitrate, but he had secret instructions from the Holy Father to support Donati, who seems to have promised Boniface the addition of Tuscany to the Papal States. The *popolo minuto,* armed with crossbows, attacked the cardinal in his lodging. His Eminence promptly placed the city under an interdict and returned to Rome in a fury. The Donati, the Pazzi, and some other nobles then retaliated on the masses by assaulting a procession of the White guilds. The government, which included Dante and the historian Dino Compagni, banished the most offensive members of both parties. The Bianchi obeyed without protest, the Neri only after vigorous resistance. Accordingly, the Whites were soon recalled, but the most distinguished of the exiles, Guido Cavalcanti, had already died of a fever.

The outlawed Neri, desperate by now, resumed their communications with Pope Boniface, alleging in self-justification that the Bianchi were actually all Ghibellines, supporters of the Empire against the Papacy. The Whites, alarmed lest Boniface be taken in by this transparent appeal to papal self-interest, dispatched their own embassy (of which Dante probably was a member) to plead at the papal court. Boniface, however, was not quite ready to act, and he contented himself with the making of pious speeches to both sides. Then, in the autumn of 1301, he judged the time ripe for action. Dangling the crown of the Holy Roman Empire before a French prince, Charles of Valois, son of King Philip III, the Pontiff induced that gullible young man to march on Florence with a large army. In the royal purse was a mandate from the Pope, authorizing Charles to bring the "Ghibelline" Bianchi to heel.

The Florentines had not expected so formidable a military action. After some hesitation they opened their gates to the prince. He was enthusiastically acclaimed by the Neri and invited by the Signory to assume administration of the city. In reply, he swore on the honor of a prince to preserve the peace. Nonetheless, he had been in touch, from the start of his expedition, with the exiled Corso Donati, and, a few days later, that implacable aristocrat burst into Florence at the head of his retainers, broke open the prisons that held the Blacks who had not been banished, and forced the White priors out of office.

The Whites hastily ordered the bells to be rung for a rising against both Charles and Donati, but it was too late. Corso's men were already behaving like foreign invaders, massacring armed and unarmed citizens alike, raping, looting, and burning. The tumult raged for five days. A Medici, wrote the municipal annalist, attacked and left for dead a Bianco during these wild scenes. But the chronicler does not otherwise name the culprit. Nor does another White who wrote: "They came during the night to our house in the Old Market and stole everything that they could find. But on the previous evening we had removed the most precious of our possessions. We men were not there, for we had escaped with our portable property. That same night there came another troop to our house and stole all that the others had left. And when they had finished stealing, the Tosinghi and the Medici demanded the persons of our women. . . . The children, both male and female, were left naked, lying upon the straw, for all their furniture and garments had been carried away. Worse deeds were not done even by the Saracens in Acre." These passages do not, of course, afford positive proof that all the Medici took the Black side. Their record as a family had been the reverse of an aristocratically oppressive one so far. The most that can be deduced is that the household of the Medici, like so many others, was divided against itself during these disturbances—and it is quite possible that both chroniclers had private reasons for hating the bearers of the name.

The next year, Charles, leaving the Neri in power at Florence, returned to Rome to quarrel with the Pontiff over the promised reward. The Frenchman had banished, among at least six hundred other Whites, Dante Alighieri. The poet happened to be in Siena at the time and was sentenced, in contumacy, for non-appearance. The savagery of his opponents—he had been a prior in the summer of 1300—was such that they ordered him to be burned alive if he ever set foot in the city again. He never did.

Meanwhile, Corso Donati had alienated by his arrogance many of his own party, including the powerful Pazzi clan, who kept him from attaining the supreme authority at which he was aiming. Anarchy followed. Order was restored only after armed intervention from Lucca, the prosperous wool manufacturing town in north-west Tuscany. Ardingho de' Medici was again prior during this confused period, and it may well have been his Medicean common sense and practical realism, in addition to his business connections, that suggested a deal with Lucca, some fifty miles away, instead of an intensification of internal military resistance to so experienced a soldier as Donati. But peace did not last long. Although Corso was now sulking quietly, other noble families took up the struggle in his name, while the Cavalcanti replaced the Cerchi on the other side. Fighting in the streets hardly ever ceased, and so fierce was the contest that no foreign *podestà* could be induced to arbitrate between such bloodthirsty antagonists.

It is interesting to find that the historian Villani, in dealing with this period (1302–3), affirms that by this time the Medici were mainly Neri. However divided their allegiance may have been in the time of Charles of Valois, they had evidently for the most part now switched to the winning side, like the shrewd traders they were, anxious only for a settled administration of any color. But it would probably have been impossible for Villani or anyone else to be certain where, for instance, the true sympathies of Ardingho de' Medici lay. On the one hand, as a merchant, he must have stood for stable political conditions. On the other hand, like all self-made men of property, he must have distrusted demagogues working ostensibly for the concentration of official power in the hands of the masses, since such a policy would almost inevitably lead to his own impoverishment. If it came to a choice between a good shopkeeper and a good general, Ardingho would probably have opted for the latter in the special circumstances of contemporary Florence. But these circumstances were to alter towards the end of the century, and such Medicean statesmen as Ardingho would then change their policies accordingly.

By 1304, with Corso Donati playing the part of Achilles brooding in his tent, the Whites under the Cavalcanti family were gaining ground against the Medici and other Blacks. But on June 10 a fire kindled by a priest destroyed much of the property of the Cavalcanti, as well as some of their leading adherents. These losses of the Bianchi enabled the Neri to turn the tide. Once again they climbed into the saddle of authority. Corso Donati and most of his lieutenants, however, were soon summoned to Perugia to appear before Pope Benedict XI, who was dissatisfied with their independent attitude. While the Black chiefs were away, the banished Whites, assisted by some Ghibelline exiles, attacked Florence from the west. They were repulsed with ease when the *popolo minuto*—the support of which the Whites had expected—spotted the hated Ghibelline banner and joined the Black defenders, as did also a number of Whites who had remained in the city. The old party watchwords by now had almost lost their meanings, causing the struggle to assume the character of an opposition between entrenched citizens and those they had ejected from residence. Both sides included *grandi* and *popolani,* Bianchi and Neri, in their ranks at this date.

The following year the government assumed the offensive, clearing its enemies from the rural castles in which they had taken refuge. Most of the exiles, however, had gathered in Pistoia, which was duly besieged by the official Florentine forces allied with Lucca. Pistoia fell in 1306, but only after turning out its women, children, cripples, and old men when food ran short. The besiegers brutally mutilated these wretched outcasts and then drove them back to the walls of the town to die of starvation.

The new Pope, Clement V, had ordered the Florentines to discontinue the siege of Pistoia. When they disregarded his command, he sent a force, in 1307, to teach them a lesson. But Ardingho de' Medici, now again *gonfalonier,* showed such energy in resisting this invasion that the papal army withdrew from Tuscany. This first of the family to be mentioned by full name in the chronicles of the time thus added military laurels to those he had gained in the counting-house and the council chamber. Such distinction was rather rare in this mercantile family, though the Medici had for some time now taken a serious part in politics. In addition to Ardingho's *gonfalonier*ship, his cousin Bernardo, of the junior branch, was elected to the priorate in this year. It was, however, largely through the efforts of the energetic Ardingho that the Medici were rising to eminence in the city. A later historian —the client of a sixteenth-century Medici duke—wrote with remarkable candor of the bygone ancestor of his patron: "It was alleged that his extraordinary mode of life, the great number of bullies and ruffians that he kept around him, his house ever open to all sorts of people, his immoderate munificence, his friendships with many Italian princes, and, in short, as is always the case when malicious rumours get about, his presence, his style of speech, his stately bearing, his walk and indeed his every gesture, word and movement, savoured of sovereignty."

The year of Ardingho's victory over the Pope was notable for the appointment of an executor of justice to enforce the Ordinamenti. The Signory decreed that this officer must come from outside Tuscany and hold office for only six months. The measure serves to demonstrate that Florence, in modern terms, was moving to the left. But the new post soon became hardly necessary, owing to dissensions among the *grandi,* which greatly weakened their aggressive capacity. The Bardi, Frescobaldi, and Buondelmonti joined Corso Donati. They were opposed by their former friend Rosso della Tossa, who also controlled the bulk of the *popolani.* Most of the citizens were now beginning to distrust Corso, so long their hero.

When Corso Donati married, as his third wife, one of the daughters of Uguccione della Faggiuola, a fanatical Ghibelline, the experienced husband was immediately condemned to death by the Signory for conspiracy "to betray the people and overthrow the government." But the strong force sent to his house to arrest him found chains and

barricades up in every street as they approached. The veteran, when
he found after some hours that no relief of his besieged mansion would
be forthcoming, ordered the gates to be opened, mounted his war-
horse, drew his sword, bellowed his rallying-cry, "A Donati!" and rode
out at full gallop, followed by a few of his kinsmen and retainers.
Leaping the barricades, he cut his way through the municipal forces
and miraculously escaped, though hotly pursued, from the city. The
government troopers caught him in the main street of the nearby
village of Robezzano. Disarmed, bound, and led back to Florence to
undergo public execution, he at first tried to bribe his guards. Then,
when they refused to be corrupted, he contrived, in a characteristic
fit of fury, to fling himself from his horse. Before he could get to his
feet, the nearest lancer had run him through. "So died," Machiavelli
wrote long afterwards, "Messer Corso, to whom his country and the
Neri owed much good and ill fortune. Had his spirit been less restless
his memory would have been more honoured. Nevertheless, he deserves to be placed among the most distinguished of Florentine citizens."

Shortly thereafter, in 1309, there appeared on the Florentine scene
another Medici of the junior branch of the family, one Averardo, of
whom hardly anything is known other than that he was elected Prior
in that year, and *gonfalonier* in 1314. These offices indicated the continuing hold that the Medici exercised on the esteem of their fellow
citizens, and point to a not inconsiderable talent on the part of Averardo,
who, in addition to his political success, was regarded as the true
founder, by virtue of his capacity for boldness in commerce and good
judgement in finance, of the fortunes of the family. He is also remembered as the ancestor of that most magnificent of all the Medici, Lorenzo.

While the star of the Medici was thus beginning its ascent, the political
situation of Florence remained as turbulent and unsettled as ever. A
new Pope, this time a Frenchman, had mounted the throne of St.
Peter. Clement V, though an admirable man in many respects, was
not a model of decisiveness. The throne of the Holy Roman Empire was
vacant, and the Pontiff seemed unable to make up his mind which
candidate to support. Initially, his compatriot, Charles of Valois, had
been the papal favorite. Clement soon perceived, however, or was soon
persuaded, that if the imperial crown became an appanage of the
House of France, that kingdom would be in a position to reduce the
Papacy to total dependence. Consequently, Clement finally chose, after
having seemed for a time to favour the candidacy of Robert of Naples,
Henry of Luxembourg, and the latter accordingly was crowned at Rome
in 1312.

Florence, as always, regarded the existence of any emperor as a
threat to her freedom, and she made no exception for Henry. Moreover, the Signory, Guelf though it was, was not on the best of terms

with the Holy See, and the Popes responded in kind by repeatedly placing the city under a papal interdict. Florence, therefore, in a gesture of contempt towards both Pope and Emperor, refused to send ambassadors to make obeisance to Henry. Instead, the Signory ostentatiously cultivated the friendship of that disappointed imperial candidate, Robert of Naples, and entertained him lavishly when he visited Florence in the autumn of 1310. After his departure, the city prepared for a siege. The fortifications were repaired, and some of the exiles, but not Dante, were recalled, so as to prevent their conspiring with either Henry or Clement. By June 1311, all of the Guelf cities of Tuscany had formed a league to resist any attempt to subvert the independence of the province. After Henry's coronation, he moved northwards, defeated a Florentine army near Arezzo to the south-east of Florence, and encamped at the very place where Corso Donati had met his death four years previously. But the Emperor's health was already failing. Within a few weeks he raised the siege of Florence and turned south. On August 24, 1313, he died at Buonconvento on the road to Siena. It is not impossible that he had been poisoned at Rome, weeks before, by Florentine emissaries. But he may just as well have succumbed to malaria, as was more generally believed.

The imperial threat to Florence, during Henry's lifetime, had served to recall the city to its pristine and vehement Guelfic commitment. With Henry's death, the Guelf political clique who had rallied their compatriots to the anti-imperial cause were strongly entrenched; moreover, they had no intention of relinquishing one iota of their power simply because Florence was no longer in imminent peril. Neither the *podestà* nor the *gonfalonier,* Averardo de' Medici, was able to restrain their tyranny, and the city was threatened by an autocracy from which even the pretext of democratic sentiment was missing. These Guelfic oligarchs met their doom the following year (1314), however, in the person of one Uguccione della Faggiuola, the son-in-law and avenger of Corso Donati. The forces of the Florentine autocrats, abetted by those of Bologna, Siena, Perugia, and a few other cities, met Uguccione's army at Montécatini, near Pistoia, and were easily overcome by the Ghibelline upstart. Florence, in panic, recalled to the city some of her Ghibelline exiles. Even those whose political convictions had won them the title of "unpardonable" were told that they might return if they would agree to pay substantial fines and do public penance for their offences. Among those in the latter class who refused to degrade themselves by betraying their principles was Dante, who chose to withdraw from Tuscany altogether and take refuge at Verona. He was soon joined there by Uguccione, whose arms had failed to fulfill the brilliant promise of their beginnings and who was now, like Dante, an exile at the court of a foreign—i.e., non-Florentine—prince.

Florence, now at peace both with herself and the world, proceeded to conclude treaties of alliance and friendship with Lucca and Pisa and, thus fortified, settled down to a short respite from political excitement.

At this propitious moment, the city seemed to be at the beginning of an era of intellectual, artistic, and economic promise. Giotto de Bondone (1267–1337), the genius of dramatic naturalism, was in the midst of a brilliant career. Dante—who, as prior, had sat for a portrait by Giotto—was at work on the *Divine Comedy*. Giovanni Villani, the first in a long line of eminent Florentine historians, was at work on his famous *Florentine History*. As the streets of Florence—indeed, of all Italy—ran with blood and echoed to the cries of contending factions, as palaces went up in flames on all sides, these Florentines, and many others, went on coolly working on their paintings, frescos, chronicles, histories, treatises, and poems. Most of these men fell short, to be sure, of the level of genius of a Giotto or a Dante; they represented, nonetheless, a remarkable aggregate of talent drawn from an area less than half the size of the state of New York and populated by slightly more than a hundred thousand souls.

At the same time, at the beginning of the fourteenth century, Florentine prosperity kept apace with Florentine intellectual activity. Florence's financial dealings influenced the civilised world from the dreary banks of the Thames to the sparkling palaces of Constantinople and the exotic domains of the Caliphs. The family of the Medici—including Bernardo, who was re-elected prior in 1317—were already playing a conspicuous part in the growth of this network of mercantile and political interests. Under the aegis of the Medici and comparably prosperous families of the city, Florentine cloth, Florentine loans, and Florentine opinions were valued as much in Amsterdam as on the Bosphorus. Similiarly, no European artist or writer with any claim to fame could afford to be ignorant of the labor of Florentines in his field.

But wealth and talent on the part of some Florentines did not automatically render Florence, as a whole, any more stable or reliable, politically and diplomatically, than those Italian states that, less happy in the gifts of their citizens, were ruled by secular and ecclesiastical princes who were unblushing despots. In this respect, Florence was no less self-seeking—though possibly she was less ostentatious about it—than Milan or Rome. It was, in fact, because of the former that Florence once more found herself embroiled in a dispute in 1318—the year during which Conte di Averardo de' Medici, son of that Averardo who was *gonfalonier* in 1314, was elected to the priorate. Matteo Visconti, Duke of Milan, had thus far managed to maintain himself in power by craft and prudence rather than by the violent methods favoured elsewhere on the Italian peninsula. In 1318, however, contrary to his usual practice, he was so emboldened by his previous successes, or so maddened by desire for the wealth of Genoa, that he moved against that city with all the force that Milan could command. Since the cities of the North—except for Venice—were generally regarded as Ghibelline in sentiment, Florence felt called upon to take up the gauntlet on behalf of her fellow Guelf, Genoa, and she formed a league of Guelphic cities to prevent Milan's further expansion southwards.

It is difficult to understand that the labels "Guelf" and "Ghibelline" could evoke such violent emotions in Italians of the fourteenth century. The great medieval battle between Peter and Caesar, between the Papacy and the Empire, had long since been settled, and neither Pope nor Emperor now had need of Guelf or Ghibelline supporters. Indeed, the Pope was now happily living on the banks of the Rhone, at Avignon, far from the bickering of the Italian states; and there was, at the moment, no Holy Roman Emperor. All the same, Ghibellines continued to wear the feathers in their caps on one side and to loathe all Guelfs, while the Guelfs wore their feathers on the other side and could not abide the sight of a Ghibelline. Ghibellines cut fruit at table horizontally, Guelfs vertically. Ghibellines drank from smooth goblets, Guelfs from decorated ones. Furthermore, like the rival English factions of the second half of the fifteenth century, Ghibellines wore white and Guelfs red roses. Ghibellines and Guelfs actually had their carefully differentiated manners of yawning, walking, dicing, gesticulating, and swearing. Even the battlements on their castles were pointed for Ghibellines and flat for Guelfs. They hated each other more by custom and according to the rules of *vendetta* than on the basis of positive political principle.

In any case, the Ghibelline forces of Milan were defeated in 1318 by combined forces of Florence, Naples, and Bologna. The next year the Florentines, for good measure, seized the Lombard city of Cremona from its suzerain, Can Grande della Scala of Verona, then called in Philip of Valois, brother of King Louis X of France, to hold the ambitious Milanese in check. Matteo Visconti replied by an alliance with the best soldier and statesman in Italy, Castruccio Castracane, lord of Lucca, a veteran mercenary of King Edward I of England. Castracane at once raided the Arno Valley, causing panic in Florence. He then unaccountably dashed first to Genoa, then back to Lucca, then back to Florentine territory once more. Bernardo de' Medici, again elected prior in 1320 and 1322, must have had his hands full during these dangerous years. By 1323, Castracane was besieging Prato, only twelve miles from the walls of Florence. The town was eventually relieved, but the situation remained perilous. Castracane now represented much more of a threat to Florence and to all Italy than

Matteo Visconti ever had. On September 23, 1325, he inflicted a re-sounding defeat on the Florentine army near Altopascio, a town be-tween Pistoia and Lucca. This third rout of the Guelfs in battle, following the disasters of Montaperti and Montecatini, could easily have given the Visconti—now represented by Galeazzo Visconti—control of Florence. But that was evidently not Castracane's object. After some contemptuous and insulting demonstrations outside the walls of the helpless city he returned to Lucca, trailing the captured banner of the Republic in the dust behind its official war-chariot.

Castracane seems, in fact, to have cared more for war than for the fruits of victory. He was soon ravaging Florentine territory again, with-out attempting to lay siege to the city itself. The Signory paid the Duke of Calabria, son of King Robert of Naples, to keep him out, for this purpose conferring on the Duke the lordship of their Republic for ten years. In 1326 his vicar, Walter de Brienne, a Frenchman popularly known under the exotic title of Duke of Athens, turned up in Florence. The two foreigners, with substantial mercenary forces, had no difficulty in parrying Castracane's fugitive feints against the city.

Then, in 1327, King Ludwig of Bavaria, who had just defeated Duke Frederick III of Austria, his rival for the imperial crown, rallied the Ghibellines at Milan. Ludwig needed their support for his claim to rule as Emperor against the will of the rapacious and dissipated Pope John XXII. In October, allied with Castracane, the Bavarian King captured Pisa and conferred its lordship, together with that of Pistoia, of Volterra, and of a neighbouring bishopric, on his wily general. By the new year, Ludwig had been crowned as Emperor in Rome.

Fortunately for Florence, the restless and incalculable warrior Cas-tracane died of a heart attack, from over-exertion on an exceptionally hot day in September of 1328. So successful a soldier, with Ludwig's support, would soon have rendered the Guelf republic defenceless against the Ghibelline faction. As it was, the Signory took advantage of this breathing-space to enact several democratic amendments to the con-stitution. They excluded all Ghibellines from office and created both a Council of the People, numbering three hundred members headed by a captain, and also a Council of the Commune—i.e., of Florence's extra-mural territory—with two hundred and fifty seats, half of them for nobles and half for *popolani,* under the *podestà.* Priors and other officials were elected by lot after their names had been approved by a board of ninety-eight citizens, including the *gonfalonier* and the outgoing priors.

Castracane's heirs were now quarrelling, and Florence was accord-ingly able to regain control of Pistoia. Villani records that he personally advocated the purchase of Lucca, which had fallen to a band of free-booters. But he was overruled, whereupon the mercenaries sold the city to a Genoese exile. A Florentine army proceeded to lay siege to Lucca, but this operation was crushed by a relieving force despatched by King John of Bohemia. John, a handsome, chivalrous, and eloquent sovereign, declared that he had no designs on the Empire. He made a success of ruling a number of Lombard and even Emilian towns— for example, Cremona, Bergamo, and Pavia in the first category, and Parma, Reggio, and Modean in the second. But elsewhere John's popularity and success aroused alarm. The Ghibelline despots of Milan, Verona, Mantua, and Ferrara joined the Guelfs of Florence and Naples to resist his further expansion on the peninsula. John was not the sort of man to risk a conflict with so strong a combination. By 1333 he had liquidated his Italian possessions and left the country, to die thirteen years later in battle against the English King Edward III and his son the "Black Prince."

Florence in the 1330s was stronger and more prosperous than she had ever been. The urban population exceeded ninety thousand. An even larger number inhabited the rural districts. The churches numbered a hundred and ten, the monasteries and convents thirty-nine, the clothiers' shops over two hundred. Florentine bankers and merchants could be found occupying responsible positions all over Europe. Fine buildings, pictures, and libraries of manuscripts abounded. Thousands of children were being taught, at six schools, to read and count. Four more schools specialised in grammar and rhetoric.

The Medici family of course shared in and contributed to the wealth that rendered all this splendour possible. But they were for the most part quiet, hard-working traders and financiers, members of the well-to-do bourgeoisie. They kept out of the limelight. But in 1336 a certain Salvestro di Averardo de' Medici, a son of Averardo de' Medici, *gonfalonier* of 1314 and a brother of the former prior of 1318 and 1324, Conte di Averardo de' Medici, was chosen to go on an embassy to Venice. The envoys were to negotiate, if possible, an alliance with that Republic against Verona, for the lord of Verona had made himself master of the especially industrious, and therefore useful, town of Lucca, of which Florence considered herself the rightful proprietor.

This Salvestro de' Medici was one of the several Medici at this period and earlier who had married into the nobility. The family of his wife was that of the famous, but never economically successful, Donati. Most of them were gifted as well as blue-blooded, but they were apt to be temperamentally perverse in the aristocratic manner. Lisa Donati and her husband, Salvestro de' Medici, are likely to have suited each other about as well as colours from opposite ends of the spectrum, her hot red or orange balancing his cool green or blue. However that may have been, the Florentine embassy to Venice gained its object. The hitherto scornfully aloof Venetians for the first time agreed to an alliance with another Italian state, and the Florentines were delighted with the tact and perseverance of their ambassadors.

The ensuing campaign proved victorious only up to a point, for the Venetians, after an initial victory, lived up to their reputation for cynical perfidy by making a premature peace with the Veronese. Lucca itself did not change hands, but Florence acquired a good slice of its territory. Venice always in fact preferred intrigue to warfare as a means of maintaining and even advancing its already considerable prosperity, derived chiefly from overseas trade. The well-named Most Serene Republic never hesitated to break a treaty if the Doge could see no point in prolonging hostilities. The hard-headed citizens, in so many respects, especially in their mercantile abilities, resembling Florentines, entirely lacked the latter's frequently aggressive militarism; indeed, with their talent for diplomatic double-dealing, they did not need it.

But Florence, in spite of failures in this direction, remained determined upon the acquisition of the hard-working and flourishing little town of Lucca. Walter de Brienne, the so-called Duke of Athens, who had been in 1326 deputy for the Duke of Calabria in the latter's protectorate of Florence, had successfully commanded a Florentine contingent during the recent abortive attempt to wrest Lucca from the Pisans. He was now appointed captain-general of the Republic. De Brienne, a bold and clever soldier but as utterly unscrupulous and as ambitious as he was dissolute, undoubtedly meant his new post to be the first stage in abolishing the city's constitution and substituting for it a despotism, with himself in sole charge. He began by inciting both the nobles and the masses against the wealthy merchants, including the Medici, who held some power for the moment but had fallen into general disfavour owing to their mismanagement of the latest project for absorbing Lucca. Before long, Walter arrested two of the most prominent of the wealthy burghers, Bernardo's son, Giovanni de' Medici, who had twice served as *gonfalonier,* and one Guglielmo degli Altoviti, on suspicion of bribery and speculation. Both were executed, on questionable evidence, in 1343. Others of their class only escaped a similar fate by the payment of enormous fines. Then Walter, cheered by the populace for this savage behaviour, coolly demanded "the lordship of Florence in perpetuity" as his reward. The Signory at first refused to grant this insolent request, but the aristocratic party enforced their acceptance of the tyrant.

De Brienne at once threw off all pretence to benevolence. He proceeded to disgust all reasonable citizens not only by renewed assaults on important banking families, such as the Bardi, but also by the reckless elevation to the priorate of labourers and adventurers of the lowest social rank. He simultaneously introduced "French fashions" in debauchery and encouraged prostitution. Finally, and most unforgiveable, he formally ceded Lucca, which he had originally vowed to capture for Florence, to the Pisans for a term of fifteen years. The vilest features of a cruel autocracy followed in Florence. Political prisoners were tortured in public, women were raped with impunity, and property both private and belonging to the state was confiscated for the use of Walter and his ruffian adherents.

Three separate plots to get rid of the Frenchman by assassination were soon organised with the utmost secrecy. The Bishop of Florence headed one, which included members of such powerful families as the Bardi, Frescobaldi, and Altoviti and was backed by Pisa itself, as well as by Siena and Perugia. A second conspiracy relied on the Donati, Pazzi, Cerchi, and Albizzi, among others. Francesco di Ardingho de' Medici, with his wife's family, the Adimari, and such other clans as the Bordoni, Rucellai, and Aldobrandini, led a third scheme. But this latter plan, by chance, came to the knowledge of de Brienne. He imprisoned Antonio Adimari but prudently refrained, for the time being, from executing him. Instead, he summoned three hundred of the most eminent Florentine citizens to the Palazzo Vecchio, announcing that they were to deliberate on what was to be done with Antonio Adimari.

It was known throughout the city, however—or at least it was thought —that Walter's real intention was to massacre these assembled "advisors," and the tyrant forthwith found himself besieged in his palace by a mob of enraged citizens. It seemed, indeed, to the alarmed Duke of Athens and his followers that the whole city was in arms. Some of his most intimate associates were seized in the *piazza* and slaughtered. The next day, on Sunday, July 27, 1343, foreign detachments arrived to reinforce the besiegers. The bishop set up a provisional government of seven nobles and seven *popolani*. The latter group included Francesco de' Medici—significantly enough not regarded as an aristocrat, though he had married the Countess degli Adimari, whose kinsman Talano served in the other half of the fourteen members of the bishop's emergency administration.

In the subsequent negotiations with de Brienne and his now half-starved adherents, numbering about four hundred, the Duke surrendered after sacrificing two of his most notorious accomplices to the fury of the people, who promptly hacked them to pieces in the *piazza*. Villani adds that slices of their flesh were cut off and devoured, both raw and cooked, by their maddened assailants. Such savagery contrasts with the disdainful punishment meted out to de Brienne. In the small hours of August 6 he was escorted as far as Poppi, in the region known as the Casentino, east of the city, and warned never to re-enter Florence on pain of instant death. This remarkable clemency may have been due either to the Christian spirit of the bishop, fear of the displeasure of the

154,627

LIBRARY
College of St. Francis
JOLIET, ILLINOIS

Duke of Calabria, or both. It is perhaps indicative of the standard of civilisation reached by responsible Florentines of this period, by no means so evident elsewhere.

When the republican constitution was re-established after Walter de Brienne's fall, a number of democratic measures were passed. Indeed, they were too democratic to suit the disfranchised nobles, who made yet another bid for administrative power. After several days of bloody street-fighting and arson, the Medici and other chiefs of the *popolo grasso*—the Bapponi and Strozzi, for instance—forced the *grandi* to yield. No fewer than twenty-two of the nobles' palaces, belonging to such families as the Donati, Pazzi, Rossi, Cavalcanti, Bardi, and Frescobaldi, had been burned to the ground by the populace during the course of the struggle. The masses, after a century and a half of almost incessant conflict, had won an almost complete victory and extinguished the aristocracy politically. Villani wrote of the autumn of 1343: "We are now under the rule of the artisans and the *popolo minuto*. I pray God that it may exalt and benefit the Republic. But I fear that it will do otherwise, because of our sins and imperfections, because our citizens are devoid of love and charity, and because our rulers continue the accursed practice of promising one thing and doing another." The historian's pessimism was not altogether unfounded. Florence's future would be as restless as her past. Yet the spirit of the city did not comprise solely the impulses of class hatred and personal ambition, lawlessness and suspicion. The intuitions of high-minded criticism and imagination, the intellectual curiosity and vision that account in part for the persistent political experiments, co-existed with the horrors of reiterated civil war, the blazing houses, shrieking women, and trampled corpses in lane and *piazza*. Both the ferocity of the Florentines and their urbanity were the setting for Giotto's painting, sculpture, and architecture, for the splendid festivals of century after century, for the traditional Florentine gayety, for the judicious chronicles of Giovanni Villani, and for the meditations that gave rise to the *Divina Commedia*.

Between 1343 and 1345, many aristocrats who had fought for the popular cause were exiled. Others had fled to the courts of foreign Ghibelline lords and were declared public enemies. All grants of money made to a *grande* as a reward for service to the Republic were revoked. Early in 1345, the great banking houses of the Bardi and Peruzzi suspended operations, chiefly owing to the repudiation of loans they had advanced to King Edward III of England. Financial chaos ensued. Villani, like many other prosperous citizens, lost everything he possessed and was imprisoned for debt. The King of France ejected all the Florentine merchants from his country, where Walter de Brienne, as it happened, had taken refuge.

The Medici and their friends devised the only possible plan to meet this situation. Their scheme was one that had been imitated in similar circumstances ever since. They created the first national debt ever heard of by the expedient of funding into one consolidated stock all the loans made to the government in the past. The stock, called *Monte Commune* or "Common Pile," bore interest at 5 per cent secured on the city's revenue, and was marketable at prices dependent on the condition of municipal credit. This reform was proclaimed to be "in defence of liberty." The same announcement was made with respect to other measures passed at this time in order to curb the power of the clergy, to prevent excessive expenditure on luxuries and dowries, and to facilitate, by a system of registration, the transfer of real estate. Nevertheless, all these enactments were really aimed at the rich, who soon counter-attacked, not by arms this time, but by subtle legislation designed, under the cover of selfless patriotism, to reduce representation of the *popolo minuto* in office.

A disastrous failure of the harvest of 1346 was followed by good crops the next year. But in 1348 the great plague of the "Black Death," which drove the gay, cultivated young men and women of Boccaccio's *Decameron* from Florence, burst upon all Italy. Three fifths of the population of Florence, including Giovanni Villani, perished in the midst of those scenes of inhumanity and desperate dissipation that have been associated with such calamities ever since the time of Thucydides. Boccaccio's brief description of them, though vivid, does not match the Athenian's terrible picture.

By 1351, Florence had recovered from the stunning blows of the past few years sufficiently to block an invasion of Tuscany by the Visconti of Milan. The fighting lasted two years before Pope Clement VI's intervention brought it to a halt. The Medici were prominent both just before and in the course of these Milanese campaigns. Giovanni di Conte de' Medici had been *gonfalonier* in the year after the Black Death. He must have been largely responsible for the social and political reconstruction that followed it. His cousin, Mario de Talento de' Medici, who married first a Bardi and then a Strozzi, won public acclaim by relieving the little town of Scarperia, some thirty miles northeast of Florence, by gallantly cutting his way through the besieging lines at the head of only a hundred men, and he was elected *gonfalonier* in 1354. Still another member of the family, whose Christian name is charitably withheld in the chronicles, disgraced himself. While holding a strong position in the Apennines whence he could easily have trapped the advancing Milanese, he fled ignominiously.

It was at this time that a new mode of warfare first appeared in Italy. It can be traced as far back as the year 1300, but by the mid-fourteenth century it had begun to affect adversely every city on the peninsula. In former ages, the mounted *grandi* had been the backbone of any army. But for decades before 1350 these nobles had been losing their ascendancy in all the states. The Guelf cities had become republics. The policy of the Ghibelline despots inclined to keep their turbulent aristocracies militarily weak in the interests of an autocratic monarchy. Yet, personal ambitions, commercial schemes, political rivalries, and the removal of the Popes from Rome to Avignon in 1309 continued to demand and encourage the use of force. It could not now be supplied by the old *grandi.* The new mercantile plutocrats had neither the time nor the wish to undergo training in warfare. Simultaneously, the pacific spirit of the industrialists was reinforced by that of intellectual circles, though the disciples of Giotto and Petrarch had different reasons for evading martial service. Finally, the temper of the masses of the people, especially the peasantry, had never in Italy been so committed to the feudal system, with its military obligations, as in northern Europe. Mercenaries had therefore to be employed by both Guelf republics and Ghibelline autocracies. The first half of the fourteenth century had seen squadrons of German lancers and French knights, brought into Italy by the Emperors and by princes such as Charles of Anjou and Charles of Valois. Not infrequently these foreign troops, after deserting or being disbanded, remained on the peninsula and sold their services to the highest bidder. Their leaders then became known as *condottieri,* "conductors" of mobile forces that would go anywhere and fight for anybody if well paid. Towards the end of the century, Italian as well as German and French *condottieri* entered the market.

The main objects of these freebooters were to start wars between communities, keep hostilities in being, avoid heavy casualties, capture rather than slaughter wealthy adversaries who could be ransomed, and eventually to acquire territory that could be used as a base for supplies and winter quarters. If such aims did not appear practicable for the time being, the *condottieri* acted as mere brigands, plundering whatever district they happened to occupy at any given moment and terrorising its inhabitants until the latter, if rich enough, paid them to go elsewhere. In 1353, for example, a German mercenary commander named Werner, who called himself, like Attila, "the enemy of God, of pity and mercy," blackmailed the Bolognese in this way. Shortly afterwards Monréal, a knight of Provence whom the Italians sarcastically nicknamed "Fra Moriale," as if this appalling ruffian were a monk, extorted huge sums from Florence and Pisa by promising that his so-called "Great Company" would cease its depredations on their property for a while. But Monréal tried this game once too often. Playing it in Rome on that reincarnation of an ancient Roman tribune, Cola di Rienzi, he was suddenly seized and executed by Cola's adherents.

Monréal was followed in 1356, a year in which Giovanni di Conte de' Medici was again elected *gonfalonier,* by one Conrad, who had gratuitously adopted the title of Count of Lando. Conrad returned to his predecessor's policy of blackmailing Florence, and the city paid him sixteen thousand florins in exchange for a guarantee that he would stay out of its territory for the next three years. Nonetheless, in 1358 Conrad applied for permission to pass through Florentine dominions on his way from Emilia to join the ruler of Siena, who had just hired him to attack Perugia. The Signory gave Conrad leave to take the desired route on condition that he marched only through an outlying district of the Apennines to the north-east of the city, by way of Dicomano and Bibbiena. The mercenary agreed, but demanded that his troops should be fed by the priors while on Florentine soil. Rations were accordingly sent him from Florence. Nevertheless, the foreign soldiers, either out of sheer habit or because they considered the rations inadequate, plundered the mountain villages. The infuriated peasants, daring to do what the timorous Signory scarcely dared conceive, attacked Conrad's squadrons in a narrow gorge, first breaking their ranks by hurling down rocks from the hillside and next assaulting them with scythe and axe. Three hundred of the riders were killed, and Conrad himself was captured. The hardy mountaineers then proceeded to starve the rest of the band into submission by preventing their escape from the gorge. Now the Signory, in an effort to placate these bandits, had despatched an embassy to escort them with honour through the territory of the Republic, and the ambassadors, including Giovanni di Conte de' Medici, had been caught in the trap with the mercenaries. Giovanni and his colleagues saw no reason why they should share the fate of the foreigners to whom they had been accredited, although they had not been able to stop the soldiers from robbing the villagers. The Florentine officials accordingly attempted to use their authority to persuade the grimly vengeful men of the mountains to let the surviving brigands go. The peasants agreed to allow the main body of bandits to leave, but they utterly refused to release Conrad. As soon as the detachment moved out, one of the envoys galloped off to Florence to report these events to the Signory. A message was returned ordering the embassy to take a separate road back to the city. Official protection was to be removed from the now leaderless bandits. They would henceforth have to take their chance of further ambushes, and no more rations, in any case, would be sent. Giovanni and his little group had no choice but to disobey this command, for the desperate mercenaries threatened to kill the Florentines if they ceased to attempt to control the local inhabitants. The ambassadors accordingly consented to escort the hungry troops until they reached Vicchio, about fifteen miles north-east of Florence, where provisions could be obtained without violence. The so-called Count of Lando had meanwhile been transferred, under guard, to a castle belonging to the

Ubaldini family, Ghibellines, who soon released him in the belief that so expert a bandit and soldier would be a better friend than enemy.

Such a series of events vividly illustrates the commingled sentiments of respect, fear, and hatred that the cities generally felt for the *condottieri*. They were slightly more popular with the quarrelsome owners of large rural estates, but the civic authorities, both Guelf and Ghibelline, detested the barbarity, perfidy, and rapacity of these ruffians. All the same, no force could be raised strong enough to suppress them. Moreover, no one could guess when an urgent occasion for their services might next arise. For the settlement of disputes between these same authorities, a mercenary captain, however extortionate his terms and whatever damage he might inflict on the countryside, could be a decisive factor.

Sometimes, however, the insolence of the roving freebooters broke all bounds and had to be checked, usually by confronting them with a rival fraternity of the same sort. In 1359, for instance, Florence defied the Count of Lando's renewed threats of invasion by sending Pandolfo Malatesta, Lord of Rimini, who himself behaved very much like a *condottiere,* to teach the blackmailer a lesson. Conrad fled before this dangerous opponent and was never again seen in Tuscany.

* * *

Shortly after the Milanese war, the corruption of the Florentine government again caused the organisation of a conspiracy by some of the Medici and other leading families. In 1360 Salvestro, the eldest son of one Alamanno de' Medici, who had been knighted for his services to the Republic in 1314, was in office. Salvestro knew nothing of the plot, but his brothers, Andrea and Bartolommeo, were implicated. One or both of them revealed their secret plans to Salvestro, perhaps in the hope of persuading him to resign and save his skin while there was still time. They found, however, that Salvestro did not share their views. He instantly had two of the ringleaders of the conspiracy beheaded, whereupon the whole movement collapsed. But Salvestro, now duly warned against the corruption of his colleagues, played a prominent part in curbing official misconduct during the next few years.

War was being waged at the time between Florence and her old enemy, Pisa, mainly on commercial grounds. The Pisans, after two defeats, hired the so-called "White Company" of English mercenaries, commanded by a famous veteran of the French campaigns of King Edward III, Sir John Hawkwood. When the Treaty of Brétigny brought temporary peace to France in 1360, Hawkwood, a flexible gentleman, took service successively with the Marquis of Monferrato against Milan, with the Pisans against Florence, with Perugia against the Pope, with the Visconti of Milan against both Pisa and Florence, then against his original Italian employer, Monferrato, and finally with the Pope against the Visconti. At this point (1375) of Sir John's chequered career, while the Pope was pressing him to attack Florence, the Signory bought him off with a lavish bribe. Then, in 1377, when Salvestro de' Medici was for the second time *gonfalonier* of the city, Hawkwood entered its service.

But in 1363, before Hawkwood's arrival in Pisa, the Florentines won a third victory. Nevertheless, the Englishman's reputation stood so high that the Signory resorted for the second time to the services of Pandolfo Malatesta. He began operations, though with disappointing negligence, in August. For in fact Pandolfo meant to take over, if possible, the lordship of Florence from his present employers. With this purpose he allowed Hawkwood to send him flying back to that city, where he announced that the only hope of its defence against Pisa and the White Company would be to confer absolute authority on himself. The priors saw through his game and sent him back disconsolately to face the enemy in his former capacity, but he did so little thereafter that Hawkwood and his men soon gained the nickname of "lions" from the country people, a reference to the savagery, speed, and indifference to weather conditions shown by the robust islanders from the North Sea. After helping themselves to all the booty they could carry, the "lions" contemptuously turned their backs on the timorously hovering Malatesta and departed, with much satisfaction, to see what they could find to do in the territory of those who had hired them.

Pandolfo Malatesta was dismissed from his command and replaced by his uncle Galeotto, who in July 1364 attacked and defeated Hawkwood near Cascina, only seven miles from Pisa. Peace was then concluded. But the mercenaries on both sides had cost so much that neither city gained substantial advantage from the war. Hawkwood's *Inglesi* (Englishmen)—a name used at this time by North Italian nurses to frighten children—revenged themselves on the Florentines by routing, in 1369, an army sent by the Signory into Lombardy. The object of this expedition from Florence had been to punish the Milanese for helping rebels against Florentine rule in San Miniato, a town about halfway between Florence and Pisa.

In 1370, Salvestro di Alamanno de' Medici was elected *gonfalonier* of Florence. He proceeded to move cautiously into opposition to the leaders of the Guelf faction, the so-called "captains." They had been growing more and more corrupt, tyrannical, and even treasonable in their intrigues with the Papal States, which were then actually aiming at the annexation of their rich and powerful Florentine neighbour. It is likely that Salvestro's influence may have been at work in the Florence's decision to detach Hawkwood, who was in Emilia, from the

Pope's service to their own. But the negotiations proved delicate and took time. It was not until 1377 that the English *condottiere* joined the antipapal league headed by Florence and Milan, who were for once united in their antagonism to Rome.

The "captains," i.e., the *capitani del popolo* originally instituted in the thirteenth century to protect the populace against the nobles, has long ceased to deserve their name. Salvestro's firm stand against their double-dealing and oppression of the people whom they were supposed to defend had rendered him so popular that it was thought certain he would be re-elected *gonfalonier* in 1378. The *capitani,* in order to counteract this probability, resorted to a statute of 1357. This law, originally directed against Ghibellines, provided for sentence without trial of disaffected persons in office. The preliminary actions taken under the measure were called "admonitions," meaning that the individual thus admonished must vacate any public office he happened to hold. The representative of the quarter in which Salvestro lived received such an admonition from the ingenious captains. They hoped that, as a result, Salvestro would be elected to the post thus rendered vacant, for by occupying it he would become ineligible, under existing law, to stand for the *gonfalonier*ship. Salvestro, however, parried this move by contriving to delay choice of a representative from his quarter until after votes for candidates legally qualified to become *gonfalonier* had been counted. Consequently, he was duly elected *gonfalonier*. It was no surprise that, some weeks later, he proposed to the priors that the 1357 Statute of Admonitions should be repealed. But, feeling certain that his suggestion would be turned down from fear of the captains, he had prudently summoned an assembly of the citizens to hear the outcome of his motion. On its rejection, as expected, he told this gathering that he had found it impossible, as *gonfalonier,* to remedy the abuses that were disgracing public life. He added that for this reason he intended to resign. With that abrupt statement he ended his speech and left the Council chamber. In the uproar of amazement and indignation that followed his departure, one of his opponents, Carlo Strozzi, endeavoured to address the meeting. He was not only howled down, he was manhandled by the mob. Terrified and struggling in the grip of several stalwart citizens, Strozzi was emphatically given to understand that the day of the captains was over. One of the friends of the Medici cried, *"Viva il popolo!"* from a window overlooking the *piazza.* The crowd outside the chamber roared back its approval. In a few minutes the shutters came clattering down to close the shop-fronts. Swords were drawn. The mob in the square stampeded to storm the Signory Palace.

Salvestro had meanwhile returned to his colleagues in the building. He met the rush of rampaging revolutionaries with upraised hands.

The priors, he said, had now changed their minds and passed his motion to do away with admonitions. He would therefore remain *gonfalonier*. At once the shouting and the clash of weapons died down. No doubt the whole affair had been pre-arranged, with typical Medicean dexterity, by himself, and approved by the leading families in league with his own. It was good statesmanship, at that place and time, to put an end to insufferable official tyranny by a show of proletarian violence. But in fourteenth-century Florence political passions, once aroused, were slow to cool. On this occasion, Salvestro had miscalculated their strength and durability. On the morning of June 21 the Companies of the Guilds marched into the Piazza della Signoria armed to the teeth, with their banners flying, as if to meet a foreign enemy. Soon the palaces of the Albizzi, Pazzi, Strozzi, and other Guelf adherents of the captains burst into flames. By the evening the houses of the rich were being plundered indiscriminately, together with sundry churches and monasteries. It was all the well-armed guildsmen could do to afford protection, so far as possible, to the property of the Medici and their friends.

Some degree of order was at last restored on July 1 by the appointment of a new Signory. But the poorest of the artisans were not yet satisfied. Led by the *ciompi* (wool-carders) who, although they belonged to the wealthiest of the guilds, that of the cloth manufacturers, were wretchedly paid, they began to lay plans for a more thoroughgoing revolution, one designed to give the masses a decisive share in the government. Wealthy and educated men, the labourers declared, had shamefully betrayed the trust reposed in them by the populace. The honest toilers in the workshops and factories would at least not cheat and bully their fellow citizens.

Salvestro may or may not have been privy to these intentions, but he was being hailed in the streets that summer as the "liberator" of his native community. A later critic of Medicean political methods, Michele Bruto, asserted that the *gonfalonier* of 1378 was "the first of his family to teach his posterity how, by courting the rabble and oppressing noble citizens, the lordship of the Republic could be acquired." There is no evidence, however, of schemes by Salvestro in this direction. Certain informers were found, nonetheless, who swore, under torture by the Signory, that Salvestro de' Medici was responsible for a conspiracy, to be acted on immediately for subversion of the government. The accused man, summoned by the priors to answer this charge, admitted immediately that he had heard vague rumours of such a plot, but asserted that he had considered them mere gossip. Having satisfied the Signory that he was not implicated in any way, Salvestro was acquitted with a mild reprimand for not having reported the "gossip" sooner.

Yet, that very night (July 19), the whole city rose once again in armed revolt. Shrieks and oaths, racing footsteps, and the ring of steel and thundering hoofs resounded in the stifling streets. Fires broke out, and the roar of the flames mingling with the cheers of the populace kept respectable citizens cowering in their beds, behind bolted doors and barricades of furniture. Before dawn, the Signory called out the guild companies in an attempt to intimidate the rebels, but only two of the *arti* appeared, and these, when they found that the rest had refused to intervene, retired to their quarters. Fires sprang up anew, and all the registers and account books of the cloth manufacturers were destroyed. But now there was no looting, for the insurgents, as daylight overtook them, had assumed a self-righteous mood. They were already masters of Florence.

The first act of the revolutionaries was to confer knighthood upon Salvestro, perhaps to his embarrassment, and upon sixty-three leading citizens known to share his view on the sins of the captains. In these circumstances the priors and the *arti* could only side with the *popolo minuto* and grant their petitions. These demands turned out, on the whole, to be surprisingly moderate. The revolutionaries insisted only upon a quarter share in the government, the establishment of some new guilds, and the reinstatement of citizens who had suffered under recent legislation. Their final demand was that the rents of all the shops on the Ponte Vecchio be allotted to Salvestro de' Medici, the "liberator." This last stipulation certainly seems to indicate a closer connection of Salvestro with the revolt that he was willing to confess. But it remains possible that his attitude was simply one of benevolent neutrality. His popularity was secure enough, considering his previous efforts at political reform, to make tangible gratitude to him appear quite reasonable. His already proved caution renders it unlikely that he had assumed leadership of the insurrection before it had succeeded. In any case, no one in the priorate, which was now thoroughly cowed, raised the slightest objection to the rent of six hundred florins per annum from the Ponte Vecchio shops being settled on Salvestro. Whatever the truth of Salvestro's involvement in the early stages of the conspiracy, it is highly probable that he took a decisive hand in subsequent events. After the current priors and *gonfalonier*—Salvestro having only been appointed to that office for the usual short term—had been forced to resign, the gates of the palace were thrown open. A mob charged into the building, headed by a bare-legged wool-carder named Michele Lando. He was carrying an official flag, seized from the house of the executor of justice, whose duty it was, like that of the *capitani,* to ensure obedience to certain laws passed long ago to prevent oppression of the populace by the aristocracy. Michele was then and there declared, by acclamation, "Lord of Florence."

A worse choice might have been made. The wool-carder soon showed his courage, prudence, and broad-mindedness by having a gallows erected in the *piazza* to string up any citizen clearly convicted of theft or arson. Then, according to the chroniclers, he turned his hand to the framing of a new constitution. It is highly unlikely that any artisan in fourteenth-century Europe, however intelligent and well-meaning, could have done any such thing. The author of the constitutional amendments in question must have been at the very least an experienced lawyer with the previous history of the city at his fingertips. The most reasonable conjecture is that Salvestro de' Medici did most of the drafting.

The new system of government would have been considered thoroughly democratic by any trained administrator. But, in the eyes of the *popolo minuto,* it did not yet go far enough. The labourers set up a rival body, again backed by force. Their former idol, Michele Lando, was now suspected of favouring certain of the nobility, and he had to be protected by the sword from these rude competitors. Once more order was restored for a while, and Salvestro and his cousin, Vieri de' Medici, had their knighthoods confirmed. But, to Salvestro's mortification, the generous movement he had so carefully sponsored, if not actually engineered, ended in riot and anarchy. In 1382 the guild companies banished Michele and beheaded or expelled from the city most of his more impetuous followers, leaving the political field to a gradual resurgence of the old Guelf families. Salvestro's experiment in democracy had failed. He was exiled for a time and, on his return, renounced all political ambition. By 1388, he was dead, an honourable man who, both morally and intellectually, appears to have been well in advance of the average politician of his time.

The hour of full Medicean ascendancy had not yet struck. The relatively pacific Vieri, Salvestro's cousin, took command of the family in politics after his more active senior's death, but Vieri had neither the ambition nor the ability to ensure the rise of his house to unqualified eminence. In 1393, for example, he was asked to assume absolute control of a majority of the citizens to act against the Guelf party. It is likely enough that, as Machiavelli long afterwards asserted, he could have acquired a constitutional lordship of the city. But he refused to take so conspicuous a position, devoting himself until his death in 1395 to restraining the schemes of others to destroy the rule of the great families. Yet, the Medici had long been so important a clan in Florence that, according to Filigno di Conte de' Medici, writing in 1373, the phrase, "You are behaving like a Medici" was commonly used in accusations of complacency. He added, probably with some family complacency himself: "We were feared by all. When a citizen deals roughly or insolently with others who get in his way, the usual comment is, 'What would people say if he acted so to a Medici?' "

More solid achievements were soon to come. The branch of the house descended from Salvestro di Averardo de' Medici, ambassador to Venice in 1336 and husband of Lisa Donati, was to supply, in the next generation, a mercantile oligarch whose political skills exceeded even those of Salvestro di Alamanno de' Medici, his uncle.

* * *

In 1393 Maso degli Albizzi, the current *gonfalonier,* withdrew all civic rights from the entire family of the Alberti, at this date close associates of the Medici. This arbitrary act led to a pitched battle in the *piazza* between one group of citizens who shouted "Long live the people and the *parte* Guelfa!" and another who retorted, on behalf of the Medici and the Alberti, "Long live the people and the guilds!" The defeated Medici partisans fled to the Medici Palace, where they called upon Vieri de' Medici to follow in the footsteps of his deceased cousin, Salvestro, and demolish the tyranny of the nobles. But Vieri would consent only to negotiate. His arguments restored order for the time being, but they did not succeed in bringing the Albizzi to reason. Banishment and heavy fines were imposed upon the leading Medici and Alberti, and for some years Maso degli Albizzi remained in practice, although not always in theory or in name, absolute master of Florence. It was not until after his death, in 1417, that the Medici regained effective influence in the city. In the interim, the family did not remain wholly aloof. In 1397, an armed band, despatched by the Medici and other exiles in Bologna, with instructions to cause an insurrection and murder Maso, burst into the *piazza* yelling *"Viva il popolo!"* and "Death to the tyrant!" But the *podestà* and his guards forced the rebels back to the environs of the cathedral and then cut them to pieces. The attempt at revolt seems to have been both ill-organised and premature— or else, as so often happened in Italian political history, the outlaws' plans had been betrayed beforehand to the government. Treachery certainly accounted for the failure of a second enterprise of this kind three years later, which was revealed before it could proceed to action at all. As a result the entire family of the Medici was officially declared "rebellious," together with many members of its adherent clans, such as the Alberti, Adimari, Altoviti, and even the Strozzi—some of the latter house having changed their minds during the past few years.

The Guelf faction had for long comprised numbers of the middle classes as well as of the old aristocracy, but the merchants and artisans of Florence now showed a courage and efficiency by no means always characteristic of members of a despotic government. Their tyranny could be weakened neither by the plague, which returned in 1400 and killed between six hundred and eight hundred citizens every day, nor by the renewed warfare that ravaged Tuscany in 1402; for the death of Gian Galeazzo Visconti and the ruin of the empire he had built up with such infinite care and cruelty, did not bring peace to Italy.

During the next few years, the Medici remained, for the most part, in exile. If the Medici were in enforced and relative quiescence, however, Florence and the rest of Italy were participating in great events. In 1406, Florence, in a complicated series of manoeuvres involving bribery and subtle diplomacy as well as the use of force, subdued Pisa, her ancient and bitter rival, so effectively and finally that that unhappy city lost all significance. Even its famous university was allowed to decay until a more felicitous era, that of Lorenzo de' Medici, "the Magnificent," would call it once more into sprightly existence. In 1417, the "Great Schism," which for forty years had rent Christendom into two and sometimes three mutually hostile parts by setting up Popes and anti-Popes according to the whim of the moment, was resolved at the Council of Constance by the election of Martin V as sole and legitimate Pope. During all of these extraordinary events, the old anti-Medicean despot, Maso degli Albizzi, had been playing a brilliant game for Florence, gaining advantages, territory, concessions, and privileges for the Republic from all and sundry and giving nothing, or as little as possible, in return. It was a game that ceased, however, in 1417, shortly before the election of Pope Martin, when Maso, exhausted by his efforts and weakened by his eighty-four years, succumbed to the plague. The Medici, along with most of Florence, heaved a sigh of relief. The Florentines, while appreciative of the political benefits that had accrued to the city during Maso's reign, had long been restless under the heavy financial burdens that their ruler's quest for glory had imposed upon them, and they had come to consider that the taxes they had to pay were hardly worth the candle of political advantage. The Medici, both those still in exile and those resident in the city, heartily shared these sentiments, and Maso was no sooner decently buried than the family began to exert an influence, more or less secretively, based on the persistently growing wealth and personal popularity of their house. The target of these surreptitious pressures, of course, was the aristocratic Signory, which had succeeded to Maso degli Albizzi's omnipotence.

It is indicative both of the characteristic resilience and the imperturbable discretion of most of the men of this house, and also of the self-confidence of Maso's regime, that Giovanni di Averardo de' Medici had been a prior in the years 1402, 1408, and 1411. Giovanni had thus repeated the achievements of his great-grandfather Averardo, prior in 1309. The grandfather, Salvestro di Averardo, ambassador to Venice in 1336, also had a distinguished career. Little, however, is known of

Giovanni's father, Averardo (commonly called, for some reason that remains obscure, "Bicci"), other than that he had married two aristocratic wives, first a Bonguisi and second a Spini. Giovanni, son of the latter lady, now proceeded to cultivate the friendship of Niccolò da Uzzano, the most influential and respectable member of the government since Maso's death.

Queen Joanna II of Naples was at this time in possession of Rome, in defiance of Martin V, through her *condottiere* Giacomo Sforza, a former peasant with a genius for military command. The homeless Pope was therefore invited by the Signory, early in 1419, to take up his abode for the time being in Florence. Both Giovanni de' Medici and Niccolò da Uzzano wished to please the new Pontiff, who continued to fear trouble from his deposed rival Baldassare Cossa, formerly Pope John XXIII and now a prisoner in Bavaria. The two Florentine statesmen therefore offered to fetch the ex-Pope to their city in order that he might make his formal submission to Martin's papal authority.

Giovanni and Niccolò had each experienced Cossa's charm while that equivocal personage was acting as papal legate at Bologna. The three men had remained on good terms through all the dramatic chances and changes of the past few years. Cossa, they assured Martin, now appeared genuinely repentant. It may really have been so. In any case, Giovanni and Niccolò, as such, could see that it was more important for Florence to earn Martin's gratitude than to censure the misdeeds of an alleged penitent, who might well be, after all, now perfectly sincere in his devotion, tardy as it may have been, to the principles of current Christianity. Martin himself, in his position, could do no less than act in accordance with their wishes. When he declared that he would deal gently with Cossa, the two Florentine patriots, for once able to serve both religion and policy by a single initiative, ransomed the captive for thirty-eight thousand ducats and brought him, not without a certain amount of fear and trembling on his part, into the Pope's presence. The Holy Father in fact proved generous. He received Cossa's abject apologies in a truly Christian spirit of forgiveness. It may even be thought to have gone rather too far when he appointed the delinquent a cardinal. But the fallen adventurer was a broken man, and he died quietly at the end of 1419.

In 1421 Giovanni di Averardo de' Medici, at the age of sixty-one, was elected *gonfalonier*. His former friend Niccolò da Uzzano opposed the election on the ground that no member of so rich and popular a family should be allowed a share in a government that had tried to resist its influence for nearly fifty years and might therefore now be exposed to its vengeance. Referring to the once dangerous career of the "demagogue" Salvestro di Alamanno de' Medici, he insisted that Giovanni would be far more subversive to stable administration, since he was so much cleverer and so much more persistent than his long-dead uncle.

Niccolò's advice was quite reasonable, from the standpoint of ideal Florentine republicanism. But it could not prevail against the opinions of those citizens who respected the candidate's intelligence, enjoyed his genial manners, and perhaps suspected Niccolò himself of undue ambition. In the event, Giovanni's election began a course of Medicean supremacy in the city that lasted, with few and brief interruptions, for rather more than the next three centuries.

He began by heading the peace party, which deplored any steps to suppress the resurgent power of Milan. Filippo Maria Visconti, head of that duchy, had seized Forlì, a town in Romagna and an unofficial dependency of the Republic. The duke had also reconquered Lombardy through his capture of Brescia and had added Genoa to his dominions before the end of the year. Martin V, now back in Rome, had been teased by the Florentine gossips during his stay in the city for being kept out of the Vatican by a troop of Neapolitans. He therefore supported Visconti and so found himself, though for a different reason, on Giovanni's side. Notwithstanding the *gonfalonier's* sentiments, the Signory, enraged by the fate of Forlì, declared war on the Milanese. Giovanni at once loyally accepted his government's decision. He gave his whole attention to the problem of the inevitable discontent that he knew would follow the imposition of extra taxation to meet military expenses. The war lasted for five years, and for the first three it went against Florence. Then Venice came to the rescue, and the tide turned. Filippo Maria was forced to make a humiliating peace in 1427. In that year Giovanni, assisted by his son Cosimo, then aged thirty-eight, introduced, though with the greatest possible discretion, avoiding every sign of personal responsibility, a new system of taxation. It was devised to ensure that demands by the authorities would be distributed according to each citizen's capacity to pay. Liabilities were assessed by a registration of estates determining the wealth of every individual in residence. Hitherto such taxes had involved much hardship for the poorer Florentines, but after the new measure—called a *catasto*—had been passed, the *popolo minuto* grouped themselves solidly behind the Medici.

The lower orders nevertheless deeply resented the renewal of hostilities with Milan in the same year, though this time the outcome was victorious after a few months. The fighting in the two campaigns was estimated to have cost three and a half million florins, and despite the efforts of Giovanni and Cosimo, the city found itself greatly impoverished. In these circumstances, the action of the Medici in themselves paying up the arrears of taxation owed by their friends, in persuading families associated with them also to contribute, and in forcing the nobility to pay its own share, further enhanced Medicean popularity.

If the people were pleased, the *grandi* of the aristocratic faction were infuriated, and these measures were considered by the conservative patriots who had ruled Florence for so long to be nothing but a subtle plan to acquire absolute control of the city. Rinaldo degli Albizzi, son of the despot Maso, did not mention these suspicions in public, but he sternly warned Giovanni de' Medici that the city was heading for a dictatorship of the mob. The latter coolly replied, in effect, that the tyranny of a clique of nobles was equally detestable. Rinaldo said nothing more at this time. He does not seem to have felt much personal animosity towards Giovanni, by that time, at sixty-six, almost a patriarch by the standards of the period, a sort of "grand old man" in Florentine politics, and no doubt more charming than ever in his mellow serenity. But Cosimo, obviously more ambitious than his father, was a different proposition. He had travelled more than Giovanni, was better informed on abstract subjects, and possessed a noble wife, the Countess Bardi. The Albizzi and their friends continued to watch the Medici family closely and took what steps they could to reduce its influence. They were rather disappointed than otherwise when Giovanni firmly refused, like Vieri de' Medici in the previous generation, the request of his party to assume sole charge of the government. If he had been reckless enough to accept, the *grandi* would have had every excuse to dispose of him by violence.

No such crime was necessary. Giovanni di Averardo de' Medici died, from natural causes, on February 20, 1429. He was the first of that famous house who can clearly be recognised representative of the Medici in their peculiar ability to attract certain people with irresistible force and to repel others as decisively. Ardingho and Salvestro di Alamanno seem shadowy by comparison with the calm and courteous old banker-statesman, the very epitome of common sense, who does not appear ever to have made a false step. Yet, even Giovanni's contemporaries and the immediately succeeding generation were divided into opposing camps in their estimates of his character. In later times the contradiction has been still more marked, not only in his case but in those of all his descendants whose activities are recorded. To writers like the English historian William Roscoe (1753–1831) and the Swiss economist Jean Charles Léonard de Sismondi (1773–1842), every Medici was a smooth-faced demon, as Giovanni himself had been to certain chroniclers of his own day. But Cavalcanti and Machiavelli found Giovanni di Averardo angelic in his generosity and impartiality of judgement, as well disposed to the rich as to the poor, tactful in charity, appreciative of the virtues of his political adversaries, and indulgent to their failings. He could not be described, these critics affirmed, as an eloquent speaker in formal debate. But his natural sagacity in dealing with intricate affairs set him apart from the born political intriguers of his time, and he appeared to avoid such men as much as he was able. The public gratitude he gained was never, it seemed even to the usually cynical Machiavelli, of his own seeking.

Other authorities, both of the fifteenth and sixteenth centuries and later, ascribe every administrative step taken by Giovanni to a sedulously concealed design to elevate his family by undermining the liberty of the state. They label his every action as self-advertisement for the same purpose, as though he were a medieval devil trying to win souls in the Florentine microcosm.

It may well be, of course, that Giovanni understood the value of personal popularity in a political career. It is also likely that he tried to show others, including his two sons Cosimo and Lorenzo, how to make themselves agreeable to all and sundry, whatever the matter in dispute. His smiles and the polite gestures, it is true, may well have seemed suspect to citizens already determined to oppose his policy, for there were many contemporary scoundrels about who behaved in the same way. But incontrovertible historical testimony proves that Giovanni di Averardo never obtained power by unconstitutional means, never used his authority to inflame the passionate party prejudices that had been the bane of Florence for centuries, and never diminished or even endangered civic freedom. It is equally certain that he relieved poor men from unjust taxation and regularly obstructed the schemes of those with autocratic ambitions. Among the *grandi* who felt bound to withstand him, his old rival Niccolò da Uzzano went out of his way, after Giovanni's death, to praise him unreservedly. On the whole, then, one may conclude that both the fourteenth-century Salvestro di Alamanno and the fifteenth-century Giovanni di Averardo were outstanding in their respective periods for public spirit, and that their methods of ensuring its effective operation, though they may have departed somewhat from the absolute standard of public morality, were no more reprehensible, and considerably less offensive, than those habitually employed by those charged with the responsibility for public affairs in medieval, as well as in modern, times.

II

COSIMO THE ELDER
(*1429–64*)

Giovanni's elder son Cosimo, forty years old in 1429, had been his father's right hand for many years in the struggle for the political rights of lower- and middle-class citizens under the government of Maso degli Albizzi. Cosimo de' Medici showed in this work much of his parent's common sense, if less of Giovanni's caution and something more of personal ambition. Faction in Florence had, by this time, been reduced to a more or less undisguised struggle between aristocrats and democrats. The latter, however, included, in addition to the Medici, other wealthy mercantile families and certain nobles who had quarrelled with the rest of their caste. This circumstance gave the popular party rather more strength than it could have expected if it had been composed only of artisans and a few liberal-minded bankers. Its leaders, after Giovanni's death, were Cosimo, and a certain headstrong cousin of his named Averardo, the son of Giovanni's brother Francesco, as well as Puccio Pucci, a highly intelligent proletarian. They were opposed by Maso's son Rinaldo degli Albizzi, and Niccolò da Uzzano, also men of contrasting temperament and outlook.

Rinaldo and Niccolò, for instance, disagreed over a proposal by the former to bring the friendly city of Lucca, some fifty miles west of Florence, under Florentine administration. The soberly judicious Niccolò considered the idea not only unjust but dangerous in view of the probable intervention of Milan on behalf of Lucca. But his arguments were discounted, and the war was undertaken. It dragged on without success into the summer of 1430, when, as Niccolò had foreseen, the Duke of Milan, Filippo Maria Visconti, sent his *condottiere* Francesco Sforza to the relief of Lucca. Sforza began the campaign, as mercenaries of the day often did, by coolly accepting a bribe from Florence to withdraw. Eventually, the siege was renewed, but Filippo Maria contrived to keep the Lucchesi supplied with food. The war lasted until May 1433, when Pope Eugenius IV persuaded the combatants to cease hostilities.

The peace treaty brought advantage only to the Venetians, who were formally allied with Florence in their capacity of hereditary enemies of Milan, though they had done very little. Consequently, Rinaldo's whole enterprise proved in the end an expensive failure. Cosimo had supported it, though without much enthusiasm, and attended the conference at Ferrara, which ended the war. It was now obvious that the aristocratic party had lost face. Averardo de' Medici in particular became virulent and positively mendacious in the charges of mismanagement and fraud that he brought against the nobles.

Cosimo sat quietly on the fence through all this, but the *grandi* recognised that he, rather than Averardo—whose reckless bluster was already making him unpopular—was their most dangerous enemy. The elderly and discreet Niccolò da Uzzano, while he lived, prevented violent action against Cosimo. But the old patrician, by far the best of the aristocrats at this period, died in 1432, before the Milanese war ended. His comparatively rash, and certainly ambitious, colleague, Rinaldo, determined to have done once and for all with the equivocal head of the house of Medici. True, Cosimo pretended to take no interest in politics and insisted that he was only a tradesman, but he was too rich and too popular with a majority of the citizens to be allowed a chance of growing more influential in Florence than the professional statesmen. Rinaldo and his closest adherents began to consider how best to be rid of the man.

Meanwhile, in July 1431, a Church council had been convened at Basel in Switzerland to discuss, among other things, the means of tightening ecclesiastical discipline, its relaxation in recent years being thought to be largely responsible for the spread of theological non-conformity. The delegates, however, could agree neither with the Pope nor among themselves. As the wrangling seemed destined to go on forever, the matter of discipline was abandoned in favour of a different project: the settlement of the differences that had divided the Greek and Latin churches for many centuries. The conclusion was ultimately reached that representatives of both confessions should meet at Ferrara, where they sat from January 1438 for a whole year. In January 1439 this council, ostensibly on account of an outbreak of plague, was removed to Florence, with interesting consequences for the Medici family, which will be described in due course. The origins of the council and its sittings at Basel were, however, contemporary with the Milanese war over Lucca and the anti-Medicean activities of Rinaldo degli Albizzi.

In the summer of 1433, at Florence, Rinaldo had ample cause for anxiety. The pro-Medicean opponents of the government had grown very considerably in numbers and audacity during Averardo's fiery attacks upon the oligarchs, but Cosimo saw no point at the time in taking advantage of this situation. He could not yet be sure of the outcome of a revolution by force, though it is highly probable that for both patriotic and commercial reasons he thought it was time to put an end to the military policy, both at home and abroad, of an aggressively aristocratic government. For even if a revolt were successful, it would be unlikely to endure against the enormously enhanced thirst for vengeance in a party dethroned by unconstitutional means. The aristocrats would be able to rely, moreover, on sympathy elsewhere, among nobles in Lombardy and Romagna in the north and in the south at Arezzo, Siena, and Perugia. Cosimo, a merchant in his bones and a politician only in his brain, much preferred the arts of peace to those of war. He meant by the former chiefly financial operations at a distance, and by the latter, in this case, the horrors of street fighting, burning palaces, and the pillage of good marketable property by such ruffians as always come to the front in an armed revolution.

The War Committee, on which Cosimo had served during the hostilities against Lucca, was dissolved in June. He promptly retired to his farm in the Mugello hills north of the city, giving the impression that he meant to devote himself wholly to private business—not a difficult impression to make for a man so naturally aloof and taciturn. He had often enough been heard to say in intimate conversation that he did not trust the "masses," believing that, even when some good resulted from communal action, such action was not undertaken unselfishly or with true courage, but always in pursuit of benefits for the poorest and largest group of citizens or from fear that this group would be still further exploited. This opinion was probably correct enough in its day, though it could be applied equally or nearly as well to parties that should have known better.

As a thoroughly practical politician, Cosimo had moved to the Mugello farm mainly to allow the mild criticisms he had made, as one of the so-called Ten of War Committee, concerning Rinaldo's conduct of the Lucca campaign, to be forgotten. If he had stayed in Florence, his comments would only have sharpened the already dangerously acute accents of the party debate, since he would have been obliged to defend his attitude in the actual presence of the Signory. He certainly foresaw trouble, and he may even have feared personal assault. Messages coming and going between Mugello and the Palazzo Vecchio at least took more time than an appeal to violence in the Council chamber. During his absence, moreover, the situation might well change. If it changed for the worse, he would be nearer the frontier; if it changed for the better, he could quickly gallop to Florence.

Rinaldo, for his part, whether or not he understood Cosimo's motives in retreating from the city, remained nervous. So much angry talk against the government could foreshadow a shift in the elections of the late summer. He meant in any case to prevent, by violence if necessary, any future return to the political arena of the Medici chief, whom he now assumed to be his one serious antagonist. He could only have felt relief, however aggressive his mood, when most of the new priors taking office on September 1 turned out to be in sympathy with his ideas. He was glad also when Bernardo Guadagni, whose arrears of taxes Rinaldo had paid and who could consequently be trusted to promote the latter's interests, was appointed *gonfalonier*. The problem of eliminating Cosimo could now be solved by constitutional means. Rinaldo proceeded to adopt such means at once. The very next day, a messenger from Florence trotted into the forecourt of the Mugello farm. He bore a politely phrased message from the Signory that no patriotic citizen of Florence could ignore. Would the illustrious Ser Cosimo de' Medici be good enough to attend the opening session of a committee that had just been formed to discuss certain important affairs of state arising from the recent election? The matter was considered urgent by the government. Cosimo gave the required assurance, and the messenger departed.

Some close friends who were staying at the farm or in the neighbourhood—members of such families as the Tornabuoni, Cavalcanti, and Strozzi—warned their leader that the Signory's order might be a trap. The *gonfalonier*, they said, and some at least of the priors who had signed the summons, were known to be of Rinaldo's party. Furthermore, that nobleman's recent language in debate had been far from conciliatory, and Cosimo might well be putting his head into the lion's mouth by going into Florence at this stage. In the view of his advisors, his freedom, and possibly his life, would be in danger. Cosimo, they suggested, might easily excuse himself on the grounds of ill-health. Everyone knew he suffered from fierce attacks of gout, especially at this autumnal season of the year, and a local doctor could be bribed to certify him as unfit to travel.

The imperturbable banker's fixed expression of amiability did not alter as he listened, without apparent interest, to his agitated colleagues. Perhaps only the deeply set eyes twinkled a little, and the great hooked nose twitched almost imperceptibly at the corners, as he answered that, having a perfectly clear conscience, he could not see why he should fear to face any investigation of his past conduct, if that was in fact what the new Signory had in mind. To evade the summons would only be playing into the hands of his enemies. He could best prove his innocence of any subversive intention by boldly submitting to an enquiry, if it should come to that. A few plain, resolute statements, which could be supported by evidence, would be enough to confound the most subtle of insinuations. Cosimo concluded his brief observations with a rather broader smile than he had permitted himself so far, and a slow handshake. His colleagues, realising that they had made no impression on him, could only sigh anxiously and shrug their shoulders.

The risk was actually more serious than Cosimo had guessed or had been informed. He was not really a very brave man, nor was he at all eloquent. But at this date he never took a strong line until the last moment, when nothing less than a vigorous counter-attack, preferably with financial weapons, would serve. Accordingly, it was not until September 4 that he rode slowly into the city with a mere handful of friends and attendants, going straight to his town house and thence notifying the Signory of his presence. Three days later, he was called to the *palazzo,* where he found Bernardo Guadagni, the *gonfalonier,* and the eight priors awaiting him. He already knew that, although only two of them, the officers next in seniority to Guadagni, were supporters of his party, the others all owed him money. Friendly greetings were exchanged all round, and the *gonfalonier* then requested Cosimo to wait for him in another room, as he wished to discuss some purely personal affairs with him. Cosimo bowed courteously. So far he was not alarmed. At that moment, however, armed guards entered the Council chamber and Guadagni indicated to the now apprehensive Cosimo that they would escort him to the private apartment mentioned. He was taken to a cell halfway up the tower of the palace and locked in alone. It was a small place, with a tiny window affording a view over the *piazza.*

For the next two days, during which he saw only the gaoler who brought him food, Cosimo watched with great anxiety the comings and goings on the square below the window. On September 9, the great bell of the *palazzo* began to toll. The entrances to the *piazza* were manned by armed sentinels. These preparations, quite familiar to Cosimo, meant that the ancient procedure of a Parlamento—in theory a popular open-air assembly called to approve or repudiate important political measures—was being revived. The Parlamento had long been a farce in practice. Now, as usual, the sentinels prevented anyone who was not already a supporter of the government from entering the square. Few people, in any case, bothered to attend. Most of those who did had been for decades the dregs of the populace, vagrants with no voting rights as householders. They came simply out of curiosity to watch a ceremony of purely antiquarian interest; or else they hoped, usually in vain, to witness some dramatic incident; or perhaps they merely wished to be offered bribes.

Cosimo heard the resonant tones of the Chancellor of the Republic duly addressing the score of loungers in the square. "O people of

Florence! Do ye say that on this day two thirds of you are here assembled?" The ritual response came solemnly back. "We do!" "Are ye then content that a *balia* [a committee] shall be set up to reform your city for the good of its people?" This time the reply fairly thundered. The proletariat was beginning to enjoy itself. "Aye, aye!" The chancellor then read out, one by one, with pauses for the invariable acclamation, the names of the persons proposed as members of the *balia.* This performance took a considerable time, for there were no fewer than two hundred such persons, but every successive item was welcomed with a louder roar of approval. When all the hoarse cheering was over, the audience made a concerted rush for the taverns.

The news of Cosimo's arrest reached the adjoining countryside in a few hours. His brother Lorenzo, his sons Piero and Giovanni, and many of his other relatives and friends at once fled to Venice with all their movable property. Lorenzo, aged twenty-eight, the husband of Ginevra Cavalcanti, was to found the younger branch of the family. Piero, a boy of seventeen, had not yet married the wholly admirable and accomplished Lucrezia Tornabuoni, the future mother of Lorenzo the Magnificent. Giovanni, only nine years old, was to live no more than thirty years longer, dying a year before his father. He had always been Cosimo's favourite, though in fact he was distinguished for little but his good nature and an enormous appetite.

The Contessina de' Bardi, Cosimo's wife, a solid and worthy woman, stayed where she was, assuming quite correctly that the government would not interfere with the domestic arrangements of a housewife who took no interest in her husband's activities outside the dining-room and bed-chamber.

He was, in the second week of September 1433, much perturbed. His prison window only gave him a view of part of the *piazza,* but he could guess that, beyond it, the *balia* would be discussing whether to kill or merely to banish him. The masses of the people, so often the recipients of his charity, would be grumbling over the arrest of their champion, but he knew they were helpless without a highly placed leader. On the other hand, his friends in the Tuscan countryside and abroad might even now be taking military measures to rescue him. The rulers of Venice and Ferrara, he knew, preferred his party to Rinaldo's, if only because they liked him personally. All the same, an armed raid on Florence could well provide an excuse for his own assassination by the government. He hoped that his more impulsive adherents would see this point in time.

On the whole, Cosimo felt that he could only sit still and pray for the best, taking care to eat nothing but bread in case the *balia* should decide to poison him. After a while his chief guard, one Federigo Malvolti, noticed the prisoner's abstemiousness and understood the reason for it. By way of reassuring Cosimo's fears, the good-natured turnkey offered to share his own meals with the prisoner. The captive banker was greatly relieved by the officer's friendly attitude. It proved that poison, at any rate, if not the dagger, was out of the question for the time being. Beginning to recover his old form as a result of this lighter atmosphere, the Medici chief proceeded, in his usual discreet fashion, to hint at the power of money, but Malvolti did not respond to these carefully veiled suggestions. He would only go so far as to invite one of the *gonfalonier's* servants, well known to be good company at supper parties, to join them at table. The inference was obvious. Cosimo was not only to be cheered up, like any condemned prisoner awaiting punishment, but also to be given a line of communication with Bernardo Guadagni. A sum of one thousand florins accordingly found its way into the *gonfalonier's* pocket, and Guadagni, who was not a wealthy man, at last arrived for the visit he had promised just before the captive's arrest. After this conversation, the *gonfalonier's* attitude at the *balia* meetings changed from severity to relative benevolence. Other members of the committee, perhaps also susceptible to bribery by Cosimo's supporters in the city, followed suit. Nevertheless, some of Rinaldo's party remained implacably resolved upon the prisoner's death. They sounded out Malvolti, but he refused either to poison Cosimo himself or to admit assassins to the cell.

Finally, on September 29, sentence was pronounced. The detained man was to be banished to Padua for ten years. His brother, Lorenzo, and other prominent Mediceans were also formally exiled to various cities throughout Italy. Venice was asked to take charge of Lorenzo, and Naples of Averardo. Less dangerous but still distrusted members of the popular party were allowed to stay in Florence, but they were disfranchised.

The verdict might have been worse. Cosimo received the news with his usual tranquil amiability. He declared that he hoped to be of use to his country wherever it might require him to reside. After spending the night of October 2 at Guadagni's quarters in the *palazzo,* he set out the next day, under guard, for the frontiers of the Republic. The guard proved serviceable even before he reached the city gates. The populace did nothing but utter a cheer or two, but Rinaldo's son Ormanno, followed by a dozen armed retainers of the Albizzi, made a determined rush at the escort of the prisoner as it issued from the palace into the *piazza.* For a moment or two pike and sword clashed, and Cosimo trembled. He could read murder in the faces of the assailants. The guard stood firm, however, and the Albizzi withdrew, cursing as they clutched at wounded arms and legs. The official party reached its desination on the Emilian border without further incident.

It had been hoped by Cosimo's opponents that, by thus enforcing his absence from commercial and financial activities in Tuscany, they would ruin him. But all through the long journey north, by way of Bologna and Ferrara, he received assurances of loyalty to his cause. At Padua, only some twenty miles west of Venice, he found that the Venetian government was pressing Florence for his further removal to Venice itself, where his brother Lorenzo was awaiting him. Rinaldo, after some hesitation, granted this request, for he was in no position to resist a reasonable demand from a power so much stronger than his own. In any case, he felt confident that Venice would not try to restore Cosimo to Florence by force, for the Venetians, like Cosimo, had the reputation of being more addicted to devious negotiations than to war. At the game of diplomacy, moreover, the Florentines believed they could at least match their Venetian rivals.

From Venice the distinguished exile wrote to a Tuscan friend: "It will hardly be believed that, having been driven from my house, I should find so much honour." In fact, the Venetians treated Cosimo as though he were a reigning prince, and they assured him they would see to it that his business interests would not suffer from his confinement to their city. Bankers themselves, and not over-scrupulous, they were fascinated by their guest's eminence in that profession, a position apparently that he had reached as much by magnanimity as by ingenuity, and they hoped to profit from his advice.

In Florence, meanwhile, the position of Rinaldo's faction was already deteriorating. The arrest and subsequent expulsion of Cosimo proved from the first less decisive than either leader had expected. The opposition to that measure was widespread and deep, though confined for the time being to classes with little or no power and no able leaders. In these circumstances, Rinaldo, nothing if not energetic, took drastic steps to strengthen his hold on the state. He granted the captain of the people much wider scope for his functions, and he appointed ten citizens whom he considered reliable to control—in the interests of the current government, of course—the drawing of names from the election bags, for his domination of the city depended on the members of the Signory, who were elected every two months.

Despite such measures, Rinaldo continued to feel uneasy. Perhaps he guessed that he had already lost his high stake. Nonetheless, he made one more effort to retrieve the situation. At a secret meeting of the aristocratic party, he proposed an alliance with the whole of the disfranchised nobility, to be followed by a sudden *coup d'état* aimed at overthrowing the system of administration he now believed to be slipping from his grasp. But the majority of his adherents, led by Mariotto Baldovinetti—he who had once approached Malvolti with the suggestion to poison Cosimo—would not agree to Rinaldo's desperate plan. Baldovinetti frankly declared that he preferred the unknown perils of democratic rule to the only too manifest terrors of government by blue-blooded oligarchs. Rinaldo at once accused his colleague of being in Cosimo's pay. The charge may well have been true, but the *grandi* saw clearly enough that the time was not ripe for such action as Rinaldo recommended. Although the Milanese war had just broken out again and the forced public loans required to finance it were increasing the unpopularity of the party in power, its replacement by a clique of aristocrats at this stage could not be expected to mend matters.

Cosimo, in Venice, was maintaining at this time a busy correspondence with his supporters in Florence and elsewhere. Most of them believed that his restoration might lead, if not positively to peace with Milan, at any rate to a relaxation, through his well-known generosity and sympathy with the lower social orders, of the intolerable burden of taxation laid on humble citizens. The two factions struggled on stubbornly for months, the Albizzi men clinging resolutely to their crumbling fortress, while the Medici and their friends tried to force their way into it. At last, nearly a year after Cosimo's arrest, and because of Medicean intrigues as well as the growing decline of their opponents' determination, a *gonfalonier* and Signory almost entirely favourable to the Medici party's interests were elected.

Rinaldo, resistant to the end, called for Parlamento and a *balia* to prevent the newly elected Signory from taking office, as they normally would, three days after the public announcement of their election. But again he was outvoted by his own party, and the new *gonfalonier* and priors duly entered upon their duties, unopposed, on September 1, 1434. Almost their first act was to arrest the outgoing *gonfalonier* for embezzling public funds. Next, on September 26, Rinaldo degli Albizzi, Ridolfo Peruzzi, and Niccolò Barbadori were summoned to defend themselves before the Signory on charges of treason. They responded by marching eight hundred of their armed retainers to the *palazzo*. This menacing attitude terrified the priors, who promised that any reasonable request by Rinaldo would be complied with if he would forthwith dismiss his followers. But Rinaldo refused to discuss terms, and it seemed that the palace would be sacked and its occupants massacred momentarily.

At that moment, however, a message was handed to the enraged nobleman that caused him to hesitate. The despatch bore the seal of Pope Eugenius IV. The Pontiff had recently taken refuge at the monastery of Santa Maria Novella in Florence to escape a riotous council in Rome that was demanding his abdication. He now ordered Rinaldo's immediate presence at the monastery. It was impossible to ignore a command from the Vicar of Christ, and Rinaldo wheeled his horse, gesturing to his little army to stand easy. After he had galloped off, his men gradually dispersed.

The Signory breathed again, ordered the row of its guards outside the *palazzo* to lower their pikes, and unbarred the doors. At the monastery, the interview between the stately Eugenius and the rebellious nobleman lasted a long time, and what actually was said has never been fully revealed. It is certain, however, that the Pope had no wish to find himself involved in another riot, and he may have suspected Rinaldo of Milanese sympathies and realised that papal policy would be better served by seeing Florence tied to Rome by gratitude than in the hands of Filippo Maria Visconti. In any case, when Rinaldo at last left the papal presence he went home and shut himself up in his palace. For the moment he made no further attempt to interfere with the government.

The priors, having ascertained that they had the Pope behind them, regained their courage and sent to Pistoia for mercenaries. On receiving these reinforcements, which arrived on September 28, they ordered tolling of the bell of the Palazzo Vecchio, the recognised signal for a Parlamento. Armed supporters of the Medici poured into the *piazza*, and the time-honoured procedure ensued. The largest *balia* on record, with 359 members, was accorded practically dictatorial powers.

The next day Cosimo's recall was decreed by an overwhelming majority, and Rinaldo and his chief lieutenants were banished. On October 6, Cosimo re-entered Florence. He did not, as was alleged long afterwards, ride in "like a triumphant conqueror," but in his usual unobtrusive fashion.

Cosimo de' Medici, the "father of his country," was now to embark upon three decades of virtually unquestioned supremacy in Florence. The city whose lord he was to become remained, during the first years of Cosimo's sovereignty (from 1429 to 1435) as politically difficult as it had always been. In other respects, however, there had been almost immeasurable progress. The intellectual and artistic movement that was to culminate, in Italy, in the maturity of Raphael and Michelangelo in the first part of the sixteenth century, had begun to develop in the first years of the fifteenth with a widespread revival of interest in the culture of antiquity. This revival had followed, at a distance of half a century, the more specialised researches of Petrarch and Boccaccio into the possibility of a less inhibited, a more naturalistic or "humane" approach to human nature than that currently offered by medieval Christianity. It was a movement that found its first, or at least its most evident, expression in Florence, in the work of the architect Filippo Brunelleschi (1377–1446), whose work clearly showed a blend of the traditional Gothic style with that of the classical and foreshadowed that style that eventually came to be known as "Renaissance." Brunelleschi's most famous work, the dome of the Florentine cathedral Santa Maria del Fiore, was completed during this first period of Cosimo's rule (1434).

The study of the ruins of the temples of the ancient Romans and of their writings on architecture had resulted in a new emphasis on proportion, on balance, and on measurement. A study of antique sculpture had a corresponding effect on the work of the sculptors of Florence. Lorenzo Ghiberti (1379–1455), Donatello (1386–1466), and Luca della Robbia (1400–82) all concentrated on bringing to their work the greatest possible naturalism and vigor in representations of the human body. Under their hands, the almost Byzantine rigidity and monotony that had hitherto been considered appropriate to the depiction of religious subjects gave way now to life-like mobility. Ghiberti's masterpiece, the great bronze doors of the baptistry in Florence, facing the cathedral, were executed according to the rules of perspective and create a vivid illusion of depth, while the figures themselves reflect a careful fidelity to nature. Their beauty, elegance, and delicacy of execution moved even Michelangelo, it is said, to declare that they were "worthy to be placed on the gates of Paradise." Donatello likewise freed his art from the mannerisms of the Gothic style and put into practice what he had learned from the study of antique sculpture. His famous "David" is renowned for its modeling and classical inspiration, and also because it was created to stand in the open air, and not in a niche, as was traditional—thereby taking a large step in liberating the sculptor's art from that of the architect. Della Robbia, though his work does not possess the vigor of that of either Ghiberti or Donatello, achieved enduring fame chiefly through the eight panels he made for the choir loft of the Florentine cathedral, for its figures of dancing and singing youths and maidens are of a beauty so extraordinary as to have pleased every generation since.

The Florentine painters of this period, in their largely instinctive rejection of the unnaturally stiff conventions of ecclesiastical tradition, had no models from the era of antiquity to study. They were forced, therefore, to do what their much-admired predecessors, the artists of the classical period, had done—i.e., to achieve realism by copying as closely as possible the world they saw around them, the trees, flowers, animals, and humans. Giotto had done much the same thing over a century before, but a purely religious sentiment remained paramount in his work. Now, in the frescos of Masaccio (1401–28) and of Uccello (1397–1475), the glories of earth were made to rival those of heaven, and even religious subjects—such as Masaccio's greatest work, "The Tribute Money"—were treated in a manner markedly superior to that achieved by Giotto's innovations. Uccello's "Route of Romano," while it indicates that the artist did not share fully the bold genius of his contemporary, does show that he had successfully worked out one of the important problems indicated in Masaccio's work, that of perspective, of which Uccello made a specialty. Different in spirit was the work of Fra Angelico (1387–1455), who combined the techniques of his contemporaries with the values of the vanishing Middle Ages in the depiction of religious subjects. Although the backgrounds of his pictures are natural and his figures exhibit a well-developed knowledge of the human form—and therefore remind one somewhat of the paintings of Masaccio and his school—in his heart the humble Dominican friar was an artist of the Trecento, the fourteenth century, rather than of the fifteenth. His best work, the "Annunciation"—a fresco executed for the Convent of San Marco in Florence—has an aura of sweetness and piety; the colours are fresh and jewel-like, and the whole gives the impression that the artist took infinite care with it. Indeed, he must have, for according to Vasari "it was Fra Angelico's custom to abstain from retouching or improving a painting once it was finished . . . for he believed, as he said, that such was the will of God. . . . He is said never to have painted a crucifix without tears flowing from his eyes. In the countenances and attitudes of his figures it is not difficult to find proof of his sincerity, his goodness, and his deep devotion to Christ."

Such sentiments, however—and perhaps such goodness, too—were on the wane. By 1434, it must have been clear even to the unpracticed eye that the contribution of Florence to the intellectual life of the age was to be in the direction of sober reflection rather than in that of ecstatic vision. Fortuitously, such was Cosimo de' Medici's own approach to life in general, and to politics in particular as well as to business. Unlike his father, however, he had long taken a considerable interest in matters that had nothing to do with politics or business except, coincidentally, insofar as their development might improve the prospects of both by attracting the respectful attention of other states. The artists whom Cosimo now patronised to an ever-increasing degree all exemplified—even the radiant mystic, Fra Angelico—the realistic spirit coloured the two deepest impulses of Cosimo's being: his steadfast love of Florence, and his genuine Christian faith.

The "father of his country" did not regard himself as an intellectual; nor would he have been justified in doing so. He had, however, an intelligent and abiding interest in art and literature, and this characteristic probably sharpened his equally authentic patriotism. Moreover, he was far too intelligent a man not to have been aware that cultural avocations might serve to refute the allegations of his enemies to the effect that he was merely a businessman, a money-grubber to whom the refinements of statecraft must remain ever an impenetrable mystery.

That his enemies were mistaken in this estimate of his character,

Cosimo took an early opportunity to demonstrate. It was not expected that the Medici would be particularly merciful to their vanquished antagonists. The past history of the city had repeatedly proved the folly of such indulgence, and tradition, if not morality, would have sanctioned a discreet averting of the eyes on the part of the populace while the restored Cosimo disposed permanently of his enemies in the most expeditious and effective way possible. Such was not the way, however, of the head of the Medici, who combined an apparent disinclination to violence with an acute sense of political prudence. If he had proceeded in the expected manner and had his enemies murdered or, on some pretext or other, executed, the people might have asked— and not without good reason—"How are we better off under the government of the Medici party than under that of the Albizzi, *père et fils,* Maso and Rinaldo?" Cosimo's men, therefore, were not allowed to resort to bloodshed; instead, they resorted to the practice of exile, an expedient that was adopted with such assiduity that, before long, Florentine exiles were a familiar feature of most Italian cities. This method of ridding oneself of one's opposition had, in addition to the avoidance of bloodshed, other advantages. Among them was the consideration that a murdered man leaves an estate, and heirs who may legally lay claim to that estate; while, in the case of exile, the victim's fortune and property were automatically confiscated by the state. The members of the anti-Medici faction who were allowed to remain in Florence did not escape with impunity. As time passed, it became clear to them, if not to the people at large, that a well-organised system of financial persecution was under way, a method of retribution in which the Medici bankers undoubtedly played a decisive, though clandestine, part. Such vindictiveness was probably the idea of the relentless demagogue Puccio rather than of the more kindly and cultivated Cosimo, though the latter must necessarily have acquiesced in order for Puccio's methods to be put into effect. He is said, in any case, to have been more than once reminded by the sterner associates of his party that he owed his position to them, rather than the other way around. Nevertheless, certain cynical remarks have been attributed to Cosimo at this time. For instance, he observed once that "a city crushed is better than a city lost," and again that "plenty of citizens can be manufactured with a couple of yards of scarlet cloth"—alluding to the fashion for red cloaks in Florence at this date. Less cynical, but equally realistic, were the aphorisms that "states are not maintained by paternosters" and that "envy is a plant that should not be watered."

Cosimo at forty-four was a lean, olive-skinned man of something over medium height, with largely moulded features that generally bore a dignified, benign expression. Unlike most Florentines, he talked but little. His easygoing manners and the complete absence of snobbery pleased the majority of the citizens, as did his tactful and expert handling of difficult political crises. His obvious sympathy with the turbulent proletariat was less appreciated in administrative circles, but only the most irredeemable aristocrat could ever call him a demagogue, an opportunistic politician. He never held high office, apart from three short terms as *gonfalonier*. He never showed any desire to dominate the city. He seemed, rather, to be ready to retire at the moment that a man of superior capacity should appear to replace him. But no such person appeared at Florence in Cosimo's lifetime.

Nor did Cosimo de' Medici share the usual bloodthirsty vengefulness of Italian statesmen of his day, including such Medici as Averardo. The *pater patriae*, during his 1435 *gonfalonier*ship, for instance, could not bring himself to sanction the execution of a single Florentine citizen. In the case of one prominent Florentine, however, his normal charity and benevolence failed to operate. That citizen, Palla Strozzi, rivalled Cosimo not only in wealth, but also in virtue. In fact, though perhaps not quite so rich as Cosimo, the high-minded chief of the great banking house of Strozzi might well be considered, at sixty-two, his ethical superior. Palla had played no part in the banishment of Cosimo's relatives and friends. He had never wholeheartedly supported Rinaldo. He even had actively promoted the recall of the latter's apparently meek antagonist from Venice. Strozzi had also, in 1396, as an enthusiastic humanist, paid most of the cost of bringing the scholar Manuel Chrysoloras from Constantinople to Florence to teach Greek. Palla had, in fact, done as much as anyone of his generation to lay the foundations of the classical revival in Italy.

The official career of this model aristocrat, as intelligent and industrious as he was physically strong and handsome, had been as exemplary as his private life was blameless. He shared Cosimo's dislike of the limelight, but he did not incur the suspicion—which afterwards fell on Cosimo—that such modesty might be a pretence adopted to mask secret political ambition. Palla Strozzi's whole behaviour, in short, bore a strong resemblance to what appeared to be the Medici leader's. The latter had lent him large sums, for even the huge Strozzi fortune did not suffice to meet the heavy taxes—which he always insisted on paying in full—to which Palla's financial position rendered him liable. Nevertheless, in 1434 Palla Strozzi was exiled, as Cosimo once had been, to Padua for ten years. Cosimo could have spared him this punishment, decreed by the *balia* appointed in November. The blow must have been utterly unexpected. But its victim never breathed a word of complaint, even when the sentence was renewed again and again, till at last he died, at the age of ninety-two, still barred from his native city. The treatment of Strozzi was generally deplored in Florence. But no one dared propose this wholly admirable old gentleman's recall, since it was known that Cosimo was dead set against it. There is no specific evidence of his reason for this uncompromising attitude. One can only surmise that Cosimo desperately feared competition for the favour of the public by so heroic a figure, probably felt to be more of a symbol, at his advanced age, than a boisterous adversary like Rinaldo. The return of the exile with a halo of undeserved martyrdom, of course, would have only aggravated this situation—which was very undesirable from the standpoint of preserving civil peace in the republic, a peace Cosimo no doubt identified with his own uninterrupted control of the administration.

The episode indicates that, whatever the Medici leader's real political attitude may have been at the start of his career, when he regularly proclaimed that he preferred business to politics, at its climax he was already determined to ensure its permanence in his lifetime and perhaps its continuance after his death. As for his motives, his general character hardly supports a theory of selfish ambition. It is likely enough that he loved power as much as any other man in like circumstances. But it is also probable that he believed, from personal experience, that the fate of Florence would be better guided by such an outstanding merchant as himself than by any other available ruler. He knew his countrymen. They were mostly very like himself, hating military despots only slightly less than they hated soft-headed idealists, and Palla Strozzi might, in his view, tend to be of the latter sort. But no one could accuse Cosimo de' Medici of dreams of conquest, either ideological or geographical. He made it clear that, while he lived, he meant to make sure that no such adventures would obstruct the Florentine pursuit of glory, wealth, and power through commerce.

The quest for glory was hardly hindered, during the first two years of Cosimo's ascension to power (1434–36), by the presence in Florence of the refugee Pope, Eugenius IV. The papal presence served not only to reflect a benevolent view of the Medici regime on the part of the spiritual head of Christendom, but also to furnish an active and impressive collaborator in some of Cosimo's plans. In addition to the consecration of the splendid cathedral of Florence in 1436, Eugenius was called upon to reorganise, with almost equal solemnity, several of the religious houses of the city. Among these was the Convent of San Marco, which was entrusted to the Order of St. Dominic. Cosimo's favourite architect and sculptor, Michelozzo di Bartolommeo (1396–1472), who had been with him in Venice in 1433, built the new San Marco edifice, containing a library similar to that which he had designed for the Venetian convent of San Giorgio Maggiore. Cosimo paid for the San Marco construction and supplied most of the manuscripts for its library. He also reserved for himself two cells in the building, which he engaged Fra Angelico to decorate. They were to form the setting for his private meditations and for conversations with the prior and the monks. The anti-Medicean faction in Florence—not a serious feature by this time in the city's political life—of course described these acts as a penance for the sinful methods by which Cosimo had acquired his wealth. But whether twinges of conscience, or mere policy, dictated the many commissions for new ecclesiastical, educational, and charitable establishments that Cosimo bestowed at this period, there were so many of them—ranging from Tuscany to Paris and even to Jerusalem—that the attention of all Italy was drawn to the munificence of a Florentine citizen who remained unadorned by any official title.

In the sphere of practical politics, Cosimo did not venture to change, except in one important respect, the system of government in vogue during the Albizzi regime. The central element of the latter's control had been the recurring scrutiny of the election bags, an operation authorised by a *balia* that derived its powers, which no one dared to question, from the traditional farce of a Parlamento. The only weakness in this arrangement had been shown in the elections of 1434, when the men passed as reliable by Rinaldo's party had suddenly changed their minds and recalled Cosimo. In order to obviate this possibility for the future, the returning Mediceans caused their own *balia,* also appointed by a Parlamento, to set up, as had Rinaldo's, a sub-committee of ten *accoppiatori* (assemblers), to hold office for five years. This body, however, was accorded by Cosimo the privilege of choosing, not by lot, but by hand-picking (*a mano*) the new priors, every two months, from the candidates whose names had been placed in nomination. The intention was to reappoint the *accoppiatori,* at the expiration of their five-year term of office, for another five years. Cosimo's supporters hoped to assume in this way a Signory permanently favourable to the Medici interests.

The device was not so tyrannical as it may seem. The original idea of resorting to chance in the nomination of magistrates had not worked well. Inevitably, a high percentage of incompetent officials had been elected. Moreover, the periodical withdrawal, every two months, of executive officers and the substitution for them of men often inexperienced in the duties required, had for a long time rendered stable government practically impossible. The recognition of this fact eventually caused any party in power to attempt to manipulate the recurrent drawings by lot through a variety of subterfuges. The Medici of Cosimo's day merely perfected a practice that had been current for several decades. Strictly speaking, it was illegal; yet, common sense and civic order both demanded that an arrangement so glaringly ineffective be circumvented, for the intensely conservative bias of the citizens made impossible a radical reform of their ancient laws.

Cosimo took care not to serve among the *accoppiatori* with his friends Neri Capponi, Agnolo Acciaiuoli, and Diotisalvi Neroni. He knew that, although he was now the leader of a victorious party, the other members of it regarded him essentially as their equal in the civic field, and hardly even as the "first among equals." Everywhere in Italy, except in Florence (and to a limited degree in Venice), a single autocrat held sway. The peculiarly rugged independence of mind in Cosimo's compatriots repudiated the slightest outward suggestion of any such dictation by an individual. At the same time, the "father of his country," bearing a title to be regarded, of course, as purely honorific, had no intention of allowing his collaborators to harden into a monolith, as Rinaldo's had hardened, thereby offering a compact target for opposition. The Medici chief kept his party fluid by admitting to its ranks social inferiors whom he regarded as especially able and energetic. This infusion of new blood not only prevented the ossification of a ruling class but also gave employment to the very men who might be expected, if opportunity offered, to oppose the government.

Much of Cosimo's own success, and the general popularity of his family at this time, was based on the favour that the Medici had usually extended, both by their easy accessibility and by their political and social measures, to the masses of the people. This attitude had by now become traditional, and it presented a strong contrast, as a rule, to that of other old banking groups, such as the Bardi, Frescobaldi, Pazzi, Peruzzi, Strozzi, and Tornabuoni. The lower classes still counted as a political force in Florence, though they had long ceased to participate directly, as a representative body, in the government of the city. Their grumbling at oppressive or arrogant behaviour on the part of bureaucrats could easily rise to obstructive or even subversive action. But such murmurs could, in those days, often be hushed by means of a casually genial familiarity with artisans and shop-keepers, and by harmless rhetoric about freedom and justice. Cosimo had no difficulty whatever in fulfilling such requirements, for he was as genial as he was accessible, and, though he was no orator, he had a store of political aphorisms that the people found as satisfactory as the thunders of public oratory. Above all, his sedulous care in preserving the outward structure of the ancient Commune intact, while actually destroying much of the complex internal mechanism that he regarded as an impediment to efficient administration, pleased the majority. In the fifteenth-century Republic of Florence, the hallowed forms of titular authority—the solemn procedures, for instance, in the opening of conciliar assemblies and public works, the reception of foreign rulers, or the visits of its representatives abroad—were sacrosanct in the minds of most of the community.

If it was true, therefore, that Cosimo's wealth had put him where he was, it was his character, his unassuming manner, and his grasp of the volatile temperament of the Florentines that kept him there. Moreover, his native generosity and patriotism—as well as an instinct common to all dictators, disguised or otherwise—caused him to gratify the people of Florence by a show of cultural grandeur in the building of churches, the establishment of monasteries, and the foundation of libraries. Thus the beauty and fame of Florence under Cosimo grew as steadily as its wealth and political stability.

Such was Cosimo de' Medici's position at home. Abroad, where potentates expected to deal with foreign spokesmen on their own hierarchical level, Cosimo did not feel that his policies could be entrusted to committees and embassies, which were constantly subject to changes of personnel. He therefore steered his way, with his own hand, through the perilous shoals and unpredictable gales of the approaches to Milan, Venice, Rome, and Naples. Despatches to other states were written in the name of the Signory of Florence, but they issued from Cosimo's palace in the Via Larga. Even so, there had to be the appearance of frank consultation, and the *gonfalonier* and the priors, who understood something of the world beyond the city walls, generally agreed with his policies. But the numerous councils and committees of government, where domestic concerns loomed larger than the exigencies of diplomacy directed to the rest of Italy, often proved harder to convince. Cosimo could not, however, afford to quarrel seriously with such bodies, and that he never did so is a measure of his mastery of the art of tactful persuasion.

The second sphere in which the great banker took personal charge was, naturally enough, that of finance—which in Florence centered upon the administration of the national debt. Cosimo insisted upon being a permanent member of the board of directors, for public funds were too important a broth, in his view, either to be stirred by too many cooks or to be secretly seasoned by one, as might well be desirable in, for instance, foreign policy. He was perfectly aware that his unconcealed control of the treasury would almost necessarily be the occasion for insinuations of dishonesty. In fact, it soon began to be alleged—not to his face, but by spreading of rumours—that he regularly helped himself to the monetary resources of the Republic. No such accusations were ever made formally, but the whispers served to call Cosimo's attention to the continued existence of an underground resentment of his unique position in the government. His reaction was to redouble his native caution.

Such discretion proved even more necessary in dealing with external affairs. In the peninsula as a whole, the one feature of which everyone could be certain was the territorial ambition of Filippo Maria Visconti, Duke of Milan. Rinaldo's expedient for meeting threats from Lombardy had been an alliance with Venice; Cosimo had good friends in that city and, for the time being, he could see no better plan. But the need to repel the repeated raids of the duke's *condottieri* in Tuscany and in Romagna, where the Papacy could do little to defend this northern province of its dominions, put a permanent strain on both Venetian and Florentine strength. It was highly desirable for both republics— though more so for Florence than for Venice—that the Pope be able to hold Romagna as a buffer state against Milan. At present, however, the liberties of Romagna, and even those of Tuscany itself, were being seriously impaired. And, once the mercenaries had succeeded in establishing themselves in lands administered from Rome, it could only be a question of time before they moved, as Filippo Maria's vanguard, on the Holy City itself, taking in Florence on the way. Pope Eugenius IV had not yet left his quarters in Santa Maria Novella, and there seemed little hope of his regaining the rebellious Vatican or of obtaining reinforcements from the distracted metropolis. Nor could any help be expected from the Kingdom of Naples, where war had broken out between two rival claimants to the throne left vacant by the death of the childless Queen Joanna, in February 1435. A Spaniard, King Alfonso of Aragon, and a Frenchman, the Duke of Anjou, were fighting for the crown.

Cosimo, therefore, in the year 1435, with his back to a crumbling southern wall, had to face an even darker menace from the north. Fortunately, Florence itself seemed prosperous and quiet, despite occasional rumblings below the surface. Everything depended, as usual, upon the availability of plenty of money. In this sphere, which he understood so well, the head of the house of Medici remained uncompromisingly determined that there should be no drain on the finances of the Republic except as authorised by himself. Defence came first. But he could see that the preservation of the city depended to a very large extent upon its prestige.

For several generations now, Florence had not been an object of fear, least of all to the warlike Milanese, on the field of battle. Everyone knew that they preferred the counting-house to the camp. But everyone also knew that their mercantile ramifications extended all over Europe and beyond. Foreigners who drew profit from the ingenious operations of the expert Florentine bankers in their countries would not care to see the offices of the latter given over to the sword. Florence might be a rich prize—but it was also the goose that laid golden eggs. The splendour of the buildings; the jovial confidence of the citizens in their luxurious environment; the absence of embittered social and political intrigue; the presence of great artists and scholars; the endless pageants and entertainments that exceeded even those of Rome in refinement; and last, the continued residence of the majestic Eugenius IV, a Pope still deeply revered, all contributed to a respect not accorded to any other city in Italy, not even to imperial Venice. (The Serene Republic at this date had a bad reputation in the rest of Italy for treachery and arrogance in politics, gross debauchery in its private life, and a cynically oppressive domestic government.)

With Cosimo de' Medici at the helm of government, however, Florence could feel rather more than less secure in a world of fiercer, though less able and less resourceful princes. Cosimo understood the situation far better than those of his contemporaries on whom war and ambition had already conferred an ephemeral glory. He was acutely aware that something would have to be done, and done soon, about Filippo Maria Visconti, if the rule of law, respect for reason and the defence of justice, if gayety and learning and the amenities of social intercourse, were not all to be overwhelmed in an orgy of greed and violence. And in Cosimo's subtle brain a plan took shape. Milan might be dealt with, he knew, in much the same way that competitors had often been dealt with in the Medici banking operations: by a bold, utterly unexpected stroke—by offering to Milan nothing less than an alliance with Florence. But these were public affairs, not those of a private business, and the Florentines were extremely sensitive about maintaining the appearances of democratically consultive government. The essential daring of what he planned to do, therefore, must be disguised as an act of common sense and, even more important, the citizens of Florence must be convinced in the end that the plan had originated with them. Such an accomplishment would require careful preparation, and there was not much time available. Cosimo, therefore, immediately set out to find a suitable starting point for his plan, a starting point of flesh and blood.

Now, it happened that, towards the end of the year 1435, a formidable personage—and one destined to become an intimate friend of Cosimo and greatly to influence his development as a diplomatist— visited Florence. Count Francesco Sforza, then aged thirty-four, had inherited his title from his father, a peasant mercenary named Giacomo, who had been ennobled by Pope Martin V for his military exploits. Francesco, by now the most dreaded *condottiere* of the day, had led the Milanese in the Luccan war, a conflict that he would have won if the Florentines had not prudently bribed him to retire. He had just defeated and killed in Romagna, on behalf of Pope Eugenius, his only serious rival in the free-lance profession of arms, Niccolò Fortebraccio. Niccolò was supposed to be in the service of Milan at the time, but he was actually engaged in carving out principalities for himself, which he might or might not place at the Milanese duke's disposal, depending on the price offered by the latter. Francesco Sforza was himself engaged in the same sort of enterprise. For the moment, the Pope was bidding highest for the prize, and it was to receive the thanks of

Eugenius, and perhaps to see whether the almost equally rich Florentines had any more use for him, that Francesco, whose mother happened to have been born in Florence, rode peacefully into the city.

The victorious *condottiere* and the most powerful citizen in the Republic immediately appreciated each other's talents. It is probable
that, during the few days they were in physical contact, the mercenary
general's conversational account of his roving depredations in Italy
served to alert Cosimo to the importance of a careful and consistent
foreign policy for so considerable a community as Florence. Such a
policy, to be successful, would have to be based on force, not necessarily
aggressive, but recognised abroad as available at need. Sforza's reputation would do the trick. It ought not to be too difficult, now that he and
Cosimo were on such good terms, to detach him from the Milanese
service, like any other *condottiere,* by the offer of a higher salary.

Both Venice and the Pope had been of great assistance to the movement for Cosimo's recall after his exile. Cosimo was therefore maintaining for the moment, out of gratitude to these major pieces on the chessboard of the peninsula, friendly relations with them. Their alliance with
Florence had originally been formed against the ambitions of the
Visconti in Milan, whither Rinaldo degli Albizzi had recently betaken
himself in the hope of persuading Filippo Maria to restore him to
Florence on the tide of war. Indeed, the fiery exile dared to warn
Cosimo, in a contemptuous message, that the "hen" was "sitting." His
supplanter calmly retorted that hens do not hatch if they are away
from home. The marriage had been repeatedly postponed, for Filippo
Maria feared the count's unscrupulous ambition if he once got permanent hold of the girl's person, dowry, and prospects. He would be quite
capable, the duke believed, of turning his father-in-law out of Milan
and himself assuming the ducal title. On the other hand, this argument
ran, while Francesco remained merely an accepted suitor, the menace
of a cancellation of the engagement would keep the *condottiere* loyal
to the plans of his patron.

Sforza therefore pointed out, in correspondence with Cosimo, that he
could only come to the latter's rescue by abandoning all hope of alliance
with the mighty Visconti family. He did not fail to add that in such a
position of solidarity with Milan, he could do far more for Cosimo than
by merely taking for him the small, if commercially prosperous, town
of Lucca. An extraordinarily tortuous series of negotiations began
among Florence, Venice, Francesco Sforza, and Filippo Maria. At
last, the professional soldier brought it to an end with characteristic
bluntness. He refused point-blank to fight against his future father-in-
law. Thus, for the third time in a century, Florence's attempts to seize
Lucca had to be abandoned.

Relations between Cosimo and his former close associates, the Venetians, became increasingly strained. He turned to cultivate the Pope—who, by now, had returned to Rome—and induced the Pontiff in 1438 to remove to Florence the important Church council that was sitting at Ferrara in the attempt to resolve the differences separating Eastern and Western Christianity. An outbreak of plague at Ferrara was announced as the cause of the transfer, but in reality Eugenius had arranged it in consequence of a promise by Cosimo to advance money for the expenses of the Greek delegates to the Council if the Pope would consent to hold it in Florence. Great ecclesiastical councils, of course, always meant greatly increased commercial opportunities for any city extending hospitality to the prelates concerned, with their numerous and wealthy retinues. Cosimo felt that this return from his investment would cover the cost that faced him, now that Sforza would not act, in holding down the aggression of the Duke of Milan.

Accordingly, on January 10, 1439, the Council began moving south, from Ferrara to Florence. The Byzantine Emperor John Palaeologus VII, his patriarch, Joseph, and twenty-two Eastern bishops were carried at the head of the stately procession, followed by hundreds of minor dignitaries and accompanied by a strong military escort. The rear was brought up by crowds of interested persons, including a small army of prostitutes, peddlers, artisans, and others who hoped to cash in on the presence of so many free-spending and excited visitors to the famous Tuscan city.* Venice, of course, got wind of Cosimo's dealings with the Pope. The Serene Republic grumbled to its ambassadors that "the Medici money-grubber," after putting the Holy Father and the Great Council in his pocket and trying to add Lucca to them by violence, would soon be stuffing half Italy into that insatiable receptacle. Cosimo could afford to ignore such childish envy. To jeer back would only be, in one of his favourite phrases, to water the weed of envy.

While Venice fumed and Florence stuffed its coffers with the gold of the conciliar Fathers, Pope Eugenius himself returned in state to the Republic to preside over the council. The months of tedious deliberation in the Church of Santa Maria Novella led, for practical purposes, to very little. An agreement was indeed reached, and the articles of the settlement were read out in Latin by Cardinal Cecarini of Rome and in Greek by Patriarch Bessarion of Constantinople. Then the two distinguished prelates embraced, and Emperor John Palaeologus and all his train knelt and made obeisance to Pope Eugenius, who was then

---

* A few years later this gathering of magnates was commemorated by the painter Benozzo Gozzoli, Fra Angelico's most distinguished pupil, in a series of remarkably beautiful frescos in the Medici Palace. John Palaeologus, the patriarch, and also by artistic licence, the renowned Lorenzo de' Medici, though he was not there at all, not having been born until 1449, have been supposed to figure in these works as the three wise men who visited the infant Jesus.

proclaimed the sole head of a united Christian Church. The arguments of the Fathers, however, the Latin and Greek proclamations, and the prostrations of the Byzantine Emperor, were all in vain. No sooner had Palaeologus returned to Constantinople than the "agreement" was repudiated by the infuriated clergy and people of the Greek Empire, and things returned to their pre-conciliar state.

The Council of Florence may not have succeeded in uniting Christendom, but it did give a distinct impetus to the new humanistic movement, of which Florence now became the center. Greek art and Greek philosophy became, more than ever, the fashion of the moment, and many learned Greeks—attracted equally perhaps by the splendour of Florence and by the haven it offered them from the imminent threat of extinction by the Mohammedans under Sultan Murad II—came to Florence and to all Italy. The Byzantine sage Georgius Gemistus Pletho (c. 1355–1450) settled at Florence in 1439. He is thought to have induced Cosimo to found the famous Platonic Academy in the city, a body that was later to exercise a decisive influence on European thought when Marsilio Ficino and Pico della Mirandola in Italy, and Reuchlin and Melanchthon in Germany, dethroned Aristotle from his place in the schools and substituted in his place the spirit of free enquiry, which eventually led to the Reformation. Thus, a Council originally intended to unite Christianity actually paved the way for its further dismemberment.

Patriarch Bessarion, for his part, prudently stayed on in Italy, union or no union. He was gratefully accorded a cardinalate by Pope Eugenius, and in this capacity, the sage, who lived until 1472, helped to ensure, by both scholarly and diplomatic activities, that the spirit of ancient Greece would never again be forgotten in Italy. His move to Italy and his travels in it amply compensated for the departure of his aged master, Gemistus Pletho, who had so impressed Cosimo by the almost pagan zest of his lectures on the philosophy of Plato.

Cosimo showed a praiseworthy interest in the new learning, and, with his encouragement and example, scholars were regularly treated in Florence with a deference elsewhere only conceded to ruling princes. Leonardo Bruni, for example (1369–1444), Chancellor of the Republic from 1427 until his death, and an extremely haughty and avaricious pedant, was followed by admirers wherever he went. The bookseller Vespasiano da Bisticci once saw the Spanish ambassador kneel in the street to "the best Latinist of the age," as Bruni stalked past in his sweeping red robe without even glancing at the obsequious nobleman from the proudest nation in Europe. Cosimo would hardly have done as much as the Spaniard. At most he would have given the chancellor the wall, stepping into the gutter, as he did for far less notable compatriots.

He was more intimate with the genial book-collector Niccolò de' Niccoli, who never, unlike most bibliophiles, refused to lend a volume to a friend. Niccolò had inherited a fortune at the age of twenty-five. But he had spent it all, mostly on manuscripts and on the new-fangled printed works that now began to come into the market, before he died. Of the eight hundred items in his library, no fewer than two hundred were found by his executors to be out on loan. Handsome and "invariably cheerful," with great charm of manner and always fastidiously dressed, Niccolò passed most of his time in the centre of a group of scholars at Vespasiano's shop or in the Medici Palace. He left his library to Cosimo, who presented the bulk of its contents to the San Marco monastery, only keeping a few of the best manuscripts and books for himself.

Of this group of scholars, Poggio Bracciolini was the oldest. He had been friendly with Cosimo at the Council of Constance in 1415 and lived to become Chancellor of the Republic, under the Medici wing, in 1452, dying in that office seven years later. In the interval, however, Poggio's indefatigable search for ancient manuscripts kept him out of Florence for most of his life.

In the midst of these intellectual preoccupations, Cosimo, and Florence, were recalled to the ruder realities of life by a message from Venice. In 1440, it was Venice's turn to apply to the Tuscan republic for aid against an attack by Filippo Maria on the Venetian possessions of Bergamo and Brescia. Again Count Francesco Sforza became the chief centre of intrigue. Cosimo now made up his mind to act decisively on the plans he had long been considering for a complete reversal of traditional foreign policy.

Ever since the days of the great Matteo Visconti, early fourteenth-century Milan had been regarded as the main threat to the security of the Republic. Only the relatively weak provinces of Romagna and Emilia lay between Milan and Florence, forming a kind of no-man's-land of small states that had not the faintest hope of resisting serious aggression from their much more powerful and united neighbours, if either Lombardy, Venice, or Tuscany should ever feel strong enough to ignore the other two. The sentiments of the Florentines with respect to the Milanese were those of a community of relatively cultivated merchants with regard to feudal militarists who had the advantage of them in physical force and bellicose temper. The contrast of a feeling that may fairly be called democratic in Florence, conspicuously exemplified by the Medici, with the undisguised autocracy of the Visconti, which they never dreamed of modifying, hammered home an utter incompatibility between the two regions that seemed destined to last forever.

Cosimo's sense of realism forced him to conclude that this was an intolerable situation. The accident of his friendship with Francesco Sforza, an unscrupulous cosmopolitan soldier whose abilities off the field as well as on it he had instantly recognised, but who had hitherto been identified mainly with Filippo Maria's ambition, showed him a possible way out. The opposition would come both from Francesco Sforza himself, betrothed to the tyrant's daughter, and from Cosimo's fellow-citizens, with their rooted distrust of what they considered Lombard craft, ferocity, and dictatorial system of government. As for Sforza, he was a man who, without being as subtly realistic as Cosimo, had shown himself in previous negotiations to be able to appreciate the main points of a strategic position if they could be proved by sheer logic. The native Tuscan prejudice against Lombardy might be found more difficult to dissipate. But the Florentine genius for trade had again and again overcome personal distaste for a customer. If Cosimo could persuade his fellow-bankers that it would pay them to shake hands with Milan, at any rate diplomatically, the Republic could be rendered infinitely safer from interference than it was at present.

Venice, preoccupied with the Turkish advance and in any case never interested in domination of the peninsula but only in maintaining a maritime empire based on commerce, could be ignored. Rome and Naples were at the moment helplessly in the grip of contending factions. Only Milan counted. An alliance of Milanese strength with Florentine intelligence could hold at least the North of Italy free from the constant demands of war on the resources of the cities, and leave them in peace to pursue their commercial, cultural, and political ambitions.

It was useless, of course, to approach Duke Filippo Maria Visconti himself with overtures of friendship, for that despot shared with his ancestors a love of conquest that excluded, for practical purposes, anything more than an armed, and temporary, truce with Florence. The duke's ambitions in the North of Italy were well known; indeed, it was rumoured that he envisaged for himself and his descendents nothing less than the crown of all Italy. In the face of such prospects, Cosimo's proposals for a permanent peace in order to allow for economic and cultural development would seem tame indeed. Since the Visconti were hopeless, it remained only to conclude that, if peace between Milan and Florence were to be made possible, the Visconti would have to be disposed of and replaced on the ducal throne by a more reasonable and pacific dynasty. And fortunately, one had not far to look for a man capable of mounting just a throne; for, in Cosimo's view, Count Francesco Sforza was suitable in every way.

Cosimo therefore applied himself immediately to winning over Sforza to his plan, although he was careful not to divulge the entire plan. He played on Sforza's fears, jealousies, and ambitions, knowing that the count himself had, on more than one occasion, cast lustful eyes on the splendour of the ducal crown of Milan, and that Bianca Visconti, Sforza's betrothed, was to be the stepping-stone to that eminence. Cosimo therefore proceeded to prove to Francesco's satisfaction that the Visconti autocrat had not the slightest intention of allowing his sole heir to marry a mere *condottiere,* and one who was the son of a peasant in the bargain. It was the plan of the Visconti, Cosimo demonstrated, instead to use Francesco to establish Milanese domination over the entire peninsula, and then to pension him off, in his old age, with, at best, some musty castle in remote Umbria or in the Marches. In the meantime, Bianca would have been married off to some effete Roman or Neapolitan princeling. If, on the other hand, Sforza were willing to seize the present opportunity, he might, with the backing of Florence and Venice, first drive the Milanese from the territory of the Venetians, and then pursue them into Milan itself, overthrowing the tyrannical Visconti duke and taking the throne for himself. Then marriage to Bianca—of whom Francesco apparently was genuinely fond—would confer at least the appearance of legitimacy on his rule.

Sforza, like Cosimo, was a realist; and, like him, he was rarely troubled by the morality of an act once the possibility of success had been demonstrated logically and convincingly. Cosimo's proposal— which, of course, was to be kept secret from everyone—therefore appealed to him immensely. He consented to take command, under those circumstances, of the combined forces of Florence and Venice, and immediately began to study the terrain of Brescia and Bergamo. Cosimo, in his turn, lost no time in communicating the good news to the Florentine Signory and to Venice, and when the news was announced publicly in those cities there was great rejoicing in the streets. Indeed, Neri Capponi, the Florentine ambassador in Venice, informed Cosimo that the grave senators of Venice had literally "danced with joy" at the news. So moved had they been, in fact, that they agreed to bear two thirds of the expenses of the war, while Florence guaranteed the remaining third.

The arrangement having been made, the money raised, and the men found, Sforza proceeded with alacrity to the task at hand. By the spring of 1440, he had ejected the usurping Milanese, under the command of the Viscontis' *condottiere,* Piccinino, from Bergamo and Brescia. But, at that point, the unexpected occurred. As Sforza's men were holding the mountain pass of San Benedetto, in the south-eastern corner of Lombardy, against Piccinino, the latter managed to break through—by bribing or otherwise suborning a Florentine officer—and headed due south, straight for Florence. Bypassing Bologna, he entered Tuscany east of Pistoia, and by the early summer he had occupied the heights of Fiesole, from which he could see the cathedral dome and the towers of Florence below him in the Arno Valley. The ease of the *condottiere's* progress in so short a time illustrates the military weakness, which Cosimo had deplored, of the loosely held papal dominions in this part of Italy, and the inability of the Republic of Florence to control the northern approaches to the city through Tuscany. The difficulty of communications overland in the fifteenth century has also to be borne in mind. Sforza, moreover, heavily engaged in eastern Lombardy, did not pursue his rival's rapid thrust southwards. Nor had Florence enough strength to risk an engagement north of the urban boundaries, for most of her forces were with Sforza, and what was left sufficed only to man the walls. Moreover, Florence had no means of knowing for certain how things were going in the North, how powerful a force Piccinino had, how fierce his temper might be, or whether Piccinino would judge the rich booty of a sack preferable to a bribe to withdraw.

Cosimo was probably more dismayed by the position than his truculent henchman, Puccio, but both kept up a bold front. When the summons came to surrender or perish, they advised the Signory to send back a sternly contemptuous answer. Such insolence disconcerted Piccinino, who had been given to understand by Rinaldo that insurgents would open the gates as soon as he reached them. The exiles urged him to attack, but his scouts reported that the walls seemed strong and well defended, without a sign of disaffection. The prospect of a prolonged siege did not attract the mercenary, who preferred easier prey. He knew it was to be had in the Casentino, the countryside to the east, whence he received encouraging messages from the most powerful despot in that quarter, the Count of Poppi, a friend of Rinaldo's who bore a grudge against Cosimo for having disallowed the bethrothal of his eldest son Piero to Gualdrada, Poppi's daughter. Piccinino thought he might persuade the Count of Poppi, in these circumstances, to join him in an all-out assault on Florence. Consequently, to the fury, at first, of the impatient Albizzi contingent, he began to retire eastwards.

Some light is thrown on Cosimo's strange mixture of realism and idealism by the preliminaries to this campaign. Sforza, on losing touch with Piccinino, had sent a rider into Florence to say that he would be ready to relieve the city if required. But Cosimo requested the count to stay where he was, strongly entrenched in Lombardy and threatening Milan. The position, the banker-strategist wrote, was too good to give up, and he himself had sufficient troops in Florence, under an able and experienced commander, Neri Capponi, to hold off Piccinino, who would certainly be recalled soon if Francesco continued to press the duke's defence of his capital. This cool view of the situation reflected Cosimo's undeviating eye on the long-term objective of ensuring the future of his republic through alliance with Sforza and, ultimately, with Milan, rather than the immediate danger to his own person and government through the approach of the Albizzi—for he already had information that Rinaldo was in Piccinino's company.

The Medici luck held. Rinaldo in the end grudgingly agreed to apply for Poppi's support. But Piccinino, the mercenary captain, once he had reached the Casentino, seemed to be able to talk to the Albizzi chief's great wrath only of castles in Umbria and even of the lordship of Perugia. Piccinino, accordingly, advancing the pretext that he was running short of provisions, began moving still farther south-east instead of manoeuvring back north-west to Florence with such reinforcements as Poppi could supply.

At that moment Duke Filippo Maria, as Cosimo had foreseen, recalled the *condottiere* to Lombardy. He turned in his tracks. Rinaldo snatched at the chance this second approach offered to the city he coveted. As the army jogged north in order to avoid interception from Arezzo, scouts came galloping back to report that the Florentine garrison had sallied and was encamped, together with a papal contingent, at Anghiari, north-east of Arezzo and close to the Umbrian border. Rinaldo urged a surprise attack. He had information, he said, that Neri Capponi was quarrelling with his second in command, Cosimo's cousin Bernardino de' Medici (1393–1465). The Albizzi chief went on to declare that he knew the forces from Florence to be a hastily assembled lot, at odds with the Pope's men and on the point of mutiny. Piccinino had only to strike hard and fast, and victory would be certain.

The mercenary leader, who stood in some awe of his aristocratic ally and respected his fiery energy, believed there might be something in what Rinaldo proposed. A disunited army camped in the open was a different proposition altogether from a compact, strongly fortified, and well-defended city that was likely to stand a long siege in order to protect its people and its treasury, the wealthiest in all Italy. And it was true that if he could route Capponi and pursue him to the walls, it was likely that either traitors could be found among the terrified citizens who would admit the Milanese, or that the Signory itself, having lost its best men, would then be amenable to terms.

As it turned out, however, Neri Capponi, a member of a family well known for its administrative, political, and even literary ability, and himself a soldier of proved capacity, had been underestimated by Rinaldo's wishful thinking. Capponi may indeed have quarrelled with Bernardino de' Medici. If the latter was a typical representative of his house, he probably knew little and cared less about military affairs, and owed his position simply to his name. In any case, Piccinino's sudden onslaught on June 29, 1440, found the Florentine camp well prepared and full of fight. It also happened that Capponi had at his disposal a minor *condottiere* named Baldaccio, who greatly distin-

guished himself in the ensuing battle, which lasted four hours. It was
largely due to Baldaccio's tactics that the assailants were driven off,
their commander himself narrowly escaping capture. Casualties were
comparatively light on both sides, but this Florentine victory finally
extinguished the hopes of the Albizzi exiles. Rinaldo himself died two
years later. Baldaccio became the hero of the Republic, which accorded him a splendid reception, full of the pageantry in which the
citizens so delighted.

Cosimo's strength, and his own confidence in his position, were
greatly increased by this success. It was a great step forward in his
far-sighted plan to ally Florence, through Sforza, with her hereditary
enemy. When Filippo Maria, after hearing Piccinino's report, put out
peace feelers to both the Venetian Senate and the Florentine Signory,
Medicean influence in both bodies made sure that a united front was
maintained. The duke's tentative suggestions for an armistice were
rejected, and the war lingered on indecisively for some months in both
Lombardy and Tuscany, though without major engagements. This con-
tinuation was not unpopular in Florence, for the Pope was meeting a
good proportion of the cost, and in order to help raise the funds required,
His Holiness sold to the Signory the town of Borgo San Sepolcro, on
the Umbrian border, for a good round sum, thus adding to Florentine
property and revenues.

Cosimo felt his position in the Republic now to be so strong that it
would not be indiscreet to signalise it by moving into the new palace
that Michelozzo had just completed for him in the Via Larga. He went
to live there with his wife, Contessina, and his two sons, Piero and
Giovanni, then aged respectively twenty-four and nineteen. But it was
at about this time that he suffered the first of his family bereavements.
His younger brother Lorenzo, a rather feeble copy of himself, died on
September 23, 1440, aged forty-five. Lorenzo, a conscientious businessman without much interest in politics, had devoted himself almost
entirely to his partnership in the Medici bank. Francesco Filelfo
called him a "cow," as compared with his brother the "fox" and his
cousin Averardo, the "wolf." There may have been a kernel of truth in
these crude metaphors, for Filelfo was no fool, although he habitually
expressed his opinions with a categorical pungency that excluded qualification.

The most powerful of the semi-independent nobles of that region,
Francesco Guidi, Count of Poppi, Rinaldo's friend and Piccinino's
potential ally, had been obliged to make formal submission to the
Republic. But Cosimo decided that he was not to be trusted. His relations with the Albizzi were too close, in view of the Medici, to permit
his continued residence in territory under Medicean jurisdiction. After
Piccinino's retreat to Lombardy, therefore, the count was banished and

his lands were expropriated. The prestige and economic benefits arising from these annexations, and that of San Sepolcro to the south-east, further consolidated Cosimo's steadily growing authority.

The hero of the movement, however, was the Florentine statesman-turned-general, Neri Capponi (whose father had been the conqueror of Pisa). It was under his guidance—with the assistance of the *condottiere,* Baldaccio, rather than that of Bernardino de' Medici—that the Milanese finally had been defeated and the prestigious new territories annexed to the Republic. Cosimo and Capponi had been collaborators in the past in matters diplomatic, and the latter's appointments as ambassador to Venice and then as commander of the Florentine forces are evidence of the respect in which he was generally held. Yet, Cosimo could not bring himself to approve of Neri's new popularity. Such excesses, in his view, might well render the man dangerous. Neri, moreover, in civil politics showed a tendency to obstruct such violent Mediceans as Puccio Pucci and Luca Pitti, the latter a man of decidedly aggressive, if also vain and boastful character, whose wealth had recently brought him to the front in municipal affairs. It was Cosimo's policy, on the contrary, to let these talkative fellows have their heads in certain matters, since they favoured an increase of his own authority— a position that he himself could not assume out of respect for public opinion.

A certain tension, therefore, gradually developed between Cosimo de' Medici and Neri Capponi. The former often snubbed his potential rival by opposing Capponi's suggestions in small matters and encouraging the younger and more reckless Mediceans to criticise such ideas of rather more moment that occasionally emanated from Neri's circle. But the object of these tactics declined to be drawn. Capponi, however, was not a military man for nothing. He remained outwardly as imperturbable as Cosimo himself, and bided his time. It was clear to him that an open breach with his resourceful chief at this stage would ruin the purpose he had in mind—to suppress, before it should be too late, any movement towards personal aggrandisement on the part of Cosimo.

As Cosimo and Neri were jockeying for position in Florence, manoeuvres of another kind were under way in Lombardy, where Francesco Sforza had been forced into a strategic trap, with all of his men, by the Milanese mercenary chief, Piccinino. Before pressing his advantage, however, Piccinino decided to try his hand at a form of diplomatic extortion, for he could not banish from his mind certain visions of castles and coronets. He therefore sent a despatch to the Duke of Milan, informing him that the troops of Florence, Venice, and the Papacy lay in the hollow of his hand, awaiting certain destruction. Whereupon, the wily soldier assured the duke, no one would remain to dispute Milanese supremacy in Tuscany. "All I ask in return," he added, "is your excellent town of Piacenza. You will understand, of course, that should you not see your way to granting me this trifle, then I shall let the rats out of their hole without lifting a finger to stop them."

It was an adroit bit of blackmail, for Piacenza was indeed an "excellent town," being strategically located among Milan, Cremona, and Genoa, for which position it would, in the hands of an ambitious master, control any movement in and out of Lombardy towards the south. But Filippo Maria Visconti was not a man to be cowed by a mere *condottiere*. On the verge of apoplexy at the insolence of his employee, he immediately sent a confidential message—not to Piccinino, but to Sforza, offering generous peace terms and renewing the promise of the fair Bianca's hand.

The result of this move, as Filippo Maria had foreseen, was heartfelt relief in the minds of both Sforza and the allies he commanded. The count could reckon that the prize of Milan was now almost within his grasp. Venice and the Papal States had long been sick of the protracted war, which seemed to lead nowhere. Their treasuries, and that of Florence, were nearly empty. Cosimo, informed of the offer, felt himself to be a step closer to the new alliance with the northern duchy, which he was convinced could be the only guarantee of the Republic's future, and he at once authorised Sforza to represent Florence at the peace conference. It was decided that the lands conquered by the count for Venice, and those acquired by Capponi in the Casentino, should remain the property of the two republics concerned. Francesco was to receive not only Bianca, but also Cremona and the cathedral town of Pontremoli in the extreme north-western corner of Tuscany.

It might have been anticipated that the prospect of the Visconti-Sforza marriage—which actually took place in the following November and which was attended by Cosimo's amiable younger son Giovanni—would create a calmer atmosphere in northern Italy. Cosimo and the count were now thinking and acting almost as one man. Venice had nothing more to complain of. The formerly implacable enemy of both republics appeared finally to have drawn in the horns. But quite apart from the temperamental antipathy between Francesco and Filippo Maria, who could never see eye to eye for very long, unexpected developments in the South soon came to trouble the waters of peace in the North.

The protracted battle for the throne of Naples between Alfonso and Aragon, supported by Milan, and René of Anjou, backed by Florence, had at last come to an end. To the dismay of the Medici and the delight of the Visconti, the Spaniard contender had driven the Frenchman from the country and proclaimed himself undisputed King. Then Alfonso entered into negotiations with the Duke of Milan and with the Pope, Eugenius IV, who, at the time, was still living in Rome. The new King of Naples, not satisfied by that fair kingdom, had cast a greedy eye on certain territories and principalities in the Marches that Eugenius had granted, in payment for military service, to Francesco Sforza. Now Eugenius' great wish was to be able to return to Rome, the only fit place, in his view, for the successor of St. Peter. The Spaniard therefore promised support in this project if the fugitive Holy Father would revoke his gifts to Sforza and transfer them to Naples. This proposal was approved by the Duke of Milan who, although he trusted neither the Pope nor the Neapolitan monarch, trusted Sforza even less.

Cosimo's opinion was not asked, but he soon discovered what was happening and saw that it constituted a threat not only to the rise of the man he privately designated as the warrior-champion of Florence, but also to the prosperity of the Republic itself, which would be caught between the ambitions of Filippo Maria in the North and a possible coalition of Naples and the Vatican in the South. The Florentine ruler therefore humbly requested an interview with Eugenius, and there exerted all his diplomacy in arguing against the project; but the Pope, bent only upon resuming residence in Rome, met all Cosimo's representations with the stern, unyielding, and unresponsive majesty for which he was famous.

Cosimo de' Medici, however, was not a man to be intimidated by the cold eye of spiritual authority. He stated with equal firmness that, if Eugenius insisted on leaving Florence, the forces of the Republic could not protect him against Sforza's opposition. They would be inadequate for such a purpose and, in short, the Pontiff would be lucky not to find himself held for ransom long before he reached Rome. Then the visitor, having reaffirmed, with every sign of obsequious deference, his utter devotion to the person of His Holiness, departed, leaving the Vicar of Christ with the infuriating impression that he was being forcibly detained in Florence.

At this point, Filippo Maria Visconti once more sent Piccinino to deal with Sforza, while Cosimo sent his cousin Bernardino (sometimes called Bernardetto) to the count with urgent instructions to avoid hostilities and to point out to both the Pope and the duke the danger from Alfonso that he, the count, was determined to resist on their behalf. Bernardino twice succeeded in persuading the combatants to agree to an armistice, but twice the peace was broken by Piccinino, with papal support. The key to this absurdly complex situation was, of course, the permanent need felt by every state in Italy to contain territorial expansion of the power of the Holy See, which could only weaken them in their confrontation with other enemies. The Popes, for their part, knew perfectly well that their spiritual supremacy, the only structure that prevented practical anarchy in Europe, depended in the last analysis upon a temporal strength that must be at least worthy of respect and, if possible, formidable.

Bernardino now reported that Eugenius, apparently dissatisfied with Piccinino's lack of success in the field, had just hired, for eighty thousand florins, the mercenary captain Baldaccio, who had practically won the Battle of Anghiari in 1440 for Neri Capponi and who was now in high favour at Florence. He commanded the infantry of the Republic and had remained on terms of intimate friendship with Capponi, whom Cosimo had begun, with some reason, to distrust. Baldaccio, it seemed, was intended by the Pontiff to evict Sforza, once and for all, from the Marches.

On the receipt of this news the Florentine *gonfalonier,* Bartolommeo Orlandini, summoned Baldaccio to his private apartments, undoubtedly with the connivance, if not on the specific instructions, of Cosimo. It was a natural step for the latter to take. He had no interest in multiplying Sforza's difficulties and probably meant to keep Baldaccio in safe custody on some trumped-up charge or other until the Pope and the Visconti could be brought to see reason from the Florentine point of view. But it was unfortunate for both Cosimo and Baldaccio that Orlandini happened to be the *gonfalonier* in office. That gentleman, in 1440, had been in charge of the strong mountain pass at Marradi in the extreme north-east corner of Tuscany when it was assaulted by Piccinino. The place could easily have been defeated, but Orlandini either bribed or, in panic, had ordered his men to retreat and had abandoned the post to the enemy. Baldaccio, never a man to mince his words, had afterwards publicly denounced this desertion in the strongest terms, stigmatising it as an act of cowardly incompetence.

Orlandini, however, much better educated than the soldier in the arts of civil dispute, had somehow or other managed to make up this quarrel outwardly with his accuser. Otherwise, he would not have phrased his invitation to the *palazzo* in such seemingly polite and innocent fashion, merely requesting the popular commander to attend him "under the garb of friendship," to discuss certain military affairs. Baldaccio was seen to enter the palace in his usual bold and confident style, without a sign of uneasiness. Probably he was unaware that his arrangement with Eugenius had already come to the knowledge of the government, since the bargain apparently had been concluded only the day before. Half an hour later, however, people passing under the windows of the *palazzo* were startled to see a corpse hurtle from one of them to the pavement. The body had no sooner been identified as that of Baldaccio when a detachment of the *gonfalonier's* guard marched up and formally beheaded it. The officer in charge explained to the crowd that his action was one of military justice, Baldaccio having been found guilty of disobedience to orders during the Milanese campaign of the previous year.

As no one believed this unlikely tale, the wildest rumours immediately became current. Most people believed, not unreasonably, that the Signory had felt it necessary to get rid of a dangerous enemy (for the news of his proposed employment by the Pope had soon leaked out) of their only martial champion, Count Francesco Sforza. That Cosimo could have been ignorant of such an intention was hardly credited, although he had never yet been known to assassinate rather than bribe an irreconcilable enemy. Some gossips, however, asserted that he wished to humiliate Neri, who happened to be in Venice at the time, in this dramatic and drastic way. Others retorted, with better judgement, that even on this hypothesis the operation had been too fast and furious to be characteristic of so discreet and deliberate a statesman. Then it was remembered that the *gonfalonier* had been openly reprimanded, to say the least, by Baldaccio for an act of weakness or treachery that had nearly resulted in the capture of Florence by Piccinino from the heights of Fiesole. Had Orlandini now used his official authority to take a base revenge for his exposure in a way that was bound to relieve the minds of the Signory, however much they might detest their *gonfalonier's* methods?

When Machiavelli, later in the century, came to consider this still mysterious episode, his naturally cynical disposition inclined him to believe in Cosimo's guilt. Analysing the struggle for power in the city at that time, he found that the steadfast and prudent Neri Capponi, who had proved himself so conspicuously able in both military and political spheres, constituted the only real threat to Medicean domination of Florence. Capponi could certainly count on the sole troops of the Republic worth talking about, those of his colleague Baldaccio. It was out of fear, in Machiavelli's view, that Cosimo kept the ominously popular statesman constantly in office, for while in office he was always within sight. The Medici leader's fear, Machiavelli thought, may have prompted him to arrange the violent removal of the only soldier in the city capable of overthrowing a pro-Medicean government in the name of democratic freedom as represented by Capponi.

This realistic opinion is entitled to respect. But a certain doubt remains, one based upon Cosimo's character, admittedly enigmatic in some ways but clearly the very reverse of bloodthirstiness or of selfish ambition. He more than once remarked, when complimented on his material splendours, his buildings particularly: "Aye, they will outlast us, both those of us alive to-day and our posterity." No would-be dictator, as Machiavelli supposed Cosimo secretly was, could have said such a thing. Cosimo's fundamental cynicism, the kind found in any born financier, matched that of his analyst, which had developed on more abstract grounds. The former did not live to read the latter's *Prince,* but if he had, he would not have approved, it is fairly safe to say, the principle of political assassination therein advocated as necessary in certain circumstances. He would probably have commented, in his wry way, that only those who cannot outwit their adversaries resort to murder.

The whole episode eludes elucidation. Baldaccio's real motives and behaviour may have been more objectionable than they appear on the evidence available. He is unlikely, as a fifteenth-century *condottiere,* to have been over-scrupulous. Yet, he was able to command not only the respect of the honourable Neri Capponi, but also the passionate affection of the kind of woman who does not often marry a coarse mercenary, however successful. Annelena Malatesta, a member of the ruling dynasty of the cathedral town of Fano in the Marches, moved the Signory by her eloquence, after the murder of her husband Baldaccio, to ensure that his possessions would not be confiscated but inherited by the infant son she had borne to him. Unfortunately, the little boy soon died, and the young mother used the legacy to turn her house into a nunnery. On her own death at sixty-four, she bequeathed the care of the institution to Lorenzo de' Medici, the Magnificent.

But whether or not Cosimo de' Medici had been instrumental in contriving the treacherous assassination of a soldier who might have been used by either Eugenius or Capponi, or by both, to check the Medicean policy of retaining Count Sforza in the Marches, the gossip that subsequently went the rounds weakened the popularity of both the rival statesmen, to say nothing of that of the more or less captive Pope. Cosimo increasingly realised that his control of public affairs, such as it was, required constant vigilance to preserve it from erosion. Capponi, for his part, dared not risk further political activity in Florence for the next two years. As for Eugenius, the Florentine children sang ballads in the streets ridiculing his helpless condition and his base and blundering interventions, so recently frustrated, in Florentine external diplomacy. The stately Pontiff needed all his Christian fortitude not to be overcome by fury in these circumstances. As it was, he never forgot, and never forgave, Florence. He became, for the rest of his life, a thorn in Cosimo's side.

Cosimo, meanwhile, in his growing anxiety, proceeded to take certain steps he considered necessary for the security of the Republic. Some of these were unconstitutional, but nonetheless proved beneficial for everyone. Others openly packed key posts with his friends and prevented his enemies from competing for them. No one, of course, expected him or any other powerful citizen to do anything else; still, there was regular, if unsuccessful, opposition to his proposals. Owing to the typical

Florentine resentment of war taxation, the names of many anti-Mediceans were found as candidates for office in the 1444 election bags.
Cosimo put up Puccio Pucci to crush their objections to his plans. The
loyal, daring, and ingenious ex-shopkeeper took drastic measures. He
raked up excuses to deprive some 250 of his chief's critics of their
political rights, and saw to it that 10 of his best men were elected
accoppiatori. They included Alamanno Salviati, Diotisalvi Neroni, and
Tommaso Soderini, all of whom were to become important figures during
the next few years. In 1445, Cosimo marked this crucial period of
his influence by himself accepting the *gonfalonier*ship, a post that he
had only bothered to fill twice before, in 1435 and 1439, and that he
never needed to occupy again.

Throughout this period, from the marriage of Bianca Visconti and
Francesco Sforza in the autumn of 1441 until the death of Filippo
Maria in 1447, underground resistance to the rule of the Medici in
Florence, which began to be noticeable after the rise of Neri Capponi
to political significance and the murder of his friend Baldaccio, came
more and more into the open. Cosimo was in fact tightening his control
of the state in all directions, but especially in the fields of finance and
action abroad, where the fragmentation of public authority so often
leads to confusion. When, for instance, the government refused to in-
demnify him, by a special tax, for thirty thousand florins that he had
advanced to the insatiable Francesco Sforza, Cosimo forced through a
law empowering the national debt commissioners to call in all the
moneys owed to that fund, thereby recovering his own expenditure.

Skillful financial operations had by this time proved to be Cosimo's
most effective weapon against his political antagonists. His treatment
of the *catasto,* the register of landed properties first introduced by his
father Giovanni de' Medici, is another case in point. The system had,
to begin with, worked smoothly in favour of the large majority of
citizens and so increased the popularity of the Medicean party. But
it had always been resented by the wealthy merchants. As Cosimo came
to depend more and more upon men who made money by the same
methods that he himself had used in accumulating his own fortune,
he allowed the adjustment of taxation through the *catasto* virtually to
lapse. Consequently, his present friends were enabled to pile up very
substantial profits. Puccio Pucci, for example, who had started as a
silk-mercer in a small way, made fifty-four thousand florins in seven
years by buying up at a low price claims on the state by citizens in
arrears with their tax payments. If such embarrassed persons were not
Medici men, they could not get their debts promptly honoured by the
government. Such victims of the arbitrary assessments of the *catasto*
on landowners tended to retire from the city itself to their rural
villas, where such taxes were lighter. In this way the Medici decreased

the influence of their opponents. But such practices, as the sixteenth-century historian Guicciardini commented, were at least preferable to the daggers of hired bravos. All the same, some good men were barred from public office by the iron gate of levies on real estate.

The abuse of the *catasto,* coupled with the extravagant subsidies to Count Sforza, finally impaired Cosimo's public image to such an extent that the names of many of his adversaries began to appear in the election bags. Accordingly, when the *balia* that had been appointed on his recall was dismissed on the expiration of its term of office in 1444, he contrived to have a new one nominated, though not, as hitherto, by an assembly of the people. The men in this second *balia* were chosen by the councils he had packed with his own adherents.

Throughout all of this, Cosimo remained intent on his policy of maintaining Sforza's peculiar position in the Marches as an ally of Florence alternately attacked and cajoled by his suspicious father-in-law on the throne of Milan—the Republic's traditional enemy, but a state that Cosimo wished to see dominated by the count one day, so that he and his friend could stand together to resist pressure from the South. But the prosecution of this perfectly justifiable plan cost a great deal of public money, and thus it caused much complaint among those not already committed to support of the Medici. The leader of the latter party consequently resolved to render such opposition powerless by coolly violating the Constitution—a lesser evil, in his view, than losing the great *condottiere's* favour. In any case, he must have reflected, the Parlamento that customarily voted for a *balia* had been a notorious farce for many years now. Packed councils were at least not composed of a rabble of irresponsible loafers, but of serious politicians whose experience and capacity had long since been proved.

Accordingly, the new *balia* and *accoppiatori* suppressed for a while the more or less inarticulate opponents of the government. Yet, the underground resistance to the Medici was still to be feared. When Pope Eugenius left the city in 1443 to replace Florentine with Neapolitan support in his designs to clear Sforza out of the Marches, pious conservatives in the Republic declared that a Pope and a King were not to be sacrificed, by the will of the Medici traders, to a ruthless brigand who stood on the steps of the ducal throne of Milan and who was determined to enslave both Lombardy and Tuscany. The judicious Guicciardini, however, when he came to write his history nearly a century later, saw that Venice, a community of subtle and unscrupulous merchants backed by the most stable government in Europe, consisted a far more dangerous threat to both regions than the life of a single boisterous soldier, uncommonly ambitious and able as he might be.

It may be assumed that this was also Cosimo's opinion. Moreover, his experiences with the Venetians since his exile had not been such as to encourage him to trust them, whereas Count Francesco, besides being personally congenial, would be highly unlikely to desert such a prompt and generous paymaster. All the same, Cosimo would not have been the good banker he was if he did not occasionally warn the *condottiere* that Florentine pockets were not bottomless. His admonition, as so often, took the form of a jest. "You must not eat all the cake yourself," he told his greedy friend, "Leave a few crumbs for me, just to cheer me up a little. You are as bad as my son Giovanni." For Giovanni, whom Cosimo had sent to Sforza's wedding in 1441, and who was now twenty and the Florentine ambassador in Rome, was already famous as an eater of tremendous capacity. In fact, he did little else in Rome.

Nor did he have to. King Alfonso of Naples over-awed the dissidents with his new dignity and restored the Pope, who was now more angry with Florence than with his unruly cardinals and Roman subjects. Eugenius and Alfonso formed an alliance against Sforza and engaged Piccinino to make a supreme bid to dislodge him. The count, taken unawares, got the worst of it for a while. Then the Duke of Milan intervened, having been disquieted by Piccinino's growing prestige. He recalled the latter, informed Francesco that he had done so, and then succeeded in poisoning King Alfonso's mind against the Pontiff. The allies quarrelled, and Alfonso withdrew from the field and signed an armistice. Sforza instantly flung himself on the leaderless papal troops and inflicted a resounding defeat on them. Piccinino, at Milan, realised that he had been made to look a fool and a traitor by the cunning Milanese despot. His career was ruined, for no troops would follow a *condottiere* who had so blithely abandoned to its fate a hitherto victorious expedition. Whether the disgrace killed him or not is uncertain, but he died shortly afterwards, and no other rival appeared to challenge the military glory of Count Francesco Sforza.

Cosimo urged Sforza to strike while the iron was hot and invade the Papal States, promising the support of both Florence and Venice. But Sforza was satisfied for the moment with his possessions in the Marches. He represented to Cosimo that Naples and Rome, whether together or apart, could no longer be considered dangerous to the North. Cosimo bowed to the opinion of the man on the spot and began negotiations with both Alfonso and the Holy Father. A treaty was drawn up at Perugia legalising the status quo.

Another step forward in the realisation of Cosimo's grand design had been taken, and he could now turn with confidence to the arts of peace. In 1444 he founded the first public library in Europe, open to all scholars. At first it was housed in the Medici Palace and contained manuscripts only. Even six years later, when printed books became generally available, it was noted that "those who owned these rare and costly manuscripts of the past, with their beautiful calligraphy, disliked the crude and ugly reproductions thereof by a mechanical process." The Duke of Urbino, Cosimo's contemporary, who followed his example a little later in their field, declined to have any printed book whatever in his new library.

Even now, however, the political situation remained tense in northern Italy. It shifted continually with the subterfuges employed by Filippo Maria and Alfonso, Florence and Venice, to gain petty advantages on the chessboard dominated by the formidable figure of Sforza, who had planted his headquarters at Cremona, a strategic point between Piacenza and Mantua in southern Lombardy. He was officially friendly to Venice and had even been fighting for that city against his father-in-law in Emilia, where the Milanese were beaten at Casalmaggiore in September 1446. Then, in his absence, the Venetians tried unsuccessfully to seize Cremona, which they had always coveted, by a trick. The count was naturally furious, and it required every ounce of Cosimo's diplomatic talents to avoid a disastrous clash.

By this time, a majority of conservative Florentines, led by Neri Capponi, who was now back in politics, were growing weary of Sforza, whom they regarded as an ambitious climber responsible for all the wars and crippling taxation from which they had suffered in recent years. This party stood uncompromisingly for the traditional alliance with Venice against all comers. The events of 1446 seemed to justify their policy. This year was marked by a sudden, unexpected coalition among Duke Filippo Maria, Pope Eugenius, and the King of Naples, which culminated in the Battle of Casalmaggiore, won by Venice, Florence, Genoa, and Bologna under Sforza against the duke and his allies. Cosimo then again managed to separate Alfonso, the easiest to deal with, from the other two members of the hostile block, and so enforced an uneasy peace.

The five years that followed the murder of Baldaccio in 1441, of which crime many Florentines still considered the *pater patriae* guilty, had been the most difficult experienced by Cosimo since his return from exile in 1434. His initial brilliant inspiration to substitute Milan for Venice as an ally against southern aggression had been obliged to meet two obstacles that would have been insuperable by a man of less prodigious gifts as a diplomat. In the first place, most Florentines had detested the Milanese and admired the Venetians for centuries, chiefly because the former represented a military autocracy and the latter a mercantile republic. Second, the contemporary Duke of Milan, Filippo Maria Visconti, happened to be one of the most unsavory despots, utterly unscrupulous in his inordinate ambition and diabolically ingenious in his methods of advancing it, that even the Lombards had ever produced.

It was most fortunate for Cosimo, in these circumstances, that he and Sforza had struck up such a close friendship. They admired and respected each other. Cosimo recognised at once his friend's military genius, a quality entirely absent in himself, yet always an essential prop for any political scheme. The Medici leader also saw that the count was by no means simply a rough soldier. He could be a practical realist off the field as well as on it, and this was naturally the basis of the sympathetic Cosimo's high estimate of him. Sforza understood, too, as he was to prove at a later date, the value of such elements in the maintenance of power as good manners, accessibility, and a care for the promotion of more civilised preoccupations than fraud and slaughter. Neither he nor Cosimo could be described as intellectuals. But they both enjoyed listening to the talk of intellectuals, and they both could see that, once some sort of tolerable order was restored to society, artists and philosophers might be of the greatest importance in preserving it. Sforza, for his part, was lost in wonder at the Florentine's typical banker's patience and subtlety. He seemed to be able to retrieve any situation, however desperate, by means that would have occurred to no one else. In short, it is probable that each guessed correctly that neither of them could have succeeded as they did without the other, resolute and able as they both were. It was an ideal partnership, up to a point. But it needed luck, which eluded them for a long time. In 1447, however, two strokes of good fortune, which neither of them had worked for, changed the situation radically to their advantage.

* * *

On February 23, 1447, Pope Eugenius IV, the implacable enemy of Florence ever since the murder of Baldaccio in 1441, died. His death came at a time when the Medici-Sforza-Venice coalition had just defeated that of the Pope and Naples. It was therefore unlikely that the Pontiff, if he had lived, would have resumed the offensive. The danger from that quarter was over for the time being. All the same, the elimination of this particular Holy Father must have brought a certain relief to the minds of Cosimo and his friends, for Eugenius had unquestionably been a power to be reckoned with in his lifetime. But the relaxation of the Medici leader's anxieties in this direction turned to positive pleasure when he heard the news of the succession to the Chair of St. Peter of the new Pontiff, Nicholas V. Nicholas was a Tuscan by birth, having been born in 1398 at Sarzana in the extreme north-west of the region. He was therefore some ten years younger than Cosimo himself. He knew Florence well, having worked there as tutor to the sons of Rinaldo degli Albizzi and Palla Strozzi. He was also an eminent humanist, scholar, and bibliophile, had assisted Cosimo in the formation of his library at San Marco, drawn up its catalogue, and founded the Vatican Library in imitation of it. Nicholas, a lively, eager intellectual, quite different in manner and presence from his predecessor, had made himself popular in bookish circles at Florence and already owed Cosimo a good deal of money. Great things were accordingly expected of him by the Medicean party.

An even more important weakening of Florence's enemies occurred in August, when Duke Filippo Maria died childless, apart from Bianca, and unregretted even by his own subjects. The ruthless and shifty character of the duke had bedevilled Italian politics for thirty-five years. Feared for his cruelty and ridiculed for his physical ugliness, about which he was extremely sensitive, Filippo Maria had nevertheless displayed great political talent, perhaps second only to Cosimo's at that time and accordingly constituted the most formidable opponent of that statesman's plan to secure the Duchy as an ally of Florence. The despot's death seemed, therefore, finally to clear the way to the realisation, at long last, of this project. But no sooner had the duke been interred than complications arose. Claims to the succession were staked by Alfonso of Naples (whom the duke himself had named as his heir, in preference to Count Francesco Sforza, whom he had recently come to detest); by the Duke of Orléans (a brother of René of Anjou, Alfonso's defeated rival for the Neapolitan throne); by the Duke of Savoy; by the German Emperor; and, most seriously of all, by the Venetians. In these circumstances, the Milanese, who did not care for any of these foreign candidates, declared their city a republic and sent for Sforza to defend it. The redoubtable *condottiere,* heartily encouraged by Cosimo, at once dashed North and inflicted a crushing defeat on an invading Venetian force.

Venice called for aid from her still official ally, Florence. Cosimo accorded it, but continued in secret to back his old friend, Sforza. At the same time he sounded out the French about cover for his rear against Naples, and struggled to bring about an understanding between Sforza and Venice. He wanted to make sure that the count would be freed from menace in that direction, so as to be able to deal with possible opposition from the republicans in Milan itself. The Venetians saw the point, but naturally from their own platform, and they hoped that the equivocal *condottiere,* who was not everybody's favourite, would be firmly resisted by the new republicans in Milan.

Cosimo, while continuing to assure Francesco, in the most absolute secrecy, of his unwavering support in the aim agreed by the two friends, that of securing the Duchy for the soldier, managed to persuade the Venetians that their best policy would be to allow Sforza to dash himself to pieces against the rocks of Milanese republicanism. Hostilities therefore ceased for the time being. The Duke of Orléans did nothing but make vague promises to restrain Alfonso. But Nicholas V could be relied on for that purpose. The bright-eyed, excitable little man had the virtue, rare in a scholar, of resolution in enforcing his authority without malice or snappishness. He would brook no contradiction and was capable of terrorising his servants. But his wit, like his erudition, remained highly polished, and he had yet to meet his match in argument.

The Medici statesman's long view and cool head correctly foresaw that for the next few years, whatever happened, he would have nothing to fear from Rome. He was, in fact, shortly to become the papal banker, to his very great material profit. Meanwhile, his policy in keeping up the Sforza connection also paid off, despite great difficulties with the Signory, which did not like Sforza and insisted in fulfilling its treaty with Venice to the letter. Nicodemo da Pontremoli, the count's agent in Florence, wrote to his master on June 18, 1449: "I cannot say that people here are troubling themselves much about your problems. Cosimo alone is indefatigable in urging the justice of your case. But the greater zeal he shows, the more sluggish his audience becomes." In fact that stauch republican, Neri Capponi, stood inflexibly for a united front of the three existing republics against the upstart mercenary captain, who showed, according to Neri, every sign of being as intolerable, because intolerant, an autocrat as the late Filippo Maria himself.

The Medici chief, coming out into the open at last, retorted in and out of season that it was Venice, not the *condottiere,* that was the dangerous, selfish imperialist, and that Sforza was the only man who could counter the Serene Republic's arrogant ambition. Cosimo contrived eventually to secure a conference with the count's representatives at Reggio in Emilia. But when the Florentine ambassadors arrived in that city early in 1450, they found that Francesco Sforza had already been proclaimed Duke of Milan. He had characteristically broken the peace terms, marched on Milan, side-stepped the Venetians when they tried to intercept him, and held them off while he laid formal siege to the city. He discovered that, as he had shrewdly guessed and as Cosimo, perhaps, had hardly expected, he had plenty of friends within the walls, and these allowed him to take over without much trouble.

Cosimo was naturally delighted with this resounding triumph of the plan he had so patiently and ingeniously worked for ever since 1435. Though the very opposite of a fiercely truculent prince, he had his own private doubts about the efficacy of republics. In his view, they had to be directed by an exceptional leader, of equal resolution and discretion, to succeed. He could congratulate himself on the possession of both these qualities, in addition to far-sighted political vision, now proved in their practical results. A great change in the Italian balance of power had taken place, substituting a clearly recognisable order for the chaos thrown up by the mutual jealousies, suspicions, and selfish greed to rival dynasties. He knew that he himself had been mainly responsible for the establishment of this equilibrium. Without the Medici money, all Sforza's diplomatic acumen and military prowess could never have solved so intricate a problem as the eradication of disturbing factors in the political structure of northern Italy. Neri Capponi would have preferred to see the Serene Republic of Venice outwit the openly despotic Sforza in the struggle for Milan; but in Cosimo's mind practical consideration of expediency outweighed political principle in this case. He knew as well as anyone that the *condottiere's* loyalty followed the highest bidder as unswervingly as a bloodhound the scent of a quarry. Well, he was able and willing, for the sake of Florence, to make the highest bid. The Venetians theoretically might be able to compete with it, but in Cosimo's view they were too crooked ever to follow a straight line, in political competition as in commerce. They would never keep faith with Sforza or anyone else—and the count could be trusted to react violently if they tried to deceive him.

Now the only dangerous enemy to the liberties of Florence, Cosimo believed, was Naples; for he now had good friends both in the Duchy of Milan and in Rome. As for Venice, that city was simply not interested in Neapolitans at present. The lagoon republic would only seek an alliance with so remote a kingdom if the Doge and his advisors, as a permanent corporation not dependent on the genius or imbecility of one man and as persistent commercial rivals of the Medici network, ever decided to strike seriously at the other two powers of the North, Milan and Florence. In such circumstances, Cosimo calculated, the latter states, with the growing strength of France—full of respected Florentine merchants—behind them, could well hope to tip the scale against the haughty and devious island-dwellers and such excitable and restless auxiliaries as the Neapolitans, governed by foreign kings, in the South.

He expected this balance, which he had built up by sheer statesman-like foresight, iron will, and unremitting uphill work, to become traditional and permanent. Hardly anyone but himself at first wanted it. Most Florentines liked the Venetians, their old allies, simply for being republicans. Support of Sforza had cost astronomical sums. Nearly everyone in Florence feared him as an obvious future tyrant. But Cosimo had got his way in the end, probably at the risk of his life.

His luck held out. When Venice called furiously upon the Signory to aid in the expulsion from Milan of the "vile usurper," Cosimo de' Medici, still officially a plain citizen, was asked to compose a suitable reply to the raging ambassadors, who had every legal, political, and ordinary human consideration on their side. It was on this occasion that he was addressed by the deputation of his fellow Florentines as "head" (*capo*) of the Republic. Cosimo was neither a good writer nor a good speaker, though he could show an amusingly acid wit in casual conversation. It is likely that he got a committee of his ablest intellectual friends to draft so important a speech for him. They probably also rehearsed him in its delivery; for like many men accustomed to deep reflection on controversial subjects requiring immediate practical decision one way or another, Cosimo spoke shyly and hesitantly in public, capable as he was of ruthless and instant action in directives passed on by a secretary.

In any case, he managed to perform his difficult task, to the satisfaction, at least, of those who shared his views. An almost equally arduous step that he also took with success was to form a war committee, which included Neri Capponi, to support the new regime in Milan.

King Charles VII of France—who had in his youth been helped to his crown by Joan of Arc—had already promised Cosimo his support if either Florence or Milan should be attacked from any quarter before 1453, by which date the Florentine "head of the state" considered that his position would be impregnable. The French interest was largely due to the increasing Florentine business undertakings in that country, which by then exceeded those of Venice in influence. Trade, once more, had paid off.

In another direction, too, Cosimo and his friend, Pope Nicholas V, had attracted the Holy Roman Emperor, Frederick III, to their side. Nicholas crowned Frederick in Rome on March 19, 1452. The Habsburg monarch, on his way to the Vatican, was given a truly imperial welcome in Florence. Cosimo lodged him at the convent of Santa Maria Novella, to the serious depletion of the city treasury, for Frederick had fifteen hundred knights with him who spent little or nothing out of their own pockets, while even he himself appears to have arrived almost penniless. But while the Medici investment on this occasion was a loss in purely financial terms, in the political sphere the visit of the German Emperor had a calming effect on the recent explosive situation between the Florence-Milan axis on the one side and that of Venice-Naples on the other. It was by no means the first time that such ceremonial advents in Italy of the titular sovereigns of Europe had put everyone in a good temper.

But no sooner had Frederick III departed, richer than he had come and with a Portuguese wife into the bargain, to face seething indignation in the rebellious German Church, than the Neapolitans suddenly burst into Tuscany, plundering and ravaging. Cosimo had in earlier years shown signs of panic on such occasions, his mercantile conscience outraged by so much senseless destruction. But now he kept his head admirably. When an excited citizen rushed up to him to report that a couple of villages had been seized by the invaders, he raised his thick eyebrows. "You don't say so," he remarked coolly. "Where has René got to, then?" the reference was to René of Anjou, the discomfited claimant to the throne of Naples, who was interested in fighting any official representatives of that kingdom. The Duke of Anjou in fact soon appeared, and he drove his erstwhile competitor's forces out of Tuscany, but the desultory campaigns promoted by Venice and Naples against Florence and Milan dragged on for another two years. Then suddenly, in 1453, the year that Cosimo had predicted to Charles VII as that of decision, the dramatic fall of Byzantium to the Sultan of Turkey, Mohammed II, frightened not only the combatants in Italy but all Europe. The Eastern Empire, the ecclesiastical deputies of which had seemed ready to accept union with the Western Empire only a few years before, when they had done homage to Eugenius IV at Florence, abruptly vanished.

Many contemporary observers believed that the Western Empire must soon follow. They did not suppose that it would necessarily be obliterated by oriental fanatics; but its fragmentation into rising nation-states beyond the Italian peninsula appeared probable. France and Spain, newly self-conscious countries that closed the Italian horizon to the west, seemed to be preparing to take over the last remaining territory of the old Roman dominions.

Nicholas V peremptorily commanded all Christians, including Charles VII, who had been too busy with revolts at home to come to Florence's assistance in 1452, to cease squabbling and form a united front to crusade against the insolent Muslims. Much talk and many processions, especially in Florence, ensued, but in the end no active measures whatever were taken to expel the Turks. Venice, however, the Italian state in most immediate peril of a heathen invasion by land from the south-east, decided to call off an Italian war that showed no sign of concluding in either victory or defeat. It was merely preventing due attention to the menace of Islam, Nicholas never tired of insisting. The Venetians accordingly opened negotiations for a peace settlement with Milan, their most formidable opponent. A treaty, with the blessing of the Pope, was signed at Lodi in south-west Lombardy on April 11, 1454. Naples and Florence signified their adhesion to the terms, which almost amounted, under the shadow of the Turkish advance into Europe, to the establishment of an Italian federation. The signatories eventually comprised representatives of practically every state in the peninsula, large and small. They swore to stand together against any member community guilty of unmistakable aggression.

The Peace of Lodi did not, of course, rid politics of its internecine rivalries; but it did improve, for the next ten years, the aspect of that troubled scene in Italy, at any rate so far as Florence and the Medici were concerned. The views that had been maturing in Cosimo's mind for nearly a generation, he now saw incorporated into an international treaty. He was sure now that an essentially commercial re-public like his own could not afford attacks on others by force of arms. Cosimo was perhaps the first important Christian statesman to believe that a proudly civilised community could have no interest in territorial expansion. This principle henceforth guided, with very few hesitations, the policy of Florence so long as it lay under the rule of the senior branch of the Medici.

During the past five years, Cosimo's private life in everything except the health of the family, which apart from Contessina's proved uni-formly bad, had been going on as well as might be expected. Piero, his gouty eldest son, already half an invalid, had married in 1443 a mentally, if not quite physically, superb specimen of womanhood. The lady, Lucrezia Tornabuoni, was destined to play a part in some of the most splendid episodes of Florentine history. Women in Italy at this date acted mostly behind the scenes; so did Lucrezia. The age of the great courtesans had not yet arrived, and in any case she was not cut out either by looks or temperament to be one of them. Her in-fluence remained quiet, but strong and continuous. It was always exercised for the good of her native city, in which the Tornabuoni, one of its most powerful mercantile families, had regularly supported the Medici. In 1449 she bore Piero's first son, Lorenzo. He became not only the most eminent of all the men of his house, but also one whose name will never be forgotten when the capacities of human character for arousing general admiration are discussed.

The marriage of Piero to Lucrezia Tornabuoni was followed in 1453 by that of the stout and carelessly jovial Giovanni—both his father's and his mother's favourite—to Ginevra degli Albizzi. The couple had one son, named Cosimo, or Cosimino, after his grandfather, but the child only lived five years. A characteristic story of the elder Cosimo, related by a contemporary chronicler, throws an agreeable light on Giovanni's sensibility to phenomena other than those of the banqueting table. The young man was planning a villa near Fiesole. He showed his father the chosen site, on a barren, precipitous hillside. "You won't be able to grow anything there," observed the practical-minded old merchant. "Oh, but look at the view," cried his son ecstatically. "Don't you think it's marvelous?" "I know a better one," retorted Cosimo in his usual dry tones. "Impossible! Where?" "Why at Cafag-giuolo, from our villa there." "But that's all flat!" "Yes, but everything in sight belongs to our family. That's more than one can say of this place."

*   *   *

It was at this time, and in the midst of these domestic considerations, that it occurred to Cosimo that perhaps the time had come for him to relinquish the reins of power to other men. He was now an old man according to the standards of that day, and crippled by that occupational disease of princes, the gout. It seemed that the moment was propitious for such a move. Italy at that time was enjoying a respite from war. The crusade against the Turks, which had been the subject of general and enthusiastic lip-service shortly before, had been recognised all along as an impossible dream, and now it was allowed to die of its own inert weight. More immediately, the failure of either Florence and Milan, on the one hand, or of Venice on the other, to achieve a definite military advantage in their confrontation, had enabled the pacific Nicholas V to mediate successfully between the two sides in 1454.

It was also at this moment, it seems, that some of Cosimo's own adherents, released from the anxieties of a foreign conflict, suspected their leader of coveting the formal "lordship of Florence." The death of Neri Capponi in 1457 offered to these disenchanted partisans an opportunity to put Cosimo's ambition to the test. Now that the most formidable challenge to Medicean domination had passed from the scene, they proposed a series of enactments designed to abolish the supremacy of the head of the state. When Cosimo, however, with his customary fondness for self-effacement—and probably with one eye already on the pleasures of retirement into private life—let it be known that he would enthusiastically support such measures, they were quietly dropped. For Cosimo knew his Florentines. So long as they were allowed to argue freely and violently, and not compelled to go down on their knees and recognise one of themselves as prince, they would put up with anything. The Medici chief had owed his long record of success to his ability to say very little while doing very much, and by being ready always to listen for hours on end to anyone, foolish or wise, who took it into his head to offer advice. Far from being a dazzling figure, he had never, unlike most Italians of his time, struck a theatrical pose in his life. But he had done wonders, though no one but his closest associates realised the fact. He had found Florence a muddle of hotheads, and he was leaving it a pattern of civilised behaviour, as that term was understood in the middle of the fifteenth century.

The great object on which he had set his heart had been achieved. The Republic of Florence, now backed by the two great autocracies of the North, Milan and France, need fear no one and could get on with the work that best suited its citizens, the weaving of a strong texture of international finance and trade to support a world in which the pen, whether in counting-houses and council-chambers or in the study and the studio, would be mightier than the sword.

Or so at least Cosimo, now an old man of sixty-six, may have felt as he turned to leave the limelight, which he had not always been able to avoid as much as he might have wished, to others.

The most annoying of these others turned out to be Luca Pitti, *gonfalonier* for the third time, in 1458. In virtue of that office, he was therefore calmly charged by Cosimo to revive the Parlamento, and thus to incur the odium this antiquated and rather disgraceful mockery of rule by majority invariably aroused among the more conscientious Florentines. For Cosimo did not care for Luca and considered that it would benefit the city to give him enough rope to hang himself.

The Pitti family had been eminent—in fact, almost world-famous— though no more so than the Medici, in the early fourteenth century. The Pitti bankers and money-changers, like other members of similar houses, had helped foreign potentates to gain or hold their crowns, and generally they acted as the Rothschilds of their day.

Luca, as *gonfalonier* also in the previous year, 1457, had kept up this reputation with a great deal of swagger and personal display. He possessed, however, distinctly less intelligence than most of his relatives and, perhaps for that very reason, more audacity. His colorful exploits culminated in the forcible imposition, after the second of the two Parlamenti he held in 1458, of his own committee of tyranny. It was appointed by the time-honoured methods of a *balia,* but on this occasion one that could only be regarded as a rigged election, promoted by intimidation. Yet, with superb impudence, Luca named it the "Priorate of Liberty."

Cosimo, now crippled by the incessant pain of the gout, let things take their course. Neither he nor his most intimate friends were consulted about the situation. Nor were they even covertly threatened. No doubt, he thought that Luca, who treated him with a deference that scarcely veiled contempt, would not last long. But he was wrong. Luca lasted eight years. The Florentines, formerly so quick to resent intrusions upon their civic rights, seemed to be as hypnotised by Luca's executions, sentences of exile, and outrageous fines, as by his huge projected mansion—still known today as the Pitti Palace—and almost royal entertainments.

The generous and energetic humanist Pope Nicholas V, Cosimo's old friend, who was so fond of frightening people and then laughing at them, had died in 1455, his last years darkened by disaffection at Rome and the failure of his attempts to launch a crusade. "As Thomas of Sarzana," he muttered on his deathbed, "I had more happiness in a day than I now have in a whole year." His successor, Calixtus III, a Spanish lawyer, found it no easier than had Nicholas to organise a crusade, and he is otherwise notable only for reasserting the claim of the Holy See to Naples and for introducing his infamous nephew, Rodrigo Borgia, afterwards Pope Alexander VI, to the Roman court.

But the next Pope, Aeneas Sylvius Piccolomini, who took the name of Pius II, installed on the death of Calixtus in 1458, proved to be a

typical humanist of the budding Renaissance, and divided his time about
equally between classical studies and ecclesiastical affairs. He had already published a number of works of considerable literary distinction.
His surviving output includes poetry, fiction, a play, speeches, and particularly a Latin History of his own times, which is a model of its kind.
This versatile Pontiff—known to students of fifteenth-century literature
as Aeneas Sylvius—visited Florence in 1459 on his way to preach a
crusade at Mantua. Luca saw to it that he was received with the kind
of lavish and tasteful pageantry, the manuscripts and the learned dis-
courses, and finally the wine-parties with resplendent courtesans, that
he loved best. Galeazzo Maria Sforza, the adolescent son and heir of
Duke Francesco and his Duchess Bianca at Milan, enjoyed similar
junketings when his father sent him at the same time to make the acquaintance of the Pope, and also of the sick but still imperturbably
courteous old man who had made the duke's fortune. No doubt Galeazzo Maria took more interest in the much livelier Holy Father.

Pius II was carried by four nobles in a litter covered with silk brocade
from one of the city gates to his quarters in Santa Maria Novella. The
hall known as the Mercato Nuovo, close to the Piazza della Signoria,
in which an entertainment had been prepared, was provided with a stage
for dancing by sixty young men and sixty girls belonging to the cream
of Florentine society. Their gorgeous costumes and graceful evolutions
were admired by a vast audience, which was also regaled by a pageant
presented by twelve boys, including Lorenzo de' Medici, aged eleven,
Cosimo's grandson. Knights jousted by torchlight in the Piazza Santa
Croce. Huntsmen baited wild animals in the Piazza della Signoria. A
great banquet was given at the Palazzo Vecchio. Young Sforza received silver ewers and goblets worth two thousand florins. The somber
Florentine chronicler, Cambi, wrote of the special ceremonies in honour
of the gay and scholarly Vicar of Christ: "The business was characterised by pride, not by holiness, and it cost us a treasure."

Cosimo may have privately agreed with him. Even Galeazzo Maria,
if he had his wits about him, could have seen that Luca Pitti had become the effective ruler of Florence.

In 1458, three days before the Parlamento of August 11, Sforza's
ambassador in Florence, Nicodemo Tranchedini, had written to his
master: "The lord of Faenza [a *condottiere* in the pay of the Signory]
will arrive tomorrow with three hundred cavalry and fifty foot-soldiers.
There will also be the troops of Simonetta [another mercenary captain
employed by the Florentine government]. . . . On the morning of the
day fixed for the Parlamento these forces will be drawn up in battle
array on the *piazza*. The people will arrive without arms. Then the
priors will read a list of the citizens to whom *balia* [i.e., membership
of a provisional committee of administration] shall be given to re-

form the town and will ask the people whether they agree. The partisans planted in the square will shout 'Ay, ay!,' and the common people will join in the cry according to custom."

The old soldier on the ducal throne of Milan must have been relieved to hear of such docility among "the people," who were supposed in theory to run the republic of Florence, his indispensable ally, all by themselves. Sforza could hardly conceive of a government that allowed the orders it gave to be disputed by those to whom they were given. But he knew from past experience that he could trust Cosimo to act, in the end, like an absolute ruler, without appearing to be anything of the kind. It is probable that Nicodemo's report caused Francesco to marvel afresh at the miraculous resourcefulness of his level-headed friend.

After the comedy of the Parlamento had in fact been played out and ten new *accoppiatori* had been appointed to name a Signory, Luca Pitti basked, for the moment, in reflected glory. Cosimo did not realise, at first, how long that glory would last. He smiled his enigmatic smile. He knew, at any rate, that the old Florence of Guelfs and Ghibellines, of high-handed magnates whose excesses had had to be restrained by Ordinance of Justice, and of powerful guilds with complicated regulations and internal rivalries that clogged every attempt to simplify domestic policy, had gone forever. Pitti, the megalomaniac capitalist, would never be able to bring back this state of affairs. Cosimo, the veteran merchant-banker, though now apparently overshadowed in his gout-ridden retirement by the hero of the hour, had laid certain foundations very firmly indeed. They upheld the reign, essentially, of one man. But that man had necessarily to be an autocrat of the utmost discretion, one who went out of his way to preserve the traditional republican forms. Then there would be every prospect of his family's permanent ascendancy, provided that his posterity, first Piero and then Piero's son, Lorenzo, understood and practised, if and when their time came, the principles in which they were being educated. The hospitality afforded to the new Pope, Pius II, in 1459 was stage-managed by Cosimo in this way.

By the time of Pius II's visit in 1458, Cosimo's arthritis had immobilised him to such an extent that he could neither rise to greet the Pope nor kneel to kiss his foot. Pius II wrote, after this meeting, of the physically rigid but mentally alert old gentleman: "He it is who decides peace and war and controls the laws, being not so much a citizen as the master of the country. Political questions are settled at his house. The men he chooses hold office. He is a king in all but name and ceremony. Such is his influence that everything is referred to him. He is unassuming to a degree, being accompanied by only one servant when he walks abroad, giving the wall to older men or to men on horseback, and showing the utmost deference to the magistrates. He knows all that goes on in Italy, and most of the cities and princes take his advice. Nor is he less well informed about foreign countries, since his business correspondents sent him the latest news."

The shrewd Pontiff was evidently far less impressed by Luca Pitti's ostentatious bluster.

Yet, as time went on, Cosimo kept more and more to his bed, conducting his affairs, as briefly as possible, from his pillows. He rarely attended meetings of the Signory. His real power was just as great as that of the frankly despotic Duke Francesco Sforza of Milan, but he had fewer enemies. His three favourite virtues—prudence, temperance and fortitude, symbolised by the three feathers of his crest—always remained conspicuous. His politeness, self-control, and inscrutability became almost proverbial.

He could put sound moral and business counsel together in a nut-shell. When a notorious chatterbox of a Florentine citizen, going as *podestà* to a foreign city, came to him for a final word of advice, he told his honest but loquacious compatriot: "Dress in red, and keep your mouth closed." Both Machiavelli and Guicciardini, cynical as they were, sincerely admired Cosimo. He preferred the games of commerce and finance to those of politics, and he went on working away at money-making schemes long after the practical need for such activity had ceased. He often said that trade united mankind and brought glory to the community that initiated it, whereas to gamble with the freedom of one's fellow-citizens as a politician could only stir up dissension in the world at large, to the ultimate disgrace of the power that began it.

To the charges alleged against him, both in his own lifetime and since, of excessive prodigality to the "bandit" Sforza, to architects and other artists, and to scholars and philosophers, who all had to be paid very largely from the proceeds of "ruinous" taxation, Cosimo might have replied that if he had not set a personal friend on the throne of Milan, and if he had not called the attention of all Italy to the intellectual eminence of Florence, Florentines would have been dominated by Venetians or by Neapolitans or by the Papal States, and they would have cut a miserable figure in the progress of civilisation. Cosimo was not, however, a man to defend his actions in this way. He was content to allow such conclusions to be drawn by the intelligent majority of his responsible compatriots. If these inferences had not, in fact, been the common opinion, he would probably have lost his position, if not his life, long before the star of Duke Francesco rose in Lombardy.

One day Luca Pitti, who was careful to stay on good terms with

Cosimo, asked Cosimo what he thought of the huge new Pitti Palace rising on Mount San Giorgio. Cosimo warned him, in characteristically pictorial terms, against immoderate ambition. "You aim at the infinite; I am the finite. You stretch your ladder to the sky; I plant mine firmly upon the earth, so as not to risk a fall by extending it too far. You and I are like two big dogs. When we meet we sniff each other. Then, when we see that we both have teeth, we each go our own way." The tone was friendly, even flattering; but the sense was the very opposite of surrender. Luca, of course, remained quite impervious, except to the flattery. He saw no reason whatever why he should not come to be an even bigger "dog" than Cosimo, who surely could not last much longer now.

In fact, the older man's health continued to deteriorate steadily, and neither of his two sons Giovanni and Piero was in much better case. All three were often in bed with arthritis at the same time, and all three were inclined to be snappish about it—Piero being on the whole the sulkiest.

In 1463 the younger son, Giovanni, died, aged only thirty-nine. He had seemed to most people who came in contact with him—including his parents and Francesco Sforza—abler than Piero, less of an invalid, and altogether of a more agreeable character. His bust by Mino da Fiesole in the Museo Nazionale at Florence, strongly resembling his brother's by the same artist, certainly shows an attractive physiognomy, although to the temperate Cosimo's annoyance, he had always eaten and drunk too much. His early death was naturally a bitter blow to his doting father and mother. "This house," Cosimo muttered sadly, while being carried in a litter through his great new palace, "is too large for so small a family." All his hopes now centred upon the somewhat unpromising Piero.

Cosimo had only one other child, a young man whom he had named Carlo, born of one Maddalena, a Circassian slave bought in Venice as a certified virgin. The young women of his Caucasian tribe, mostly Mohammedans, were greatly prized in the markets of the East for their good looks and good humour. Neither they nor their parents had the slightest objection to their being sold off to the highest bidder, for they regarded the transaction as involving no degradation whatever for anyone concerned. The girls, however, were not very good servants, being inclined to laziness and argumentation. The buyers had to be content, as a rule, with the decorative qualities, often superb, of such acquisitions. Carlo, who took after his mother in looking extremely Slavonic, apparently inherited from his father something of the latter's industrious disposition. But there could, of course, be no question of a Medici inheritance in business or politics. Cosimo had the boy trained for the priesthood, in which he seems to have made a satisfactory career for himself. At any rate, posterity heard nothing more of him worthy of historical note.

The old man's health was now quite broken. When Contessina asked him why he so often sat with closed eyes, he answered, with his usual smile, that he wanted to accustom them to the darkness of the tomb. His long silences made her uncomfortable. "What do you think of all the time?" she demanded one day, hoping to rouse him from his apathy. "Are not you, too, silent, my dear," he replied, "when you are preparing to go on a journey?"

He knew he was dying, and did not resent the fact. He told Ficino that he regarded death as a release from the tormenting contemplation of the miseries of life and of the evil deeds of men.

On July 26, 1464, Piero de' Medici wrote from Careggi to his sons Lorenzo and Giuliano at Cafaggiuolo:

"I wrote to you the day before yesterday, telling you that Cosimo was worse. I think he is sinking, and he is of the same opinion. On Tuesday evening, therefore, he ordered everyone out of the room but Madonna Contessina and myself. . . . He spoke of the government of the city, of its trade, of the management of the family property, and of you two, taking comfort in the thought that you have brains. He said I must bring you up well, as you would be a great help to me. He regretted two things, that he had not done all that he wished and might have done, and that he was leaving me in poor health and with much trouble on my hands.

"Then he said that he would not make a will, that he had never meant to make one, even when Giovanni was alive, because he saw that we were united in love and mutual esteem. . . . He wished for no pomp or display at his funeral . . . and to be buried in San Lorenzo. He spoke with such calm deliberation, wisdom, and courage, that it was a marvel to hear. He told us he had enjoyed a long life, and that he was quite ready to depart when it should please God. Yesterday morning he rose, dressed completely . . . confessed to the Prior of San Lorenzo, and heard mass, uttering the responses as if he were quite well. Then, being questioned about the articles of faith, he answered correctly and received the sacraments with all possible devotion, after asking pardon of everyone. All this has increased my courage and my hope in the Lord God. Though according to the flesh I am grieved, yet seeing the greatness of his soul and his good disposition, I am almost resigned to watch him approaching the end we must all reach.

"Yesterday he seemed well and passed a good night. But in view of his great age I have not much hope of his recovery. Have prayers said for him by the friars, and see that alms are given as it seems good to you. Pray God to leave him with us for a time, if it be for the best. And do you, who are young, take example from him and bravely shoulder your share of trouble, since God wills it, and see that you act like men, though you are but boys, since your position and circumstances demand it. Above all, look to everything that can do you honour and help you. For the time has come when you must rely on yourselves. Live in fear of God, and hope for the best. I will write again about Cosimo. We are hourly expecting a doctor from Milan, but I put my trust in God rather than in anything else."

The doctor had been sent by Cosimo's old friend, Francesco Sforza. But by this time medical ministrations could not save the patient. Cosimo de' Medici the Elder died on August 1, 1464, aged seventy-seven. The funeral was a simple one, by his own request. But everyone who was anyone, and a great concourse of the humble citizens of Florence, crowded the approaches to the church of San Lorenzo. The words *Pater Patriae* were inscribed by public decree on his tomb in that edifice, in recognition of the fact that, during the greater part of his life, Cosimo had enjoyed a position probably unique at the time in political history. At any rate, no record exists of a plain citizen, with no hereditary or official claim to eminence, wielding almost absolute authority in public affairs.

He undoubtedly amassed a huge fortune during his years of power, but it was not inordinately larger than those of many families of Florence, such as the Pazzi, Strozzi and Pitti—not to mention houses that never achieved any political power at all. The true secret of Cosimo's astonishing ascendancy lay in his peculiar mentality. He had, in a rare degree, a certain moral rather than intellectual distinction, resembling that which, in a much narrower and lower sphere, enables some men to exercise an uncanny sway over women, often without deliberately intending to do so. In Cosimo's case it amounted to an extension, perhaps barely conscious, of his innate courtesy and forbearance, backed by an exceptionally resolute and subtle intelligence, to rivals and even open enemies in business and politics. Yet, like many men who succeed, as the popular phrase goes, "without really trying," Cosimo never used his wealth, popularity, or commercial acumen as means to personal enjoyment. He detested debauchery, luxury, and ostentation as much as any of his sternest critics. It can hardly be doubted that his strongest passion was patriotism, but his keen practical realism prevented even this obsession from becoming either as ridiculous as it tends to be in simple minds, or as harmful as it becomes in the fiercer type of nationalist. His banking and mercantile experience had shown him both the folly of unthinking excitement and the force of envy and resentment that can be aroused by over-confident leadership. He saw that if his beloved, passionately self-willed mother, Florence, was to be protected against both herself and against the outsiders who coveted her beauty and her glory, then her champion must never appear to be her master, but at the same time, he must make it obvious to foreign monarchs that he in person ruled her as effectively as they did their own dominions.

It was an extremely difficult assignment, especially in the domestic problems it raised. Abroad, Cosimo could easily be understood by the surrounding autocrats. The only other strong republic, Venice, on the whole a pacific community, could do no more—if he played his cards carefully—than face his own singleness of purpose with what was after all a mere committee of oligarchs, each as argumentive as the other. But in Florence every outward sign of his essentially free hand had to be discreetly veiled.

One way of doing this, he found, was to appoint to office capable men who in one way or another were genuinely grateful to him. The able proletarian Puccio Pucci, for instance, proved a most useful ally when promoted by Cosimo's influence. As for opponents on principle, like the honest but stubborn Neri Capponi, they could be flattered into acceptance of embassies or other important posts in foreign countries. Within his own family, he carefully suppressed any action that might be construed as a step toward a Medici "lordship" in Florence. He would not allow Piero, for example, to marry a feudal noble's daughter, and he rejected Brunelleschi's design for the new Medici palace as too magnificent.

The Medici bank was an effective, if occasionally surreptitious, instrument in securing the kind of popularity that Cosimo desired at home. It often happened that dangerous individuals among his adversaries lost ground financially, and that his friends found it easy to obtain loans if they got into debt, especially to the state, through excessive taxation. Openly, he gave away large sums to charity, and he spent even larger ones on splendid churches and convents, thereby earning the devotion of the powerful and numerous clergy and the still devout Florentines. The intellectual élite, meanwhile, were drawn to him through his enlightened patronage of art and learning—a patronage concerning which he invariably sought their advice—and he commanded even his business correspondents to collect statues, jewellery, coins, and manuscripts for him throughout Europe and the East. Almost as many objects of cultural interest as consumers' goods filled his ships and wagon-trains.

The Swiss art historian Jakob Burckhardt (1818–97) was impelled by Cosimo's close intimacy with such artists as Donatello, Angelico, and Lippo Lippi to comment: "A man in Cosimo's position, a great merchant and party leader, who also had on his side so many writers, thinkers, and scholars . . . was to all intents and purposes already a prince." Perhaps he was not, as Burckhardt also suggested, either the most nobly born or the most eminent in mind of the Italians of his day. But he was certainly the most versatile in his combination of commercial invincibility, subtle statesmanship, respect for creative imagination in fields remote from business and politics, and in the mysteriously effective charm that he radiated without design or effort.

The craft and the lack of scruple that often accompanied the exercise of Cosimo's virtues were common to his era, and they elicited no comment from any of his contemporaries other than the unduly pious. Under his rule, Florence prospered and was widely respected, even by professed moralists. The great majority of the citizens were happier then than they had ever been before. It would be hard to find a single clear instance in Cosimo's career when he deliberately subordinated patriotism to self-interest. He genuinely hated violence and bloodshed, and the one case in which he may have been privy to it, the murder of Baldaccio, has yet to be proved against him. So earnestly virtuous a Christian philospher as Marsilio Ficino wrote: "To Plato I owe much, to Cosimo no less. He realised for me the values of which Plato gave me the conception."

The very worst that can be confidently alleged of the *pater patriae* as a politician is that he deprived his community of a certain fragile semblance of freedom in exchange for a stable and efficient government. Most Florentines were perfectly well aware that he had done so, and they were glad of it, for the countless experiments that they had made in representative government, ingenious and honourable as they had been in intention, had all failed.

Florence may perhaps be regarded as the most interesting of all proto-democracies, and Giovanni and Cosimo de' Medici as the most fascinating of the leaders of such constitutions.

The problem they attempted to solve, the search for a means of harnessing personal liberty to national prosperity, of training a team of brilliant individualists to collaborate as a smoothly working whole, is recurrent in human history. For Cosimo was to reign, as it were, in plain clothes, from the wings of the political stage, and to depend entirely on his own special diplomatic gifts and on the psychological limitations of contemporary Florentines. A contemporary book-seller, Vespasiano da Bisticci, summed up his methods succinctly:

"He acted with the greatest skill to preserve his control. Whenever he wished to achieve some measure, he took care, in order to avoid envy as much as possible, that the initiative appeared to come from others, not from himself."

Cosimo had felt, at the age of seventy, that the foundations of his system had been laid firmly enough to resist the antics of his unofficial successor, Luca Pitti, who, after all, was doing the Republic no very great harm as yet. Consequently, in the last few years of Cosimo's life, he paid more attention to his sons Piero and Giovanni than to affairs of state. When his favourite, Giovanni, died comparatively young, without surviving issue and without ever having shown clear signs of reaching his father's level of intelligence and determination, the old man could only concentrate, with some misgiving, upon Piero, who at least had a stronger character.

But Piero's health was even more uncertain than Giovanni's. A variety of the Medicean gout kept him almost immobile, and incapable of work, for weeks on end. In these circumstances Cosimo's melancholy, as his life drew fast to its close, is understandable. The prospects of a struggle between the Pitti and Piero, the playboy and the invalid, could only depress the man who had done so much to give the city the stability and prosperity it then enjoyed.

III

LORENZO THE MAGNIFICENT
(*1464–92*)

Florence, along with Cosimo the Elder, doubted that Piero di Cosimo de' Medici was of the stuff that would enable him to use, for the benefit of the Republic, the power and prestige bequeathed to him by his father. It was true, people said in the streets, that Piero had served the state adequately, if without distinction, as ambassador to Milan and to Venice, as prior in 1448, and finally in 1461 as *gonfalonier* —the last of the Medici to hold this office. Still, he had no legal title enabling him to succeed to his father's authority, and his temperament seemed to exclude the geniality and tact that had been his father's key to success; moreover, the parlous state of his health—he was nicknamed *il gottoso,* "the gouty one"—precluded the possibility of strenuous political activity. Yet, as aware as was the public, and even Piero's family, of his shortcomings, there was no evidence that Piero himself shared this general opinion of his abilities; indeed, there was considerable evidence that the heir of Cosimo had no intention of relinquishing without a struggle a single iota of the Medicean authority in Florence.

Under these circumstances, a crisis was inevitable, and it was not long in coming. Three of Cosimo's friends were so alarmed at the son's pretensions that they joined Luca Pitti in a plot to eliminate Piero from politics entirely. These three were Agnolo Acciaiuoli, Diotisalvi Neroni, and Niccolò Soderini, all scions of distinguished and wealthy Florentine families. All of them felt themselves to have been slighted, in one way or another, by the Medici: Acciaiuoli, because his son's offer of marriage to Piero's daughter had been passed over in favour of a more advantageous match; Soderini, because he was a political idealist whose supernal notions of government the Medici, though they listened courteously, made no move to implement; and

Neroni, simply because he was an ambitious man who aspired to re-place Piero at the centre of Florentine power.

This Neroni, moreover, was an astute, rich, and influential citizen whose judgement had been much respected by Cosimo right up to the latter's death. He was sadly misjudged not only by the usually sagacious *pater patriae,* but also by his eldest son.

For Piero, in perfectly good faith, made a dangerous mistake. He asked Neroni, as Cosimo's most trusted counsellor in the past, to examine the Medici account books. The new head of the firm may have been influenced to take this step by rumours that his family had been helping itself to public funds. It was easy to make such charges in view of Cosimo's intricate methods, rarely known precisely to anyone but himself, of financing his policies abroad. Neroni at once saw his chance, in this assignment, to reduce Medicean popularity. He reported that the bank's affairs were in a critical condition. In order to restore their stability, he added, Piero's best course would be to call in all outstanding loans advanced by the firm immediately.

Piero innocently acted on this advice. There were, however, hardly any Florentines of note to whom Cosimo had not lent money; consequently, resentment of the required repayments reached proportions among the debtors that imperilled the political authority of the nominal head of the Republic. He was accused by many, both in private and in public, of harshness and avarice.

In these circumstances Luca Pitti suggested to the other three conspirators that the time might now be ripe for an armed insurrection. Niccolò Soderini, however, always the idealist, would not agree to violent measures, although he strenuously affirmed his opposition to anything like the rule of one man in Florence. He favoured the method, he said, of letting Piero's now damaged reputation bring him, of itself, to political ruin. This attitude was eventually adopted, with some reluctance, by the others. Accordingly, at the end of 1465, when Niccolò Soderini was elected *gonfalonier,* he promptly proposed various constitutional reforms and certain committees of enquiry into the recent administration; but all these motions were rejected by the Signory. For the moment, the four conspirators were baffled.

In the spring of that same year, Piero sent his eldest son, Lorenzo, aged fifteen, to Milan to meet the thirteen-year-old Prince Federigo of Aragon. Federigo was on his way to Milan to fetch the duke's daughter, Ippolita Sforza, and escort her to Naples to marry his elder brother Alfonso, Duke of Calabria and heir to the throne of the kingdom. The two teen-age boys, Federigo and Lorenzo, struck up a warm friendship. It was a relationship that was to prove of much service to Lorenzo in later life. On the leisurely journey North, which took in Bologna, Ferrara, and Venice, Lorenzo was everywhere welcomed as if he were the heir to a reigning prince rather than to a prominent citizen already the object of conspiracy in his native community. The boy's father had instructed him "to act like a man," and do all he could to promote the credit of his family with the Duke of Milan. In spite of the zealous reception accorded to Lorenzo as the grandson of Cosimo, Piero was well aware that Sforza and his fellow-princes might be losing confidence in the stability of the son of that great man. Nicodemo Tranchedini, the Milanese ambassador, had already warned him, in the duke's name, that he must be wary of antagonising the anti-Mediceans in Florence. Piero, in his turn, warned his son not to be importunate with Francesco, for the ex-*condottiere* was growing old and infirm, and in any case Francesco would be wholly occupied with the details of his daughter's wedding. "You must expect," the anxious parent of Lorenzo went on, "to be treated by His Highness like a servant or one of his household."

But Lorenzo pestered neither the Duke nor anyone else. He enjoyed himself hugely, not only in the marriage festivities but also in cultivating the society of Ippolita, whom he found to be as intelligent and even learned as she was beautiful. In this instance, as in so many others, the Medici boy's irresistible charm and tact at this early age easily outweighed his less than prepossessing appearance, clumsy movements, and the nasally harsh voice in which he uttered his flow of light-hearted, prematurely sophisticated courtesies. Ippolita at once respected his already wide, if not deep, erudition, and especially his ready susceptibility to anything elevating or amusing, whether material or mental. The two young people promised to write regularly to each other, and they did so over a long period.

Early in 1466, Piero despatched Lorenzo to Rome. Lorenzo was in the first place to do homage, on behalf of the family, to the new Pope, Paul II, an irascible Venetian who required tactful handling. For Florentine policy remained devoted to preserving the Milanese alliance at all costs, together with the Sforza dynasty, while the Venetians were known to want a republic in Lombardy on the Venetian pattern, and one if possible under Venetian influence. In the second place, Lorenzo was to seek instruction from his uncle, Giovanni Tornabuoni, the brother of his mother Lucrezia and manager of the Roman branch of the Medici bank, in the mysteries of trade and finance. Finally, Lorenzo, now a youth of eighteen, was to secure a contract for working certain alum deposits recently discovered near Tolfa, some thirty miles north-west of the Holy City. The mineral was important in the processing of Florentine cloth, but very little alum could be obtained anywhere in Europe except at Tolfa. Lorenzo and Tornabuoni between them duly extracted the alum contract from the Pope, to whom Medici capital was indispensable.

On the very day, March 8, of Lorenzo's arrival in Rome, Duke Francesco Sforza, who had been in poor health for some time, died. Piero's party favoured the continuance to the duke's son and heir, Galeazzo Maria, of the subsidy hitherto paid to Francesco in pursuance of the fixed Medicean policy of maintaining the closest possible ties of friendship with the powerful northern duchy. The late duke, since his accession, had proved that he was no ordinary military tyrant by using the money to make his court one of the most splendid in Italy, and a haven for Italian scholars and exiled Byzantine sages. Ippolita, at any rate, had benefitted remarkably from their company, acquiring a Latin style, as even foreigners noted, of impeccable elegance.

Luca Pitti led a strong and certainly not unreasonable opposition to the subsidy. The character of Galeazzo Maria did not appear to be such as to encourage trust in his reliability. Now twenty-two, he had long shown signs of moral weakness and a quarrelsome character under a veneer of the refined manners now fashionable at the Milanese court. The respectable Niccolò Soderini, disappointed at his own failure to introduce constitutional reform in the previous year, proceeded to throw the weight of his much-admired ethical idealism into the scales of the Pitti faction. A rising against the government of Piero was again plotted, but the conspiracy was quickly revealed to Piero by no less a person than Luca's own secretary. With characteristically Medicean discretion, the head of the Republic took no overt steps to suppress the activities of Pitti and his fellow-plotters. He simply made the schemers aware that he knew of their plans, and added that his own party would be strong enough to resist them.

Lorenzo had by this time, early in April, gone on to Naples, where he renewed his friendship with Federigo and Ippolita. He also did what he could to counteract in the mind of the King, Ferdinand I, the insinuations of Piero's enemies at the court. Don Ferrante, as the monarch was more familiarly known, took an immediate fancy, like most foreigners, to the Medici boy. About a month later, Lorenzo returned dutifully, if reluctantly, to report to his parent.

On August 27, Piero was lying ill at his Careggi villa, unable to move his gouty foot, when news was brought to him through an old friend of Cosimo's, Ercole Bentivoglio, Lord of Bologna, to the effect that the Duke of Ferrara was approaching the Florentine city of Pistoia in arms. The object was said to be—in a phrase that later eras were to work to death—to "liberate" Florence from an oppressive government. The message added that the famous *condottiere* Bartolommeo Colleoni ("Lion-heart"), in the employ of Venice, was about to take the field for the same purpose. It seemed that Luca Pitti had arranged for Colleoni's intervention. The conspiracy already disclosed in the city had in fact taken a more vicious turn. The plotters intended, Piero was told by the same informant as before, their secretary, to remove the senior member of the house of Medici by assassination.

In these terrifying circumstances, a further report that Galeazzo Maria Sforza, the new Duke of Milan, had despatched fifteen hundred horsemen to help Piero withstand the Ferrarese, did not overly console the prospective victim very much. But Piero displayed a courage and an energy worthy of the best of his ancestors, setting out, with Lorenzo, at once for Florence in a litter. The sixteenth-century historian Niccolò Valori alleges that Lorenzo, riding some distance ahead, encountered some peasants who told him that the main road into the city was blocked by a body of armed men. The boy instantly retraced his steps, galloping at full speed back to the litter. He persuaded his groaning but indomitable parent to take another route. Lorenzo then coolly trotted back, straight on by the main road, met the soldiers from Florence, pretended he thought them to be a guard of honor sent to welcome his father, and announced that Piero would be arriving very shortly. Then he smiled amiably at the unfriendly faces surrounding him, thanked the commander for his courtesy, waved his hat, spurred his horse, and cantered on with a few attendants into the city.

This incident, if true, attests to the precocious intelligence and daring of a budding political genius. But other early chroniclers do not mention it, and it is likely enough that the part played by the young Lorenzo in this affair was much more modest. Piero, in any case, reached Florence safely later in the day. He mustered and armed his party, and then called for help from Galeazzo Maria's commander, who had reached a point in Romagna near the north-west border of Tuscany. Finally he gave the Signory documentary proof that Ercole d'Este, brother of Borso, Duke of Ferrara, was leading an army towards Florence with subversive intent.

Niccolò Soderini now showed more intractability than his chief, Luca Pitti. The former demanded immediate and forcible coercion of the priors to compel them to act against Piero. Pitti, however, hurried off to see Piero, who was in bed again, and had a long chat with him, showing every sign of affection for the man he had plotted to kill and who had so disconcertingly acted with more resolution than his adversary. Perhaps Luca also now realised that there were far more Medici men about in Florence than he had thought. At the bedside interview the invalid head of the Republic treated his unexpected visitor with gracious magnanimity, apparently promising that he would later on betroth Lorenzo to one of Pitti's daughters.

With Pitti soothed, it was possible to elect a new, pro-Medicean Signory, which promptly ordered both parties to disband their forces. Niccolò Soderini, still furiously intransigent, actually persuaded Luca— though the latter was now secretly reconciled with Piero—to send an urgent despatch to Ercole d'Este, requesting him to cross the Tuscan frontier with all speed and, at the same time, to assure the revolutionary faction that he planned immediate and violent intervention on their behalf.

Nothing came of all this. No doubt Ercole received other more realistic assessments of the situation in Florence. Luca, whose mind was far more practical and pliant than Soderini's, saw that the game was up. By making his peace with Piero, he saved himself from the death sentence passed on all four conspirators by the Signory. Piero commuted the penalty to banishment in the cases of Niccolò Soderini, Diotisalvi Neroni, who had been lying low for some time, and Agnolo Acciaiuoli. He pardoned Luca Pitti, who was by this time over seventy years old, but he also retracted his promise to betroth Lorenzo to the aged rebel's daughter. The old man had at last overreached himself, thereby belatedly fulfilling the expectations of the dead Cosimo.

Henceforth, Machiavelli wrote, "when he [Pitti] appeared in the streets, his friends and relatives not only feared to accompany him but even to salute him . . . now, when it was too late, he began to repent that he had not taken Niccolò Soderini's advice and died honourably, sword in hand, rather than live dishonoured among victorious foes." It may be doubted whether Luca, at any period of his long life, would have preferred a hero's death, in the ancient Roman fashion that Machiavelli was so fond of representing, to dishonour. But he must have gone through all the agonies of finally frustrated ambition and cursed himself for over-estimation of his own power and underestimation of Piero's. The punishment of living on as a disgraced figure among those who had so often trembled at his nod was perhaps worse than exile. But there can be no question that in the general opinion of his fellow-citizens he deserved to die a traitor's death. Merely to be ignored, and to see his great, half-finished palace abandoned by the workmen under his very eyes, seemed to the majority of Florentines too light a penalty for his sedition.

It would perhaps have been better for Florence if Piero had acted in the style of Machiavelli's ideal prince and executed all four of the conspirators, elderly though they were. But he had been so far from even dreaming of such a thing that when Acciaiuoli, from Siena, promised submission if he were recalled from exile, the head of the Republic replied that he personally bore his correspondent no grudge and even felt like a son to him. It was Florence, not Piero de' Medici, he declared, which had decreed the exile of rebels against the state, and the city's sentence therefore must stand. Piero may or may not have foreseen the consequences of his clemency. He was a brave as well as a humane man, and not easily frightened. In any case, he now had to face outright war. Venice, alarmed by the consolidation of the Milan-

Florence axis, and encouraged by Soderini and Neroni, sent an army across the Po on May 10, 1467, with Colleoni in command. His orders were first to reduce Florence, and then Milan.

Bartolommeo Colleoni, already a veteran sixty-six years old, had learned his trade under Francesco Sforza. In the past he had served Venice and Milan, alternately, and had beaten the Milanese in three pitched battles, although he had never yet fought the Florentines. For the past twelve years he had been captain-general of the Venetian forces, and his army was a large one for the period, consisting of eight thousand horse- and six thousand foot-soldiers.

Piero obtained auxiliary troops from Naples, and appointed Federigo da Montefeltro, Lord of Urbino, commander-in-chief of the Florentine forces. Federigo, by then in his forties and the husband of Battista Sforza, one of the daughters of Francesco, had a reputation as a soldier at least equal to Colleoni's. But he was known, too, as a highly enthusiastic patron of art and literature. He had collected a fine library and was the patron at this time of one of the most influential painters of the fifteenth century in Italy, Piero della Francesca. This artist at a later date executed a double portrait of Montefeltro and Battista, which hangs now in the Uffizi gallery. Federigo's court, one of the most refined on the peninsula, was destined to be important in the future history of the Medici. In the present campaign, his staff included young Galeazzo Maria himself, at the head of a Milanese contingent, and Alfonso, Duke of Calabria and husband of Ippolita Sforza, in charge of the Neapolitans. The ghost of the great Duke Francesco Sforza accordingly overshadowed in more ways than one the cautious manoeuvres of the two armies in Romagna.

For some time, Colleoni eluded every attempt by Montefeltro to engage him in battle, but at last Federigo manoeuvred him into a corner and prepared to attack. At that moment, Galeazzo Maria perversely declined to obey orders, and, in the delay, Colleoni slipped away. Montefeltro complained passionately to the Signory of Florence. The priors tactfully invited Galeazzo to visit them in the city in order to discuss "urgent business of great importance" to both Milan and themselves. The capricious young man, weary of Federigo, whom he regarded as a pedant, and perhaps remembering the good times he had enjoyed in Florence as a boy—when he came to meet the genial humanist Pope Pius II there in 1459—accepted the invitation with alacrity.

Federigo, thus relieved of his insubordinate ally, again outwitted his veteran opponent. Colleoni's Venetians were caught in retreat at the village of La Molinella near Imola, where they fought so stubbornly under their wily old leader that the battle went on for two hours after dark, by the light of torches. Then, at last, they were compelled gradually to abandon the field to their almost exhausted adversaries. The engagement had not been decisive, for the white-haired "Lionheart" had dextrously evaded annihilation. But Venice, disappointed at this result and at the absence of the expected anti-Medicean rising in Florence, recalled Colleoni, and a peace treaty was signed on April 27, 1468, re-establishing the former situation. Piero now felt reasonably secure from further foreign interference; but to make doubly sure, he purchased the fortresses of Sarzanello and Castelnuovo, commanding the roads from Genoa and Lombardy, respectively.

With the Medici now as powerful as ever in Florence, the citizens seemed to be in a docile mood, ready to return to their peacetime amusements of public pageants and celebrations. Piero decided to signalise in this way Lorenzo's arrival at maturity. The boy was now twenty years old. He had been in love for several months with a girl of the Donati family, named Lucrezia. The object of Lorenzo's affections, unfortunately, had already been married for about three years to a certain Niccolò Ardinghelli, a merchant with interests in Asia Minor. Lorenzo, when asked by his father what sort of ceremony he would prefer, begged for a grand tournament to be held in the Piazza San Croce in order to entertain Lucrezia Donati, whose husband had left for the Orient a month after his marriage and was still there. Accordingly, on February 7, 1469, this affair duly took place.

It was subsequently described in a somewhat pedestrian poem entitled *La Giostra* [*the joust*] *di Lorenzo de' Medici,* written by one of Lorenzo's household, the Florentine Luigi Pulci, famous at a later date for his burlesque epic of Carolingian chivalry known as the *Morgante Maggiore.* Everyone taking part in the titling, including Lorenzo's younger brother Giuliano, was gorgeously dressed. Lorenzo wore a velvet surcoat, a silk scarf embroidered with pearls, and a cap studded with diamonds and rubies. He carried a banner painted by Verrocchio, and rode horses presented to him by the King of Naples and the dukes of Milan and Ferrara, who also supplied his armour. He wrote, not long afterwards, with characteristic irony: "Although I was young and of no great skill, the first prize was awarded to me, namely a helmet inlaid with silver and surmounted by a figure of Mars." Everyone concerned had, of course, made sure that the brilliant young heir to the now generally acknowledged head of the state would carry off all the honours of the tournament and thus please his beautiful Lucrezia.

Despite Lorenzo's attachment to Lucrezia, the festival at which he cut so fine a figure was officially a celebration of Lorenzo's betrothal to Clarice Orsini, of the powerful Roman family so named. He had caught a glimpse of the girl during his last visit, on Piero's behalf, to the Pope, but had taken no particular notice of her. The proposed match was unpopular in Florence, where Romans were generally disliked for their alleged excessive pride, turbulence, and insensitivity to civilised values. Piero may have planned the spectacle of the tournament to some extent in order to console his compatriots for a union he considered desirable on political grounds, since Florence had so few friends in Rome at this period. Lorenzo himself did not seem greatly pleased at the prospect of marrying the Orsini maiden. He noted curtly in his memoirs that "I, Lorenzo, took to wife Donna Clarice, daughter of the lord Jacopo Orsini; or rather, she was, in December 1468, placed at my disposal." This last phrase, however, did not necessarily mean that the young man resented the marriage. He may merely have thus indicated his acknowledgement that he was not in a position at his age to speak in this regard as though he were acting on his own initiative, but could only signify his acquiescence in the proposal made to him by his own and Clarice's parents. He could see no object to the project in this case, and he knew perfectly well that he would be at liberty, whether married to her or anyone else, to make his own arrangements, according to the custom of the time, for extra-marital diversions.

His mother, the truly estimable Lucrezia Tornabuoni, wrote to her husband Piero from Rome: "The girl is above the middle height, of fair complexion and pleasing manners. She may be less beautiful than our own daughters, but she seems very modest. So she will, I think, be easy to train. She is not a blonde, for there are no such girls here. Her thick, dark hair has a reddish tinge. Her face is of a circular shape, but not objectionably so in my view. The neck is quite beautiful, though on the thin side, or, perhaps one should say, delicate. I could not see the breasts, as here they are entirely covered, but so far as I could make out they are decently formed. She does not hold her head up proudly, as our young women do, but bends it forward a little, a mannerism which I ascribe to her extreme timidity. The hands are very long and slender. On the whole the girl appears to be well above average. But she cannot be compared with Maria, Lucrezia, and Bianca. . . . Lorenzo himself has seen her, and if he approves of the match you will hear from him accordingly."

The marriage of Lorenzo to Clarice, which took place on June 4, 1469, turned out reasonably well, as might have been expected with so even-tempered a husband. The first two days of these remarkable festivities were entirely devoted to the reception, in the Medici Palace, of gifts from the villages and towns of Tuscany, including 150 calves; over 2,000 brace of capons, geese, and other birds; casks of native and foreign wine; and various additional tidbits. These Lorenzo shared generously with the ordinary citizens of Florence. During the next three days no fewer than five banquets were offered to friends of higher social standing. The loggias and gardens of the palace in the Via Larga were filled to capacity by these guests. Separate tables were laid for fifty young bridesmaids, who served as dancing partners for the gentlemen. Older ladies were presided over by Lorenzo's mother, Lucrezia Tornabuoni.

On the first day of this feasting, a Sunday, the bride, riding the mighty war-horse presented to Lorenzo by the King of Naples, left the palace of the Alessandri, where she had been lodged, and escorted by a long train of nobles, entered her new abode. On her arrival a symbolic olive branch was hoisted at the balcony, to the accompaniment of ecstatic music. When the revels ended on Tuesday morning, the party adjourned for Mass at the Church of San Lorenzo, Clarice carrying one of her hundreds of wedding gifts, "a little book of Our Lady, most marvellous, written in letters of gold upon blue paper, the binding decorated with designs in crystal and silver."

This "modest and timid" daughter of the relatively uncouth Roman aristocracy must have been quite overwhelmed, as even more sophisticated foreigners were, by the evidences of material power and esthetic sensibility everywhere conspicuous in the Republic. Countless treasures of ancient and contemporary art met her gaze. Few of the great merchants, unlike the rich men of Rome, took much trouble to display their wealth; instead, its proofs imposed themselves almost casually in the splendour of even utilitarian objects. The wit and the gayety, the good, or at least striking, looks of nearly everyone, the general air of ease and happiness—so different from the Roman atmosphere of dark antagonisms, fierce religiosity, scandalous rumour, tragic incidents, and the contaminations of fever and plague—might have been supposed capable of transforming Clarice Orsini. But nothing of the sort happened. Clarice, married to the most brilliant man in Italy, perhaps in Europe, remained throughout her life in a state of morbid melancholy, which was never modified by anything that Lorenzo could do for her. It was not due to an intelligent insight into the fatal flaws of early Renaissance society, and it had nothing in common with her husband's later sadness at the perverse, incorrigible fraud and violence that seemed to rule the world. Clarice's gloom was constitutional. It was lucky for Lorenzo that, though by nature as kindly as his father Piero, and a good deal more so than his grandfather Cosimo, he was also too naturally exuberant and too level-headed to grieve over a dull and querulous wife. Once or twice he lost his temper at her silliness, but, as a rule, he treated her with the greatest courtesy and consideration, so far as the growing multiplication of his business and his pleasures, neither of which had anything to do with her, would permit.

Piero's adherents were now beginning to exploit his increasing infirmity by behaving, in Machiavelli's pungent phrase, "as if God and fortune had given them the city for a prey." The plucky invalid reacted by summoning the most prominent offenders to his bedside. He warned them that he knew perfectly well what they were doing and that, if they persisted in their misdeeds, he would soon force them to change their tune. They professed astonishment at the severity of his tone, swore that he had been misinformed, protested their entire devotion to his leadership, and retired with many compliments and good wishes. Then they coolly continued their depredations and excesses.

The head of the state sent emissaries secretly to invite Agnolo Acciaiuoli to Caffagiuolo. Piero regarded that allegedly repentant conspirator, who was some years his senior, as the least dangerous of the men he had banished three years before. He thought that perhaps the agile old gentleman could now be trusted to return to Florence and check the indiscipline that prevailed in the government. The recall of exiles had long been a feature of Florentine domestic politics, and it was not in fact such a desperate measure in this case as it might appear at first sight. Acciaiuoli, a patriot in his way, like nearly all his fellow-citizens, would at least, Piero conjectured, have introduced some confusion into the ranks of the trouble-makers. But when the exile returned, his worried host could not make up his mind either to give him definite instructions or any definite promises. Death put an end to the discussions. Piero de' Medici finally fell a victim to his malady on December 2, 1469, aged fifty-three. The funeral, at the church of San Lorenzo, was not the occasion for much pomp, although the Florentine sculptor Andrea del Verrocchio, who had just executed his bronze figure of David for the Bargello, was called in to design the tomb.

Piero de' Medici, like his father Cosimo, was one of the most attractive members of the family. He resembled his parent both in his aversion to ostentation and in his tactful tenure of a political position that had no foundation in law and that would have tempted most men of his day to tyranny. Piero's temperament was innately humane, his moral character firm, and his intelligence, though inferior to Cosimo's, adequate for its difficult task.

He showed much courage in his endless struggle against ill health, talking sound common sense even when he could move neither hands nor feet. He also carried on, like his father, the Medici tradition of encouraging intellectuals without actually presuming to join their circles, though he was undoubtedly of a more scholarly disposition than Cosimo. Foreigners had a high opinion, also, of Piero's political judgement. No less an authority on that abstruse subject than the stern and indefatigable King of France, Louis XI, indicated his appreciation of the Florentine's diplomacy by permitting him, in 1465, to stamp the three royal lilies of France on one of the six red pellets constituting the Medici coat of arms, and to change the colour of the ball so stamped from red to blue.

The bust of Piero by Mino da Fiesole in the National Museum of Florence presents "the gouty one," as he is usually called by Italian historians, as a fine-looking man, with confident determination, but not much else, in every line of his strong features. No more of an esthete than his father, and with far less humour and subtlety than Cosimo—as well as less cynicism—the second Medici to deal on equal terms with kings and dukes deserves simply the admiration that has at all times been accorded to an unmistakably decent and resolute personality. He did not fail to solve his main problem of holding on to his patrimony and handing it on intact to his subsequently illustrious son. Nothing more could have been expected of an invalid.

* * *

Under the guidance first of Cosimo and then of Piero, both sedulous patrons of art and letters, Florence rose to exceptional eminence as an intellectual centre, far exceeding in this respect such courts as that of Urbino and of Milan itself in Duke Francesco's time. During the period from 1434 to 1469, Florentine architects such as Brunelleschi, Michelozzo, and Alberti, such sculptors as Ghiberti, Donatello, Luca della Robbia, and Mino da Fiesole, the painters Fra Angelico, Filippo Lippi, Gozzoli, Uccello, Andrea del Castagno, Antonio and Piero Pollaiuolo, Domenico Veneziano, and Baldovinetti, together with such authors as Poggio, Filelfo, the historian Giovanni Cavalcanti, and the architect Alberti, were all active in the city. Most of them were in the service of one or other of the Medici, and some of them, like Michelozzo and Donatello, Lippi and Angelico, and in Piero's time Botticelli himself, were closely intimate with the head of the state. A practical result of this munificence was that in these fields, what is generally known as "Renaissance culture" began earlier in Florence than elsewhere.

The Venetian Leon Battista Alberti (1404–72) did not spend much of his time in Florence. He preferred Rome and Mantua. So far as is known, he had little to do with the Medici. But he did once, in 1441, long before Cosimo's death, persuade the young Piero to take part in a poetry reading contest. It was held in the cathedral in the presence of the Signory, the archbishop, and the Venetian ambassadors. The poems were to be on the theme of friendship and composed in the vernacular, and not, as was generally the case at that time, in Latin. Poggio acted as one of the judges. Alberti himself—but not, needless to say, Piero de' Medici, who merely stage-managed the affair—competed. But Piero probably paid for the valuable silver crown, shaped like a laurel wreath, which would be presented to the victor. It was typical of Florentine society at this period that an enormous jury of ordinary citizens packed the cathedral to deliver the ultimate verdict on the competition. First, the judges spoke to the Florentines. Both these and the rival poets were humanists. But the judges, naturally enough, tended to be of the old-fashioned sort, considering Latin literature to be infinitely superior to anything that could possibly be composed in Italian. So they themselves, backed by the jury, appropriated the crown. The enraged younger poets appealed to Pope Eugenius IV, who was in the city at the time, but he refused to intervene. Only Alberti shrugged his shoulders, commenting dryly, "I think the subject of the next competition had better be envy."

The ensuing generation was to change its mind about the vernacular. Even in 1441, many of the audience on this occasion demanded copies of the poems written in a language they could understand. Thus, the final result of the meeting promoted by Piero de' Medici, and no doubt approved by Cosimo, was a popular success. In the end, it consolidated the popularity of their family, a consequence that it is very likely they had foreseen when agreeing to Alberti's proposal.

If Alberti had stayed longer in Florence, he would certainly have been of great, if indirect, assistance to the Medici; for he was an exceptional man, one of the first of those versatile men who typify the Renaissance. Eminent as an architect, painter, and musician, a writer of both verse and prose in the vernacular as well as in Latin, a philosopher, mathematician, and engineer, Alberti also was a brilliant conversationalist. In addition, he could execute a six-foot high jump, throw a coin to the top of a tower, and tame the most obstreperous of horses. Nevertheless, he did not, like so many men of superlative energy, indulge in sexual debauchery, heavy drinking, or intrigue.

His buildings constitute his chief title to fame today. His paintings and musical compositions have disappeared, but much of his verse and prose survives, including his well-known treatise on architecture. But the merits of these works, though high, are rather those of scholarship and practical preaching than of elegant style, wit, or imagination. It is in architecture, both secular and ecclesiastical, that he can be regarded as almost the equal of Brunelleschi. Another sculptor famous for his refined and delicate effects, as well as his pious feeling, Mino da Fiesole (1431–84), carved many tombs, busts, and portraits in low relief remarkable for their precise finish and expressive power. His extremely lifelike bust of Piero de' Medici has already been mentioned.

In Florentine painting of this period realism was gaining ground, even in the later works of Cosimo's favourite, Fra Angelico. It is also conspicuous in Benozzo Gozzoli, the decorator of the Medici Palace in the

Via Larga. The close imitation of natural appearances also came wholly to absorb Uccello, Andrea del Castagno, and the Pollaiuolo brothers. Angelico's majestic frescos in the San Marco convent, the intensity of grief, excitement, or meditation he could convey in the faces of his figures, and especially in his Virgins, a suavity and spirituality never hitherto attained in the medium, attest the genius of this great and humble painter.

Cosimo's impartial admiration for technical achievement was also extended to a friar of a very different sort, Filippo Lippi (1412–69), who displayed a more progressive idealism than Angelico, as well as a decidedly more earthy character when not professionally engaged, despite the mystic, marvellously chromatic grace of his painting. The humanity of both Cosimo and Piero, neither of them frivolous men, appears in their steady nursing of the incorrigibly susceptible monk's artistic genius. Jacopo Sellaio, one of his pupils, as was also Botticelli in the year 1465, considered that none of the Sienese, nor even Angelico or Masaccio, could match Lippi's Virgins for sheer natural beauty, so wondrous as to make the very miracle of Christ's birth intelligible.

Lippi had been left to starve in the streets of Florence almost before he could walk. He had become a monk at the age of eight, an artist at ten, a brawler and fighter at fourteen, and at seventeen, after he had run away with a girl to Ancona, he was picked up by Moorish corsairs and carried off as a slave to Africa. There he drew so fine a portrait of the local pasha on the prison wall that he was set free. Soon afterwards he was in Naples, then in Florence again, paying his way with portraits of the men and women he met in brothels and taverns, till at last he attracted the attention of Cosimo de' Medici himself and was presented as a potential painter of sacred subjects to the Holy Father, Eugenius IV. But Cosimo soon found that Fra Lippo had to be locked up while he produced his saints and madonnas, to keep him away from less edifying company. All the same, he was forever escaping, if necessary from high, barred windows, into nights of carnivals. His patron, in an attempt to tame the friar, appointed him chaplain to the Franciscan convent of Santa Margherita in the little market town of Prato. There, according to Vasari, the new chaplain immediately abducted a beautiful novice or boarder at the convent, one Lucrezia Buti, and with her co-operation became the father of Filippino Lippi, later himself a distinguished painter.

This scandal naturally led to the chaplain's ignominious expulsion from his post. But the Pope, who at the time was the genial humanist Pius II, Aeneas Sylvius, pardoned the offence, at Cosimo's request, on condition that the seducer marry his victim. Lippi had not the slightest objection. He went through the ceremony, and then set to work first on

Cosimo's and then on Piero de' Medici's commissions. He grew famous and respected, but continued to live as boisterously as ever. He died in 1469, the year of Piero's death, of poison administered—so the story goes—by relatives of Lucrezia Buti, or possibly of some other young woman whom he had loved and left.

Another contemporary was Benozzo Gozzoli (1420–97), who was an assistant to Fra Angelico until 1449. By the late 1450s, he had begun his most celebrated fresco, "The Journey of the Magi," in the Palazzo Medici. It took him three years to finish it. In 1464, when Cosimo died, Gozzoli left Florence and returned only in 1496, to end his days in the following year. His peculiar attraction as a painter comes from his lively blending of the celestial with the mundane. His gay cavaliers mingle with solemnly gliding angels against a rich but conventionally treated landscape. Lorenzo de' Medici, Piero's eldest son, has been considered by some authorities, on the strength of the assertion of a French guide-book of 1888, to figure in this splendidly decorative scene—the "Journey" fresco—as one of the Magi, despite his ingenuously childish appearance. This prettiness may be the result of Gozzoli's tactful idealisation, in his master's manner, when Lorenzo was about ten years old in 1459, of features that could not have been so ethereally angelic even at that age. But Lorenzo in fact had ridden a white horse, as he does in the painting, during a torchlight procession along the Via Larga at the time in April–May 1459 of the visits of Pope Pius II and Galeazzo Maria Sforza to Florence. The Medici boy may then have seemed quite appealing, among the alternate gleams and shadows of such an occasion, to so romantic a stylist and devoted a Medicean as Gozzoli. The other two Magi have been supposed, on the same dubious evidence, to represent the Greek Patriarch, Joseph, and the Byzantine Emperor, John Palaeologus, who had both come to Florence twenty years earlier, when the artist was about nineteen.

Literary activity under Cosimo's and Piero's patronage concentrated more on scholarship than on original production. Classical manuscripts were hunted down and edited with almost fanatical zeal. But while Cosimo had merely provided the money, mainly for reasons of political prestige, his son, much more studiously inclined—owing partly to the amount of time he had to spend in bed—took a more technical interest in the movement to promote the learning of the ancient pagans. Both men were probably rather bored by the tedious wrangling of domestic politics, and they both preferred foreign diplomacy, where the atmosphere in general was more polite and leisurely. But whereas Cosimo would usually be occupied with balance sheets on his journeys, Piero would be more likely to be found poring over the latest edition of Cicero, Livy, Caesar, or Seneca.

The difference was reflected in Florentine society under their respective rules. Though the reign of Cosimo was much longer, there were more literary gatherings and inspections of studios in Piero's, from the poetry competition promoted by Piero and Alberti in the cathedral to less formal discussions in book-shops or with Luca della Robbia or Gozzoli. Women, too, inspired by the example of Lucrezia Torna-buoni, were taking a more active part in the progress of civilisation, though not as yet in so striking a way as during the next half-century. In many respects, Florence was growing more cosmopolitan, and Machiavelli noted the popularity of Piero, like his father, at foreign courts. Piero was liked, however, less as a remarkably accessible banker than as a sort of Solomon in disputes between, for instance, Milanese and Venetian policy, as well as an admirer of fine works of art wherever they were found.

There can be no doubt that the five years of Piero's tenure of power had strengthened, despite the opposition of less determined and incisive characters than his own, not only the political entrenchment of his house in Florence, but also the city's reputation abroad. Rome, Venice, Milan, Urbino, and even Naples looked to the Tuscan capital for intel- lectual inspiration. Mantua and Ferrara, under the Gonzagas and Estes respectively, were soon to do their best to rival Florentine art, erudition, humane ideals, wit, and gayety. But a chapter in the history of the Medici was now about to begin that would far exceed in glory all the previous achievements of that extraordinary family. It was in fact to mark at once a climax and a beginning in European civilisation.

* * *

At the time of Piero de' Medici's death, Lorenzo was a mature young man of twenty-one years who had already demonstrated con-siderable political acumen. As already noted, when only a youth he had represented his invalid father at Milan, on the occasion of a visit to that city of Federigo of Aragon, heir to the crown of Naples; in ad-dition, Lorenzo had personally negotiated successfully with Pope Paul II in Rome and with King Ferdinand in Naples. Moreover, Lorenzo had undoubtedly been of considerable assistance to his father in dealing with the conspirators who were intent on toppling Piero from his un-official throne.

Despite the vigour of youth, Lorenzo, from the physical standpoint, was not prepossessing. His nose was long and flat, his complexion sallow, and he had a high-pitched and grating voice that must have made an unfavourable first impression on strangers. But if nature had denied him beauty of form, it conferred on him everything else: the exquisite courtesy and tact of his grandfather, Cosimo; the gentle disposition of his father, Piero; and, in addition, the erudition of the intellectual and the poet's feeling for beauty. Much of this brilliance was due to Cosimo's far-sightedness; noting Piero's ill health, Cosimo had done his best to prepare Lorenzo for the early assumption of power. The boy had studied Greek under Joannes Argyropoulos and philosophy under Ficino, and he had been exposed continuously, from his earliest years, to the conversation of statesmen, churchmen, poets, artists, and humanists. During his long and splendid life he was to make many enemies; but not even the most vicious of those critics would ever, in the midst of bitterest invective, accuse Lorenzo of being dull, or a bore, and his opponents, like his friends, all coveted the pleasure of his company.

It was not to be expected that the susceptible Florentines could resist this paradigm of the virtues. And, indeed, they did not. A few hours after Piero's death, Tommaso Soderini, brother of the banished Niccolò but himself always a good Medici man and high in the esteem of the Florentines, easily persuaded an assembly of six hundred prominent burghers to transfer to Lorenzo the authority that his father and grandfather had possessed.

"The second day after my father's death," wrote the new head of the state in his memoirs, "although I, Lorenzo, was very young, that is to say, twenty-one years old, the principal men of the city and of the state came to our house to condole with us on our loss, and to encourage me to take upon myself the care of the city and of the state, as my grandfather and father had done. I consented to do so, but unwillingly, since, considering my age, the burden and danger were great in the task of protecting our friends and our property. For it fares ill in Florence with the rich who do not govern."

Giuliano, Lorenzo's younger brother, was not considered, either by the Florentines or probably by Lorenzo himself, for a share in the power that had just been conferred upon the elder son of Piero; for Giuliano, healthy, robust, very handsome, was fitted by character and inclination for the role of playboy rather than for that of statesman. Giuliano could scribble passable verses and turn a graceful compliment, he was good at games and could hold his own in the tiltyard. He was neither selfish nor extravagant; he was modest without being shy, humourous without a trace of vulgarity, and he possessed, in a superlative degree, those external graces that providence had denied to Lorenzo. Yet he had but little of his brother's wit, less of his originality, and nothing at all of his resolute ambition. Giuliano was content, therefore, to leave affairs of state to Lorenzo, and the latter and Florence were equally content with that arrangement. Florence, in return, took Giuliano to her heart, and he became the idol of the city at every social and economic level. It would be scarcely possible to imagine anyone more likeable or more harmlessly decorative.

For the moment, therefore, the city was at peace under the hand of

Lorenzo de' Medici, seconded by the able Tommaso Soderini. But such tranquility could not endure and, in the spring of 1470, the news was brought that an ambitious Florentine named Bernardo Nardi—who had been banished with Niccolò Soderini, Neroni, and the other conspirators of 1466—had seized the little cathedral city of Prato in the hills about twenty miles north-west of Florence. It was further related that Nardi, inflated by his success, was preparing, with Neroni's backing, to march against Florence herself. The Signory, alarmed at this threat from a base so close to the city, immediately despatched troops to crush the rebels. Before they could reach Prato, however, the *podestà* of the town had already regained control of it, captured Nardi, and promptly executed him, together with many of his followers. According to a letter written at the time by a respectable Florentine matron, Alessandra Macinghi-Strozzi, over forty men suspected or proved guilty of participating in the rebellion were hanged during the next few days, to the terror of all Prato.

This bold and efficient *podestà,* Cesare Petrucci, was to be heard of again, greatly to his credit, in Florentine history. A man of humble birth, he had been promoted to important offices by the Medici in pursuance of their traditional policy of raising talent from the ranks. They had long since discovered that such men developed qualities of unquestioning obedience to those who treated them decently. Shopkeepers or artisans who had proved themselves capable, in their ordinary vocations, of some degree of organisation and command, were often found to be much more reliable and honest than the argumentative and astute gentlemen of superior education who had, on several occasions, intrigued dangerously against Medicean ideas of government.

The quick suppression of the Prato rebellion indicated that Lorenzo's installation as head of the Republic had been congenial to the masses both in and beyond its capital. The troops would never have marched if it had been otherwise, nor would the Prato population have supported a foreign *podestà* at the risk of their lives against Florentines bent on a change of constitution in Florence—a matter that could hardly have greatly affected an obscure highland community twenty miles away. The first serious test of loyalty to the existing government in Florence had therefore been passed by Lorenzo with flying colours. He now felt that he could count on instant military action being taken against subversion if he ordered its suppression by force.

In the spring of 1471, Duke Galeazzo Maria Sforza and his wife, Bona of Savoy, made a ceremonial visit to Florence. Their arrival might be interpreted both as an act of courtesy between ostensible allies and as a reminder that Milanese power and wealth were not to be despised by the proud Florentines. The duke, who remained more or less an insolent child throughout his short adult life, brought with him twelve litters covered in gold brocade, containing the ladies of his retinue. In addition, he was accompanied by councillors, courtiers, chamberlains, and vassals, forty of whom wore ornamental chains worth at least a hundred gold florins each. There were fifty war-horses with saddles of gold brocade, gilded stirrups, and bridles of embroidered silk. Huntsmen and falconers with their hounds and hawks, trumpeters and other musicians, a hundred knights each in the uniform of a captain, and column after column of infantry, marched after the main body. This horde of peaceful invaders rode two thousand horses and two hundred mules. The sharp-eyed Florentine merchants promptly estimated the ducal equipage alone to have cost two hundred thousand gold florins.

All the visitors except the duke and duchess were lodged at the expense of the Signory. Lorenzo looked after the two principals in his palace in the Via Large, the magnificence of which filled the visitors with wonder and envy. They had certainly never before beheld such a collection of pictures and sculptures, vases, gems, intaglios, and rare, richly illuminated manuscripts. Galeazzo Maria, who genuinely loved such things without having much idea of their esthetic value, had the decency to acknowledge that, in comparison with such treasures, his piles of gold and silver were so much rubbish.

The festivities in the palace and elsewhere included the eating of meat in public, a practice strictly forbidden by the Church during this season of Lent, in the middle of March. Many Florentines, both priests and laymen, were deeply shocked at this breach of ecclesiastical law. But it could carry no very serious penalty in the case of a master of ceremonies who was practically a sovereign prince. In any case, Lorenzo made up for it by having three liturgical dramas performed in three different churches for the edification of his guests. Unfortunately, during the *Descent of the Holy Ghost,* acted in the Santo Spirito building, with real flames to represent the miraculous phenomenon described in the title of the play, the fabric caught fire and the church was burnt to the ground. Not only the elegant audience, but humbler citizens who had gathered to stare at the conflagration fled panic-stricken in all directions. They were convinced that the vengeance of heaven, in punishment for the flesh-gorging and wine-bibbing during the holy fast, was being visited upon them.

In the summer of that same year, Lorenzo turned his mind to more serious matters. He had previously been markedly cautious and conciliatory in his domestic policies, but now he began to assert himself more vigorously. In July, with the assent of Soderini, a temporary council was appointed to scrutinise the list of candidates for the magistrate over the next five years. Fifty of the *gonfaloniers* who had held office since 1434—the year of Cosimo's recall from exile—and the forty members of the existing *balia,* chose men to serve on a Council of One Hundred. The new councillors could accordingly be relied on for their loyalty to Medicean interests.

A Council of this size had previously been created by Cosimo in 1458. But in July 1470 it had refused to appoint forty-five *accoppiatori,* all supporters of the Medici who were to scrutinise the candidates for public office and, if they thought proper, to exclude certain names. Between 1458 and 1466, *accoppiatori* had been appointed by a *balia.* Since the latter date, that of the conspiracy against Cosimo's son Piero, the right to appointment had been transferred, to guard against such plots for the future, to the Council. But after the Council had declined, in July 1470, to sanction Lorenzo's proposal for the constitution of a permanent body of forty-five trusted Mediceans to act as *accoppiatori,* he obtained, a year later, conciliar consent to the less openly dictatorial arrangement noted above. The Signory and five *accoppiatori* now named forty citizens, who in their turn elected a Great Council of Two Hundred. At the same time five *accoppiatori* and these forty electors set up a committee of eighty men, which would henceforth choose men to serve on the Council of One Hundred. Both this last body, therefore, and the Great Council, could be relied on in practise to carry out Lorenzo's directions without argument. The ancient Councils of the "Commune" and the "People" became purely administrative corporations.

Lorenzo explained that this constitutional change would facilitate dealings with foreign potentates by ensuring a higher degree of consistency and stability in this field than could be contrived by more democratic means. Soon, however, Council of One Hundred came to assume supreme authority, and at the same time, the Otto di Guardia (Eight Custodians) constituting the court of criminal appeal were equipped with extended powers diverted from other branches of the judicature. Steps were taken, of course, to make certain that the "Eight" would henceforth always be Medici men.

These measures followed the principles laid down by Cosimo in private conversations with Piero. It was only long afterwards that they were formulated in writing by Lorenzo's own son Giovanni, when that shrewd family patriot, as Pope Leo X, entrusted another Lorenzo, his nephew, with the government of Florence. In the first place, Leo wrote, his young relative must take care to have an absolutely trustworthy and intimate friend on every executive council. Second, though a non-Medici man might well be allowed to hold the office of prior or *gonfalonier,* that office must never be filled by a man of strong personality or exceptional ability. Third, the Board of the National Debt, on which financial prosperity always depended, should be staffed solely by wealthy and respected citizens. Fourth, all important boards, of whatever description, were to have a clear Medicean majority.

The perusal of such principles of contemporary statesmanship tempted one to conclude that it was not possible, in the circumstances of fifteenth-century Italy, to rule without subterfuge and occasional force, including the slaughter of rebels prepared to take the ultimate risk of political defiance. Certainly fraud, and, if necessary, bloody violence, were often employed. They were common forms at a time and place that encouraged the development of separate principalities over a restricted area. In that circumstance, patriotism was liable to quickly degenerate into a narrow, unbridled selfishness, accompanied by consuming envy, which, as Cosimo himself said, "should never be watered," and by a greed ready to take instant and inordinate advantage of the least concession by a rival.

Lorenzo's clear vision and Latin logic recognised this situation automatically, as did all the other outstanding minds of his day. But he differed from most of his contemporaries by his parallel supposition that it need not always be so. Like the best of the clergy and humanists—a rather small percentage, it is true, in both cases—he felt in his bones a detestation of controversy, pugnacity, and ferocity. He was also possessed by a love of speculative thought, which seemed to promise a feasible intellectual Eden. This paradise, however, would be only partially Christian. It would retain the refreshing fruits of charity and the salutary herbs of humility recommended by the Church in its official injunctions, but this would be a setting, above all, for the pursuit of those secrets so often suggested by a manuscript by Plato, a passage in Virgil, a picture by Fra Lippo Lippi, or even by the notes of a lute. The young head of the Florentine Republic felt sure that nothing else was really worth the gravest attention of a civilised man. But he happened to be a ruler with a sense of practical duty to his fellow-citizens, at least, and perhaps to all mankind. The opinions of his mother, Lucrezia, and of the sages of ancient Rome, he found, repeatedly endorsed that sentiment, in any case innate in him.

Yet, for all the strength of his convictions, Lorenzo knew perfectly well that neither Florence nor Italy was ready for such an intellectual and esthetic Utopia. Although manners were steadily achieving more social importance in Italy than in the rest of Europe, although refined diction, elegant attitudes, and an informal appreciation of luxury and agreeable objects in general had become the ideal of all classes of society, as in ancient Athens, yet in the fifteenth century even the highest social levels fell far short in practise of Periclean theory. Mediterranean passions had been exacerbated by over a millennium of Christian austerity. They could not be restrained, always and everywhere, by a curb that lacked the terrors of supernatural sanction.

Under the brilliant surface of Lorenzo's world, therefore, there existed a seething ferocity, continuously threatening to erupt, generally when least expected, in cynical fraud and merciless violence. In these circumstances the whole peninsula, a mosaic of mutually antagonistic yet relatively weak states, presented an inextricable network of ceaseless diplomatic intrigue without parallel in Europe at that time.

The smaller world of Florence was no exception. The Tuscan intelligence awed foreigners like Galeazzo Maria of Milan by its quickness, but it was also more eagerly contentious than theirs. Republican pride in Florence, unlike the smug complacency of that in Venice, never rested on its laurels. It remained permanently suspicious of such autocracy as prevailed beyond its immediate frontiers, from Bologna, Ferrara, and Milan to Rome and Naples. Classical erudition, especially that nourished on the history of consular Rome, reinforced this feeling in a city that then led the whole Christian community in its studious attention to Livy and Cicero. Such preoccupations made the inhabitants constantly suspicious of a government that had to be strong in order to keep non-Florentine despots at bay, and that therefore never ceased, itself, to incur the charge of despotism.

The careers of Cosimo and Piero had 'taught Lorenzo how best to defend himself from such dangers. But the latest Medici ruler was also beginning at this period to develop tactics of his own, which he owed less to his father and grandfather than to his own ingenuity. He asked advice frequently, once remarking that he could thus employ other people's brains as well as his own, but he consulted individuals separately and never committed himself there and then to their opinions. He took his decisions later, in isolation. The counsellors he approached were usually men not yet socially eminent but of marked practical ability. He generally, like his grandfather, preferred to send members of high-ranking families on diplomatic and business engagements abroad. Other citizens of distinguished lineage, like Tommaso Soderini, whose influence, he felt, might prejudice his own, he prudently restricted to subordinate tasks; for he remembered, as he commented in later life, that his father Piero had nearly lost his political authority, in 1466, by allowing Luca Pitti and his adherents too much administrative power.

The visit of Duke Galeazzo Maria Sforza and his wife, Bona of Savoy, to Florence in the spring of 1471 was returned by Giuliano a few months later. Giuliano enjoyed splendid entertainment in the Milanese duchy, and thereafter the two courts kept up a regular correspondence on fairly intimate terms. But the duke's repeated requests for loans and his manifest jealousy of King Ferdinand of Naples—with whom Lorenzo also maintained friendly, if more surreptitious, relations—embarrassed the wary Florentine leader. Nevertheless, Lorenzo dared not antagonise Galeazzo Maria, who was encouraged by his ambassadors to continue the pressure so as to hold down a potential rival. "May he see," the Milanese envoy wrote to his master, "what will happen to him if you withdraw your support. He will learn then to be more humble, and not to have a foot in every camp. . . . Perhaps the difficulty he has in meeting your demands will bring him to his senses and teach him gratitude."

During the following year, 1472, an event as ominous for Florence as Galeazzo Maria's rumblings occurred in the election of Pope Sixtus IV as successor to Paul II, who had died on July 26, 1471. Sixtus had been born Francesco della Rovere, son of a poor fisherman at Albisola, in the province of Savona, near Genoa. Against this simple background, however, the new Pontiff had developed a far from simple character, mingling true generosity and enlightenment with a relentless and devious ambition. Eventually, he was to bring Lorenzo de' Medici into deadly peril, but, for the moment, Sixtus trod cautiously and received the customary delegation from Florence, bearing congratulations on his elevation to the tiara with much affability. Lorenzo, who accompanied the embassy, acquired from Sixtus, for the Medici firm, charge of the banking account of the Holy See. The young Florentine leader also obtained from the Pope further concessions in the matter of the Viterbo alum mines and, as a personal gift, marble busts of the pagan Roman Emperor Augustus and his son-in-law, Marcus Vipsanius Agrippa, who had won the Battle of Actium against Marc Antony. There, however, the Pope's generosity ceased, and Lorenzo was unable to obtain a favour dear to his heart, the conferral of a cardinal's hat upon Giuliano.

Sixtus and Lorenzo parted, to all appearance, the best of friends. The immediate gossip about the unusual displays of mutual affection that had marked the meeting between these two important rulers aroused, of course, the jealousy of Duke Galeazzo Maria. Ever since the profound impression made on him by the splendours of Florence during his visit to the city, the duke had been striving to out-do Lorenzo in all things. Galeazzo had hitherto believed that he himself occupied the first place in the Medici chief's non-Florentine attachments. Now, this low-born priest of fifty-seven, Galeazzo complained, had come between two glorious young princes of similar tastes and destiny. In this reaction, however, the petulant duke was badly mistaken on three counts: Lorenzo had no personal sympathy with him whatever; Sixtus was more afraid of Lorenzo than fascinated by him; and, finally, the careers of the hated Sforza despot and the generally admired head of the Florentine Republic were to be as diverse as possible.

The ostensible papal favour encouraged Lorenzo to undertake certain measures at home with a view to further reinforcement of his personal authority. More Mediceans of proved loyalty were added to the controlling machinery of the government, and citizens like Tommaso Soderini, who had acquired influence that might one day threaten Lorenzo's own, as Piero's had been threatened in 1466, were sent on missions abroad. The *parte* Guelfa, formerly the mainstay of the aristocratic Albizzi faction, and still representing traditional political opposition to the Medici, was dissolved. Its disappearance caused hardly a ripple, for the Guelfs, as a party of doctrinaires, had long ceased to have any meaning in the contemporary world.

Lorenzo also abolished, at the same time, the ancient office of captain of the people, which dated from 1252 and to which it was customary to be granted extraordinary powers during civil disturbances. Again, no one but a few unredeemed conservatives objected. It was obvious to most Florentines that they no longer needed a special officer to unite them in resistance to aristocratic arrogance. The old families were now subject to the law, like anyone else. The captain's post, if it continued, would not only be a sinecure but a permanent temptation to its holder to rouse an irresponsible rabble of short-sighted revolutionaries.

As regards foreign affairs, the head of the Republic succeeded, like his grandfather Cosimo, in keeping them, to a large extent, in his own hands. He himself signed a great deal of the correspondence; and therefore despatches from Rome, Naples, Milan, or Venice tended to be addressed to him by name rather than to the Signory. King Ferdinand of Naples, for instance, was so well aware of the situation that he wrote to Lorenzo: "If we wish to obtain any favour from the illustrious Republic of Florence, we hope for no other mediator and representatives than your Magnificence."*

Lorenzo knew from his own experience, and from his reading of modern Florentine and ancient Roman history, how important the respect of others is to a rising state. Such deference might often be elicited by prowess in war, but it is more solidly based on peaceful penetration and, best of all among civilised peoples, by the personal character of a ruler. In the case of fifteenth-century Florence, charm and intelligence, combined with the rarer quality of that sincere idealism more often found among artists and philosophers than in men of action, accounted for much of Lorenzo's reputation in Italy and other European countries during his lifetime.

Despite Lorenzo's high standing in the eyes of Florence and of Europe as a whole, events occasionally dimmed his luster momentarily. Such an event occurred in 1472 because of certain mining concessions

---

* This honorific title was employed quite frequently, though not always, in addressing contemporary rulers. It was only in later times, after Lorenzo's death, that his unique position and talents, as well as the unvarying splendour, not only of his formal entertainments and the solemn ceremonies he arranged, but also of his everyday life, caused him to be referred to consistently as Il Magnifico.

in the Florentine town of Volterra. In 1470, a combine of Florentine citizens had obtained a concession, on behalf of a Sienese trading company that they owned, to work the recently discovered alum mines of Volterra. In 1472, however, the Signory, upon reviewing the terms of the concession, declared the arrangement to be illegal, and ordered the mines to be closed and the Sienese company ejected. The real reason for this high-handed action apparently had nothing to do with the legality of the contract. The fact was that the alum being mined— which was an indispensable item in the dyeing of Florentine cloth— had proved to be far more profitable than originally expected, and the Volterran Signory, regretting the terms of their original contract with the Sienese company, had decided that Volterran alum should be dug up—and the profits made—by citizens of Volterra. The mining company, outraged, and encouraged no doubt by two major stockholders who were well-known Medici partisans, appealed to the superior authority of the Florentine Signory. The latter body ruled in their favour, stipulating that their judgement was subject to the personal approval of Lorenzo who, after all, had dealt with alum mines before, and who might be presumed to know something about an element so necessary in the cloth trade in which, among so many other interests, the Medici were actively involved.

The citizens of Volterra, of course, objected strenuously to the matter being laid in the lap of Lorenzo de' Medici, as though he had some sort of title to omnipotence in their affairs. A strong republic, they admitted, might dictate to a weaker one, but they would not be ordered about by a single man. They staged a violent riot in the streets, rushed the Florentine *podestà* palace, nearly killed him, and actually killed two Florentine members of the firm who had taken refuge in the building, as well as two of their Volterran colleagues. The rebellious citizens were joined, as usual on such occasions, by a mob intent only on plundering the rich. The Volterran Signory, however, eventually suppressed the tumult. They sent a delegation to Florence signifying their acceptance of Lorenzo's personal authority.

Tommaso Soderini saw no reason why any further action should be taken. The status quo had been restored, the town was now under control by its local officials, and the company could now return to its exploitation of the mines. But Lorenzo argued that to overlook the seriously insubordinate behaviour of Volterra, involving the murder of Florentine citizens, would set a dangerous precedent. It might encourage other dependencies to revolt; and it might even cause Volterra to intrigue with Venice or Naples—which were full of disgruntled Florentine exiles—for assistance in the overthrow of the present regime in Florence. He spoke so forcibly—and with such authority—that the priors accepted his advice. Troops were accordingly sent, under the command of the veteran soldier Federigo da Montefeltro, Lord of Urbino, to undertake the formal submission of Volterra.

It seems clear that nothing more was actually intended than an enquiry, supported by a show of force, into the recent disturbances. Volterra had been part of the territory of the Florentine Republic for over a century, and, in legal terms, federal soldiers had been despatched to occupy a region legally subject, though somewhat insubordinate, to the central administration. The element of difference in this case was that the local government had already reported that it had regained mastery of the situation and that there was no question of repudiating the supreme power of the capital. Even so, Lorenzo's position remains intelligible. His position was not formally that of a sovereign with the right to demand uncompromising loyalty from those who owed him allegiance. He was merely a highly respected advisor to the state. Moreover, he had only exercised personal power for a short time, and he knew that he had implacable enemies traditionally opposed to his house. What was more, the Volterran Signory might not be sincere. If not, the glitter of "foreign" arms in their streets was the only way to overawe them. Finally, Lorenzo, still in his early twenties, had not yet achieved the mature discretion of his later years. His great energy tended at this date sometimes to manifest itself in impulsive and irrevocable action. At any rate, that he had assessed the temper of the Volterran citizens as a whole, if not of its Signory, correctly, is proved by the fact that Montefeltro found the gates of the town closed against him. He had to engage in a siege of it, which lasted a month, until June 18, when surrender was made.

The sequence of what next occurred is not clear, but it seems that a councillor was robbed by one of Montefeltro's mercenary soldiers, that other mercenaries, hired by Volterra, came to blows with the occupying forces. Some of the latter, who had the advantage in numbers, escaped the control of their officers and began to butcher the Volterrans and plunder their goods. In these activities they were soon joined, characteristically enough, by the mercenaries who had previously been defending Volterra. The level-headed Lord of Urbino, a much more cultivated and reasonable man than is the wont of military commanders, tried in vain to stop the fighting. He rode down in person some of his own men and attempted to protect at least the women and children. He even hanged on the spot two alleged murderers. But he could do little more, and for some hours Volterra suffered all the horrors of a fifteenth-century city in the hands of its enemies. When the news of the sack reached Florence, Lorenzo immediately galloped off, with a few attendants, to Volterra. He restored order and compensated, so far as was possible, the victims of the pillage and destruction that had taken place.

Such are the facts that are clearly discernible in this lamentable affair. The rest is speculation. Lorenzo cannot be proved to have been responsible in any way for the savagery visited upon the rebellious town. There is indeed much evidence that neither he nor Montefeltro would ever countenance such barbarity, common as it was at that period. The "chastisement" that Lorenzo had advocated in the previous debate on the subject could only have meant the trial and sentence of such ringleaders of the riots against the *podestà* of Volterra as could be apprehended and found guilty of treason, and possibly the imposition of certain fines on individuals and on the city as a whole, accompanied by the withdrawal of a few civic privileges. He was understandably nervous in his still unofficial position of practically absolute authority. He knew from his own family's history the reckless violence to which the Tuscan temperament had been repeatedly driven at the mere suggestion of a menace to political freedom. This inclination, moreover, had been greatly reinforced during the past fifty years by study, in Florence particularly, of the pagan civilisations of ancient Greece and Rome.

It was doubtless his intention to show that he could not be intimidated, and in the Italy of 1472 he can hardly be blamed for that purpose. Nineteenth-century historians have sternly censured his severity on this occasion, but twentieth-century historians, rather better acquainted than their grandfathers with the consequences of turning the other cheek, are hardly justified in condemning Lorenzo's peremptory retort to the original lawlessness in Volterra, simply because it had so deplorable an outcome due to circumstances he could not have foreseen. This rare instance of an arguable failure in magnanimity need not today do more than lightly shade the image transmitted to posterity of the greatest of the Medici.

A more agreeable aspect of it almost immediately appeared. At the end of the year, Lorenzo paid a prolonged visit to Pisa—once the hated rival of Florence, now the principal seaport of the Florentine Republic—in order to rehabilitate the decaying Pisan university, already two hundred years old. The Signory of Florence felt, with as much common sense as generosity, that the main Tuscan centre of learning might better be situated at Pisa than in the administrative capital of the Republic. The university at Florence had experienced both a shorter and a more chequered history than that of the Pisan establishment. In the metropolis, the incessant visits of lay and ecclesiastical magnates and their elaborate retinues, as well as the regular arrivals of commercial delegations and the series of conferences on all sorts of subjects requiring the attendance of authorities from abroad, rendered scarce suitable lodgings for students not already resident in the city. Pisa was also a healthier site than Florence and easier to escape from by sea—an important consideration at this period of recurrent epidemics. Lorenzo subscribed from his personal fortune a large contribution to the necessary funds. It enabled stipends equal to the highest in Italy to be paid to the professors at Pisa.

This munificence could be compared with Cosimo's in similar directions. Lorenzo, however, possessed neither his grandfather's aptitude for finance nor that plain-living citizen's austerity in private life. The wealth of the Medici was therefore beginning to decline, while Lorenzo characteristically took no notice of this situation, but continued to spend more than ever on his household, on hospitality, on charity and public entertainments, on his collections of works of art and literature, and on personal luxuries. He himself always dressed soberly, if richly, generally in black and gold. But where others were concerned, it was a different matter. For example, in 1475 he arranged a gorgeous tournament, partly to celebrate a recent treaty among Florence, Milan, and Venice, signed in November 1474, but mostly for the amusement and honour of Giuliano, to whom he had never ceased to be deeply attached. Politian (1454–94) was moved to record the tournament in verse. *La Giostra di Giuliano de' Medici,* as the work is known, refers frequently to *"la bella Simonetta,"* presumably Giuliano's current favourite, born Simonetta Cattaneo, who is also celebrated in some of Lorenzo's verses. There are grounds for believing that this young lady—who died of consumption in 1476, at the age of seventeen—was the wife of an agreeable nonentity, Marco Vespucci (a cousin of Amerigo Vespucci) of the wealthy and prominent Florentine family. Botticelli is thought by some authorities to have painted Simonetta Vespucci in the half-length portrait of a slender, long-necked girl of somewhat prudish and stolid aspect. The canvas today hangs in the Prometheus Room (No. XX) of the Pitti Gallery in Florence. The manner of execution certainly resembles Botticelli's. But there is little trace of that unique poetry of feeling, so impressive in all Botticelli's clearly authenticated works, in this one. It is more probably by a pupil or imitator, and it is not even certainly a representation of Simonetta.

The tournament of 1475, however, was specifically dedicated, like that of 1469, to Lucrezia Donati, probably the woman whom Lorenzo always loved best, apart from his mother. Simonetta, however, was styled "queen of beauty" of the day, being the acknowledged toast of all the younger generation. Giuliano wore a suit of silver armour. Verrocchio painted his banner and designed the helmets of both brothers, and no fewer than three of Botticelli's chief pictures refer to the occasion.

The shock of Simonetta's death in the spring of the following year was mourned by all Florence. Lorenzo was at Pisa, superintending the reorganisation of the university, whence he had sent his own private physician to attend the dying woman. After receiving the news of her end, he is said to have gone out into the calm spring night with his friend Federigo of Aragon and, seeing a particularly brilliant star, to have exclaimed: "Behold, the soul of that most gentle lady hath either been transformed into that new luminary, which I have never seen before, or fused with it."

A few months after the removal of this adored young matron from the world, Florence and the Medici had to face the equally sudden and more violent destruction of a young man whose friendship was politically important to the Republic. The manner of his elimination also seemed ominous to every prince, responsible or otherwise, in Italy.

On the day after Christmas 1476, at Milan, three youthful nobles— Carlo Visconti, Girolamo Olgiati, and Gianandrea Lampugnani—suddenly set upon Duke Galeazzo Maria Sforza as he was entering the church of Santo Stefano in Milan. Before any of the duke's bodyguards could intervene, the duke's assailants had fatally stabbed him. Two of the assassins were killed on the spot. The third, Olgiati, escaped and hid for a day or two, but he was eventually captured and subsequently quartered by the public executioner.

A majority of the Milanese population were loyal to the tyrant's widow, Bona of Savoy, and she was installed with Lorenzo's backing, as regent of the duchy until her infant son, Gian Galeazzo, should come of age. But the intrigues of the child's four uncles at once began to render the government unstable, and the role of Milan in Italian politics, hitherto of much concern to the rest of the peninsula, gradually declined.

At the same time, many influential Italians approved the murder of Galeazzo Maria, not so much on account of his conspicuous vices or because his assassins had acted in the name of liberal aspirations, as because the scene on the steps of Santo Stefano reminded them of others they had read about in Greek and Roman history. Thus Harmodius and Aristogiton, they exclaimed, those two noble Athenian youths, had slain Hipparchus, younger brother of the despot Hippias, in 514 B.C., after Hipparchus had insulted the sister of Harmodius. Thus, too, Brutus and Cassius had publicly stabbed Julius Caesar, who had wished to make himself alone lord of the Roman world. Such evocations of the past became very fashionable south of Lombardy, both in private conversation and in official debate. A Bolognese professor, Cola Montano, whose lectures on political history had been attended by all three assassins, announced that the tyrannicide was "holy." A Florentine humanist, Rinuccini, declared that the murder of Galeazzo Maria was a "worthy, laudable, and manly deed, which should be imitated by all who live under a tyrant or any similarly oppressive government." This last phrase was received by Lorenzo, in the company of his friends, with an outward expression of calm assent.

Attempts were soon afterwards made to assassinate another of the Sforzas, and also Ercole I, Duke of Ferrara. Despots all over Italy redoubled their bodyguards and police precautions. Such rulers were themselves being multiplied at this period, owing to the persistent and open nepotism of Pope Sixtus IV in carving out petty fiefs for his relatives. As a priest, he had been more notable for preaching and theological learning than for ambition. But with the conferral of a cardinalate upon him by Paul II—which had come as a surprise to everyone, including himself—he then turned more and more to secular intrigue. On his elevation to the throne of St. Peter he concentrated upon building up the power of his family both in Rome and elsewhere. His nephew Pietro Riario, for instance, a dissolute young ruffian of twenty-five, was treated to a cardinal's hat and the archbishopric of Florence, where he soon became notorious for the practice of supplying his mistresses with gold chamber-pots. He perished three years later, in 1474, as a result of his excessive debaucheries.

Pietro's brother, Girolamo Riario, who had started life as either a grocer's assistant or a customs clerk, was created Lord of Imola in the Romagna. The Pope had purchased that strongly fortified town from Galeazzo Maria in 1473, though that prince had acquired it, with Lorenzo's approval, for the very purpose of keeping papal aggression out of Tuscany. When the question of sale arose, Lorenzo had offered to buy Imola from the duke, but Sixtus' bid—forty thousand ducats— was more than the Florentines thought the place was worth. This vast sum also covered the betrothal of Girolamo Riario to the duke's natural daughter, who grew up to be the redoubtable Caterina Sforza. She was then only about eleven years old.

The money had naturally to be raised through the Curia, the temporal Court of the Holy See. Lorenzo had obtained control of the financial affairs of Sixtus during his visit to Rome in 1471. But since that agreeable occasion, when the two men had got on so well together, the Florentine's eyes had been opened to the Pontiff's dangerous territorial ambitions for his kindred, which had included the appointment of the insufferable Pietro Riario to the archbishopric of Lorenzo's own city. Lorenzo accordingly took discreet steps to obstruct release of the funds required for the purchase of Imola by the Holy Father. At this point, the powerful Florentine family of the Pazzi, which also had a banking agency in Rome, offered to advance to Sixtus the amount he needed, telling the Pontiff—probably with truth—that the Medici had asked them not to do so. The Pope gratefully accepted their proposal and immediately, in his wrath at Lorenzo's opposition, transferred the papal finances from the Medici to the Pazzi. A struggle thereupon began between the Pope and the Medici that nearly proved fatal to the uncrowned king of Florence.

The Pazzi had been prominent in Florence for two centuries, and they had taken part in every domestic feud and plot during that time. Their wealth and influence was second only to that of the Medici. They had not, however, hitherto been especially opposed to the Medici. In fact a Guglielmo, son of the house, had married Lorenzo's sister, Bianca. But the traditions of the Pazzi were aristocratic rather than mercantile, and the manners of most of them were considered arrogant by the Florentine masses. In that quarter, therefore, they had not acquired much popularity. For this reason Lorenzo, always respectful of the potential weight in politics of the man in the street, had kept members of this rival clan out of office. He had also contrived that Guglielmo's brother, Giovanni de' Pazzi, should lose a suit brought against him on the death of his wife's father by the nephew of the deceased, Carlo Borromeo, for possession of the estate that would normally have gone to Beatrice.

These manoeuvres gave a sour turn to the formerly more or less good-natured rivalry between the two banking firms. Giovanni's younger brother in particular, Franceschino de' Pazzi, manager of his family's bank in Rome, conceived a furious hatred of Lorenzo and became intimate with two other important personages who also had reason to detest him. These were Girolamo Riario, the Lord-designate of Imola—a city that Lorenzo would have preferred to see remain in Milanese hands—and Francesco Salviati, nominated by Sixtus to the archbishopric of Pisa, after Lorenzo had refused to admit him to such an office in Florence. This Salviati had been described by Politian as "known to all the world to be an ignoramus, contemptuous of both human and divine law, steeped in crime and disgrace of every kind." Yet an older cousin of the man, Jacopo Salviati, had been a great friend of Cosimo's and one of Giuliano's tutors.

Nonetheless, Lorenzo had tried hard to keep on good terms with the aggressive Sixtus, who was perhaps almost as able as himself in politics and diplomacy. Just before the transfer of the papal monies to the Pazzi, the Pope accused the Florentine ruler of lending money to Niccolò Vitelli, the defender of Città di Castello, a town in the extreme north-west of Umbria that was under siege by the papal troops. Lorenzo, in denying that he had done so, wrote: "Be assured, Holy Father, that I reckon the favour of your Holiness to be among the greatest of my treasures. I have no desire to lose it for the sake of Messer Niccolò or anyone else."

Despite such protestations of respect, both Lorenzo and Galeazzo Maria Sforza had done all they could, short of actual armed intervention, to prevent the fall of Città di Castello to the Pontiff's general, who was no other than that Federigo da Montefeltro, who had acted for Lorenzo at Volterra in 1472. When the city finally fell, the Lord of Urbino was promoted by Sixtus to ducal rank, while Vitelli, the legitimate ruler, took refuge, significantly enough, at Lorenzo's city of Pisa. It was in fact vital to Florentine security to keep the Papacy out of such towns as Imola and Città di Castello, near the Tuscan border, and Lorenzo was pulling every diplomatic string at his disposal, including the greasy one of obsequious flattery of Sixtus, to achieve this object. The assassination of Galeazzo Maria at the end of 1476, after the loss of these two towns, weakened the Medicean stand against the Pope's secular ambitions.

Outwardly, the chief Italian states still remained friendly, but the inner tensions were beginning to approach breaking point. By 1477, a general war on the peninsula appeared imminent. In that year the *condottiere* Carlo Fortebraccio attacked Perugia and devastated Sienese territory. Carlo was the son of a famous military adventurer, Braccio Fortebraccio, Lord of Perugia in 1420. This Braccio, after being ejected from Rome by Francesco Sforza, had been invited to Florence and grossly flattered, so as to ensure that he would not oppose the return of Pope Martin V to Rome. Now, nearly sixty years later, the son, Carlo Fortebraccio, was suspected by Rome and Naples of connivance with Florence in a project to extend its authority and territory southwards. Papal and Neapolitan troops marched North. But Lorenzo, almost certainly innocent of the design attributed to him, which would have been contrary to his normal policy, managed to avert the threatened catastrophe by persuading the *condottiere* to withdraw his marauders.

Italy breathed again. But already a new conspiracy was being hatched in Rome by Franceschino de' Pazzi, Girolamo Riario, and Francesco Salviati, who envisaged nothing less than the overthrow of the Medicean regime in Florence. This feat could only be effected, the conspirators decided, by the murder of both Lorenzo and his brother Giuliano. Several different plans were considered. It was first proposed that Lorenzo should be called to Rome on some colourable pretext and that his death should be contrived there, while Giuliano would at the same time be assassinated in Florence. Girolamo Riario accordingly sent a fulsomely worded and pressing invitation to Lorenzo to visit him in Rome. But Lorenzo, without declining this request, did not immediately comply with it. He was, no doubt, making secret enquiries in the Holy City as to what Girolamo, whom he had no reason to love, wished of him.

The conspirators grew impatient. A new, more openly violent, course of action was propounded. This time both brothers were to be simultaneously assassinated in Florence during some public ceremony, while a professional military force stood ready outside the city to occupy it in the ensuing surprise and confusion. The extent of domestic support for the Medici was not considered wide enough to resist a resolute invasion by their external enemies, and it was imagined that much underground opposition to Lorenzo existed within the walls. The purely military action was thought to be safe in the hands of one Giovan Battista Montesecco, a mercenary captain in the Pope's pay who was indebted to Girolamo for a lucrative rise in the world. But the soldier only agreed with reluctance to play his part, pointing out that he was supposed to take up arms only on direct orders from the Pope. He also declared that he did not share the conspirators' view of the ease with which Medicean power in Florence could be crushed. The others assured him, however, that they had reliable knowledge of Lorenzo's weakness, and that the support of Sixtus for the plan would be forthcoming. Montesecco, however, demanded a personal interview with the Pontiff, declaring that he would not stir without definite instructions from the Holy Father himself. The conspirators agreed to introduce him to the Pope in a private audience as requested.

A very remarkable conversation then took place during that audience. Montesecco began by warning Sixtus that the project in view would entail the deaths not only of Lorenzo and Giuliano, but also of many other Italians. The Pontiff replied: "I will not on any account have the death of anyone, for it is not our office to consent to the death of any person. Lorenzo had been uncivil to us and treats us badly. Yet I will not on any account have his death, but only a change of government in Florence."

Girolamo Riario then assured His Holiness that every effort would be made to avoid killing people. If, however, any lives should be lost, he trusted that the Pope would pardon those responsible for any such unfortunate occurrence. At once, so Montesecco wrote afterwards, Sixtus called out angrily, *"Tu sei una bestia!"* ("Idiot!") He probably meant that he was not to be trapped into condoning murder in advance. The spiritual head of Christendom was in fact a far more intelligent man than either Riario or Montesecco. Sixtus added sternly: "I say that I will not have the death of anyone. I only desire a revolution. I am very anxious for the government of Florence to be changed and taken out of Lorenzo's hands. For he is uncivil, and an evil man who does not respect us. If he were removed from Florence, we could do as we pleased with the Republic and that would be a good advantage to us." Both Riario and Francesco Salviati, who was also present, nodded vigorously. One of them exclaimed that in such a case the Papacy could control half Italy and would be courted by every power in the peninsula. "Your Holiness may therefore be content with everything that is done to achieve such a situation," the speaker concluded hopefully. But Sixtus set his jaw grimly. "I tell you I will not have it. Go and do what you will, so long as no death is occasioned."

The three visitors, who had been kneeling before the Pope's throne, then stood up. Each one of them was now sure that Sixtus desired the death of Lorenzo, though he would not say so. Salviati asked, staring hard at the Pontiff's fierce countenance: "Are you content that we steer this ship, and that we steer it well?" The Holy Father seemed to incline his head slightly. His heavy eyelids drooped. He answered in a steady voice: "I am content."

The trio of conspirators, after taking their leave, discussed the matter further from various points of view. The *condottiere* unexpectedly advanced moral considerations, stating bluntly that it would be "a bad deed" to kill Lorenzo. The two nobles shrugged their shoulders over this unsophisticated reference to ethics. "Great deeds cannot be otherwise accomplished," they assured Montesecco contemptuously. The soldier frowned. He still did not like this affair, he said; but he was persuaded by the others that Sixtus' words had been tantamount to a command.

Eventually, the squeamish *condottiere* agreed to go so far as to visit Florence on a preliminary reconnaissance. He was instructed by Riario to seek an interview with Lorenzo on the subject of a claim by the former to an estate near Faenza in Romagna. During the conference, he was to observe carefully the temper of his proposed victim. Giovan Battista was also directed to call on an elderly knight, Jacopo de' Pazzi, head of the family, who had previously refused to have anything to do with the plot, and try to make him change his mind.

Lorenzo received the mercenary commander graciously, and said that he thought Girolamo's claim to the Faenza lands sounded reasonable. But, he added, he would have to consult his lawyers in the matter. The visitor, impressed by the genial courtesy and calm confidence of his host, felt less and less inclined to obey what seemed to be the will of the Vicar of Christ in this matter.

As for Jacopo de' Pazzi, he at first reiterated his negative attitude. Lorenzo was his friend, he said. Moreover, if Count Riario and Archbishop Salviati, who were not resident Florentines, thought that the Florentines would acquiesce in Lorenzo's overthrow, let alone help to bring it about, well then, he, Jacopo de' Pazzi, a Florentine born and bred, who had lived in the city for seventy-odd years, could tell them they did not know what they were talking about. The old knight habitually expressed himself, with many oaths, in this forcible manner. Montesecco, a little awed by this example of the fashions of an earlier day, then deferentially repeated, so far as he could remember it, what had passed at the recent interview at the Vatican between the conspirators and Sixtus. There could be no doubt, the soldier added finally, with as much firmness as he could command, that both the Pope and the King of Naples would reward anyone who got rid of Lorenzo, with or without violence.

At last, Jacopo, with a groan and a heartfelt blasphemy, indicated that the Romans could count on him. After all, his family held the purse-strings of His Holiness. If the plot succeeded and he, Jacopo, were known to have opposed it, the Pazzi would certainly lose that highly remunerative office, which was fast enabling them to catch up with Medicean financial resources and the political influence they entailed. Accordingly, the final arrangements in this discreditable affair were made.

As a first move towards Lorenzo's death, Giovan Battista Montesecco posted troops at Città di Castello, Perugia, and Todi in Umbria, to the south-east of Florence, and at Imola in Romagna, to the north-east, ready to converge on the Tuscan capital the moment news came that Lorenzo had successfully been assassinated. Then conspirators were enlisted in the plot. They comprised the archbishop's brother Jacopo Salviati; Bernardo Bandini, the black sheep of his family; and Jacopo Bracciolini, the unworthy son of the gay and learned humanist Poggio Bracciolini, who had owed so much of his fame to Medicean encouragement. Jacopo himself had strenuously cultivated it, for he had some literary ability, having dedicated a book on Petrarch to Lorenzo in fulsome terms during the previous year. The other three were Antonio Maffei, a priest from Volterra, who believed Lorenzo to blame for the sack of that town in 1472; another priest, Stefano da Bagnone, formerly employed in the household of Jacopo de' Pazzi; and finally Napoleone Franzesi, a rogue as desperate as Bandini.

In April 1478, Archbishop Francesco Salviati appeared in Florence. His task was to prepare the ground both for the assassination and for his own seizure of power after it. Already there was Jacopo de' Pazzi, who was to be responsible for inciting the populace to support the revolution. This choice alone demonstrates the conspirators' unawareness of Florentine political realities, for Jacopo was every shopkeeper's and artisan's idea of an aristocratic nuisance.

Jacopo's first assignment was to send for a boy who was intended to play a certain part, of which he was no doubt kept in ignorance, in the execution of the plot. This was one of Girolamo Riario's nephews, a lad of sixteen named Raffaello, who was attending the University of Pisa, recently reorganised by Lorenzo. Raffaello had already been appointed a cardinal by that indefatigable promoter of family fortunes, Sixtus IV, so the proclamation of the youthful prelate's arrival in Florence "on a visit to the Pazzi family" was generally held to be a compliment to Lorenzo. The hospitable head of the state, as had been anticipated, at once arranged for a Solemn High Mass to be held in the cathedral to welcome the child cardinal.

As soon as the conspirators had ascertained details of the forthcoming ceremonies, they set the order of their own procedure. Montesecco was to stab Lorenzo. Franceschino de' Pazzi, assisted by Bandini, was to make sure of Giuliano. The moment the deed was done, the archbishop would lead an armed detachment of Perugians to the palace of the Signory and take forcible possession of it. At the same time, Jacopo de' Pazzi would rouse the masses of the people of Florence to rebellion. The assassination of Lorenzo was to take place at the entertainment planned for the cardinal at the Medici Palace, after High Mass in the cathedral on Sunday, April 26. It became shortly known, however, that though Lorenzo would attend the Mass, he would be absent from the celebrations following.

The conspirators, however, considered it dangerous to wait any longer. Too many persons now knew the secret for those most deeply involved to be certain that it could be kept. Moreover, the approach of the troops from north and south had already begun. The alarm of their advance might be given at any moment. It was hurriedly resolved —since to kill Lorenzo, but not Giuliano, would be to invite serious resistance to the usurpation of government—that the crime should be perpetrated in the church itself, at the moment of the elevation of the Host.

Montesecco refused point-blank to commit such an appalling sacrilege. He would not budge from this position, and he was impatiently dismissed, with a fierce warning to hold his tongue till all was over. The two priests, Antonio Maffei and Stefano da Bagnone, had no such scruples. They coolly offered to take Montesecco's place and were duly appointed to murder Lorenzo.

On the appointed Sunday, however, it was noticed that Giuliano was, after all, absent from the Church. Franceschino de' Pazzi and Bernardo Bandini, his allotted killers, went off to fetch him from the Medici Palace. On arrival, they subjected the good-natured young man to much hearty chaff over his alleged indisposition. They even administered, with facetious enquiries, some playful body blows to his stomach and chest. These thumps were really designated to discover whether he was wearing chain-mail under his surcoat. At last they succeeded in persuading their prospective victim to accompany them to the cathedral.

Talking and laughing together, the ill-assorted group of three entered the crowded church. The tall, regular-featured Adonis of a Medici, just then looking romantically pale—for he was in fact suffering from some kind of indigestion—linked arms with the lithe, restless little Franceschino, bearing, as usual, a cynically waspish expression, and the coarse profligate Bandini, squat and muscular, the very type of a hired bravo of the streets.

Everyone made way for Giuliano as soon as he was recognised. The three newcomers joined the group of conspirators, who were standing at the entrance to the choir, situated immediately underneath the dome and surrounded at that date by a low wooden balustrade. Lorenzo stood on the south side of the opening in this barrier, with the two priests, Antonio Maffei and Stefano da Bagnone, close behind him. Giuliano, followed by Franceschino and Bandini, made his way, as custom demanded, to the north side.

For some minutes nothing could be heard but the chanting of the choir and the tinkling of silver bells. When these sounds ceased for a moment or two, the whispering and stirring of the congregation, the subdued clank of scabbards, the rattling of bracelets and rustling of silks and brocades, took their place. At last the utter silence fell that precedes the elevation of the Host. The celebrant of the Mass, erect before the high altar, lifted his arms slowly.

At that instant, a handful of gorgeously dressed figures at the entrance to the choir suddenly surged together spasmodically, then parted, scuffling, with a violently scraping swish of shoe-leather on the tessallated pavement. A blood-chilling cry of *"Prendi, traditore!"* ("Take that, traitor!") rang through the great church. Immediately afterwards a wild uproar of yells and shrieks, beginning in the choir, spread throughout the building and echoed far up into the towering cupola.

Bernardo Bandini had rapidly stepped forward and plunged a short sword, with all his strength, into Giuliano's heart. As the young man went down, Franceschino de' Pazzi flew at him, stabbing him with lightning speed, again and again, even after the collapsed figure had ceased to move. Simultaneously, Maffei and de Bagnone had attacked Lorenzo. But only one of their daggers, that of Bagnone, reached him, inflicting a slight gash in the throat. Lorenzo leaped away quickly, and immediately his cloak was round his left arm and his sword out. Parrying other blows from the daggers, he vaulted the balustrade of the choir and fled past the altar into the sacristy.

Bandini, leaving the dead Giuliano to Franceschino, rushed after the fugitive. One of the Medici bank managers, Francesco Nori, who had been with Lorenzo at Milan in 1469 for the baptism of the duke's infant son, stopped the pursuer for a moment, only to drop under a thrust as well-aimed and fatal as that which had killed Giuliano. But Nori had saved Lorenzo's life. By this time there were half a dozen of his friends, including the poet Politian and two members of the Cavalcanti family, between the assassin and the heavy bronze doors of the sacristy through which Lorenzo had just vanished. Before Bandini could tug his sword out of Nori's corpse, Lorenzo's friends had barred the doors securely.

More Medici supporters now poured into the choir, already filled by the terrified choristers of the Mass, who were trying to get out of the enclosure. In the inextricable tumult of roaring or screaming laymen and priests, Bandini the murderer managed to escape by mingling with jostling congregation in flight from the naves. Franceschino and the other conspirators also contrived to reach the street in the confusion.

Meanwhile Lorenzo, in the sacristy, after having had his wound sucked in case it should be poisoned, ordered a youth named Sigismondo della Stufa to climb up the organ loft, from which he could look down into the choir. Sigismondo shouted that Giuliano was lying motionless in a great pool of blood, but that only men of his own party could now be seen. Cardinal Raffaello, he added, was cowering in terror on the steps of the altar, defended by some Medici loyalists and being menaced by others who evidently believed him guilty of collusion with the killers. Lorenzo then directed that the doors of the sacristy should be opened. On emerging, he instantly had the cardinal arrested, and thereupon he turned to examine his brother's lifeless body.

By this time the archbishop, Francesco Salviati, had reached the Palazzo Vecchio with his detachment of some thirty Perugians. He demanded an interview with the *gonfalonier,* no other than Cesare Petrucci, whose prompt and resolute action had crushed Nardi's rebellion at Prato in 1470, when he was officiating as *podestà* there. Petrucci did not like the prelate's manner, which was simultaneously nervous and arrogant. Nor did the *gonfalonier* believe that his visitor had an urgent message from the Pope, as Salviati declared. The civil officer therefore made a sudden excuse to leave the room. After crossing the threshold and without another word, he locked the door on the outside, leaving the archbishop alone and a prisoner. On the stairs Petrucci came upon Jacopo Bracciolini, one of the conspirators, a man he thoroughly disliked and who had no business being there. Bracciolini addressed him insolently. The *gonfalonier,* alarmed and angered by these extraordinary intrusions, knocked Bracciolini down and called loudly for help. At once the great bell of the *palazzo* began to toll wildly. Petrucci's staff and the palace guard flung chains across the main staircase, overpowered the Perugians, and held the gates against a rush of men from the street, who were shouting *"Liberta"* and the Pazzi war cry.

Old Jacopo de' Pazzi had been summoning the populace to arms, as arranged. Helmeted and breast-plated, with his sword drawn, he was riding towards the palace with a hundred of his retainers, all bristling with weapons. But this force was met by counter-shouts from the Medici supporters, charging into the street from all sides. As soon as really dangerous fighting began, the rabble that had assaulted the *palazzo* fled.

Jacopo, seeing he was outnumbered, drew off his personal following and disappeared.

Soon the adherents of the government were bursting into the houses of the Pazzi. They found Franceschino in bed with a deep wound in his thigh, self-inflicted by accident during the blind fury of his stabbing of Giuliano's dead body. The indignant citizens, some of whom must have been aware by this time that Giuliano had been killed, dragged Franceschino, bleeding and clothed only in his shirt, to the palace of the Signory, where he was imprisoned with the archbishop and the Perugians who had survived the previous struggle with the priors' guards.

Almost at the same time, the news of what had occurred in the cathedral reached the *gonfalonier*. He immediately had Salviati hanged from one of the windows of the *palazzo,* together with the prelate's brother Jacopo, who had also been captured; then Franceschino de' Pazzi and Jacopo Bracciolini were strung up beside the Salviati brothers. The other surviving members of the archbishop's party were massacred or flung out of the windows, over the four dangling corpses, to be cut to pieces by the raging mob in the *piazza.*

Lorenzo by now had returned to his own palace, where he addressed his supporters from the balcony, despite the wound in his throat. He begged them to restrain their desire for vengeance, but he probably knew well enough, to his secret satisfaction, that the request would be disregarded. Everyone, in fact, who was even suspected of complicity in the plot and dared to venture into the streets was lynched on the spot. About eighty persons are believed to have perished in this way.

The veteran Jacopo de' Pazzi, cursing the bunglers who had forced him into a hopeless position and the God who had allowed such a thing to happen, had galloped off to a neighbouring mountain village. There he was seized by the local peasants, brought back to the city, and hanged—a disgraceful means of death for a man of his rank. His corpse, however, was duly buried in the Pazzi chapel at Santa Croce, but when the Signory heard that the dead man had uttered a torrent of dreadful blasphemies in his fury and despair, while the noose was being adjusted, the shocked priors ordered his body to be exhumed and buried, as that of a heretic, outside the city gates. There it was again dug up, this time by a mere horde of roughs, and dragged by the rope still secured to its neck to house after house of the Pazzi family and their supporters to the accompaniment of a yelling chorus: "Open to Messer Jacopo de' Pazzi!" The Signory, however, soon sent a detachment of its guards to put an end to these scenes. The now mangled remains of the proudest of the Pazzi were at last pitched into the Arno and pelted with filth, as the body floated downstream, by the vengeful crowds on the embankment.

Two days later, the sacrilegious priests, Maffei and Bagnone, were run to earth in a monastery, and their mutilated corpses quickly were swinging beside those of their leaders from the windows of the Palazzo Vecchio. After the bodies had begun to putrefy and been removed, the Signory ordered representations of them to be painted on the wall, hanging head downwards, as traitors to the state. Botticelli executed this work, which remained visible for several years.

Of the rest of the Pazzi family, which was almost ruined financially by these events, Renato, old Jacopo's nephew and a *gonfalonier* in 1462, knew of the plot but had refused to join. Nevertheless, he was executed for not having revealed this information. Lorenzo could have reprieved this unfortunate man, and that he did not do so must be ascribed to his implacable grief at the treacherous murder of his beloved brother. Of Renato's six brothers, none except the second eldest, Niccolò, was aware of the conspiracy, but they were all either imprisoned or banished. Even Guglielmo de' Pazzi, Jacopo's grand-nephew, Franceschino's eldest brother and Lorenzo's brother-in-law, was exiled. Giovanni de' Pazzi, Franceschino's next eldest brother and the husband of Beatrice Borromeo, whose fortune Lorenzo had diverted to her cousin Carlo, suffered incarceration for life.

The *condottiere* Giovan Battista Montesecco, who had declined at the last moment to kill Lorenzo, was captured during his escape from the city. After a long trial, he was sentenced for treason and beheaded. While awaiting execution he wrote, in prison, an account of the conspiracy that is the chief source of the details later noted by historians.

The Pazzi, in addition, were deprived of their coat-of-arms and all their lands and houses. Those who married into the family, it was decreed, would be excluded from the public service. The grim scoundrel, Bernardo Bandini, got away and fled as far as Constantinople. In due course, Sultan Mohammed II heard of the events that had culminated in the cathedral at Florence on April 26, 1478. He did not care for the assassins of heads of state, whatever their religion, and he sent Bandini, after negotiation with the monarch, back in chains to Lorenzo, who had despatched Antonio di Bernardino de' Medici, son of the joint commander at the Battle of Anghiari in 1440, to extradite the criminal. The brutal slayer of Giuliano was duly and deservedly hanged, with little ceremony, before the public of Florence. One result of this episode was the deep impression made in Florence and elsewhere in Italy by Lorenzo's evident high standing with the fearful Turkish sultan.

The only conspirator who escaped unpunished was the most insignificant of the chief participants, Napoleone Francezi. This ruffian, who died fighting for the King of Naples in the following year, had been befriended by Piero Vespucci, a cousin by marriage of the fair Simonetta and, of course, also related to the adventurous Amerigo. The story eventually came out, and Piero had to serve two years in prison for the reckless compassion or mere folly of this act. His daughter implored Lorenzo, in vain, to remit her father's sentence. The letter throws an interesting light on the relations of Lorenzo with his subjects:

"Beloved lord, I write on behalf of a good father . . . yesterday I was not able to speak with you as I desired, to recall the love and good will you once bore to this house, the words you spoke, the promises you made me and your kindness in calling me sister. . . . I now pray you to have mercy upon us all. May it please you to consider the condition of my father, to look upon him through my eyes and not judge him alone for what he has done, since others were guilty with him. I entreat your grace most urgently to restore him to me without further injury. Let the punishment he has already suffered for his offences suffice. He is old and in feeble health. He has long been feverish and is now so again. At the thought of where he is, with chains upon his feet, my heart breaks. If these lines weary you, pray have patience. Remember that those who are merciful shall be shown mercy. I beg you to send me a favourable reply by the bearer of this letter. May God move your heart to restore my father to me this night. I am sure you would do this if I were with you now. A moment ago news was brought to me that he is being tortured again. I conjure you, keep us no longer in despair. From Ginevra the unhappy."

No answer is recorded. Lorenzo was not the man to be stunned by grief. But the tragic outcome of the Pazzi conspiracy had hardened him, in spite of its political failure. He could see, after Montesecco's confession, that the vile murder of his brother had been the climax of schemes originating in the almost pathological secular ambition of a Pope distinguished by his learning and public spirit. The men used by Sixtus to promote the subjection of Florence to his power were, for the most part, utterly contemptible. The best of them, the professional mercenary Montesecco, and the choleric old gambler Jacopo de' Pazzi, had been over-awed by the papal prestige. Or perhaps they had genuinely shared the declared view of the Pontiff that the Medici were impious dangers to Italian freedom. But all the rest were, at bottom, unscrupulous self-seekers, however much they might talk of the nobility of Greek and Roman tyrannicides. No doubt the boy cardinal, Raffaello Riario, remained entirely innocent of any complicity in the affair. Lorenzo, at any rate, soon allowed him to leave Florence for Rome. There, after he had got over his fright at his experiences on April 26, he proceeded to enjoy himself in the usual gay fashion of youthful Italian cardinals of the Renaissance era. By 1513, however, he had reformed sufficiently to be considered as a candidate for the papacy eventually acquired by Leo X.

The Pazzi plot had failed conspicuously to achieve even its secondary object of discrediting the Medici. The behaviour of their most active representatives, Lorenzo and Cesare Petrucci, was exemplary, if decidedly severe. Their party, now regarded as the heroic victims of Roman and Neapolitan aggression—for King Ferdinand was known to have been implicated in the over-all design to crush the Medici— became stronger and more popular than ever. The exceptionally independent spirit of the average Florentine remembered how the family had always stood, in the main, from the time of Salvestro, the challenger of oligarchs in the middle of the fourteenth century, right down to the present, Lorenzo's first decade of government, for a degree of political liberty unknown anywhere else in the world.

By the summer of 1478 the pride, hope, and courage of the city had risen to a point they were never to reach again. It was felt in the *palazzi,* the banks, the shops, the factories, and even in the soldiers' barracks and the artisans' and artists' humble dwellings, that Florentines were all brothers in the service of an ideal humanity. More or less inarticulately, they looked forward to a culture, an intelligence, and a moral stature unequalled since Cicero had exemplified them. Few of the citizens believed that such qualities could not make their way against all the ferocious bigots who were understood to be seething with rage against them in the autocratically ruled lands to the south and north of Tuscany.

* * *

Although the domestic situation of Lorenzo and his city was now more stable than it had ever been before, both Sixtus and King Ferdinand of Naples were exasperated at the failure of the Pazzi conspiracy, while the fury of Count Girolamo Riario, in particular, drove him to violent action in Rome. If the Venetian and Milanese ambassadors had not intervened, he would have thrown into prison Donato Acciaiuoli, the Florentine envoy—whose family had been restored to Medicean favour after Piero's recall in 1469 of the aged exile, Agnolo. Donato, a learned author as well as an experienced diplomat, had been an intimate friend of both Cosimo and Piero. To the latter, indeed, he had dedicated certain of his writings. No one could have been a more devoted Medici man, and this circumstance was enough to render Riario his deadly enemy.

Certain other powerful Romans, taking their cue from the Pope, also proceeded to various arbitrary acts, on one excuse or another, against Florentine businessmen resident in the Holy City. Many such merchants were arrested, and many had their stock in trade and other property confiscated. Meanwhile, the inexorable Pontiff ordered the Florentine Signory to decree the banishment of Lorenzo. This demand was purely spiteful, for Sixtus could not have supposed that it would be complied with. When it was ignored, however, he followed it up with a bull of excommunication against Lorenzo. Such documents, excluding offenders from the rites of the Church, had become the usual weapons of the Papacy in its quarrels with Italian and other European states. The present bull threatened, in addition, that if Florence did not deliver the person of Lorenzo to the Vatican within a month to answer for his conduct, the archbishopric conferred upon the Tuscan capital would be withdrawn.

In this missive, by tradition couched in very abusive language, Lorenzo is termed a "child of iniquity" and "nurseling of perdition" guilty of encouraging mercenaries—for instance, Carlo Fortebraccio, in 1477—to attack the Papal States. It was also charged that the Medici ruler had prevented Archbishop Francesco Salviati from taking possession of his see, and had subsequently hanged him. Furthermore, Lorenzo had dared to arrest a cardinal (Raffaello Riario) at the most sacred moment of High Mass in the cathedral. Worse still, the unoffending dignitary in question had been cast into a foul dungeon at Lorenzo's command. The Pontiff coolly attributed all these events to family feuds arising from the tyranny of the Medici. He ignored the murder of Giuliano, regarding it, by implication, as due to the same cause.

On receipt of the bull, Lorenzo immediately took counsel with an assembly of Tuscan prelates and theologians, presided over by the Bishop of Arezzo in the cathedral at Florence, and, upon their advice, the head of the state publicly declared the bull of excommunication invalid. He also sent statements of the facts, accompanied by copies of Montesecco's confession, to every court in Europe. He then prepared to resist by force the papal military invasion that he knew would follow.

Venice, never famous for its piety, approved Lorenzo's attitude in a letter to its ambassador in Rome: "The Holy Father must not flatter himself," the Doge wrote, "that he can conceal the purpose of his evil thoughts by asserting that he does not intend to chastise Florence itself, but only Lorenzo. For we all know perfectly well that he is attacking not only Lorenzo, who is entirely innocent of the false charges brought against him, but also the present form of government in the city. It is this which the Pope desires to overthrow and replace by one subservient to himself, with consequent ruin upon all Italy."

The Serene Republic would never have taken this line if it had not been assured of the support of most of the powerful northern states against the intolerable passion of Sixtus to dominate the peninsula. Milan, still more boldly than Venice, menaced the Pontiff with war if he did not withdraw his bull. The last thing Lombardy wanted was to see her wealthy buffer community to the south humiliated and robbed by the Vicar of Christ. Ferrara and Mantua indicated at least their sympathy with Lorenzo. Even King Louis XI of France, a strong monarch very interested in merchants and bankers and therefore, as he had often shown in the past, friendly to the Medici, professed himself scandalised at the Pope's conduct. The French ruler sent the historian Philippe de Comines, his chamberlain, to warn Sixtus that an Ecumenical Council would be set up to examine his fitness for his office if he persisted in stirring up hostility against Florence.

Nevertheless, the Pope and King Ferdinand despatched two expeditionary forces into Tuscany. One was commanded by Federigo da Montefeltro, whom Sixtus had made captain-general of the Papal States, as well as Duke of Urbino, after his capture of Città di Castello in 1474. Federigo's army entered Florentine territory from the east, while Alfonso, Duke of Calabria, led other troops, which appeared in the south. Both these generals had a high reputation at the time. Urbino had formerly been much trusted by Lorenzo, who had always found his cultivated tastes congenial. The Neapolitan was a different sort of fellow, though Lorenzo, as already mentioned, kept up a friendly correspondence with his wife and younger brother. The Duke of Urbino had of course to accept the favours of a man, the Holy Father himself, whose territory bordered on his own and who could have ruined him in a few weeks.

Lorenzo put the Florentine forces, which included contingents from Milan and Venice, in the charge of Ercole d'Este, Duke of Ferrara, who though not an ineffectual soldier, was not so good as he thought he was. On July 11, 1478, the Calabrian duke sent a herald into Florence to announce, on behalf of Sixtus, that he was not making war on the Republic, but only, as Rome had already several times declared, on Lorenzo. All the same, the herald went on, if the Signory did not at once expel their "tyrant," they would be rightly stigmatised as the enemies of Christianity.

Although these messages invariably stressed ecclesiastical aspects, the repeated branding of Lorenzo as "anti-Christian" probably alludes to his personal character, which was considered impious by conservative churchmen on account of its philosophic bent, literary culture, gayety, and love of luxury. There were many other men in Italy at this time, both princes and prelates, who more or less privately exercised free speculation in metaphysics and ethics, wrote humourous and amourous verses, kept mistresses, collected works of art, and spent much time with hawks and hounds. But most of them were careful—and Lorenzo was not—to quote orthodox doctrine both in and out of season. In point of fact, Lorenzo was as sincere a Christian as the next man. He was not, however, ostentatious about his faith, and he therefore incurred the suspicion of heresy among the theologically rigid, both ecclesiastical and lay, and among those who pretended to be such.

After hearing the duke's herald, the head of the state summoned an assembly of some three hundred leading citizens and told them he was perfectly prepared to suffer death or exile if they thought either penalty desirable in the interests of the imperilled Republic. No doubt, Lorenzo felt he knew what their answer would be, and he was correct. "Your Magnificence must take courage," the burghers answered, "for it behooves you to live or die with the Republic." The meeting prudently proceeded to appoint a bodyguard of twelve professional soldiers to protect Lorenzo from any further attempts at assassination. Such attacks were considered by responsible citizens, with some reason, to be now highly probable.

The fighting between the dukes of Calabria and Urbino on one side and that of Ferrara on the other remained desultory for some months. The only serious losses were those of the peasantry in the destruction of their crops and dwellings and the callous, occasionally outrageous, treatment that they experienced at the hands of the troops on both sides. Nothing is more striking in this episode, and at this period, than the reluctance of Italians to accept the first principles of warfare. Conflicts on the peninsula were rarely fought out to the bitter end. The opposing commanders sought rather to entrap and starve out their opponents than to destroy them. Terms of unconditional surrender were therefore never imposed. Casualties remained light, and peace treaties, temporary. It must be remembered, in trying to account for this peculiar method of campaigning, that warfare was almost wholly in the hands of mercenaries, both foreign and Italian, who did not so much hate, as desire to get the better of, their antagonists. Such hired armies were not, as a whole, animated by abstract ideas of freedom or loyalty to one particular state. In defence, they acted more in the spirit of a householder confronted by a burglar than in that of a determined rebel against occupation. The object was simply to force the enemy to retreat. In attack, again, they concentrated more on outwitting the foe and holding him for ransom than on eliminating forever the danger that the enemy represented.

The futility of fifteenth-century battles on the peninsula also derived largely from incessant fluctuations in the political situation. In the present case, for instance, not all the Northerners thought Sixtus in the wrong. Siena openly took his part, while Lucca seemed unable to make up its mind. Meanwhile, both Genoa—attacked by seaborne Neapolitan troops—and Pisa—which feared a similar surprise—clamoured for Florentine assistance. King Louis of France himself gradually adopted a less truculent tone, and supported by embassies from England and

Germany, he contented himself with asking the Pope to come to terms with Lorenzo.

By this time, the Pontiff realised that he had exceeded the limits of the possible in setting his objectives so high, and he relented somewhat. In April 1479 he suspended the interdict on Florence, cancelled hostilities, and said no more about arresting the head of the Republic. His terms still remained too severe for acceptance, and they were rejected by the Signory. In June, war broke out again.

Towards the end of that month Roberto Malatesta, Lord of Rimini, defeated the papal forces near Lake Trasiemeno, on the very ground where Hannibal had routed the ancient Romans in 217 B.C. during the Second Punic War. The engagement had no important effect, and a few weeks later an absurd dispute over some plunder caused the Duke of Ferrara and the Marquess of Mantua actually to come to blows in person. While they sulked, the main Florentine army was badly beaten by Neapolitan troops at a place called Poggio Imperiale in southeastern Tuscany. The victors marched west, bypassing friendly Siena, captured Poggibonsi, Vico, and Colle, in the Val d'Elsa, and halted dangerously close to Florence. A siege would undoubtedly have ensued but for the autumn rains.

Lorenzo demanded a truce, which was granted on November 26. Since the defeat at Poggio Imperiale, he had grown seriously alarmed about his prospects of continuing to defy Rome and Naples. He was no soldier himself, but he could see that his chief officers, with the possible exception of Malatesta, were no match for the dukes of Urbino and Calabria. Both of these naturally wary commanders had learned by bitter experience, unlike the Ferrarese and Mantuan princes, to discipline both themselves and their armies, a notion that at this period rarely occurred to the average Italian captain, mercenary or otherwise.

Apart from the unfavourable military situation, the ruler of Florence did not like the look of affairs at Milan. His agents there had reported that Bona of Savoy was allowing her brother-in-law, Lodovico Sforza, called Ludovico Il Moro,† fourth son of the late Duke Francesco, to take over much of her administrative duties. In his new capacity as head of the Milanese foreign office, Ludovico now informed Lorenzo that Milan was not prepared to render further aid to Florence in the war, at any rate so far as it involved Ferdinand of Naples, whose friendship Milan was now cultivating, for the reason that the military

† As a child, Lodovico, now aged twenty-eight, had been called Il Moro (The Moor) by his father, simply because Moro was the boy's second baptismal name. Ludovico's complexion was not, in fact, as dark as a Moor's. He was fair in colouring, like many northern Italians; but as he grew up he took the secondary meaning of his name as a joke, and adopted as his devices a Moor's head and a mulberry tree, which in Italian is also called *moro*.

laurels of the southern kingdom were beginning to shine more brightly than those of any other state in the peninsula. Lodovico advised his correspondent, if he wished to save his skin, to do the same.

On the whole, the shrewd head of the Republic felt inclined to agree with the Milanese. He was well aware that, as usual after a serious setback in the field, the citizens of Florence were growing weary of the expense of maintaining hostilities. He knew that some of them were wondering why they should be ruined for the sake of a single individual who happened to have incurred the enmity of the Pope. Sixtus, indeed, was still telling all the world that he had no quarrel with Florence, but only with its objectionable autocrat. This last word was no more popular in fifteenth-century Florence than it had been in the preceding centuries. Its mere utterance caused people to frown and lay their hands on their daggers. In these circumstances, Lorenzo decided he must act fast.

As early as November 29 he despatched a trusted messenger, Filippo Strozzi, on a secret mission to King Ferdinand of Naples. The Pitti family had been exiled by Cosimo in 1457, but they had long since been recalled and were now staunch allies of the Medici, as they were to prove often enough in later years. Filippo had been an eye-witness of the murder of Giuliano, and he left for posterity an account of that event. The fact that he could see so much proves him to have been one of Lorenzo's closest friends at the time, standing near to the brothers at the fatal service in the cathedral.

Filippo Strozzi was to tell the King of Naples that Florence would consider any proposal that might emanate from his court with a view to ending the war. The emissary had no sooner left than the head of the Republic called some forty of his most devoted followers together and, after earnestly begging them not to repeat what he was about to say, announced that he himself was setting out for Naples very shortly. He had already, in fact, arranged for news of his visit to be conveyed to Ferdinand before Strozzi's arrival at the court. Lorenzo went on to instruct the astonished assembly that, in his absence, the affairs of the Florentine state were to be conducted by Tommaso Soderini, formerly one of the best of Piero de' Medici's men and now the most confidential advisor of the present head of the Republic. Only the privileged forty knew that Lorenzo was leaving Florence, but, on the seventh, after travelling west in order to avoid the left wing of the papal troops in Tuscany, he wrote officially to the Signory from San Miniato al Tedesco, on the road to Pisa, where he intended to take ship: "In the dangerous circumstances in which our city is placed, it was more necessary to act than to deliberate. . . . I therefore mean, with your permission, to proceed directly to Naples, conceiving that, as I am the person chiefly aimed at by our enemies, I may, by delivering myself into their hands, perhaps be the means of restoring peace to my fellow-citizens."

As he had no doubt anticipated, this communication did much to reinforce his waning popularity, not only with government but also, when the news was made public, with those citizens who had been grumbling over the expensive and inconclusive war. At Pisa, he received a formal despatch from the priors authorising him to negotiate in their name, in any way he pleased, with the King of Naples.

So bold, even reckless, a move certainly exposed Lorenzo to personal risks. He might be assassinated, either during the journey or at Naples. The step also entailed the peril of a revolution in Florence while he was away. He knew that some Florentines—and those by no means the least powerful—would remain implacably opposed to his authority even if they had proof of his courage in staking both his liberty and his life on an attempt to regain peace and prosperity for the Republic. But it was characteristic of the man that he could not only weigh a situation in which he was subject to pressure from Ludovico Sforza, the Pope, and the papal allies, but that he could also come to an almost instant decision to reverse a previous policy and could implement it with equal speed.

Once in Naples, Lorenzo found that he had not much to fear. On December 18, King Ferdinand received him courteously, and a few days later affectionately. The visitor took advantage of this warmth to urge upon his host the attractions to a Neapolitan monarch of a politically stable Florence as contrasted with the shifting sands of Milan— with a woman on a throne besieged by four jostling brothers-in-law— and the unsteady policies of the Vatican, which changed every time a Pope died.

The King temporised, pretending that he could not bear to let his enthralling guest go. In reality, he was reluctant to face the break with Sixtus entailed by a reasonable treaty with Florence. Moreover, many of Ferdinand's court, who knew little about the true state of affairs in Florence, kept stressing Lorenzo's unpopularity at home. The monarch could not help reflecting that the longer the head of the House of Medici stayed away from Florence, the more chance there would be of a revolution that would improve the Pontiff's present temper. On the other hand, the King was impressed by Lorenzo's insistence on the decline of Florence's traditionally amiable relations with France, for the Neapolitan sovereign feared renewal of the Angevin claims to his throne. He also appreciated his visitor's representation of the somewhat restless Ludovico as a good friend of both Florence and Naples for the time being, but only so long as the Republic discouraged his attentions to France, which the Milanese inclined to regard as unreliable.

Yet Ferdinand perceived with some wonder, in view of what were supposed to be Lorenzo's difficulties with his own people, that Lorenzo seemed in no hurry to leave. Apparently, he found Neapolitans on the whole gayer than Florentines, if less intellectual. The frank, carefree side of his nature, the keen simplicity of his reactions to sensuous stimulation, which comes out so clearly in his lyrics, whether light or melancholy, had less inhibited scope in the comparatively riotous bounty of Campania, which made him too feel more generous than usual. He began to throw his money about, entertained lavishly, presented dowries to poor girls, and bought out criminals condemned to the appalling slavery of the galleys—a punishment often inflicted for trifling misdemeanours.

This prodigal expenditure and revelling may simply have been assumed to mask real anxiety, for it was not easy to guess what the King might actually have in mind. It was obvious that Sixtus was exerting a relentless pressure on him either to lock Lorenzo up or send him in chains to Rome. Moreover, external events were also making it difficult to settle the terms of the treaty under consideration. Two subordinate commanders in the forces of the Duke of Calabria had broken the armistice by capturing and plundering a town that had been held by Florence since 1468, as a key point strategically, the strongly fortified little city of Sarzana in the extreme north-west of Tuscany. The duke, it seemed, had looked the other way while this operation was in progress. Again, certain lords of Romagna, who had helped Florence during hostilities, were clamouring for a clause to be inserted in the peace treaty providing for their immunity from papal vengeance. Meanwhile, Sixtus himself was insisting tirelessly that no agreement should be signed until Lorenzo had personally presented himself in Rome to beg the Pontiff's forgiveness.

At last, in February 1480, Ferdinand's agents in Florence reported that a revolt against Medicean control appeared out of the question, so long as Lorenzo lived. The King, who genuinely admired Lorenzo, respected his power, and believed him sincerely devoted to the pacific development of civilisation throughout the peninsula as well as in Florence, decided that his violent removal, however much it might please the Vicar of Christ, would really betray the cause that the Pontiff himself was in theory bound to support. The royal signature was therefore rather suddenly affixed to the draft treaty, and a duly reasoned explanation of this act was despatched to the Pope. Sixtus flew into a rage, but he did not, for the present, resort to either threats of hell-fire or of the sword.

Lorenzo's courage, tact, and patience, exercised imperturbably for two months, had achieved an object that hardly anyone but himself had believed attainable. Peace had triumphed over the threat of general war. Pallas Athene had tamed Mars. Sandro Botticelli painted a fine canvas to immortalise this event. It represents the goddess, crowned with olive and armed with a great halberd, cornering a discomfited centaur. The fingers of her right hand are firmly entangled in the monster's bushy hair, suppressing his fidgets with absolutely calm, almost maternal, confidence. The face of Pallas, as so often in the case of this highly romantic artist's delineations of women, conveys an effect of specifically female intelligence, quite devoid of severity. In this picture it illustrates a kind of superhuman tenderness, much more Christian than pagan, which might be that of an ideal feminine administrator of this world, a being illimitable in wisdom as in power. The picture attributes to the Magnificent Lorenzo's feat a nobility, in allegorical form, that goes far beyond the merely defensive common sense that inspired it. The comparatively modest recipient of this indirect offering may have been slightly embarrassed by so much transcendental glory, for Lorenzo's very real pride was never simple vanity.

However that may have been, more usual expressions of gratitude greeted the uncrowned monarch of Florence on his return to the city, on March 7, 1480, and the terms of the alliance that he had secured between the hard-headed Tuscans and the volatile Neapolitans were published ten days later. The towns that Florence had lost to the papal forces during the war were to be ceded to Siena, a loyal supporter of Rome. The members of the Pazzi family in prison at Volterra were to be released. The Duke of Calabria was to be paid an annual retainer by Lorenzo to guarantee Neapolitan military services if the two newly allied states had to combine against an outside aggressor. The treaty did not mention either the protection demanded by the lords of Romagna, since Ferdinand had given his visitor a private assurance in that direction, or the restoration of Sarzana.

These conditions were rather humiliating to Florence, but a price had to be paid for such powerful support as that of the ruler of Naples. There was some grumbling, nonetheless, especially about the retention of Sarzana by Lorenzo's former foes. Nor, as time went on, did it seem quite certain that Pallas Athene had permanently tamed the centaur. Venice expressed dissatisfaction with the martial aspect of the agreement, which appeared aimed at states in the North, and Sixtus therefore snubbed Ferdinand and came to an understanding with the Venetians. Lorenzo promptly negotiated an understanding with Milan. The Holy Father, however, neither cancelled his prohibition of religious rites in Florence, nor withdrew his demand for Lorenzo's presence in Rome to make personal submission to the Holy See. Moreover, the ambitious Duke of Calabria had gone to live in Siena, with the evident intention of acquiring the lordship of that city.

But at this dangerous juncture a decisively distracting event occurred far to the south of the peninsula, at the port of Otranto. The genial but frequently rapacious Sultan Mohammed II, who captured Constantinople in 1453, and had subsequently conquered most of Greece and defeated the Venetians, was now determined to add Italy itself to his dominions. He began with a raid on Otranto that proved alarmingly successful. The port was burnt to the ground and its male inhabitants were massacred. Ferdinand at once recalled the Duke of Calabria from Siena to eject the invaders, a project that Alfonso was bound to attempt but that he considered a great nuisance at this stage of his plans, which were concentrated just then on the northern region of central Italy. The Turkish attack had been quite unexpected. It suddenly drew the attention of Italy in general to the dreaded prospect of Moslem domination, which had been almost forgotten—except by the Venetians—while Mohammed was engaged in the Balkans. The Pope also turned his whole attention to this new approach of Islam, which he judged a menace to all Christendom.

As an item in his endeavours to call all Italians into a common front to face the terrible infidels, he told the Florentine priors that if they sent him a delegation to sue for pardon it would be accorded them, whether Lorenzo came in person or not. Twelve ambassadors were immediately despatched to St. Peter's. They knelt in the portico before Sixtus, exhibiting every sign of contrition for the city's offences to the Pontiff and imploring the papal forgiveness. It was the kind of scene that the Pope relished. He gave the embassy absolution and altogether promised to remove the already suspended interdict. But Florence, he added severely, must in return supply fifteen galleys to operate against the Turks so long as the heathens remained on Italian soil. The envoys humbly assented, but they knew that, since their city was not a naval power, the Holy Father could hardly insist on this face-saving imposition. In fact, he did not do so.

While Alfonso of Calabria marched reluctantly southwards, the Turks gradually withdrew from Apulia. Their long-term project had been postponed. Mohammed II died in the following year, and his successor proved a man of peace, or at any rate, a man less interested in Italy than in adventures to the north-east of his empire, where he anticipated less effective resistance. It was not until the very end of the century that Islam was to turn west again, and then only to attack Venetian power.

Lorenzo could now, accordingly, apply himself with renewed confidence to domestic affairs. He found that his position at home, despite some obstinate malcontents, had definitely improved. It was generally recognised that he could not have hoped for better peace terms from Ferdinand and Sixtus than he had actually obtained. After all, Rome and Naples plausibly could be considered to have won the recent war. The Neapolitan visit, all the same, had greatly advanced Lorenzo's reputation for bold and successful diplomatic ability.

He determined not to risk a deterioration in his popularity by attempting, as almost any other fifteenth-century Italian ruler would in such circumstances, to make himself legally as well as practically a monarch. He already possessed the substance of power in the city, and there was no advantage further in acquiring merely the forms of sovereignty. In spite of his truly Italian love of luxury and display, Lorenzo understood perfectly from his study of Florentine history alone—to say nothing of more ancient models—the perils of personal arrogance in a constitutional prince. He resolved to imitate for the rest of his life the admirable discretion that had served his grandfather Cosimo so well. He also took steps at this time to introduce such popularly acceptable constitutional measures as would remedy the post-war financial depression that had set in. In April 1480, the three existing councils at Florence—that of the One Hundred, representing the masses only; the Council of the People, with its captain and 300 members drawn from the lower ranks of the population; and finally the Common Council, under the *podestà,* comprising 125 nobles and an equal number of their social inferiors—all passed a resolution appointing a *balia,* or provisional government, of 258 members representing all classes and districts as equitably as possible. The duties of this Grand Council (Consiglio Maggiore), as it came to be called, were to nominate candidates for public service, to enquire into reports of abuses in the management of the national debt and in the assessment and collection of taxes, and to relieve distress in the areas that had suffered during the war. The Grand Council in its turn created a Council of Seventy, ostensibly for five years, though in practice the members sat for life. This arrangement inaugurated a novelty in Florentine politics, where brief tenures of office had hitherto been the rule. But, as a safeguard against irresponsibility, all the councillors had to be over forty years old, to be either guildsmen or distinguished in some other way, and to represent at least forty families. The Council of Seventy—of which the *gonfalonier* was an *ex-officio* member—appointed the priors and otherwise took a leading part in the administration of the state. The Committee of Eight (the *Otto di Pratica*) controlled military and foreign affairs. The Committee of Twelve (*Procuratori*) dealt with the crucial subjects of finance and commerce. These two committees held office for six months only and were not eligible for re-election.

It was agreed that every approach to the Seventy, whatever the question, must always be made through the Signory. But the three original Councils—that of the One Hundred, that of the People, and that named the Common Council—retained their legislative functions.

Each new bill, before it became law, would have to be approved by a two-thirds majority of a quorum of two thirds sitting in council.

Although Lorenzo took care not to pack any of these councils exclusively with Mediceans, and although the introduction of the new bodies implied no departure from the previous administrative structure except for the tenure of seats for life by the Seventy, this last practice had considerable importance for the preservation of the existing regime of his house. A majority of the Seventy supported Lorenzo and, since they customarily sat for life, government by Medicean oligarchs was ensured. Yet none of these men, all chosen for their exceptional intelligence and high degree of education, would have found it easy either to assume despotic authority himself or to allow Lorenzo to do so. They represented of necessity all the urban districts, the lower social classes as well as the middle and upper. They could, in theory, oppose Lorenzo's advice whenever they pleased. In other words, the elaborate machinery that Lorenzo de' Medici had contrived to maintain his personal power could, at any moment, be used to destroy it. Every one of the Seventy recognised this fact. Some of them would have been prepared to take advantage of it if the head of the state had ever given them a pretext to work in that direction.

He never did so. Under the arrangements of 1480, Florence remained, until Lorenzo died, less troubled by faction and family feuds than she had ever been before. After that year, Sixtus would have not been able plausibly to ascribe a murder, undertaken with his connivance to promote his own ambitious schemes, as a mere squabble between tribal chiefs. For the next twelve years, experienced and efficient administrators were continuously in charge of the Republic. Art and trade, industry and public works, all flourished to an unprecedented extent. Whatever objections in principle to oligarchy may have been cherished by political theorists at that time or may, for that matter, be upheld today, Florentine oligarchy in Lorenzo's last period proved a great practical success.

A plot to assassinate him, which was discovered in June of this same year, merely increased the popularity of a leading citizen who was royal in all but name. The conspiracy can probably be attributed to the implacable Count Girolamo Riario's machinations in Rome, though there is no documentary evidence of his complicity. Proof exists, however, that a certain Battista Frescobaldi was implicated. His family earlier had served Cosimo de' Medici well, but Battista considered that he had been inadequately rewarded for his part in negotiating the extradition from Constantinople of the unconscionable ruffian Bernardo Bandini, who had stabbed Giuliano. This descendent of the honourable line of the Frescobaldi discovered in due course three other gentlemen who fancied they had equal grievances against Lorenzo. The quartet eventually decided that the head of the state, like his brother, should be murdered in a church, either the cathedral or Santa Maria del Carmine. Ascension Day was fixed as the date of the crime; but Frescobaldi and two of his fellow-conspirators were arrested in good time and beheaded. The Signory then passed a law designating any attempt on Lorenzo's life as high treason. This was the first official recognition that the *de facto* ruler of Florence, technically a private individual, could be regarded as equivalent in rank to the dynastic sovereigns with whom he so often corresponded or conversed on terms of practical equality.

Apart from the constitutional reorganisation noted above, Lorenzo continued in other ways to follow his father's and grandfather's policies of elevating able men of low social position to responsible officers. It is also true, however, that like nearly all other Italian rulers of this period, Lorenzo also found major or minor posts, if only clerkships, for his less talented dependants of humble origin.

In fiscal affairs, Lorenzo's record is less satisfactory. Unlike Cosimo, he had little understanding of, or interest in, finance. Yet he needed large sums both to meet war debts and to maintain his influence and prestige both at home and abroad. A task almost equally urgent and expensive, and one that he tended to neglect, was that of keeping the family business on an even keel. When he failed in the latter objective, he was apt to supply this private deficiency from public funds. It is not at all clear, in the absence of the accounts—which disappeared after his death—just how serious these depredations were, and they have been variously estimated by different historians. Some commentators who put the figures high have suggested that records of such transactions may have been deliberately destroyed by Lorenzo in order to shield his own reputation or to protect his family and friends. The truth probably is that Lorenzo, like most men with keen esthetic interests and a fastidious taste in such matters, was naturally extravagant. He certainly loved, and wished to acquire for himself, all sorts of beautiful things, from the masterpieces of the fine arts to textiles and furniture. His personal expenses are therefore likely to have been beyond his immediate means. His credit, on the other hand, was far from restricted. He could order what he liked, in other words, but could not always pay cash for it within a reasonable time.

Exceptionally generous in the ordinary sense of that word, as well as magnanimous, Lorenzo spent a great deal of money on friends. No doubt, they often exploited his ready prodigality, so unlike that of a typical merchant in its lack of prior calculation. Yet, despite all these calls upon one's private purse, no man in his position and of his family could descend to borrowing from individuals who might try to obtain a hold upon one by such obligations—just as Cosimo had obtained control of potential opponents by lending them money. Still less would it have been advisable for Lorenzo to borrow from rival mercantile corporations, which would thus be apprised of or likely to assume a decline in Medici resources.

According to the poet Alessandro de' Pazzi, son of Lorenzo's sister Bianca and Guglielmo de' Pazzi, the Medici bankers had already begun to experience difficulties in the 1470s. Alessandro wrote in 1522: "When their credit fell, they would have been driven from their position but for the events of 1478, which gained new friends for the Medici, confirmed the attachment of those who already favoured them, and in every way strengthened their power. The same events enabled Lorenzo to use both his own fortune and the funds of the Republic, which he would not have dared to touch formerly, to pay his debts and rebuild his political influence on a permanent foundation."

It was certainly Lorenzo's constitutional distaste for financial administration, shared also to some extent by his father, that had allowed the enormous wealth bequeathed by Cosimo to the family to erode. It is also true that, as Alessandro suggests, the general sympathy aroused by the cowardly and treacherous murder of the inoffensive Giuliano, and by Lorenzo's firm and dignified attitude in the face of this terrible affliction, rallied the Republic as a whole to his side. In these circumstances, few people may have seriously objected at the time to his raiding the treasury in order to re-establish his own fortune and, consequently, the state's economic position. It may be said, therefore, that the conspirators' aggression had resulted, not in the ruin but in the triumph of its prospective victim. Lorenzo's own personal popularity, which he could not have acquired in so vigilant a community as Florence had he been merely a cynical opportunist, had saved him. Alessandro's view, which was that of a man who belonged, in Medicean eyes, to a guilty family, was endorsed by his contemporaries, Machiavelli and the historian Guicciardini, who both admired Lorenzo with certain reservations. A modern critic must conclude that, whether or not that daring and ingenious statesman diverted a proportion of public funds to entirely private purposes, he undoubtedly applied a large part of such moneys, in secret, to a patriotic end, that of subsidising the allies of the Republic. His own and his bank's resources, so depleted since 1469, when he first came to power, would never have sufficed to supply such huge sums, essential to his foreign policy.

In order, therefore, to reinforce the capital required for purely political purposes, Lorenzo began by raising forced loans, secured mainly on the private property of rich citizens. But this expedient was found to be bad for trade. Consequently, the bulk of the incidence of the new taxation was transferred to real estate, where it did not affect the poorer classes. The method of collection, however, as usual in those days, was certainly inequitable, causing much more damage to known adversaries of Lorenzo than to his supporters.

In addition to such dubious practices, Lorenzo was responsible for the introduction of certain abuses into the administration of the Dower Fund. This latter was an institution, founded in 1425, through which parents, by making small payments during their daughters' infancy, could provide these girls at a later date with substantial marriage portions. Lorenzo's recently established Grand Council decreed that four fifths of any such capital accumulation in any individual case should be retained by the state, bearing interest at 7 per cent, and only one fifth paid to the girl on her marriage. The figure of interest quoted being much lower than that which any level-headed Florentine merchant could obtain on his ordinary investments, this conciliar machination caused a reduction in the number of annual weddings and a consequent increase in sexual licence, thereby weakening in the Republic the foundation of contemporary Christian society, the family. Lorenzo must be blamed for the adoption of this desperate expedient in his efforts to raise money in order to promote political security. Quite apart from its ethical and social aspects, it remained an error of judgement on practical grounds, for it led immediately, as might have been foreseen, to a diminution in the quality and quantity of the personal loyalty extended to him by the citizens at large. It was, moreover, on this feeling that in the last analysis his influence depended.

Lorenzo, if faced with accusations of embezzlement, or at least of bad judgement, would doubtless have pleaded the exigencies of maintaining his foreign policy. He laboured incessantly all his life, as had Cosimo, to preserve a balance of power among the five powers of the Italian peninsula. In addition, and unlike Cosimo, he worked untiringly to keep the peace between Florence and her immediate neighbours, such as Siena, Lucca, Bologna, Ferrara, and Perugia. The task, as a whole, proved far from easy. In particular, Ferdinand of Naples, Ludovico Sforza, and the Venetians were all thorns in the diplomatic side of the Florentine Republic. In 1480 Ludovico, for instance, had persuaded the Milanese nobles—the commoners having little or no say in the matter—that he would make a better regent for the eleven-year-old Duke Gian Galeazzo than the boy's mother, Bona of Savoy, Ludovico's sister-in-law. He then forced Bona into exile and proceeded to rule the duchy himself in the name of Gian Galeazzo, the legitimate heir. Lorenzo found the new regent evasive, for no one—least of all Ludovico himself—seemed to know what he really wanted. But one thing was clear: Ludovico did not propose to continue the friendly policies of his father Francesco, and of his brother Galeazzo Maria, towards Florence. No doubt, he felt that the Medici were growing too powerful, and he meant to present himself in due course as a rival to what he conceived to be their territorial ambitions. Such was not, in fact, Lorenzo's objective, but the misunderstanding, which he found it impossible to remove, introduced a vexing factor into the delicate balance that he was trying to maintain.

Finally, the overweening pretensions of Pope Sixtus and his nephews constituted a perpetual menace to everyone. In 1481, for example, the Pope installed his nephew, Count Girolamo Riario, as Lord of Forlì in Romagna, an obvious first step towards the Duchy of Ferrara in north-eastern Emilia; and, in fact, the count soon started negotiations with Venice for support in his Ferrarese design. The Doge, who had an eye on Ferrara himself, picked a quarrel with the duke of that city over some salt mines and, with papal support, invaded Ferrarese territory. This performance aroused hostility not only in Florence, which was traditionally friendly to Ferrara, but also in Milan, Bologna, Mantua, and even Naples.

Sixtus was at this time experiencing difficulties, not only in Rome, where a scarcity of food was causing popular riots, but also in Germany, where, the Pontiff believed, his authority was being disputed by the last Holy Roman Emperor to be crowned at Rome, Frederick III. These worries induced Sixtus, for all his furious energy, to realise that he had bitten off more than he could chew in the north-east of the peninsula. On December 12, 1482, he concluded peace with Florence, Ferrara, and their allies. He also summoned Venice to desist from hostilities. The Venetians felt strong enough to disobey, but, after a year of fighting, they were decisively defeated by a force that included contingents from almost all the rest of Italy. Even then, the Doge took advantage of a quarrel between Ludovico Sforza and the Neapolitan Duke of Calabria to sign a separate armistice with Milan. With Sforza's encouragement, Venice also induced the formidable King of France, Louis XI, vigorously to press the claims of the French Duke of Lorraine to the Neapolitan crown.

By now, everyone except the Pope was tired of the war. A treaty was finally signed at Bagnolo on August 7, 1484. Its terms were found by Sixtus, who had been seriously ill for some weeks, to be so disadvantageous for his own side that, in a paroxysm of rage, he died on the following day. He had, in his time, done much to reform the Church, to found or revive useful secular institutions, and to patronise art and letters. But there can be no question of his unbridled greed in money matters, or of his determination to ignore moral considerations in his almost pathological pursuit of worldy glory for himself and his family. A Roman wit observed that the late Holy Father had been so warlike that the very word "peace" killed him.

Meanwhile Lorenzo's mother, the grave and pious intellectual Lucrezia Maria Tornabuoni, had succumbed on March 25, 1482, aged fifty-seven. Her health, always as precarious as her advice in political affairs had been sound, her modesty, and her plain looks, had prevented her from being as conspicuous a figure in Florence as she might have been. She kept regularly in the background, often at a spa near Volterra, which she frequented to relieve her rheumatism and eczema. Still, everyone praised her prudence, her good counsel, and her charity. In Piero's time, about 1465, the beauty of her expression, if not of her features, had inspired Botticelli's splendid picture "Madonna of the Magnificat," where her two sons appear as angels kneeling to her, the handsome Giuliano being tactfully rendered by the artist as the more prominent of the two. The ugly Lorenzo had inherited both her poor physical health and her outstanding mental ability, while Giuliano had taken more after his father Piero in his bodily aspect.

That Lucrezia was no mere devotee is proved by her special encouragement of the gifts, not only of Botticelli, but of that incorrigible improviser at parties and remorseless mocker of the solemn Platonic Academy, Luigi Pulci. But no doubt she preferred "Gigi's" essays in folklore to his ribald epics and ditties. She is said to have commissioned *Morgante Maggiore,* though she is likely to have been scandalised, eventually, by its more outrageous passages. Botticelli's portrait in the Staatliches Museum of Berlin probably shows this calmly intelligent lady at her best. The self-possessed, slightly melancholy countenance, with the peculiar nose, so conspicuous in Lorenzo, barely indicated, conveys a remarkable impression of imperturbable feminine dignity, proof against almost any shock. One instance of her good sense and lack of nervousness appears in her treatment of Giuliano's illegitimate male infant by Fioretta Gorini. When the existence of this bastard came to light after Giuliano's death, Lucrezia took the child into Lorenzo's household, gave him the name of Giulio, and educated the little boy in exactly the same way as her own sons had been brought up, to such effect that this Giulio de' Medici was eventually to attain the throne of St. Peter.

Lorenzo wrote to the Duke of Ferrara, when Lucrezia died, that "plunged into grief, I have lost not merely a mother, but my only refuge in many troubles and the comfort of my labours." He was warned by his ambassador in Rome to be on his guard against conspiracies, "now that your mother is no longer here to save you from them, as she was wont."

The opinion of the Florentine poet and novelist Franco Sacchetti (1335–1400) that "the understanding of women is keener and more quick than that of men" receives considerable support from the quiet but influential career of Lucrezia Tornabuoni. As the wife of Piero, a strong-minded invalid called to high office, she had shown a great deal of insight and tact. As the mother of the most remarkable personality in the greatest period of her native city's history, she had carried, it was universally agreed, these qualities to an exceptional level. It is very probable that Lorenzo's obituary tribute to her, and his ambassador's even more respectful estimate of her political acumen, were not exaggerations.

The death of Lucrezia removed from Lorenzo's life an irreplaceable influence for good. That of Sixtus was less malignant in its effects. The sacred conclave had elected, to replace the deceased war-maker, Giambattista Cibo, a native of Genoa, who took the title of Innocent VIII. The new Pope was, to the relief of everyone, of comparatively equitable temperament and without worldly ambitions either for himself or for his family. Indeed, so devoid was Innocent of dreams of personal power that he allowed himself, and, to a large extent, the Church, to be ruled by the energetic Cardinal Giuliano della Rovere, a nephew of the late Pope Sixtus. Lorenzo, hoping to re-establish more friendly relations with the Papacy during Innocent's pontificate, sent his thirteen-year-old son, Piero, with the customary Florentine embassy to offer official congratulations on the new Pope's election. The boy was given characteristic instructions by his cautious parent: "Whenever you find yourself in the company of the other young men of the mission, behave with gravity and courtesy. Treat them as your equals, and take care not to claim precedence over anyone older than yourself, for, although you are my son, you are no more than a citizen of Florence, like the rest." As for the new Pope, young Piero was to assure His Holiness that Lorenzo was determined ever to obey him, knowing what it would mean to lose his favour, and to convince Innocent that the Florentine autocrat could not believe himself to be wholly to blame for the animosity shown to him by the late Pope Sixtus. Piero was instructed to add that Lorenzo commended to the Holy Father his son, Giovanni, who was being trained in such a way as to bring honour to the priesthood for which he was destined. Finally, Piero, quite apart from everything else, was to obey his uncle, Giovanni Tornabuoni, the manager of the Medici office in Rome, and never to speak unless expressly authorised by him to do so.

Piero seems to have played his part creditably. Innocent VIII was pleased by the articulate young emissary and charitable in his interpretation of Lorenzo's troubles with Sixtus. The embassy returned to Florence carrying a message of benediction for the erstwhile excommunicate, Lorenzo, and for all the city.

* * *

With Italy pacified, at least for the moment, and with a new Pontiff who, it seemed, could be counted on at least not to be a fomentor of discord on the peninsula, it appeared to all observers that the Italian states were now to enjoy a moment of unaccustomed tranquility. In fact, it was hardly more than a moment. In June 1485 the nobles of the Kingdom of Naples suddenly rose in revolt against King Ferdinand, whose rule the southern barons had long found as oppressive as it was expensive. The other states of Italy chose sides according to the dictates of self-interest, policy, or whim. The Papal States sympathised with the rebels, as did Venice. Milan, under Ludovico Sforza, sent encouraging messages, but not much else, to King Ferdinand. Florence, however, after some hesitation, decided, at Lorenzo's instigation, that the peace of Italy might be permanently endangered if Ferdinand were dethroned. After much debate and only after a great deal of argument by Lorenzo—for the councils regarded as untrustworthy both Ferdinand and his son, the Duke of Calabria—it was decided to send a contingent of troops to help the harassed King retain his throne.

Despite this war-like act, Lorenzo continued to negotiate with Innocent in the interests of peace, for he regarded the situation as extremely perilous for Florence, far more so than an uprising of disgruntled aristocrats to the south would seem to warrant. He feared, for one thing, that the new French king, Charles VIII, who was sympathetic to King Ferdinand, might retaliate for Florentine intervention in the South by persecuting the numerous Florentine bankers and merchants established in France. Moreover, one might realistically expect treachery of some kind either from Ferdinand or from his unpredictable son, and trouble of some kind was likely, as always, from Ludovico in Milan. Finally, Lorenzo's health was declining, and gout was beginning to cripple him, as it had crippled his father and grandfather. But, fortunately for everyone except the insurgent barons, the war proved something of a military farce, owing to the Pope's attention being distracted by the resurgence of civil disorders in Rome. Eventually, on August 11, 1485, a peace treaty was signed. Ferdinand granted an amnesty to the leaders of the revolt, but soon afterwards, by his express command, most of them were lured into a trap and massacred.

The Neopolitan war seems to demonstrate both the stubborn opposition to his foreign policy that Lorenzo could still encounter in Florence itself, and the grim determination with which he nevertheless followed it, always with a view to saving Italy from a collapse into anarchy. He stood practically alone in this unswerving devotion to the interests of all Italians in general as well as to those of his own city. When Lorenzo in private conversation expressed the wish that Italians would become capable of uniting themselves into a nation like France or Spain, by resolving at least the worst of their differences, his friends usually laughed at what they considered his fanciful naïveté. He would join in the laughter. "Oh, the idea does no harm," he is said to have observed on more than one occasion. "Fancies don't pay taxes!"

It was true enough that the citizens of the Tuscan Republic, as a whole, had the double superiority over their rivals of being both far-sighted traders and reflective idealists. But it was Lorenzo himself—whose commercial abilities were mediocre—who ensured that Florence, at this climax of a career that the quite different mentalities of other members of his house had so notably influenced, would always be remembered with respect by posterity. He was the only true intellectual and esthete among contemporary rulers on the peninsula, though they all pretended to share his enthusiasm for creative thought, good manners, and works of art. The situation was one endlessly repeated in history and especially noticeable in periods of unusual cultural advance. Sensible and sensitive persons both in and out of responsible posts abounded in Renaissance Italy, as they had abounded in the Athens of Sophocles and the Rome of Catullus and Lucretius. But such people never acquired effective political power, which regularly falls into the hands of comparatively short-sighted and unscrupulous opportunists. Lorenzo de' Medici was perhaps unique in his combination of a commanding administrative position, diplomatic genius, and the nature, fundamentally, of a speculative artist.

Lorenzo soon recovered the popularity in Florence that had been shaken for a while by his reluctant championship, on grounds that few other statesmen could appreciate, of the tyrannical Ferdinand. The town of Sarzana in north-western Tuscany, purchased by Florence after the Venetian war of 1468 and seized by adventurers from the Duke of Calabria's army while Lorenzo was in Naples early in 1480, had not been alluded to in the treaty with the King signed in 1485. This omission may have been due to the influence of Ludovico of Milan, who was interested in the place as a strategically important strong point. Nevertheless, Lorenzo seized the chance of an attack by the Sarzana garrison on a neighbouring fortress under Florentine jurisdiction to retaliate by a punitive expedition. This campaign resulted in the capture of the town in June 1487. He himself took care to be present at the final stages of the assault. On his return to Florence, the citizens cheered him for inflicting such summary vengeance on those who had insulted him in 1480.

In the autumn of the same year, two of Lorenzo's children were betrothed to non-Florentines. The father's choice in each case was dictated by his desire to increase Medicean influence in Rome with a view to ensuring success for the future careers of both his sons. He arranged for the elder of the two, Piero, to marry Alfonsina, a member of the great Roman house of Orsini, from which Lorenzo himself had taken a wife. A similarly inspired step had already been taken in Florence by the marriage of his eldest daughter, Lucrezia, to the Florentine Giacomo Salviati, a harmless relative of that infamous archbishop who was hanged in 1478 for his leading part in the Pazzi conspiracy of that year. The head of the state had deliberately intended, by this union, to wipe out the memory of bad blood between the Medici and Salviati and so to leave his son Piero as solid an edifice of power as possible in the city. Experience had proved that such structures were best built with the cement of matrimonial alliances. He now allotted his second daughter, Maddalena, to Franceschetto Cibo, a son of Innocent VIII, the fruit of that Pontiff's early, and indiscreet, years. The papal scion, a profligate and gambler, who was about forty years old to Maddalena's fourteen, was taught, but probably did not appreciate, a much-needed lesson when entertained by his prospective father-in-law in Florence. There, Franceschetto commented rather ruefully and in some mystification to his host on the contrast between the rich fare supplied to the guest's retinue and the simple dishes set before the guest himself. "Why, I am treating you as a member of the family," Lorenzo rejoined lightly. "I myself, my wife and my children, of whom I now regard you as one, have never believed in encouraging indigestion. We leave such risks to be run by our staff."

It is doubtful whether Franceschetto felt much gratitude for this particular compliment. But his father the Pope unquestionably had a higher regard for Lorenzo's principles, for Innocent immediately began to show himself amenable to Medicean influence, with results of much benefit to Florence and the rest of Italy. The Orsini connection also made for peace, since that family maintained friendly relations with Ferdinand. Consequently, Lorenzo's dealings with the untrustworthy but necessary Neapolitan despot could now proceed with less friction.

To these plans Lorenzo's wife, Clarice Orsini, contributed little. She was basically a dull, proud, bigoted woman, querulous and spiteful. Politian, when staying with her at the Cafaggiuolo villa as tutor to her children, found her very boring and cantankerous. On her side, she considered him vulgar, irreligious, and cynical. Finally, she dismissed him. Lorenzo himself could never get on with her. He occasionally, during their long separations due to her ill-health, wrote her a sharp letter. But though they saw each other rarely, he must have been attracted to her physically, for she bore him no fewer than ten children, and there was never the slightest suspicion that she might have taken a lover.

In 1487 she accompanied her daughter Maddalena to Rome for Maddalena's wedding to Franceschetto Cibo, and in July of the following year she died in that somewhat unhealthy city. Lorenzo mourned her demise in the eloquent prose he could always command. No doubt he was grateful for her fertility in providing so many offspring to make good marriages for her son Piero's sake. Nor had her sexual or social conduct, though she could be brusque with her social inferiors, ever given him substantial cause for complaint. He could have wished only for a more intelligent consort, not for a more respectable one.

The wedding of Piero and Alfonsina took place in Florence, with great splendour, in May 1488. In other directions, however, this year proved one of private grief to the bridegroom's father. His third daughter, Luisa of Luigia, perhaps named in honour of the French King Louis XI, died suddenly that summer, aged only about twelve, soon after her betrothal to Lorenzo's cousin Giovanni de' Medici. Luisa's death preceded by but a few weeks that of her mother. Meanwhile, Lorenzo's gout continued to grow steadily worse. He probably realised that it was incurable. Neither in the fifteenth century nor at any later period have doctors been able to do much to ameliorate the recurrent pain of this condition in its various arthritic manifestations, though it is remarkable how little it seems to affect the energy of a constitution otherwise resistant to common ailments. At any rate, in Lorenzo's case none of the depressing events of 1488 weakened seriously either his vitality or his political idealism.

He continued to labour tirelessly to pacify the incessant quarrels between Pope Innocent and King Ferdinand and to make head or tail of the devious schemes of Ludovico Sforza. He also kept careful watch on the occasionally dangerous disputes of the smaller states. His extant correspondence reveals an astonishing mastery of complex situations and an unusual skill in reconciling conflicting ambitions. It was no wonder that one day he was heard to remark that he wished he could go away and bury himself in some inaccessible region to which no rumours of Italian political affairs could ever penetrate.

Before the year 1488 ended, Lorenzo's old enemy Count Girolamo Riario was stabbed to death at Forlì. This violently covetous nephew of Sixtus IV had married, some years before initiating the Pazzi conspiracy, Caterina Sforza, the illegitimate daughter of Galeazzo Maria, the Duke of Milan assassinated in 1476. By 1484 Girolamo and Caterina had acquired the lordships of Imola and Forlì in Romagna, as well as great wealth, by means of one fraud or murder after another. As neither husband nor wife had the faintest concept of decent government, their subjects soon began to intrigue for their replacement by Franceschetto Cibo, the future husband of Maddalena de' Medici. Three of these conspirators, as a last resort, put a violent end to the life of Riario and imprisoned his widow and children. But Caterina Sforza was not so easily disposed of. She had already proved her martial prowess in Rome when she defended the castle of Sant' Angelo on her husband's behalf against a faction of the cardinals that attacked it on the death of Sixtus in 1484. She now escaped from her confinement in Forlì to the citadel of the town, which had not yet been captured by the rebels. Once more in her element, this Amazon exultantly trained the guns of the castle on the surrounding streets and refused to surrender, even when the insurgents threatened to cut her children's throats. The intervention of her uncle, Ludovico Sforza, for some years now in effective control of Milan, finally re-established her power over her dominions, and she immediately exterminated all the leaders of the rebellion.

Lorenzo's cool discretion, as he watched these events, induced him to support Caterina in her triumphant return to the lordships of Forlì and Imola. He considered that these lands would serve Florentine interests better as an independent state than in the hands of Milan or of Rome. The private morals of a foreign ruler never influenced Lorenzo de' Medici in his public conduct if the foreigner's position kept Milan and the Papacy out of Tuscany. In the present case, he considered, neither Caterina's blood relationship to Ludovico nor the Pope's sympathy with his son's claim to her possessions would lead either power to move against the Republic. The lady, in Lorenzo's judgement, would be too formidable an opponent to the Roman side and too untrustworthy an ally of the Lombards, for active aggression on Florentine jurisdiction, whether by the Pontiff or the Milanese regent, to have any prospect of success.

In two other cases, however—those of Bologna and Perugia—the ruler of Florence felt compelled to intervene in order to keep peace. He arrested and held in prison for a number of years the Lord of Bologna, a despot who had been instrumental in the assassination of the legitimate feudal chief of Faenza, a cathedral city some thirty miles to the south-east of Bologna. The Bolognese tyrant had coveted Faenza for the usual reasons of its strategic importance and wealth. At Perugia, during a struggle between two leading families, Lorenzo had supported, and thereby ensured the decisive victory of, the faction he himself preferred.

Yet, in the midst of all this political ferment, according to Florentine historian and statesman Francesco Guicciardini, "the city enjoyed profound peace. The members of the government were in close agreement with one another. Their power appeared to be so firmly established that no one dared to oppose it. Every-day spectacles, festivals, and all kinds of novelties were arranged for the entertainment of the masses. Everyone was well fed, for provisions were plentiful and cheap. Industries of many different sorts were flourishing. Men of genius and even those of less talent in every branch of culture were subsidised and institutions established for the promotion of their labours. Within the walls of Florence an almost perfect tranquility reigned. Abroad, the city's reputation was everywhere acknowledged to be great and glorious."

In 1489, in the midst of the happy prosperity, Lorenzo's second son, Giovanni, aged thirteen, a plump little fellow with his father's nose but little of his charm, was created a cardinal by Innocent VIII. The news, however, was not made public for three years, owing to the boy's immaturity. He had been receiving ecclesiastical training, under his father's directions, for some time, the choice of the Church as a career for the second son of an eminent man being quite usual at this period. Giovanni already held the archbishopric of Aix in Provence and other valuable preferments assigned by the Kings of France and Naples. Although the recipient of these honours perhaps looked a bit foolish, with his mouth forever open, due to a jutting lower lip, he was showing the greatest promise in his studies. Such outstanding scholars as Politian and the philosophers Pico della Mirandola and Marsilio Ficino were instructing him. It was clear enough that young Giovanni had inherited far more of Lorenzo's intelligence and firmness of purpose than had his elder brother Piero.

The latter, now seventeen, took after Giuliano, up to a point. He was nearly as good-looking, a notable athlete, and could scribble verses. In other respects, his personality fell short of his murdered uncle's. He tended to be inconsiderate, vain of his social standing, and such a blunderer that he soon acquired the nickname "Peter the Unlucky." He was not too popular among the more thoughtful of his companions, but it was supposed that the passage of years and the usual careful education of a youthful Medici would improve him.

Meanwhile, the deepening of religious sentiment in Florence consequent upon Giovanni's elevation to the cardinalate, the favour of Innocent VIII, and the pacific fostering of intellectual culture by genuinely pious writers such as Pico della Mirandola (already well known in Rome for his earnest reconsiderations of orthodox doctrine), began gradually to revive the domestic anxieties of the government. People were becoming argumentative, especially on questions of the relations between the Church and the state, instead of, as before, being absorbed about equally in their businesses and their pleasures. In keeping with this spirit, Pico, who had heard much about a Dominican friar of Florence named Giorlamo Savonarola, who was then preaching in Lombardy, suggested to Lorenzo in 1489 that the summoning to Florence of so remarkable an orator might benefit both the newly created cardinal, Giovanni, and the city as a whole. As it happened, this same Savonarola had, ten years before, preached a series of Lenten sermons at the Church of San Lorenzo in Florence, where his talk of sin and repentance, and his rhetorical clumsiness—more reminiscent of the street-corner than of the pulpit—had made his audience yawn with boredom. But Lorenzo, who may or may not have known of Savonarola's previous fiasco in Florence, was amenable, and the Dominican accordingly was induced to give a course of lectures in the gardens of St. Mark's Convent. The Florentines who before had laughed at, or slept through, the friar's commonplace words and unharmonious cadences, now came to San Marco, where they sat entranced as Savonarola expounded the mysteries of the Apocalypse. The preacher's frail body and thin face did not detract in the least from the deep impression made by his preternaturally burning eyes and by the inspired, almost frenzied, expression of his face. Many of his listeners swore that never before had they witnessed such power in a man of religion. Those who could remember his failure as a preacher nearly a decade before were amazed at the change that time had wrought. Savonarola's name sped from lip to lip, until the garden of San Marco could no longer contain those who came to hear him preach.

By Lent of 1491, the fiery monk's fame had so grown that he was asked to preach at the cathedral during the holy season, an honour customarily reserved to the finest preacher of Florence. The great church was packed each time that Savonarola spoke, for the friar's command of terror and pathos in his phrases could by this time thrill and persuade even an audience of sophisticated Florentines. They especially appreciated his persistent attacks, in the most bitter terms possible, on established authority, both civil and ecclesiastical; and one may imagine the simultaneous horror and delight with which the good citizens heard their Lorenzo described as a "tyrant" and as a man of immoral habits. Such daring, in a city habitually adverse to the dictates of authority in any form, was quick to capture the imagination and the emotions of the Florentines. Before the end of Lent, Savonarola was the moral arbiter of the city. Wherever one went, the litany of "Savonarola says" and "the friar says" was heard, in the mouths of vagrants and aristocrats alike. Lorenzo had, if not a challenger, then at least a rival, for the obedience and respect of the people.

The head of the state, however, as might have been expected, considered such recklessness undesirable from the standpoint of good government—already under indirect fire from other quarters—and even good literature. He found a number of Savonarola's verbal conceits, effective as they were, lacking in taste. He therefore sent five of his friends to the thundering monk, begging him at least to show proper respect in his references to a man—viz., Lorenzo himself—who had nothing but the protection and advancement of civilisation and Christian principle at heart. The friar merely answered, glaring sternly at the deputation: "Tell Lorenzo to repent of his sins, for the Lord spares no one and fears not the princes of the earth." The spokesman of the group warned him that he might be banished. He retorted scornfully: "I fear not your exile . . . though I am a stranger and Lorenzo the first citizen, I must remain here and he must depart." After the men had gone, he added, to his own circle, that such despots as the chief of the Medici, and his associates, Pope Innocent VIII and the King of Naples, would soon die. This cool insolence, which the master of Florence, Lorenzo, would never have allowed himself, demonstrates Savonarola's entire confidence in the position he had so swiftly gained as practical dictator to the city, if not by formal proclamation, at any rate in the sentiments he had implanted there. Perhaps only a religious zealot could be so utterly certain of himself. But long before the end of his career Savonarola was to prove that he was much more than that. His Christian beliefs were held with absolute sincerity and all the force of an imperious moral personality. But he also possessed the subtle brain of a born tactician. He could see that his most dangerous enemies were the humanists, and that they could only be defeated by those who thoroughly understood them. He therefore took the trouble to acquaint himself with their learning, so that he could meet them with their own weapons. He could speak of certain artists and philosophers with authority, even with eloquence and affection, so long as their mentalities could be plausibly represented as being essentially of a Christian sort. He thus escaped the charge of bigotry so often levelled in those days against outstanding churchmen and so carefully evaded by the ablest of the Popes. Nor did Savonarola despise the easy victories to be gained by methods bordering upon those of a charlatan. His prophecies, for instance, which later caused such a sensation, of the approaching deaths of Lorenzo, Innocent, and Ferdinand, could have been made by anyone who realised, as everyone did, that the hereditary malady of the first-named was increasing in severity, and that the other two were old men.

In July of 1491 the friar was elected prior, or superior, of St. Mark's Convent, an establishment that owed its very existence to Cosimo's rebuilding of the fabric and Lorenzo's munificent endowment of its functions. It would have been the usual practice of a new prior to present formal homage to the head of the Republic, but Savonarola retorted to those who urged this step upon him that it was not Lorenzo, but Almighty God, who had promoted him to his present office. He added that he considered Lorenzo responsible for what every true Christian must judge to be the corruption of Florentine society. To such a man, he asserted, he would not render homage. When this attitude was reported to the alleged tyrant, Lorenzo commented sadly: "You see, gentlemen. A stranger has entered my house, and yet he does not think me fit to visit." The tone must have been more disconcerted than contemptuous, for the speaker, whose manners were always perfect, continued to treat his unmannerly prior with what may have been quite genuine respect. Lorenzo's morals, in the scale of absolutes, may have left something to be desired, but he was no atheist. He probably reverenced so unhesitatingly pure a faith as Savonarola's, and he may well have felt secret astonishment at its consistent firmness in so furiously sinful an environment as Renaissance Italy.

At the same time Lorenzo was undoubtedly also exercising his usual conciliatory technique with strenuous competitors for his authority. He often called at St. Mark's, but its prior deliberately avoided meeting him. The head of the Republic might easily have persuaded his friend, the Pope, to rid Florence of this troublesome and rude monk, but Lorenzo, with his usual acumen, had correctly diagnosed the present mood of the citizens. A majority of them were enthusiastically devoted to the prior. Savonarola's removal, however disguised as further promotion, would probably cause, if not a revolution, at least a serious decline in the popularity of the Medici. It would have been easy then for the influential new block of Savonarola's adherents to represent the ruling family and its supporters as a set of irresponsible semi-pagans.

The great Lorenzo was, in fact, so unwell as to prefer the course of least resistance. Indigestion plagued him almost uninterruptedly. His inherited gout grew so painful that, by 1492, he found himself unable to attend effectively to business. He felt too ill even to be present at the celebrations held when his son Giovanni came of age, at sixteen, and entered upon his duties as a cardinal. Lorenzo's doctors would only allow the proud father to contemplate for a few moments, from a litter, the splendid evening banquet given at the Medici Palace in honour of the boy.

On March 21 in that year the now desperately sick ruler of Florence retired to his villa at Careggi, where his grandfather had died in 1464. There Lorenzo took leave of his eldest son Piero in a long interview relating to the young man's future activities on behalf of the Republic. Neither of the participants doubted that the accession of Piero to power was now imminent. Then Politian and Pico della Mirandola came to see the last of their dying friend and benefactor. "I wish," he told them, "that death had spared me until I had completed your libraries." He was so weak that he had to receive Extreme Unction lying down.

Then Savonarola entered the room. It is generally assumed that Lorenzo had sent for the prior in order to make peace with him at this final moment. In any case, it was later stated that the prostrate head of the Republic asked his stern visitor for absolution. The latter refused it until three conditions were met: "First, you must repent and feel true faith in God's mercy." "I do so." "Second, you must give up your ill-gotten wealth." To this demand Lorenzo did not reply for a while. There cannot be any doubt that, despite his condition, he was thinking only of the future of Florence. Finally, however, he assented. "Third, you must restore the liberties of this city." At this impertinence, Lorenzo turned his face to the wall and said nothing more. Savonarola stood motionless for a few moments, then abruptly he left the room. Shortly afterwards Lorenzo, unabsolved, drew his last breath. The date was April 8, 1492.

Such is the version given by the pious Pico della Mirandola of the last minutes of the life of Lorenzo de' Medici. But Pico, a subtle and learned theologian, soon afterwards became a devoted disciple of the prior. Even if this had not been so, the account of the scene as recorded above would have been partisan to the point of incredibility. Savonarola, though no doubt fanatical in his religious views and peremptory in affirming them, was no fool. He would never have forced such preposterous second and third requirements for absolution on a man in Lorenzo's political position. It was neither practicable for the Medici chief to beggar himself since his son was to succeed him, nor to "restore the liberties" to a city that had been better governed and, for the most part, happier under his direction than ever in its previous history.

Politian described the conversation more acceptably. Unlike the hot-headed Pico, he never showed any tendency to mysticism, and he had the true poet's respect for what he could see, hear, and touch. According to this sensuous realist, Pico had left the room before Savonarola arrived. Nor was there any question of a confession and absolution, since Lorenzo, like any other Catholic gentleman of substance in his day, had his own private confessor. Politian affirms that the dialogue between the healthy ascetic and the mortally sick statesman ran as follows:

"Hold fast to the faith."

"I do so."

"Amend your life."

"I will try so to do."

"Meet your death, if it must come to that, with courage."

"Most readily, if it be God's will that I should die."

"Then your sins will be forgiven."

"Give me your blessing, Father."

The two men then prayed together, as if alone in the world, while the others in the chamber broke into uncontrollable sobbing. The prior then solemnly departed. Lorenzo died soon afterwards while attempting to kiss a crucifix held to his lips.

There may be some poetic licence in this record. But it is much more plausible than that of Pico della Mirandola. Savonarola, though he could be overbearing with those he considered sinners, was too genuine a Christian to persecute them on their death-beds. Lorenzo, though the least superstitious of men, unquestionably believed the essence of Christianity to be true, revered its honest expositors, and loved his country and the civilised ideals he had tried so hard to encourage, more than he loved himself and his appetites for material enjoyment.

The usual rumours of poison became current. One of Lorenzo's doctors had been sent to him by that dubious character, Ludovico Sforza. The Medici family physician, Pierleone, was found dead the next day at the bottom of a well. He had probably committed suicide in a paroxysm of grief and remorse, but it is not impossible that he may have been murdered for suspected incompetence or for the acceptance of a bribe to kill his patient. Nevertheless, although the medical treatment administered to Lorenzo may have hastened his end, no proof was ever forthcoming that it was intended to do so.

Both of those convinced republicans, Machiavelli and Guicciardini, writing in the next generation, recognised the impact of Lorenzo's early death as disastrous not only for Florence but for all Italy. "No Italian of his or any earlier time," the former commented, "had so high a reputation for prudence, or was so regretted by his fellow-citizens." Guicciardini, who elsewhere remarked that Lorenzo had acted like the isthmus of Corinth in keeping the raging seas of foreign aggression from all quarters at bay, declared, "He was mourned as a public father and patron of the city. Florence had been happy, all things considered, while he lived. After his death, such great calamities and misfortunes ensued as to multiply to infinity the sorrowful remembrance of his personality and achievements."

Even the reprobate King Ferdinand of Naples, in a burst of genuine feeling, wrote: "This man has lived long enough for his own immortal fame, but not long enough for Italy. God grant that now he is dead men may not attempt that which they dared not do while he lived."

* * *

Any appraisal of the rule of Lorenzo de' Medici in Florence must, of necessity, take into account that revolution the consolidation of which occurred in Italy, and particularly in Florence, during the latter part of the fifteenth century. The term "Renaissance," or "re-birth," which is customarily applied to that revolution, leaves a great deal to be desired from the standpoint of historical exactitude. It was not so much a re-birth of pagan learning in the fourteenth, fifteenth, and sixteenth centuries as a period of new achievements in the plastic and literary arts, in science, philosophy, politics, and religion. It is true, of course, that the foundation of many of these achievements was the inspiration afforded by the best minds of pagan antiquity, but

it is also true that progress soon went considerably beyond the boundaries of Greek and Latin influence. The Renaissance, moreover, introduced into the world the hierarchy of values upon which the subsequent
civilisation of the West is generally regarded as resting. Chief among
these ideals was that of humanism, which, in its widest sense, signifies
the exaltation of the human and the natural, of the world, as opposed
to the glorification of the divine and the supernatural, of the "other
world," and which implies such corrolary ideals as optimism, naturalism,
and individualism.

This new world of humanism was obviously at sharp variance with
the spirit of the Middle Ages that it followed and into which it was
subtly dove-tailed. The universe was no longer a collection of spheres
revolving around the earth and created for the edification of Christendom; it was a treasure-house of knowledge, of which the earth was a
small part—but a part that must be explored and investigated and
examined until it had yielded up its secrets. The fit object of human
intelligence was no longer solely the God of the Christians; now it was
man himself and his world. The social and intellectual culture of the
Middle Ages, expressed in chivalry, on the one hand, and Scholasticism, on the other, now fell into general disrepute. The medieval
condemnation of the profit motive in business, and of the practice of
collecting interest on loans, was now ignored by the hard-headed
businessmen and bankers of Europe. The persuasive medieval belief
that man could exist happily only when submerged in an identity
greater than his own—in a church, a guild, a fixed social order—was
replaced by an almost fanatical faith in the autonomy of every individual man.

This conviction, translated into political terms, spelled the end of the
old order in Europe. By the middle of the fifteenth century, feudalism
was showing clear signs of decay, while the ideal of European unity
under the dual domination of Holy Roman Emperor and Roman
Pope was fast vanishing. The post-medieval state, like post-medieval
man, believed in total freedom from external control. This spirit was
manifested, in France, Spain, and England, by the coalescing of their
peoples into identifiably national groups and by the emergence of
fiercely independent nations. In Italy, however, culturally the most
advanced section of Europe, the various and diverse traditions of Venice,
Milan, Florence, the Papal States, and the southern part of the peninsula were already almost violently contrasted. These geographical en-
tities amounted, in their varying institutions, psychology, and special
interests, to separate nations. The common language of Latin among
the upper classes united them no more than the same phenomenon
had previously united England and Spain, or France and Germany,
since the dialects of the masses of the people on Italian soil differed

in adjoining areas and even from one isolated village to another. The ease of communications across contiguous land frontiers, or by coastal shipping, helped no more than Latin to achieve Italian solidarity; for such a development was paradoxically prevented, through the very simplicity of inter-regional transport, by incessant warfare.

At the intellectual level, a less inhibited approach than Dante's to the understanding of human nature had been introduced about the time of his death in 1321, with Petrarch's addition of pagan literature to Christian theology in his studies. Slowly, and at times painfully, the former abyss between the classical and medieval civilisations was bridged. The education of Lorenzo de' Medici and his social equals demonstrated to them that Homer and Plato, Cicero and Virgil had probed the predicament of mankind at least as deeply as, and perhaps more widely than, the saints who had laid the foundations of religious orthodoxy. The early humanists had founded classical philology and established editions as accurately as their scholarship would allow of all available ancient Greek and Latin manuscripts. They had set up these works as the basis of secular education, gradually superseding the training in dialectics and Christian dogma that was the standard curriculum of the schools. They had multiplied texts and collected libraries, and they had proved that pagans as well as churchmen could be philosophers.

Their own creative efforts, however, being composed mostly in a dying language, Latin—then in the course of being imperceptibly ousted by the colloquial speech of their pupils—lacked vitality. They composed pedantic and soulless imitations of Livy and Virgil. They were doing their very best to reflect, not their own age, but that of a spirit that had perished in Europe when the ancient Empire of the Romans had given way to the depredations of the barbarians a thousand years before. Even the brilliant Politian, the embodiment of a critical and liberal temperament that was, in many ways, very like that of the best of the ancient Romans and Greeks, was admired less for his own sake than for theirs. But, in fact, the polished glitter of this facile scholar's odes, elegies, and epigrams concealed a sensitivity, a sagacity, a tolerance, and a humour that became evident at a more personal level. On September 20, 1478, he wrote to his patron, Lorenzo, from Pistoia:

"God save you, for it seems to me that everything depends on that. Do not worry about us here. We are very careful. For myself, I shall fail neither in vigilance nor in good will. I know how much I owe your Magnificence, and my love for Piero and the other children is hardly less than your own. If at times I am subjected here to disagreeable or unkind treatment, I shall try to bear it for love of you, to whom I owe everything."

In November of the same year, at Cafaggiuolo, Clarice was in poor health, rain fell incessantly, and Politian was reduced to playing at ball games indoors with his young pupils, the Medici children. "Our stakes," he then told Lorenzo, "are generally the soup, the sweet, or the meat, and the loser goes without. Often, when one of my pupils loses, he pays tribute to the Lord Humidity (i.e., weeps). I stay indoors by the fire in slippers and mantle. If you saw me you would think me the picture of misery . . . for I neither do nor see nor hear anything that amuses me . . . asleep or awake, our wretchedness haunts me. Two days ago we began to spread our wings, for we heard that the plague was gone. Now we are depressed again, for we learn that it still lingers. . . . Ser Alberto di Malerba drones prayers with the children all day long, so I am left alone . . . no one with whom to share my forebodings, no Madonna Lucrezia in her room for me to confide in. Truly, I am bored to death." The self-mockery and more or less burlesque complaints of the behaviour of dull people, together with the writer's obvious affection for his correspondent's mother and children, show clearly through the depression of a scholar to whom politics was nothing but a vexation.

Politian's influence led later on to the ideal of the "gentleman" that governed the best minds of succeeding epochs. This notion already coloured the outlook of many Italian artists, scientists, philosophers, and moralists. Administrators and traders, even certain churchmen, gave at least lip-service to it. The result was a general softening of manners, the cultivation of refined diction and elegant attitudes, accompanied by attempts at informed appreciation, especially of works of art, but also of pleasing objects in general. Even such soldiers as the Duke of Urbino worked hard to acquire a semblance of cultural sophistication.

Yet Renaissance society, from any point of view, fell short of the ideal. More than a millenium of Christian moral coercion had sharpened the ancient Italian addiction to intrigue and vengeance. Such impulses, by this time, could not always and everywhere be suppressed by fears of hell or death, for it was almost universally believed that a death-bed repentance could rescue the sinner from eternal torment. Accordingly, men like Lorenzo, combining stern pride and determination in practical affairs with high imaginative capacity and a perfectly sincere love of beauty and philosophical speculation, could, at times, be guilty of fraud and violence. Nor did many of his contemporaries regard such conduct as seriously objectionable—unless they were themselves the victims of it. Lorenzo, however, rarely erred in this way. He was far more unexpectedly frank and gentle with his opponents, as notably in the case, eventually, of the murder of his beloved brother. It is true that coolly calculated policy as much as impulsive generosity was regularly responsible for such restraint in him, as well as for such apparently magnanimous acts as the reform of the Pisa university. His heredity being strictly mercantile and political, the arts of persuasion, not to mention those of deception, were in his blood; but his whole career demonstrates impatience with that selfish opportunism that never looks beyond personal advantage.

It is equally clear that Lorenzo understood those values that make for the happiness of a community. He worked tirelessly to achieve them rather than such popular effects, military glory and territorial expansion—though he was sometimes obliged to seek those up to a point, in order to satisfy the wishes of his fellow-citizens. He never himself wanted, like so many Popes and princes of his day, to force an antagonist—the Duchy of Milan, for example, or the Republic of Venice, or the Kingdom of Naples—to submit to his authority. He genuinely preferred peace to war, and he genuinely believed himself to be the only man in Florence capable of securing peace.

His treatment of Pisa illustrates both this aspect of his character and his practical care for cultural advancement. The Pisans had hated their Florentine conquerors ever since the early years of the fifteenth century. Lorenzo's reaction to this sentiment was in the first place to buy a house in Pisa and live in it for extended periods at frequent intervals. Second, he revived the ancient university, older than that of Florence, and divided the education of Tuscan undergraduates between Pisa and his own city. He directed students at the former city to concentrate on law, medicine, and theology, reserving Florence for students of the classics and of secular philosophy. Thus Pisa became a center mainly for avid careerists and Florence for scholars and theorists.

In politics, Lorenzo again proved his possession of an imagination that surpassed merely material ambitions by obtaining for his Republic a degree of internal civil equality unknown anywhere else in the world at that time. This goal had been present in the minds of many Florentines before Lorenzo was born, from Gian della Bella, promoter of the Ordinances of Justice at the end of the thirteenth century, to Neri Capponi, the most vigorous opponent of what he felt to be Cosimo's designs for acquiring personal ascendancy in the city. Lorenzo was, therefore, well aware of a native sentiment of resistance to special privileges in his community. He knew that such a feeling might in certain circumstances work to the detriment of efficient administration as he understood it. Nevertheless, he deliberately strengthened the formal opportunities for expressing this kind of opposition. His example certainly influenced the rest of Italy, but the other states never entirely adopted it.

Having been born to power himself, Lorenzo could not help developing certain despotic traits of character; but these were constantly countered by his delight in matters that had nothing to do with schemes for the suppression of enemies. Literature, art, and the society of such pacific scholars as Politian, Pico della Mirandola, and Marsilio Ficino drew his attention indefatigably to the virtues of self-control, logic, and sympathy with less talented people.

For various reasons, democratic forms had a far better chance of acceptance in Lorenzo's time than in previous generations. For one thing, his accession to power in Florence coincided with the sudden multiplication of printed books. The first such had appeared at Subiaco, about thirty miles east of Rome, only four years before Piero de' Medici's death, and thereafter cheap volumes were readily available to persons of modest means, whereas previously the acquisition of books, in the form of painstakingly copied (and therefore expensive) manuscripts, were the prerogative of the wealthy. Even the relatively poor citizens of Italy now could cultivate their minds and their emotions either by the purchase of their own books or by frequenting the public libraries endowed by the rich for the use of the poor. The commoners of the later fifteenth century therefore became more and more capable of judging questions of government on a level that entitled their views to consideration.

The formal intellectual life of Florence, however, was in the hands of the scholars, professional or otherwise, rather than in those of private citizens of studious habits. That life tended to center upon the so-called Platonic Academy founded by Cosimo de' Medici. This institution was an institution only in the broadest sense; it had neither a specfic organisation, a recognisable staff, nor an income. It offered no lectures, nor did it publish a record of its proceedings. It was simply a symposium of irregular membership, whose adherents met occasionally to talk informally about the philosophy of Plato and to hear the thoughts of the most eminent Platonist of the time, Marsilio Ficino. Lorenzo himself, and his most intimate friends, were the most faithful attendants at these convocations.

Lorenzo's interest in Platonic thought had been come by honestly. His grandfather, Cosimo, had been much taken by the octogenarian Byzantine philosopher Georgios Gemistos Pletho in 1439, when the latter had visited Florence as a representative of the Greek Church. It is likely that Cosimo, whose tastes were less speculative than those of his grandson, understood little of that transcendental mysticism, today known as neo-Platonism, that Gemistos expounded as a substitute for Aristotle's more pragmatic vision of the world. But Cosimo could recognise mental ingenuity wherever he found it, whether in a counting-house, the court of a prince, or an ecclesiastical assembly. He was impressed by the earnestness of the learned Greek, though he could not for the moment see what good it was likely to do Florence or the

Medici family—these two phenomena being by this time nearly identical in his mind. His personal physician, however, had an attractive son, Marsilio Ficino, who soon gave evidence of a passion for erudition, and of an intelligence and an industry equal to Gemistos Pletho's own. Cosimo saw that this unassuming and remarkably selfless young man, who asked for nothing but permission to spend his life in the service of the enlightenment of mankind, might reflect great prestige, in the changing social conditions of the mid-century, on Medicean eminence in Italy, and the Medici according encouraged and supported this endeavour.

The first instalments of Ficino's Latin translation of Plato's works were presented to Cosimo a few months before the latter's death in 1464. The dedicated scholar toiled on under Piero and Lorenzo until, in 1477, he wrote the last sentence. By 1491, the entire translation was in print and on sale. The wheel had come full circle. The early Fathers of the Church—Augustine, for example—had been captivated by a somewhat fanciful interpretation of Plato's philosophy; as the Middle Ages advanced, however, an intense scientific curiosity took its place, enthroning the thought of Aristotle in place of the mysterious concepts of the disciple of Socrates. Now, at the climax of Lorenzo's influence in Italy, neo-Platonism was again in control of the leading minds of the peninsula. They found it, as it had been found by the first Christian thinkers, peculiarly compatible with the religious vision of contemporary Europe. As the century closed, the logic-chopping arguments for the Christian faith propounded by the Aristotelians became less and less fashionable.

The revived philosophical theory was known as "Platonic Love" by the Academy. The phrase meant simply that, as a later axiom would have it, and as Dante implied in the last line of *Paradiso,* "Love is all." Physical beauty, the doctrine continued, is love's visible emanation, and so identical with it. The ecstasy of love, however, occurs only at the beginning of its long journey, with the recognition of such a symbol in the flesh. This amourous passion must end with the contemplation of the deity, the only absolute and transcendental good. Human beings are therefore capable, through love, of progress from animal passion to spiritual desire. Botticelli's "Spring" and "Birth of Venus," respectively, have sometimes been supposed to illustrate the inception and the culmination of this pilgrimage of the soul. Michelangelo's sonnets and Castiglione's *Courtier,* together with much of Renaissance art and literature, take their fire and force from such ideas. Indeed, one is perhaps justified in preferring the poets and artists to the philosophers in this connection. Ficino, and still more Pico della Mirandola, misconstrued from the start the ancient Greek whom they studied so eagerly. Politian and Lorenzo himself in their idyllic verses, whether erotic or pastoral, come much nearer to the pagan sensuousness constantly evoked by Plato's prose, even at its most abstract. Such artists as Botticelli, his master Lippo Lippi, and such sculptors as Luca della Robbia and Mino of Fiesole come nearest of all, for they transcend the senses and appeal to imaginative constructions of essentially religious import.

Yet Lorenzo embodied the ideal of what may be called "the Renaissance man"—that is, the man to whom nothing human is foreign—to a far greater extent than they. He was famous as a poet, and still more famous as a statesman. In the domain of agriculture, as well as in that of music and of architecture, his interests went beyond contemplation to action. He could judge a painting or a sculpture as well as any professional of his day. He collected books and manuscripts with taste and discrimination. He bred race-horses expertly. He loved hunting, pageantry, and also less pretentious forms of entertainment. He could work all day and half the night at the problems of public affairs. He could turn easily from a romp with his children, who were characteristically encouraged never to call him anything but "Lorenzo," or his boon companions, to attend Mass or to debate with a grave theologian. And whether the head of the Republic was being ribald or deadly serious, he expressed his views with a grace and precision that few of his contemporaries, not even Politian, could rival. In private he lived simply, but his public appearances were usually ceremonious in the high Renaissance manner, although they consistently avoided flamboyance in manner of dress. He rarely put on anything but black and gold in a world where others wore clothing in all the colours of the rainbow. Finally, the practically effective help, in particular financial relief, that he gave to friends in trouble is illustrated again and again in contemporary chronicles.

It is difficult, on the evidence, to think of Lorenzo as the "unbridled profligate," or as "infamous" as the "pernicious and cruel tyrant," or as the "embezzling usurper and usurer," as he has been represented by some contemporary and later censors of his character and acts. He certainly had a long love affair with a married woman, Bartolomea Nasi, wife of Donato de' Benci. He punished the Pazzi family for their conspiracy, as well as some other active opponents of his regime, with merciless severity at first. But many of them were subsequently pardoned and their families re-admitted to his favour, as when he married Giacomo Slaviati to his favourite daughter, Lucrezia. He also made arbitrary decisions, not free from the suspicion of self-interest, in one or two legal disputes. Nor had he any documented title to hereditary rule, but he was appointed head of the state of Florence by the free vote of its citizens. He left the city's constitution very much as he had found it, and he sedulously guarded the republican forms of government.

He probably did secretly remove funds from the Treasury, but mainly for public, not private, purposes. These aims included rescue of the Medici banks from insolvency; yet, had they suspended payment, the Republic itself, which so largely depended upon them for its prosperity, would have been more than half ruined.

The conclusion can scarcely be evaded that Lorenzo, in comparison with such rulers as Ludovico Sforza or the Malatesta of Rimini—by no means the worst of contemporary heads of state—acted more like a President than a sovereign. His vaguely defined powers, actually illicit, were unquestionably used without much scruple, though more often for diplomatic than for purely personal ends. It is difficult to understand what else a trusted and popular, but quite illegal, administrator of an unusually organised but key community in the tangle of Italian politics could have done. It was necessary for the survival of Florence that foreign princes should regard Lorenzo as their equal, which meant, in their eyes, that he must govern, like themselves, ultimately by his own will. Their spies reported quite truly that this was the case. So Ferdinand of Naples and the Duke of Milan, the Pope and the Doge, felt at ease in communicating with him. They would not have been so polite, as non-belligerents, if they had supposed themselves dealing with a mere businessman, even one who was Medici.

In that respect, it is certain that Lorenzo clearly saw the political dilemma of fifteenth-century Florence. On the one hand, the popular demand for a republican form of government could not be resisted. It had always been characteristic of Tuscans and Venetians, if not of the still half-Teutonic Lombards and the thoroughly mixed populations of the South. On the other hand, Lorenzo's fellow-citizens were equally determined to secure an efficient administration, without which their wealth and a culture, on the whole superior to those of their neighbours, would have been overwhelmed by the cupidity of Milan, Venice, Rome, or Naples. The two thorns of the dilemma impaled both monarchy and a legally constituted oligarchy on the one side, and genuine democracy, which could only have been chaotic at that time and place, on the other.

By the date of Lorenzo's accession to power, every solution had been tested. All had failed, from the autocracy of the Duke of Athens in the early fourteenth century to the modified feudalism of Charles of Valois or the Duke of Calabria; from the steersmanship of the great or small merchants in Florence itself, or of the well-meaning aristocrat Maso degli Albizzi, down to the rule of mere artisans like the wool-carder Michele Lando. Despite the institution of innumerable representative councils, committees, and boards of managers, with innumerable methods of electing their members, despite the appointment of individual controling officers, consuls, *podestà,* captains of the people, and *gonfa-*

loniers, and despite a Signory of changing priors but permanent functions, experiment after experiment had collapsed into incompetence.

At last, Cosimo de' Medici devised, and Lorenzo de' Medici perfected and maintained, a solution: a disguised and safeguarded dictatorship that reconciled apparently irreconcilable requirements. It worked well for sixty years, but it depended in its essence on outstanding ability in a single holder of the office that pretended to be unofficial. Moreover, a tolerable integrity of character, and far more than average intellectual capacity, were essential to the central figure of the system. Lorenzo must have hoped that his descendents would continue to repeat his own eminence in these aspects, and he laboured earnestly to ensure that his son, Piero, understood what would be needed in his own person for the stability of the Republic. But Lorenzo must also have realised that, sooner or later, an unworthy Medici would take over. The fundamental weakness of the solution he had evolved lay there; yet no other could have been worked out in the circumstances of the era.

Such were, in Florence, the political circumstances in which occurred that splendid cultural climax known as the Renaissance. No subsequent age has ever surpassed the subtlety and range of the painting, sculpture, and architecture created at that period. In other activities, in originality of thought that could be expressed in words, and in technology of all kinds, the mind of man was reaching out to encompass—for it was then thought possible to do so—the whole of the knowledge available in his environment and age. Under the impetus of this ambition, new information poured into Florence. Lorenzo almost doubled the library that Cosimo had formed. The monasteries, by this time, had realised that the "heathen heresies" filling their chests and cupboards, and sometimes their garbage heaps, and often scribbled over with the figures of their accounts or their commentaries on Jerome or Augustine, could command high prices from rich laymen's agents. Among such emissaries, Lorenzo's representatives were conspicuous. They seldom bargained like those from Urbino or Milan, and they generally paid hard cash for whatever parchments caught their fancy. They even examined the papers kept in the privies, and once or twice they carried off such a bundle with shining eyes, while the abbot cursed an unhappy monk for letting the treasure go for a few coppers.

The scribes in the Medici Palace and the convents of San Marco, Fiesole, and San Gallo, all expert archeologists earning generous fees, pieced these foul fragments together with an awe they rarely showed in church or chapel. Many of the scrolls had been written out centuries ago on sturdy materials. Sometimes the younger scholars believed they might be dealing with a manuscript that had actually been touched by the hand of Tacitus or Juvenal. This was probably never the case, but at least some of the grimy pages surviving in the monks' storerooms had once lain in libraries saved by Justinian or Constantine or Charlemagne from the flames of the barbarian incendiaries of old.

Now new libraries were springing up all over Italy, beginning in Tuscany. The university at Pisa, for instance, which Lorenzo had resuscitated in 1472, now possessed one of the most famous collections in Europe. There was no excuse for a professional writer being ignorant of his great predecessors, for even schoolboys could now read them. They were discussed at all social gatherings, by ladies as well as by gentlemen. They were repeatedly referred to in political debate and diplomatic negotiation. Lawyers and physicians checked their principles from pagan practices. Even churchmen carefully studied the heathen philosophers in order to refute them. Savonarola, for example, carried Plato and Seneca in his head, as well as the early Christian Fathers.

In patronising artists, Lorenzo went far beyond Cosimo's and Piero's example. He associated as easily with poverty-stricken painters and sculptors as he did with Politian and Pico della Mirandola, who was born a prince. Lorenzo, moreover, took pains to understand something of the trade of these humble artisans, as they were usually considered. The painters Signorelli and Leonardo da Vinci, handsome men and autodidacts, put on great airs, but the sculptors Donatello and Verrocchio looked and behaved like ordinary workmen. The architects, labouring on such a huge scale, were generally more cultivated and articulate. Lorenzo found them easier to talk to and learn from, till he could himself, without assistance, design a cathedral front. But whether artists could express themselves in words or not, he recognised all his life that their work required an intelligence and sensitivity that Providence had denied to most of mankind. He was almost unique in his time in seeing that lack of formal intellectual training need not necessarily prevent a man from exercising imagination, sometimes to the extent of conceiving visions at least as impressive as those of the philosophers and poets; his attentions to Botticelli are a case in point. Moreover, the Medici ruler's esthetic sensitivity had a range and a variety denied to all but the greatest artists of his time, such men as Alberti, Leonardo da Vinci, and Michelangelo. The work of the latter, while Michelangelo was still in his teens, was noticed by Lorenzo in the studio of Ghirlandaio. The boy genius was at once transferred, by the direction of the head of the state, to the museum of sculpture that had been established in the gardens of the Medici Palace. The aged Bertoldo, a former pupil of Donatello, ran the establishment, which was filled with antique marbles and bronzes, exhumed, like the antique manuscripts, from the dust and rubbish of centuries.

During the three years that Michelangelo remained in Bertoldo's establishment, under the indulgent eye of Lorenzo, who only laughed at the lad's rugged looks and scornful unsociability, he was allowed to attend the meetings of the Platonic Academy. He never forgot them, remaining a Christian Platonist till his death. This crucial period in the great artist's development ended with Lorenzo's death in 1492. It is doubtful whether the sculptor, under any other ruler, would have reached maturity as soon and with so little upheaval in his extremely difficult temperament.

The plastic arts in which Lorenzo so delighted differed in his day from the poetry that he himself practiced, in having developed as much from the traditional theory and practice of medieval artificers as from the inspiration of classical antiquity. Many sculptors, Michelangelo in particular, were certainly highly conscious of the latter. But the painters were less familiar with it, owing to their usually defective literary education, which deprived them of accounts of their pagan predecessors' styles and also of course to the rarity of heathen examples of the treatment of colour and design. In the same way the sculptors and architects, though they could see fragmentary evidence of the character of ancient Roman civilisation here and there in their environment, generally looked at it through eyes uninstructed by the theories of Pausanias and Vitruvius. The artists of the early Renaissance were still most at home with the skills in handicraft bequeathed by their Christian ancestors. These had only improved gradually during the long centuries that stretched between the reign of the first Christian Emperor, Constantine the Great, in the fourth century A.D., and the outburst of inventive capacity around the year 1450.

The mounting complexity and interaction of social levels in the fifteenth century affected the architects to begin with, for the important practical nature of designing buildings brought them into close touch with the ruling classes of their communities. Filippo Brunelleschi (d. 1446), the first and greatest of the Florentine architects to rise under Medicean patronage, went off with the sculptor Donatello to study the surviving remains of classical structure in Rome. The Romans themselves at that time took so little interest in the ruins of the pagan temples, palaces, baths, theatres, aqueducts, and villas that they imagined the two amateur archeologists from the North to be looking for buried treasure. They were; their treasures were those of marble, brick, and bronze, not gold and silver. Brunelleschi discovered the Doric, Ionian, and Corinthian principles of pillar construction. He noted the various motives of the antique style of decoration. But he could not use his new knowledge in the erection of Christian religious and secular edifices. He could only recognise, behind the prevalent Gothic fashions he found in Florence, the older Romanesque tradition, itself derived from pre-Christian models. He introduced new energy and elegance into the aspects of loggias and cloisters. He transformed the massive Romanesque architecture into something altogether novel, into what in fact may be called early Renaissance idiom. It immediately attracted the attention of Cosimo de' Medici, who proceeded to employ Brunelleschi regularly. The church and sacristy of San Lorenzo and the dome of Santa Maria del Fiore, the cathedral, arose to substitute urbanity and restraint for the ponderous majesty hitherto in favour.

Such works strongly influenced the pioneers of the next generation, Michelozzi and Alberti, who both lived on into 1472. Michelozzi, of a more equable temperament than Brunelleschi, became Cosimo's favourite architect. He was commissioned to produce both the graceful cloister of San Marco and the great Medici Palace in the Via Larga, almost a fortress in contrast with the ecclesiastical structure mentioned. The versatile Alberti went much farther than either Brunelleschi or Michelozzi in returning to antiquity. In his façades for the Rucellai Palace and Santa Maria Novella, the medieval inheritance has been almost wholly discarded. Alberti's style came to dominate Italian architecture in the following century, though his buildings, so far as originality and accurate expression of the great Medicean age are concerned, are not the equals of those of his two predecessors.

In sculpture, Lorenzo Ghiberti designed the north and east gates of the Baptistery. Like Brunelleschi in architecture, he combined the spirit of the Middle Ages with that of the Renaissance, adding some, though fewer, classical features. The over-all impression of these panels, depicting scenes from the Old and New Testaments, respectively, is one of harmonious and animated motion. It produces a feminine and flowing, rather than a masculine or monumental effect. The constructions of Donatello, Ghiberti's younger contemporary, supplied the latter type of style, but less in the classical spirit of serenity than in that of the virile naturalism of his own restless era, his immediate environment.

The variety and extent of Donatello's achievement would be most remarkable in any age. The pungent Christian idealism of the marble figure of St. George, originally destined for an exterior niche of Or San Michele and afterwards transferred to the Bargello, conveys at the same time lifelike heroism and youthful male elegance. The sculptor's portrait busts fairly throb with animation. His representations of children gayly dancing and singing, as in the relief decorating the organ loft at the cathedral in Florence, seem actual living flesh. So does his equestrian statue of the *condottiere* nicknamed Gattamelata ("Honeycat") at Padua. Donatello's zestful genius inaugurated a school of sculpture that was to dominate the art until the twentieth century.

Cosimo, as already suggested, was devoted to the man in spite of his untidy private life. Yet, after the artist's death in 1455, his extraordinary feats were followed by a series of masters of equal accomplishment. Luca della Robbia made a counterpart to Donatello's relief in the cathedral organ loft. It is comparable for its sheer beauty to the older man's, yet utterly different in what may be described as a species of intonation, affirming an exquisite musicality as compared with the other's lusty sense of physical pride and enjoyment. Antonio Pallaiuolo surpassed even Donatello in the depiction of furious vigour when he modelled the small bronze group of Hercules wrestling with Antaeus. Andrea Verrocchio, another unassuming member of Lorenzo's circle, could show in his bronze of a boyish "David" the attractive embarrassment, as well as the daring, of a teen-age hero. Verrocchio also rivals both Donatello and the far less productive, but practically faultless, carver Desiderio da Settignano in his marble bust of a girl, where the tranquil dignity of the sitter, every feature instinct with refined delicacy, makes an impression at once intensely personal and secretly withdrawn. Verrocchio's famous equestrian bronze of Bartolommeo Colleoni—who actually was not a very good mercenary commander—is, by comparison, a mere rhetorical gesture, if perfect of its kind, symbolising fierce military self-esteem.

Of the painters patronised by the senior Medici before Lorenzo's time, Fra Angelico is the most important. Under Cosimo, he produced frescos at San Marco in the cloister, chapter house, and cells. Though Angelico was a Dominican friar, his religious sentiment recalls rather the tenderness of St. Francis than the austerity of St. Dominic. This ecstatic suavity characterised very few of the generally hard-bitten, sharp-witted, and realistically minded natives of Florence. Angelico is unique in this respect among their more renowned painters, whether older or younger than himself. But in his technique, the rapturous visionary proved that he had a grasp of uncompromising craftmanship. The perspective, for instance, of the garden in his "Annunciation" is much more typically Florentine than his figures. His bright, long-lasting colours are another proof of his proficiency in the mere handling of paint. He was quite clearly concerned above all in making sure that his pious joy in the divine world of innocent dreams should affect to the full both his contemporaries and future generations.

Masaccio, dead at twenty-seven in 1428, the year before Cosimo came to political power, cannot be ranked as a painter patronised by the Medici, but his influence on subsequent work in this medium was the greatest since Giotto's. He learned naturalism from Donatello's sculpture, and perspective from Brunelleschi's architecture. Yet, in painting, his mastery appears entirely original. He lived long enough only to complete a single work, the frescos of the Brancacci Chapel in the Carmine Church. Here, the dignity and grouping of the figures can be compared with Giotto's, but the bodies are fully three-dimensional. They are precisely articulated anatomically even when clothed. Furthermore, the calm presentation of nudes, in defiance of ecclesiastical prohibition at this period, constitutes a daringly creative step forward. Again, landscape is more realistic in these paintings than ever before. Tone largely takes the place of line to indicate mass and distance. Masaccio thus invented the technique of *chiaroscuro* (light and shadow), the basis of European pictorial art down to the end of the nineteenth century. The technicians Uccello (d. 1475), preoccupied with perspective, Castagno (d. 1457), and Domenicao Veneziano (d. 1461), who added oil to the current medium of tempora, extended and exploited Masaccio's concentration on anatomy. The more conventional artists who followed could not have reached, without this example, their accuracy in depicting scenes of everyday life, whether agreeably familiar and homely as in Lippi's pictures or gorgeous as in Gozzoli's pageantry.

It was under Lorenzo de' Medici, however, that Florentine painting approached its zenith, in the masterpieces of Leonardo da Vinci, Sandro Botticelli, Andrea del Verrocchio, Domenico Ghirlandaio, and many others. Leonardo da Vinci (1452–1519), in the popular estimate of posterity—though not necessarily in that of the *cognoscenti*—was head and shoulders above the rest. Of this man, Vasari, the historian of artists, says: "Sometimes according to the course of nature, sometimes beyond and above it, the greatest gifts rain down from heavenly influences upon the bodies of men, and crowd into one individual beauty, grace, and excellence in such superabundance that to whatever that man shall turn, his very act is so divine, that, surpassing the work of all other men, it makes manifest that it is by the special gift of God, and not by human act. This was true of Leonardo da Vinci, who, beside a physical beauty beyond all praise, put an infinite grace into whatever he did, and such was his excellence, that to whatever difficult things his mind turned he easily solved them." Although he was a Florentine by birth, Leonardo spent only half of his sixty-seven years in that city, and his most important work was done after Lorenzo's time. As a youth, he assisted the subtle Verrocchio (he painted the kneeling angel in his master's "Baptism of Christ"), and, by 1477, he showed such unusual talent that he was patronised by Lorenzo. During this period, he produced a "Madonna and Child," an "Adam and Eve" (unfinished), an "Adoration of the Magi," a miniature "Annunciation," and a bust of St. John the Baptist—for by now he had added sculpture, as well as anatomy, astronomy, botany, mathematics, engineering, and music to his accomplishments. In 1482, while on a mission for Lorenzo to the court of Ludovico Sforza in Milan, he entered that despot's service, and Florence was to see no more of him until the year 1500. It was in Milan that he painted his masterpiece, "The Last Supper."

Sandro Botticelli (1444?–1501), the greatest of all the Florentine painters except Leonardo and Michelangelo, was the favourite of Lorenzo, and he was, for his part, the most devoted to the Medici until his patron's death in 1492. A clean-shaven, massive man with brooding grey eyes, luxuriant brown hair, and a manner by turn awkward and impulsive, he was as eccentric and erratic as he was gifted. He seemed to wander around half in the world of reality—which he ill understood and depicted badly—and half in the world of fantasy, which he understood and portrayed superlatively. His two best-known masterpieces, "Primavera" (Spring) and "The Birth of Venus" illustrate this imaginative facility, which was Greek—as the Florentines understood that term—in its inspiration. The glory of dawn, the freshly unveiled beauty of the world that the Greeks had seen, Botticelli saw also. But into this innocent contemplation of beauty, a new and more complicated element is introduced, the idea of a moral order. On the face of Venus, and in the figure of Primavera, there is the hint of a presentiment that they must leave the ocean haven and the magic wood in which they find themselves. The result is a touch of sadness, the recognition of an opposition between two beautiful things, or perhaps the knowledge that all things pass. These two works were followed by a preoccupation with wholly Christian mysticism that culminated in Botticelli's complete subservience to Savonarola and, after the monk's execution, in a period of sterile passivity, which endured until his death. Such unpredictability characterised the painter's entire life and career. One never knew whether he was about to produce an illustration for the New Testament, a classical allegory, a portrait, or an episode in the life of a saint. What he did, however, reflected a fastidious and fragile vision of unmistakable quality, the significance of which was often so rarified as to seem inexplicable.

Another master spirit of this generation, Andrea del Verrocchio (1435–88), displays a subtle and complicated conception of life. In his work, there is always a joy in beauty, with which another element is super-added. His "Boy on a Dolphin," which stands in the courtyard of the Palazzo Vecchio, is a personification of the grace and carelessness of childhood—but the face of the boy reflects an impish scepticism. The same is true of the bronze "David" who, having just subdued Goliath, exhibits an odd, mischievous sprightliness. Both statues reflect an attitude of tolerant amusement, of scepticism, towards the seriousness of life that had characterised Florence in the days before Lorenzo. Concerning Verrocchio's paintings there has been much dispute, not with respect to their quality but with regard to their authenticity, and today only the "Baptism of Christ" (in the Uffizi of Florence) is ascribed to him with certainty, although a "Madonna and Angels" and a "Tobias and the Angel" are probably authentic. An entrancing subtlety is Verrocchio's chief characteristic, and it was from Verrocchio that Leonardo learned the smile, if it be a smile, on the faces of his portraits of women.

Domenico Ghirlandaio (1449–94) was born in Florence, began work as a goldsmith, and, in 1472, first turned his hand to painting. His now lost work in the Vespucci Chapel and in the church of Ognissanti was followed by crowd-filled scenes for the church of San Gimignano. After working in Rome on the Sistine Chapel ("The Resurrection" and "The Calling of the Apostles"), he remained in Florence until his death, completing figures of Roman statesmen for the Palazzo della Signoria, and frescos on the life of St. Florence for the Sassetti Chapel in Santa Trinitia and for the life of St. John the Baptist and the Virgin for the Tornabuoni Chapel in Santa Maria Novella. Among the frescos of the Sassetti Chapel is perhaps the best surviving portrait of Lorenzo. Ghirlandaio used contemporary persons for his faces, dressed his figures in Florentine costumes, and arranged them in rooms reflecting the structural and decorative tastes of his own time. He was no intellectual, like Leonardo, nor a mystic, like Fra Angelico or Botticelli, but he was a superb technician, expert in perspective, composition, anatomy, and *chiaroscuro*. It was Ghirlandaio who formed the talent of his youthful disciple, Michelangelo, and it was in his studio that the latter first came to the attention of the Medici. One day in 1489, the story goes, Lorenzo happened to visit Ghirlandaio's studio, where he caught sight of the sculptured mask of a grinning fawn. He asked the artist whether the fawn was his own work. "Oh, no, Magnificence," Ghirlandaio answered. "That is the work of one of my apprentices, Michelangelo Buonarrotti. Do you think he has talent?"

"I am sure of it. How old is he?"

"Fourteen."

"Send him to me, then."

Lorenzo took the heavy-featured, sulky lad, whose nose had already been broken by a fellow-student in exchange for unsolicited criticism, into his household. The boy was paid an allowance of five ducats a month and was given the run of the Medici gardens, where he could study the works of Donatello and of the ancients, and listen to the discussions of the Academy and to readings from the *Divine Comedy*.

The mere names of those whom Lorenzo patronised and who rendered Florence illustrious by their works would fill pages, but a few must be mentioned in addition to the masters given above: Andrea della Robbia, nephew of Luca and almost his uncle's equal in the charm of his Madonnas; Benozzo Gozzoli, who painted the three generations of Medici (Cosimo, Piero, Lorenzo, and Giuliano) in the Riccardi Palace; Antonio Pollaiuolo, sculptor as well as painter, who was notable as a leader in the new school of realism, and Filippino Lippi, Lippo Lippi's son, who completed the frescos in the chapel of Santa Maria del Carmine that had been left unfinished by Masaccio.

The only art in which the period of Lorenzo's rule fell short of the preceding fifty years, at least so far as Florence was concerned, was that of architecture. The Palazzo Strozzi, by Benedetto da Maiano (who was also a sculptor, as witness his exquisite pulpit in the church of Santa Croce), with which Lorenzo had nothing to do, was the only edifice undertaken during his reign that rivalled the work done, in Cosimo's and Piero's time, by Brunelleschi, Michelozzi, and Alberti.

In sculpture, however, Lorenzo's favourite, Andrea del Verrocchio, proved as excellent a practitioner as he was in painting. This calm, taciturn man, with his huge spectacles and unprepossessing physique, looked more like a shop assistant than an artist; yet, in true Renaissance fashion, he not only painted and sculpted but also composed creditable music. In 1472 he completed the monument to Lorenzo's father Piero, and the latter's brother, Giovanni, in the church of San Lorenzo. In 1476, the bronze "David" was cast; it is not a work comparable for classic beauty to Donatello's version of the same hero, but it is strikingly vivid in its realistic portrayal of the victorious shepherd boy. Verrocchio's masterpiece of design, pose, and execution, "Bartolommeo Colleoni," greatest of equestrian statues, which stands in Venice, was modeled in 1488, but it was not cast for another eight years. In addition to the formidable talent of Verrocchio, Laurentian Florence also abounded in sculpted beauty from other, less famous and perhaps less talented, but nonetheless memorable, sources: Benedetto da Maiano, whose pulpit in Santa Croce has already been mentioned; Mino da Fiesole, who is remembered for his bust of Piero de' Medici; and Antonio Rossellino, who created a famous tomb for a Portuguese prelate in the church of San Minato.

The literature of the Laurentian age did not reach the level of its painting and sculpture. Some modern authorities have plausibly argued that, although Lorenzo and his good friend, Politian, were poets, Lorenzo paid more attention to the plastic arts than to literature because he feared that men expert in the expression of ideas might incidentally damage the carefully framed system of government he had developed as the only reliable support for his Republic's special character and circumstances. He thus prevented, it is maintained, the rise under his egis of authors of the stature of Machiavelli and Guicciardini, or in poetry of such figures as Boiardo, Ariosto, Michelangelo, and Tasso.

It can readily be admitted that Lorenzo's deepest preoccupations were political, and that he tolerated with reluctance such excursions into this field as did not merely complement his own. The free play of speculation about what Plato, Aristotle, or Virgil may have meant was thoroughly congenial to him, but he did not care for discussions of fifteenth-century political or ethical principles that disregarded current notions of human nature or religion. Such talk might be dangerous to

Medicean conceptions of these matters. Literary genius of the first order—that is, constructive genius—tends to a synthesis. It would therefore offend both his essentially analytical and sceptical cast of mind and his determination to keep a firm hold upon his city. It may well be for this reason that his own verse and prose, which the age in general naturally imitated, were on the whole distinguished rather for perfection of form and elegance of diction than for ardor or depth of inspiration. In a word, Lorenzo's idealism, though vividly imaginative and sympathetic to that of others, in the sense that he could easily enter into their thoughts and feelings, nevertheless lacked the breadth and insight of, for instance, those Greek philosophers he studied in so decidedly amateur a spirit, without ever troubling to learn their language.

For all Lorenzo's delicacy of observation and phrasing in his compositions, one has only to look at Ghirlandaio's portrait of him in the Sassetti fresco to see that in life, as contrasted with literature, a certain coarseness and blunt vigour accompanied his outstanding intelligence. He never, in fact, concealed his tastes for women and sport, ceremonies and luxury, the company of simple men and of frivolous women. In his position, and at his time and place, no one, not even Ficino and Landino, thought any the worse of him for such frank exuberance.

A similar practical and forthright strain also caused Lorenzo to see to it that Florence took the lead at this period in substituting the vernacular speech for the Latin which, since the era of Petrarch and Boccaccio, had resumed its ascendancy as the language of written communication. This innovation may almost be said to have been stage-managed by Lorenzo. He repudiated vigorously the contention of the older humanists that Italian could not command the grandeur and lucidity of the tongue of Horace, Virgil, Cicero, and Seneca. Indeed, he gave the reactionaries an example in his own works of what he meant. The early love-songs were the outcome of his affection, rather than passion, for Lucrezia Donati, heroine of the 1469 tournament. But in all his productions, a large vocabulary, an excellent ear for rhythm, and skill in composition are evident. Occasionally a poignant melancholy mingles with playful exhortation somewhat in the Horatian manner. The first stanza of the celebrated *Song of Bacchus* runs:

> *Quant' è bella giovinezza*
> *che si fugge tuttavia.*
> *Chi vuol esser lieto, sia.*
> *Di doman non c'è certezza.*
> ("How fair is youth, yet gone
> how soon. Ere fades to-day
> let him who wills be gay.
> To-morrow is unknown.")

Politian, undoubtedly the somewhat lonely Lorenzo's most intimate friend, strenuously seconded the movement to replace Latin with Tuscan at high social and intellectual levels. Politian himself, however, still preferred classical literature. He had made excellent translations of parts of the *Iliad* into the idiom of Virgil before he was eighteen, and before he was thirty his lectures on the pagan writers were attracting students to Florence from all over Europe. His own compositions in Latin verse were never surpassed in his own time or since. But Lorenzo, fortunately for Italian letters, turned Politian's attention, at last, to his native speech. The younger man then outdid even his patron's efforts. The exquisite charm of the Tuscan lyrics that Politian turned out, the half-romantic, half-humourous ballads and occasional pieces, seem to be light-weight improvisation, but carefully cut and polished to perfection.

This style was almost at once carried into epic by the Emilian Ludovico Ariosto (1474–1533) with a wonderfully natural vivacity of fancy and wit that soon enthralled a far wider audience than Politian ever reached, but he unquestionably owed much to the Florentine humanist. The latter, physically an unprepossessing little fellow with coarse and bristling dark hair, could only impress those who met him for the first time by the extraordinarily forceful mobility of his cherubic features; sparkling, greenish eyes; and dandified dress. It is probable that he was homosexual. He never married or took a mistress, and the death of Lorenzo, his only associate, in 1492, broke his heart. He died himself two years later, at the age of only forty.

Marsilio Ficino (1433–99), an authority on Plato and yet a Christian mystic, looked the part of the scholar-mystic with his puny stature, ragged beard, harassed and furrowed countenance, shabby clothes, and fanatically glaring eyes. His translations into Latin of Plato, Plotinus, and many other Alexandrian writers, his Italian version of Dante's *De Monarchia,* his life of Plato, moral essays, and *Theologica Platonica* are now unreadable except by specialists. Yet he was one of the most learned, if also one of the least logical, philosophers of his day, and an honest man.

The enlightenment of Lorenzo's Academy may be gauged by the fact that the next most important member of it presented a complete contrast with Ficino. The burlesque poet Luigi Pulci, whom everyone called "Gigi," a neat, merry, keen-minded, and ruthlessly impudent personage in private life, looked like a popular comedian, and in fact anticipated *Don Quixote* by making all Europe laugh at his *Morgante Maggiore,* an erudite but almost uninterruptedly ludicrous unmasking of the chivalrous ideals prevalent in former centuries and concentrated by Pulci in the legends about Charlemagne. The frivolous bard, decidedly philoprogenitive and always in some kind of financial difficulty, gave his giant, "Morgante," a fir-tree for a toothpick and a cunning dwarf named Margute for a Sancho Panza. This deliberately absurd fairy-tale drew smiles even from the strait-laced Lucrezia Tornabuoni and fascinated both scholars and playboys.

The personality of Pico della Mirandola appears to have been less striking than either Ficino's or Pulci's. A handsome man of unimpeachable morals, he owned great estates and possessed an awe-inspiring range of scholarship in Latin, Greek, Hebrew, Arabic, and even Chaldean. The mysteries of science—except those of astrology, which he ridiculed—also deeply attracted him.

Perhaps it was the exclusively intellectual cast of his mind that prevented him from being wholeheartedly adored by the Medicean circle, as devoted to art and the life of the senses as to abstract argument. But Florentine society, for its part, began by idolising Pico. It was much amused, for instance, when it heard that he had once run away with a grocer's widow, an affair that brought about his arrest. Lorenzo came to the rescue by declaring, probably more in jest than an earnest, that Pico's secretary, having a grievance against his high-born and learned master, had contrived the whole business in order to bring discredit on the polyglot nobleman. The grocer, incidentally, was a member, though a very humble one, of the house of Medici. No one, Lorenzo is said to have exclaimed, could possibly be unfaithful to a Medici.

At a later stage, however, the leading citizens of Florence were repelled when Pico announced that he had burnt five books of his Latin verses because they were "amourous in character." Nor did everyone approve of his nine hundred theses offering evidence from Jewish and Arabic sources in support of Christianity, for these essays brought him under the ban of the Church for seven years after 1486.

Pico's best-known contribution to the literature of the Renaissance is his *Oration on the Dignity of Man,* which reflects Ficino's ideal of the unity of all things. He believed that the principles of Platonic philosophy could be traced to the Mosaic code of the Old Testament and that the philosophic truths of antiquity were but fragments of the one, eternal—that is, Christian—truth. It was because of this breadth of vision, as well as because of Pico's immense erudition, that Machiavelli was moved to describe Pico as "a man almost divine."

A man of another sort was Cristoforo Landino, Lorenzo's former tutor and a professor of poetry and rhetoric at the University of Florence. The very type of a serene and courtly sage, outwardly epicurean and inwardly stoic, Landino was imagined by his contemporaries to be almost a reincarnation of Cicero in looks and mentality. He was reputed to understand the works of Dante and Petrarch better than any other scholar of his day. He is remembered chiefly for his edition of the *Divine Comedy,* published in 1481, which was illustrated by Botticelli in a series of drawings of no particular merit.

* * *

Such were the leaders of that intellectual and artistic revolution that was to set the pattern for the civilisation of the next four centuries. It was a revolution endorsed, supported, and encouraged by successive generations of Medici who, in turn, were largely responsible for its peculiar blend of commercialism, devotion to intellectual pursuits, moral egalitarianism, earthy sensuality, humour, and a passion for pageantry and entertainment. The movement spread, of course, to the rest of Italy, and then to all of Europe. Yet none of the states to which it came could appreciate the spirit of Florence that had inspired and promoted it, a spirit manifesting itself in a violent dislike for autocracy, an equally violent passion for liberty, and a wholehearted devotion to superiority in diplomacy and trade.

It was, of course, this typically Florentine tolerance and pacifism that brought the May of the spirit so soon to November in the city. Lorenzo was born within a year of the appearance of the first printed book in Europe; he died almost at the moment of the discovery of the New World, which immensely enlarged the scope of Western man's material concerns at the expense of his spiritual preoccupations. Lorenzo, the last of the great Medici of Florence, had stood for moderation in judgement and tranquility in social relations, even more firmly than for—if also because of his delight in—both philosophic speculation and natural or man-made beauty. The tragedy of European humanity has always been the pitifully brief illuminations of its mind between the prolonged phases of violence in its blood. The antitheses remain endless. Even if Lorenzo had been a soldier of genius as well as an extremely subtle administrator, he could not have rescued his continent forever from its dark inheritance, for the pure compound of soldier-statesman at its best tends to lack the grace of twin qualities that so often act together, poetic insight and cosmopolitan generosity. These two in their turn, it is true, are seldom accompanied by the will to meet a big stick with a bigger one. Accordingly, hatred, not love, despite all that religious can do, rules, in the long run, the communities of men.

Florence's run was to be shorter, though so vigourous while it lasted, than most.

It would seem that the Medici, up to the climax of their power under Lorenzo, had always been aware of this circumstance. Cosimo, the plain, good-natured, yet formidably shrewd merchant, successfully creative in both commerce and diplomacy, suffered from an incessant strain of melancholy. Perhaps he could see far enough to understand that his work would not endure in a material sense. But it is doubtful whether he realised how much influence it would have, under the egis of his grandson, on the mentalities of future statesmen all over the world. "Our buildings will outlive us," he said once. "This house is too big for so small a family," he had murmured sadly when the news of the death of his son Giovanni was brought to him. He himself then lay dying at his grand new palace in the city, and he may have meant more than appears on the surface of the phrase he uttered. He may have foreseen a time when the numerous Medici he had made so powerful and so admired would be few and insignificant on pages of Florentine history rendered significant by others.

Cosimo's son Piero, plagued by gout all his life, at the heart of affairs for only five years and dead at fifty-three, nevertheless held on stubbornly to the authority and glory of his inheritance. He was not lacking in the energy, the basic equanimity, the sagacity, or the respect for learning, literature, and art that had marked his father's career. Piero, moreover, unlike Cosimo, had the luck to marry a woman, Lucrezia Tornabuoni, who combined high intelligence with domestic virtue. The gloom that occasionally overcame him, especially towards the end of his life, came only partly from his persistent ill-health. Certain traits in the temper of his fellow-citizens, the ineradicable prejudice against even the shadow of monarchy, the tendency never to forget a real or an imagined injury, the idealism and the love of intrigue alike, all of which were liable to exceed the bounds of common discretion, depressed him.

The conspiracies, which he crushed without bloodshed, organised by Luca Pitti, Niccolò Soderini, Agnolo Acciaiuolo, and Diotisalvi Neroni, showed him how precarious was the position of a *primus inter pares,* more than a figurehead but less than a dynast. But he could never bring himself to suppress lawlessness by violence, and to that extent he must be regarded as a tragic character, more truly "Peter the Unlucky" than the second Piero, his grandson, had ever been at school. He may well have been conscious of an impending catastrophe in his house, merely to be averted for a while by the brilliant promise of his son Lorenzo.

The promise was in fact magnificently fulfilled. Florence became the Athens of Italy in the twenty-odd years that followed, and perhaps superior to ancient Athens in the discretion of its politics. The superlative social charm of the new head of the state obliterated the bodily disadvantages, so obstructive in an age that prized perfection above all, of a sallow complexion, little peering eyes, a flat nose, a harsh voice, and clumsy movements. Lorenzo made little of them himself, once observing, when twitted about his defective sense of smell: "Never mind. Most smells are unpleasant, aren't they?" The portraits generally reveal some evidence of a dauntless self-confidence, as well as a patience, in the irregularly jutting features. But the liveliness and superb tact that so impressed his contemporaries, even the worst of them, the smile that, breaking through the dark, twisted mask, had won so many cruel hearts, have to be imagined. Apparently no one could have been more suitable, except in face and form, to lead a nation to deserve the gratitude of mankind.

Yet this very versatility and unorthodox outlook on most of the questions that confront the occupant of a highly responsible post made enemies for Lorenzo. There were fewer people who censured him unfairly than adored him uncritically; but strict moralists had some excuse for considering him unscrupulous in money matters and even ruthless in taking advantage of the folly or weakness of honest men. There was something hard to define about the Medici in general that often scandalised naïve persons. It was, however, at this date nothing so reprehensible as the rascality commonly disclosed in Renaissance princes such as the Visconti of Milan or Ferdinand of Naples. It was rather that cool disregard, as afterwards positively recommended by Machiavelli, of ordinary ethical principle, in circumstances judged by the perpetrator of these dubious acts to be of more public moment than justice to individuals. No doubt all men entrusted with the welfare of nations are open to this kind of accusation. The first three Medici, however, and particularly Lorenzo, have aroused peculiar animosity in the historians of later generations. It seems clear today that these scholars were wide of the mark in their adverse verdicts on Lorenzo. His virtues, in fact, on the evidence, far outweighed his faults. But his piercing intelligence and sincere idealism must have made him uneasily conscious not only of the hopeless immorality of most able and resolutely ambitious persons of a practical turn of mind who achieve great influence, but also of his own ethical shortcomings in this respect. The characteristic Medicean melancholy, to which he was as subject as his father and grandfather, might well have been deepened by such reflections, maintaining a shadowy counterpoint to his temperamental gayety and optimism. At any rate, such thoughts, and the natural dejection of a chronic invalid, may account for his rather baffling restraint with respect to the fanatic Savonarola after 1489. The prior stood for so much that Lorenzo disliked—apart from both men's respect for religion—in the shape of bad manners, intransigence, and recklessly aggressive fits of fury, that a secular ruler who had won authority largely by opposite traits would normally have been repelled by the preacher's personality. But the fatally sick and, to an extent, conscience-stricken Lorenzo treated the uncompromising priest more in the

style of the devoted suitor of an obstinately hostile princess than in
that of the practically omnipotent autocrat of a loyal, energetic, and
cultivated community.

Lorenzo's end at forty-three was therefore even more tragic than
his father's at fifty-three, the more poignant on account of the sparkling
success that preceded it. He knew better than Savonarola what the
Florentines were really like. He understood more accurately the moral
and political forces that were at work in Italy, undermining the ideas
of democratic freedom in the religious sphere as well as in theories of
government. He realised, as the friar did not, that mere pious zeal
would never make headway against these sappers of civic strength.
Only a raising of the general level of culture, he seems to have
thought, could counter, if not wholly eradicate, the degeneration of
humanity into a horde of self-seeking opportunists and voluptuaries.
But, as usual, the intellectual, betrayed from within by his own reluctance to give and take hard knocks, retreated before the doctrinaire
ideologist.

Lorenzo failed therefore to achieve his long-term objective of a
rational civilisation, uniting the best elements of classical paganism and
the Christianity of his own day. The truth is, indeed, that Laurentian
Florence fell a long way short of perfection. The philosophers were not
so wise and deep as they thought they were. The pedantic Ficino was in
no sense the equal of Socrates or St. Thomas Aquinas, although he
would have been outraged at the merest hint of this inferiority. Neither
Politian nor Lorenzo, elegant as they were, could rival the lyrics of
Euripides or Horace, or even the anonymous *Pervigilium Veneris*
(probably of comparatively decadent fourth century A.D.), or even the
great thirteenth-century hymns such as "Dies Irae" and "Stabat Mater."
Only the best of the painters, architects, and sculptors of Renaissance
Florence can survive comparison with both their heathen and Christian
predecessors and with many of their famous successors. Nor did less
distinguished Florentines of this period regularly reach such intellectual,
spiritual, or moral heights as have been characteristic of certain small
and short-lived European communities before and since their time.
Some of the *dramatis personae* in the plays of Aristophanes had a
bolder and more incisive wit than any of Luigi Pulci's. Patriots, saints,
and martyrs were in rather short supply among the hard-headed Florentine merchants and artisans of the second half of the fifteenth
century, while fraud and sexual license, without perhaps being quite
so rife as in contemporary Rome, Naples, Milan, and Venice, prevailed
sufficiently to justify the warnings, if not the fanaticism, of Savonarola.

Nonetheless, during the twenty-odd years of Lorenzo's undisputed
leadership in Florence, he set an example to humanity that no one
who has ever even glanced at European history can cease to revere.

It was not Savonarola alone who brought down that fabric. External events over which Lorenzo, for all his influence in Italy and elsewhere, could not have exercised control, came in the next few years to inflict ruin upon his Republic. The catastrophe coincided, ironically enough, with an expansion of Western material and intellectual, if not spiritual horizons, which no one in the year 1492 could have been in a position to foresee.

IV

THE LOSING BATTLE

(*1492–1530*)

1. Piero di Lorenzo de' Medici and
Fra Girolamo Savonarola

The mourning for Lorenzo de' Medici was not confined to Florence.
Men and women who had never known him personally lamented him,
chiefly on political grounds, and most thoughtful Italians realised that
the main prop of peace on the peninsula had been withdrawn. They
felt apprehensive, not of absolute catastrophe but of wearisome hostilities that might lead to economic and cultural decay. Yet there was some
reasonable hope that Piero, the eldest of Lorenzo's three sons, would
at least attempt to follow in his father's footsteps. In 1492 he was
twenty-two, a year older than Lorenzo had been on his accession to
power in 1469. Piero seemed to most people a passably decent young
man, despite a certain blundering arrogance, which perhaps was pardonable in one of his years and social position. This quality, moreover,
proved highly congenial to the Roman relatives of his wife Alfonsina
degli Orsini, who were themselves not remarkable for their humility.

The citizens of Florence did not care greatly, on what may be called
purely nationalistic grounds, for this marriage between the Medici heir
and the Roman princess. It had been deliberately arranged by Lorenzo
in order to obtain a political footing in Rome, an area peculiarly liable
to instability because of the unpredictability of the Popes and the
comparative rapidity with which, in the natural course of events, they
were replaced. Neither Romans in general, nor the Orsini in particular,
were popular in Florence, where the pride of both was considered
ostentatious and their culture reactionary. In general, the businesslike
and decidedly individualistic Florentines had no time for the languid
swagger and suspiciously aggressive piety of most of the Romans they
met, which seemed based on nothing but the presence of papal pomp

in their metropolis, and certainly not on military achievement, intellectual eminence, or moral virtue. Yet, after all, the great Lorenzo himself had married into the Orsini clan, with no ill effect for the state; rather the contrary. In any case, Florence felt, Piero would have a better start than anyone else in exercising secular authority in the Republic. The second son of Lorenzo, Cardinal Giovanni de' Medici, had the better reputation for academic distinction and general intelligence; but even if Giovanni had not already been a churchman, he could not, as a younger son, have been regarded as the natural successor to his father. The third son, Giuliano, was only thirteen.

Piero, therefore, now that Medicean supremacy had lasted for three generations, was regarded by Florentines almost as their hereditary prince. At least he was tall, strong, and handsome, like his uncle Giuliano, and adept at such field sports as wrestling. He had received an excellent education, which enabled him to improvise light verse, somewhat in his father's manner, and to speak well both in public and in private. He could not, however, be described as easy-going in the typical Medici fashion. His pride was easily wounded, and on such occasions his temper became dangerous; yet, with all this, the new Medici ruler could rather suddenly be brought to change his mind.

Many incidents indicate, however, that Piero had inherited something of his father's dexterity in governing his touchy compatriots. When, for instance, Alfonso II of Naples, the former Duke of Calabria, who had succeeded the deceased King Ferdinand in 1494, offered Piero de' Medici a title and estate, the Florentine merchant-prince retorted coolly:

"Your Majesty knows that my ancestors have lived as private citizens by their trade and their estates. Nor have I myself any desire for a station above theirs. I have no intention of falling short of their ideas in this connection. Forgive me for declining your offer. If you still wish to confer a favour upon me, pray do so in whatever way you think best, through my bank managers. . . . I do not feel myself to deserve such high recognition as you suggest. I have no wish to become a baron." Piero was perfectly well aware that acceptance of Alfonso's compliment would have infuriated all Florence. The head of the Republic needed no such ennoblement as a Neapolitan barony could confer. To bear the name of so potent a family was already more than enough. Nevertheless, Piero was also sufficiently typical of his line not to be able to resist mentioning that his bank would be glad for any favours Alfonso might care to confer upon it.

Yet the handsome, peremptory, articulate, and athletic Piero, unlike his plump, studious, vague, and hesitant younger brother Cardinal Giovanni, took no interest in state business, which he left to his chancellor. Nor had he more than an occasional trace of his father's suave discretion. Generally he gave any orders that occurred to him on the spur of the moment, and he expected them to be obeyed without argument or even comment.

The street-corner gossips muttered: "That's his mother and his wife coming out." In fact, both Lorenzo's pious consort, Clarice degli Orsini (d. 1488) and his much more able but equally haughty daughter-in-law Alfonsina, of the same house, invariably kept ordinary Florentine citizens at arms' length. Florentines who did not consider themselves to be ordinary observed with regret that Piero, although he had been educated by Politian and surrounded by artists and intellectuals throughout his adolescence, appeared to prefer the company of grooms and acrobats to that of scholars or even businessmen. There was one exception. Michelangelo, an inmate at that time of the Medici Palace, pleased Piero for some reason, perhaps on account of the sculptor's combative temper and fierce energy. In any case, the new ruler of Florence gave the stalwart stone-cutter nearly as much of his time as he accorded to a certain good-looking Spaniard, by occupation a stable-man, to whom Piero seemed to have a homosexual attachment.

These matters are not related by the chroniclers in very convincing detail. It is clear that a good deal of malice and exaggeration were involved in the accounts of these historians, who could not help being conscious of the deplorable episodes in Piero's later career. But the conclusion cannot be avoided that his character rapidly deteriorated after he succeeded his father.

On July 26, 1492, only a few months after Lorenzo's death, the worthy but not conspicuously intelligent Pope Innocent VIII, whose son Franceschetto Cibo had married Lorenzo's second daughter, Maddalena, also died. The Pontiff had, for the most part, remained on excellent terms with Florence. In 1486, it is true, he had prohibited, on pain of excommunication, the public recitation in Rome of the nine hundred Propositions of Pico della Mirandola, a member of Florence's Platonic Academy. It is doubtful, however, that this edict greatly disturbed Lorenzo, who, though quite keenly interested in the problems of religion, could not be held responsible for the opinions of a learned friend who was not often in Florence. Nor is it likely that the Pope thought any the less of the head of the Republic for not interfering with the theological activities of a man with no political influence and one whose estates were in Romagna, not in Tuscany.

Innocent was succeeded by a very different sort of man, the Spaniard Rodrigo Borgia, who took the name Alexander VI. His election emerged from a conclave in which separate candidates were supported by the King of Naples and Ludovico Sforza, regent of Milan. Piero did not think much of either of these potentates, but he feared Ludovico more than he mistrusted the seventy-year-old Ferdinand, who was to die eighteen months later. The senior Medici therefore instructed his brother, the young Cardinal Giovanni, to vote for Ferdinand's man. Giovanni, however, rather resented Piero's imperious attitude and turned to Cardinal Ascanio Sforza, Ludovico's brother, for advice. Ascanio knew that he had no chance himself, and he therefore recommended that Giovanni vote for Rodrigo Borgia, who was sure to win, as he was bribing every cardinal who would listen to him. But Giovanni, in his youthful innocence and probity, had strong objections to the purchasing of the Papacy. He therefore voted for Ascanio in order to deprive the Borgia of at least one voice. This admirable step failed to keep out Rodrigo, for that astute, wealthy, and utterly unscrupulous prelate obtained the majority and consequently the tiara.

Piero, when he heard the news, lost his temper. He ordered the Florentine ambassador in Rome, Filippo Valori, to keep an eye on Giovanni and see that he did not make such a fool of himself again. The young cardinal, on his discovery of these directions, dashed off an indignant reply to his brother about this high-handed action. After complaining of being placed in charge of a tutor, the aggrieved lad went on:

"Piero, all these things, together with this cursed election, have upset me so much that I do not think there is a more wretched man alive. I am in the right, and would to God these complaints of mine were as idle as yours of me. I wish to tell you these few things, first, that I could manage our business here as well as anyone. I am also a cardinal, and you should treat me with some respect, at least for the sake of my dignity, when giving orders to me. You should remember, and not imitate Signor Ludovico in his treatment of Ascanio, because I am a cardinal as much as Ascanio I do not think you are or want to be Signor Ludovico. I am very annoyed at all this because I see you show so little regard for me."

Giovanni was really quite loyal to his elder brother, as his later conduct showed, but the two young Medici were of quite opposite temperaments, bound to misunderstand each other.

At this juncture Girolamo Savonarola, the prior of St. Mark's, whose popularity in Florence had been rising rapidly during the past four years and was now at its apex, began to concentrate the weight of his preaching against Ferdinand of Naples. Now, Piero had no love for the treacherous old schemer on the Neapolitan throne. In fact, he despised him. But it was no part of his policy to quarrel with firmly established sovereigns, and he resented the prior's trouble-making fulminations against tyrannical governments and the evil lives of great princes—i.e., Ferdinand—and prelates. Of the latter, Savonarola obviously had Pope Alexander in mind, for the Borgia's vices were already notorious. But the Pontiff was very far indeed from being a weak debauchee. His brains and his financial resources were equally well known to be as abundant as his moral weaknesses. He could be a formidable enemy, and he would respect only a formidable friend. Piero had determined, therefore, for the sake of self-preservation, that Alexander VI should respect Florence.

The prior's passionate calls, moreover, for the repentance of sinners, and his terrifying prophecies of future disaster if the citizens of Florence declined to follow his precepts and back him against every power in Italy, were also found objectionable by Piero. It was the sort of thing that, in his opinion, might weaken the hold of the Medici, hitherto regarded as the champions of the majority of Florentines, upon the city. For the moment, Savonarola did not mention Piero by name, as he had once mentioned Lorenzo. Nevertheless, the present head of the state had this troublesome preacher quietly transferred to Bologna for the Lenten season of 1493. That year, a rival preacher entertained society in the cathedral of Santa Maria del Fiore with much more mellifluous and less disturbing orations.

Despite this move, the prior of St. Mark's and the senior Medici remained on outwardly good terms. Piero supported Savonarola's petition to Rome for the separation of the Tuscan Dominicans from those of Lombardy, for the current Florentine civil policy of keeping Ludovico at a distance would be promoted by such a measure. All the same, it would consolidate the commanding position of Fra Girolamo in Tuscany. The political situation was also being complicated by the plans of Duke Alfonso of Calabria, heir to the throne of Naples, to evict Ludovico from the regency at Milan in favour of a non-entity, Gian Galeazzo Sforza, now aged twenty-three, who had a legitimate claim—being the son of Galeazzo Maria Sforza and Bona of Savoy— to govern the duchy. Alfonso's point here was the existence of his own daughter, the far from negligible Isabella of Aragon, who was married to Gian Galeazzo. Once he could be rid of Ludovico, he would have all Lombardy, as well as Naples, in his pocket.

It was in these circumstances that the leading states of Italy, in accordance with custom, sent embassies to congratulate the new Pope, Alexander VI, on his election. Ludovico Sforza cannily suggested to Piero that one ambassador might do for Milan, Florence, and Naples combined. Perhaps he meant to confront Alexander with the hint of a strong potential combination against any territorial ambitions that he might, in the style of so many of his predecessors, be cherishing. But Piero, with characteristic arrogance, not only declined Ludovico's proposal, but contrived that the Florentine embassy should be noticeably more splendid than that of the Milanese. The regent realised at once that Lorenzo's successor was a very different sort of man from his father. The policy of Milan was accordingly rearranged by Ludovico, with catastrophic results for the whole peninsula.

Ferdinand of Naples chose the moment, at the instigation of his son and heir Alfonso, to demand the abdication of Ludovico as regent of Milan. Ludovico, after his long taste of power, was not prepared to give in so easily. He explained that it would be a betrayal of the duchy to hand it over to such an imbecile as Gian Galeazzo, legitimate duke though he might be. Ferdinand, after consulting Piero, regarded Ludovico as a great danger to all Italy, and threatened openly to put matters on a legal basis in Milan by force, aided by Florence. Ludovico appealed to both Venice and the Pope, but received only vague promises. Neither power wished to uphold openly a usurper, whose continued existence could bring them no foreseeable advantage and might well cause them to lose profitable Medici business. What Cosimo had always feared, while labouring so long to establish his friend Francesco Sforza on the Milanese throne, and what neither Cosimo's son nor his grandson had ever dreamed could happen in their lifetime, after the foundations of the Milanese-Florence axis had been so well and truly laid, now occurred. With the political isolation of Milan, the balance of power in Italy was destroyed, and Ludovico took the fatal step of seeking a foreign ally.

Charles VIII, King of France, had a somewhat nebulous claim to the crown of Naples through René II of Anjou, Duke of Lorraine, who had died in 1480. Charles himself combined two characteristics which, taken together, were an explosive mixture. He possessed a mediocre intelligence and he was also a megalomaniac. His subjects, not only soldiers but also statesmen and scholars, had long been inflaming his imagination by depicting the glory and the rich plunder awaiting the conqueror of Italy. Ludovico's ambassadors were therefore received with much sympathy in Paris, and the excitable King resolved, from one day to the next, on the seizure of Naples as a preliminary to the recovery of Constantinople, Jerusalem, and the whole Near and Middle East for Christendom.

When the news of Charles' intended expedition reached the Italian states, neither universal consternation nor martial defiance, but merely increased diplomatic activity, ensued. The men of the Christian centuries, up to that time, had, in general, little sense of patriotic devotion to this or that geographical area. Venice openly announced neutrality in the coming upheaval. The Pope also declined to commit himself either way. On the one hand, he owed his election mainly to Cardinal Ascanio Sforza, Ludovico's brother, but on the other hand, the new Pontiff had no wish to fall out seriously with so near and powerful a neighbour as the Kingdom of Naples.

Ferdinand, for his part, feeling himself to be Charles' main target, called urgently for assistance from Florence and the cities of the Romagna states, including Bologna. The request was somewhat reluctantly granted. Florence, at any rate, had a traditional inclination to sympathise with the claims of the French Anjou against those of the Spanish Aragon, dating back to the ecclesiastical schism of the fourteenth century, when the Spanish family had been favoured by the anti-Popes and the French one by the solid citizens of the Tuscan Republic. The latter also had good reason to detest the Duke of Calabria, though Lorenzo had gone out of his way in the past, typically enough, to placate Alfonso's hostile attitude to the Signory.

King Ferdinand made the situation even more uncertain by dying, on January 25, 1494. He was the last of the trio of "tyrants" to fulfill Savonarola's prophecy that they would all soon perish, for both Lorenzo and Innocent had expired in 1492. The forecast had been, as already noted, a fairly safe one, in view of Lorenzo's bad health and the advanced ages of the other two. But the prior's reputation for seeing into the future immediately soared. He was commonly credited with supernatural powers, and the masses were ready to heed his words on any matter, political as well as religious. Even such distinguished Mediceans as Politian and Pico della Mirandola became his vociferous disciples and proclaimed the rather fatuous Charles VIII to be a saintly hero, moved by God to deliver all Christians from the hideous burden of their sins.

It was at this moment, in the spring of 1494, that a quarrel over a dancing partner broke out between Piero de' Medici and his cousins, the grandsons of Cosimo's brother Lorenzo. Giovanni di Pierfrancesco de' Medici, the younger of these cousins, then aged twenty-seven, even better looking than Piero and just as arrogant, in his quieter way, as the latter, is supposed to have been slapped by his mighty cousin at a ball, for presuming to make advances to a girl in whom Piero was interested. It was impossible for Giovanni, in the circumstances, to retaliate in the usual fashion. He could only bow and grind his teeth. But Piero was not done with him yet. On the pretext that both the Pierfrancesco brothers were in the pay of France, now Ludovico's friend and Florence's enemy, the senior Medici had them arrested for treason. It is not unlikely, indeed, that the French court and Ludovico were bribing the two young men not to cause any trouble if Florence had to be disciplined by the prospective invaders, or perhaps even to oppose Piero if he should object to any such French interference. But it seems that of all the Medici, the sons of Pierfrancesco were the least likely to be dangerous, as they had never hitherto shown any interest in politics and were content to live as country squires of a distinctly luxurious cast. The innocuousness was so well known that Piero, in the end, had to let them go, with a great display of magnanimity, accompanying them home himself, no doubt hoping in this way to prevent them taking sides definitely with Charles and Milan. He was enough of a Medici to be nervous about the present reversal of his ancestors' unvarying policy of cordial relations with Lombardy, whatever his fellow-citizens, under the spell of Savonarola, might feel about it.

The French expedition, led by Charles in person, crossed the Alps in September. Alexander VI hurriedly entered into a close alliance with the threatened King of Naples, now Alfonso II, the former Duke of Calabria. That sovereign, himself an experienced campaigner, marched North to meet the invaders. He heard disquieting news of them. The foreigners numbered some sixty thousand; they were armed and disciplined to a degree well beyond that of which the Italians had any knowledge in their small citizen armies and bands of mercenaries. The Swiss infantry of the French army could shatter any charge of cavalry, the manoeuvre by which most battles in the peninsula had hitherto been decided. The light, mobile French cannon discharged not stone, but iron balls that could break up any close formation before it could be brought into effective action. And, in fact, the reports were not exaggerated. The French routed Alfonso at Rapallo, in Liguria, and he at once withdrew to concentrate on defending his own territory.

Meanwhile, Charles had been obsequiously entertained at Milan by Ludovico, and at Pavia by Gian Galeazzo and his wife, Isabella of Aragon. That lady's eloquent plea to the King to spare her father's dynasty was disregarded. The foreign soldiers marched on to Piacenza, on the border between Lombardy and Emilia, where they heard that Gian Galeazzo had suddenly perished, and that Isabella had been imprisoned with her four children. The regent, Ludovico Sforza, had thereupon proclaimed himself Duke of Milan. He may well have poisoned the debauched Gian Galeazzo, whose existence had been the pretext for the Neapolitan intervention in the affairs of the duchy. But this rumour had always lacked corroboration, for Ludovico was not the sort of man to be easily caught out in his intrigues.

Now Florence alone, of the major powers of Italy, stood in the path of the French invaders. King Charles was joined at Piacenza by the Pierfrancesco brothers, an event that proves their continuing hostility to Piero, despite his act of grace in releasing them from their captivity. It was the first time that the Medici had split into irreconcilably opposed groups. Piero saw that he was losing ground, for, in addition to the junior branch of his family, many prominent Florentines were clearly showing signs of sympathy with France. Such an attitude was traditional in the city, as a counterpoise to the power of Milan and earlier, against the aggressions of the Emperors against the Popes. Nevertheless, Piero, much to his credit, refused Charles' command to surrender Florence to his forces, which were already approaching north-western Tuscany on their way South. Ludovico, the usurper Duke of Milan, thereupon cunningly persuaded the disconcerted King to evict the Medici bankers from Lyons. It was the intention of the new duke, by this move, to give the Florentines the impression that it was Medicean supremacy, not the Republic itself, that was being challenged by the Swiss and the artillery. Charles obeyed, and, as Ludovico had anticipated, the atmosphere of hostility to the Medici darkened in Florence. Piero met this danger characteristically, with a show of haughty indifference, designed to convince everyone that he was invincible. He took care to be seen playing *pallone* in public with his cronies, while the French prepared to assault Sarzana, just inside Tuscan territory.

Yet, on the fall of Sarzana to the French gunners, Piero seemed suddenly to lose his nerve. Late in October, he made a secret dash to Charles' camp before the stronghold of Sarzanello, which was being stubbornly defended by a Florentine garrison. The autocrat of Florence there fell on his knees to the Frenchman, whose throne was backed by a forest of Swiss pikes, and begged his pardon for having dared to oppose him. Ignominious terms were accordingly offered and at once accepted, much to the contemptuous amazement of Charles' advisors. Sarzana, Sarzanello, Pisa, Leghorn, and some neighbouring towns were to be administered by the invaders until Naples had been taken. A loan of two hundred thousand ducats to finance further operations to this end was to be forthcoming immediately from the treasury of the Republic.

If sheer stupidity is more pardonable than cowardice, it is possible to take a lenient view of Piero's behaviour. He was not really fit, temperamentally or intellectually, to hold a responsible office. He could judge the flight of a ball on the *pallone* court, or the points of a racehorse, to a nicety, but he could not gauge the gravity of a political situation. It was one thing for a superb negotiator like Lorenzo to go in person to another Italian ruler, however shifty and dangerous, and win him over by imperturbable tact from animosity to friendliness. It was quite another for an impatient playboy, who was bored by anything that was not amusing, to throw himself on the mercy of insensitive foreigners at the head of an army of sixty thousand greedy professional soldiers whose lust for plunder had already been raised to inordinate heights by a series of easy victories. But Piero could not see the difference between these two sets of circumstances. Having little imagination, his only method of dealing with difficulties, if he could not crush them in a physical sense, was to yield to whatever pressure they exerted. This procedure sometimes paid off in gymnastics and wrestling, but the fate of several large, highly civilised communities could not be successfully manipulated in the same way. It was perhaps Piero's misfortune, rather than his disgrace, that he was incapable of distinguishing between a life-and-death struggle and a wrestling match.

When, after about a fortnight's absence, he returned to Florence on November 8 and announced the conditions on which he had secured peace, the wrath of the Signory genuinely astonished him. The Council of Seventy had been called together as soon as his departure and its object had become known. One of the members, Piero Capponi—a descendent of Cosimo's old antagonist, Neri Capponi—had declared bluntly that the head of state had proved himself unequal to that office. It was time, Capponi went on, to have done with such childish control and recover liberty under a government of the mentally adult. The Council had been resolved to send five ambassadors, including Capponi and Savonarola, to treat with the King of France. Piero's report, therefore, of his dealings with the monarch was heard in scornful silence. He flung out of the chamber in a rage, and when he returned the next day at the head of an armed detachment of his personal attendants, he was refused admittance at the public entrance to the Palazzo Vecchio. The officer on duty told him that he could only enter the palace alone and unarmed, by a side-door. Even Piero understood what that meant. If he obeyed, it was unlikely that he would ever be seen alive again. He withdrew, fuming, to the Medici Palace in the Via Larga. There, he started a discussion with a few men of influence who still remained loyal to him, as to the chances of regaining his authority by violence. They did not seem very favourable. The debate grew tiresome and repetitive, without coming to any definite conclusion. Then it was dramatically interrupted.

The great bells of the cathedral began to ring tumultuously. Ferocious roars could be heard from a huge crowd gathered in the *piazza*. Piero's spies reported that the Signory had proclaimed Piero di Lorenzo de' Medici a rebel and an outlaw. All the citizens his scouts had met in the streets were armed. Even the old men were flourishing the rusty swords and halberds that had been used against Venice in Cosimo's time. But encouragement came from an unexpected quarter. Piero's brother, the nineteen-year-old Cardinal Giovanni, was present in the Medici Palace. He had returned to Florence both because he deplored the rule of Alexander VI and because the news of Piero's clumsy diplomacy had perturbed him. While the insistent tocsin pealed and the cheers from the *piazza* grew more and more deafening, Giovanni showed more spirit than the despairing head of his house. The young cardinal led some of the family retainers, with weapons at the ready, into the Via Larga. The little party set up the once dreaded Medici war-cry, "Palle! Palle!"

This ancient rallying-call referred to the balls (*palle*) or pellets on the Medici coat-of-arms. It had been enough, for a century now, to rouse the populace against the enemies of that family. But this time, it was answered only by far louder and more numerous yells of *"Popolo e libertad."* Giovanni saw that he could do nothing against the dense throng of menacing citizens advancing towards him in the street. He ordered his handful of partisans to retreat, and he retired to the palace. Piero had already left the building. With his younger brother Giuliano, and a few grooms and other cronies, he had hurried through a back door, taken horse, and spurred through the Porta San Gallo onto the Bologna road, intending to make, ultimately, for Venice.

Cardinal Giovanni's youthful courage was now reinforced by a wisdom beyond his years. He disguised himself as a monk, transferred the most valuable portable treasures of the palace to the St. Mark's Convent, and then, still monastically garbed and cowled, left the city, trotting quietly off in the wake of his brother. Both men soon afterwards heard that the Signory was offering a reward of four thousand florins for the head of Piero and two thousand for that of Giovanni.

The palace in the Via Larga and the Medici villa at Careggi were sacked. Two houses belonging to Piero's ministers were burned to the ground. The exiled anti-Medicean clans of the Pazzi and Neroni were recalled, together with the Pierfrancesco brothers. After two years of Piero's rule, the revulsion against the rule of the senior branch of the Medici, which had conferred upon Florence the greatest power and glory it had ever known or was ever again to know, was complete. The importance of character in the hereditary head of the house could not have been proved more spectacularly than by the utter ruin, in so brief a period, of an authority that had lasted almost unquestioned for over sixty years, simply because its contemporary representative had fallen short of his three notable predecessors in political judgement and personal dignity. Piero di Lorenzo, by the ordinary standards of his time, was neither a fool nor an unmitigated scoundrel. He simply committed the sin, unpardonable in a Florentine chief of state, of having no diplomatic or administrative talent. It was enough, in his particular circumstances, to humiliate and injure the honour of his city and of Italy, among foreigners, for nearly four hundred years.

*   *   *

As Florence was repudiating the Medici, the invaders from the North entered Pisa. Charles declared that city free of Florentine control, as he had agreed with Piero, and the reluctant Signory could do nothing but endorse this ominous proclamation. The French King graciously replied to their rueful message that the position would be regularised as soon as he reached Rome. A few days later, the indomitable Girolamo Savonarola strode into the presence of Charles. He thundered out that his terrified listener was no more than an instrument in the hands of

Almighty God intended solely for the reformation of the Christian Church. If Charles violated that mission, the speaker continued, by offering harm to the Republic of Florence, then heaven, which he was privileged to represent in this context, would take a terrible revenge upon the monarch for such perfidy.

It must be acknowledged that this boldness testifies to a genuine love in the Ferrarese friar for his adopted community, a love that no one else at the time would have dared to express in such uncompromising terms. Savonarola was a mere local prior, not even a bishop. Charles commanded the allegiance of the most powerful nation in Europe and of the largest and most efficient army Italy had seen since the days of ancient Rome. The Dominican also showed, unquestionably, that he knew how to bypass physical strength so as to pinpoint the moral weakness of an opponent. He played with absolute confidence, like a master, on the cowardly superstition of a King who could have hanged him on the spot without the slightest trouble and with perfect impunity. Savonarola knew what the result would be. In fact, his performance made an enormous impression on the whole French court. No one dared to speak or lay a finger on the unarmed and unescorted figure as his last sentence rang through the room. The slightly built priest turned his back on the victorious King of France and stalked out of the presence as unhesitatingly as he had entered it.

Whatever may be thought of Savonarola's fanaticism and his impetuous judgement of the Medicean regime he chose to live under, the courage and sincerity of his determination to defend Florence, not only against vice but also against foreign aggression, cannot be doubted. It is highly probable that his stern and dauntless attitude in the French camp, when he warned Charles, in effect, that God was keeping an eye on him, saved the Tuscan capital from the irretrievable disaster of sack and massacre.

When the invaders of Italy were at last sighted, on November 17, from the walls of the city, the Signory decided, on the prior's advice, to open the gates. A ceremonious entry took place, in pouring rain. The long procession included twelve thousand men-at-arms, artillery drawn by horses—not by oxen, as was usual on the peninsula—and magnificently caparisoned cavalry. As often in French armies at this period, an exotically garbed Scottish contingent rode among the other squadrons. Although King James IV of Scotland was trying at this date to end the tradition by which his country had for centuries encouraged French rivalry with England by putting Scottish troops at the disposal of France, the practice was dying hard. It also happened that just then, during the relatively peaceful negotiations between James and King Henry VII of England, warlike Scots had no active employment at home.

The feeble little French sovereign, his insignificance disguised by a vast white hat, a voluminous blue cloak, and an imposing black charger, brought up the rear of the tramping and clattering ranks, their swaying banners soaked in the incessant rain. The King rode in full armour and with lance at rest, the very model of a contemporary conqueror. He was cheered hopefully by the populace, for Savonarola had blandly assured all the inhabitants of the city that Charles would prove a remorseless prosecutor of wickedness in high places. In other words, the most popular man in Florence, Girolamo Savonarola, believed—with some reason, it seems—that he had the foreigners in his pocket.

The soldiers had deeply impressed the citizens—who were now in a somewhat chastened mood after their recent excesses against the Medici —by a dashing appearance and up-to-date equipment, as they marched in towards the *piazza*. But while the people of Florence admired the French, the Swiss, the Germans, and the Scots, the Northerners were positively amazed at Florence, at the massive grandeur of the private palaces, the striking architecture of the public buildings, the splendour of the official reception in the *piazza* and at the Palazzo Vecchio, at the rich dress of even the shop-keepers and artisans, and last but not least, at the refinement of manners everywhere evident. All these phenomena, they noted with awe, far exceeded anything they had seen at home.

The Signory appointed Piero Capponi and three other commissioners to come to terms with the French. The latter, both officers and common soldiers, were beginning to realise, owing to two or three rather startling incidents, that their situation in Florence was not quite so authoritative as they had been led to believe. One day, for instance, the great bell of the Palazzo Vecchio suddenly boomed out over the *piazza*. At once all the shutters of the shops came clanging down. Barricades went up at a great pace in every main avenue. Armed citizens came running from their houses. The occupying forces hurriedly prepared for trouble, though they could not imagine what had gone wrong. They were not conscious of having offended the population in any way. But a few minutes later the bell ceased tolling and the streets quickly resumed their normal appearance. Enquirers at the Palazzo Vecchio were told that Piero de' Medici had been reported on the march a mile or two from the walls. This rumour, afterwards proved to be false, had caused a typically Italian reaction in the preliminaries for street warfare, unfamiliar at first sight to other Europeans. A few days later, again, as the result of another unfounded report, the royal bodyguard of Swiss pike-men left their quarters by one of the city gates and began moving up, in battle formation, towards the *piazza*. The detachment had scarcely got into motion before every conceivable kind of missile, hurled from windows and roofs, came clattering down on to the soldiers' helmets, in such quantities and so well aimed that the unhappy Swiss were forced to take cover. It was fortunate for Florence that orders reached these well-disciplined troops before they were battered into retaliation. They retreated imperturbably to their quarters. As soon as they were seen to do so, the rain of tiles, domestic utensils, and furniture from the housetops and balconies ceased. Such episodes made it clear to the invaders that they were not to presume too far on Florentine hospitality, either in attempting to suppress disagreements by force or in manoeuvres to restore the Medici. Against such experienced street-fighters as the Florentines, casualties among the foreigners would be heavier than they could afford at this stage, when the main object was only to get into Naples with as little trouble as possible.

Nevertheless, the conditions that the King's advisors proposed to the Signory's commissioners were found unacceptable. The Florentines began with a mere remonstrance. But Charles, who was present, could not be restrained from exclaiming petulantly: "Submit! Or we shall sound our trumpets!" In an instant, Piero Capponi sprang to his feet. Holding aloft the paper on which the terms had been written, he tore it furiously in half, retorting at the top of his voice: "Sound, then! And we shall ring our bells!" He flung the two fragments of the draft treaty to the floor and turned on his heel, with a violent movement, to leave the room. He was apparently about to put his threat into immediate execution. This could not be allowed to happen. Someone whispered urgently to the tactless monarch. Charles broke the tension with a nervous laugh, assuring Capponi that he did not mean to be taken seriously, and the commissioner reluctantly returned to the conference table.

At last, more reasonable arrangements were worked out. They contained provisions for a close alliance between France and Florence and for an indemnity of 120,000 ducats to the invaders. In return, however, Florentine jurisdiction over Pisa, Leghorn, Sarzana, and Pietrassant would be restored after conclusion of the French expedition.

Two days later, on November 27, the French forces left Florence for Rome. The King took with him, in his baggage train, a great deal of portable Medici property that had remained after Cardinal Giovanni had removed the most valuable items to St. Mark's Convent and the subsequent pillage of the palace in the Via Larga had been stopped by the Signory. The booty carted off by the Frenchman was estimated, however, to be worth at least 7,000 ducats. It consisted of many small but costly articles, in particular a bronze unicorn and some ornamental cups, cameos, and medals. Apart from these petty thefts from a discredited family, there does not seem to have been any substantial plundering of private property by the invaders. In this respect, at any rate, the decidedly firm attitude of the officially friendly city to its temporary occupiers had paid off.

The King's triumphal progress through Rome to Naples, which he entered on February 22, 1495, met no resistance. Pope Alexander VI signed everything he was asked to sign without the slightest intention of keeping his promises. Alfonso II of Naples simply fled Italy as soon as the hostile troops approached his frontier. Charles was crowned in his place on May 12. This ceremony was all he had really wanted, in addition, of course, to the usual plunder of a conqueror, despite all his former grand talk of bringing Eastern infidels to heel, which he had completely forgotten during his revels at Naples in the spring. He was then advised, in view of certain ominous developments in Italy, to return home as fast as he could with the treasures he had collected during his march through the peninsula.

In the first place, a movement of resistance had begun. The fugitive King Alfonso had not altogether wasted his time abroad. As a member of the House of Aragon, he had gone straight to the Spanish court. The greatest captain of the day, Gonzalo Fernández de Córdoba, who had been conspicuous during the recent wars to expel the last of the Moors from Spain, was allowed by Queen Isabella to lead an expedition to restore the Aragonese dynasty in Naples, and his forces had landed in Sicily. Farther north, the Pope and many Italian princes were busy with plans to clear the French from the whole country.

Second, an extraordinary event with consequences for European history that have even yet not been adequately assessed was already in operation. It affected the Medici no more than anyone else, and therefore cannot be dwelt on in the present context. But it played its part in Charles' decision to abandon his Italian enterprise and therefore indirectly caused a certain change in the plans of Piero de' Medici. The fact was that the army of King Charles in Naples was being decimated by a new disease called syphilis. It is not yet quite certain whether the seed of *spirocheta pallida* had long been latent on the Continent or whether it had been newly imported through the regular communications established with the West Indies by Columbus during the past two years. In any case, the turbulence and debauchery of the foreign soldiers in Campania, the panic and venality of the local population, and the overcrowded and insanitary living conditions of that time and place caused the population, both permanent and temporary, to reap an appalling harvest of acute fevers, racking headaches, intense pains in the joints, ulcers, hideous lesions, delirium, paralysis, and death. These dreadful symptoms, exceeding anything since recorded of syphilis, spread unchecked, like wildfire from a supernatural source, and sealed the determination of the invaders to depart with all speed from so unappealing an environment. Charles turned North, to fight his way, if necessary, back to France, content with his material spoils and ready to surrender only those that existed solely on paper. It appears to have been at this time that Piero de' Medici joined him, no doubt expecting to be reinstated in Florence with the aid of French military power.

The hurrying army had reached Siena without opposition before the Florentine Signory took steps to remind the King that he was formally, by the treaty in the previous year, their ally. Savonarola was the obvious choice as ambassador in this connection. He met Charles at Poggibonsi, a few miles nearer Florence than Siena, and repeated his threats of divine wrath. It is hardly probable that Piero was present at this audience, though he may have been a sullen onlooker, warned by the French courtiers, who were anxious only to see the last of Italian politics, not to weaken his possible chances of a restoration by intervening.

Naturally, the Dominican found it easy to score his main point. The royal troops turned away from Florence, westward to Pisa. It was not until they had pushed on a hundred miles farther north, to Fornovo in Emilia, east of Parma and Reggio, that they had to fight. Forces raised in common by Venice, the Papal States, and even Milan—where Ludovico considered that Charles had betrayed him by his mild behaviour in Florence—had been joined by those of King Ferdinand of Spain, intent on the reconquest of Naples for Alfonso, and a contingent from the so-called King of the Romans, Maximilian of Habsburg, son of the Holy Roman Emperor, who was far from desiring a French Italy. At Fornovo, this mixed host confronted the homesick and weary French and Swiss, now reduced by syphilis and desertion to no more than nine thousand men.

The allies numbered forty thousand. They would have gained a resounding victory if their combination of military incapacity, mutual jealousy, and greed for plunder had not permitted their opponents to struggle out of range on the night of July 6. The French by now had but one object: to escape. Strict discipline enabled them to achieve it. By mid-July they were at Asti in Piedmont, where they were reinforced by twenty thousand more Swiss pike-men. In spite of this relief, no one wished to start a second campaign. The King and his officers had all the treasure they wanted; they had no more interest in Italy. A few days later the entire army crossed into French territory. Piero de' Medici did not accompany the troops. After his discomfiture by Savonarola at Poggibonsi he had returned to Rome, to be welcomed by his wife's family, the Orsini, and to forget his sorrows in a round of dissipation and games.

Meanwhile, in the absence of the family that had ruled Florence for so long, the city returned to the constitutional experiments, the class hatreds, and the popular riots of the pre-Medicean years. On December 9, 1495, the Council of Seventy was abolished and replaced by a Council of Twenty. But this expedient, since no master-mind arose to direct it, failed. There were but two men of note in the new Council. Piero Capponi, a soldier of some distinction, had already proved his patriotism and courage by denouncing the blunders of Piero de' Medici and standing up to Charles VIII. Francesco Valori had directed the sack of the Medici Palace after the flight from Florence of the head of the state. But Valori, though an energetic demagogue, could no more be called a statesman than the bold Capponi. Neither really understood how to manage a large community or control its dissensions.

The prior of St. Mark's, Girolamo Savonarola, was the only public figure at this time who had any influence with the restless populace. He suppressed the most dangerous of their outbreaks, but he could not save the life of an honourable civil servant, Antonio di Bernardo, formerly chief of the National Debt Office under Piero de' Medici. This unhappy functionary, believed responsible for the financial chaos of this period, was seized by a yelling mob and hanged from a window in the Bargello.

A powerful Medicean faction, in touch with the exiled Piero, still resided in the city, but it operated so discreetly, though supported from both Rome and Venice, that its members were named Bigi (Greys), since they appeared to be neither white nor black. This group was obstinately persecuted by another party, backed by Ludovico Sforza, Duke of Milan, and known as the Arrabbiati (Crazies) for its senseless and violent conduct. The members came almost exclusively from the old nobility and were intent on seizing for themselves the authority so long held by the Medici. The Arrabbiati detested the Francophile Piagnoni (Whiners), as the followers of Savonarola were nicknamed, the Bigi, and the new popular government with impartial ferocity.

The prior had only recently pronounced on political principle from the pulpit of the cathedral. He now turned, probably under pressure from the distracted Signory, to proposing practical political action. The measures he suggested smacked of the Venetian Constitution, but this approach did not shock the Florentines. Most of them had always admired the only stable republic in Italy. They had never ceased to wonder how it was that those Northerners, so difficult to deal with in both commerce and diplomacy, contrived to keep their vessel of state steady on the lagoons.

The Signory decided to give Savonarola's plan for a Grand Council, on the Venetian model, a trial. Like that at Venice, it was designed to have a small Senate of Eighty attached to it. Membership of the Council itself was to be limited to citizens thirty years old or more who had paid their taxes and had magistrates among their ancestors. At the first election, thirty-two hundred inhabitants of the city qualified. It was resolved that approximately one third of them should hold office for the next six months, another third for six months thereafter, and the last third for a final period of six months. The Senate of Eighty would be elected every six months, from such members of the Grand Council as were then over forty years old. These arrangements were duly made, the Signory itself retaining its functions but being obliged to consult the Eighty at least once a week.

Savonarola took an active hand in framing the laws passed under the new government. They included tax reform, political amnesties within reason—i.e., no dangerous Mediceans to be recalled—and the establishment of a new court of appeal. This last enactment ran into trouble. The Dominican had suggested that appeals from the sentences of capital punishment in both political and criminal cases should be heard by a court of eighty or a hundred members chosen by the Grand Council. Those who had opposed the setting up of the Council thereupon cunningly tabled an amendment. The whole Council, they maintained, not just a tenth part of it, should hear such appeals. This apparently democratic proposal was designed to discredit the Council, for in view of its great size it would be bound to commit errors of judgement in appeal cases and so render itself liable to abolition. To the delight of these ingenious schemers, and to the chagrin of the shrewd prior, who had seen through their manoeuvre almost immediately, the amendment was adopted and became law.

Savonarola then realised for the first time that it was not going to be easy for him to step, for all practical purposes, into the shoes of Lorenzo de' Medici, the man whom he had so sternly censured for "tyranny" a few years before. But the priest-turned-legislator, who was probably moved at this date as much by real affection for Florence and a determination to secure social justice for the citizens, while upholding their Christian piety to a high level, as by secular ambition, did not lose heart. Still resolutely self-confident, he pushed through certain other measures, in themselves admirable enough—such as the creation of a chamber of commerce—without serious opposition. In this legislative field his undoubtedly great practical ability was not impeded by his religious evangelism, but when he interfered in foreign affairs, his obsession with the foolish and immoral King of France, who had been cast by Savonarola for the part of a redeemer of mankind, proved disastrous. It seems incredible that a man of such undoubted intellectual capacity as the prior could have been so deceived in his reading of the King's character. Savonarola no doubt recognised in Charles a weakling who commanded immense strength in a royal inheritance that was generally believed at that time to be of divine ordination. Fra Girolamo had apparently made up his mind to use that strength, since it was greater than any other available, to promote the ends of God and the plans to realise them that he felt he alone could contrive. Such speculations are mere conjecture, unsupported by documentary evidence. The fact remains that, however obvious the French monarch's personal weaknesses were to everyone else, the prior would never budge from the decision he had taken to side with Charles and France in all political matters.

The King, however, had not kept any of his promises to Florence, except that relating to Leghorn. Pisa remained under the control of the league of allies that had so nearly defeated the French at Fornovo. Pietrasanta had been sold to Lucca. Sarzana and Sarzanello had gone, for a good price, to Genoa. In view of Charles' cynical disregard of his obligations under the treaty with Florence, the most logical step would have been for the city to join the league against France. The prior of St. Mark's nonetheless advised the Signory to demand the restitution of Pisa before committing themselves to anti-French proceedings. He knew that the League would never consent to this condition, and counted on its refusal to throw the Republic back into the arms of that bizarre saviour of Italy, King Charles. "If you return to virtue in this way," Savonarola promised, "I will see to it that your reward shall be Pisa." He can only have meant that he felt confident of being able to persuade the French King to eject the league from Pisa by force. Nothing could have been more unlikely, for it was obvious to any unprejudiced observer that France had lost interest in Italy altogether.

More and more Florentines now began to wonder whether their adored preacher was really the inspired prophet, capable legislator, and fiery Christian they had thought him to be. They asked in what way the depredations and atrocities committed by the huge host of merciless brigands under French command had set a moral example to Italians, as foretold by the prior before the invasion. He could still excite a majority of emotional men, and most women and children, to hysterical frenzy by his burning rhetoric, which included the softer notes of calls to decency, tenderness, and charity, as well as rousing challenges to the devil. But cooler heads recognised in his sermons the immemorial arts of those who in every age lead passionate simpletons to destroy, to their own ultimate misery, the scaffolding of civilisation. To other critics, the style of Savonarola's addresses, an important consideration in the fifteenth century, seemed offensive, and his theology suspect. The powerful and worldy-wise religious orders hated him as a needlessly severe and authoritarian priest. Rome objected to his impudent strictures on the behaviour of Romans, from the Pontiff downwards. Milan and Venice were angered by the prior's perverse exclusion of Florence from their league against France. Half a dozen Florentine factions arose from among the holders of such views. They included some Mediceans, now back in the city as a result of Savonarola's own generous amnesty laws, who were plotting industriously to have Piero de' Medici recalled from Rome. The hostility between these enemies of the preacher and his adherents grew steadily more implacable.

In these circumstances, it seemed to Pope Alexander that the moment was favourable for an attempt to restore Piero de' Medici, who by this time had been joined in Rome by his faithful cadet, Cardinal Giovanni. Accordingly, an army was raised and placed under the command of Virginio Orsini, Piero's brother-in-law, who was to lead it from Rome in an invasion of Tuscany. After some delay, this force marched northwards, until it came to the city of Perugia. There, the troops pitched camp to await reinforcements from Bologna. In Florence, however, Savonarola had persuaded the government and the people that a Medicean restoration would result in the moral and political ruin of the city, and the Florentines were working strenuously, and with much publicity, to prepare for the defence of the Republic. The Bolognese, of course, heard of these preparations, and had second thoughts about joining in an attack on a city known for its ferocity in defending itself and for its skill in taking vengeance on its enemies. Far from sending reinforcements to Virginio Orsini, therefore, they expelled from their city Giuliano, Piero's sixteen-year-old brother, and Cardinal Giovanni de' Medici, who had joined Giuliano there. Meanwhile, in Perugia, Virginio's army waited, and waited, while its funds melted away and its troops, unpaid and therefore unhappy, vanished into the countryside. The mortified Orsini commander left in disgust to take service with the French in Naples; and, finally, Piero de' Medici was obliged to creep back to Rome.

Under the burden of shame of this double rejection, first by the Florentines and then by his allies, Piero's character—never, even at its best, a model of probity—deteriorated rapidly, and he embarked on a routine of dissipation that scandalised even the cynical Romans. Lamberto dell' Antella, a former associate of Piero's, who had left the Medici service in disgust at his erstwhile master's excesses, described Piero at this period as starting the day with an enormous meal and much heavy drinking. Ordinarily, Piero would then retire to his chambers for a time in the company of a prostitute, either male or female according to his mood. After this diversion, he gambled until nightfall, and then set out with a few companions to visit various disreputable houses and taverns in Rome, where he continued his dissipations until dawn. This account, no doubt, is coloured by the natural vindictiveness of a disappointed courtier; still, there is little doubt that Lamberto's stories had more than a little foundation in fact. Piero loved to eat and drink and to gamble, and he had never learned to discriminate between the attractions of male and female in satisfying his sexual appetites. He did retain, however, something of his Medicean pride, despite his humiliating reverses. A poem, written during this period by this debauched son of Lorenzo the Magnificent indicates that Piero was determined to return to Florence one day and there "to take no advice from anyone"—a phrase he used to a friend who had suggested that it might be well for him, once re-established in Florence, to govern with the aid of "an experienced council of twenty or thirty citizens."

Piero was watching, in fact, with malicious pleasure, the rising tide of Florentine discontent under Savonarola's administration. More than one attempt on the prior's life was made during 1495 and 1496, although it remained impossible for even his political foes to believe him a bad man. He sometimes advanced ludicrously inapposite proposals, such as the erection of a theocracy under the presidency of Jesus Christ; but he just as often toiled for the practical good of the citizen. He diverted, for instance, the wildness of the city's children into more productive channels by organising pageants and processions in which they sang like angels instead of throwing stones at their elders. Few respectable citizens, moreover, could find fault with the Dominican's intrepid denunciations of Alexander VI and his rascally associates. Their conduct was already alienating Catholic France, Germany, and England, as well as ultra-Catholic Italy, if not the Pope's native Spain. All the same, Alexander was known to be not only a villain but also fiendishly clever. Certain of the anti-Savonarola factions thought the Pontiff might be able to rid France of their arch-enemy. Deputations from these bodies accordingly represented to Alexander that the prior of St. Mark's was beginning to be something more than a local nuisance. He might well end, they hinted, by shaking the Holy Father off the Chair of St. Peter and taking it for himself.

The Pope was impressed. With characteristic subtlety, he invited the prior, in very friendly terms, to come to Rome to explain why he thought himself inspired by Almighty God. Savonarola suspected, with good reason, a trick to deposit his person in the dungeons of Sant' Angelo, and he humbly notified his august correspondent that, for the moment, he felt too ill to visit him. Alexander, with an abruptness as typical of him as his flattery of a prospective victim, changed his tone to one of menace. In September he prohibited the prior from preaching until an enquiry into the nature of his tenets had been concluded. The Pontiff also took this opportunity to make his own political position clear to the Signory. He warned the government of Florence that it ran the risk of excommunication if it continued to support King Charles of France.

This threat was a blow to Savonarola's plans. He felt, however, that he could safely defy the prohibition of his preaching, and he con-

tinued his sermons until, on October 16, he received a second mandate
to the same effect as the first. Alexander could easily have excommunicated the disobedient priest forthwith, but he probably wished to provide his critics, both present and future, with evidence in this way of
his own patience. The Dominican, with a somewhat similar motive,
obeyed this second order. He foresaw, at any rate, that he would not
lose by yielding ostentatiously to the Vicar of Christ. As he had anticipated, popular agitation began the moment that he stopped preaching.
A substantial majority of the citizens clamoured for the renewal of
his thunders against the sins of their social superiors. The Signory, in
alarm, pleaded with the Pope to withdraw his decree. Once again
Alexander, with superb tactical acumen, acted cautiously. The prior of
St. Mark's, he benevolently announced, might celebrate Lent by a
course of sermons. Accordingly, on February 17, 1496, Savonarola
again appeared in the pulpit of the cathedral before an enormous
congregation. He mentioned no names, but it was clear that his in-
vectives were aimed at the spiritual head of Christendom.

The object of these recriminations saw that it was time to strike
everyone dumb by an act of such apparent magnanimity to a relentless
political as well as moral foe, as would put the rebellious priest permanently in the wrong. He sent the superior of the Dominican Order
to the prior with the intimation that, if the preacher would cease proph-
esying the doom of the Christian Church, he might expect a cardinalate.
In that office, it was pointed out, he could set himself to the more
sensible work of reforming ecclesiastical administration—with every
assistance, naturally, from the Chair of St. Peter. Savonarola gave
his answer in his next sermon, which the superior attended: "I seek
neither cardinal's hat nor bishop's mitre. I desire only, O Lord, what
Thou hast given to Thy saints, martyrdom. Give me a hat, I pray
Thee, a red hat, but red with blood!"

The chips were down with a vengeance. The open duel between
Pope and prior was watched with breathless interest throughout Italy
and with anxious attention in the rest of Europe. Behind the religious
issue loomed the even more explosive political situation. Florence still
stood formally allied with France, which had ravaged the Italian peninsula and treated the spiritual authority of Rome with contempt, while
the Signory still suspected the league, openly hostile to the French, of
intending to restore the egregious Piero de' Medici to command the
destinies of the Republic.

In October 1496 the league, in collusion with Alexander, took the
bold step of inviting to Italy Maximilian I, the current Holy Roman
Emperor. The real purpose of this move was to force Florence into the
league, but the ostensible reason was to confer on Maximilian a
ceremonial coronation at Rome. The Emperor applied pressure on

Florence by besieging Leghorn, while the Venetian fleet blockaded the harbour of the port. Piero Capponi, the best of the Florentine generals, had died in the previous month, and the Florentine forces had been obliged to retire from before Pisa. Papal troops were threatening Florentine territory from Siena. It looked, for the moment, as though Savonarola had lost the game. But then he had a great stroke of luck.

On October 30, he organised a penitential procession to intercede with heaven on behalf of the stricken city, surrounded by triumphant enemies and already running short of food. While the mournfully chanting, white-robed adherents of the prior passed along the streets, to the jeers of less pious citizens, a despatch rider dismounted at the western gate. He brought news that Florentine ships, laden with provisions, had broken the Venetian blockade during a storm and were now anchored in the harbour of Leghorn.

Maximilian, who had trouble at home and, in any case, though a decent monarch in many ways, could never persevere in one project for very long, abandoned the siege and returned to Germany. In Florence the sudden recovery from a desperate position within minutes, so to speak, of the prior's personal petition to the Almighty, greatly raised his declining prestige.

The Pope, energetic and dextrous as usual, counter-attacked at once. He ordered the Dominican convents of Tuscany and Rome to be united in a single congregation under a Roman vicar. This meant that Savonarola, as prior of St. Mark's, would be rendered subordinate to the new vicar, who could, and almost certainly would, remove him from Florence to some small provincial post, where his spiritual arrogance would be less dangerous to ecclesiastical and civil authority than in the Tuscan capital. But the prior was as quick and as vigourous as the Pontiff. He sent a formal remonstrance to Alexander, indicating that he intended to remain where he was. This defiance could be misinterpreted —either by the Pope himself, or by those who considered that papal commands, even if they involved no question of dogma or morale, must be obeyed to the letter. Savonarola's reckless arrogance lost him nearly as much support as he had recently gained though the retreat of the Holy Roman Emperor.

The Holy Father, however, was less afraid of the Dominican's religious revolt than of his political influence on the officially Francophile, but unofficially Francophobe, Signory of Florence. For this reason, he still held his hand, hoping that in the new year, 1497, one of the prior's opponents would be appointed *gonfalonier*. In fact, the very opposite happened. An unscrupulous rabble-rouser, Francesco Valori, a believer in armed force and violent revolution, was elected to the post. He proceeded to banish the Franciscans, who were hostile to Savonarola;

to enrage substantial citizens by a graduated income tax; and to lower to twenty-four the age at which candidates for the Grand Council would be eligible for election, thus introducing a vociferous section of hotheads into that supposedly grave assembly. He took all these measures under the cloak of a pious adherence to those Christian principles of personal humility, decency, and justice for all that were so sincerely professed by his leader, the Dominican prior.

The shrewd Savonarola, however, was not altogether happy over his ardent disciple's political exuberance. Guessing that it might lead to serious disturbances that his own secular power would be inadequate to check, he determined to re-assert his purely moral influence. He demanded that Florentines should give tangible proof of having taken to heart his incessant denunciations of material luxury. It had long been a custom in Florence, according to Giorgio Vasari, "to erect cabins of fire-wood and other combustibles in the *piazza* at carnival time. On the night of Shrove Tuesday these huts were set ablaze and the people danced around them. Men and women joined hands, in pursuance of an ancient tradition, and encircled the burning shanties, dancing and singing." Savonarola conceived the idea of converting these revels into a religious ceremony, and his plan was approved and assisted by the government. Organised bands of children were sent from house to house to collect all objects that ascetics might suppose to contribute to worldliness or sin. Sometimes such articles were voluntarily surrendered, but on other occasions the indignant house-holders drove the rudely clamourous boys and girls away with blows and kicks, so that eventually the youthful collectors had to be accompanied by armed bodyguards. The demands were for table-games, playing-cards, dice, chessmen, hand- and foot-balls, musical instruments, masks, wigs, carnival dresses, rouge-pots, depilatory tools, cosmetics, curling-irons, hairpins, nail-files, mirrors, perfumes, powders, jewels, transparent garments, sumptuous clothes and ornaments of all kinds, brocades, tapestries, pictures, sculptures, and books, unless these last four or five categories could be judged to be edifying to a Christian. Some of the objects thus collected had been made of precious materials by master craftsmen. Many of the books and pictures, no doubt, were merely frivolous, but others were of great value. They were all burned on Shrove Tuesday night (February 7), 1497, in the form of a cone sixty-feet high and 240 feet round at the base, set up in the middle of the Piazza della Signoria. The cone, like certain Egyptian or Mesopotamian pyramids, had seven steps or stages, corresponding to the seven deadly sins. On the lowest were piled the masks and other paraphernalia of former carnivals. Then came books by such pagan authors as Anacreon, Aristophanes, Ovid, and Lucian and by Christians such as Boccaccio, Pulci, and even Petrarch. Above the books lay toilet articles and accessories, then musical instruments and the apparatus of indoor and outdoor games. Still higher towered drawings, paintings, and statues of courtesans and profane subjects, the figures either nude or else in deliberately seductive costume. Last, on the summit of the pyramid, there could be dimly described images of the gods, heroes, and sages of heathen antiquity, made of wood and coloured wax. Above all sat a grotesque effigy with goat's legs and a long, wild beard. It represented Pan, Satan, or Old King Carnival, according to the taste of this or that individual in the vast concourse of spectators.

A Venetian merchant had offered 22,000 florins, cash down, for the whole lot, but his tender was proudly refused. All the same, this production of the "chattering friar," as Pope Alexander called him, found a mixed reception. Cultivated citizens were distressed by the senseless destruction of so much beauty and learning. Economic experts condemned the disappearance of marketable assets. Many of the more thoughtful inhabitants of Florence, as more than once on previous occasions, doubted Savonarola's judgement in morals as well as in politics. The glorious days of the Medici, when no one dared to despise, much less burn, works of art were often recalled.

The prior's position was also weakened soon afterwards, on April 28, by the sudden appearance of Piero de' Medici, with an army of some 1,300 men, at the gates of the city. He was there, no doubt, at the suggestion and with the blessing of Alexander VI, who hoped that Savonarola's Lenten spectacle had sufficiently discredited him as to encourage open opposition to his rule in Florence. That hope was sustained by the fact that the new *gonfalonier,* Bernardo del Nero, was a secret Medici partisan; but Bernardo was a discreet man, and he knew his fellow-citizens. The gates were not opened, and Piero waited vainly for some hours for signs of a popular uprising in his favour. When none came, he could do nothing but withdraw to Siena.

This fiasco served to exacerbate the rage of Savonarola's enemies, for they believed that the Dominican friar himself had arranged the affair in an attempt to discredit them, by giving the impression that it was they who had encouraged Piero to show himself once more in Tuscany. The new Signory of that month, many of the members of which had no love for the prior, indicated their displeasure by prohibiting all preaching on and after May 5, on the pretext that large public gatherings were conducive to an outbreak of the plague.

On May 4, the Feast of the Ascension, the date of Savonarola's last permitted sermon, a riot occurred in the cathedral. A group of young men had organised a plot to assassinate Savonarola, and the disturbance was to be the signal for their attempt. The friar, however, had been informed of the conspiracy, and he was prepared. An armed guard of his followers, who had mingled with the congregation, fought off the potential assassins and escorted Savonarola, his sermon only half completed, back to San Marco. This scene convinced Alexander that he could now safely excommunicate the prior without hopelessly antagonising a Signory already furious with the Holy See for its fancied dealings with Piero de' Medici. But Savonarola, as before, publicly denounced the sentence. He contrived, furthermore, that the next Signory, appointed in July, should be packed with his friends. Once more, the battle seemed to be turning in his favour.

In August, Bernardo del Nero, Lorenzo Tornabuoni (a member of the family to which the mother of Lorenzo the Magnificent had belonged), and three other citizens of high social standing were convicted of treasonable correspondence with Piero de' Medici. Francesco Valori pressed for capital sentences, and all five prisoners were duly beheaded. They were probably guilty, in the technical sense. There were some irregularities in the trial, however, and Savonarola was suspected of culpable, interested negligence in letting the letter of the law take its course. His enemies were by this time permanently embittered against him, and they repeatedly blocked the efforts of his party to have the sentence of excommunication lifted. Both the growing Medicean faction and the government, firmly anti-Medicean at this time, were now plotting his overthrow.

On Christmas Day the prior calmly preached again in the cathedral despite the papal ban, and even administered the Eucharist with his own hand. It was remarked, however, that the congregation appeared noticeably smaller than usual on this occasion. On Shrove Tuesday of 1498, a second "burning of the vanities" was held. This time, the participants in the event were publicly and loudly insulted by the people, and some of them were waylaid and badly beaten by young men of the anti-Savonarola faction. The March elections to the Signory reflected the same sentiments, and power seemed now to rest in the hands of the friar's enemies.

The papal court was soon apprised of these developments, and Alexander was encouraged by them to proclaim that, unless the rebellious Dominican was delivered up by Florence to stand trial in Rome, the Tuscan capital would be laid under an interdict. The Signory was in dread of the papal ban, but in even more dread of the possible uprising that might accompany the deliverance of Savonarola to his enemies. The government therefore chose to compromise, and simply forbade Savonarola to preach. The indomitable friar had no choice but to submit, and on March 18 he bade farewell to his dwindling congregation in a sermon alternately pathetic and menacing—but not before he had made Alexander quake on his throne by calling upon France, Spain, England, and Hungary to convoke an Ecumenical Council for the purpose of deposing the Pontiff.

The Franciscan order, believing that the hated Dominican rival now had his back to the wall, closed in for the kill. One of their order, Fra Francesco de Puglia, challenged the prior to prove the truth of his doctrines by the ancient ordeal of fire. Francesco declared himself ready to walk through the flames beside the Dominican; the survivor would be the man whom God truly favoured. An acceptance of the challenge by a substitute Dominican friar, Domenico Buonvicini da Pescia, a leading spirit in the "burning of the vanities," was contemptuously rejected. Then Savonarola himself, with equal contempt, publicly denounced the whole idea of an "ordeal" as a proof of innocence or guilt.

The matter would probably have ended there if the younger and fiercer secular opponents of Savonarola had not seized on the idea. They clamoured for the ordeal, which they expected would give rise to a riot, during which the prior might be arrested or even killed. The Signory perhaps shared these hopes, for they sanctioned the ceremony, naming April 7 as the date for its enactment. In view of Savonarola's persistent objection to submit to anything so degrading, and Francesco's equally resolute determination to enter the fire with no one but the prior, two other members of the rival orders, Domenico Buonvicini as a substitute for his leader, and Fra Giuliano Rondinelli replacing Francesco da Puglia, were appointed to undergo the test. The government announced that, if Domenico perished in the flames, Savonarola would be exiled. They did not say what would happen if Giuliano succumbed.

These dramatic arrangements, an official cover for a purely political manoeuvre, collapsed in fiasco. On the day set for the ordeal, the Franciscans, perhaps now doubtful of its outcome, lodged an immediate protest. They alleged that Savonarola had rendered Domenico's robes fire-resistant by devilish incantations. In the midst of the angry recriminations arising from this accusation, the wilder elements of the opposition to the prior tried to storm the Loggia dei Lanzi adjoining the Palazzo Vecchio, where the Dominican, with two hundred companions of his order, had assembled to watch the proceedings. Savonarola's personal bodyguard, however, repulsed this assault. Then a sudden thunderstorm drenched everyone and terrified the superstitious masses. After it had subsided, the Franciscans further postponed operations by manoeuvering the prior into a long theological argument. The Signory saw that nothing would be gained, in these circumstances, by forcing on the programme. It intervened brusquely and put a stop to the whole affair.

Although Savonarola had played a dignified part in this absurd and yet tragic charade, his enemies immediately charged him with cowardice. Even his friends felt that he had betrayed them. He was stoned as he left the *piazza,* and he would not have reached San Marco alive if his pike-men had not held the mob at bay with cold steel. On April

8 the populace, now as vengefully hostile as they had formerly been hysterically devoted, assailed the convent. The defence, a stout one, was led by Francesco Valori, but that acute realist soon perceived that it could not last without reinforcements. He pluckily went in search of military aid, after escaping from the convent by a back window, but he was recognised in the street and cut to pieces on the very door-step of his house. His wife, as she came to one of the windows in alarm at the disturbance below, was at the same time shot dead by a crossbow-man.

That night an enraged multitude, joined as usual in times of rev-olution by a formidable contingent of blood-thirsty marauders intent on plunder rather than religious or political issues, fired the gates of the convent. When the ferocious rabble burst into the courtyard, making for the doors of the sacristy, the stalwart friars, wielding lighted tapers, candlesticks, and heavy crucifixes to great effect, actually drove the onslaught back into the open, where stones and hot embers hurled by other monks on the roof rained down upon the aggressors.

For a few moments the discomfited mob wavered, and the fighting clergy began to cheer defiantly. Within minutes, however, a message arrived from the Signory ordering the convent to surrender. Even then two friars, one of them a gigantic German, standing on the high altar of the church, fired arquebuses, with stentorian yells of *"Viva Cristo!"* into the surging ranks of laymen, keeping them at bay until Savonarola himself appeared at a side door. He beckoned to the surviving defenders to follow him into the library, where he had been at prayer. There he was arrested, with Domenico Buonvicini, by the captain of the Palazzo Vecchio guard. Another close associate of the prior, Fra Silvestro Maruffi, was seized the next day. All three were imprisoned in the very dungeon where Cosimo de' Medici had once played cards and discussed bribes with his gaolers.

At Rome, Pope Alexander praised the "holy zeal" of the Francis-cans, absolved the city for having stormed a convent, and commended the Signory. He added that the three captives, after sentence, should be sent to Rome for punishment. By a sinister coincidence, the wretched King Charles of France, the prior's one remaining powerful supporter, had died, almost certainly of syphilis, on the very day before Savonarola was arrested.

On April 9 the once illustrious prisoner was tortured on the rack, but no clear confession of heresy, political misconduct, or fortune-telling could be extorted from him. All through the week of the trial, which ended on the nineteenth, he was repeatedly tortured, but to no more useful effect. A garbled report of his alleged confessions was submitted to the Signory, but the lawyers were not satisfied with it. The rack and red-hot coals were applied again, from April 21 to April

25, but the result still remained less than clear to the jurists. Nor would Fra Domenico, after even worse torments than his master had endured, renounce his belief in Savonarola's divine inspiration. There was no need to torture Fra Silvestro. At the mere sight of the rack, he declared himself and his two fellow-captives guilty of every crime that the inquisitors suggested to him.

Some delay ensued before execution of the capital sentences imposed. The Signory wished the condemned men to suffer in Florence, while the Pope insisted on being at least officially represented at the death of his old enemy, though he was now prepared to forego the witnessing of it himself in Rome. In the end, he sent two commissioners to Florence. They arrived on May 20 and staged a third mock trial, during which Savonarola was again subjected to rack and fire; but he would say no more than before. On May 22, the papal commissioners confirmed the death sentence, and the next day the three prisoners were hanged in the *piazza* as "heretics and schismatics." Immediately after the strangulation, faggots beneath the gallows were kindled, and the corpses were burned to ashes, which were then thrown into the river Arno from the Ponte Vecchio.

There is no clear evidence that the exiled Medici played a significant role in this judicial murder. Piero's sporadic attempts to re-establish himself as unofficial dictator of Florence had little chance of success once King Charles VIII had decided definitely to withdraw from Italy. Others in sympathy with Medicean ideas of government, whether members of the family or not, and whether abroad or at home, could do little to advance their cause in the atmosphere prevailing in the city. The Tornabuoni and other descendents of the circle of Lorenzo the Magnificent behaved with extreme discretion during this period, except when they knew the Signory was behind them. Sometimes it was— but never to the point of elevating a Medici to supreme power.

The emergence in 1494 of the Bigi (Greys) is only marginally symptomatic, though many of them, like Bernardo del Nero, were Mediceans who professed to support Savonarola, while actually plotting to reinstate Piero. They were certainly neither "Black"—i.e., wholehearted adherents of the prior—nor "White"—i.e., unsympathetic to his personality while not objecting violently to his policy. Fourteen years, in fact, were to pass before the Medici were again cheered in the streets of Florence. And that would only be because the individuals in question had been brought to the city by older relatives more masterful and ingenious than themselves.

Of these successors the seductive Giovanni di Pierfrancesco de' Medici was not destined to be one. The Signory of 1496 had sent him to Rome as Florentine ambassador. There Caterina Sforza, widow of two murdered husbands and as licentious and merciless as any male *condottiere* of her day, soon carried him off, as her third spouse, to her court at Imola. It was a marriage, so her nervous uncle, Ludovico Sforza, Duke of Milan, was informed, consummated solely to satisfy the lady's entirely physical lust for this exceptionally well-favoured member of the house of Medici. Ludovico was alarmed by the union, as were also the Venetians, on political grounds. So martial a ruler as Caterina, so firmly established, with a Medici partner, at Imola and Forlì in Romagna, constituted a distinct threat to the northern regions of Italy.

But Giovanni, perhaps worn out by his extremely exhausting conjugal duties, died in 1498, the year of his son's birth. Ludovico breathed again, and he proceeded to combine with Florence in order to defend his niece from Venetian aggression. Yet, when in the following year Caterina refused to allow the betrothal of her son, Ottaviano (fathered by her first husband, Riario) to the Pope's daughter, Lucrezia Borgia, the Pope, who was looking for fiefs for his own son Cesare, sent that dreaded commander with an overwhelming force against her. Caterina's splendid fight to hold off her terrible antagonist was heroic but in vain. Her youngest son, Giovanni, equally terrible, though much more jovial and gifted, was to become a Medici simultaneously more loved and feared than any member of the extraordinary house since Lorenzo the Magnificent.

2. *The Return of the Medici*

The death of Girolamo Savonarola, despite the treachery and cruelty it involved, considerably improved the political position of Florence. Internally, the city was now comparatively free of those violent emotions that had erupted so often, and so publicly, under the impact of the friar's denunciations of princes and prelates. Externally, Florence was on cordial terms with that equivocal Milanese despot, Duke Ludovico Sforza, and she was at least at peace with the equally unpredictable Pope Alexander VI. Piero de' Medici seemed to be content, for the moment, to spin away the hours at the wine-parties of Rome, and he did not appear a serious threat to the stability of the Florentine Government. The city that Piero had lost for Florence, Pisa, had yet to be recovered, but there was no doubt in the public mind that that omission would soon be rectified.

The schemes relating to Pisa, however, were blocked for a while by foreign enterprises to both north and south. Louis XII, the new King of France, had in his veins a strain of Visconti blood, through his great-grandmother. On this pretext, he lodged a claim to the Duchy of Milan, a move that was secretly encouraged by Alexander. The Pope needed the Swiss pike-men of the French army, whom he had come to know in

Rome during King Charles' expedition. The mercenaries in question were required to further the ambitions of the Pontiff's favourite son, Cesare. An invasion of Italy by Louis would therefore suit the papal book admirably.

In May 1499, the most able general of the Florentine Republic, Paolo Vitelli, failed to take Pisa. The Signory, enraged at this setback, accused Vitelli not only of treason in the military sense but also of political intrigue with Venice and with Piero de' Medici, who was not now quite so innocuous, it seemed, as had previously been reported. It is likely that Vitelli, a professional soldier, bored when not fighting, would not have objected to a general war involving both the Doge and Piero, but whether he had discussed with Piero any definite projects cannot be ascertained. All the same, the Signory tortured him, failed to extort a confession, and nevertheless brutally beheaded the tight-lipped general.

In the same month of May, the French again crossed the Alps, and in September, with the aid of Venice and the Pope, they expelled Duke Ludovico from Milan. After receiving aid from Emperor Maxmilian, Sforza regained possession of the duchy . He was able to hold it only for a short time. In April 1500 he was meditating a second flight when his Swiss troops betrayed him to the French, who kept him a captive in France for the eight years that remained of his life. The elimination of Ludovico from Italian politics may perhaps be regarded as a happy end to a career not without interest. Modern estimates of his character have sometimes been more favourable than those of his contemporaries. In spite of his native arrogance and disconcerting unreliability in diplomacy, he at least patronised humanists and artists with some show of enlightenment and generosity. He revered Leonardo da Vinci and supported him for sixteen years, until December 1499. An enormous amount of work by the greatest genius of the day resulted, which would have been even more extensive if the fastidious temperament of the executant had not continually revised it. But not much more can be said for Ludovico. His political influence on the peninsula, especially during the earlier part of his life, can only be called pernicious.

The Florentine reaction to his capture was dictated by the traditionally French sympathies of the Republic, which had been dimmed during the last days of Savonarola. Now this sentiment revived, but at the cost of ingratitude for Ludovico's help in the siege of Pisa. In the end, Florence drew little profit from the resuscitated French alliance. Louis XII indeed sent an army to help the Signory to regain Pisa, but his commanders secretly favoured the Pisans and never intended the expedition to succeed. Soon it was withdrawn, to the impotent anger of Florence.

Meanwhile, Cesare Borgia, also disposing of French Troops, had found them more amenable to his designs. He took Imola; Forlì, which held out for a while under Caterina Sforza; then Faenza; Rimini, in south-eastern Romagna; and Pesaro, near Urbino, in the Marches. Next, he appeared at Campi, some twenty miles north-west of Florence, and gave the Signory to understand that, if it did not willingly restore Piero de' Medici to the government of the city, he himself, Cesare, would force them to do so.

The Borgia can hardly have meant this threat seriously. As a resolute man of action, he had the greatest contempt for Piero's repeated failures to recover his power, and Cesare did not rely on him in the very least. The Pope's son was merely applying pressure in his usual style, to the civic authorities in Florence. He knew perfectly well that they were desperately afraid of him, not only as a successful military commander, but also as representing his papal father, with whom Florence simply could not afford to quarrel. The Signory in fact hastened to placate Cesare by appointing him captain-general of the forces of the Republic at a salary of thirty-six thousand florins a year. They did not refer to Piero, whom they, in common with their rascally correspondent, now thoroughly despised.

By now, the rulers of Florence were almost at their wits' end. Apart from the Borgias, a deadly external peril loomed, not from Piero, but from the other exiled Medici, Cardinal Giovanni, the prior Giulio, and young Giuliano, who might easily win the fickle affections of the Florentine populace. Giuliano obviously had much of the Medici charm, though his ability had not yet been put to the test. Both Giovanni and Giulio, in any case, were known to have the brains to advise him, if Giuliano did not develop intelligence of his own. They could also depend on their connections by marriage, the powerful and energetic Roman family of the Orsini.

From another direction, Vitellozzo Vitelli, brother of the general executed in the previous year, was known to be implacably determined on vengeance for his brother's death. He was in close touch with Cesare, and also with every Medicean he could find who had a grievance against the existing government of Florence. Internally, the Pisan war and subsidies to Louis XII had almost drained the city exchequer even before the huge retaining fee to Cesare had been decided upon. The Grand Council, like most large popular assemblies, obstinately declined to sanction expenditure for purposes it did not understand. It understood the awful menace of Cesare Borgia, only twenty miles away, but it constantly interfered to the detriment of foreign affairs farther afield. The majority of the councillors had never left Tuscany and could not appreciate the mentality of "foreigners" or the significance of events that took place on the rest of the peninsula. The Venetians were also peculiarly aloof in this way. But they could afford to go in for democratic experiments at this period of Italian history. Venice, built on marsh and lagoon, was militarily almost impregnable. But Florence, exposed to the advance of land armies in all directions and surrounded by despotic rulers who objected to the publicity that the Signory was constitutionally obliged to give to its negotiations, enjoyed no such immunity.

In these circumstances Florentines of honest good will, ability, and influence grew less and less inclined to participate in public affairs. The legal tribunals in the city took bribes, and factions flourished, creating endless talk and enfeebling action. The Bigi no longer made any secret of their Medicean sympathies and called for a reversion to the political principles of Lorenzo's time. These had, in practice, led to a plutocratic oligarchy masked by republican formalities, but with a single leader from whose authority there could be no appeal when questions proved intractable by conciliar debate. Under the shadow of the ambitious Cesare and of the exiled Mediceans, the Republic finally resolved, in the interests of unity, to make the *gonfalonier*ship a life appointment.

On November 1, 1502, Piero Soderini, not a member of any recognised party, was elected to this post. He belonged to an old family that had opposed Savonarola and the more extreme democrats, but he himself had always upheld the theory of free government, respected the Grand Council, and insisted on the maintenance of orderly constitutional procedure. In private life his conduct was irreproachable. He represented, in short, the ideal of quiet, respectable men with a little property or a steady business. Such citizens have invariably been the backbone of any prosperous and confidently independent state. But in the first decade of the sixteenth century Florence could not be defined in those terms. In desperate financial straits and threatened by foreign invasion, the city could no longer be safely left to the advice of its honourable but only too parochial lower middle class, even if led by a man of distinguished political ancestry. The wits of social levels other than that of small tradesmen soon began to laugh at Piero Soderini. A few years later Machiavelli's wicked tongue presented their views in a famous epigram:

> *La notte che mori Pier Soderini*
> *l'alma n'ando dell' Inferno alla bocca.*
> *E Pluto le grido, "Anima sciocca,*
> *che Inferno! Va' nel limbo dei bambini!"*

> The night that Peter Soderini died
> his ghost went trotting to the mouth of hell.
> "Off with you, silly fellow," Pluto cried.
> "Your place is where the souls of babies dwell!"

All the same, the new *gonfalonier* proved a capable administrator. With the instinct for figures typical of a solid merchant, he did not take long to restore some degree of order to the chaos of the Republic's finances. He also had a great stroke of luck in the death, on August 18, 1503, of Pope Alexander VI. The Pontiff may have been poisoned, but more probably he succumbed to malaria, the most prevalent of Roman diseases. He was seventy-two. The inordinate territorial ambitions and intrigues of this Pope had been perilous to Florence ever since his accession to the Holy See a few months after the death of Lorenzo the Magnificent. Papal aggression had been especially conspicuous after the humiliation the Vatican had endured at the hands of Charles VIII, the Tuscan city's ally. Alexander had, furthermore, been more than ever hostile to the Signory during Savonarola's attacks on Roman iniquity, and again when Cesare invaded Romagna, which Florence also coveted.

Even before the Pope died, however, Soderini's reforms had so strengthened the position of the Republic that it was able to take a very different line with Cesare when the latter renewed his blackmail from Urbino, which he had recently captured from the reigning duke, Guidobaldo da Montefeltro. The Borgia then summoned Florentine envoys to his court in the captured city and informed them they would have to change their form of government if they wished him to remain their friend. But Soderini's embassy, which included Niccolò Machiavelli, then aged thirty-four, coolly replied that they would see what could be done in this line, but that such revolutions could not be arranged from one day to the next. Cesare, disconcerted by this calm retort, contented himself with somewhat vague menaces of fearful vengeance if his orders were not soon obeyed. He then returned to Rome to deal with the Orsini, who were conspiring against him, and almost at once fell seriously ill of the same disease that was about to carry off his father. On his recovery, he found his newly seized dominions in other hands, and, with his father now dead, his power in Italy at an end. He left the peninsula for Spain, where Alexander had been born, and was killed in 1507 while fighting for the King of Navarre.

These events were a great relief to Florence. At the very end of the year, another notable occurrence still further heartened Soderini's government. On December 28, the outstanding Spanish soldier Gonzalo de Córdoba, in the course of the long quarrel between Spain and France over the division between them of the Kingdom of Naples, almost annihilated the French army on the banks of the river Garigliano on the frontier between Latium and Campania. In the precipitate flight of the French survivors across the fast-flowing waters, Piero de' Medici, who was serving in their ranks, sank aboard a barge heavily overloaded with four cannon and perished in the torrent.

He had never been a competent leader, either in Florence or out of it, but his mere existence, after he left the city, constituted a rallying point for persons dissatisfied with the various Florentine governments that had succeeded one another after 1494. In spite of his shortcomings he was, after all, the son of the great Lorenzo, and he might have reformed sufficiently, if reinstated, to have given the state a tolerable figurehead. His death, accordingly, removed in the opinion of most of the citizens of Florence a very real source of anxiety for the survival of the Republic. It did not seem that any other Medici had the power, the ability, or the will to replace Piero. His brother, the cardinal Giovanni, now twenty-eight years old, was clearly the most efficient and resolute of the family, but he appeared to be devoted to an ecclesiastical career in Rome, where he had already achieved considerable influence. His younger brother Giuliano, aged twenty-five, somewhat resembled his murdered uncle and namesake, and he was universally admired for his ingrained generosity and gentleness, his courtesy and tact, his expressed distaste for bloodshed and debauchery, his personal accomplishments, and his genuine appreciation of literature and the arts. But Giuliano was neither ambitious nor an intriguer, and his detachment from practical politics served to discourage the Florentine exiles in Rome who looked to him for the future.

In Florence itself, meanwhile, a rather different personage, in fact a genius, but one curiously ineffective in his tireless practical activities, was now coming to the front. In 1498, a month after the execution of Savonarola, a sharp-featured, bustling young man of twenty-nine, short and slightly built, with black eyes and a lean countenance, had been given charge of the Second Chancellery and also appointed secretary of the War Committee of Ten. In these capacities Niccolò Machiavelli, scion of an old but impoverished family, soon came to know a lot about affairs of state, both domestic and foreign.

He was sent on important missions to neighbouring cities, and Piero Soderini, later to be the victim of his malicious wit, thought highly of him. In the autumn of 1502, Machiavelli accompanied the embassy that interviewed Cesar Borgia at Urbino. After Pope Alexander's death and Cesare's illness, the astute secretary was despatched to Rome, France, and Germany in turn. He thus made the acquaintance of the new Pontiff, Julius II; the King of France, Louis XII; and the Holy Roman Emperor, Maximilian, not to mention various cardinals and minor rulers both in Italy and elsewhere.

Soderini asked Niccolò what he thought should be done about the interminable Pisan war. The secretary suggested the establishment of a native militia instead of the unreliable and inefficient mercenary troops hitherto employed, who were only interested, Machiavelli affirmed, in Florentines as paymasters and could easily be bribed to betray them. Soderini pulled a long face. He knew that the great majority of his fellow-citizens, absorbed in trade, detested military service. They had not performed any for nearly two hundred years. But in the end the worried *gonfalonier* decided to give his brilliant subordinate's idea a trial. He started with the peasantry, always the first to suffer in war. They willingly agreed to take a personal hand in defence of their fields. On December 3, 1506, the Signory passed a bill to conscribe the rural population, and a force of ten thousand men was raised in this way. Machiavelli was entrusted with its organisation.

The Republic now faced a clearer horizon in all directions. The Borgias were gone, the exiled Medici quiet, and the foreign aid previously accorded to Pisa was being withdrawn in consequence of the entirely different schemes of Pope Julius II. In 1509, the starving Pisans capitulated, largely owing to the activities of Machiavelli's newly formed militia. It was the secretary's finest hour. On June 8, 1509, one of his colleagues in Florence wrote to him: "Everyone without exception has gone mad with exultation. There are bonfires all through the city, though it is still afternoon. Think what it will be like at night! If I were not afraid of making you too vain, I would say that you have arranged matters so well with your battalions that you alone have restored the fortunes of the Florentine state."

Julius, a highly militant Pontiff—in fact, a born soldier—had accompanied the expedition of Charles VIII in 1494. This Pope, a nephew of Sixtus IV, now began to disturb the peninsula. His first object was to recover the cities of Romagna for the papal dominions. Venice had seized some of them and others had declared independence. The triumphs in war and diplomacy of the impulsive yet far-sighted Julius, a typical Ligurian in the energy that Sixtus IV had also exhibited, had very little to do with the Medici or indeed Soderini's Florence until the year 1510. It was then that the Pope withdrew from the so-called League of Cambrai formed by France, Milan, Spain, and Germany, as well as himself, against Venice. He then made peace with the Venetians and called upon all Italy to expel the "barbarians"— i.e., the French—from its soil.

Louis XII did not care to face the warrior-Pontiff in arms. Instead, he proposed a council of cardinals to deliberate on policy towards their majestic firebrand of a chief. The King requested permission from the still traditionally friendly city of Florence for the council to meet in Tuscany. The *gonfalonier* and the popular party wished to accede to Louis' demands, but their aristocratic opponents, including some more or less crypto-Mediceans, feared retaliation by Julius for any such concession. The opposition argued fiercely against falling out with a Pope who had shown himself to be not only a genius in war but an inspiring believer in the superiority of Italian to foreign civilisation. Nevertheless, Soderini gained the day, and the council met at Pisa on

September 1. The Pope immediately laid Florence under an interdict and sent Cardinal Giovanni de' Medici to Perugia to supervise the papal interests. This prompt action caused Piero Soderini to change his mind. He pressed Louis to take his schismatic council elsewhere, and at last he succeeded in having the assembly transferred to Milan.

Spain, Venice, and Rome then proceeded to declare war on the French King, who was feebly supported by Florence. At the Battle of Ravenna, fought out between French and Spanish troops on April 11, 1512, the French finally held the field, but their best commander, Gaston de Foix, was killed. Before the end of June, the allies had achieved the Pontiff's object. The French fled across the Alps, and their military power in North Italy had ended for the time being.

Julius then turned his attention to Florence. He sent an army under the Spanish general and viceroy of Naples, Raimundo de Cardona, accompanied by Giovanni de' Medici and his brother Giuliano, to demand the dismissal of Soderini, the reinstatement of the Medici as private citizens, and an indemnity of one hundred thousand florins. The aristocractic party had been right in the debate over the location of the cardinals' council, and retribution had followed Soderini's decision to obey Louis and let it meet in Tuscany. Nevertheless, the *gonfalonier* felt strong enough to refuse in peremptory terms compliance with what amounted to an ultimatum. Cardona immediately stormed Prato, scattering Machiavelli's militia with the greatest ease, and allowed the victorious veterans to do as they liked with the unfortunate town. The sack was the first experience by Italians of the "Spanish fury" that afterwards became so notorious. Every building was pillaged. The male inhabitants of all ages were ruthlessly massacred. The women and children were raped and tortured in the churches to which they had fled. A contemporary Italian chronicler, Jacopo Modesti, affirmed that the nuns of the invaded convents were forced to submit to the unnatural as well as natural lust of the soldiers. In the streets, mothers threw their daughters into wells and jumped in after them. Men cut their own throats. Girls flung themselves to death from balconies and roofs. Such scenes raged for twelve days and nights.

At last, the Medici brothers permitted female refugees to take shelter in their quarters. The condition in which the wretched women arrived to receive this belated charity may be imagined. It is unlikely that either Giovanni or Giuliano, both basically good-natured men, ever forgot the horrors that accompanied the restoration of their family, by foreign troops, to power in Florence.

The news of the rape of Prato caused a panic in the capital city. Soderini was compelled to resign his office. He fled into exile, first to Siena, then, in order to evade the papal agents in pursuit of him, to Castelnuovo, a port on the east coast of the Adriatic. The government that succeeded him at Florence in 1512 undertook to reinstate the Medici, to join the league against France, to pay an indemnity of 150,000 florins, and to conclude an alliance with King Ferdinand of Spain. In other words, all and more than all Julius' demands had been met, in surrender to enormously superior physical power.

On September 1, 1512, Giuliano de' Medici and his twenty-year-old nephew Lorenzo, son of Piero and brother of the Clarice de' Medici, who had married Filippo Strozzi, entered Florence in state. The two young men were greeted with cries of *"Palle!"* by the aristocratic party. A nobleman named Atonfrancesco degli Albizzi, whose family had been bitter enemies of the Medici in the past, lodged the pair in his palace. The tactful Giuliano, now aged thirty-four, set an excellent example to his nephew in not appearing in any way to exceed his specified status as an ordinary citizen, even shaving off his beard to conform with Florentine fashion, which differed in this respect from that of France and most other courts of the day. Giuliano, however, was almost immediately invited to join a debate on the future constitution of the Republic. He gave his consent to the abolition of a life *gonfalonier*ship, and it was agreed that the office should be held henceforth for one year only.

A fortnight later, Cardinal Giovanni de' Medici arrived in the city. He was accompanied by a young, robust, black-browed cleric, the brothers' cousin Giulio, a bastard of the murdered Giuliano, brother of Lorenzo the Magnificent. The two Medici ecclesiastics were attended by Filippo Strozzi, who had so far been keeping discreetly in the background. The Florentine provisional government told these visitors that more had been expected from their easy-going relative Giuliano than a tame acquiescence in Savonarola's ramshackle constitution. Giovanni agreed that the city had been in a sad state of weakness, corruption, and lawlessness during the past years. He himself proceeded, with bland assurance, to disband the Grand Council, to reduce the term of office of the *gonfalonier* to two months, and in other ways to return to the arrangements that had been current under the great Lorenzo, his father. The populace registered no objection, for the restored Medici had executed no one, confiscated no one's property, and banished only a few of Soderini's relatives.

The cardinal, at thirty-six, had developed, since the days of Piero and Alexander VI, into a relatively charming and capable prelate, recognised as one of the leading patrons of art and literature in Rome, where he soon installed in his sumptuous palace the books that had been preserved by Savonarola at St. Mark's in Florence. Giovanni's other Medicean traits were a love of music—nearly all the Medici, good, bad, and indifferent, sang well—and hunting, though his figure rendered him somewhat unwieldy in the saddle. The cardinal's friend,

Giulio, served as confidant and keeper of the treasury, keeping his exuberant cousin's expenses almost within the bounds of his large income. Others intimate with Giovanni in these years included Bernardo Dovizi, who had accompanied him on his travels in northern Europe before 1500; Pietro Bembo, the Venetian humanist and expert on Tuscan dialect; Baldassare Castiglione, the mirror of every Italian gentleman; and Raphael, who painted Venus and Cupid on the walls of the cardinal's bathroom, to the great scandal of more conventional Christians.

In these circumstances, it was evident to the Florentines that Giovanni de' Medici would be a distinct improvement on his deceased elder brother as an advisor to the city. The populace, on all public occasions, roared its approval for the anticipated return to the great days of the late Lorenzo, the Magnificent One.

It was from the aristocrats, who had been the first to shout *"Palle!"* on September 1, that trouble came. A youthful classical scholar of distinguished family, one Pietro Paolo Boscoli, who so adored the ancient Roman Republic that he considered civilisation to have ended with the suicide of Brutus, one day accidentally dropped a scrap of paper. It was picked up by a passer-by and found to be a list of eighteen names, including that of Niccolò Machiavelli and also that of Agostino Capponi, a close friend of Boscoli, about his age and of similar rank and opinions. The list was turned over to the Signory, and all the persons named on the list were arrested and racked. Boscoli and Capponi confessed that they were preparing a plot to murder both Giuliano de' Medici and his nephew Lorenzo; but they declared that none of the other men mentioned yet knew that they were to be approached in connection with the conspiracy. Nevertheless, most of them, under torture, acknowledged that they had already heard of it. Machiavelli, however, swore that he was completely ignorant of the plan, and he managed somehow to convince the inquisitors of his innocence. Boscoli and Capponi were executed on February 22, 1513. Of the rest, some were banished, and a few, including Machiavelli, discharged as innocent.

Giuliano and his nephew realised, despite the public uproar, that the plot did not present a serious threat to their authority. The obsession of a group of young fanatics with pagan tyrannicide could not rank as a major political tendency. The two Medici therefore resorted to the great Lorenzo's usual expedient for calming the overwrought city. They provided festive amusements for the citizens almost every day, themselves appearing as conductors of the joyous celebrations and pageants.

As Florence was thus feasting under the watchful eyes of the Medici, Pope Julius II quietly died in Rome, in the midst of his preparations to eject his former allies, the Spaniards, from Italy, as he had ejected the French. The news of the old warrior's death reached Florence on the very day of the executions of Boscoli and Capponi. Cardinal Giovanni de' Medici, who was widely regarded as a strong candidate for the now vacant papal throne, left immediately for Rome in the company of his cousin Giulio. On March 11, 1513, Giovanni was duly elected, taking the name of Pope Leo X. No doubt the cardinal-electors anticipated the new Pope's early death, for he was much over-weight and known to be suffering from ulcers and a fistula. Otherwise, they would hardly have voted for so young a man—he was only thirty-eight—who would normally have postponed their own chances for the Papacy for another generation. Giovanni, moreover, who pos-sessed all of the Medici charm and much of the Medici guile, took care to bribe his chief rival in the stuggle for the tiara. The prelate in question was Cardinal Soderini, brother of the ex-*gonfalonier* of Flor-ence. Giovanni accordingly promised Soderini that, if elected, he would recall Piero Soderini from exile and allow him to live in Rome, though not in Florence. The Medici candidate's affability, a pleasant contrast to the irascibility of Julius, finally turned the scale in his favour among the necessary majority of the Sacred College.

On April 11, the new Pope, the first member of the House of Medici to occupy the Throne of St. Peter, was crowned. In the pro-cession concomitant with the ceremony, Pope Leo rode the white Arab charger that had carried him at the Battle of Ravenna twelve months before. The Duke of Ferrara, who had been obliged to flee from Rome in Pope Julius' day, held the papal stirrup. The route of the procession was lined with arches, tapestries, flags, and banks of flowers. Altars, surrounded by priests and monks, stood at intervals along the streets. Shouts of *"Leone!"* and *"Palle!"* echoed in the ancient streets. The statues of antiquity were displayed along with those of contemporary artists, and Christ and Apollo vied for the attention of the roaring mobs. The Medici emblems of lions, diamond rings, and feathers, with the *palle* spouting water and wine, flanked all the decorations. Figures of Mercury and Pallas Athene, divinities of peace, suggested the dawn of a new epoch of civilisation, a golden age.

In this new era, it seemed that the Medici were destined again to play a dominant role on the Italian stage. Pope Leo almost at once con-ferred the cardinalatial dignity on his cousin, Giulio de' Medici, and on his nephew, Innocenzo Cibo, the son of his sister Maddalena. Giulio was, in addition, created archbishop of Florence, a move designed to give that shrewd prelate a voice in the affairs of the city. Giuliano, Pope Leo's brother, was made *gonfalonier* of the Roman Church, per-haps to his secret embarrassment, for the office was a military one and Giuliano was a man of peace. The new *gonfalonier* of the Church now had to join his brother in Rome, and his nephew, Lorenzo, became virtual head of the Florentine Republic.

Pope Leo, the fount of this new magnificence, began his pontificate with excellent intentions. He forgave the cardinals who had staged the anti-Julian council first at Pisa and then at Milan. He reduced taxes, and he introduced some badly needed ecclesiastical reforms of a minor nature. He wished to undertake a more radical program of reform, but he was so vigourously opposed by prelates of the Roman Curia in this matter that his plans were quietly dropped. Leo's comment on that occasion was characteristic of him and his reign: "I will further consider this matter," he said, "to determine how I can best satisfy everyone."

Leo's most striking quality was his good nature. He never stopped smiling; he spoke quietly and pleasantly and, unlike the great Lorenzo, in a beautifully cultivated and musical voice. He was tactful in the extreme, and careful never to offend. He could refuse petitions in such a way that the petitioners were honoured rather than offended, and when such refusals became necessary, he was genuinely distressed. He was delighted when he could grant what was asked, and in such instances he always apologised for not being able to do more than was asked. His inherent dignity of person and his conscientious fulfillment of his religious responsibilities were humanised by the stout man's shortness of breath and tendency to perspire, and by his habit of putting people at ease by little jokes.

In foreign policy, Leo was cautious and generally prudent, and his diplomacy was, on the whole, noted for its honesty, although the new Pope could lie like a veteran when he felt that it was for the good of the Church to do so. He began his reign by declining, out of deference to Louis XII, to join the League of Malines, which had been concluded between Henry VIII of England and Ferdinand I of Spain, in 1513. But when King Louis led his Frenchmen into Lombardy, the Pope, without formally adhering to the Spanish, Milanese, and English troops that offered resistance, lent their commander money to pay the Swiss pike-men, and it was the Swiss who decided the Battle of Novara in Piedmont against the French on June 6. A reconciliation between Rome and France followed, constituting a triumph for Leo's diplomacy.

Meanwhile, the Pontiff's eager interest in the new age he was supposed to have inaugurated, which included unprecedented geographical discoveries by Europeans, appeared in his delighted reception of an embassy from Portugal, headed by Admiral Tristan da Cunha and his three sons. The deputation was accompanied by Persian horsemen, and brought to the Pope African leopards and rare birds from Asia, together with the first elephant seen in Italy since the era of ancient Rome. The beast came from India, but had a Carthaginian name, Hanno. In 1516 the German humanist Ulrich von Hutten, who was in Italy at the time, wrote with disdainful sarcasm to a friend: "You have all heard how the Pope had a great animal, an elephant, which he held in high honour and loved much. You must know that this animal is now dead. When he was sick the Pope was filled with woe. He summoned many doctors, saying, 'If it is possible, cure my elephant.' They all did the best they could. They examined the elephant's urine and gave him a great purgative, which weighed five hundred ounces. But it did not take effect and so he is dead and the Pope greatly grieves. They say that he would have paid five thousand ducats to anyone who cured the elephant, for he was a remarkable animal and had an enormous nose. He always knelt down when he came into the Pope's presence and trumpeted loudly the syllable, 'bar, bar, bar!' "

Leo ordered Raphael to paint a life-size picture of the dead monster on the wall below which it had been buried. The Pontiff himself composed a grandiose epitaph in Latin. All Rome was still talking, with discreet laughter, of these events, when innumerable copies of a printed pamphlet began to be offered for sale at every street-corner. It was entitled *The Last Will and Testament of the Elephant*. The text related that Hanno, having realised that his end was near owing to the unhealthy air of Rome and the short rations on which he was kept by his miser of a trainer, Gian Battista of Aquila, had commissioned the anonymous author to make copies of a will drawn up by the consistorial court lawyer Mario de' Previchi. The document continued:

"Item, to my heir, the workshop of St. Peter, I give the golden covering which I wear on festal occasions, on condition that the alms given to the said workshop are not put to unholy uses. . . . Item, to my heir Cardinal San Giorgio I give my ivory tusks, so that his thirst for the Papacy, as intense as that of Tantalus, may be moderated. . . . Item, to my heir Cardinal Sante Croce I give my knees so that he can imitate my genuflections, but only on condition that he tells no more lies in council. . . . Item, to my heir Cardinal Volterra I give my wisdom, if he will promise to be generous for a change. . . . Item, to my heir Cardinal Santi Quattro I give my jaws, so that he can devour the revenues of Christ the more readily. . . . Item, to my heir Cardinal Medici I give my ears, so that he can hear the doings of everyone. . . ."

The cardinal referred to at this point was Giulio, whose activities as Leo's private agent were thus indicated. But the reference is quite good-natured as compared with those to the other cardinals, proving the popularity of both the Medici ecclesiastics at this date. The satirist, in any case, had no need to be afraid of either, since he had covered his tracks so carefully.

Between guffaws, every reader speculated about the author of this scathing document. Before long, one Pietro Aretino, at that time employed as a lackey in the palace of the millionaire banker Agostino

Chigi, let it be known that he, a footman in that magnificent establishment, had written the "will."

Leo in fact loved a joke at the expense of the ambitious fops, clerical or lay, who surrounded him. He had already permitted the greatest freedom of speech often enough in his fairly frequent moments of relaxation. As a Florentine, too, he had no objection to seeing pompous Romans having their legs pulled. Aretino, whose moral courage and mental dexterity in self-defence exceeded those of any of his contemporaries, rightly guessed that the elephant's death had been a heaven-sent opportunity for personal advancement. He confidently awaited favourable reactions to Hanno's "last will and testament."

They soon came. It was not only Chigi and his guests who heartily congratulated their bold servant on his literary talent. The Pontiff himself sent a request to the banker to release the jester to join the papal household. Such a demand could not be refused. Pietro hastened to present himself before the jovial Vicar of Christ, who asked him facetiously: "Which would you rather be, *messere,* Virgil or Camillo Querno, my poet laureate?"

"Your Holiness's laureate of course," retorted Pietro instantly. "For he can drink more good mulled wine in the Castello in July than old Virgil could have got from Emperor Augustus for two thousand fawning *Aeneids* and a million *Georgics.*"

The answer was characteristically cunning, both in its notification to Leo that he had acquired a learned henchman, worthy of promotion and indulgence, and in its implied sharing of the Pope's taste for strong liquor. Actually, Pietro cared no more for wine than any addict of good living. He was never drunk in his life, though he often pretended to be if occasion warranted it. Leo was delighted with him. Aretino's scurrilous and in the main highly successful career thus started under Medicean patronage. It was to continue for nearly twenty years, off and on, to be protected by the same egis.

The Pope's reconciliation with King Louis of France was cut short by the latter's death on New Year's Day 1515. Louis was succeeded by a very different sort of sovereign, the young and dashing Francis I. The new King at once laid claim to the Kingdom of Naples, an act in which he was encouraged by Pope Leo; for Leo, always with an eye to Medicean glory, desired to oust the Spanish incumbent and secure that throne for Giuliano de' Medici, *gonfalonier* of the Roman Church. As a further step in that direction, the Pope quietly arranged the latter's wedding to King Francis' sister, Filiberta.

The French monarch, however, proved to be more aggressive than the Pope had bargained for. He alarmed Leo on September 13, 1515, by defeating the hitherto irresistible Swiss, employed by Spain and the Emperor, at the Battle of Marignano, a few miles east of Milan. The

Pope decided to meet the advancing French army and its royal leader at Bologna. On his way North he stayed for three days, beginning on November 30, in Florence.

The contemporary historian Landucci wrote afterwards that the grandeur and expense of the preparations for the reception of the first Florentine Pontiff beggared description. No other city in the world, he declared, could or would have done anything like it. Vasari seconded this opinion, speaking with all the authority of a practising artist, well aware of previous efforts in this line. Certainly the details recorded are imposing. More than a thousand labourers and craftsmen were employed on the decorations for a month beforehand. They toiled all through the various feast-days that fell within the period. Churches were converted into workshops. Triumphal arches, reproductions of celebrated buildings, and allegorical devices and statues were produced by architects, painters, and sculptors whose reputations have survived into the present time. To give only one example, a wooden structure executed by Jacopo Sansovino, to a design once sketched by the great Lorenzo himself, was painted in *chiaroscuro* by Andrea del Sarto. The purpose of this grandiose but merely temporary façade was to screen the still not completely finished cathedral, founded in 1298 on the plans of Arnolfo di Cambio, brought almost to completion by Brunelleschi, and consecrated in 1436.

At the Bologna conference between Leo and Francis, the chief question discussed was the fate of the Duchy of Urbino, at this date held by a great friend of Giuliano's, Francesco Maria della Rovere, a nephew of the late Julius II and, like him, an eager man of war. The present Pope desired Urbino for his nephew Lorenzo, already nominally in charge of Florence, but no definite decision on this point was reached at Bologna.

The Pontiff, on his return from that city, again visited Florence, from December 30 in this year until late in the following February. But on this occasion murmurs were heard about the extent to which the vast and splendid papal retinue had sent up food prices. The Holy Father might at least have arranged for the import of corn to his native city, the malcontents groaned. It was the first time anyone had found much fault with Leo. The decline in his popularity was offset a little, though not much, by his gift to the cathedral chapter of a jewelled mitre worth ten thousand ducats.

Two weeks later, on March 17, 1516, Giuliano de' Medici, who had been seriously ill with tuberculosis for some months, died at Fiesole. He had gone there for fresh air, to counteract the fever-stricken atmosphere of Rome. Everything recorded about the life of this gentleman, one of the best if not one of the most able of the Medici, makes an agreeable impression. His death at the age of thirty-eight is almost as tragic an event as the assassination of his equally admirable uncle and namesake in 1478, the very year of the younger Giuliano's birth. Michelangelo's magnificent, though highly idealised, statue of him, made for Leo's tomb in the church of San Lorenzo at Florence at the express command of that Pontiff himself, may afford some consolation to posterity. The meditative pose, far more than the conventional armour, rendered with superb aptitude the character of one of the best-loved and ill-fated members of the House of Medici.

One of Giuliano's last acts had been to thwart his brother Giovanni's design to seize the Duchy of Urbino. Guidobaldo da Montefeltro, Giuliano's indulgent host during his exiled youth, had bequeathed the property to the Francesco Maria della Rovere just mentioned, whose military ability had been much appreciated by his warlike uncle, Julius II. Giuliano foresaw trouble if Leo attempted to deprive Francesco of this inheritance, but the Pontiff, within a few days of his invalid brother's death, summoned the duke to Rome to answer a charge of murder. Francesco ignored the papal mandate and was excommunicated and dispossessed of his capital by Leo's troops. On August 18, the Pope created his nephew, Lorenzo, Duke of Urbino.

Lorenzo di Piero de' Medici, like his father an excellent rider and good at all sports, also resembled the late Piero in never being able to make up his mind or take a resolute initiative in matters that required prolonged attention. In politics, accordingly, he was more or less ruled by his domineering mother, Alfonsina degli Orsini. Her ideas of government tended to be despotic and did not appeal to the still obstinately republican citizens of Florence. Lorenzo meant well, but Alfonsina, who adored him, was determined to make him a powerful ruler in the only sense in which she understood the term, that of absolutism. It is certain that she stimulated such ambitions in the mind of a high-spirited young man without much capacity for serious reflection; but it is doubtful whether her son ever wished to go so far in that way as she would have liked.

The campaign for the capture of Urbino had succeeded, and for a while Lorenzo maintained himself in the field against the dispossessed duke, who had immediately attempted to regain his city. In 1517, however, Francesco Maria fought his way back into the capital with the aid of Spanish and German mercenaries, and Lorenzo was expelled. This result satisfied everyone—including perhaps Lorenzo himself— except the Pope; for Leo's somewhat frivolous nephew, no more interested in war than he was in art, literature, or music, had not enjoyed himself in the fighting, during which he had been wounded. He therefore declined to return to the scene of hostilities or to meet Francesco Maria in a duel, as that expert fencer suggested. Nonetheless, financial considerations eventually settled matters in Leo's favour. The unpaid foreign mercenaries dispersed. Terms were agreed on between the combatants. The Pontiff and the Signory of Florence paid Francesco Maria's debt, and the twice-deposed duke retired to Mantua, confident that his loyal subjects would soon expel Lorenzo, a man who cared neither for books nor for artillery. These articles were the duke's favourite possessions apart from his personal sword, a weapon that easily slipped from its sheath into the bodies of such of his enemies as dared to come near him.

Another swordsman of at least equal calibre, Giovanni di Giovanni de' Medici, Caterina Sforza's son by her third husband, a member of the junior branch of the Medici family whom she married in Rome in 1496, was now nineteen years old. Both parents were by this time dead. The young Giovanni had taken part in the first attack and final seizure of Urbino by Lorenzo's forces. There can be no doubt that of all the officers on the Medici commander's staff, this adolescent cousin of his was by far the most remarkable. At eleven he had already looked like a miniature but lean and athletic *condottiere*. Hardly ever out of the saddle, when in it he usually rode at full gallop. He swam rivers in the depth of winter, hunted his grounds, raided neighbouring villages, and robbed passing travellers in the spirit of a medieval baron. At twelve he visited a brothel for the first time, and at the same age he killed his first man. At fourteen, after his cousin Leo had assumed the tiara in 1513, he was sampling Sienese, Roman, and Neapolitan courtesans. At sixteen, he unhorsed eight antagonists, one after the other, in a tournament in Florence.

In 1516, this terrifying youth married Maria Salviati. The girl's father Giacomo (sometimes called Jacopo) had been married as a young man to Lucrezia de' Medici, the eldest daughter of Lorenzo the Magnificent, in order to renew the close relations formerly maintained between the Salviati and Medici families. By the will of Caterina Sforza (d. 1509), her son Giovanni had been confided to the care of Lucrezia and Giacomo. The latter could never control the precociously headstrong child, but his tougher wife gradually came to acquire an influence over Giovanni that she never lost. The boy was about the same age as her own daughter, Maria, and it seemed perfectly natural to Lucrezia, perhaps even desirable in view of the girl's peaceable and submissive disposition, that the two young people should marry. They had of course known each other well for years. Maria's devotion to Giovanni was already obvious. He for his part always treated her with courtesy, both before and after their marriage. But he never at any time dreamed of admitting her to the impassioned intimacy he extended so freely to male friends and feminine companions of a gayer temper.

During the second Urbino campaign of the spring of 1517, Lorenzo put Giovanni di Giovanni de' Medici in command of a hundred light horsemen, Corsicans whose "sombre courage" he was ever afterwards to swear made them the finest soldiers in the world. These troops, under such leadership, proved more than a match for Francesco Maria's Spanish arquebusiers, even in the Apennines, and contributed largely to the recapture of the city.

On the conclusion of this affair, Pope Leo set about marrying Lorenzo, as he had married Giuliano, to a French princess. Madeleine de la Tour d'Auvergne, a connection of Francis I, became the wife of the second Lorenzo di Piero de' Medici in 1518. The wedding guests noted with more or less sympathy, according to their characters, that the bridegroom showed signs of the ravages of syphilis. Next year the unlucky young wife died in giving birth to a daughter, known to history as Catherine de' Medici, who was to become the most famous of the Medici women.

A few days after Madeleine's death, Lorenzo himself perished. He had begun his adult life, under his uncle Giuliano's influence, with typical Medicean discretion. But after being left in sole charge of Florence when Giuliano went to Rome as *gonfalonier* of the Church, Lorenzo apparently had changed for the worse. He was criticised by the citizens for ostentation, insolence, and ambition, no doubt due largely to the pressure of his mother Alfonsina degli Orsini. But this failure to win popularity in Florence may also have resulted as much from his absence during the war with Francesco Maria, and from the taxes he imposed on Florentines to pay for it, as from any serious faults of personality. He had much of the Medici charm and good nature. But again, in the last year of his life his marriage to a Frenchwoman and his adoption of French manners and dress, including the beard so disliked in the Republic, led to much malicious gossip about his morals. He was certainly weak in mind, yet not so stupid, ill-mannered, treacherous, or criminally selfish as some of his contemporaries asserted. The truth is probably that this Lorenzo was simply a young man who had been led from the first to believe himself extremely important, and who seemed delightful and quite clever as an adolescent, and somewhat inscrutable and reserved as he grew older. He left the post of mentor to the Florentine Government vacant once again, after enjoying that peculiar office for scarcely five years.

Cardinal Giulio de' Medici at once hurried to the city in order to assess the situation. This prelate was destined to be one of the most celebrated and complex representations of the family, typical in many of the contradictory strains that characterised its members from this time on. As a child, though illegitimate, he had been accepted at once into the household of his uncle and great-aunt, Lorenzo the Magnificent and Lucrezia Tornabuoni, a matron who combined unimpeachable virtue and the warmest of hearts with a penetrating intelligence and worldly understanding. Giulio soon showed, as he grew up, by his pleasant manners and lively wit, as well as by his dark, strongly marked features, much of the personal attraction of his murdered father, Giuliano. A certain incalculability and shiftiness in later life caused him to be nicknamed "the Chameleon."

In 1519 Giulio had already been acting for some years as the trusted assistant of his cousin, Pope Leo X. The cardinal gave the impression to most people of honest industry, courage in adversity, and true piety. He was also found more accessible, generous, and cultivated than most busy churchmen of high rank at this period. After the death of the second Lorenzo di Piero, Giulio soon became quite popular in critical Florence. He gave himself no airs, lived simply, listened attentively to the orations of the leading citizens, and kept public expenditure at a minimum. Accordingly, in a short time the cardinal acquired more effective control of the city than anyone had possessed since the height of Savonarola's influence. Under Giulio the financial situation of the Republic, which had deteriorated in the brief reign of his predecessor, young Lorenzo, was restored to order. Taxation was lightened, the administration of justice reformed, and the rights of the elective corporations, which Lorenzo had cut down, were reinstated.

The Florentines were the more ready to put up with Cardinal Giulio because they considered him essentially as regent for the infant Caterina, Lorenzo's daughter. Meanwhile Machiavelli, now restored to official favour, advised the cardinal on constitutional policy. In his plans, he took it for granted that Medicean views—by which he meant those of Leo and Giulio—concerning the degree of liberty desirable, should be final word. Those views strongly emphasised at least the external forms of republicanism. The aristocratic faction in the city was less tactful, and their extreme opponents in the popular party—which included some young nobles desirous, under the influence of Machiavelli's own indiscreet adulation of ancient Rome, of emulating Marcus Junius Brutus—also gave some trouble. Despite such resistance, Giulio's firm and bland management of the potential forces of disruption in the councils finally left Florence, on his departure five months later, as quiet, prosperous, and hopeful as it had ever been. Even Cardinal Passerini, his fumbling deputy for the next two years, did no lasting harm to the system thus established.

During this interval, Pope Leo had problems more urgent than those of the Florentine Republic to deal with. In the first place, his formidable young cousin Giovanni di Giovanni de' Medici, on his return from the Urbino wars, proved a source of much irritation. He quarrelled with everyone older than himself who presumed to know something about fighting. He lived with the extravagance of a ruling prince. He seldom sat down to a dinner for less than fifty, and he kept thirty horses in his stables. Moreover, the stubborn violence of his unending personal disputes, some of them with respectable people, had passed beyond mere comment. On November 25, 1517, for example, he had written to a military officer of good family, one Camillo degli Appiani, then in residence at the Tuscan port of Piombino opposite the island of Elba: "Lord Camillo. Recently a man in my service, who is called Il Corsetto [the little Corsican], arrived at Piombino and asked if you had any message for me. After making him wait a while in your house, you inflicted five or six wounds upon him. You call yourself a gentleman. The greatest rascal in the world would not have done such a shameful thing. I summon you to meet me in arms, when I will punish you for your ignoble behaviour. If you have any honour left, you will not fail to meet me, though I doubt if you will dare to fight me. I will send you word of a safe meeting-place, suitable for persons of our rank. If you do not accept battle, I will treat you as such cowardice deserves. I will give you fifteen days from that on which you receive this letter to reply to it."

Friends and relatives on both sides intervened to prevent a duel, but Camillo degli Appiani eventually retorted to a second, and equally offensive, challenge by pointing out to his excited young correspondent that the alleged "Corsican" was a Calabrian vassal of the Appiani family named Antonino da Cola, and that he, Camillo, had been obliged to chastise the fellow, by the sword, for insufferable impudence. Giovanni, beside himself with fury at being given the lie in this fashion, rushed, with his "Corsetto," to the Glove Inn at Florence, where he had been told that Camillo's chancellor and clerk were staying. Bursting into their quarters, he wounded both men so seriously that they subsequently died. The two assailants galloped off to Ferrara, beyond Florentine jurisdiction. From that city, Giovanni issued another frantically abusive challenge to Camillo.

Even in sixteenth-century Italy, this excessively aristocratic behaviour could not be ignored. The young Medici found that everyone was against him, including his cousin, Pope Leo, who summoned him to Rome to explain his conduct. At last, early in March 1518, Giovanni sullenly condescended to apologise. He was then sentenced to five years' banishment from Florence. The "Corsetto" confessed, under torture, that he had in fact baited Camillo, and he was duly beheaded for his part as prime mover in this somewhat mysterious affair. Apparently, he had merely posed as a Corsican in order to enlist Giovanni's help in revenging himself upon Camillo for some real or fancied injustice.

In December 1518, the stormy petrel of the House of Medici again appeared in Florence, over-awing the magistrates, using his irrepressible sword in street brawls and then contemptuously apologising, piling up debts, writing letters to everyone except his appalled wife, sending the worried Leo a present of falcons, and being generally such a centre of disturbance—since for the moment, there was no war in which he could be usefully employed—that in March 1519, the Pontiff again summoned him to Rome, paid his debts, and gave him a hundred men-at-arms to drill. The story goes that once Giovanni had occasion to rebuke one of these fearless mercenaries and strode up to him in his usual menacing fashion. The fellow laid a hand on his sword. "One step nearer, Captain, and you die!" Giovanni, enraptured by this prompt exhibition of ferocity, promoted the soldier on the spot to command a company. The man, needless to say, was a Corsican.

Troubles of wider import than the insubordination of a fire-eating young cousin engaged Pope Leo's attention. First, both King Ferdinand of Aragon and Emperor Maximilian of Germany had died. Charles of Habsburg, a young man with a long nose, a hanging underlip, and an eager but solemn expression, was elected Holy Roman Emperor as Charles V. Moreover, a learned and able German monk named Martin Luther was making a name for himself by denouncing the sale of indulgences. The Pope sent for Luther, requiring him to explain in Rome what his intentions were. The interview never took place, for the monk advanced one excuse after another. Finally, in 1521, Leo felt compelled to excommunicate the rebel theologian.

In addition to this outbreak of heresy and much uncertainty as to how Charles would act, the Pontiff had been plagued by actual schism at the Vatican. A plot was discovered among the younger cardinals to kill him. He executed the ring-leader, Alfonso Petrucci of Siena, imprisoned several of the other conspirators, and created no fewer than thirty-one loyal new members of the Sacred College to replace them. The Pope was further preoccupied in this last year of his life with schemes for the aggrandisement of the domains of the Holy See. He added Parma and Piacenza, officially, to his unofficial control of Florence. His worst fears were confirmed by the war that broke out in June between the austere young Emperor, Charles V, and the recklessly ambitious King of France, who considered that he himself should have been chosen to fill Charles' position.

In this combat Giovanni di Giovanni de' Medici greatly increased his already high reputation for dashing heroism in the field and for shocking outbursts of ill-temper against elderly generals at councils of war. Like Horatius, he crossed a river in full armour, though on horseback. On the road to Milan, while hurrying to meet the imperial troops marching to relieve the city from the close pressure of the French, a mob of Italian refugees fleeing in the other direction brought his horse down. Far ahead of his men, he fought off this attempted interference single-handed. His sword whirled, witnesses declared after-

wards, in all directions at once. In the end, Milan was saved from
the French, and the restored duke of that city, Francesco Maria
Sforza, the second son of Ludovico, personally thanked Giovanni de'
Medici for his conspicuous part in the victory.

Leo lived just long enough to hear of the victory of Milan and of the
annexation of Parma and Vicenza to the Papal States. He caught a
chill while sitting at an open window to watch the festivities celebrating
the capture of Milan. Complications developed, and the Pontiff expired
on December 1, 1521, at the age of forty-six.

Pope Leo X had been a typical Medici, in the patronage of learning
and art as well as in the precariousness of his health and in the
brevity of his life. Humanists had greeted his election with enthusiasm,
and they were not disappointed in him as a patron or as a paradigm
of refinement in his taste for art, manners, and social intercourse. Any
man with a claim, however tenuous, to literary merit could, if he chose
to live in Rome, find employment in the papal Curia. Pietro Bembo
(d. 1457), a Latinist of almost Ciceronian grandeur, flourished under
Leo as a papal secretary. Although a Venetian by birth, Bembo had
been educated in Florence and had enjoyed the friendship of Lorenzo
the Magnificent—doubtless a double recommendation in the Pope's
eyes. He was joined in the papal secretariat by Jacopo Sadoleto (d.
1547), a humanist of comparable reputation and similar Ciceronian
tendencies, and under the influence of these men and others like them—
for by now the Curia had become famous as the refuge of otherwise
unemployed scholars—Rome emerged as the focal point of a vigourous
literary life. Writing in all its forms was cultivated, and Italian poetry
was cultivated as assiduously as were the ancient classical models of
Latin literature. The best minds of the day were invited, at prodigal
salaries—for Leo was munificent in all things—to accept posts at the
University of Rome. The study of classical archeology was stimulated
by Leo's client, Raphael, when the latter proposed to make a huge map
of the ancient city based upon careful study of the old structures and
of the Latin classics.

Behind all of this intellectual and artistic activity was Pope Leo, the
Maecenas of his time. The Leonine Age—as his pontificate is often
called—had it most noticeable effect, however, upon the world of art.
The Pope's favourite was Raphael (1483–1520), and he employed
that painter more than any other artist in projects dear to his heart.
Among those undertakings were the decoration of the Vatican by
frescos, and Raphael took delight in complimenting the Pope who had
entrusted to him such an important and profitable task. In the room
of Heliodorus, for example, is a fresco representing Leo I confronting
Attila the Hun, in which the face of the hero-Pope is a portrait of
Pope Leo X. The Vatican frescos of Raphael reflect exactly the spirit

of Leo and his age, for they combine Christian and classical, or pagan, themes and figures without any awareness of contradiction.

Another client of Leo's was the surly young sculptor whom Lorenzo the Magnificent had taken into his household many years before, Michelangelo. The artist's most famous work had been done under Leo's predecessor, Pope Julius II, the fiery Pontiff whose temper was a match for Michelangelo's own. Indeed, the early years of Leo's reign found the artist occupied with the execution of Julius' tomb; later, however, the Pope employed Michelangelo to undertake a façade for the Florentine church of San Lorenzo. When that project was dropped some time later, the sculptor was retained to create appropriately monumental tombs for the Medici family in the same church. The Pope also engaged the sculptor Andrea Sansovino (1460–1529), also known as Andrea Contucci, to decorate the sacred house of Loreto.

Such projects, despite the eminence of the artists, were comparatively minor ones, and it is true that under Leo the sculptor's art did not play so prominent a role as might have been expected. The same cannot be said of architecture. Bramante was appointed to carry on the construction of the basilica of St. Peter's, and, when he died in 1514, he was replaced by Raphael. Work on the basilica, however, was not to be completed for a long time, for Leo's prodigality had, it was found upon his death, virtually emptied the papal treasury. Indeed, his carelessness with money was so well known during his lifetime that the Roman bankers would consent to lend him funds only at an exorbitant rate of interest—sometimes as high as 40 per cent—since they felt sure that, under Leo's hand, the Papacy would end in bankruptcy.

That sentiment was not far from wrong. Indeed, Leo's financial exigencies required that he do violence to his own upright character and to the well-being of the Church. His lavish gifts to friends, relatives, artists, and entertainers, his sumptuous court, the bottomless hole that was St. Peter's, the expenses of war, and the effort to organise a crusade against the Turks, all combined to exhaust even his enormous income. To raise money, Leo resorted not only to ruinous loans, but also to the sale of ecclesiastical offices and to the hawking about of indulgences throughout Europe. Although much of the money thus raised was used for charitable and religious ends, the methods by which it was found served only to exacerbate the discontent of much of Europe with the Roman Church. And it was upon that discontent that the great reformers of the North were about to capitalise.

Despite Leo's fiscal scandals, his good intentions and his piety were never seriously questioned in his own time. He could, in true Italian style, be charitable and compassionate in private, while practising cunning and fraud in public affairs. In diplomacy, he was skilled, and the end of his reign found the Papacy to be the dominant political power in Italy. Yet Leo was no more successful than Pope Julius II in ridding the peninsula of foreign invaders, and, despite Leo's power and influence, he was unable to awaken sufficient support to enable him to contain the aggressive Turks. In religious affairs, his faith and devotion were exemplary, and his personal life was innocent of those sexual blemishes peculiar to Popes of his era. Yet his desire to please all men blinded him to the real needs of his Church, and he failed utterly to effect those reforms that might, even then, have prevented the rupture between the northern and southern halves of Christendom. Even in those things he loved best, in art, sculpture, and literature, he was not without fault. He was the most generous and understanding, but not the most enlightened, of patrons. He could appreciate a fine turn of phrase, and the elegance and wit of Bembo and Politian pleased him immensely; yet the subtleties of Machiavelli and the grandeur of Ariosto escaped him completely. He encouraged Raphael and rewarded him lavishly, but he had little respect for Leonardo da Vinci and little understanding of Michelangelo's greatness.

Despite these faults, Leo was not without greatness, either personal or historical. He was a happy man, and his ambition was, insofar as he was able, to bring happiness to others. It was Leo who brought to Rome the tradition of patronage that existed in Medicean Florence, and so provided, for the world to see, an example that was soon to be copied throughout Europe. The Italians knew him as one of themselves, and they esteemed him at his basic worth. When he died, he was mourned as no Pope had been mourned for centuries. Even at a distance of twenty years, one of Leo's scholarly survivors would lament,

> *Deliciae humani generis, Leo Maxime, tecum*
> *ut simul illusere, interiere simul.*

> (Mankind's delight with thee, O greatest Leo,
> no sooner made us sport, than it was gone.)

Bankers, too, to whom the late Pontiff had owed vast sums at his death, and cardinals and bishops who had staked their careers on his continued existence, were all inconsolable. Petty minds, however, recorded the papal demise in less complimentary, though memorable, terms: "He came to the throne like a fox," wrote one such, "he ruled like a lion, and he died like a dog." Alfonso of Ferrara, on whose domains Pope Leo had always had designs, was beside himself with joy when he heard of the Pope's death, and he had a medal struck that proclaimed that he had been delivered *ex ore leonis* ("from the jaws of the lion").

Such judgements are too simple for a man so complex as Pope Leo X, who seemed to combine in himself virtues that were sometimes faults, and faults that were often virtues. For so human a Pope and a Medici, perhaps the most accurate epitaph is that assigned to him by Will Durant: "He was a good man ruined by his virtues."

* * *

Most of Italy expected that Cardinal Giulio de' Medici, though only forty-three, would succeed his cousin as Pope. He himself was determined to do so, not only on grounds of personal ambition, but also as a Florentine patriot. He had heard with anxiety, as the year 1522 began, that anti-Mediceans in the North were taking advantage of the confusion in Rome, for the deliberations of the Sacred College on the succession were being unprecedentedly prolonged. In Florence, too, the adversaries of Giulio's family were exploiting the greed and stupidity of his deputy, Cardinal Passerini, with a view to overthrowing the government so recently and successfully established. Hostile troops from Perugia and exiles from Urbino were moving West.

Worse still, Giulio found the French cardinals and Cardinal Francesco Soderini obstinately determined to vote against him. Francesco belonged to a Florentine family that had often in the past opposed the Medici, and he now insisted that a Pope whose birth was illegitimate would be a scandal to Christendom. The older cardinals, too, wanted a Pontiff who could be expected to die soon and give one of their number a chance of election. Giulio, fit as a fiddle and only just approaching middle age, did not suit this scheme. In desperation he resorted to a wild gamble. With every sign of self-effacement, he proposed a candidate so obscure that it might be supposed his name would be rejected immediately, and, in the reaction he himself, obviously the most distinguished of the cardinals, might be elected.

To Giulio's intense mortification, the prelate he mentioned, Adrian of Utrecht, received the necessary two thirds majority of votes. Adrian, a Fleming of sixty-three, had risen from humble origins to become tutor to Charles of Habsburg, now the Holy Roman Emperor, Charles V. Thereafter he had been appointed, through imperial influence, to his cardinalate. An extremely modest, worthy, and learned man, though otherwise quite unremarkable, Adrian had not even troubled to attend the conclave on this momentous occasion.

When his name was announced from the balcony of the still unfinished basilica of St. Peter, the crowd in the square below at first greeted the news in shocked silence. Then catcalls, whistles, and finally a roar of jeers broke out. For a while, the Roman populace seemed at the point of revolt. They would have cheered for a Medici or for a Colonna. They might have accepted a Spaniard or even a Frenchman. But a Dutchman! The Venetian ambassador wrote home that he was "stunned" at the result of the election and could hardly believe his ears.

The cardinals themselves seemed to regret their decision as soon as they had taken it. When they emerged from St. Peter's after the announcement, they looked, according to the Roman poet Tebaldeo, "Like ghosts from limbo, so white and distraught were their faces. . . . Almost all are dissatisfied and repent already of having chosen a stranger, a barbarian and a tutor of the Emperor, a monarch most dangerous to the temporal power of the Papacy."

But nothing could be done about it. Giulio de' Medici left Rome at once for Florence. There he hired Swiss and German mercenaries, led by the *condottiere* Guido Rangoni, to repulse the troops advancing on Siena, the first obstacle in their march towards the Tuscan capital. Rangoni, assisted by the Sienese, who were now friendly to the Medici, successfully blocked this invasion, which had originally been inspired by the implacable Cardinal Soderini. Giulio then resumed his former control of Florence. He had no difficulty in consolidating his old position there, especially as he proceeded to conciliate the exiled from Urbino by appointing Francesco Maria della Rovere, their leader, captain-general of the Florentine army. This honourable post, unfortunately, was coveted by that now experienced soldier, Giovanni de' Medici. This firebrand—who is better known to history as Giovanni delle Bande Nere (John of the Black Bands) because of the black bands that he and his men had adopted at the death of Pope Leo— felt that he was the logical, indeed, the only possible choice. He had proved his mettle in the campaigns against the French, and indeed against that very Francesco Maria della Rovere when the latter was Duke of Urbino; and, moreover, he was a Medici. Quite apart from the incompatibility of temperament between the turbulent young Giovanni and the sober Giulio, the long-standing jealousy between the older and younger branches of the Medici family still existed. Lorenzo the Magnificent had tried without success to eradicate it by betrothing his daughter Luigia, who had died while still a girl, to Giovanni's father. But it had been resuscitated by the intrigues of the two Pierfrancesco brothers against the late Piero de' Medici. In Giulio's mind, the ill-feeling had no doubt been increased by his recognition that the only legitimate representatives of his blood, except the baby Caterina, were now to be found on Giovanni's side of the house.

The disappointed candidate for the Papacy had some excuse for not wishing to put Giovanni delle Bande Nere in official charge of Florentine troops. The amusements of that young man, when not fighting, which he much preferred to anything else, were hardly edifying. He was at that moment at Reggio, in Emilia, indefatigably pursuing the courtesans and officers' wives of that merry garrison town. According to Pietro Aretino, who joined Giovanni there early in 1523, these ladies compared most favourably, at any rate, with the women the two young men had cultivated in Rome, where they had become boon campanions in the intervals of Giovanni's campaigns. The Roman girls had been, Pietro considered, glamourous enough, but possessed of "the faces of angels and the hearts of devils." At Reggio, however, ". . . joy filled the hearts of all. For the young leader had just given his soldiers a night of liberty. Torches were blazing everywhere. The whores of the city had come to the camp in great numbers. Some of the troopers were leaping from their horses, having just returned from foraging. Bottles of wine, hams, baskets of fruit, and even bleating lambs were slung across their saddle-bows. Such provisions had cost them nothing, for they had robbed everyone for ten miles around. A few of the women in the plundered families wept and tore their hair, while their husbands and fathers clamoured and argued, pleading for the restoration of their wives, daughters, and livestock. But the male peasants were beaten back with the flats of daggers and halberds. Enormous camp-fires gleamed in the oak-groves. The shadows of the soldiers drinking, gambling, or making love were cast hither and thither in the ruddy light of the cressets."

While Giovanni delle Bande Nere was thus occupied in overcoming his disappointment, Cardinal Giulio de' Medici was discovering, in restless Florence, that mere courtesy, conciliation, unremitting attention to public business, and almost superhuman tact were not enough, unless one possessed the irresistible personality of Cosimo or the Magnificent Lorenzo. Those originally most enthusiastic of Giulio's supporters, the aristocrats, suspected that he was likely to reintroduce the Grand Council, while the opposition party doubted his promises of constitutional reform.

One group of young intellectuals mostly Mediceans by tradition, grew so dissatisfied with the cardinal's leadership that they actually conspired with the anti-Mediceans of Rome, headed by Cardinal Soderini, to murder him. Once more the example of Junius Brutus and the rugged republicans of ancient Rome appears to have been at work. Machiavelli was a member of the party to which the Florentine conspirators belonged, and he was fond of talking with admiration of the assassins of Julius Caesar. But there is no evidence that he had the slightest idea of what the dissidents, all younger than himself, intended.

Someone else had. One of the plotter's couriers was arrested, and treasonable correspondence was found on him. This discovery caused the arrest of one of the ring-leaders, Jacopo da Diaoceto, who confessed that he and his friends meant to kill Giulio because he had not kept his solemn oath to introduce a truly republican form of government. All the suspects were given a fair trial, and only Diaoceto was beheaded. Those of the others who had not already fled were banished. The cardinal had, as usual, behaved with remarkable clemency, and there were many who opined that he had acted too mercifully for the good of Florence. Giulio, however, was unperturbed. Mercy, he believed, was the quality that distinguished the Christian from the pagan, the enlightened prince from the despot.

3. Pope Clement VII

The cardinal was soon to have the opportunity to put his principles into practice on a much wider scale than that afforded by the limited horizons of Florentine affairs. On September 14, 1523, all Rome was relieved to hear of the death of Pope Adrian IV, that austere, tight-fisted, reform-minded Dutchman who, at the previous conclave, had unwittingly deprived Giulio of the papal tiara. The Romans had never forgiven Adrian, first for being Pope, and, second, for being what a Pope should be. He had caused an economic catastrophe in the city by abolishing the ecclesiastical sinecures by which a vast number of citizens supported themselves and their families. He had put an end to the sale of offices and to bribery of curial officials. He had ordered the vast multitude of bishops and cardinals, who idled away their days in Roman pleasures, to return to their dioceses and conduct themselves as Christians. When scholars came to him seeking a living, he had told them to go back home and find an honest job. He put an end to the expenditure of public monies on such non-Christian frivolities as art, literature, music, and carnivals. He was a Pope in the manner of a Hildebrand, or of a Gregory the Great; and Rome, from the most eminent cardinal to the lowest beggar, never forgave him for it. After Adrian's death, his physician was hailed in the streets as Liberator Patriae ("Liberator of the Fatherland").

After such a taste of other-worldliness, the cardinals of the conclave were more than ready to return to earthly realities, and their choice fell upon the man who seemed to promise most in that direction, Giulio de' Medici. The new Pope, who took the name of Clement VII, was only forty-five, handsome, genial, pious, wealthy, erudite, an admirer of art, literature, and learning, and experienced in the ways of princes. Rome greeted the new Medici Pope as a reincarnation of Leo X, and Bembo, in that spirit, forecast Clement's reign as one of the most glorious that the Church would ever know.

Roman optimism was shared by many who were less inclined to hasty judgement. The Venetian ambassador at Rome wrote to his masters that "His Holiness is temperate in every human action, particularly in eating and drinking. He sets an example of sexual continence that nowadays—though I cannot speak of the past—no one can censure him in that respect. He indulges in no kind of vice, nor does he spend anyone else's money, sell any offices, or practise simony. He gives much to charity. Since his election, he had not been to Leo's hunting-lodge more than twice, nor does he care for music or buffoons." It is hardly likely that an ambassador of the Most Serene Republic could have been deceived in his estimate of the new Pope. Venetian emissaries were famous for their discretion, judgement, critical sense, and knowledge of absolutely everything that went on anywhere in Europe. Moreover, they always told the truth to their masters, though they were believed never to have told it to anyone else. There is, then, no reason to doubt this portrait of Clement in 1523. It conforms to his career as the Cardinal de' Medici, when he was known for his hard work for the benefit of those whom he wished to please, and his avoidance of complications with those whom he had reason to fear or distrust.

Such discretion and prudence seemed indispensable virtues at the inception of Clement's pontificate. In politics, there loomed the menacing problem of the rival ambitions of Francis I of France and Emperor Charles V. In this connection, the Pope had promised the French cardinals to favour Francis and to be wary of Charles. Thus far, however, he had taken no definite steps to do either. In northern Italy, in Naples, in the Netherlands, and along the Pyrenees, the opposing generals of France and Spain were still vainly guessing which way the enigmatic Pontiff would eventually jump. It is probable that Clement himself had not yet made up his mind, for the future of Florence, where he had just re-established the Medicean power, preoccupied him at this time. Both Francesco Guicciardini and Niccolò Machiavelli, the two most acute political philosophers in Italy at this period, urged Clement, with passionate earnestness, to take a frank and positive stand in public affairs. But he was constitutionally unable to do so. Unending subterfuge, his only answer to the complexity and menaces of international relations, were to mark his conduct for the next four years, until at last he was reduced to a sort of petrifaction.

There was no legitimate representative of his family whom he could appoint to look after Florentine matters except the "Great Captain" or "Great Devil," Giovanni delle Bande Nere. Giovanni, however, was hardly on speaking terms with his senior relative since the latter had made friends with Francesco Maria della Rovere, now re-established (by Adrian IV) as Duke of Urbino and still Giovanni's deadly enemy. In any case, the "Great Devil" had no talent for civil administration, and he had already shown by his brawling in the streets of Florence itself, as well as elsewhere, that he was of far too impetuous a character to be entrusted with anything of more consequence than horses, foot-soldiers, and artillery.

In these circumstances, a Florentine embassy, perhaps prompted by the Pontiff himself, drew Clement's attention to two young Medici bastards. Ippolito, fathered by the amiable and sexually uninhibited Giuliano de' Medici, who had died in 1516, was now thirteen, a handsome and intelligent lad, who might go far with the right guidance. The other boy, Alessandro, officially declared to be a son of the second Lorenzo di Piero de' Medici, the usurping Duke of Urbino, was a year older than Ippolito but decidedly less promising. His dark skin, low forehead, thick lips, and crisply curling hair gave rise to the rumour that his mother had "Moorish blood." In any case, he was considered a hopelessly vicious little monster by the adults who knew him best. His legitimate sister, Caterina, only four years old at this date, was hardly in a position to give an opinion.

A majority of the ambassadors suggested that these two boys should be sent to Florence as accredited representatives of the family, accompanied by Cardinal Silvio Passerini, who would govern the city during their minority. Clement, who apparently had no other recourse, agreed to this extremely rash proposal. The choice of Passerini was especially ill-judged, for that prelate had already incurred the detestation of the citizens for his avarice and boorishness while deputising for Clement, then Cardinal Giulio de' Medici, at Florence between October 1519 and January 1522. But no other Medici of the senior branch were available, and the Pope was determined to keep that illustrious name before the eyes of the Florentines. As for Passerini, though personally unpopular, he at least knew the city, and he had managed to hold the government together during his tenure of power for well over two years.

Ippolito, the younger and much more presentable of the two young Medici boys, reached Florence on July 31, 1524. The other, Alessandro, followed him a year later. Clement had spent the interval in having the uncouth lad rigorously trained for his future duties, and in securing certain revenues to his person to enable him to perform them. The procedure seemed normal to some contemporaries and ill-advised to others. It had no justification in law, but only in a custom already once broken by the expulsion of Piero di Lorenzo in 1494. To many impartial judges, the Pope seemed to be assuming a hereditary right of the direct descendents of Lorenzo de' Medici to rule Florence. Some thought his enthusiasm for the uncouth Alessandro to be inordinate, and they did not hesitate, in the fashion of those days, to hint at a homosexual relationship. They were quite wrong. Clement's affection was perfectly "natural" as was to become more and more evident over the next few years.

On Alessandro's arrival at Florence in the summer of 1525, now thoroughly coached in the part he had to play and already a rich landowner, he was immediately accorded formal honours, the title of Magnifico, and seats in the Assembly and the Council of Seventy. Passerini, as usual, gave offence by his crude manners, but both the boys behaved well, and factions in the city had grown so chaotic that no party felt strong enough to stage a revolution. The old Medici supporters, now called Palleschi from the family crest of Palle, had split into two groups. One side advocated a Medici as president of a tight oligarchy; the other preferred to have such a man as hereditary chief of a constitutional administration. Among the anti-Mediceans, some simply hated the very sound of the name, while others were uncompromising republicans. A third section thought only in terms of their personal ambitions. No one but a stern disciplinarian like Giovanni delle Bande Nere could have united such diverse elements, but he, owing to the Pope's attitude, was beyond consideration.

Clement was in fact very much afraid of Giovanni, and with good reason. In the autumn of 1524, Francis I had invaded Lombardy. He was eventually trapped at Pavia, about twenty miles south of Milan, on February 25, 1525, defeated by Spanish and German troops, and then captured and carried off to Spain. In the previous year, Giovanni had been fighting for Emperor Charles' generals, but they had not paid him adequately, in his own opinion, for his services. He therefore rode off, with his black bands, to the port of Fano in the Marches, where he took to piracy in the Adriatic in order to maintain himself and his company. Giovanni was distinguished from other pirates by his family connections and by such outstanding military ability that he was becoming more and more regarded, while aggression by France and Spain increased, as the only possible saviour of Italy.

Clement, at once alarmed at his young cousin's lawlessness and hard pressed by the French cardinals, had then sent a rider to Giovanni at Fano recommending him to put himself at the disposal of the French King, who was in those days still at liberty. No doubt the Pope also hoped to prove by this gesture his official neutrality in the existing struggle between France and Spain for secular domination of the peninsula. The move might, furthermore, rid him, without giving rise to censure, of an uncongenial and potentially dangerous member of his family.

Giovanni had been only too delighted to comply with the Pontiff's suggestion, which afforded the prospect of regular employment under a mighty sovereign on land instead of hazardous and intermittent seaborne attacks on Venetian and Turkish shipping, in which the special qualifications of his men had little scope. He joined the vigourous and jovial French monarch at once and got on well with him. Soon afterwards, the "Great Captain," hit in the leg by an arquebus ball, found himself in a hospital in Piacenza when the decisive Battle of

Pavia was fought. If he had been in the field and could have persuaded the impetuous young ruler of France to take his advice, he would probably have turned the tables on the expert Spanish arquebusiers. He had beaten them before, with his Corsicans, skirmishing in the Apennines against Duke Francesco Maria. But he now knew, to his cost, that only cannon, not old-fashioned cavalry charges, could get the better of them in pitched battles.

Clement had long been submitting to the Emperor's endless demands for subsidies, in the expectation that Francis and Giovanni, between them, would drive the Spaniards and Germans out of Italy. After the defeat of the French at Pavia, however, he realised that he, himself, like the King, was a prisoner. He did his best to encourage optimism in both the French and the Italians, but to little effect. Then in March 1526, Francis came to terms with the Emperor by relinquishing to the Holy Roman Empire the rich province of Burgundy, in exchange for his release. Back in France, the King immediately entered into communication with Rome, and all the rest of Italy, with a view to ensuring a spectacular revenge for the humiliation of Pavia. As a result, the League of Cognac was formed among France, Venice, and the Papal States.

The Papacy raised ten thousand troops, almost half of which were placed under the command of Giovanni delle Bande Nere, and this force was reinforced by a substantial Venetian contingent. To Giovanni's dismay, however, he found the over-all commander of the combined Italian forces to be his old enemy, Francesco Maria della Rovere, the reinstated Duke of Urbino. These troops assembled at Marignano, a strategically important village near Milan, to await the troops promised by King Francis. The constant friction between Giovanni and Francesco Maria did not make the period of waiting an easy one for their officers and men. The duke was all caution and prudence, while Giovanni was famed for his audacity and daring in matters both personal and military. Before matters could come to a head between the two commanders, however, King Francis' Swiss mercenaries arrived, and personal differences were forgotten in a flurry of preparations for an assault on Milan.

The attack, when it came, was a fiasco. A small army of hardy Milanese and Spaniards emerged from the walls of the city and drove off Francesco's men in panic. Giovanni, cursing the Duke of Urbino, fought on courageously until almost surrounded by his enemies; then, gathering his men, he withdrew in good order. To his infinite disgust, there was no more fighting that summer, and so he retired to Mantua to share the company of the ladies of that town for a while. Soon, however, he was back in service in the approaches to Milan, harassing the imperial and Spanish troops in the vicinity during the day, and writing to King Francis at night to beg for funds with which to pay his troops.

Francis, for his part, earnestly begged Giovanni not to risk his life needlessly in skirmishes, and carefully refrained from encouraging him to believe that any French money was forthcoming for Italian troops.

Giovanni was soon too occupied even to worry about French gold. In February of 1527, the commander of the imperial forces in Milan— a renegade French duke, Charles de Bourbon—led his men southwards to Piacenza, where he joined forces with the *Landsknechte,* or German mercenaries, of one Georg von Frundsberg. These combined forces then continued the southwards trek, heading, it was rumoured, towards the Eternal City itself. Only Giovanni delle Bande Nere, with his few thousand men, stood between this imperial horde and the capital of Christendom. The opposing armies met at Governolo, a small town about eight miles south-east of Mantua. Giovanni gave the command to charge, but the first volley from the imperial troops broke his right leg and he fell from his horse, unconscious. His men, in general consternation at this casualty, broke off their assault and withdrew. The wounded man was carried to a nearby village, where his leg, by now gangrenous, was amputated. He died a few days later, as he had lived, laughing and cursing the luck that had brought him to such a pass. Pietro Aretino, Giovanni's boon companion, was quick to foresee the effects of the great soldier's death. "I only wish that I were lying," he wrote, "when I declare that Florence and Rome will discover what it means not to have this man among the living."

The Aretine was not without a prophetic gift. As soon as the imperial army was free of Giovanni's obstruction it attempted to seize Florence but was turned away by a force under the command of Francesco Guicciardini, a historian turned general. Enraged at the resistance of the Florentines and urged on by the promise of unlimited loot in the Holy City, the horde turned once again towards Rome. There, Pope Clement was in desperate straits, attempting alternately to arrange a truce with the Emperor and to raise funds by the sale of cardinal's hats. Neither expedient worked. By May 6, Bourbon's men were at the gates of Rome. They stormed the city with heavy losses, and Bourbon himself was killed in the attack, but eventually they broke through and slaughtered Pope Clement's Swiss guards and the Roman militia. The Pope and the cardinals took refuge in the impregnable tower of Sant' Angelo, but the rest of Rome was at the mercy of the invaders, and not a house was spared. Men, women, and children were killed indiscriminately. Wives were raped before the eyes of their husbands, and daughters in the sight of their horrified parents, and then all were killed. Nuns were subjected to orgies of lust in their convents or hauled off to become the common property of the soldiers' camp. Hardly a house was not plundered, hardly a church not ruined, hardly a man not held for ransom, hardly a palace not burned. For eight days, the sack of Rome continued, while Pope Clement looked on from the tower of Sant' Angelo, until at last order was restored among the soldiers of the Holy Roman Emperor, Charles V.

The Emperor himself, who was in Spain, was delighted to hear that Rome had fallen to his good Germans, though he expressed pious indignation at the savage treatment of the city and its inhabitants. His devout nature, however, did not prevent him from taking full advantage of Pope Clement's predicament. On June 6, 1527, his representatives compelled Clement to sign an ignominious peace. The Pope agreed to pay an immense indemnity, to surrender to Charles the cities of Piacenza, Parma, and Modena as well as several fortified castles (including Sant' Angelo), and to remain virtual prisoner until it should please the Emperor to release him. It seemed that the structure of the Church itself was on the point of collapse, and all Europe—even those who had little sympathy with the indecisive Clement and who deplored the iniquity of the Curia, the sins of the Papacy, and the perfidy of the hierarchy—was shocked at the brutal rape of the capital city of Christendom and at the humiliations to which the Vicar of Christ had been subjected by a Christian Emperor. Erasmus of Rotterdam, the greatest scholar of his age, reflected popular sentiment when he lamented that "Rome was not only the temple of the Christian faith, the guardian of noble souls, and the home of the Muses, but the mother of nations. To how many was she not dearer than their own land? . . . Truly, this is not the ruin of one city, but of the world."

The misfortunes of the unhappy Medici Pope were amply shared by his Florentine relatives. Early in 1527, the imperial forces had entered Tuscany, where they were closely watched but not impeded by the Duke of Urbino, who had been freed by the death of Giovanni delle Bande Nere from that soldier's importunate demands for military action. On April 26, Cardinal Passerini, with the two Medici lads, Alessandro and Ippolito, whom he was supposed to be training for the control of Florence, visited the duke's camp. Immediately, the strictly republican party in Florence noted their absence and leaped to the conclusion that the Medici had fled. They roused the masses, and the ominous roars of *popolo e libertà* resounded once more in the streets. But already the Medicean faction had despatched a messenger to Urbino's quarters, and Passerini, who was no coward, at once returned to the city with a detachment of professional soldiers headed by Francesco Guicciardini. His arquebusiers took up positions covering the Palazzo Vecchio, but Guicciardini, before giving the command to attack the palace, stepped forward to address the rioters who had taken possession of the building. His sincerity and eloquence shortly persuaded them to capitulate. Cardinal Passerini did not proceed to extreme measures.

No doubt Guicciardini—whose brother Luigi happened to be *gonfalonier* at the time and was in the palace, either held there by the rebels against his will or in sympathy with them—advised against executions. The ring-leaders were merely fined.

Such clemency made the Medicean party uneasy, for it encouraged, they felt, the increasingly articulate and growing group of malcontents in Florence to attempt yet another *coup d'état*. It may well be that they were better advised in their wish for severity than was the cardinal in his act of leniency. Only a few days later, on May 11, news reached Florence of the fall of Rome to the new barbarians, and an irresistible anti-Medicean reaction immediately erupted. With Pope Clement, the head of the House of Medici and the true ruler of Florence, in the hands of the Emperor, the Florentines saw no reason why they should continue to submit to the rule of an incompetent cardinal and two children. Passerini, incompetent though he was, was not blind, and he recognised that the situation was virtually hopeless. He and the two young Medici accordingly left the city a week later and established themselves at Pisa, while Piero Capponi—a representative of that house that had so often opposed the Medici, and the son of the Piero Capponi who had defied Charles VIII to his face—established an oligarchy in the city of Lorenzo the Magnificent.

During the few days that elapsed before the departure of the cardinal and his charges, events had occurred that cast a vivid light on the unique position of the Medici family in Florence, even during their political eclipse. In 1508, while the Medici were still exiled from Florence, one of its richest citizens, Filippo Strozzi, a banker, had married Clarice de' Medici, daughter of the unfortunate Piero the Second. By 1527, Strozzi had returned to Pisa, where he remained neutral, without committing himself to either Mediceans or their adversaries. He had family connections with both, for his sister had married Niccolò Capponi. After the news of May 11, he was faced with a dilemma, for both Cardinal Passerini and Capponi had sent urgent requests to him to attend them. The cardinal needed Strozzi's money to pay his troops, who had mutinied on account of the arrears of their wages, but the banker had now no reason to love Clement or Clement's dependents, and he felt vaguely inclined to back Capponi. Before making up his mind, however, he despatched Clarice, who had much of the typical Medici courage, intelligence, and debating ability, to judge the situation in Florence.

Now, Clarice was a devout wife, who did not care for bastards, whether in her own family or elsewhere. She also disliked ill-mannered prelates. She therefore gave Passerini a lecture on the evils of misgovernment, and then told the two Medici boys that, if the citizens did not want them, they had better leave Florence. She behaved, in short, very like her father, Piero, in one of his tantrums, haughtily reminding the two cowering lads of their low-born mothers and of her own utterly irreproachable social position as the last remaining senior and legitimate representative of her great house. She expressed the bitterest contempt for their feeble conduct in the responsible office with which they had been imprudently entrusted. She reviled their frivolous misuse of Medicean power, to which their contaminated blood gave them no justifiable title. They had no right, she finally cried, to sit there in the palace of the Magnificent Lorenzo, and the farther they removed themselves from its glories the more all decent people would be pleased.

On the day after Clarice's diatribe, Strozzi himself arrived in the city. He called on the cardinal and pretended to be quite unaware of his wife's uncompromising attitude. On hearing of it from Ippolito, the more articulate of the two youths, he expressed great regret. He promised to try to undo the "mischief" she had caused and went off to the Palazzo Vecchio to consult the members of the new oligarchy.

There, he found that the desposition of the Medici had been agreed upon, but that Ippolito, Alessandro, and the latter's eight-year-old sister, Caterina, would retain Florentine citizenship and that they would be free to stay or leave the city, as they wished. Moreover, if they remained in the city, they would be exempt from all taxation. As the discussion progressed, however, this original and rather generous arrangement was amended to the effect that the Medici children were to be informed that their departure from Florence would be "agreeable to the people" of the city.

Strozzi was asked to convey this decision to Ippolito and Alessandro. He did so, but to his amazement the children expressed their unwillingness to comply with "the people's views" on where they would live. The banker, therefore, perhaps at a loss before the idiosyncrasies of adolescents, left the room and went in search of his wife. "See what you can do with them," he suggested.

The virago needed no encouragement. She strode into the chamber where Cardinal Passerini was in conference with the young Medici, leaving the door open so that her husband might hear, and launched into a tirade that left little to the imagination of her disconcerted audience. Clarice pointed out, at the top of her voice, the difference between Passerini administration and that of her renowned ancestors. She once more gave her listeners to understand that, in her opinion, bastards—even a bastard who was a Pope—could not be expected to handle affairs with the competence of persons of legitimate birth. She then peremptorily ordered the cardinal and the children—all clients of the "papal bastard"—to "leave a house and a country to the possession of which you have no right, either by descent or by intellectual capacity."

This torrent of aristocratic eloquence quelled the last protests of Passerini and his wards. On May 17, they trotted out of Florence, escorted by Capponi and Strozzi. The latter was instructed not to part from the group of exiles until the garrison commanders at Pisa and Leghorn had recognised the new government. Capponi returned to Florence before the party reached Pisa. Sometime after he had left, young Ippolito vanished, and it was generally supposed, when Strozzi professed ignorance of his whereabouts, that the banker, who was known to be bisexual, had fallen in love with the handsome young man and allowed him to escape as the price of surrender to erotic intimacy.

However that may had been, Ippolito made his way to Rome. Some two years later, after Clement had paid his ransom to Charles, the young Medici was created a cardinal. He died, probably poisoned, in 1535. Strozzi rejoined his wife in Florence, where he found her living in the Medici Palace and intriguing for all she was worth to oust Capponi in favour of her husband and sons. The pleasure-loving banker was not politically ambitious, however, and he raised no objection to Capponi's request that he take himself and his family off elsewhere. He withdrew to a country life, and ultimately to exile in France, at Lyons.

Niccolò Capponi, despite his family traditions and the leading part he had played in the recent expulsion of the Medici from Florence, had originally been a Medici partisan himself. He showed much discretion in his republican reforms, for which he returned more or less to the constitutional ideas of Savonarola. He re-established the Grand Council, the Council of Eighty, and the so-called Ten of War with a Signory of eight priors, presided over by a *gonfalonier,* to hold office for a year only but to be eligible for re-election.

The new head of the state took no reprisals against the Medicean party. Instead, he betrothed his son to a daughter of that loyal Medicean, Francesco Guicciardini. Capponi even entered into a conciliatory correspondence with the captive Pope in Sant' Angelo. The anti-Mediceans, however, were so enraged at this moderation that they pulled down the Medici emblems from public buildings and destroyed wax effigies of the family in the church of the Annuziata. Niccolò's careful cultivation of Clement, however, was a prudent move, for he guessed that a reconciliation with the Emperor was bound to come, and he laid his plans accordingly.

The main supporters of the revised system of government had been the small shopkeepers, who revered Savonarola's memory. The moderate members of the numerous, though now quieter, Medicean faction recognised the new *gonfalonier's* obviously sincere desire to keep the city peace, so they also stood by him. Even the few surviving representatives of the old nobility felt more at ease with Capponi, whose family was more ancient and distinguished than many of theirs, than they would have felt with an upstart demagogue. On the other hand, the extreme left wing of the democrats—implacable foes of all wealthy men, and in particular of the Medici, whose power had been founded on the accumulation of commercial profits—detested Capponi and all he stood for, both as an aristocrat and a time-server. These "Crazies," as they were called, like the Arrabiati of Savonarola's day, were insignificant numerically, but they included several aggressive, able, and ambitious young men who exercised a good deal of influence, owing to their vigour and eloquence.

On the whole, the generally democratic temper of his last stage of the Florentine Republic cannot be judged too severely. The governing councils had much vitality and many admirable ideals. The Republic's ultimate failure, like that of so many experiments in popular rule, resulted from the confusion of irreconcilable opinions held by theoretically equal counsellors at a time when swift practical action was necessary, when everyone, on principle, has to be allowed his say and not everyone is capable of judging a situation with complete objectivity, and the moves finally made tend to be either too restricted, too late, or wrongly directed. The ancient Roman republicans so admired by the Florentine humanists had taken account of this danger by providing for "dictators," at critical moments, whose function it was to "save the Republic," but these comparatively few figures too much resembled kings to have much appeal for sixteenth-century Florentines.

In the special case of the problem of Medicean or anti-Medicean government at Florence in 1527, it was hard to conjecture what would be the outcome of the thirty-year-old struggle between France and Spain, in which the control of a Medicean Pope hung in the balance. Clement was the prisoner of an Emperor whose subjects, even after the revolt of Luther, remained Catholic enough to be horrified at the ignominious captivity of the Vicar of Christ. The Pontiff himself furiously resented his detention, and he would make no concessions to the almost apologetic Charles until it became clear that Francis would not act against the victorious imperialists and that no one else was in a position to do so. The French King did promise rescue of the prisoner by force, but he had previously betrayed Clement by remaining passive when the Germans and Spaniards descended upon Rome with such catastrophic effect. It would be a waste of time, the Pope considered, to trust him again.

In these circumstances, Clement called on Florence for support. The city was, of course, too weak to be able to afford a rescue force in military terms. But from Capponi's point of view, a formally expressed solidarity with the incarcerated Holy Father might brighten the future of the Republic, whether Francis or the Emperor eventually emerged triumphant from the struggle. At the same time, Capponi knew enough about the recent military history of Italy to incline to the Emperor's side. Ever since the days of Gonzalo Fernández Córdoba, veteran of the conquest of Granada from the Moors in 1492 and of the immediately succeeding Neapolitan wars, the Spanish pike-men and arquebusiers had been more than a match for the Swiss. Moreover, the *gonfalonier* reasoned, if Florence contracted an alliance at once with the Emperor, he might, as a reward, allow the Republic to continue; whereas it would soon be doomed if Clement, with or without the aid of France, regained his liberty. Clement's first act would undoubtedly be to reinstate the Medici and to confer on them powers more despotic than ever. The Francophiles, and the masses who remembered Savonarola's popular reforms—which he had always prophesied could only survive under French protection—opposed to Capponi's views the long tradition of friendship with France, which meant so much to the wool traders and bankers. But their appeals were overwhelmed by Niccolò's more reasonable calculation. On June 22, 1527—the day, as it happened, of Machiavelli's death—Florence agreed to contribute a force of four thousand infantry and four hundred horses to the imperial cause. Some six weeks later, as though in answer to Florence's decision, Francis' capable general Odet de Foix, Vicomte de Lautrec, swept across Lombardy. The following year, Lautrec marched into the Kingdom of Naples and besieged the capital, but plague decimated the French camp and, in August 1528, Lautrec himself fell a victim to the disease. The remnant of the French were trapped in the neighbouring hills and surrendered.

Meanwhile, as Niccolò Capponi had foreseen, Emperor Charles released Pope Clement, who departed to Orvieto in south-west Umbria. There he watched, with an anxiety which, as events turned out, need not have troubled him, the discomfiture of Lautrec's forces. By the autumn, it was clear to Clement that he would have to acquiesce in the pacification of Italy under the Emperor, who might chastise, but would never dethrone, a Pope.

The imminent restoration of the Pontiff to liberty, and therefore to power, heartened the Medici faction in Florence, while the republicans of the city prepared for an armed attempt to restore that family to power. Michelangelo was called in to supervise the fortifications, and four thousand urban Florentines joined the ten thousand men of the rural militia. The question of hiring mercenaries was also seriously debated.

Then, in April 1529, a letter from an agent of the papal secretary in Rome, addressed to Capponi, was found in a corridor of the Palazzo Vecchio. It was couched in vague terms, merely suggesting a meeting outside Florentine territory between Capponi's son Piero, married to the

Medicean Francesco Guicciardini's daughter, and the writer of the note, "to discuss important matters." But this discovery sufficed to bring down the *gonfalonier,* who had been re-elected against considerable opposition in the previous year. He was arrested and tried for treason, but the sentence imposed was only that he must not leave Florence for six months—i.e., he could not be allowed the opportunity to reveal abroad the secrets of republican defence. It remained clear throughout that the disgraced man was much more a sincere republican than a Medici man, though he was dangerously conciliatory to that family, now mainly represented by the restored Pontiff.

At the end of June, Pope Clement came to terms, remarkably favourable to himself, with Charles. The Emperor, despite his formal alliance with the Republic, which had sent him troops to serve against the French, promised to reinstate the Medici in Florence. He even contracted to marry his illegitimate daughter, Margaret, to Alessandro de' Medici, also illegitimate, but now the only lay representative of the house available, since Ippolito had been created a cardinal in the previous month. This treaty was followed by another, in August, between France and the Empire. King Francis thereby undertook, to the rage of the Florentine republicans, not to interfere with the forthcoming reimposition of Alessandro upon the city.

4. The End of the Republic

The new *gonfalonier,* Francesco Carducci, was as thoroughly democratic and uncompromisingly patriotic a statesman as it was possible for a sixteenth-century Italian to be, and he began strenuous preparations to resist the combined strength of Pope and Emperor. He tried hard to convert the Medicean faction to his way of thinking, but times had changed since the Medici had put political freedom before personal interest. Their supporters were solidly against Carducci. The small-scale traders who believed they would be ruined by the effects of a prolonged siege, the poor who hoped to improve their fortunes by a change of government, and finally a substantial section of the almost destitute masses, which had loved the gay spectacles provided under Medicean rule, all followed the rich and influential Palleschi in more or less secretly calling for an agreement with Clement.

All the same, Carducci controlled a majority of the citizens. His most numerous adherents were the so-called Frateschi ("Friar-lovers"), who venerated the memory of Savonarola. Their support enabled the *gonfalonier* to raise a forced loan and to lay in stores of grain. The Florentine military commanders were Malatesta Baglioni of Perugia, who was reputed to be an irreconcilable enemy of the Papacy since his father's execution by Pope Leo X, and Stefano Colonna, a member of the great Roman family of that name, which was perennially at odds with Pope Clement.

These preparations were made none too soon, for in the summer of 1529, Emperor Charles ordered his commander, Philibert, Prince of Orange, to attack Florence. When this news was made known in the city, an embassy was immediately despatched from Florence to the Emperor, who was then holding court at Genoa. The ambassadors— Niccolò Capponi, Tommaso Soderini, and Matteo Strozzi—presented themselves before Charles in due course and pleaded, not without dignity, for the salvation of the Republic of Florence. Charles listened courteously and gravely, as was his custom, until they had finished. Then, with a wave of his hand, he said, "Plead your cause before His Holiness, Pope Clement." The ambassadors withdrew in despair. Strozzi and Soderini had not the courage to face their Florentine compatriots with failure, and they fled, respectively, to Venice and Lucca. Capponi, who had inherited his father's courage, started out for Venice, but his health had been destroyed by his struggle to preserve the Republic, and he got no farther than Castelnuovo, in north-west Tuscany. There he died on October 18, saying, with his dying breath, "Alas! To what straits have we reduced our fatherland!"

On September 29, the Prince of Orange and his army, carrying the banners of Emperor Charles and of Pope Clement, entered Tuscany, and quickly took possession of Cortona, Arezzo, and the upper valley of the Arno. By the middle of October, the prince's forces were encamped at the foot of the walls of Florence, where they were joined by another imperial army under the command of a Mantuan, Ferrante Gonzaga. Now the Florentines were perfectly willing to fight; they were even eager to do so. Still, they were a city of shopkeepers and merchants, albeit patriotic ones, and they could not refuse to attempt a last-minute negotiation.

The *gonfalonier* felt it advisable, as recommended by the Emperor in August, to send an embassy to Clement. The Pope received this deputation at Cesena, in south-eastern Romagna, while on his way to meet Charles at Bologna. The Pontiff, in an unexpectedly gracious mood, declared that, if the Florentines would readmit his nephews as citizens, he would preserve the existing government of the city almost intact. But this ready answer aroused the suspicions of Carducci, the *gonfalonier*. He believed that once Ippolito and Alessandro had again entered the city, the papal promises would be thrown to the winds. He therefore shrewdly ordered the ambassadors' report to be suppressed, in case it should mislead the Signory and the councils into taking Clement at his word, and it was never submitted to those bodies. The siege of

Florence therefore began, on October 24, with a bombardment of the fortress-church of San Miniato, south-east of the walls. The building was repeatedly struck, but Michelangelo had encased it so thoroughly in bales of wool that it suffered no serious damage.

There cannot be much doubt, in the light of later events, that Carducci's distrust of Clement was justified. The Pontiff was no longer, since his terrible defeats and humiliations, the man who had been so well-intentioned and reasonable before his indecisive ways had involved him in so many miscalculations in dealing with the combined spiritual and temporal crisis that confronted him. Both his resolution and his honesty had given way under the strain. It was perfectly clear that he was now the mere puppet of Charles, who understood no form of government but dictatorship.

In November the Emperor and the Pope met at Bologna. Florentine ambassadors were again in attendance, but Clement's attitude had now changed to open severity. He told the embassy that he would accept no terms from Florence other than unconditional surrender. It was, of course, the actual presence of Charles, in command of a strength no city would hope to defy for long, that had encouraged the long since enslaved Pontiff to throw off the mask of clemency.

In December, Venice joined Genoa, Milan, Ferrara, and Urbino in submission to the Emperor. The abandonment of Florence was complete. Yet Carlo Cappello, the Venetian ambassador in the city, reported to his government, "The spirit of the citizens is rising every hour. They are becoming more and more desirous of measuring their strength against the enemy. Nor can it any longer be said with truth that the farms they own are hostages for them in the hands of the besiegers. For so many magnificent and lovely villas have been burned down by their possessors themselves as well as by the invaders, that it is difficult to say which is the greater, the barbarous ferocity of the enemy or the noble determination and fortitude of the citizens. Although it is impossible not to grieve over such widespread ruin, it is nevertheless a satisfaction transcending sorrow to behold the greatness of mind manifest in the general promptitude and readiness to suffer all these losses, and indeed any other calamity or peril, for the sake of liberty."

In fact, for the time being the Florentine sallies and sorties against their besiegers were as a rule successful. Assault after assault on the walls by Philibert's troops was repulsed. Stefano Colonna was proving a better soldier than Baglioni, for, strange as it may seem, that shifty officer, who had surrendered Perugia to the enemy without a fight and had been disgraced, had been able to argue his way back into his post. It is certain that, despite the heroism of the majority of the defenders as reported by Cappello, many of them were of two minds about their best policy. It is significant in this connection that Carducci failed to gain re-election to the *gonfalonier*ship in January 1530. Raffaello Girolami, an aristocrat and former Medicean, but now a foe of Clement on grounds of republican principle, was appointed to the office; but he showed less energy than his predecessor, a sign that the anti-Mediceans were slowly losing their hold on the city.

Whether or not the Pope had become aware of this so far barely perceptible change, he suddenly withdrew his former demand for unconditional surrender. He indicated that he was prepared to consider terms. Another Florentine embassy, empowered to negotiate, was despatched to Bologna, but on February 7 it returned with depressing news. Both Clement and his cardinals, the envoys reported, had treated them with contempt and refused to listen to them. Nor had Charles' attitude been any better. It is quite evident that the Pope, who crowned with his own hand on February 24, as Holy Roman Emperor, the man who had so cynically humbled him in the past, could not make up his mind for more than a few days at a time whether to act like a supranational Pope or a Florentine prince with ambitions for his family. The ambassadors could do nothing but return to their besieged city with empty hands.

In these desperate straits, the sole chance of Florence's salvation seemed to rest in the hands of Francesco Ferrucci. With the collapse of negotiations with Clement, Ferrucci embarked on a plan that, though as daring as it was precarious, seemed to have a chance of success. He made a tour of Tuscany, collecting every soldier and every man of courage who was willing to fight for the Republic, with the intention of attacking the Prince of Orange's camp outside Florence and forcing the imperial forces to raise the siege. The movement of his men, however—which by now amounted to three thousand infantry and five hundred cavalry—did not pass unnoticed, and soon the Prince of Orange himself, with part of his army, was in full pursuit. The armies met on August 3, 1530, at the mountain village of Gavinana, and the battle was fought furiously in the streets of that place. Orange himself was soon killed by a double shot. (According to the autobiography of Benvenuto Cellini, the prince was killed by Cellini himself; but Cellini, superb sculptor that he was, was also an incorrigible liar and reckless swashbuckler.) Despite this loss, the imperial troops pressed the attack against Ferrucci and his men so severely that, before long, two thousand Florentines lay dead in the streets of the hamlet. Finally, Ferrucci himself was seriously wounded, and the forces of the Republic, or what remained of them, fled in disarray. Ferrucci then was carried, bleeding and at the point of death, into the presence of one Fabrizio Maramaldo, a personal enemy, who commanded the imperial light cavalry. Maramaldo, a Calabrese, by origin and a hothead by temperament, was

thrown into a rage by the sight of the Florentine commander and, drawing his dagger, he stabbed Ferrucci until the latter died. Ferrucci's last
words were, "Would you kill one who is already dead?" With him died
the last hope of the Republic of Florence.

Still, the beleaguered city fought on. A contemporary chronicler
wrote admiringly: "The shops were kept open. The magistrates ad-
ministred justice. Business was transacted in the government offices.
Services were held in the churches. The squares and market-places were
crowded. There were neither brawls among the soldiers nor disputes
among the citizens." Despite this appearance of calm, the mood of the
war party had hardened. Lorenzo Soderini, for example, belonging to
a family so often opposed to the Medici in the past, was hanged simply
for communicating with Baccio Valori, a Medicean in the imperial
camp. Panic and desperation had come to becloud the judgement of
the government. In that atmosphere, it is difficult to understand why
Malatesta Baglioni, who repeatedly was suspected of being a traitor,
was allowed to remain in command of the besieged troops. But the
Perugian, a jocular opportunist, sat triumphantly on the fence. He
talked of liberty to one faction, of peace to another, of the virtues of
the Pope to a third, and of the advantages of oligarchy to a fourth.
He affirmed openly to his friends, when they asked why he visited
the council with a bodyguard, that he feared "to take the leap of
Baldaccio"—i.e., the rough but gallant soldier Baldaccio d'Anghiari,
murdered and thrown from the window of the *gonfalonier's* private
room in 1441, for reasons still not wholly clear. Baglioni, in fact, was
to be the instrument that finally brought Florence down. In the panic
that followed the news of Ferrucci's defeat and death, the Perugian, in
defiance of the orders of the Signory, began openly to negotiate with
Ferrante Gonzaga of Mantua, who had replaced the Prince of Orange
as commander of the imperial army. When the republican militia of
Florence, at the command of the Signory, attempted to arrest the
traitor, he turned his cannon on them. With their commander and his
men in open mutiny, and with the imperial forces as strong as ever,
no hope remained for Florence, and at last the starving city capitulated.
Envoys were sent to Gonzaga's camp, and articles of surrender were
signed on August 12, which stipulated, among other things, an indemnity of eighty thousand florins and the return of all exiled members of
the House of Medici and their supporters.

Baccio Valori, a Medicean of the imperial camp, took charge of
Florence for the time being, while the old cry of *"Palle! Palle!"* echoed
in the streets. Retribution was simple and straightforward. Francesco
Carducci was executed, and Girolami, the current *gonfalonier,* was imprisoned. The only other victim was a half-deranged monk of the
convent of San Marco who envisioned himself as a reincarnation of

Savonarola. This poor man was allowed to starve to death in the Roman dungeon of the Castle Sant' Angelo.

The next year, on July 5, Alessandro de' Medici entered the city. On July 6 he was declared head of the Republic—though the Republic by now existed only in name. In 1532, the Signory was abolished, and Alessandro was appointed *gonfalonier* for life.

The great days of Florence had long been over, but even after the death of Lorenzo the Magnificent, in 1492, the list of great names in the city's intellectual life had continued to grow. The architects Jacopo Sansovino, Raphael, and Michelangelo all worked at various times in Florence, following Bramante, who was born in Urbino and was active mainly in Lombardy and Rome, Bramonte survived till 1514. New sculptors, including Sansovino and Michelangelo, succeeded Verrocchio.

One of Michelangelo's outstanding masterpieces, the Nuovo Sagrestia, or New Sacristy, at the church of San Lorenzo in Florence, was commissioned by Clement VII early in his pontificate. The Pope, who showed so little judgement in other matters, was a great admirer of the sculptor and treated him with the respect that he would ordinarily have accorded a sovereign prince. "When Buonarotti comes to talk with me," Clement recorded, "I always sit down and then ask him to do the same, for I am certain that he would sit whether I asked him to or not." Despite the caution that Clement exercised in the presence of the temperamental genius, the New Sacristy was not, nor was it planned to be, an architectural masterpiece. It is a simple quadrangle, divided by pilasters and crowned by an unimposing dome. Its function was merely to serve as a backdrop for the statues that were to stand in the niches along the walls. The Sacristy—known also as the "Medici Chapel"—was completed in 1524. Clement, however, was eager for the crowning work, the sculptures. "You know," he wrote to Michelangelo, "that Popes are not blessed with a long life, and we wish, more than anything else, to see the chapel with the tombs of our kinsmen, or at least to know that it has been finished. . . . Neither commissions nor rewards will you lack so long as we are alive."

Of the six tombs planned—for Lorenzo the Magnificent, his brother Giuliano, Leo X, Clement VII, the younger Giuliano, and Lorenzo di Piero de' Medici—only two, those of the younger Giuliano and Lorenzo di Piero, were ever completed. These, however, are generally regarded as the crown of Renaissance sculpture, as the Sistine Chapel—executed by Michelangelo for Julius II—is considered to be that of Renaissance painting. The statues make no effort to reproduce the actual features of the two dukes. Perhaps the somewhat insignificant personalities involved would not have suited the solemnity of the setting; or perhaps it simply did not matter. Michelangelo himself observed, in this respect, "Who will care, a thousand years from now, whether or not these are

their features?" Giuliano is represented as a young man of heroic proportions, armoured, bare-headed, and apparently on the point of
rising to his feet to issue a command. Lorenzo, also dressed as a warrior, sits in a meditative attitude, chin in hand, his face shadowed by
his helmet. The two figures face each other in recesses that rise behind
their respective sarcophagi, the coffins resting on the floor. Each of the
stone tombs carries two recumbent nudes, one male and the other female. According to an old, and not necessarily accurate, tradition,
the nudes represent Dawn and Twilight in the case of Lorenzo, and
Day and Night in that of Giuliano. The sculptor is said to have remarked that, taken together, the figures illustrate "time, which con-
sumes all things."

Raphael, Botticelli, Filippino Lippi, Leonardo da Vinci, Perugino,
Lorenzo di Credi, Piero di Cosimo, and Fra Bartolommeo worked on as
painters after the great Lorenzo's death. Only in literature did memorable names grow fewer, after Politian, Ficino, Pulci, Pico della Mirandola, and Landino. The statesmen and historian Niccolò Machiavelli
and Francesco Guicciardini in prose, and the universal artist Michelangelo in poetry, then first acquired fame in those fields.

Of these last three, the two first were closely associated with and
admirers of the Medici family. Machiavelli, born in Florence, began his
adult career in 1494, the year of Piero's exile. It was not until the
revival of the Medicean influence that Machiavelli, already an experienced diplomat and enthusiastic student of the career of Cesare Borgia,
found himself a servant of the restored dynasty, although his previous
work for the deposed government kept him out of favour until the
pontificate of Leo X began in 1513. During this period of enforced un-
employment, Machiavelli devoted his talents, in a rustic and poverty-
stricken environment, to history and theoretical politics. His letters on
public affairs were not directly addressed to the Medici, but these
documents were meant to be brought to the attention of the family.

Machiavelli was a true Florentine democrat, in the sense that he
believed the ultimate strength of a people to reside in its masses, not
in its nobility and clergy; but he did not believe that this popular
energy could be advantageously released except under authoritarian
control. Even the earlier Medici, from Cosimo to Lorenzo the Magnificent, had recognised this principle, but they had always been careful to
disguise it in republican forms. Their successors, from Piero the Second
to Alessandro, had been less prudent.

Machiavelli wished to dedicate his most important work, *The Prince,*
to a Medici, but he was still distrusted by the existing representatives
of that house, which had by now outstripped Machiavelli himself in its
ideas of government by a single individual. Nevertheless, he exercised
enough influence on both Leo and Clement to bring them to the point

of considering a measure of autonomy for the Republic of Florence in particular. In 1519, when Cardinal Giulio de' Medici, the future Clement VII, took charge of the city, he applied for Machiavelli's advice on this subject. The political philosopher answered, in the first place, with a methodical treatise, "On the Art of War," setting forth the means by which in his view a republic could be rendered strong enough to maintain its independence. His democratic convictions appear in this essay's assertion of the superiority of national troops to mercenaries, and that of infantry to artillery. In a splendid peroration, he called upon the Medici magnates to liberate all Italy from its petty tyrants by employing such methods.

He then proceeded to write a history of Florence down to 1492, dedicated to Clement. In the spring of 1526, while the city was being administered by Cardinal Passerini on behalf of the two Medici boys, the Pope so far unbent as to nominate the historian to inspect the fortifications in existence at that time. In the summer, Machiavelli was allowed to attend his colleague Francesco Guicciardini, then acting as quarter-master-general of the papal forces in Lombardy. Guicciardini had always been a loyal Medici man. He liked Machiavelli and appreciated his ability. The two great historians accordingly became close friends, in spite of their differences in personal character. Guicciardini, a somewhat coldly critical intellectual and, at the same tme, a moral cynic, could hardly have been more of a contrast with a man who, for all his apparent cynicism in theory, was capable of a genuine nobility of sentiment. Machiavelli was also, unlike Guicciardini, a jovial, even rather dissipated figure in his hours of ease. There was a difference of fourteen years between them, and unfortunately for the development of this promising association of diverse temperaments, the older of the two friends, Machiavelli, died suddenly in the summer of 1527, at the age of fifty-eight.

Guicciardini, for his part, entered the service of Leo X in 1515, when he was thirty-two. Consequently, both these able intellectuals were in a position to observe the Medici family at about the same time. They each came to favourable conclusions, but Guicciardini showed less hesitation, or more determination, in laying plans to rise to fortune under Medicean egis. It is true that he had been given a better start than Machiavelli. By 1523, Pope Clement VII had appointed him papal vice-regent of Romagna, but nothing had been done by the Papacy by that date for Machiavelli's worldly advancement. In the fatal year, 1527, Guicciardini, as lieutenant-general of the Pontiff's army, could not induce Francesco Maria della Rovere, the Duke of Urbino, to take any military steps to defend Clement, whose family had formerly expelled that once excellent soldier from his duchy. Yet the steadfastly loyal historian did not for that reason lose the confidence of the Holy

Father, even in the ruin that the duke's inactivity had helped to bring upon him.

Guicciardini's political ideas, however, resembled Machiavelli's in their failure to correspond with the notions of government entertained by the later Medici. This result had nevertheless been reached along rather different lines by the two men. In particular it is clear that Francesco abominated the secular ambitions of Leo and Clement. His ideal, like Savonarola's, was a commonwealth on the Venetian model. Machiavelli preferred the ancient Roman Republic. Again, Guicciardini saw that the Medicean system of his day was little better than a tyranny, yet he went farther in promoting it than warranted by his beliefs.

As for the painters during this last stage of the Florentine Republic (1492–1530), Botticelli in his later life became a religious fanatic under Savonarola's influence and, on principle, practically abandoned art. He would therefore have starved if representatives of the junior branch of the Medici, Giovanni di Pierfrancesco, who married Caterina Sforza, and his nephew Pierfrancesco di Lorenzo, the cousin of Giovanni delle Bande Nere, had not come to his rescue. He died in 1510.

His pupil Filippino Lippi returned to Florence from Rome in 1493. In 1496, he painted an "Adoration of the Magi" for the Florentine church of San Donato. This altarpiece, now in the Uffigi Gallery, contains portraits of the above-mentioned Pierfrancesco de' Medici the Younger and certain other members of the junior branch of the family who had supported Filippino's master in his old age. The Dominican monk Fra Bartolommeo produced, when about twenty, the best surviving portrait of Savonarola and thereafter fell wholly under the ascetic prior's influence, flinging, like Lorenzo di Credi, all his studies from the nude into the "bonfire of vanities." But he resumed them in 1513, long after Savonarola's death, with great effect. It was then that he did his picture of Sebastian, a splendidly virile evocation of masculine beauty that much perturbed the ladies who came to St. Mark's to confess their sins. The friars were repeatedly told by their fair penitents that the painting had inspired them to commit the adulteries that they tearfully acknowledged. Consequently, this striking work was withdrawn from the convent and eventually sold to the French King, Francis I. No doubt he found it a useful instrument in his endless seductions of his feminine subjects.

The Florentine painter Andrea del Sarto (1486–1531) was praised to Raphael by Michelangelo, but he is mainly of interest in a history of the Medici for having copied in Rome Raphael's composite portrait of Pope Leo X, the future Pope Clement VII, and their cousin Cardinal Luigi de' Rossi, son of Maria de' Medici, the illegitimate sister of Lorenzo the Magnificent.

The circumstances in which this copy was made are somewhat unusual. The story begins with a plot by the rogue satirist Pietro Aretino, then in Rome, to put the Marquis of Mantua, with whom he had been staying, so far in his debt than the ruler in question would refuse him nothing.

"*Messer* Pietro Aretino," wrote Francesco Gonzaga, the Mantuan ambassador in Rome, to his cousin the Marquis, "told me that while talking to the Pope [Clement VII] three evenings ago he informed His Holiness that you had lately mentioned your keen desire to have the picture by that great artist, recently deceased, Raphael of Urbino, which is now in Florence, representing the late Pope Leo of blessed memory, our present Pope himself, and certain others, all as large as life. The Pope has ordered this picture to be sent to you at Mantua and says he would gladly do more to give you pleasure."

The picture, however, did not turn up at Mantua within a reasonable time. Francesco Gonzaga, at the marquess's urgent request, asked Pietro to investigate. The Aretine reported that Clement had commanded "a certain excellent painter in Florence" to make a copy, which His Holiness wished to keep in memory of Pope Leo, and that as soon as the copy was finished, the original would be sent to Mantua. It would be accompanied, Pietro went on, by an ode that he himself had composed in honour of the Mantuan ruler. Francesco added, faithfully transcribing the intermediary's demands in detail: "I would pray Your Excellency to have sent to the Aretine two pairs of shirts worked with gold, as the fashion now is, and two other pairs of shirts worked in silk, together with two golden caps."

The marquis never got his Raphael. Instead, the sly Pontiff sent him the copy by Andrea del Sarto, correctly anticipating that the recipient would be none the wiser. Pietro was luckier than his patron, for he got his shirts. Federigo Gonzaga was not a very perceptive art critic, but del Sarto's copy, which its bearer, one Ottaviano de' Medici, known only from this incident, assured the marquess was the original, must have been excellent. Raphael's pupil, Giulio Romano, who had actually helped Raphael with the portrait, himself could not believe that Andrea's copy was not the original.

One easel painting, or rather the cartoon for one, by Michelangelo, was purchased for the Medici Palace about 1512–13, just after the return of Giuliano the Second and his young nephew Lorenzo to the city. It represented Florentine soldiers surprised, while bathing, by Sir John Hawkwood's troops in 1364. The cartoon soon disappeared, probably during the last illness of Giuliano in 1516, but copies have survived.

Jacopo da Pontormo (1494–1556), a pupil of Andrea del Sarto, painted several excellent portraits of Cosimo de' Medici for a cell that Cosimo had intended to occupy in St. Mark's convent, where one of Pontormo's representations of him can still be seen. Jacopo also painted

Cardinal Ippolito de' Medici, a work now in the Uffizi Gallery. He decorated, too, the Medici villa at Poggio a Caiano with murals depicting pageantry. His pupil Angiolo Allori, known as Il Bronzino (1503–72), also painted several fine portraits, preserved in the same gallery, of the family, as well as portraits of Dante, Petrarch, and Boccaccio. He became court painter to Grand Duke Cosimo I of Tuscany, the son of Giovanni of the Black Bands.

By the beginning of the sixteenth century, the extraordinary cultural independence of Florence was passing away, just as her cultural domination had passed away when Rome, under the initial impact of Leo X, the first Medici Pope, transformed the Renaissance from a Florentine product into a universal possession of mankind. There had been a time when painters such as Fra Angelico and even Botticelli produced masterpieces in which a *tertium quid,* a certain something Florentine, was distinguishable. Such work was, in fact, Florentine, painted in Florence, under the patronage of Florentines, for the edification of Florentines. That time was no more. Such titans as Michelangelo, Leonardo, and Raphael were human rather than geographical phenomena, and they worked equally well, one may believe, whether in Florence, Rome, Milan, Venice, or anywhere else.

The development of literature proved less homogeneous and continuous, often broken as it was by external influences. Between the time of Dante, Petrarch, and Boccaccio and that of Lorenzo the Magnificent—an interval of about one century—there was nothing essentially Florentine in the writing of the Florentines, except perhaps in the lively tales of Franco Sacchetti (1335–1410), an imitator of Boccaccio. Lorenzo's group, however, in the latter part of the quattrocento, or fifteenth century, achieved a unique character in the gayety and brilliance of Pulci, Politian, and even of Lorenzo himself—which served to offset the artificial and rhetorical magniloquence of the prose of such men as Ficino and even of Pico della Mirandola. Thereafter, the originality of Machiavelli and of Guicciardini in their production of scientific history, and perhaps in the former's comedy, *Mandragola,* stands practically alone as a Florentine literary phenomenon against the genius of the Emilian epic poet Ariosto, who worked at Ferrara; the exquisite stylistic purity of the Venetian scholar and cardinal, Pietro Bembo, who rivalled the Florentine *literati* of the previous generation; and the Roman poetess Vittoria Colonna, revered friend of Michelangelo.

The movement of cultural inspiration away from Florence to other centers during the sixteenth century is clearly illustrated by the case of the Florentine sculptor Benvenuto Cellini (1500–71). After 1519, Cellini lived mainly in Rome, where his loyalty to Pope Clement during the tragic events of 1527 caused him to be recalled to Florence as soon as the Signory and the Pope found themselves on opposite sides of the political fence. Thereafter, he lived in Mantua, Naples, and Rome again, before returning to Florence. He worked everywhere he went, and everything that he produced was of Cellini rather than of Florence; what he produced in Rome, for example, was for the glory of Rome rather than of his native city. Such an attitude resulted from, more than it caused, the loss of that specifically regional and peculiar character that had hitherto distinguished Florentines both in action and in contemplation, including the best of the Medici, Cosimo and the great Lorenzo.

Such traits had rendered the history of Florence culturally more significant than that of any other Italian community. Strong personalities, above all those of many of the Medici, and daring experiments in political theory, repeatedly influenced by Medicean practice, combined with the dazzling artistic and literary achievements patronised by nearly all the members of that remarkable family, however objectionable they might be in other respects, make up a strange tale of imaginative triumph and moral failure, a story, therefore, essentially tragic.

Lofty administrative ideals were never realised. The incessant struggle for freedom from civic tyranny never succeeded, for the cool mentality necessary to maintain such independence hardly existed in Florence. In general, the citizens shared with other Italians of their time a recurrent and selfish egotism—elsewhere regularly repressed by despots—which manifested itself in those rivalries, feuds, factions, and conspiracies that wrecked successive governments. Neither the tact of Cosimo and Lorenzo the Magnificent, the uncompromising religious severity of Savonarola, nor the concentration of so many eminent Florentine humanists upon the virtues of the ancient Roman Republic could teach moral restraint and true public spirit to the men of Florence.

V

THE DECADENCE

(*1530–1743*)

1. Alessandro de' Medici

The entry of Alessandro de' Medici into Florence, on July 5, 1531, it will be remembered, was not an auspicious occasion. The city lay crushed under the heel of the Holy Roman Emperor Charles V, and its Constitution and laws had just been revised at the dictates of Pope Clement VII. Moreover, the city's memories of Alessandro during the time that he had "governed" the Florentines, with his cousin Ippolito, under the tutelage of the fumbling Cardinal Passerini, were as unenthusiastic as Alessandro himself was unprepossessing. Pope Clement, however, had little choice in the matter. If the Pope wished to retain control of Florentine affairs—and he certainly wished that—then he must have a Medici as the Florentine head of the state. And Alessandro, unfortunately, was the only male member of the senior Medici branch who was available. His more promising and younger cousin, Ippolito, was in Holy Orders, a cardinal, and hardly in a position to found a dynasty.

Alessandro—now twenty years old and betrothed to Margaret, the eleven-year-old bastard daughter of the Emperor—arrived in Florence, therefore, clutching in his hand a document, signed by Charles V, that declared that he and his heirs were to rule the Florentine state in perpetuity. The cautious Charles had been careful to add that the traditional Constitution—i.e., as reformed so many times—must remain in force. Perhaps the Emperor, who always set much store by the appearance of respectability, was not greatly taken by the less than refined look of his prospective son-in-law; or it may be that he had heard rumors of Alessandro's morals.

Though the Emperor's intentions in 1531 are somewhat nebulous, his intentions in the following year are not. In April 1532, Pope Clement declared, with Charles' approval, that the ostensible Republic of Florence was at an official end, and that henceforth its territory would be known as the Duchy of Tuscany. Alessandro, instead of being called the head of the state, was now the Duke of Tuscany. Moreover, in line with this new arrangement, the offices of prior and *gonfalonier* were to be abolished and replaced by that of the hereditary duke, a Council of Two Hundred, a Senate of forty-eight members, and an "inner Cabinet" of three citizens. These last were Baccio Valori, a hitherto unswerving Medicean who was, nonetheless, to desert to the republican exiles in 1535; Francesco Vettori, a solemn pedant who, in 1523, had argued pontifically against attempts to limit Cardinal Passerini's powers; and finally, Francesco Guicciardini, that judicious historian and military patriot. None of these offices, of course, from that of the new duke to the lowest, possessed more than the appearance of authority. All power rested, in the last resort, in the hands of Pope Clement VII.

In these circumstances, the new officials of the Florentine Government were agreeably surprised to find Alessandro a fairly good-natured and co-operative young man. They could detect no sign in him either of that arrogant indifference to affairs of state that had caused the ruin of his grandfather, Piero the Second, or of those undesirable personal traits that had already caused him to be described by a contemporary as "a vicious, ill-tempered bastard." The boy was certainly not a fool, they concluded, nor was he by any means devoid of a characteristic Medicean adroitness and amiability in social intercourse. They might have reflected, however, that Clement, in his early years, had displayed the same kind of promise. For a year or two, therefore, the Cabinet, Senate, and Council of Two Hundred felt that they could manage Alessandro without too much friction. Favourable reports on the situation were transmitted to the Vatican, which in its turn kept up a private correspondence, no doubt of an admonitory as well as benevolent description, with Alessandro.

It may be assumed that Alessandro felt himself to be running in harness, for when the Pope died on September 25, 1534, to be succeeded by Cardinal Alessandro Farnese, who took the title of Paul III, Duke Alessandro de' Medici, now free of the control of his anxious kinsman, began to emerge in his true colours. He shocked Florence by organising and participating in sexual orgies of a kind to which the city had hitherto rarely been exposed—unlike many other Italian cities, notably Rome—at this period. Guicciardini in particular was repelled by such behaviour, and he and other leading citizens contacted Cardinal Ippolito de' Medici with a view to sounding him about a change of government. Encouraged by this development, a number of disgruntled Florentine exiles in Rome rallied around the young prelate and complained to the Emperor. They stressed, however, Alessandro's tyrannical conduct in general, since Clement's death, rather than his excessive eroticism. Ippolito told Charles that he would be willing to take over the administration of Florence unofficially, just as Cardinal Giulio had before his election to the Papacy. The perennially impecunious Emperor was then offered a substantial bribe if he would consent to this reorganisation of the city's affairs.

The monarch, then in Tunis, which he had just captured in pursuance of his policy of forcing back Muslim aggression in every direction, did not reply at once to the cardinal's urgent despatch. Ippolito therefore set out to visit him. By August 10, 1535, the prelate had reached Itri, in the south-west corner of Latium, when he was suddenly taken ill and perished in a few days. It was rumoured, and it is not unlikely in the circumstances, that Cardinal Ippolito was poisoned at the order of Alessandro, who must have been aware of the plot to replace him.

On the Emperor's subsequent arrival in Naples he granted an audience to the Florentine expatriates. As a result of what they told him, he immediately summoned Alessandro to present himself at Naples and answer the charges brought against him. The duke obeyed, but he took the wise precaution of inviting the hitherto secretly dissident Guicciardini to accompany him. The ambitious historian, flattered by this honour, calculated that his own fortunes would be best served by reassuring the most powerful autocrat in Europe about the antics of a man who had long since been betrothed, by agreement between Clement and Charles, to the latter's illegitimate daughter, Margaret.

The case against the duke, as presented by Jacopo Nardi, leader of the republican exiles, seemed irrefutable. Alessandro was proved to have violated again and again the terms of the surrender treaty signed in 1530; to have attacked and ruined prominent members of the government and the nobility; to have forced their younger female relatives to submit to his lust; and, in every way, to have behaved more like an irresponsible criminal of the crudest type than as the representative of an illustrious house that had, in the past, made of Florence the most civilised community in Europe.

Two purely personal considerations made the verdict a foregone conclusion regardless of the evidence: first, Guicciardini was the most powerful orator in Italy; second, the Emperor, with whom of course the ultimate decision lay, had no intention of publicly acknowledging his prospective son-in-law to be an unconscionable ruffian. Charles, after hearing Guicciardini's coldly elegant repudiation of the charges, which Guicciardini characterised as no more than the malice of a defeated faction, merely promised that he would send an imperial minister to Florence to ensure that in the future the conduct of the accused in constitutional matters gave no excuse for ill-natured gossip. The allegations of murderous oppression and sexual violence were ignored. Nardi and his witnesses could only pack up their papers and leave the court in an appalled silence. Guicciardini had completely persuaded Charles—who, of course, wished to be persuaded—that Alessandro had been grossly calumniated.

The ducal party returned to Florence in triumph, and Alessandro, convinced apparently that this reprieve provided absolution for future sins, embarked on what amounted to a career of debauchery. To his delight, he found an almost equally depraved relative in the junior branch of the family, one Lorenzino di Pierfrancesco de' Medici, who, Alessandro thought, would make an excellent procurer and companion in concupiscence.

This Lorenzino was a slightly built, leering, and somewhat obsequious young man of twenty-one years, studious and delicate in appearance but subtle and resolute in the pursuit of his ambitions. From his mother, Maria Soderini, daughter of the staunchly republican Tommaso Soderini, Lorenzino had inherited an abiding hatred of tyranny. From his father, Pierfrancesco de' Medici the Younger, he had inherited nothing but a respected name and a number of illustrious kinsmen. This heritage, combining with Lorenzino's undoubted intelligence, had produced a complex of resentments in the young man. He saw, at the apex of power and honour in Florence, a young Medici, and an illegitimate one at that, with half his brains, while he himself was unknown and penniless. With the pride of his house, and none of its emoluments, he grew first sullenly resentful and then subtly aggressive.

In 1530, these sentiments had taken the form, nourished by Lorenzino's classical studies, of a fierce detestation of hereditary authority. He expressed it by an attempt to destroy the stone remains of ancient Roman grandeur, statues and other monuments still to be found in the Holy City, where he was then seeking his fortune. Like Alcibiades, he went about at night defacing and overthrowing such images, for they represented, in his view, a wickedly oppressive imperialism. He was arrested and brought before Pope Clement. Cardinal Ippolito de' Medici, barely three years older than the sixteen-year-old delinquent, generously defended this iconoclasm as mere youthful ebullience. But the Pope was not amused. He exiled the culprit from Rome to Florence.

Lorenzino did not like what he found in the city of his ancestors. He knew Alessandro of old, having lived with him and Ippolito in the Medici Palace at Rome. The angry young student of ancient literature despised the brutishness of his distant relative, but he recognised that the duke's power was at least theoretically absolute. Alessandro could as easily make a poor but proud man's fortune as he could have him assassinated. Lorenzino wanted the social position he felt to be due to his rank and capacities even more than he wanted to establish freedom and justice over the whole earth. In fact, the latter ideal, he saw, could not be attained without first acquiring the former. He determined, therefore, as a preliminary step, to gain by any means whatever, including the basest, the esteem, and if possible the affection, of his crude but ducal Medici kinsman.

By 1532, the two young men—the intellectual fanatic on the pattern of Alcibiades and Brutus, and the pitiless sex maniac on the pattern of Caligula—were getting on famously together. Alessandro knew that he was physically the master of Lorenzino, as of every male or female in Florence. Nothing else mattered to him. He remained incapable of wondering why a man who could quote Cicero and Machiavelli by the hour should trouble to make himself so exceptionally agreeable to a man who had never opened a book since he came to Florence. The chance of such a subservient and ingenious accomplice in criminal enterprises was not to be missed.

Their intimacy went far enough for Lorenzino to risk openly confessing to the duke that he was in touch with the anti-Medicean exiles in Rome, but only, he said, in order to ascertain and foil their schemes. He had in fact sounded them. But he found that, although they all hated Alessandro like poison, as did also Ippolito and the new Farnese Pope, Paul III, they could not agree on the best method of getting rid of him. Nor would they trust their correspondent, a "faithless Medici" whom they knew to be without funds or influence among secretly republican Florentines. Nor did they care for certain unpleasant tales that were now beginning to be heard about Lorenzino's morals, in his capacity as procurer for the duke. Lorenzino, more embittered than ever by such treatment, concluded that nothing was to be expected from so suspicious and timid a crew of wranglers. He resolved, come what might, to act alone. He was not yet sure, however, just how to act.

It was at that moment of indecision that the debonair Ippolito, in Rome, suddenly determined to bring the unsatisfactory position in Florence to a head at the highest possible level. Titian's portrait of him, with mace and sword and nodding plume, subtly stresses the jutting black beard, hard features, and stern eyes of the born soldier he had always wanted to be, instead of the courtly and cultivated prelate most people saw in him. No existing Medici could have been more suitable in courage and intelligence, as well as by the material resources he commanded, for the job in hand; for this unusual cardinal, sick of the hesitations of the exiles, now meant to tackle in person, as none but he could, with the whole weight of his striking personality, another formidable military man, the Emperor himself, actually the prospective father-in-law of the rascally despot he and Clement had forced upon Florence.

Lorenzino, when he heard the tragic story of Ippolito's death, was overcome by an extraordinary anger, superbly masked in Alessandro's presence by the sly gayety of a pander. He was certain the duke had arranged for the dangerous Ippolito to be poisoned, and it was this crime, combined with the failure of the formal arraignment of Alessandro before Charles at Naples, that finally caused the solitary conspirator to proceed to extreme measures. He was confident that the action he intended would be approved by every decent man in Italy, a majority that excluded Charles V and Francesco Guicciardini. This belief of Lorenzino's was reinforced when he met, by chance, in Rome, a young soldier of some renown, Piero Strozzi, son of Filippo. Strozzi had demanded impatiently, upon meeting Lorenzino, what the latter proposed to do now about Alessandro, implying that the result of the recent trial of the tyrant before the Emperor might have caused a loss of nerve in the former assiduous Florentine correspondent of the Roman refugees. Lorenzino answered darkly, between his teeth: "You'll soon know what sort of a man I am." He refused to reply to further questions, pleading that he was in a hurry to rejoin the ducal party. Piero, who had learnt discretion in war, nodded solemnly and took his leave, probably supposing the pallid civilian's remark to be a mere cover for his confusion.

Strozzi would have been very much surprised if he could have overheard his scholarly friend coolly telling Alessandro, as they jogged back together on the road to Florence, exactly what had passed at that encounter. Lorenzino related the conversation in his usual style of devoted adherent, with contemptuous amusement at Strozzi's anxiety. The duke, in the highest spirits after his triumph at the late hearing, joined heartily in his favourite's laughter.

In the spring of 1536, Charles V paid a formal visit to Florence, assuring the citizens of his good will and his plans for their future prosperity. In June, his daughter Margaret arrived for her marriage to the duke. She was accompanied by some of the Florentine exiles whom the Emperor, as promised, had pardoned. During the ensuing festivities, a comedy by Lorenzino was produced. Although the piece was merely an adequate imitation of the ancient Roman conventions in this line, Alessandro, in an exultant mood, roared with laughter and congratulated the author effusively.

For the rest of the year, time passed in Florence much as it had passed before. Lorenzino and the duke continued to be inseparable in their debaucheries, revelling in the palace, raiding convents, and storming private houses in their search for amourous adventure. Scandal after scandal came to light, but no one dared to say a word.

It was known that free speech, to say nothing of conspiracy, would be immediately betrayed and punished with ruin or assassination.

During the New Year's carnival of 1537, on the night of January 5, Lorenzino escorted the duke to his own relatively modest lodgings adjoining the palace and left him there, promising to return shortly with a certain lady, the wife of one Leonardo Ginori. The lady was actually Lorenzino's aunt, being the sister of his mother, Maria Soderini, and she was known to be extremely virtuous. Alessandro, who had as usual drunk a good deal of wine, soon fell asleep. When Lorenzino returned, however, after a short absence, he was followed not by Signora Ginori, but by a professional assassin known as Scoronconcolo, or the "Nutsheller."

The exact details of what then occurred were variously reported afterwards by Lorenzino himself and contemporary chroniclers. It seems certain, however, that Lorenzino first fastened the sleeping duke's belt and sword-hilt together in such a way that the weapon could not be drawn. He then drew out his own rapier and thrust it with all his strength through the slumbering despot's broad back, which was turned towards him. Alessandro, rolling over with a deep groan, tried to grapple with his assailant. The latter, to prevent his calling out more loudly, rammed two fingers down the dying man's throat, whereupon the convulsively struggling duke bit them to the bone. A frantic tussle began. Scoronconcolo, in these circumstances, required a few seconds to find the victim's neck with his dagger, but at last he plunged the blade in under the chin, twisting it expertly in the wound. Lorenzino wrenched his profusely bleeding fingers free and staggered back. Alessandro's head fell back, and the plump body twitched and writhed for a moment, then lay still. Scoronconcolo withdrew his dagger and stood up, grinning savagely.

The murderers drew the sheets of the bed over the blood-stained corpse. Lorenzino pinned on these coverings a paper bearing a line from the *Aeneid* (Vol. VI, p. 183): *Vincit amor patriae laudumque immensa cupido*. ("Love of country and unbounded desire for glory shall conquer.") Then the two assassins fled together to Venice.

Lorenzino, like all the men of his house, had been well educated. In Renaissance Italy, as in classical times, a well-educated man meant one who could prepare a good brief. The studious young Medici possessed the intelligence as well as the training that enabled him to do so. His subsequently written *Apology* was composed with considerable skill and eloquence, and it was probably quite sincere. He may really have been sure, like so many classical scholars of his day and before, that the murder of a cruel autocrat was a patriotic duty. He may have thought himself quite justified in engineering Alessandro's dissipations and praising his crimes in order to eliminate all prior suspicion of animosity.

Ambition of some sort, however, or at any rate the longing to make a glorious name for himself, cannot be ruled out. He knew that he had a better claim to the succession than the only other possible candidate, his eighteen-year-old cousin Cosimo, who descended from the younger son of Pierfrancesco the Elder through the two Giovannis, whereas he himself traced his descent from the first Giovanni's senior brother Lorenzo di Pierfrancesco. Yet he had good reason, as a murderer of the reigning duke, to fear the vengeance of Cosimo or his advisor. It was no doubt because he considered such a reaction likely that he decided to take leave of the city for a while.

Lorenzino had certainly also been warned by the fate of previous imitators of Brutus, who had taken people into his confidence and killed his man in public, that it would be best to rely upon himself alone until the very last moment, when a bravo could be hired and easily, if necessary, silenced forever afterwards. The *Apology* proves that Lorenzino knew the truth had already come out, or soon would, but perhaps he gambled on its remaining a mystery long enough to lead to his recall. On the whole, this incentive to the murder—the mere desire to take Alessandro's place, as a mature hero, as an extremely articulate and courageous intellectual, who had already proved his patriotism, accords well with Lorenzino's peculiar character. It was that of a cultured but wholly unbalanced voluptuary, whose genuine *amor patriae* alone, the defence he alleged in the *Apology,* would hardly have spurred him to murder.

With Alessandro's death, the senior branch of the Medici—apart from the legitimate Caterina, daughter of the dead Lorenzo, Duke of Urbino—came to an end. But Caterina had now been married for three years to the Duke of Orléans, afterwards King Henri II of France. Technically, the leading representative of the junior line, after Lorenzino himself, could be none other than Cosimo, for Alessandro had died without fathering any legitimate offspring. Yet the ingenious author of the *Apology* might well have believed that he could outwit, divert, or even poison Cosimo.

It was not to be. Guicciardini and the Senate favoured the choice of Cosimo, who was moreover immediately accessible, being then in residence at the Trebbio villa of the Medici in the Mugello hills near Florence. No one dreamed of suggesting a resuscitation of the Republic.

2. Cosimo I

The accession of Cosimo de' Medici as Duke of Tuscany seemed to the dissident Florentine republicans to afford an opportunity for a *coup* by which the new autocracy would be replaced by a more liberal regime. These republicans, most of whom were in exile from Florence, assembled a respectable force of some four thousand infantry and three hundred horses, in addition to a strong French contingent. Under Piero Strozzi (the son of Filippo) and Bernardo Salviati, this army invaded Tuscany in July 1537.

The regime of the new duke was not remiss in meeting the challenge. A force comprising foreign mercenaries and German and Spanish troops of the imperial army, as well as native Florentines, all under the command of Alessandro Vitelli, was hastily assembled, and marched out to meet the army of the republicans. The two groups clashed near Prato, to the north-west of Florence, on August 1; and Cosimo's men won a resounding victory, and a number of leading republicans were captured.

Strozzi had fallen into the error common to all who attacked Florence. He had supposed that the city was restless and unhappy under Cosimo, and that the news of a republican uprising would be greeted in Florence by an enthusiastic revolt against Medici rule. Nothing could have been farther from the truth. After the self-indulgent tyranny of Duke Alessandro, Cosimo's rule appeared to the Florentines, in the short time in which they had been able to observe it, to be a model of competence. He had come to the ducal throne with the reputation of a boyish nonentity, concerned with nothing but athletics. But no sooner had he tasted power than he grasped the reins of government firmly in his own hands, and his enemies came to realise that here, indeed, was the son of Giovanni delle Bande Nere. Among his first acts was the banishment of those citizens who were in any way suspected of resisting the ducal authority.

The severity was extended to the republicans captured on August 1, some of whom were young men of good family who had formerly been friendly with Cosimo. They were brought back to Florence and locked up in the Bargello, and four of them were publicly beheaded on four successive mornings in the courtyard. On August 20, Baccio Valori, his son, and his nephew were likewise decapitated, but the young head of the state spared the life of the handsome old rake Filippo Strozzi, who had been so generous with his money to so many Florentines, both Medicean and anti-Medicean. Cosimo merely kept the banker behind bars.

The Strozzi Palace, and as much of the family's property as the Medici could lay hands on, were confiscated. On December 18, the unfortunate Filippo, still a popular figure in Florence, was found dead in his cell, with a sword through his heart and a paper beside him, inscribed with the words of Virgil, *Exoriare aliquis nostris ex ossibus ultor*. ("Some avenger shall arise from our bones.") The presence of this note indicates that Filippo's death was voluntary, though some later anti-Medicean chroniclers insist that he was killed at Cosimo's orders.

Many have censured the new duke's conduct on this occasion, which recalls the ferocity, at the same early age, of his father. Whether a perfectly impartial contemporary observer would have found it extraordinary is doubtful. The prisoners were treasonable outlaws who had plotted to overthrow, by force, the legitimate government of Florence. If released, they would almost certainly have tried again. Their most dangerous leaders, even in prison, would have been a serious threat of disaffection. It was only to be anticipated, in the moral climate of sixteenth-century Italy, that a young man, disposed to stern measures both by heredity and by the relative insecurity of a position into which he had only recently been precipitated by the fortune of an unexpected assassination, should react to such a challenge by summary executions.

Significantly enough, the rest of Cosimo's long reign until his very last years shows a progressive improvement in his character. He never grew conspicuously merciful, but he did grow more judicious. Nonetheless, after the events of his early reign, many people came to think of Cosimo as the incarnation of Machiavelli's prince in the entirely unscrupulous and pitiless furtherance of his aims. Guicciardini, for instance, who had hoped to be able to dominate the duke, found he could do nothing of the kind. He retreated from public life, though still protesting his loyalty to Cosimo, and died among his books in 1540.

By that time, Cosimo's "Machiavellism" had made him so generally feared that rumour at once charged him with having poisoned the artful elder statesman for continuing attempts to undermine the ducal authority. Ever since the experiments of the medieval alchemists, poison had been mentioned, and was to go on being mentioned, whenever a well-known man or woman died, suddenly or otherwise, except on the battlefield. In the case of Guicciardini, Cosimo had no reason to suspect the historian—whom he knew quite well—as a naturally rebellious character. The innate cynicism of the old student of human nature and public affairs directed his mind far more to sycophancy than to conspiracy, a trait that must have been very clear to so perceptive a ruler as the young duke.

Cosimo was perhaps not interested in poisons, but he did not hesitate at this time to make free, by proxy, with the dagger. His bravos roamed foreign cities in search of anyone who talked too loudly of tyranny in Florence. Lorenzino, for example, in Venice, was suspected, probably with good cause, of plotting against his distant kinsman, and he was to be duly assassinated in 1547, at the age of thirty-two.

After his victory over the republicans, Cosimo proceeded with plans to consolidate his position under the Emperor. He first asked Charles for the hand of Alessandro's young widow, Margaret, who was the Emperor's own daughter. This request was haughtily refused, and so the duke then applied to the next most powerful man in the imperial service, Pedro of Toledo, the Viceroy of Naples. This ruler had an only child named Eleonora, aged seventeen, a personable young woman of high character and intelligence, with whom a rich dowry could be expected. Pedro agreed, and the marriage took place early in 1539, at the church of San Lorenzo in Florence.

The duke then transferred his residence from the Medici Palace in the Via Larga—which he considered inadequately protected for the ruler of a city with a long history of turbulence—to the Palazzo Vecchio, a building more like a fortress. He accommodated his bodyguard of Swiss pike-men, during their hours of duty, in the open Hall of Justice erected by the Florentine architect Orcagna in the fourteenth century and adjoining the Palazzo Vecchio. This structure therefore came to be known as the Loggia dei Lanzi, the "Lancers' Guardroom." Cosimo and Eleonora themselves lived in the Palazzo Vecchio for the next ten years.

In 1542, the struggle between Charles and the King of France, Francis I, was renewed, after a truce that had lasted four years. Cosimo at once took the side of the Emperor and supplied that sovereign with contributions from the ample funds available to the duke through his marriage to Eleonora. Charles gradually began to regard this valuable paymaster as his mainstay in Italy. Once more the characteristic Medicean genius for making money do the work of diplomacy and armies came into play. In 1544 another truce was signed between the chief antagonists. As a result of grants of territory from the grateful Emperor, Cosimo's dominions were considerably enlarged.

In 1546, Cosimo's forces drove back a hostile expedition from Lucca, led by Piero Strozzi. Cosimo, however, did not take the field in person. He was no soldier, in spite of his resolute and peremptory disposition, and he did not intend to risk impeding his ambition by submitting to capture or defeat. In 1547, the deaths of three notable personalities—Francis I, Henry VIII of England, and Martin Luther—materially increased Emperor Charles' power and consequently that of Cosimo. Between them, these two prudent leaders were easily able to check the reactionary schemes of Pope Paul III, who had been encouraged by the recommendations of the Council of Trent in 1545, and Luther's death two years later, to block the ecclesiastical reforms in favour with more liberal prelates.

Two years later, Cosimo once more was able to come to the rescue of Charles by pacifying the Sienese, who had revolted against the

Emperor and driven his Spanish garrison out of the city. The master of Florence actually persuaded his imperial overlord to allow the ancient republican form of government in Siena to be restored, on condition that an imperial officer and garrison should also be reinstated. This statesmanlike act, however, cynical in its conception, indicates that Cosimo had already begun evolving, perhaps to some extent under his sensible wife's influence, into a reasonably circumspect, and even far-sighted, sort of ruler. Yet he was still a year short of thirty.

By early 1550, the duke felt firmly enough established in power, at home as well as abroad, to anticipate a move from the Palazzo Vecchio. He began work on a new palace on the north-western slope of Mount Boboli, south of the Arno. The site was occupied, at the bottom of the hill, by the still unfinished mansion begun by Luca Pitti, in 1459, during the closing years of the ascendancy of Cosimo the Elder. The edifice, as completed by Cosimo I, is still known as the Pitti Palace, although it owes very little to Brunelleschi's original design of 1440 for Luca. The new palace, moreover, was to be greatly expanded during the next two hundred years of Medicean government in Florence. The massive structure seen today includes only a small central section constructed by Ammanati, architect to Cosimo I. The duke himself supervised the splendid gardens behind the Boboli building, for he possessed to the full the Italian love of work of this kind. He also wished to provide in this way a playground for his children, of whom there were now eight.

A further amelioration of the character of Cosimo I, whose early severities have perhaps given him too sinister a reputation among a few historians, was manifested at this time in his archeological interests. He undertook excavations in the territory once known as Etruria, and he collected both Etruscan and Egyptian antiquities. The Florentine artists Giorgio Vasari and Angelo Allori, called Bronzino, who lived at his court, were commissioned to collect pictures, sculpture, and pottery, some of which had belonged to earlier Medici and been dispersed among other families. Bronzino, according to his colleague Vasari, "painted all the great men of the house of Medici, beginning with Giovanni dei Bicci and Cosimo the Elder, down to the Queen of France [Caterina de' Medici] in that line, and in the line of Lorenzo, brother of Cosimo the Elder, down to Duke Cosimo and his children." Eleonora, of whom Bronzino produced one of his best portraits, may once more have influenced Cosimo in these cultural directions.

Politically, it was now becoming clear that Cosimo meant to bring the whole of Tuscany under his firm control. He acted with especial determination at Siena and Lucca. The former city, despite Cosimo's magnanimous treatment of it in 1548, continued as hostile to Florence as it had always been, and it was at this period a refuge for republican exiles. In 1552, King Henri II of France, the husband of Caterina de' Medici, who did not care much for Cosimo, encouraged the Sienese to revolt once more against their Spanish garrison. The citizens of Siena managed to expel the Spaniards, and, for the second time, they accepted a French garrison instead. Cosimo immediately communicated with both Charles and Henri, coolly demanding troops from each of them to enable him to recover Siena. The Emperor, who had recently been doing badly against the competitive Henri, was alarmed at the prospect of an agreement between the French King and the duke he had himself encouraged to acquire such power in Tuscany. A relief force was quickly despatched from Naples at Charles' orders, but owing to the death of the viceroy, Eleonora's father, it failed to retrieve the situation. A mixed army of the Emperor's Germans, Swiss, and Spaniards then hurried to Cosimo's assistance, under the command of an able *condottiere,* the Marquess of Marignano.

Siena was defended by Piero Strozzi, now a marshal of France, together with the French general Blaise de Montluc. In June 1554, Strozzi broke out of the city in search of reinforcements, leaving Blaise in charge. On Strozzi's return, after successful recruiting in Tuscany, the Marquess of Marignano trapped him at Marciano on August 2 and beat him soundly, through superior strength in cavalry. Strozzi, twice wounded, first by an arquebus ball and then by a pike thrust, and knowing that capture meant death, preferred flight to surrender.

Blaise de Montluc put up a stout resistance to Marignano all through the autumn and winter. The promised relief from Tuscany, for which Strozzi was now waiting at the strong town of Montalcino, some twenty miles to the south, failed to arrive. At last, after even the women and children had helped to man the walls of Siena, after only six thousand defenders remained alive out of an original forty thousand, and after everything edible had been consumed, the stubborn Sienese, fiercely republican since the eleventh century, capitulated.

Cosimo imposed remarkably generous terms on the city, and he allowed Piero Strozzi to escape to France. The Marquess of Marignano received from the Emperor the Order of the Golden Fleece for his capture of the city. The decoration was presented to him on his deathbed, for he had suddenly collapsed in November 1555, while on his way North to command for Charles in Piedmont.

In the following year, the Holy Roman Emperor abdicated, leaving his hereditary dominions to his son Philip II and his imperial title to his brother Ferdinand. Charles' virtues had, on the whole, outweighed his faults. He was a sincerely devout man, though somewhat inclined to sanctimonious hypocrisy, and he could be irresolute and even timid. But he was capable of listening to reason, and he was temperate, a first-rate military commander, and a lover of children, flowers, and animals. He was musical, and he was known to be devoted to his favourite artist, Titian. In a word, he might be thought a dull fellow compared with his brilliant adversary, Francis I, but he was a humane and conscientious man, whose chief concern in life was the glory of his realm. After his renunciation of the throne, Charles retired to the monastery of Yuste in Estremadura, Spain, and died there in 1558.

The death of Cosimo's eldest daughter, Maria, in 1557, at the age of sixteen, shortly before her intended marriage to the heir of Duke Ercole d'Este II of Ferrara, was the first of many private.calamities that were to befall, as though by way of deliberate humiliation, the uniformly successful, highly capable, now generally admired, and supremely self-confident ruler of Florence. So basically prosaic a character hardly seems to have deserved the "poetic justice" that was to plague the rest of his long reign, as if by the malice of such unappeased ghosts as those of Filippo Strozzi and other honourable political antagonists whose lives he might have spared.

The second catastrophe, this one of a more public nature, occurred shortly thereafter, when the river Arno, in an unprecedented display of natural violence, flooded and reduced Florence to a sea of mud that was, in places, twenty-five feet in depth. All of the bridges were swept away except the Ponte Vecchio. Cosimo took energetic measures to relieve the distress of the people, supplying them with both food and shelter from state resources and, later, restoring public and private property to its original condition. The new Ponte Santa Trinità, which was commissioned by Cosimo and undertaken by the ducal architect, Ammanati, remains a masterpiece of its kind.

Such disasters, both personal and civic, served to mellow Cosimo. He was no longer the ruthless, cold, and ambitious despot who had been so merciless to all opponents of his rule. Undoubtedly, the benign influence of his wife and the joys of fatherhood had also served to smooth the rough edges of a temperament that he had come by honestly enough, as the son of Giovanni delle Bande Nere. An event occurred at this time that illustrates the extent to which Cosimo had changed. Piero Strozzi died in active service in France, where he had been much respected by Queen Catherine de' Medici and protected by her against Cosimo's earlier attempts to have him assassinated. It was public knowledge that Strozzi was Cosimo's most dangerous enemy, for he was the most devoted of the Florentine republicans as well as one of the most accomplished soldiers of his day. Yet, when news of his death reached Cosimo, the duke seemed genuinely moved, and he eulogised his late enemy in glowing terms, calling him "one of the greatest gentlemen of Italy."

In such a frame of mind, Duke Cosimo undoubtedly welcomed, in 1559, the terms of the Treaty of Câteau-Cambrésis, by which an end was put to the struggle between Spain and France for the domination of Italy. The signatories (Henri II on one side, and Philip II of Spain and Elizabeth of England on the other, for the latter monarch was, at that time, a supporter of the Spanish) agreed that Spain was to control southern Italy, as well as certain parts of the North, while Cosimo, Spain's most trusted ally, was to hold the centre.

Such good news, which signified the final consolidation of Cosimo's position, was shortly followed by more. A new Pope, Pius IV, had just been elected. The Pontiff, before his election, had been Cardinal Giovanni Angelo de' Medici, a brother of the late *condottiere,* Marquess of Marignano. He was no relation to the Medici of Florence, being the son of an undistinguished family of burghers of Venice; but he aspired to a connection with the princely Medici clan of Florence, and he publicly claimed that his own family was a branch of that stately tree. Cosimo knew perfectly well that that assertion was false, and yet he made no objection, for he had plans of his own. And those plans required that he not offend the new Pope in any way. An accommodating genealogist was therefore found, who grafted the family of the Pontiff onto the Medici trunk. The Pope was delighted, and Cosimo smiled quietly.

Cosimo's purpose in this comedy was to obtain from Pope Pius the title of Grand Duke of Tuscany, by virtue of which he would be recognised as a reigning sovereign. As a simple duke, he was merely the vassal, albeit an important one, of the Emperor. The new Emperor, Ferdinand I, would be reluctant to consent to the elevation of Cosimo to the rank of grand duke; but a Pope, Cosimo knew, as the theoretical superior even of the Emperor, need not be so particular.

In 1560, the candidate for the grand-ducal dignity visited his new-found relative at the Vatican. Quite in the spirit of Cosimo the Elder, he allowed the suggestion of the prize he was after to come from the Holy Father himself, who understood well enough that his guest was now far the most important prince of the peninsula. Nevertheless Cosimo, with Medicean prudence by this time one of his most conspicuous traits, professed to believe that Pius was only joking. With a polite smile, the visitor changed the subject. He still preferred to bide his time. Europe was temporarily at peace, but he judged a new war to be inevitable between Spain and France. In that event, the claim of the duke to a higher rank, as the commander of a strong army, would have a better chance. In the meantime, with the pseudo-Medici Pope in his pocket, Cosimo felt that he could safely concentrate on the advancement of the real relatives of a prospective grand duke. He succeeded in having his son Giovanni, aged seventeen, appointed a cardinal, just as the great Lorenzo had once succeeded in the case of his own son Giovanni, who became Pope Leo X. Cosimo hoped that the identity of Christian names would prove a good omen. At this point, however, his life once again was disrupted by a series of calamities.

First, his daughter Lucrezia, who was married to the Duke of Ferrara, died at the age of only seventeen. Next, in October 1562, while the already twice-bereaved father was touring western Tuscany, his wife Eleonora, and his sons Cardinal Giovanni and fifteen-year-old Garcia, all succumbed to an epidemic of malaria.

The deterioration in Cosimo was illustrated by an act, dictated by sheer ambition, for which he was responsible in 1566. The fanatical Pope Pius V, who had succeeded the mild Pius IV in the previous year, plunged at once into a persecution of Protestants as violent as any undertaken against early Christians by the pagan Roman Emperors. One of the best-known of the Italian leaders of the reformed religion, a Florentine of good family and a consistently loyal Medicean named Carnesecchi, had been protonotary apostolic to Clement VII. He was converted to the Protestant cause in France some years after that Pontiff's death in 1534. He must therefore have been well into his fifties when in 1557 Pope Paul IV pronounced him a "refractory heretic." Carnesecchi thereupon wisely fled to the court of Caterina de' Medici, and on the death of Paul IV he returned to Florence. Under the lenient pontificate of Pius IV, he became one of Cosimo's most trusted friends and advisors.

One of the suggestions Carnesecchi made to the duke, when the intolerant Pius V succeeded Pius IV, was that Emperor Maximilian II should be induced to call an Ecumenical Council in Germany, to restrain the new Pope's ferocious assault on dissenting Christians. The idea seemed reasonable, but Cosimo, intent on his plan to be made a grand duke through papal favour and through the opportunities of war rather than peace, would not act in that respect. Worse still, when, in the summer of 1566, Pius V demanded the surrender of Carnesecchi to the Inquisition, the duke, hardened in his decision by the objections of Queen Catherine de' Medici, duly handed over the "heretic." The unfortunate old man was sentenced in Rome by an ecclesiastical court, and burnt alive there, by the secular arm, in October 1567.

As Carnesecchi had prophesied on more than one occasion, civil war soon afterwards broke out in France, while the Netherlands revolted against Spain, and both England under Elizabeth and Germany under Maximilian took sides in the general conflict. Cosimo had himself foreseen this situation, which brought about at last the culmination of his long-laid and tirelessly promoted schemes. Pius V created the ruler of Florence Grand Duke of Tuscany, and he was crowned as such in Rome by the Pontiff himself in February 1570. Both Spain and Germany refused to acknowledge the Medici's new rank, but

France and England recognised it immediately. In the course of time, the other Europeans powers, one by one, followed the latter example.

Grand Duke Cosimo thus became one of the group of sovereigns administering the continent. Clement VII had long ago aimed in vain at this elevation of his family, though he would scarcely have approved of its being conferred at last on a representative of the junior branch, the son of that Giovanni delle Bande Nere. The irony of the position was deepened by the fact that the execution of Clement's own former servant, Carnesecchi, as faithful to the junior branch as he had been to the senior, had actually hastened the acquisition of a crown by the subsidiary line hitherto despised by the main and, apart from Giovanni, so much more distinguished dynasty.

Cosimo, content with this achievement of his ambition, now transferred the government of his grand duchy almost entirely to his son Francesco, a man with little or no capacity, as it turned out, for serious work. The father retired to his villa at Castello and married again, much to the vexation of his family. His bride, a woman of humble origin named Camilla Martelli, formerly his mistress, caused him endless trouble owing to the inordinate intrusions and demands of her numerous relatives. She herself sometimes reduced her normally self-possessed husband to tears by her selfishness and neglect. The new grand duchess was of too coarse a nature to understand Cosimo's melancholy.

Cosimo, however, could still show much of his old spirit in dealing with critics of his wife. When he heard that Emperor Maximilian II, now brother-in-law to Francesco de' Medici, heir to the grand duchy, had said that Cosimo must be out of his mind to marry so far beneath him, the aging autocrat of Tuscany wrote sternly to Johanna, his daughter-in-law: "I contracted this union in order to soothe my conscience. In so doing, I have to account for my actions to God alone. . . . I am not the first prince to take a vassal to wife, nor shall I be the last. She is now a gentlewoman, and my consort. She must be respected as such. I have no desire to make trouble for anyone, but I intend to face any that may arise in my house. When I undertake any action whatsoever, I invariably go through with it, since I have already foreseen the consequences, and I trust in God and my own capacity to handle them."

Cosimo's death on April 21, 1574, at fifty-five years of age, followed three years of undignified domestic dispute and estrangement from his surviving descendents. He had been far happier before his crowning glory at the hands of Pius V than after it.

The character of Cosimo I, despite his virtues, was basically cold and cruel. He did show, however, some signs of administrative skill and intelligence typical of his family. Like Cosimo the Elder and the Magnificent Lorenzo, he promoted men of low birth but proved ability to important posts. Like his father, Giovanni delle Bande Nere, he always got on better with simple and unpretentious persons than with proud magnates. With the latter, while insisting on their presence at ceremonies, he maintained an aloof attitude. With the former, he talked frankly and easily. But he took advice from neither class on weighty matters.

It is also true that Cosimo found himself in 1537 at the head of a small, hitherto misgoverned, and insignificant state, dependent on Spanish power, its capital city half ruined by the long siege of 1530, its territory devastated by war, and its society degraded by the five years of tyranny under Alessandro de' Medici. On Cosimo's death thirty-seven years later, the grand duchy constituted an extensive and flourishing region, with its own powerful army and navy, its prosperous trade, industry, and agriculture, its towns rebuilt, its laws reformed, and its population enriched. These developments ensued under the iron hand of a man who lacked both generosity of spirit and elevation of mind, both common courtesy and common consideration for others. Such shortcomings did not matter greatly in a purely economic sense. Discipline, even if it excludes mercy, regularly makes for more practical efficiency than benevolent indulgence, at least for a while and at least in the political and military spheres.

Intellectually, the grand duke had neither the elder Cosimo's nor the Magnificent Lorenzo's interests. He realised, however, that a powerful state could not survive without learned men, well-trained officials, and duly qualified architects and engineers. He therefore restored, like Lorenzo, the once-famous University of Pisa, which had again fallen into neglect. He reorganised the system of public records and rebuilt much of the national property.

The period of Cosimo's reign (1537–74) saw the end of the Renaissance in Italy, after almost 250 years of glorious accomplishment. Similarly, the sparkling intellectual climate of Florence herself disappeared almost simultaneously with Duke Cosimo's accession. It may almost be said to have been drowned in the sycophantic cheers of the mob in the courtyard of the Bargello, on August 20, 1537, as the heads of sixteen prominent republicans rolled. It was then no longer possible for thoughtful citizens of Florence to be proud of a state that thenceforth took a minor position, intellectually if not politically, among the separate powers of Italy. Florentines now could only experience pride when they looked back on other times.

Perhaps the rank and file of the people were indeed happier and better off under the strong and unquestioned role of Cosimo I, first

Grand Duke of Tuscany. But the city, once the glory of Christendom, had now ceased to build the towers of the cultural edifice of Europe.

3. Catherine de' Medici

In 1533, Pope Clement VII, who always took very seriously his duties as head of the House of Medici, had arranged a marriage between Caterina, daughter of Lorenzo de' Medici, Duke of Urbino, and the brother of the heir to the French throne. In the fashion of his age, Clement was concerned neither about the welfare of the young girl nor about the wishes of the prospective bridegroom. His sole concern was political: to strengthen the hand of King Francis I in Italy against the overbearing Emperor Charles V. His political sentiments, however, may have been tinged with family pride, for it was not every day that the King of France accepted as his daughter-in-law a girl, even a Pope's relative, who was not of incontestably royal blood.

The union took place, and little Catherine—as she was subsequently known—was married to Henri, Duke of Anjou. It all seemed very happy, very splendid, and very promising for the future. These appearances, however, did not long survive. Catherine, for all her good will and her not inconsiderable intelligence and charm, was not popular among the French, who considered the royal Henri to have married beneath his station. She was treated coldly at court, ignored by the people, and was given the contemptuous designation, "the Italian woman." She was made the victim of endless scurrilous and unjustifiable attacks for sins that most people of the North of the Alps had come to identify—sometimes accurately enough—as practices of Italy's ruling families; sorcery, sexual mania, and murder.

The almost universal dislike of the new Duchess of Anjou was exacerbated by her childlessness during the first ten years of marriage. The duke himself probably should have borne part of the blame for this state of affairs, for he expended his not unlimited energies chiefly in the company of his durable mistress, the still ravishing, though ageing, Diane de Poitiers. Catherine loved him deeply, for her part, but with typically Medicean prudence and self-control, she stayed for long in the background of Parisian court life, a generally hated and passive, though alert, spectator of the strange scenes about her.

She hardly deserved such a fate. The last legitimate descendent of the senior branch of the Medici, she was nothing if not versatile in her mental gifts. She loved reading as much as hunting and dancing. She loved art, especially architecture, as much as the exercise of political and social power. She greatly enjoyed splendid ceremonies, serious conversation, and personal luxuries. In all these traits she resembled the

Magnificent Lorenzo, her great-grandfather. Yet she was basically as cool-minded as her contemporary, Elizabeth of England, a sovereign also significantly childless.

In 1536 the heir to the French throne, Henri's elder brother Francis, Duke of Orléans, who had always been subject to ill-health, died suddenly. It was once rumoured, as usually happened in such cases, that he had been poisoned—by the seventeen-year-old Catherine, in order to ensure her husband's succession. Neither the King nor any reasonable observer believed this calumny, but the prospect of "the Italian woman" as Queen of France intensified her unpopularity.

At last, in 1543, the reproach of barrenness, which had caused the possibility of a divorce to be discussed in court circles, was removed. In that year she bore to Henri, who had succeeded his brother as Duke of Orléans, a son, the future King Francis II of France and husband of Mary Stuart, Queen of Scotland. This belated blessing was followed by no less than ten others in quick succession. The phenomenon of sudden fertility in a wife after a barren decade was, of course, not unknown, but it gave rise to a good deal of probably unfounded gossip. The likely explanation is that some psychological or physiological change took place in one or both partners, accounting for the ensuing twelve years of a prolific relationship. It is not clear, though it is possible, that the advancing age of Diane de Poitiers had anything to do with the matter. In any case, an important objection to Catherine as a future Queen of France was disposed of.

Henri acceded to the throne, following the death of Francis I, in 1547. He was twenty-nine, and Diane de Poitiers was forty-eight. She continued to hold him spellbound—some believed by means of a magic ring or potion. He hardly ever left her side, day or night. She became the real ruler of France during this period. Catherine, as titular Queen, withdrew still farther into the shadows than she had as a mere duchess. The incorrigible Diane, as malicious as she was beautiful, took advantage of this situation to patronise "the tradesman's daughter," as she called Catherine. Diane acted as head nurse when the royal children were born, graciously accepting the doctors' compliments on her skill and benevolence in this respect. Henri actually paid her a salary "on account of the good, praiseworthy, and agreeable services she hath rendered to our dear and beloved companion, the Queen."

The wife of Henri II, bitter though she may have been, bore these circumstances with exemplary patience. The Venetian ambassador, Contarini, wrote to the Doge: "At the beginning of the reign, the Queen could not endure this love of the King for the Duchess of Valentinois [a title Henri had bestowed upon Diane] but later, by reason of the urgent prayers of the King, she resigned herself to it." Even a few Frenchmen were provoked to sympathy for Catherine. Marshal

Tavannes, talking one day to her, offered to cut off the duchess' nose if the Queen would allow it. That operation, he said, would undoubtedly alter the present disagreeable state of affairs for good. Catherine had the good judgement to pass off the proposal as a jest. Yet, long afterwards, in 1559, the year of her husband's death, Catherine showed in a letter to her eldest daughter Elizabeth, then Queen of Spain, how much she had taken this scandal to heart. "You have seen me in former days as content as you are now, and believing that I should never have any trouble but that of not being loved by the King your father as I would have wished. He, doubtless, honoured me more than I deserved. But I loved him so much that I always feared to offend him, as you well know. Now God has taken him from me . . . so think of me and let me serve as a warning to you, not to trust overmuch in the love of your husband."

In 1552 war broke out, with France on one side and both the Empire and most of Italy on the other. Henri led an army into Germany, but he did not, as was usual in such cases, appoint the Queen regent in his absence. Diane de Poitiers wished to remain at the head of affairs, as before in the King's absence. One of the courtiers informed the constable of France, Montmorency, that, on hearing the news of this public insult to her authority, Catherine "only smiled, and said that though it had not pleased the King to allow her that office, which His Majesty Francis I gave on a similar occasion to his mother, Louise of Savoy, and though she herself would have done her best with it if her husband had so nominated her, yet she did not intend to ask him to redress the wrong done her. But she hoped that the royal order [to appoint Diane de Poitiers regent] would not be published, in case it should lower respect for the Queen among the people."

In 1557, the constable of France was decisively defeated at the Battle of St. Quentin in northern France by the Duke of Savoy, Emmanuel Philibert, acting on behalf of Spain. Montmorency himself was taken prisoner. The news caused panic in Paris. Catherine, almost alone, showed courage and practical common sense. She addressed the Parlement, calling for a vigorous defence of the Kingdom and for large subsidies for this purpose. The deputies cheered her loudly. It is not recorded that Diane de Poitiers did anything more than pack her bags for flight into the country. For a while, the national prejudice against Catherine disappeared. She had acted, it was said, like a true Frenchwoman, and not as the low-born Italian she had been previously considered. Henri himself, absent in Champagne at the time, was much impressed, and for the next two years, until his death in 1559, he treated her with greater respect.

On April 24, 1558, Caterina's eldest son, Francis, was married to Mary Stuart, then aged fifteen. This girl, exceptionally handsome and high-spirited, a daughter of King James V of Scotland, and later to have as many furious enemies as passionate friends, had been betrothed to Francis in 1548. Since then, she had been educated at the court of France with the Queen's own three female children. The imposing pageantry of the wedding in 1558 culminated in an evening ball of extraordinary magnificence. Round the great hall of the royal palace, blazing with torches and jewels, gorgeous coaches and great ships on wheels, covered with crimson velvet, were drawn to the strains of martial music. Henri and Mary occupied the leading vessel, Francis and Catherine the second. In June of the following year, the victor of St. Quentin, the Duke of Savoy, married Henri's sister Marguérite, while Philip II of Spain married by proxy Caterina's favourite daughter, her eldest, Elizabeth, then aged fourteen. These last two weddings were celebrated for many days. The festivities concluded with a grand tournament held on the last day of the month, during which Henri tilted with the rest. At first, he met with success, but in a final tilt against a Captain Montgomery of the Royal Scottish Guard, the King was thrown from his horse, he was found to have been wounded in the temple by his adversary's lance, and he died ten days later.

Catherine's eldest son succeeded to the throne of France as Francis II, and the Queen-Mother, as Catherine now was, immediately grasped at the power that had eluded her during her husband's reign. The younger King, though legally of age since his fourteenth birthday, was still too much a child to govern effectively. There could be no legal regency, therefore, but there might be an actual one, and it was at this latter expedient that Catherine aimed. She was, however, thwarted by two brothers, Francis and Charles de Guise, whose niece, Mary Stuart, was the wife of young Francis and therefore Queen of France. Since both the royal couple were children, they required guidance, and this the Guise brothers were happy to furnish. Francis, Duke de Guise, therefore managed the army, and Charles, a cardinal, took care of foreign affairs. Thus, just at the moment when Catherine had seemed poised on the threshold of power, she was once more thrust aside by pretentious upstarts. And once more, with Medicean caution, she was content to bide her time.

It was not only Catherine who resented the pretensions of the Guise brothers. The Protestants, known as "Huguenots," were bitterly opposed to them. The "reformed religion," as Protestantism was called in France, had made great progress in the time of Henri II, despite numerous edicts and persecutions, among both the upper and lower classes. The more adherents the Huguenots gained among the nobility, the bolder the party became, and a spirit of opposition gradually manifested itself. Prisoners were set free by force, the condemned were rescued on the way to the scaffold, and a plan was devised for producing a change in the fortunes of the Protestants by violence. A certain Protestant nobleman named La Renaudie planned to attack the Guises and carry off the King. The plot, however, was discovered, and a number of conspirators were seized and executed. It was revealed, or at least pretended, that Louis de Condé, the youngest of the royal princes, had been implicated in the plot, and the Guises now dared to imprison and try him before a tribunal of partisans and then to condemn him to death. Catherine, the nobility as a whole, and indeed all France, were aghast. But, in the midst of this ferment, destiny intervened. On December 5, 1560, Francis II died suddenly, and his demise marked the end of the Guise supremacy, and therefore the intrigues aimed at suppressing the new religion. Catherine felt that at last her time had come. The young King had hardly breathed his last when the Queen-Mother took the person of the new King, the ten-year-old Charles IX, into her apartments, and the royal power into her hands. Charles was not more promising than his elder brother, and like him he was sickly and a weakling. Moreover, he had been neglected by the Guises, and he was consequently more attached to his mother than Francis had been. Thus armed by nature, Catherine attained the regency that had eluded her previously, and the situation changed immediately and wholly. The Guises were permitted to retain their posts and offices of honour, so as not to stir up their enmity towards the new King, but henceforth all real power was wielded by Catherine alone.

As regent, Catherine ordered the immediate release of the Prince de Condé. Her next act was to appoint Antoine de Bourbon, King of Navarre, as commander of the French armies, and Michel de l'Hôpital as her chancellor and chief advisor. This latter shared wholeheartedly Catherine's aim of abolishing the parties that were dividing the Kingdom into two parts. A wise system of religious toleration, he affirmed, would reconcile all true Frenchmen. "Let us," he declared, "do away with the diabolical names that cause so much treason —Lutherans, Huguenots, and Papists. Let us not alter the name of Christians."

By command of the new King, who was ruled by Catherine, and through the counsel of the chancellor, edicts favourable to the Protestant were issued. The Huguenots were granted freedom of worship in rural districts, and the penalties previously enacted against them were suspended on condition that they did not interfere with Catholic worship. Finally, French Protestant leaders were invited to meet with Catholic prelates and theologians at Poissy, near Paris.

While France yearned and hoped for peace under the tolerant regime of the new regent, a plot was brewing that was to plunge the country into a state of turmoil even more dangerous than the previous one. Antoine de Bourbon, a Protestant whom Catherine had appointed lieutenant-general of the Kingdom as a means of pacifying the Huguenots, announced his conversion to Catholicism. He had seen the light, he said, during the learned discussions by the Catholic and Protestant divines during the conference at Poissy. In fact, his new-found faith had been inspired by the promise to return to him the Spanish part of his little Kingdom of Navarre. Now he publicly invited the Guise brothers, who were living in exile in Joinville, to return to Paris. Almost immediately thereafter, the duke and the Cardinal de Guise led a massacre of Protestants at the little town of Vassy. And this was the signal for war.

The Prince de Condé, one of the two leaders of the Huguenot party, issued a proclamation calling for all Protestants of the country to take up arms. The other chief, Admiral de Coligny, was at Chatillon, and Catherine wrote to him there, urging him, in letter after letter, but in ambiguous terms, to take up arms in defence of the young King. Coligny, however, had already made up his mind to join Condé, and he wrote to Catherine that he would make war, not against the King, but against those who held him captive.

This first of France's "religious wars" lasted for a year. During that time the Huguenots took control of most of southern France, destroying churches and smashing statues and sacred vessels with pious fervour. Nor were the Catholics idle. Armed with the assurance that God was on their side, they slaughtered some eight hundred Huguenots of Paris, women and children as well as men, in the summer of 1562. The two armies finally met at Dreux, on December 19. Six thousand men were killed, and the Catholic commander, Montmorency, was captured by the Huguenots, while Condé, the leader of the Protestants, was wounded and captured by the Catholics. The battle, though an indecisive one, was a victory for the Catholics. The first news of it, however, described the encounter as a disaster for the royal army, and Catherine, with her usual *sang froid,* commented on hearing of it, "Well, well. We must pray to God in French."

Catherine worked assiduously during this time for peace, although it was as clear to her as possible that either side, as the victor, might well either exile her or depose her son, or both. Nonetheless, she arranged a meeting between Montmorency and Condé, and persuaded them to end the conflict by the Edict of Amboise, dated March 19, 1563. The terms of the settlement were a disappointment to the Protestants and an outrage to the Catholics. Only Huguenot "barons and lords high justiciary in their houses with their families and dependents" were granted freedom to practise their religion, and "nobles . . . for them and their families personally." Public worship was forbidden in Paris and in most other cities, and was confined to the outskirts of only one town in every bailiwick. Admiral de Coligny could not believe that Condé had consented to these terms, and when he was persuaded of the truth of the matter, he publicly charged Condé with having sacrificed the good of the people for the benefit of his own class.

Coligny himself, however, did not escape from this war without blemish. On February 19, 1563, the Duke de Guise was shot dead by a Protestant spy who had joined, for that purpose, the Catholic army besieging Orléans. At his trial, the spy swore repeatedly that he had been engaged by Coligny to commit the crime, and even at the moment of his execution—he was torn apart by wild horses—he swore by his eternal salvation that Coligny was as guilty as he. The admiral, of course, denied the charge, and, while Catherine ostensibly accepted his word, the death of Guise did much to intensify the bitterness of those whom he had led on behalf of the orthodox religion. The Edict of Amboise did little to appease their feeling, and the clouds of civil war still darkened the skies of France, although the nation was officially at peace with itself.

The regent, however, was determined to put the best face possible on a bad situation. A week of festivities following the signing of the edict. Mock naval battles, races, and processions alternated, in the evenings, with pyrotechnic displays in the gardens and torchlight dances in the galleries of the royal castle of Chenonceaux, near Tours. Troops of ladies and gentlemen, disguised as nymphs and satyrs, roamed the woods and meadows of the estate, gayly re-enacting the legends of ancient Greece.

Catherine, in her enthusiasm for the unity of France, obstinately divided as it remained, led in person an expedition to drive the English out of Rouen. The campaign succeeded, and Elizabeth's forces surrendered in July 1563. Charles IX, now fourteen, was duly crowned in the city and thereafter taken by his mother—who had now surrendered her regency, but not her power—on a prolonged tour of his uneasily pacified Kingdom. The journey lasted until the end of 1565.

But the ashes of the former conflict were still smouldering. The regent had to issue a further edict calling upon both Catholics and Protestants to respect each other's beliefs and to compose the endless disputes, often on trivial points of precedence and ceremony, that broke out between them. In the new year, however, she was able to concentrate on the amendment of secular law, on architectural projects, and the patronage of art and literature. The famous names of the poets Ronsard and Du Bellay and of the architect of the Tuileries, Philibert de l'Orme, date from this period.

In September 1567, religious hostilities burst once more into flame. The Protestants tried to seize the person of Charles IX. They failed to do so, but in the resulting Battle of St. Denis, the Catholic constable of France, Montmorency, was killed. Then the Huguenots took the port of La Rochelle, halfway down the western coast of the country. The city thenceforth became their permanent headquarters, and peace was not made until March 1568.

Catherine's difficulties throughout these turbulent years were vividly described by the highly intelligent Venetian ambassador, Giovanni Correr, who soon gained her confidence. "I do not know," he reported to Venice, "what prince would not have made mistakes at a time of such confusion. A woman, a foreigner without trustworthy friends, in perpetual fear and never hearing the truth from those about her, is in even worse case. I have often been surprised that in her bewilderment she did not yield to one or other of the two parties, a course that would have utterly ruined the realm. She alone has preserved the royal majesty, which still exists in France. I myself, therefore, have always pitied rather than censured her, when she speaks to me of her distress and the woes of the Kingdom."

A few months later, in August, the civil war started again, for the third time. In March 1569 the Prince de Condé was killed at the Battle of Jarnac, about sixty miles south-east of La Rochelle. A German army entered France to assist the Protestants, while Spanish forces marched in on the Catholic side. With the advent of these foreigners, the conflict grew still more savagely fanatical. No quarter was given. The Huguenots demolished and defiled the sacred buildings of their opponents. They dragged crucifixes and the relics of the saints through dust and mud, threw the Communion bread and wine to dogs and cattle, greased their boots with the holy oil of Catholic ritual, and burnt the bones of St. Louis the Crusader (King Louis IX) and the heart of Francis I. This vandalism, largely due to the Germans, roused all Catholic Europe to a vengeful storm of fury. The Queen-Mother herself wrote: "I do not think anyone in the world can feel more pained and horrified than I at the atrocities committed by the foreign soldiers. I am dying on my feet at the spectacle."

The population of Paris, predominantly Catholic, now cursed Catherine's protection of the reformed religion. They called her "Jezebel," and they demanded permission to leave the capital for some region where they could practise their religion without being exposed to the heretical enormities of the Huguenots. Catherine was sufficiently intimidated by this rebellious language to withdraw to Metz, in north-eastern France, with the young King.

In October 1569, Coligny was defeated at the Battle of Moncontour, about fifty miles north-east of La Rochelle. But, in August 1570, the regent succeeded in arranging the Treaty of St. Germain-en-Lays, by which the Protestants obtained favourable terms, deeply resented by Philip of Spain and by the majority of French Catholics. But Catherine remained hopeful. "If I am not to be again hampered," she wrote, "I mean to show that women are more sincerely determined to preserve this Kingdom than the men who have plunged it into its present miserable condition."

In keeping with that determination, the Queen-Mother turned her hand to the arrangement of marriages for her children. Such projects, however, were not maternal, or even romantic, exercises in match-making, but were intended to effect reconciliation between embittered antagonists. In the present instance, the purpose was to bring the French royal house into alliance with Protestant sovereigns, and hence to introduce the spirit of tolerance into France at the highest level. Charles IX, of course, as the reigning King of France, could hardly be expected to marry a Protestant, and for him a Catholic princess, Elizabeth of Austria, daughter of Emperor Maximilian II, was selected. Catherine's next son, however, Henri, Duke of Anjou, might be betrothed to Elizabeth of England, while the royal princess, Marguérite, was destined by her mother for Henri, the new—and Protestant—King of Navarre.

The first of these designs was soon put into effect. King Charles and Elizabeth of Austria were married in November. But the prolonged negotiations with the English Queen eventually foundered, mainly because of papal intervention. Pius V feared that, if the weak Duke of Anjou married the subtle and resolute Elizabeth, France might soon turn Protestant. Two more years elapsed before the wedding of Marguérite and Henri of Navarre could be agreed, for Pius also opposed this union of a Catholic princess and a heretic King. At last, however, it took place at Paris, in August 1572, in the presence of a great concourse of representatives of both religions. Yet each party was really less in favour of the marriage than appeared. Catholics could not forget the desecration and destruction in the recent war of all that they most venerated. Huguenots saw in the ceremony an attempt to entrap their leader into a papist circle. All the Protestant gentlemen ostentatiously left the church when the celebration of Mass began as part of the wedding rites. The new Duke de Guise, Henri, in particular, regarded his fellow-guest Coligny as the treacherous murderer of his father, and he was determined to take the admiral's life at the first opportunity.

In these ominous circumstances, on August 22 in a street near the Louvre, Coligny was wounded in the hand and arm by shots fired from the window of a house occupied by one of Guise's retainers. Each party at once began to plot the massacre of the other. At dawn on the twenty-fourth, St. Bartholomew's Day, armed bands of Catholic nobles and their supporters started to patrol the streets, calling upon the citizens to exterminate all Huguenots. At the same time the Duke de Guise led a detachment in battle order to the house where Coligny was lying wounded. Catherine had posted a strong guard to protect him, but her men were taken by surprise and overwhelmed by the determined rush of the Guise party, which burst into Coligny's chamber, killed him, and flung his corpse from the window.

A general slaughter of Protestants immediately ensued. Most of them were still asleep and could offer little resistance. The doors of house after house were broken down, and swordsmen stormed like packs of hounds into the rooms, cutting down and running through men, women, and children indiscriminately as they leapt in alarm from their beds at the uproar in the streets and on the stairs. The yells of the men-at-arms and the Paris rabble resounded for hours as the search for the hated heretics went on. The bodies of the victims, whether killed or only wounded, were hurled from the roofs where they had taken refuge, or from the windows of an upper chamber to the merciless violence of the mob below. It was afterwards estimated that some two thousand Protestants perished in the massacre.

Despite its ferocity and thoroughness, it appears that the onslaught had not been long premeditated. Probably both sides began only to prepare for a renewal of the war after the attempt on Coligny's life. The impatience of the Guises to avenge the assassination of their beloved chief, seven years before, no doubt broke all bounds at the spectacle of the marriage of Marguérite and Henri of Navarre. The Duke de Guise obviously made sure, by arranging the attack for the first moments of dawn, that the papists—the *papegots*—would be first in the field.

Catherine has been charged by many historians with at least connivance at the murder of Coligny and the butchery that followed. But, though she and her children were all at least nominal Catholics, her whole career as regent and Queen-Mother proves her intense longing for the peaceful coexistence of the two rival bodies of Christians. She must have known that if she allowed the most important leader of the Catholics to kill the most important leader of the Protestants as an act of private vengeance, she would have undone all her patiently calculated work of reconciliation over more than a dozen years. Nor, in view of the strength of the reformed religion outside Paris, would anyone but a fool have dreamed that a sudden massacre of Huguenots in the capital would have ensured a decisive victory for the creed preferred by the royal family. The Queen-Mother's well-authenticated understanding of human nature, as well as her indubitable political acumen and innate detestation of lethal violence, in both of which traits she resembled her great-grandfather, are enough to dismiss a theory easily traceable to religious prejudice. Even Jules Michelet (1798–1874), who came of Huguenot stock and hated Catherine de' Medici, absolved her of any complicity in these events. The equally eminent French man-of-letters, Prosper Mérimée (1803–70), wrote

a masterly work about this very period, his *Chronique de Charles IX*
(1829), which puts the case for Catherine's innocence even more
strongly. "Is not the attack on Coligny," he asked, "which took place
two days before the St. Bartholomew slaughter, sufficient to refute the
idea of a conspiracy? Why kill the chief before the general massacre?
Was not such an act just the way to warn the Huguenots to be on their
guard?"

It had, in fact, been only a question of hours, after the shots fired
at Coligny in the street, before one of the two factions decided to act.
That Guise was first was probably due to his natural impetuosity and
personal involvement, owing to the murder of his father by the Huguenots.

The Queen-Mother's own plans were destined to ruin from the same
instant. She had managed to save the lives of the new Prince de
Condé, the King of Navarre, and her chancellor, De l'Hôpital, together with some other leading Huguenots, by shutting them up in the
Louvre or by fortifying their houses with garrisons more powerful than
Coligny's. But she could not prevent the renewal of the civil war. It
was fought out for a whole year, with the same ferocity as ever, until
July 1573. A temporary truce, the so-called Peace of Rochelle, was
then patched up, once more to the advantage of the Protestants, who
had been more successful than their opponents in the field.

In February 1574, the conflict began once more. In May, Charles
IX died, leaving a daughter who only lived five years. His brother Henri
III, Catherine's favourite son, succeeded him. Henri was not stupid.
He understood something of the arts of both warfare and administration, but he was indolent and extravagantly eccentric, writing love letters to the Princess de Condé in his own blood, wearing little silver
ornaments shaped like skulls all over his clothes, even on his shoe-
ribbons, when she died, and a week later proposing marriage to a girl,
Louise de Vaudemont, whom he had seen only once before. He also
not only joined the sect of the so-called Flagellants, penitents flourishing at Avignon at this time, but insisted on all the ladies of the court, including his mother, doing the same. He married Louise de Vaudemont
immediately after his coronation at Rheims on February 13, 1575. She
was the daughter of a mere count, and by no means wealthy, but she
had an admirable character, becoming very popular, as the "White
Queen," with both her Catholic and Protestant subjects. Catherine, in
the intervals of doing the King's work for him, adored her.

The Queen-Mother's labours culminated at last in another truce, concluded at Beaulieu in April 1576, on conditions again favourable to the
Huguenots and closely adherent to the stipulations of Catherine's edict
of January 1562. For fourteen years the power of Protestantism in
France had been only too evident; yet the Catholics of that country

—except for "the Italian woman"—and also of the rest of Europe, apart from England, Germany, the Netherlands, and Scandinavia—remained implacably set on crushing the heretics. The Queen-Mother's toleration of the dissenters amazed the upholders of the old religion. Her indulgent attitude unquestionably derived from her Medicean heritage, a tradition broken only by the disastrous ambition of Clement VII. Catherine steadily refused, for example, to allow the Inquisition, then at the height of its power in Catholic lands, to be established in France. Refugees from the persecutions found safety, if they cared to take advantage of it, under the protection of a Medici, first the Queen of France and then the mother of its Kings.

No Medici had ever been, or ever would be, anything but a Catholic in religion. Before the Reformation came to a head in the mid-sixteenth century, it had not been so difficult or dangerous for the philosophic intellectuals of the Renaissance—Pico della Mirandola, for instance—to extend the traditional toleration typical of Medicean Catholics to persons of a different faith, whether Mohammedan, Judaic, Greek Orthodox, or Lutheran. Muslim, Jewish, and Christian merchants had always understood one another. Once humanism, early in the fifteenth century, had driven its originally pagan roots decisively into the Western mind, the Popes could never rouse Italy, let alone Europe, to crusades on a continental scale. To spread Christianity by the sword began to seem old-fashioned. No one dreamed of persecuting the learned and courteous Byzantines when they came to Italy to discuss religious coexistence. Even Luther, with his quaint personality and sturdy logic, long delighted such leading Catholic theologians as Erasmus of Rotterdam. It was only when Protestants, with every excuse, it must be admitted, assumed the colours of political revolution in central Europe and so opened its ranks to a massive influx of cruelly exploited peasants and unpaid mercenaries, that unforgivable sacrilege, especially after the German sack of Rome in 1527, caused first Catholic and then Protestant to abolish in practise that mercy that both believed to be a chief attribute of the divine creator of mankind.

The savagery of the European wars of religion, as primitive in sophisticated France as in the relatively uncouth regions to the east on the Continent, retarded civilisation for a hundred years. Catherine de' Medici, the descendent of a foreign family the members of which had long lost the qualities that had once raised it to exceptional moral and intellectual lustre, represented till she died the last clearly visible rock of sanity above the blood-stained, ruinous tide running from the Pyrenees to the Baltic. It was no wonder that both friends and enemies credited her with supernatural powers.

The celebrations of the Peace of Beaulieu gave Henri III, whose homosexual tendencies were always marked, the pretext for further ex-

traordinary behaviour. He received the guests at the castle of Chenonceaux dressed as a woman, wearing jewels in his hair, earrings, and a
pearl necklace. All the male courtiers, at his orders, followed his example. The ladies were allowed bare shoulders and their long hair, but
they had to dress as men in other respects. This sport was short-lived,
however. The Duke de Guise now proceeded to form the Catholic
League, and he arranged for the assembly of the States-General, on
January 1, 1577, to vote for "one religion only." Henri was forced to
annul what had come to be known as the Edict of January, i.e., that of
1562. The Protestants at once rebelled. Elizabeth of England supplied them with funds, and a sixth civil war broke out. It ended, after
nine months, with the same result as the others: the "edict" was restored
to validity.

Catherine, now nearing sixty, had grown enormously stout. Yet she
still danced and hunted, talked as wittily as ever, worked hard at administrative business, and, at times, despite an increasing cynicism, lost
her temper as fiercely as if she were half her age. Nor had her humour
deserted her through all these arduous years. On hearing that the
Huguenots called their biggest cannon, so huge that it could hardly be
moved, the "Queen-Mother," she burst into a shout of laughter. Again,
on overhearing from a window the malicious gossip against her exchanged by a couple of tramps who were roasting a goose on the street
outside, she called gayly down to them, "I can't be such a fiend, for it's
thanks to me that you have that nice fat goose to eat!" The great Lorenzo might have smiled grimly at this retort, directed at the kind of
critics with whom he was only too familiar.

In August 1578, the Catholic League again grew ominously active.
Catherine set out on a peace-making tour, through the South of her
kingdom, where the Catholic cause stood strongest. Rheumatism and
overweight now made all motion a torment to her, and the jolting litter,
the rains of spring and autumn, and the scorching heat of summer
added to her discomfort. In winter, she was sometimes snowed in for
weeks and half starved, and the risk of infection by the plague never
ceased. Everyone thought she was attempting the impossible, in any
case; yet in February 1579, she succeeded in effecting still another
agreement between the Catholics and Huguenots by virtue of which
each agreed to try to coexist without violence.

At Montpellier, where the general sentiment was known to be hostile
to her personally, a revolt was believed imminent. Nonetheless, she
reported to the King: "All showed a more friendly feeling than I had
been led to expect. I was told that my going so freely among them
encouraged their trust that there would be no war. . . . I had intended
to sleep here only for this last night, so as to escape the plague by ar-

riving in Provence a day earlier. But I felt rather tired, for I had travelled fully six leagues among the rocks of this district before dining."

From the Dauphiné, far inland, to the east of the river Rhône, she wrote to the Duchess d'Uzés in Paris: "Were it not for the plague I would bring you news of your estate. But all the country round Uzés is so infected that the very birds are said to fall dead as they fly over it. . . . We slept two nights in tents . . . my own health remains good except for a troublesome catarrh, which soon turned to sciatica. But it doesn't stop me walking, though not very well, so that I have to ride a little mule occasionally. I think the King would laugh if he could see me on it, looking just like Marshal de Cosse [an enormous officer, renamed for his weight], but if one goes on living, one must grow old. I am very lucky not to feel it more . . . tell me that I shall be welcome when I return."

Such letters, moving in their elderly courage and longing for appreciation, could not have been written by a "fiend." Both their pathos and their heroism are undeniable. Soon after this date, Catherine was in Picardy, then the most northerly province of France, where her pacific mission again succeeded. Nonetheless, in March 1580, a seventh civil war, lasting eight months, began, and continued almost as a replica of its predecessors. Then four years of national exhaustion and disorder followed, but without declared hostilities.

In June 1584 the death of the Queen-Mother's fourth son, the Duke of Alençon, left Henri of Navarre the next heir to the throne, for Louise de Vaudemont had not borne her perverse dandy of a husband any children. In July of the following year the so-called War of the Three Henrys—Henri III; Henri of Navarre; and Henri, Duke de Guise—started in spite of all Catherine could accomplish by a special journey to Champagne to see the duke. This culminating misfortune caused her to abandon public affairs for a while, but when a German army again invaded France, she set out on a final attempt to bring the nation to its senses. She met Henri of Navarre at Cognac, some fifty miles south-east of La Rochelle, but she could not induce him to take any decisive action. Returning in despair to Paris, she found the Catholic League dominating a revolutionary government.

In May 1588, the Duke de Guise besieged Henri III, the Queen, and the Queen-Mother in the Louvre. After the King had managed to escape, his dauntless parent caused herself to be carried out of the palace in a litter, telling the League sentries that she was looking for the duke. Passing barricade after barricade, where the troops in charge stood aside to let her conveyance through, she pursued her way across the city and was eventually admitted to Guise's presence. She actually succeeded in persuading him to accompany her to Chartres in order to discuss the situation with Henri III. An agreement was signed, but this time the terms left the League practically omnipotent in France.

The Queen-Mother, sixty-nine years old and worn out by so many labours, anxieties, disappointments, and personal frustrations, retired to the royal castle of Blois on the Loire. There could be no doubt that she was dying. The court, including the Duke de Guise, gathered about her. Now Henri III felt free, at last, to act on his own initiative. He issued certain instructions to his special bodyguard, a group of his intimate friends known as the "Forty-five." Then he summoned the duke to his bedchamber. As the Catholic leader strode along the corridor towards the royal apartments, some of the "Forty-five" closed in behind him, drawing their swords. The duke turned to face them, whipping out his own weapon. In the narrow, crowded passage, his assailants got in one another's way, and their intended victim, though wounded in several places, managed to reach the King's chamber alive. But he had no sooner crossed the threshold than he collasped on the floor, where he was easily despatched by his pursuers.

Henri immediately descended to his mother's quarters and told her, as she lay in bed, what he had done. She could only answer, in her weak state, irretrievably embittered at this final act of bloodthirsty folly on the part of her favourite, that he would live to repent it. Then, in a last excess of desperate courage, she roused herself, ordering her attendants to take her to visit Cardinal Bourbon in the prison to which he had been committed by Henri. The aged prelate, however, a relative of the King of Navarre, so far from consoling his mortally sick visitor, merely repeated the old charge that it was she herself, by tolerating two religions in one country, who had brought about the assassination of the duke and so prolonged the fatal conflict. Catherine's distress at the injustice of these reproaches, and her horrified anticipation of the inevitable vengeance that would be taken by the Catholic party on Henri for his treachery, caused her to succumb a few days later to a high fever. It ended her life on January 5, 1589.

Few important women in history have been so unfairly traduced as Caterina de' Medici. The archives of her correspondence and those of the Venetian embassy, which gave the true facts of her career, did not become available to scholars for three hundred years after her death. Meanwhile, she was represented by both Catholic and Protestant historians, but especially by the latter, as an utterly unscrupulous and even murderous traitor, and sorceress, responsible for every disastrous event that occurred in France during the last half of the sixteenth century. Her great-grandfather Lorenzo, whom she resembled in so many ways, has been similarly censured. In both cases the sinister accusations arose from the refusal of each of these highly intelligent rulers to act as uncompromising partisans in the political antagonisms of their age. Impartiality is always less inspiring than fanaticism to writers more concerned with dramatic contrasts between black and white, in their approach to the past, than with the intermediate shades that compose its real background, in the public as in the private lives of outstanding individuals.

Less partisan analysis, however, indicates that both Lorenzo and Caterina were consistent idealists. The former's aim was the maintenance and advance of his native city in the van of civilisation. This was no doubt a higher target than that aimed at by his great-granddaughter's transplanted patriotism, since she was simply concerned with the suppression of an internal feud in her adopted country. But "the Italian woman's" devotion to purely French interests may actually be considered more remarkable than her ancestor's concentration on the cultural and political progress of his native Florence. There can be little doubt that the daughter of Duke Lorenzo de' Medici remained, throughout her life, honestly determined to identify herself with the cause of her unsatisfactory French husband and sons.

In this project, she was faced with an unprecedented and implacable religious crisis of a magnitude far exceeding any known to the men of the later Middle Ages. It split France from top to bottom. No one but Catherine dreamed of resolving it by any method but the force of arms. She alone laboured, in a spirit that is even today rare among statesmen, to meet each adversary halfway. But her reward consisted solely of the curses and calumnies of her contemporaries, both Catholic and Protestant.

The characteristic Medicean gift on which Catherine depended, the talent of adjudicating differences between conflicting parties, had been a principal factor in the rise of the Medici to power. Catherine's task, however, was more difficult than those of either Cosimo the Elder or Lorenzo the Magnificent; for the conflict of her time was one of religion, which does not often, if ever, admit of solution by reason and compromise alone, rather that of politics or economics. And therefore, she was destined to fail in the end to resolve the crisis that was to plague France for many years after her death.

Henri IV, perhaps France's greatest King, knew intimately the problems that fate had inflicted upon Catherine's time, and therefore he judged her leniently: "I ask, what could a woman have done, left as she was by the death of her husband with five little children, and with two families in France who were reaching for the crown—ours [i.e., the Bourbons] and the Guises? Was she not forced to play strange roles in order to deceive first one and then the other, and in order to protect, as she did, her sons, who successively reigned through the wise conduct of that shrewd woman? I am surprised that she never did worse."

4. A Century of Masks

FRANCESCO DE' MEDICI

Francesco de' Medici, the new Grand Duke of Tuscany, inherited Cosimo's suspicious unprincipled and despotic nature. But, though just as aloof with his court as Cosimo had been, he had neither his parent's accessibility to his humbler subjects nor the courage and resolution to preserve the independence of Tuscany. He behaved like a vassal both to Emperor Maximilian II, his brother-in-law, who controlled Austria, and to Philip II of Spain, even to the point of imposing heavy taxation upon the Tuscans in order to keep Philip—who had an even larger empire than Maximilian to govern—supplied with funds.

Francesco surpassed his father, however, in the interest he took in learned men. He patronised literature, and he was passionately devoted to chemistry—though perhaps more for the sake of the gold-making "philosopher's stone," still sought by the alchemists of his day—than in pursuit of abstract knowledge. He also commissioned from the sculptor known in Italy as Giovanni da Bologna, Flemish-born but Florentine by residence, the marble group known as "The Rape of the Sabines," completed in 1583 and now in the Loggia dei Lanzi. Giovanni's other works commissioned by Francesco include a fine bronze of Cosimo I on horseback, and in particular the bronze Mercury in the National Museum at Florence, representing the god poised on one foot as if in the act of starting one of his aerial journeys. Francesco contributed further to civilisation by founding the Uffizi picture gallery, originally commissioned, from Vasari by Cosimo I, and the Medici theatre.

The Della Crusca Academy of Florence, moreover, was initiated during his reign, in 1582. The rather curious name of this literary establishment—*crusca* meaning bran, or chaff—refers to the members' possibly ironic view of themselves as resulting from a separation of the grain of linguistic purity from its husk. The idea had been borrowed from a previous society, with similar aims, at Perugia, the Accademia degli Scossi, or School of the Well Shaken. The *Vocabulario della Crusca,* which the Florentine institution published at Venice in 1612, set up as a model language the Tuscan written at Florence in the fourteenth century—that, for instance, of Boccaccio and the historians

Giovanni, Matteo, and Filippo Villani. The Accademia della Crusca later was to abandon its autonomy and combine with two older societies, that of the Apatici, or Impartial Ones, and the Florentine Academy.

Francesco's family circle, apart from his wife Joanna, formerly Archduchess of Austria, shared to the full the violent eroticism of so many courts of the era. His sister Isabella was strangled by her husband, Paolo Giordano degli Orsini, Duke of Bracciano, for alleged adultery. Her brother Piero murdered his wife for the same reason. Francesco himself had been keeping, since before his union with Joanna, the beautiful and ambitious Venetian, Bianca Cappello, whom he subsequently was to marry. Perhaps the most amusing episode involving his court in sexual adventure was that of his eldest daughter, Eleonora. Francesco wished to dispose of her to Vincenzo Gonzaga, heir to the Duke of Mantua, but he wished to provide a dowry of not more than two hundred thousand crowns to the avaricious duke. Another lord, the Duke of Parma and Piacenza, however, offered three hundred thousand crowns if Gonzaga would marry his granddaughter, Margherita Farnese. On March 2, 1581, therefore, Vincenzo married Margherita. He was nineteen, she was fourteen. Within a day or two, it was being rumoured—and it was eventually admitted by the sexually ambivalent Vincenzo—that the marriage had not been consummated. Vincenzo said it was the girl's fault. She was therefore examined, and declared normal, but not yet quite physically capable of indulging in full intercourse.

As time went on, Margherita's disability did not lessen, and the Duke of Mantua began to worry about the succession. He was determined to have a grandson to carry on the Gonzaga line, and he had no one but Vincenzo to perform this duty. His court physician, after exhaustive investigations, reported that an operation, which might imperil the subject's life, would be necessary before Margherita could hope to bear children. The duke, a humane man, decided instead to send the still virgin wife back to Parma forthwith. Let her own family doctors cure her, he exclaimed sulkily.

The surgeons of Parma had no better luck than those of Mantua. The question of an annulment was raised, but the Farnese family now laid the blame to Vincenzo. He was admittedly a sodomite, they alleged, and incapable of normal copulation. The girl innocently confirmed that she had submitted to unnatural connection with her husband. At last, the Pope, Gregory XIII, pronounced judgement. On the one hand, he said, he had no doubt, on the evidence, of Vincenzo's capacity for ordinary conjugal intimacy, or of the absolute necessity for continuance of the Mantuan dynasty. On the other hand, it was equally clear that Margherita would be of no use for this purpose.

Therefore, she could enter a convent, a proceeding that would automatically annul her marriage, and Vincenzo should re-marry.

The Duke of Mantua thereupon reopened discussion with Francesco de' Medici about Eleonora's availability. The grand duke said he would pay a dowry of 300,000 crowns with her, but only on the day Margherita took her vows as a nun. At last, in October 1583, two and one half years after her marriage, the unfortunate child, weeping bitterly, became a Benedictine nun. Francesco, however, and his younger brother, Cardinal Ferdinand de' Medici, now imposed a further condition before they would allow Eleonora to marry Vincenzo. The latter must prove his virility with a virgin, they insisted, and before witnesses.

After fierce theological arguments in Rome, Gregory and the Gonzagas agreed to this stipulation. The Mantuan ambassador to Ferrara found a suitable virgin, the daughter of a Roman architect's widow, in that city. The Duke of Ferrara, however, would not allow his subject to be made an exhibition of in Mantua. Eventually an Albizzi bastard named Giulia, aged twenty, the best-looking girl in the Piety Orphanage at Florence, was appointed to undergo the test, which was to be carried out in Venice. The interested parties landed in that city on March 7, 1584. Vincenzo failed in his first attempt at intercourse with Giulia, because he had indigestion; but on March 14 he triumphantly succeeded, according to the evidence of a witness who handled the organs involved at the moment of intromission.

Yet, to everyone's amazement, Giulia insisted that she was still a virgin. A third attempt was made, and this time there could be no doubt of Vincenzo's success. The girl confessed that she had lied on the previous occasion, because she wished for a further demonstration of Vincenzo's prowess. She went so far as to say she now hoped she was pregnant, and in fact, as it turned out, she was.

Towards the end of April, therefore, Eleonora de' Medici was married to Vincenzo Gonzaga at Mantua. Cardinal de' Medici visited the bridal chamber the next morning, and he was able to certify from the evidence of his own eyes, as had been stipulated, that the bridegroom had deflowered another virgin, this time without witnesses, misunderstandings, or accidents. Then, at last, the grand duke paid up the final installment of the agreed dowry. He also paid a Roman musician called Giuliano three thousand crowns to marry the pregnant Giulia.

The fate of another Eleonora, the wife of the grand duke's youngest brother, Pietro, has been painted in altogether darker colours. She was a niece of the first wife of Cosimo I, Eleonora di Toledo, and bore the same name. Pietro, a worthless profligate of twenty-two, soon tired of his bride and amused himself elsewhere. She thereupon fell in love with a more decent youth, one Bernardino Antinori. Bernardino, however, had the misfortune to kill a man in a street brawl, and he was exiled to Elba. One of his letters to Eleonora came into Francesco's hands. Her unfortunate lover was immediately recalled to Florence and executed on June 20, 1576.

On July 11, Eleonora received a message from Pietro to meet him at the Medicean villa of Cafaggiolo. There, after entertaining her at supper, he was said to have suddenly drawn his sword and killed her. In any case, it is certain that her corpse was buried in San Lorenzo the same night. But when the body was exhumed in 1608, it was found to be in perfect condition, embalmed, with no signs of injury prior to death. It was announced at the time of her burial that she had died of a heart attack, but Francesco immediately sent Pietro out of the country, to Spain, where he died in 1604, as much despised there as he had been in Florence.

Such is the only evidence of the circumstances in which the younger Eleonora di Toledo died. On the whole, the tale appears probable enough. Pietro was certainly capable of murdering a wife whom he believed guilty of infidelity. The process of embalming might have covered the traces of any wounds he inflicted upon her. Nor was it known that the dead woman suffered from a weak heart. It is unlikely that the exact, detailed truth will ever be known; but that Pietro was responsible for her death in one way or another, however, may be taken as fairly certain.

Five days later, Francesco's sister, Isabella, perished in an equally tragic affair. She was a clever, attractive, and good-natured young woman, universally popular. In 1576, at thirty-four, she had already been married for eighteen years to the head of the Orsini family, Paolo Giordano, Duke of Bracciano. But he, a good deal older than herself, had always neglected her, for he was infatuated at this time with Vittoria Accoramboni, a rapacious beauty, the wife of one Francesco Peretti. The duke was persuaded by Vittoria to get rid of both her own husband and Isabella, in order that the lovers might be free to marry. Isabella heard of this project and planned to take refuge with her hospitable cousin Catherine de' Medici, in France, who duly made arrangements to receive her. But before Isabella was ready to set out, her husband summoned her—just as Pietro, a few days previously, had summoned Eleonora—to meet him at his villa near Empoli, about twenty miles west of Florence. It was impossible, in the social conditions of the day, for a wife with any care for her reputation to refuse such an order by her spouse. Isabella therefore went, although she probably realised that she was going to her death. Orsini received her affectionately, and insisted on her retiring with him to their bedroom, alone, after supper. She found the chamber in almost complete darkness. Her husband bent forward as though to kiss her, but at the same moment he slipped a noose round her neck and, after a violent struggle, he succeeded in strangling her. A hole in the ceiling, through which the noose had been let down, was afterwards discovered. Her death was ascribed publicly to a fit of apoplexy. She, too, was buried in San Lorenzo, and it was noted at this time that the corpse was disfigured by bruises. Soon afterwards Orsini had Vittoria's husband assassinated in Rome, with the connivance of the lady herself.

Pope Gregory XIII, however, would not allow the guilty lovers to marry. Orsini defied him, staged the forbidden ceremony, and beat off with his own retainers the papal troops sent to arrest the assassins. Vittoria was imprisoned, but escaped. The criminal pair went off to live together at Bracciano, the duke's property, some twenty miles northwest of Rome but outside the Pope's jurisdiction. After Gregory's death in 1585 they returned to Rome, where they found, to their horror, that the new Pontiff, Sixtus V, was the uncle of Vittoria's dead husband. They had to fly for their lives, Orsini to Venice, Vittoria to Padua. Paolo died shortly afterwards, in despair at the utter ruin of his family, for centuries the most potent in Rome. Vittoria, to whom he had left what remained of his property, was murdered by his nearest blood-relation, Ludovico degli Orsini, for that reason. But neither he nor any other member of his once dreaded house ever achieved importance again in Roman politics.

Grand Duke Francesco's own wife, Joanna of Austria, died, of purely natural causes, in 1578, at the age of thirty-one. She had borne six children to her husband, of which the only survivors were Eleonora, who was destined to become the wife of Vincenzo Gonzaga, and Maria. Francesco mourned for a decent period, and then, in 1579, he married Bianca Cappello, his mistress of fifteen years' standing. Bianca was an unusual and gifted woman, even in that age of adventurous young women with beauty and brains. Born as she had been into a wealthy and aristocratic Venetian family, and ending as the wife of a Florentine ruler distinctly unpopular with his subjects, she was exposed to a good deal of malicious gossip on both counts, since Venice had been Florence's most detested rival for over a century at this date. Moreover, Ferdinand, Francesco's brother, had hated her from the start as a possible competitor for the succession to the Grand Duchy. Though a cardinal, he had never taken Orders, and was therefore eligible to accede to this dignity.

At seventeen, she had fallen in love with a young bank clerk, a Florentine of good family but poor circumstances. He seemed to reciprocate her affection, but marriage in Venice between a girl of patrician rank and a foreign clerk was out of the question, and the couple therefore eloped to Florence. They married there, but were obliged to live in poverty with the husband's parents. The Cappello family offered a reward of two thousand ducats to anyone who would wipe out the intolerable insult to their name by murdering Piero Buonaventuri, the seducer of their daughter.

The red-headed beauty became a household drudge and never went out, for fear of being kidnapped by her enraged father's agents. Piero also stayed at home, dreading the assassin's knife. In due course a daughter was born to the practically imprisoned couple. One day in 1563, when Bianca was twenty, Francesco, the heir to the Grand Duchy of Tuscany, happened to be crossing the *piazza* and saw her looking out of an upper window. The young Medici, then aged twenty-two, arranged for the wife of his Spanish tutor to invite Bianca to her house, which also stood in the *piazza*. Francesco, of course, was to be there when Bianca arrived, and the girl, startled by the sudden and unexpected presence, fell on her knees, declared herself bankrupt of everything but her honour, and implored Francesco's forbearance and protection.

Francesco, deeply smitten, for the first and last time in his life, bided his time. After due enquiry into her position, and confirmation on all sides of Bianca's virtue, he procured Piero a post at court. The young man, thus promoted, took advantage of his relief from poverty and terror to rush to the other extreme. He grew arrogant and dissolute, and it was not long before he had unforgivably insulted a member of one of the best-known families in Florence, the Ricci. One night he was attacked in the street by a group of their retainers and fatally stabbed.

Francesco thereupon openly took Bianca as his mistress. His marriage to Joanna of Austria at the end of 1564 did not make the slightest difference to his relations with the lovely Venetian, and when Joanna died, he made Bianca Cappello his second grand duchess. She was then thirty-five. Venice could not ignore so glorious a social elevation, and it was celebrated in that city with stately and even gay ceremonies. In October 1579, the Venetian ambassador declared the grand duchess, at her coronation, to be "a true and particular daughter of Venice." Francesco spent on this function some 300,000 ducats, a sum about equal to a year's revenue of the former Florentine Republic.

Bianca lived simply and modestly in her new rank, but she continued to be unpopular with the citizens of Florence, who could not bear their "tyrant" Francesco to be happy. They accused her of poisoning his only son, Filippo, in 1582, though the boy had actually died quite naturally. Her brother-in-law, Cardinal Ferdinand, who lived in Rome and did not get on with Francesco, called her a "witch" who had learnt magical practices in his brother's laboratory. She vainly did her best, until Francesco's death in 1587, to conciliate the animosity of the prelate and sole heir to the Grand Duchy.

During the thirteen years of Grand Duke Francesco's reign (1574–87), little changed to distinguish the city from what it had been under his predecessor and father, the first grand duke, Cosimo. So far as Europe was concerned, Florence was relegated more and more to the level of a backwater; no more did she play the part for which Francesco's ancestors had prepared her so long and so well. If she had, in her heyday, been the new Athens, now she was the Athens under the Romans: the relic of a bygone splendour.

As a ruler, Francesco was no worse than some of his predecessors, and better than some of his successors. It is true that he sacrificed to the friendship of Spain and the Empire the sovereign status that Cosimo I had schemed so long and so hard to achieve; it is also true, however, that the security provided by that sacrifice enabled Florence, under his reign, to prosper in all things, save the virtue of chastity.

MARIA DE' MEDICI

The second surviving child of Francesco and Joanna of Austria, a daughter christened Maria, had reached the age of fourteen on the grand duke's death in 1587. Short, thick-set, blond, and withdrawn, Maria took more after her bland Habsburg mother than her Medici father. She had not inherited that ruler's intellectual interests, but his despotic temper was hers, although masked throughout her life by helpless susceptibility to unscrupulous and cunning favourites. The first of these, and the most permanent, was a girl some three years older than herself, Leonora Dori, sometimes called Dianora, a sharp-featured, black-eyed, and black-haired little creature of extraordinary intelligence. Despite her poor health, bad figure, hopeless teeth, spotted complexion, and elfin appearance, Leonora seemed to fascinate everyone she met. It was probably by virtue of this gift that she had somehow wormed her way into the Medici household and thence into Maria's usually unresponsive heart. No one could fail to be interested in Leonora at first, but a good many people who encountered her in later life came to regret their original enchantment.

At sixteen, Maria, along with Leonora and everyone else of note in Florence, attended the burial service at San Lorenzo of a Queen of France, Catherine de' Medici. Leonora said afterwards that she saw no reason why Maria, too, if she laid her plans carefully, might not one day occupy Catherine's throne. The younger girl's Uncle Ferdinand, the current grand duke, Leonora intimated, was inclined to the same opinion. Difficulties in the way of this prospect did not, in fact, seem insuperable. The childless Henri III, assassinated a few months after the death of his mother, Catherine—as the latter had prophesied—had named Henri of Navarre as his successor. That monarch, it is true, already had a wife, the beautiful, learned, and promiscuous Marguérite de Valois, one of Caterina's daughters and therefore the sister of Henri III. But that lady was in the process of being divorced for her sterility.

Ferdinand, intrigued by the possibilities involved, got in touch with everyone concerned. He promised Henri of Navarre all the financial support he needed against the Catholic League, which was disputing his accession. Moreover, Marguérite, in spite, told Henri that she would only allow herself to be divorced if he would marry the Medici heiress and not, as he then wished, his much more attractive mistress, Gabrielle d'Estrées. He answered equivocally, for the conquest of Paris, which he had not entered for twenty years, since the massacre of St. Bartholomew's Day in 1572, occupied his mind at this period. The city, he now decided with celebrated scepticism, was "well worth a Mass," and early in 1594 the judicious former champion of the Huguenots declared his conversion to Catholicism and forthwith became Henri IV. Five years later, to the fury of Ferdinand, Leonora, and Maria—who was now twenty-six—he announced his forthcoming marriage to Gabrielle. Within a month, that charming young woman died in childbirth, without having become Henri's legitimate wife.

King Henri was the sort of man who had need of a mistress at all times. He had loved Gabrielle with such deep sincerity that his hair and beard turned almost white at the news of her death, but he instantly conjured up another favourite, Henriette d'Entragues, a woman ambitious, crafty, fascinating, and intelligent. She seems to have exercised a strong and permanent fascination on Henri, for the King returned to her arms time and again, long after he had become perfectly well aware of her stony heart and ruthless schemes to trap him into marriage.

One of the earliest of these schemes was to trick the King into signing a promise to marry her if she ever became pregnant by him. Otherwise, she said, all must be over between them. Henri would have signed away his soul if such a signature had been the passport to Henriette's bedchamber, and he cheerfully scribbled his name to the document she proffered. Henriette coolly sent a copy of it to Ferdinand in Florence, almost driving the grand duke out of his mind with rage and anxiety. But these feelings cooled down when the lady's communication was followed, in the spring of 1600, by the arrival of a formal French embassy to arrange the terms of their King's marriage to Maria de' Medici. Obviously, Ferdinand realised, no such sturdy amourist as Henri, with whose peculiar reputation in such matters he was now familiar, would dream of keeping even a written promise to a mere mistress.

On October 5, 1600, the "Green Gallant"—as Henri was called in

Paris, because of his perennial sexual ardour—married by proxy Maria de' Medici, twenty years his junior and almost wholly unacquainted with the French language, which was considered in Tuscany to be the "tongue of heretics." At long last, the steady purpose of Ferdinand, Leonora, and Maria herself had triumphed over all obstacles. Peter Paul Rubens, then aged twenty-three, attended the ceremony in the suite of the Duke of Mantua's party. He is certain to have noted with interest the massive proportions and creamy, café-au-lait complexion of the new Queen of France. Twenty years later he was to illustrate the highlights of her career, to her immense satisfaction, in twenty-four great allegorical paintings still preserved in the Louvre.

These glorious scenes began with her journey from Florence to Leghorn, and thence by sea to Marseilles. Henri, who was then conducting a victorious campaign in the Duchy of Savoy, had sent word that he would meet her at Lyons, where she arrived early in November. Every stage of her progress thither passed in surroundings of the utmost material splendour. Galley and coach glittered with gold, jewellery, and sumptuous tapestries. Silks and satins that had cost a fortune glimmered and rustled around and upon the stately central figure, her short stature half disguised by the luxurious amplitude of her costumes. Maria had nothing to complain of in such circumstances, and she was in fact enraptured by this lavish gratification of her ruling passion, the display of outward magnificence.

Despite this auspicious beginning, the first meeting of the King and Queen of France somewhat disconcerted both of them. Henri had already spied upon her from an upper gallery in the palace where she sat at supper, and he had expressed the opinion to a male companion that she was far from beautiful. Her bovine features, heavy body, and general lack of animation had disappointed his connoisseur's eyes. He was also connoisseur enough, however, to know that such an aspect often concealed an interesting temperament, and he looked forward, perhaps optimistically, to dealing with it at close quarters. He therefore gave orders that Maria was to receive him alone, at once, in her bedchamber. The dignified and extravagantly attired Queen, accustomed all her life to the polished formalities of the grand ducal court, saw to her amazement, when he entered the room, a rather dirty and ill-dressed little fellow, even shorter than herself, with a bristling white beard and burning eyes, who dashed at her and kissed her passionately on the mouth. It was not only this unconventional approach, the obvious preliminary to imminent copulation, that caused her to faint in his arms; the King's body, which he seldom troubled to wash, had a naturally goatish odour, as she remarked later, which asphyxiated her.

When Maria regained consciousness, she found that Leonora, who had of course accompanied her to France, was putting her to bed. Henri had left the room. The Duchess of Nemours and the Marquise de Guercheville, also in attendance, told her gayly that her new husband was striding up and down the corridor outside, "like a beast in a cage." They did their best to reassure her about his character—impetuous, no doubt, but so worshipful of women that he would never dream of hurting her feelings. In a few more minutes, as the ladies had foretold, he was kneeling at her bedside in tears, begging her pardon. Yet, the next moment he shocked her again by bluntly announcing; "Well, the sooner we make an heir to the throne of France the better." With that, he began stripping off his doublet and hose at a great pace, without the slightest attempt at decorum.

During the next few days the King appeared radiant. He was fairly well satisfied, in a physical sense, with his tongue-tied consort, and he told friends, with his usual candour, that if she were not his wife he would like to have her as a mistress. Nevertheless, he soon found that he needed a change. After warmly embracing the Queen, he rode off to Paris to join the scheming Henriette d'Entragues.

Maria—or Marie de' Medici, as she was called in France—followed him at her leisure, taking counsel with her favourite. Leonora had long since contrived to get herself adopted by the prominent Galigai family and assumed their surname. She had also become engaged, during the journey from Florence, to one Concini, the nephew of Ferdinand's Secretary of State and a handsome and calculating blackguard. He and Leonora understood and approved of each other in every detail, for Concini, an enthusiastic homosexual, took far more interest in his bethrothed's brains than in her physique. This remarkable pair of ruthless adventurers were soon married, and they began together to exercise a disastrous effect, through their mastery of the weak Queen, upon the public affairs of France.

In Paris, Henri calmly introduced Henriette, whom he had made Marquise de Verneuil, to his wife, at a reception attended by his whole court. "This lady used to be my mistress," he observed blandly to Maria. "Now she desires only to be Your Grace's most humble servant." Maria de' Medici had been taught self-control, which suited her lethargic disposition, at a very early age. She gazed imperturbably at the bent head of the curtseying marquise, which the King, with the familiar gesture of an old friend, pushed down a bit farther, till it practically touched the base of the Queen's crinoline. But Henriette, too, had been bred in the hard school of palace etiquette. When she rose after kissing her rival's skirt, as custom demanded in the case of a petitioner of less than royal birth, she began laughing and chattering to Maria as though they were intimate friends. The fashionable witticisms in French were lost on the silently outraged Florentine, but the

effect of the marquise's consummate poise, after Henri's open rude-
ness, was superb.

There could hardly have been a greater contrast than that between
the King's casual jocularity and the Queen's humourless reticence, or
between the uninhibited gayety of the Parisian aristocracy in the half-
ruined Louvre, after thirty years of civil war, and the complacent
pomp of the grand ducal courtiers in an atmosphere that Cosimo I had
protected, for about the same period, from both internal and external
unrest. The sedentary, respectable Maria hated the change. She could
only counteract it by using her money to redecorate the dilapidated
gloom of what she could hardly believe was a royal residence, and by
becoming the most splendidly dressed woman of her time. Meanwhile,
she concentrated for the most part on indoor preoccupations. Henri, on
his side, hunted, planned fresh campaigns, and went to bed with various women, just as he had before their marriage.

The King was overjoyed when, at the end of September 1601, the
Queen gave birth to a son, the future Louis XIII. At the same time,
he expressed what seemed even more pleasure at the practically simultaneous production by the Marquise de Verneuil of a male infant. At once, he made arrangements for Henriette's child to be brought
up in the Louvre, which was already overrun by a troop of his illegitimate offspring. Henriette immediately began a long and complicated
series of intrigues to enable her son to inherit the throne, which soon
culminated in the arrest and execution of a scapegoat, the Marechal de
Biron, in July 1602. In the following year, Maria bore Henri a daughter
christened Elisabeth. In 1604, another plot devised by the indefatigable
marquise—and backed by Philip III of Spain, in the hope of disposing
of the dangerously free-thinking French King—led to the trial of
herself and her whole family for treason. The evidence left no doubt
of the guilt of the conspirators, yet Henri saw to it, in the end, that the
death sentences passed on them were commuted to imprisonment, ostensibly for life. Most of them, however, were freed in a short time, and
Henriette herself was restored to complete liberty of action in September 1605.

Soon afterwards a ludicrous incident served once more to reconcile
the infatuated sovereign and his elegant mistress, whom he sometimes
called a "skinny, yellow-faced piece of merchandise." One day the
royal coach, containing the King and the Queen, their little son, Louis,
and a few courtiers, was being ferried across the Seine at Neuilly when
the vehicle overturned and fell into the river. Henri, a strong swimmer,
easily regained the bank, only to plunge into the water again in order
to rescue Maria. He had seen her being held up by one of his gentlemen, who was clutching her abundant fair hair, while her billowing
skirts helped to prevent her instantly sinking to the bottom, with her

usual imperturbability, while grasping the shrieking and struggling dauphin in her arms. In the end, no one proved any the worse for this ducking; indeed, the King of France declared that this adventure had completely cured the toothache he was suffering from at the time. The Marquise de Verneuil asked permission to be received by her royal lover in order to congratulate him on his escape. He granted her an audience in the presence of some attendants, but in the absence of the Queen. Henriette soon sent him into fits of laughter with her comments on the episode, which she professed to find a sad example of Maria's hitherto unsuspected drinking habits. The "fat banker's daughter," of course, heard all about this interview within an hour or two. Her Florentine manners had been deteriorating for some time under the pressure of her husband's coarse frivolity and the scarcely veiled contempt of the French nobility; now in an uncontrollable fit of fury, she screamed that she would not leave her apartments until "that whore" had freed Paris of her disgusting person. The King obediently despatched his insolent favourite back to her country estate; but in a few days, on October 6, he was writing to beg her for an immediate renewal of their relationship.

This extraordinary situation, with endless bickering between Henri and his consort, went on. Meanwhile, the King still professed, no doubt sincerely, to be deeply enamoured of his wife, and she, for her part, presented him with a regular, almost ritual, series of babies. The Queen gave birth to a daughter, Christine, in 1606; a son, Henri, in 1607, who died four years later; still another son, Gaston, in 1608; and finally, in 1609, Henriette, on whose name the father must have insisted. Meanwhile, the older Henriette bore a boy, whom she in her turn called Gaston, like the legitimate prince, and a girl named, like Henri's late mistress, Gabrielle. Maria was powerless to prevent this absurd, yet rather ominous, duplication of identities. Nor could she stop the "Green Gallant" from procreating elsewhere. It was no wonder that the Tuscan ambassador informed the grand duke, with fastidious distaste, that the Louvre, packed as it was with the King's prolific mistresses, resembled a brothel more than a palace.

Ferdinand thought, not without reason, that this state of affairs was mainly Maria's fault. Catherine de' Medici had been obliged to face the same sort of problem in the case of her husband, King Henri II of France, and Diane de Poitiers. The present Queen could easily have forestalled her own humiliation from the start, the grand duke complained, if only she had taken, like Catherine, the trouble to understand her royal partner. Henri IV was a simple enough sort of man, despite all his genius for war and women. But the grand duke's remonstrances did no good, and he died on February 7, 1609, embittered by his niece's failure to live up to her position as a Medici and as Queen of what had been rendered by Henri's victories the most powerful nation in Europe.

The ambitions of Henri, however, far transcended the bed-chamber. Indeed, it is clear that the French monarch had visions of nothing less than a United States of Europe, and that he saw as the chief obstacle to that dream the still apparently implacable hatred between Catholics and Protestants. As a thoroughgoing, though tactful, sceptic, who disposed of what appeared to be an invincible army, he may have felt that he was the only man capable of resolving the deadlock. He once replied, in his usual style, to the menaces of Philip III of Spain: "One of these days, you will see, I shall hear Mass in Milan, lunch in Rome, and sup in your satellite Kingdom of Naples."

Maria, a staunch Catholic and something of a bigot, to whom he confided this idea, was quite incapable of understanding it. Her only reaction was to represent it to other people, on her own intellectual level, as a device to depose the Pope and transform the Continent into a hotbed of heretics. Rather too many of the inhabitants of France, Spain, Austria, and Italy began to share this belief. In a street near the church of St. Roch in Paris, a big, bull-necked, red-bearded schoolmaster from Angoulême with a boyish, gentle, almost imbecilic face, asked a cutler to fix in more tightly the wobbling horn handle of a butcher's knife, otherwise in excellent condition. The cutler thought nothing of this routine request at the time. But afterwards he remembered that the fellow had seemed clumsy and diffident for one of his trade. This awkward manner had then been ascribed by the shopkeeper to his customer being a foreigner, a Fleming, perhaps, from his bright green cloak and reddish colouring.

In May 1610, Henri IV announced that he was going to march into the Netherlands, where the ruling archdukes in control had to be taught a lesson. Maria, whose only characteristically Medicean traits were a taste for pageantry and a longing for the real power behind it, immediately saw her opportunity. She demanded a coronation, so that she could legally act as regent in the sovereign's absence. He agreed as nonchalantly as if she had asked leave to make some slight alteration in domestic arrangements at the Louvre.

Accordingly, on the thirteenth of the month Maria de' Medici, arrayed in breath-taking splendour, was crowned Queen Regent of France. For the first time in many years, the broad-browed, normally vacant features of the leading lady in this open-air ceremony dispensed truly radiant smiles. She had never enjoyed herself so much before, and never would she again. Every evidence of a glory she had not in the least deserved came crowding about her. Cannon thundered; trumpets sounded; flags waved; magnificent personages bowed and curtseyed before her; and hymns of praise, cheers, and organ music—of which last she was very fond—rose to the sunlit sky. On a throne with nine-teen steps, far above the multitude of her subjects, she almost fainted away in a voluptuous ecstasy. Nothing possible to humanity, in her view, could exceed gratification by the presence of the material symbols of prestige there offered to her. With unwonted loquacity, for the rest of the day and half the night, she talked of nothing else but this affair, going into its most minute details.

But it was not for that reason that Henri could not sleep. He felt extraordinarily restless and inexplicably nervous, perhaps less because of a distrust of the new regent than on account of the great schemes for European unity that were fermenting in his mind and the deadly opposition he knew they would provoke. In the afternoon, he decided to ride out by open coach, since the weather was excellent, with some of his gentlemen. He impatiently refused a formal bodyguard, though he and all his immediate circle had known for some time that he had resolute enemies in France as well as beyond the frontiers.

In the narrow Rue de la Ferronerie, beside the Cemetery of Inno-cents, the carriage's progress was temporarily blocked by a hay wagon and a wine cart. A powerfully built, red-bearded fellow in a green jerkin jumped onto a stone post placed at one of the corners of the lane, and before anyone could stop him, he seized the door handle of the royal coach with his right hand and stabbed the King three times with his left. Then he stood staring at the fallen body. The withdrawn knife, of a type used by butchers, dripped in his hand.

An instant later, the gentlemen escorting the carriage on horseback had disarmed and captured the assassin. Swords were drawn to run him through, but the Duke d'Épernon, who had been seated next to Henri, roared that the assailant, who was making no attempt at re-sistance, must not be cut down but taken alive for questioning. The duke, being the senior nobleman present, was obeyed. The dying monarch and his curiously passive murderer were rushed off in opposite directions.

The Queen Regent, sitting majestically in her private apartments among her Italians, turned pale under her rouge as confused shouts and trampling resounded in the street outside and on the stairs. The chancellor, Sully, and Praslin, the captain of the royal guard, burst into the room, followed by the eight-year-old Louis. Maria, clutching her ample bosom, gasped out: "The King?" Sully, drawing himself up and laying his hand on the weeping boy's shoulder, answered gravely, "Madame, here is the King!" He added the traditional phrase, *"Le Roi est mort. Vive le Roi!"*

Marie rose unsteadily, in silence, supported by her women, and gestured to the men to precede her. Only when she saw the blood-stained corpse of her husband laid out on the bed she had so often shared with him did her self-control leave her. She fainted, recovered, and then began to scream. Even Leonora could not pacify her.

The highly complex antecedents and consequences of this crime, and conjectures as to their interpretation, belong to French rather than to Medicean history. It is almost certain that Maria, though she sometimes hated and feared Henri, had nothing to do with his murder. Most modern investigators believe that Jean François Ravaillac, the schoolmaster of Angoulême, a fanatical Catholic, had been the unwitting instrument, at several removes, of French, Austrian, and Spanish conspirators, who had sworn to eliminate the King. Their leader, the Duke d'Épernon, seems to have intended to evade suspicion by causing prolonged and atrocious torments to be inflicted on the assassin, with the utmost publicity, instead of allowing him to be summarily slaughtered on the spot.

In spite of the incrimination of d'Épernon and his friends by honest witnesses at Ravaillac's trial, the question of ultimate responsibility for the regicide was never resolved. The only certain point in a mass of contradictory reports was that Ravaillac had struck the actual blows. The prisoner himself insisted, under torture, that he had acted entirely in obedience to his "visions," without any human prompting. He had unimpeachable information from supernatural sources, he declared, that Henri intended to depose the Pope. The ex-schoolmaster evidently expected to be applauded as a hero by the citizens of Paris and to be rescued at the last moment by them, or by Spain or Austria, or even by the Pontiff himself.

No such events took place. In the end, after repeated merciless applications of steel and fire to the person of the deranged giant, each of his four limbs was riveted to a fast horse and the four animals were then ridden at furious gallops to the four points of the compass. His legs and arms were thus torn from a trunk that only ceased to writhe at the third repetition of the process. This awful spectacle was watched by an enormous crowd, including most of the notabilities then in Paris, but not by Maria, who remained closeted in the Louvre for forty days after the murder. She did see, however, from her window, a group of her Swiss guards hilariously roasting a bloody fragment of Ravaillac's body.

When the widowed regent emerged from her seclusion she began, to everyone's astonishment, to take a positively feverish interest in politics. The whole nation, distressed by the rivalries of d'Épernon, Condé, Sully, and the Duke de Guise, seemed to be rallying gratefully around her. It was, however, the adventurer Concini, Leonora's husband, together with the papal legate and the Spanish and Austrian ambassadors, all secretly jubilant at Henri's death, who exercised far more influence on her than any Frenchman. Concini, of course, hardly cared for any political or religious ideal. He engaged in state business simply in order to enrich himself, and in that spirit, he advised Maria to do whatever he calculated would be, however indirectly, to his own advantage. He judged that advantage to be bound up with the Catholic cause, which was rapidly advancing now that the only man of genius who had opposed its more reckless manifestations in the secular sphere had been removed. Among the results of this attitude of Concini's were the betrothal, in 1612, of Louis XIII to the Spanish Infanta, Anne of Austria, daughter of Philip III, and the pledging of the regent's eldest daughter, Elisabeth, to the future Philip IV of Spain.

The French Protestant nobles, led by Henri, Prince of Condé, at first objected to these arrangements, but eventually they were bribed into submission by Concini, who was now Marquis d'Ancre and a marshal of France. The new marshal, too cold and overbearing ever to be popular with either sex, and by no means congenial to the Queen herself, owed his sensational rise in the world almost wholly to his wife, Leonora, never ceasing to do what she liked with Maria, which was mainly to pour massive portions of Maria's wealth into Concini's pocket.

Essentially, Leonora was a merciless realist. Long ago she had understood that to be amusing would not be enough to bring her ugly, lively little person, through her resplendent husband, to the heights. Nor was it enough to be the cleverest woman in France. Something else was required. She therefore decided at an early stage to make herself feared, in that superstitious age, as a witch. Among other practises, she pretended to go into trances and interview omnipotent agents from other worlds. She possessed an enormous apparatus of devices for terrifying people whom she wished to influence. It was in vain that doctors of medicine talked of hysteria, and doctors of the Church alluded to the phenomenon of demoniacal possession. Leonora always knew exactly how far to go in this line, and when to present an entirely different personality so as to discredit such diagnoses. If these doctors ever began to look dangerous, she blackmailed, bribed, or simply outwitted them. Everyone knew, in any case, that she was the Queen's favourite, and no one wanted to fall into Maria de' Medici's bad graces. By these methods, Leonora, for a while, ruled France.

In purely political terms, things could have been worse. The stability of the country was now being affected less by the Queen's lack of common sense than by the fanatical Protestants among the nobility and the higher civil officials. Leonora gradually got rid of the latter on one pretext or another, without open violence, and replaced them with the more able and worldly of the Catholic clergy. She soon perceived that the most subtle and tactful of these priests was a certain Armand Jean du Plessis de Richelieu, son of a faithful servant of both Henri III and

Henri IV. In 1614, at the age of twenty-four, young Armand had already been bishop of Luçon in western France for six years. By 1616, the year in which Condé was arrested and imprisoned, Richelieu had been appointed Secretary of State to Louis XIII.

Yet all was not well. Leonora's plans were continually being checked by the inordinate ambitions of her husband, who was hated not only by the Protestant princes but also by the young King himself and a growing number of citizens. Such sentiments began to diminish the popularity of the Queen-Mother, as she was now officially called, for Maria was blamed for everything. One day Concini's house was sacked by a furious mob and a portrait of Maria was thrown out of the window. The sixteen-year-old Louis thereupon determined to assert himself against his too pliable parent's favourites.

He began by confiding in a godson of his father. Charles d'Albert, aged thirty-six, an expert huntsman but in other fields not remarkable for intelligence, was descended from a distinguished Florentine family that had been exiled to France a century and a half before. D'Albert, known as the Duke de Luynes, vented enough pressure at Louis' instigation to force Richelieu to act.

As soon as the Secretary of State understood that the wind was changing, he proceeded to obstruct certain of Concini's numerous lawsuits. A typically insolent letter from Concini to Richelieu survives: "By God, sir, I have to complain of you. Your treatment of me is intolerable. You negotiate for peace [with the Protestants] without my knowledge. You advise the Queen-Mother to persuade me to drop the suit against M. de Mountbazon for her sake. What do all the devils in hell, or you, or the Queen-Mother, think I am going to do in these circumstances? I tell you, sir, anger gnaws my vitals!"

On April 24, 1618, at ten o'clock in the morning, some of Louis' friends trapped the marshal alone in a room of the Louvre by suddenly closing the entrance door behind him and locking it in the face of his escort. As Concini's right hand flew to his sword-hilt, the group shot him down with pistols and then despatched him, as he fell to his knees, with cold steel. Louis, when he heard the news, exclaimed loudly: "Now I am King!" He refused to see his mother, dismissed Richelieu as too indulgent to the Protestant party, and then, ironically enough, adopted the dead Concini's expedient of promoting Catholics right and left. Both Maria and Leonora had followed the same policy, but during the past few days Leonora at least had seen that her husband was pressing his luck too hard. She had urged him to resign before the inevitable crash came, but for once he would not listen to her. Louis now kept both ladies under close guard in the Louvre.

A day or two afterwards, Richelieu, as he crossed the Pont Neuf on his way back to his bishopric, noticed a corpse dangling by the feet from one of the gallows set up on the bridge. A yelling mob was slashing the body with knives and axes. The imperturbable ex-minister enquired of one of his attendants, who was riding beside the window of the carriage, what was going on.

"They are taking vengeance on the earthly remains of the Marquis d'Ancre [Concini], my Lord Bishop."

Richelieu nodded blandly.

"Ah, good. *Vive le Roi.*"

He withdrew his head from the window as coolly as if he himself had ordered the proceedings. He knew his disgrace would not last long. At almost the same moment, Maria was remarking to Leonora, with apparent resignation to Concini's murder and the King's unexpectedly bold reactions to it, "Ah, well. I have reigned seven years. I ought to be thinking only of a heavenly crown now." Her subsequent activities, however, proved that she was not prepared to do anything of the sort.

Louis packed his mother off to her castle of Blois, on the river Loire in central France, where he innocently supposed that she could do no more harm. The farewell interview between mother and son is recorded as follows. Said the King: "Madame, I wish to relieve you now of the fatigue of state business. It is time for me to take this burden from you for I do not intend to allow anyone else to do so. But I shall always treat you with the respect due to a mother. You will hear from me at Blois. *Adieu, madame.* Do not cease to love me and you will find me a good son." She replied: "Sire, I regret not having acted, as regent, in accordance with your wishes. But I did my best, and I beg you to consider me in future your humble and obedient mother and servant."

She embraced the stern-faced boy for the first time in many years, but he remained rigid in her arms. Then he stepped backwards, bowed deeply, and left the room. After the door had closed behind him, the Queen-Mother, no longer regent, began to weep. Richelieu, advised of these events, followed her to Blois, with characteristic discretion, in the last coach of the long procession of vehicles.

The moment Maria's back was turned, Leonora, who had not been permitted to accompany her, was put on trial for sorcery. She set up a masterly defence, but Louis had long since resolved to have done with her once and for all. Found guilty of treason, heresy, and malversation of public funds, Leonora was duly beheaded in the Place de la Grève and her corpse afterwards burnt. She was forty-one years old. The crowd had pitied her diminutive figure, with cavernously hollowed eyes and white, drawn features, trembling with genuine fear at last, as she approached the block.

The Queen-Mother, horrified by the execution of her life-long friend, discovered that certain gentlemen—the dukes of Épernon, Montmorency, and Guise in particular—shared her indignation at the King's severity and were prepared to help her own restoration to political power. Louis' refusal to permit her to attend the wedding of her daughter Christine to the Prince of Piedmont, heir to the Duke of Savoy, in February 1619, was the last straw. On the night of the twenty-first of that month, a rope ladder was attached to the windowsill of her bedroom in the castle of Blois. Richelieu helped her to climb out, steadying her from above, while Brenne, one of her equerries, guided her feet. In pitch darkness and freezing cold, this operation and the subsequent descent of the unwieldy and terrified yet determined prisoner, tightly trussed in a huge mantle, proved extremely arduous. She appeared to faint as she reached the ground. Sentries passing at some distance merely whistled and shouted jocular encouragements at the impression they received of a pair of ruffians trying to rape a stout female. "They take me for a trollop," the Queen-Mother gasped thankfully, as her rescuers rushed her to a waiting coach, which immediately set off at full gallop, accompanied on horseback by Richelieu, the equerry, and half a dozen other gentlemen, for d'Épernon's estate in Provence.

The report of Maria's disappearance and probable whereabouts soon spread. The King made for Provence with an army, but he was persuaded by the Duke de Luynes to negotiate with Richelieu before proceeding to battle. As the result of the negotiations, the Queen-Mother was appointed Governor of Anjou. Early in September, she and Louis met for a formal reconciliation at which ceremonial embraces were exchanged.

Years of political turmoil ensued in France. Maria and the King, the Duke de Luynes, the Marquis de Vitry, the Prince de Condé, now released from prison, and the capricious, dictatorial little blond Queen, Anne of Austria, struggled for power, sometimes in actual military operations. Richelieu alone, like Catherine de' Medici in the second half of the previous century, worked for peace and made himself hated in the process. No one, however, could deny his tireless patience and ingenuity, and at the end of 1622, he was made a cardinal. De Luynes had died in the field, where he had never been much use, the year before. The obstinately spiteful Condé was eventually exiled to Italy. One after another, the Queen-Mother's worst enemies, under the cardinal's hammer blows, lost influence. He contrived at last to get Maria admitted to the Privy Council, where she made a good impression by invariably acting as he had suggested beforehand. By 1624, he himself had joined this Cabinet at the King's request. Louis had finally concluded that the prelate, like his royal master, had never in fact been anything but a true patriot and probably, unlike the well-meaning but not always judicious monarch himself, the best statesman France had even known.

The decline of religious intolerance under Richelieu's policy was manifested in the marriage arranged at the end of this year between Maria's third daughter, Henriette, and a Protestant, Charles, Prince of Wales. The cardinal had no intention of allowing the Habsburgs to dominate Europe, and he felt that an alliance between France and Britain would effectively check the Austro-Spanish designs in that direction.

Richelieu's health had never been good. It deteriorated as fast as his political star rose against the stormy sky of his personal unpopularity. He now asked permission to retire, but neither the Queen-Mother, nor the King, who was also ill, would hear of such a thing. The furrowed, bloodless countenance above the splendid robes, the austere expression, and the stately confidence that masked an inward physical torment, remained familiar at court.

Louis' absence from Paris at the siege of La Rochelle, again held by rebellious Huguenots, enabled Maria to return officially to her former post of regent. She and the cardinal, of whose power the Queen-Mother was by this time becoming jealous, had now to face three openly hostile forces, those of Spain, Austria, and Britain, all intent on destroying the unity of France. But an epidemic broke out in the supporting British ships off La Rochelle, and in October the city fell to Louis' troops. Richelieu, now admired by almost everyone of consequence, became practically omnipotent in Paris. He was well aware of his position, yet realist enough to remain cautious. At this period, his extraordinary changes of mood, from affability to austerity and back again in an instant, mystified the Queen-Mother. She began to quarrel with him again, and by 1630 the pair were at daggers drawn. When he intruded upon a private interview between herself and the King, she lost her temper and cursed the prelate in Franco-Italian at the top of her voice. He fell on his knees before her and begged her pardon. Louis intervened. He rebuked his mother in measured tones, but also ordered Richelieu to leave the room. Maria believed that the monarch meant to dismiss Richelieu, and she told all her friends so. At that moment, she felt sure that with this proud cleric out of the way, and her son sick in body and desperately worried in mind, she needed only a step to become the truly great—by which she meant entirely despotic—Queen she had always longed to be.

As usual, Maria was mistaken. The King, after giving certain instructions to a special crony, Claude de St. Simon, drove down to Versailles. Richelieu, convinced that his career was at an end, went to Le Havre. The port, which he owned, would be a convenient point for escape by sea to England, where he had reliable friends. While he waited there for definite news, St. Simon arrived to see him, with a message from Louis. The cardinal was to attend the sovereign immediately at Versailles.

King Louis could not have been more accommodating at this meet-

ing. He told the visitor that he believed unreservedly in his genius
and unshakeable loyalty. At all costs, the greatest minister France
had ever had must stay at the head of affairs. The prelate, much relieved, was emboldened to reply that he could not govern the country
adequately while Maria de' Medici remained in Paris. Louis agreed
grimly that his mother had no administrative or political sense whatever, and he promised that he would see what could be done.

What he did was to banish, imprison, or execute Maria's most effective adherents. Some of them hardly deserved such treatment, having
erred only in supposing the cardinal a sinking star and the Queen-
Mother more public-spirited than she was. Her son's unexpected and
drastic change of front appalled and infuriated her, and she swore she
would never make peace with Richelieu while the heavens remained
in position. At last, the papal legate persuaded the Queen-Mother to
attend a council at which the cardinal would be present. She sat in icy
silence while he explained his views on policy as calmly as ever.

Nevertheless, Richelieu was in for a surprise. A few days later Maria
summoned him to her presence at the house of her confessor. Probably
on the advice of the latter, she told the astonished minister that she had
never wished to separate him from the King, but only from state affairs.
Then she burst into tears. The cardinal solemnly assured the distraught
woman that, after serving her faithfully for fourteen years, he was still
ready to do all he could to regain her good will.

The reconciliation did not last. The incorrigible Queen-Mother was
found to be encouraging her son Gaston, a young man of few virtues, to
disturb France once again by seeming to aim at the throne. Accordingly, in February 1631, Louis formally escorted his mother, in the
company of his wife Anne, with whom she generally agreed at this
period, to Compiègne, some forty-five miles north-east of Paris, and
he commanded her to remain there. Since even at Compiègne she
would not listen to anyone who begged her to recognise Richelieu's
capacity and good faith, the cardinal finally lost patience and altered
his tactics. It was impossible for him, he could see, to lead his country
to prosperity while Maria persistently snapped at his heels. He resolved therefore to crush her interference, this time for good. He began
in typically roundabout fashion by stressing her faults, which everyone
knew by this time, to the monarch, speaking with great deliberation
and earnestness. He suggested, in sorrow rather than anger, that she
favoured Gaston at the expense of her eldest son, and he produced
documentary proof of her machinations in that direction. Finally, he
took God to witness that he would resign if the Queen-Mother ever
showed up in Paris again.

He was, in fact, talking to a converted judge. Louis had already made
up his mind that his mother constituted a public danger. He might

have simply sent her back to Florence, a step many of his loyal subjects considered highly desirable. Instead, after first requesting her to move farther from Paris, he allowed her to escape from Compiègne to the Netherlands, held by her friends the Spaniards. As he had anticipated, after a tearful proclamation to himself and the Parlement that she was wholly innocent of all the charges brought against her by Richelieu, whom she accused of plotting her assassination, the Queen-Mother was soon in Brussels, under the care of its ruler, the Spanish Infanta, Isabella, a granddaughter of Catherine de' Medici.

The rest of Maria's story can arouse nothing but pity for a foolish and obstinate, but not really ill-natured, woman. She has been credited with extreme "Medicean cunning" and talent for intrigue. But the plots and plans that appeared to be hers were always actually thought out and engineered by other people, at first by the Concini and later by Spanish and Austrian officials. The tales of her adulteries and cruelties are mere gossip. She was naturally chaste, and she never tried to kill anyone by direct action. It was simply her appetite for a power she was quite unfitted to exercise, and her opposition to the most astute statesman of her age, that irretrievably ruined her.

On August 12, 1631, Louis declared her a rebel against his authority, outlawed her person, and sequestrated her property. Refusing the invitation of her nephew, Grand Duke Ferdinand II of Tuscany, to settle in Florence, she wandered miserably about the Low Countries, where her presence embarrassed the Spanish Government as a potential source of serious discord with France, at this date showing signs of superiority to Philip's declining empire in both military organisation and diplomacy.

In June 1633, Cardinal Richelieu heard that Maria was lying ill at Ghent. He sent her a message of sympathy, to which she retorted bitterly that she preferred his abuse to his compliments. Yet, in February of the following year, homesick for Paris, she wrote to ask him to forgive her and forget the past. He did not answer. When she wrote again in the same strain, he merely advised her to change her mind about going to Tuscany.

In October of the following year, her son Gaston, who had been spending a certain amount of his time with her in the Netherlands, deserted her in order to comply with a courteous invitation to the French capital from the cardinal, who wanted to keep an eye on him at closer quarters. His mother proceeded to bombard the King with letters imploring him to allow her to follow Gaston, but Louis answered evasively. She could only watch, with alternately rising and falling hopes, Richelieu's over-confident defiance of Spain, the defeat of his troops in an invasion of the Netherlands, and the threat of the victors to Paris, which eventually came to nothing. When, in 1638, the French began to get the upper hand in the war, the exiled Queen-Mother, fearing that if they occupied the Low Countries she would be their first victim, fled to London, counting on a safe refuge with her daughter Henriette, married to the British King, Charles I.

But the Protestant Charles was having a great deal of trouble with his Parliament, and he made it clear to his ultra-Catholic mother-in-law that he only received her for his wife's sake. The unwelcome visitor resumed her correspondence with Louis and the cardinal in the most abject terms. To the latter she wrote: "I have forgotten the past. I only want to be friends with you. I should be so happy if you would deign to grant me the great favour of my return to France." Although she took care not to mention Paris, the King was not mollified. He again recommended Florence as the best place for her. Richelieu might possibly have relented, but he heard that Maria was once more talking, in private, about a second regency, and the news convinced him that she might still be dangerous.

Meanwhile, in London, the popular riots against Charles were getting worse. They were partially directed against Maria. Violently attacked in Parliament as *persona non grata,* she began to fear actual physical injury. The death of Rubens, almost the only friend she had left, at Antwerp on May 30, 1640, also depressed her. She abandoned the British capital, now openly hostile to its King and Queen and threatening civil war, in August 1641.

The unhappy Queen now had nowhere to go. England had rejected her. France declined to receive her. Even King Philip IV of Spain now refused to allow her to settle in his country of the Netherlands. Her pride would not allow her to return to Tuscany as a rejected Queen and mother. She eventually found a modest haven in the city of Cologne, whose prince-archbishop expressed a Christian sympathy for the woman who had been ambitious not beyond her station but beyond her means. She died there on July 3, 1642, at the age of sixty-nine, a decrepit and unhappy woman, believing to the very last that fate had destined her to be a great Queen.

FERDINAND I, COSIMO II, AND FERDINAND II

The Grand Duke Francesco de' Medici, Maria de' Medici's father, had been succeeded as the ruler of Tuscany in 1587 by his brother, Ferdinand. At the time of Francesco's death, Ferdinand, a cardinal, had hastened to renounce his ecclesiastical dignities for the sake of the grand ducal throne. His haste, however, was due not so much to inordinate ambition as to his belief in the necessity of claiming his inheritance at once, if he was ever to do so. The dead Francesco's second wife, Bianca Cappello, had been scheming for years in an attempt to displace Ferdinand as heir to the throne. The threat, as it turned out, was not a serious one, for Bianca was not sufficiently adept in the ways of statecraft for her stratagems ever to bear fruit. Nonetheless, her constant intrigues—all of which Francesco saw through immediately, and all of which he forthwith disarmed—were a source of irritation, and of some trepidation, to the nervous Ferdinand. As soon as the throne was vacant, therefore, he lost no time in claiming it and in installing himself as undisputed master of Tuscany. It was probably purely coincidental that his accession was followed almost immediately by the death of Bianca; and it is likely that, rumours to the contrary notwithstanding, malaria, and not poison, carried off the Dowager Grand Duchess of Tuscany.

Ferdinand's almost pathological hatred of Bianca during her lifetime and even after her death is the one dark spot in his otherwise admirable career as Grand Duke of Tuscany. He was a generous patron of the arts in the tradition of his ancestors, although allowances must be made for the reduced availability of great art and great artists to patronise. His most noteworthy accomplishment in this regard was the foundation of the Villa Medici at Rome, which he stocked with ancient paintings and superb statuary in great quantity.

As a statesman, Ferdinand I reformed the administration of justice and worked hard at public affairs both at home and abroad. He tolerated Jews and heretics in the port of Leghorn, which Francesco, in one of the few measures to his credit, had done much to improve materially. Ferdinand's enlightened policy towards the citizens themselves naturally led to greatly increased prosperity in that city. He also further extended the harbour facilities there and had a canal dug from Leghorn to Pisa, about fifteen miles to the north-east across the Arno. Elsewhere in the Grand Duchy, numerous works of industrial and commercial utility testified to Ferdinand's practical good sense, in strong contrast with his predecessor's idleness and self-indulgence.

The attentions to Leghorn paid off principally in the growth of the Tuscan navy, which captured, in 1607, one of the chief nests of pirates on the so-called Barbary Coast, Bona in Algeria. In the next year, the Tuscan war-galleys won an even more brilliant victory over the Turkish fleet, taking nine ships, seven hundred prisoners, and treasure to the value of two million ducats.

Ferdinand, who, even as a cardinal had never taken clerical vows, married in 1589 Christine of Lorraine, the favourite granddaughter of Catherine de' Medici. The grand duke always remained on excellent terms with both Catherine and Cristina, as the latter was called in Italy. The younger woman made an impeccable grand duchess. Only twenty-two at the time of her wedding to the ex-cardinal, she long survived his death in 1609. His eldest son, then nineteen, succeeded him as Cosimo II.

It was during the reign of the Grand Duke Ferdinand I that Florentine intellectual genius once more came to the fore in the person of a single figure, Galileo Galilei (1564–1642), who had been born at Pisa of a noble but impoverished Florentine family. Galileo seemed in his youth more likely to take up music or painting as a livelihood than science. It was not until he had left the University of Pisa without the medical degree for which his father had destined him that, at the age of twenty-one, he began lecturing on mathematics in Florence. An essay published in 1586 describing his invention of the hydrostatic balance rendered him well known throughout Italy. His subsequent achievements in astronomy and philosophy are relevant to the history of the Medici family only insofar as he spent most of his life in the Grand Duchy of Tuscany. None of the Medici except Cosimo II, who occasionally protected Galileo from the malice of ecclesiastical fanatics, and, in the last few years of his life, Ferdinand II, were concerned personally in either his triumphs or his disasters. In those days the productions of artists, both more spectacular than scientific invention and with a longer history, were considered superior to machinery and the juggling of figures and diagrams.

Cosimo II continued his father's concentration on naval affairs, but he abandoned Ferdinand's interests in commerce and finance. The latter had himself supervised the Medici banks abroad, but his son turned this labour over to others. In fact, the character of Cosimo II resembled that of his uncle Francesco in its inclination to luxury, although he was far more sociable than Francesco and cared little for either science or art. What he most enjoyed was watching pageants. Nonetheless, either he or his advisors must be credited with recalling Galileo to Florence from the University of Padua, where the scientist held the chair of mathematics in 1610. He had, in that year, discovered satellites of the planet Jupiter, which he called "Medicean stars" in honour of Cosimo, who had attended his early lectures to the Florentine Academy.

The grand duke appointed Galileo to the sinecure of court philosopher and mathematician, so that Galileo might proceed with his astronomical researches in peace. These, however got him into trouble with the Vatican. He had told the German astronomer Johann Kepler (1571–1630) in a letter dated August 4, 1597—i.e., during the reign of the Grand Duke Ferdinand I—that, although he believed Nicolaus Copernicus (1473–1543) to have been right in postulating the sun as the fixed center of the cosmos, he himself, Galileo, was afraid of being laughed at if he proclaimed this opinion to an Italian public. It was not, however, the public that Galileo had to fear. In 1616, after Ferdinand's death, the theologians of the Holy Office condemned as heretical the proposition that the sun is immobile, while the earth rotates daily about it. The Pope, Paul V, thereupon ordered Galileo, who was in Rome at this time, not to "hold, teach, or defend" such a doctrine. Galileo obeyed, and returned to Florence for seven years of almost wholly silent study.

During this period, in 1621, Cosimo II died at the early age of thirty-one. On the whole, he had been, as a ruler, an agreeable nonentity, and the happiness and prosperity of the Tuscans, founded on the wise dispositions of Cosimo I and Ferdinand I, continued without much apparent variation. After Cosimo's death—since his eldest son and successor, eventually to be Ferdinand II, was but a child of ten—the Grand Duchesses Cristina and Maddalena, Cosimo's French mother and Austrian widow (Magdalen of Habsburg), respectively, carried on the government. In 1627, the boy, then seventeen, was allowed to exercise his grand ducal authority, though at first, he shared it with the grand duchesses and, officially, with his four younger brothers Giancarlo, Mattias, Francesco, and Leopoldo, who at this time was sixteen, fourteen, thirteen, and ten.

During the awful plague of 1630, Ferdinand II showed a great deal of courage and passed several useful measures for the relief of suffering and for the prevention of such recurrences in the future. But, unlike any of his predecessors, he fell deeply under ecclesiastical influence. He allowed Pope Urban VIII to seize the Tuscan Duchy of Urbino, when the last duke died, without a sign of protest. More and more priests were seen in Florence, and many of them were appointed to high offices of state—a revolutionary proceeding that Cosimo I would never have permitted. Pope Urban's ambitions threatened next to deprive Odoardo Farnese, Duke of Parma—who had married Margherita, the youngest of the two sisters of Ferdinand II—of his duchy. Farnese therefore invaded the papal dominions and Ferdinand was obliged, since the duke was his brother-in-law, to let the Parmese army pass through Tuscany on its way South. Eventually, however, France intervened, and peace was restored.

The grand duke had reluctantly stood aside while the Pontiff's enemies marched through the Tuscan countryside, but it was too much to expect that the priest-ridden Ferdinand would choose to protect Galileo when the great astronomer, then in his seventies, was hauled before the Inquisition in February 1633. In 1632, the very year of Ferdinand's formal installation as grand duke after his five years' apprenticeship to that office, Galileo had published his famous Latin *Dialogue of the Two Chief Systems of the World,* a work hailed with admiration by everyone except conservative theologians. The old scholar duly attended his trial in Rome, recanted, was imprisoned for a few days, and did not return to Florence until December. During the remaining eight years of his life, he took care not to run afoul of the Holy Office again. The legend that he was tortured and then stamped to the floor, exclaiming, *Eppur, si mouve!* ("All the same, the earth does move!") is a romantic fabrication of later times.

At this time, however, the chief concern of the grand ducal family was not the question of whether or not the earth was stationary, but that of procuring an heir. The grand duchess, Vittoria della Rovere— an extremely haughty and disdainful lady—was unfortunate in her first two children. A boy who was born while Vittoria was suffering from smallpox, in 1639, lived only a few hours. In 1641, she gave birth again, after an excruciating labour, to a girl, who perished immediately after baptism. In these circumstances, the prospects of an heir appeared less than bright, particularly since Grand Duke Ferdinand was known to prefer the angular beauty of young men to the, in any case dubious, attractions of his frigid wife. Despite these inauspicious beginnings, however, the next year, in August, the grand duchess was finally delivered of a healthy male infant, whom the happy parents had christened Cosimo.

Ferdinand, delighted to be thus relieved of his distasteful conjugal duties, gave himself up to more agreeable pastimes. He had a natural gift for statecraft, in which he indulged in the manner of a hobbyist, and he managed to steer his country skillfully and calmly through the dangers presented by the ambitions of Austria, France, and Spain. In time, his subtlety and self-confidence at this game gained him a European reputation as something of a statesman.

His other amusements were equally well known. After the birth of Cosimo, he concentrated his affections upon the person of a young count who was the handsomest of his many handsome pages. Ferdinand was too honest a man to attempt to conceal this connection from Vittoria, although he was careful, for the sake of his wife's standing, to preserve the outward aspect of a loving husband. The Tuscans, like all Italians, approved of this conduct. They could understand weaknesses of the flesh, but they could never have forgiven that debility of the spirit known as hypocrisy. Public opinion considered that Vittoria had put herself utterly in the wrong by her attitude of icy disdain after discovering Ferdinand's dalliance with the page, and from that time on, the grand duchess was hated by her subjects.

Ferdinand's mother, Grand Duchess Maddalena, was no more sympathetic than his wife. One day she burst into his chambers and, in fury, handed him a long list of prominent Florentine homosexuals. She demanded that these sinners be punished immediately, adding that their particular offence was one of especial repugnance to good Christians everywhere. Ferdinand, who himself was a sincerely devout man, took the list in silence and studied it; then he calmly took a pen and added his own name at the bottom of it.

"Don't be absurd," his mother admonished him. "You know perfectly well that you have added your name only so as to save those guilty wretches from the punishment they deserve. I will see, all the same, that they do not escape the reward that they deserve."

"And what will that reward be, Signora?"

"The fire," the grand duchess snarled. "They must all be burned to ashes."

"Very good. It shall be as you wish." So saying, the gentle Ferdinand threw the paper into the open flames of the hearth. Then he turned again to his mother. "Behold, your sentence has already been carried out, Signora."

Next to statecraft and his young friend, Ferdinand II most loved money. An Englishman who visited Tuscany in 1654, Sir John Reresby, wrote: "He does not think it below him to play the merchant, and his great frugality makes him, not without reason, esteemed the richest prince in Italy, of which last it is evidence sufficient, I mean of his frugality, that he boards with his cook; i.e., that he agrees with him by the week to provide for him daily so many dishes of meat for his own table, most of his servants being put to board wages"—i.e., having to pay for their own food. About ten years earlier, the diarist John Evelyn had commented: "In this palace the grand duke ordinarily resides, living with his Swiss guards after the frugal Italian way and even selling what he can spare of his wines at the cellar under his very house, wicker bottles dangling over even the chief entrance, serving for a vintner's bush."

The grand duke's parsimony, however, did not extend to the cost of public entertainments. He knew that he was expected to provide them, and he did so lavishly, in the forms of fireworks, chariot races, horse and greyhound shows, football, tournaments, processions, and other pageants. Mythological fantasies were devised and played out, often to music. Recitations, accompanied by all sorts of stage effects, were given. Fountains spouted wine. Architectural scenery and machines were displayed. Concerts and dancing, drama and singing, illuminations and nocturnal regattas excited the citizens, all free of charge.

Ferdinand's own favourite recreation was hunting, but he also loved fishing and bowls, though he was not much good at either of the latter. All this gayety greatly appealed to the Tuscans, who had found opportunity to indulge in the lighter side of life during their previous history, despite all its catastrophes. Heavy eating and drinking, with their usual concomitant of sexual dissipation, became the fashion. But this wave of licentiousness did not impair the vigour, only the ultimate success, with which the community ruled by Ferdinand II cultivated art, science, and letters.

The composers of frivolous music, the fresco painters who went in for riotous subjects, the architects who played conjuring tricks with perspective and *chiaroscuro,* enjoyed immense popularity and worked at almost incredible speed. A Neapolitan, Luca Giordano (1632–1705), turned out unnumerable copies of pictures by Giulio Romano, Raphael, and Michelangelo, and he worked so rapidly that he was called the "thunderbolt of painting" and "Luca fa Presto"—Luke the Hustler. His father fed him, as though he were a nestling sparrow, while he wielded the brush, and he used to give notice of his periodic fits of hunger by shrill cries.

Scientists and engineers displayed inventions, from barometers and thermometers to telescopes and artificial incubation. Poets dashed off odes and sonnets in a moment. But of all this immeasurable cornucopia of rapid intellectual activity, less survives today than from epochs of deadly insecurity and violence. Nothing so permanent as the achievements of the men who laboured under the Magnificent Lorenzo was produced. An eccentric painter, Gio da San Gio, is typical of Ferdinand's reign as fifth Grand Duke of Tuscany. This artist, half paralysed with gout, sat in a tub to paint his outdoor frescos of attractive young men, contemporary myths such as the "Expulsion of the Sciences from Greece" and on one occasion a satyr, readily recognisable as Ferdinand's pet dwarf Ghianni, being castrated while tied to a tree by a bevy of nymphs. An indulgent abbot once called Gio "whimsical." It seems an understatement.,

Another Neapolitan painter, rather better remembered than Gio, Salvator Rosa, was called from Rome to Florence by Cardinal Giancarlo de' Medici, Ferdinand's brother, in the late 1640s. Rosa stayed in the Tuscan capital for about nine years. It must have been a distinct change for the blithe, happy-go-lucky Florentines of this period to contemplate his wildly melodramatic landscapes and battlepieces.

The versatility and productivity of these men and many others, almost unknown except in Italy, testify to the extraordinary vitality, superficial though it was, of the age. Naturalists and doctors wrote verses in complicated lyrical metres. Poets went in for chemistry, painters for stage farce. Nothing could be more different from this flashing energy than the sickly morbidity often ascribed to the Italian seventeenth century by those glutted with the glories of the Renaissance. The previous two hundred years perhaps exhibited as much coarse sensuality, bigotry, and pretentious nonsense as the era from 1600 to 1700, and possibly even more pedantry and nepotism. But the seventeenth century far outshone its predecessors in sheer ebullience and merriment, in the variety of its amusements and careers, in the simmering and shimmering of a society no longer preoccupied, as it had been in the days of Cosimo the Elder and his successors, with embittered political faction and jealousy. There is, after all, nothing like benevolent despotism, so often aimed at and so rarely obtained, for the happiness of a community not large enough to be called a nation or small enough to be honeycombed by the petty tyrannies of an inbred society.

Ferdinand II, quite as interested, despite his religious orthodoxy, as his great-uncle Francesco in scientific investigation, continued the patronage of such researches as had occasionally been exercised by Cosimo II. All Italy, and Florence in particular, fully shared the sudden new inclination of the mid-seventeenth century in Europe to prefer the mysteries of nature to those of art. The foundations were already being laid in these years for the so-called "enlightenment" of the next few generations. Both the grand duke and his excessively amorous youngest brother Leopoldo, later appointed a cardinal, studied the technical improvements in the means of elucidating mundane truth.

Galileo was given much to do by Ferdinand after the astronomer's return from Rome to Florence at the end of 1633. Orders poured from the grand ducal palace for still more elaborate telescopes and mensuration instruments of all kinds. Sir John Reresby noted in certain rooms a mathematical device for "demonstrating the perpetual motion, another that either by land or sea, if you see the fire of a cannon or hear the report and desire to know what distance it is from you, it infallibly shows it, as they say, to a quarter of a mile, by the knocking of a leaden plummet fastened by a string against the wood of the instrument." Ferdinand and young Leopoldo carried such contrivances about and hung them on the walls of every house they stayed in.

In 1657, the future cardinal, Leopoldo de' Medici founded an academy called Cimento ("Test") for discussion by the scientists attached to his family. There were ten members, and the grand duke and his relatives generally attended the meetings, which were held at the palace. Hebrew and Christian authorities, even such pagans as Aristotle and the Arabian physician Avicenna, were caught out again and again by these uncompromising Florentine intellectuals, who believe nothing that they could not see or touch. The wonders announced by contemporary globe-trotters were exposed with equal assurance. Unfortunately, the Cimento lasted only ten years. Its members quarrelled so fiercely among themselves that some could not be induced to speak if others were present. The society gradually dispersed, especially after Leopoldo had left for Rome to assume his red hat. The academy's astrolabes, quadrants, vases, tubes, thermometers, microscopes, magnets, and telescopes were abandoned to dust and cobwebs, together with a planetarium originally built in 1593 for Ferdinand I. Ferdinand II, nevertheless, had begun a direction of thought that was to dominate cultural history for the future ages of civilisation.

Ferdinand would have liked to have given his eldest son, Cosimo, a scientific education, but his sullenly bigoted grand duchess, Vittoria della Rovere, objected on religious grounds. Ferdinand, a man of peace, gave in to her prejudices, and Cosimo was brought up by a fanatical, though mediocre, theologian, Volumnio Bandinelli of Siena. But the boy did not spend all his time listening to sermons. Before he reached his teens, he was shooting like a veteran, killing geese in mid-air and pigs on the run with his toy arquebus. At fourteen, he was riding in public and seemed, with his beefy frame and complexion, cut out, like many of the earlier Medici, for an athletic career.

In 1659, however, when the heir to the Grand Duchy was seventeen, the ambassador from Lucca reported: "The prince exhibits the symptoms of a singular piety . . . he is dominated by melancholy beyond all that is usual, and in this he differs from his father. The grand duke is affable with all men, easily moved to laughter and ready with a jest, whereas the prince is never seen to smile. The people attribute this to an imperious and reserved disposition, from which they do not foresee any desirable consequences." In other words Cosimo, like many lads of his age, was undergoing a crisis in his religious sentiments and returning to the austere precepts of Bandinelli. Apparently he didn't care for girls, though he always treated them with punctilious courtesy. He loathed dancing and all music but that of church choirs. He went on several pilgrimages, heard Mass every day, and read a great deal of sacred literature.

At this point in Cosimo's development, his father parted from the handsome page, who no doubt was no longer a lad, and resumed his conjugal duties. In 1660, the grand duchess bore another son, Francesco Maria, but Ferdinand's last years were saddened by the elder boy's gloomy reserve and intensive preoccupation with martyrs and miracles, medieval scholasticism, and the question of salvation. The grand duke, earnest Christian as he was, would almost have preferred Cosimo to resemble the oldest of his three surviving uncles, Giancarlo, connoisseur of pleasure and the arts, whom the grand duchess would not receive owing to what she considered his vulgarly riotous mode of life, much concerned with hunting, gambling, and fornication. In Sustermans' portraits of this Medici, Giancarlo looks a typical "cavalier" of the period, with his long curls and the jaunty angle of his hat, even when it became a red biretta, as it did when he was thirty-four. In 1655 Cardinal Giancarlo de' Medici heartily seconded the brilliant, reckless, and dictatorial Queen Christina of Sweden, then still a spinster, when she visited Rome after her conversion to the Catholic faith and at once plunged into a whirl of luxurious dissipation. Pope

Alexander VII strongly disapproved of the ensuing scandal, and he requested Ferdinand to recall his too exuberant brother to Florence.

There the incorrigible cardinal proceeded to hold orgies in the gardens of the long defunct Platonic Academy of Lorenzo the Magnificent, transforming its decorous walks and groves into a phantasmagoria of grottos, fountains, gigantic statues, and exotic plants. Giancarlo called these plants after his various female favourites. The name of one of them, Cepparella, happened also to be a diminutive of the Italian word for an underground root. It might be supposed that if the lady lived up to her appellation, she was a delicate creature. In fact, she soon died, but it appears that even after death she continued to arouse her lover's concupiscence. According to the sexton in charge of the vault to which the body had been consigned, the cardinal, when he came to look upon the corpse for the last time, entered the coffin and ordered the man to leave the room.

The grand duke was rather afraid of this unconventional brother, who could be murderously vengeful. A lad named Luca—another charming page beloved by Ferdinand—once competed with the cardinal in a heterosexual affair. The youth was thereupon asked to dinner, with some other guests, on an islet in the academy gardens. As night came on and the diners began wandering away to amuse themselves elsewhere, young Luca, who was very drunk, walked off with a friend of his to a bridge connecting the islet with the mainland. There, he fell into the water and was drowned. Giancarlo professed to be aghast at this accident, but few of the citizens of Florence were willing to believe that he had not arranged it.

This otherwise reprehensible prelate had a genuine interest in art. It was he who, as already noted, first invited Salvator Rosa, whom he had met in Rome, to Florence and supported him there. Giancarlo also patronised the stage, providing permanent theatres for two groups of players formerly hired at intervals by his uncle, Prince Lorenzo (d. 1648), brother of Cosimo II.

No one, in short, could have been more different than Giancarlo from the morose young nephew who was to be Cosimo III. Ferdinand considered that it was high time something was done about the latter, to ensure, at any rate, that the legitimate line of grand dukes of Tuscany should continue. Marriage, perhaps, might humanise the lad. The present grand duke had long been on good terms with Louis XIV of France, owing to the craze for Tuscan singers at the French court. In 1658, one of Ferdinand's confidential advisors in Paris informed him that a niece of Louis XIII (d. 1643) "with brown hair, greenish-blue eyes, and a sweet, gentle nature," by name Marguérite-Louise d'Orléans, was in the matrimonial market. Ferdinand also heard that the great statesman Cardinal Mazarin, Italian by birth but French by choice, who had just secured a peaceful start for the reign of Louis XIV, had asked for a portrait of the heir to the Grand Duchy.

It appeared, however, that the girl's father, Duke Gaston d'Orléans, wished to marry the girl to the King himself. Louis, however, disappointed him by marrying the Infanta of Spain, and negotiations with Ferdinand were resumed. Cosimo was impressed by the flattering accounts he read of Marguérite-Louise, and he began to pay unprecedented attention to his clothes, which now all had to be of the French fashion. Then, it appeared that the dowry to be expected with this princess of the blood royal of France would not be sufficient. Gaston, who died on February 2, 1660, had left nothing but debts. His widow, moreover, warned Ferdinand that her daughter, already, at fifteen, used to a great deal of freedom and gayety at the French court, was likely to be bored in the more restricted and solemn society considered appropriate for women of high rank in Italy. But Mazarin, who wanted the support of the powerful Grand Duchy of Tuscany in his designs on the pontificate, bribed the Duchess d'Orléans and her friends to hold their tongues, and the marriage contract was signed on January 24, 1661.

Then, on March 9, Mazarin died. The duchess immediately renewed her objections to the match and recklessly encouraged an affair on which her self-willed daughter was embarking with her eighteen-year-old cousin, Charles of Lorraine. But Louis XIV overruled everyone, and the marriage duly took place, by proxy, in the Louvre, on April 17. Cosimo, in bed at Florence with measles, was represented by the Duke de Guise. Afterwards, Marguérite-Louise wept all the way to Marseilles, on the first stage of her journey to Florence, but at the French port she cheered up a little, for Charles of Lorraine, a nephew of the reigning duke of that region, had spurred after her for one more day of leave-taking. At Marseilles, moreover, costly gifts and gay festivities were presented to her by Ferdinand's brother, the soldierly Mattias de' Medici, before the party set sail for Leghorn.

At that port, since Cosimo remained measles-ridden, his aunt, the Duchess of Parma, Margherita de' Medici, did the honours. Carpets, tapestries, and pictures decorated the streets. Cannon thundered from the fortresses and the war-galleys in the harbour. Four thousand men-at-arms lined the whole way to the grand ducal palace. As evening came on, torches and fireworks illuminated the entire city, and the noise and glare kept everyone awake all night.

Then, at last, on June 15, at Empoli, some twenty-five miles west of Florence, the still sulky young French princess met her husband for the first time. Both parties preserved the most rigid decorum, Cosimo because he was neither demonstrative by nature nor yet completely recovered from his measles, and his bride because she wished with all her heart that she were somewhere else. Her doctor, perhaps at her own instigation, recommended that the young couple refrain from sexual intercourse for the time being, lest the wife catch measles from her new husband.

At Signa, still nearer to Florence, Ferdinand, Giancarlo, and his younger brother, the future Cardinal Leopoldo, met the carriage containing the silent, ill-assorted pair. The grand duke, with the stately courtesy for which he was famous, would not permit his new daughter-in-law to leave the vehicle. She must have been glad, at least, to see his brothers, both gallants of the obviously dashing, susceptible, and gayly eloquent type that she preferred.

In Florence, the coronation ceremonies began at seven on the morning of June 20. They exceeded in splendour anything seen in Italy since Pope Leo X had visited the city. Parts of the built-up area and its walls had been pulled down to make room for a new avenue, flanked by symbolical effigies, and a new gate. New porticos and triumphal arches went up everywhere, and a theatre was erected in the Piazza San Gallo to accommodate spectators of the actual crowning.

The princess wore an embroidered gown of silver cloth with a lace headdress. A chain of diamonds with forty tapering pearls hanging between them was sewn over the robe. Two pearls, each the size of a small pigeon's egg, fastened the fabric at the shoulders. She was escorted into the theatre by Cosimo and Mattias and knelt at an altar in the centre of the stage. The Archbishop of Siena handed the crown to the grand duke, who set it on her head. The old bells of the Florentine churches, which had so often toiled for war and triumph in republican days, then chimed incessantly while cannon boomed.

Then the procession to the cathedral began, headed by the twelve mace-bearers of the Senate, in vermilion livery, and the pages of the grand duke. Marquesses, prelates, more pages, heralds, and grooms followed, in black or cerulean velvet, in green or in purple and gold, riding in pairs. Next marched the Swiss guards, in two tones of scarlet, and finally Cosimo, in black, superbly mounted, with gems on his baldric, sword, and brocaded doublet, and even on his golden spurs. A hundred men-at-arms in Medici crimson thronged about him. Behind them, the princess reclined in an open litter, all white and silver, drawn by white mules similarly caparisoned and ridden by two angelic-looking children in white and gold. Thirty-two young Florentine nobles carried the heavy canopy, of gold cloth fringed with pearls. The Duchess d'Angoulême and the Countess de Belloy came next, in a carriage emblazoned with the arms of France, the lilies being rendered by topazes, and of Tuscany, the Medicean rubies gleaming on a ground of lapis lazuli. Three hundred coaches bearing the entire aristocracy of Florence brought up the rear.

At the entrance to the cathedral, the Bishop of Fiesole sprinkled the bride and bridegroom with holy water, while twelve choirs intoned the "Te Deum." Cosimo led Marguérite-Louise to the high altar, a dazzling blaze of gold. Incense filled the great church. The bishop reduced most of the congregation to tears of rapture by his impassioned oratory. As the grand duke and duchess came forward to meet the married prince and princess, the ceaselessly cheering citizens and the crashing guns drowned out every other sound.

Marguérite-Louise, despite her immense vitality, had been utterly exhausted by these proceedings. It was not until the evening of the twenty-second that the princely pair were led to their marriage-bed. The grand duchess Vittoria personally handed over the bride's night-gown. The bedposts were of solid silver, with variegated enamelling, adorned with differently coloured jewels of great value. But this gorgeous setting did not stimulate the bridegroom; he performed the conjugal rites clumsily and without enthusiasm, apologising for the weakness in which he had been left by his illness.

On July 18, Nicolas Fouquet, Minister of Finance to Louis XIV, was informed that "the prince hath only couched with her three times, and every time he does not go he sends a valet to tell Madame not to await him. The French ladies and maids are greatly surprised by this method of paying compliments . . . they try to keep her amused but are deeply embarrassed by her continuing melancholy. The prince and princess never speak to each other. Madame finds life here very strange."

The princess started the first of her long series of quarrels with Cosimo on the second night they slept together, by demanding that all the grand ducal jewels be presented to her as her personal property. Cosimo refused, politely enough, pointing out that the articles were Medici heirlooms, to be reserved for future generations. After a shrill torrent of curses, Marguérite-Louise coolly stole as many of these items as she could lay her hands on and despatched them to France. Her French couriers were overtaken, however, and forced to disgorge the plunder.

Such behaviour, Ferdinand decided, could be stopped only by keeping the lady entertained. A series of diversions of staggering magnificence and ingenuity began. They included Prince Cosimo's own specialty of ballets on horseback by night in the Boboli gardens. It is probable that for sheer spectacular glory nothing seen before ever surpassed or even equalled the stupendously radiant and grandiose scenes of pagan and Christian mythology then presented.

Yet, despite all the hard work put in to keep the utterly spoilt princess in a good temper, despite the repeated evidence of her natural charm and irrepressible high spirits, Marguérite-Louise continued to be a very great nuisance to both her husband and Tuscans in general. On July 30 the Venetian ambassador reported: "During the wedding festivities, the young princess, in wishing to display her royal grandeur and generosity, has given the grand duke and other princes of this house much cause for displeasure. For they discovered that she has despoiled herself of many precious objects for her personal use and necessity, to bestow them upon her ladies and others who have accompanied her from France. The grand duchess was very aggrieved about it, and the grand duke resented it so deeply that friction and misunderstanding have arisen between them, which persevere. The prince, her husband, is likewise affected, as he takes great exception to the freedom of his wife's behaviour, which, if customary in France, is very unusual in Italy, as the princess had previously been warned. They have had several other vexations because of the excessive licence of her household, so that the princes have been obliged to make her dismiss at once almost everyone, providing her in the meantime with Florentines. Only those of her French servants who appear the most moderate are suffered to remain."

But gradually, after all these prolonged celebrations, life at the grand ducal court settled down to its former routine. Ferdinand returned to his laboratory, Cosimo to his devotions, and Vittoria to her confessor. By 1664, the prince was only sharing his wife's bed once a week, and even then with a doctor in attendance who ordered him out of it, on medical grounds and probably by pre-arrangement, at frequent intervals. On normal occasions, though, the young man, still in his early twenties, seemed decorously happy. He looked and talked like a quiet, benign priest twice his age. He referred, for instance, with absolute horror, to the death of the Duke of Mantua, because it occurred during active sexual intercourse with a mistress. This austerity formed the stronged possible contrast with the cynically defiant frivolity of his nineteen-year-old consort.

It was at about this time that Charles of Lorraine suddenly appeared in Florence. He was given a most courteous reception by Ferdinand, who knew nothing of the visitor's former intimacy with Cosimo's restless wife. The lovers then enjoyed a number of private interviews together, but these meetings could not have been wholly exhilarating. Both partners had disagreeable circumstances to relate, Charles having quarrelled with Louis XIV, who had promptly exiled him.

When Charles left Florence in order to repair his fortunes by taking part in certain military adventures, Marguérite-Louise sent ardent letters after him. He replied with amusing but affectionate sets of verses. One of these was intercepted and perused with painful indignation by Ferdinand and Cosimo. They said nothing of this discovery to the princess, but a close scrutiny of her correspondence, even of that with her mother, followed as a matter of course. Undesirable communications were destroyed or returned to her. She complained to Louis XIV of this treatment, but he declined to intervene. An almost open war developed between the Medici family and their French princess. The young lady's tongue, in this campaign, won victory after victory. She did not even hesitate to accuse the venerable Grand Duchess Vittoria herself of a guilty association, to make up for so many years of chastity, with her swarms of priests and monks.

Cardinal Giancarlo might have relieved Marguérite-Louise of her boredom, though apparently he never wished to do so, for he preferred ladies of more agreeable disposition. In any case, he died of apoplexy in January 1663, much to Ferdinand's relief. The cardinal, as he aged, had grown increasingly lawless and unscrupulous. On one occasion he had reprieved a notorious murderer at the price of sleeping with the criminal's wife, a woman of exceptional beauty. It was unquestionably his extravagant dissipation in all directions that killed him at fifty-two. Ferdinand, in order to have a second cardinal in the family, since his sixty-eight-year-old Uncle Carlo was already senile, arranged for his brother Leopoldo, aged forty-six, to receive the red hat in this year.

On August 9, Marguérite-Louise gave birth to a son who was christened Ferdinand. Her convalescence proved slow, for she had exhausted herself by riding, in her usual impetuous style, up to the last possible moment. Cosimo, relieved that the succession was now ensured, took less notice of her than ever, but he dismissed more of her French staff. It was now clear even to Louis XIV that the marriage he had so inflexibly promoted was going from bad to worse. He wrote to the delinquent wife: "I have seen certain letters you wrote to friends of yours which have astonished and offended me to an extent you can judge of, considering the kind of ideas that pass through your head, which could not be more extraordinary. You reflect on my affection for you . . . I hope that as soon as you have had time to think better of your behaviour and to remember what blood you are descended from, you will regret ever having entertained such fanciful notions."

Nevertheless, most Florentines not closely associated with her liked the attractive, witty, and energetic Parisienne better than her moody husband. The latter decided, or was advised, to go off to Venice for a time to prevent further deterioration in his popularity. On his return for his birthday on August 7, 1664, the Venetian ambassador wrote that "the fondness the princess had proclaimed for her son, her affability towards her mother-in-law and general semblance of gayety before her husband's return" were no longer in evidence. Discord, he went on, "waxed more lively than ever . . . she has told her husband she wishes to retire to the top floor of the palace." She also told Ferdinand that she refused to acknowledge Cosimo as her husband, and that she did not wish to be "molested" by him. The birthday celebrations were cancelled.

At last Marguérite-Louise hit upon the most effective expedient she had yet tried to annoy her pious spouse. She declared that a convent would be the only way to save her soul, since she had been coerced into marriage and was therefore living in sin with a man whom she could not regard as her legitimate husband. It was in vain that Cosimo's theologians pointed out the fallacies in this argument. Plunged into gloom at the thought of having committed fornication and fathered a bastard, Cosimo kept more and more to himself, and, whereas another man might have taken to drink, he spent most of his time eating.

In 1665, Marguérite-Louise changed her mind again. She called on the grand duke, expressing her desire to resume a normal married life, and Cosimo immediately forgot his misery and welcomed his repentant wife effusively. King Louis wrote: "The best news I could hear from you is that of your reconciliation with my cousin the Prince of Tuscany and all his family. My joy is redoubled when I perceive that this has happened of your own free will, without my being obliged to assert my authority." The princess next proceeded to enchant everyone around her, from Ferdinand downwards, by her amiability and grace. When, however, she found herself pregnant for the second time, she instantly began riding all over the countryside at full gallop, obviously with the intention of ending her condition, which did not appeal to her luxury-loving temperament. She refused to eat for a time with the same object. Then she collapsed with influenza. Yet, she not only recovered in time to bear a healthy daughter, christened Anna Maria Luisa, on August 11, 1667, but was also cured of a breast ulcer and an attack of small-pox, which was treated by cutting off all her hair. It was no wonder that, as soon as she was allowed out of bed, she reverted to floods of tears and abuse of Cosimo as the cause of all her misfortunes. The wretched husband, on his father's advice, fled once more abroad. He visited Austria, Germany, and the Netherlands, returning to Florence in May 1668. But he found his incalculable wife still implacably embittered towards him. She would not see him, and she was believed to be plotting to escape to Paris.

There was nothing for it but more travel. In September, Cosimo set sail for Barcelona. He toured Spain and Portugal, then took ship for London, which he reached early in 1669. Pepys noted on April 1: "Took coach again and went five or six miles towards Brentford. The Prince of Tuscany, who comes into England only to spend money and see our country, comes into the town today and is much expected. We met him, but the coach passing by apace, we could not see much of him, but he seems a very jolly and good comely man." On April 11

the diarist added: "Going out of the Queen's Chapel I did see the
Prince of Tuscany come out, a comely black fat man in a mourning
suit, and my wife and I did see him this afternoon through a window in
this Chapel." Sir John Reresby wrote in his *Memoirs* for the same
month: "The Prince of Tuscany came to London with a retinue and
equipage suitable to his quality. The King entertained him magnificently.
After some time he kept house at his own charge, where he had all the
portable varieties of food and drink Italy could afford. I dined twice with
him. He was very kind to me, as he was to all those that had travelled
in Italy and knew the language."

From London, on June 1, Cosimo embarked for France, where
Ferdinand had told him he must make as good an impression on Louis
as he had on other potentates. There had been trouble in London, however, with the French ambassador, on a point of ceremony, and that
functionary had not come to salute Cosimo on his last day at the English
court. Consequently, the ultra-conventional Louis would not at first consent to Cosimo's crossing to the French coast. The prince therefore
spent some days in the Netherlands before reaching Paris. Once there,
however, he found the King at his most gracious and, now that his
indiscretion in London had been duly punished by a delayed arrival in
the etiquette-ridden capital of France, he satisfied its hyper-critical
monarch and court with his thoroughly Medicean gravity, which most
of the members of that family could put on and off at will.

The Duchess de Montpensier, step-sister to Marguérite-Louise and
generally known as La Grande Mademoiselle, commented that Cosimo
"spoke admirably on every topic and was very well acquainted with
the mode of life at all the courts of Europe. In that of France he
never made a single blunder. . . . His physique is rather stout for so
young a man, he had a fine head of black, curly hair, a large red
mouth, good teeth, a healthy, ruddy complexion, abundance of wit,
and is agreeable in conversation."

The grand duke's heir had certainly improved a good deal during the
extensive travels he had undertaken to relieve his wife of his detested
presence, but it is doubtful that the change was a basic one. The en-
graved portraits of Cosimo all show certain defects of feature, notably
very heavy lips, which the duchess did not mention. She had not, however, the reputation of a very conscientious observer or reporter. She
was better at military operations than at giving an impartial account
of strangers.

The heir to the Grand Duchy of Tuscany parted from the Sun
King on excellent terms. After four months in the French capital,
Cosimo understood more clearly how to deal with his very typically
French consort. He organised a ballet for her on the lines of those he
had seen in Paris, where the King himself had participated in them.

Marguérite-Louise danced the chief part in Cosimo's production, and the Florentine court suddenly acquired a sprightly aspect.

This new-found joy, however, was soon dissipated by the death of Grand Duke Ferdinand in 1670. A historian of the next generation recorded the passing in some detail: "Since the grand duke had derived no advantage whatever from the medicine he had taken on the previous day, the cupping glasses were used again, and another ounce was removed from his bladder . . . four live pigeons were ripped open and put on his forehead. A cauterizing iron was later applied to the head, but without success. His condition worsened towards midday, and the legate arrived at the palace and gave him the papal benediction . . . next morning at ten o'clock, he had several reliquaries placed about him. At a quarter of two, he expired at the age of fifty-nine, after a reign of forty-nine years."

Ferdinand II, for all his weaknesses, was greatly mourned by the citizens of Tuscany, and sincerely regretted by the princes of Europe. He had been an able statesman, a compassionate and wise ruler, and a genuinely good man. His faults, which he was the first to acknowledge, were not those that impede the prosperity of states, while his virtues had been sufficient to win for him the esteem of everyone except the women of his own household.

5. Cosimo III

Cosimo had inherited the piety though not the scientific interests of his father. He showed no trace whatever of the stern energy of Cosimo I, the respect for learning of both Francesco and Cosimo II, or the devotion to public service of Ferdinand I. The benign Ferdinand II had scored certain political and diplomatic triumphs. He had governed economically, on the whole, and he had dealt patiently with his heir's extremely disconcerting wife. And so he had finally secured the Medici succession. At the time of his death, however, certain shadows were falling upon the Tuscan scene. Heavy taxation, English and Dutch rivalry with Italy in trade and manufactures, the excessive influence of priests and monks, the multiplication of nunneries, and the prevalence of plague and malaria all combined to darken the prospects of the Grand Duchy.

At the helm of Tuscan affairs, in these circumstances, stood a blunt-minded pietist, found so intolerably boring by his spirited wife that she could scarcely contrive a smile at the coronation festivities. But Marguérite-Louise, if she could not smile, could still plot for power, a faculty that immediately brought her into conflict with her mother-in-law. Vittoria had never had much time for the capricious French-woman, who had already jeered at her, quite unfairly, as a licentious hypocrite. But the dowager grand duchess, now that her son had succeeded to the head of affairs, began to take an interest in politics and administration.

Cosimo condoned Vittoria's meddling. He had meant at first to rule conscientiously and reform the state financial system so as to cope with the deteriorating economy of the country, but he soon grew tired of this dutiful work and consulted Vittoria at every turn. She gradually took charge of the government, while he spent more and more time at his prayers. Marguérite-Louise soon found that she could not match her grave senior, who behaved more and more like a mighty abbess every day, in matters of diplomacy and business. Thus, when the Privy Council began to meet in Vittoria's private apartments, the embittered consort of Cosimo III gave up the struggle.

On May 24, 1671, Marguérite-Louise produced a second son, whom she named Giovan Gastone, after her father, the late Duke Gaston d'Orléans. She had in fact quite lost interest in the Medici family, having decided that the two representatives she knew best were insufferably dull bigots. She thought of nothing but escaping to France, and in pursuance of this plan, she informed Louis XIV that she was again suffering from cancer of the breast and must have a French doctor. The King sent her a venerable specialist, who soon saw that her malady was psychological rather than physical; but, like everyone else except Vittoria, he could not resist his patient's overwhelming personal fascination. He told Cosimo that the grand duchess's constitution stood in need of medicinal waters that could only be obtained in Burgundy.

The grand duke, though not the most intelligent of men, was not a fool. He naturally pointed out that the waters in question could easily be brought to Florence. The doctor hastened to agree, was generously remunerated, and took his leave. Marguérite-Louise, defeated again but indefatigable, nagged both her husband and the august Sun King interminably, usually on the most trivial grounds. Cosimo was accustomed to it, and he found consolation with his confessor. Louis, however, grew tired of his obstreperous young cousin and ceased to answer her letters. The lady, in fact, had nothing to complain of except the inability of her consort and his court to cater for her passion for such amusements as she had known in Paris. Finally, by the end of 1672, the grand duchess's ennui reached the point where she was moved to extreme action. She wrote to Cosimo:

"I have done what I could until now to gain your friendship and have not succeeded. The more consideration I showed for you, the more contempt you showed for me. For a long time, I have tried to bear it, but this is beyond my power. So I have made a resolution which will not surprise you when you reflect on your base usage of me for nearly twelve years. It is that I declare I can live with you no longer.

I am the source of your unhappiness as you are of mine. I beg you to consent to a separation to set my conscience and yours at rest. I shall send my confessor to discuss it with you and shall here await the orders of His Majesty [Louis XIV] to whom I have written craving permission to enter a convent in France. I beg of you the same, and assure you that I shall forget the whole past if you grant me this favour. Do not perturb yourself about my conduct. My heart is as it should be and it will never let me perform a dishonourable action, seeing that I have the fear of God and horror of this world ever before my eyes. I believe that what I am proposing to you is the surest means of affording us peace for the remainder of our days. I recommend my children to you."

Cosimo replied immediately, with austere dignity: "I do not know if your unhappiness can have exceeded mine. Although everyone else has done justice to the many signs of respect, consideration, and love which I have never tired of showing you for nearly twelve years, you have regarded them with the utmost indifference. I ought to be satisfied with universal approbation, but I continue to hope that Your Highness will also recognise this truth. I await the father confessor you are sending to learn what he has to say on your behalf. I shall acquaint him with my own sentiments. Meanwhile, I am giving orders that, in addition to proper attendance and convenience, Your Highness will receive at this villa all the respect which is your due."

Actually, Cosimo was beside himself with rage at her insolence. It is probable that his ancestor, Cosimo I, would have had his grand duchess quietly assassinated. Cosimo III did not care for this way of dealing with problems. The "respect" to which he referred in his letter took the form of ordering the closest possible confinement of his wife at Poggio a Caiano. She was never to leave the house except for short rides or walks under military escort. No one from outside the villa was to be allowed access to her quarters without his own written permission. There were to be no more parties. She was to communicate with him only through the Prime Minister.

This situation, and the bombardment of speeches for both prosecution and defence with which Louis was assailed by the contestants, caused the French King in the spring of 1673 to send the Bishop of Marseilles to talk matters over with Cosimo and his wife. The prelate, a man of the world, visited the lady first. She appeared delighted to see him, but whenever he tried, during the next few days, to give the conversation a serious tone, he found himself interrupted by violinists, by songs from Marguérite-Louise in person, by jovial portrait painters, by dancing, and by other uproarious diversions. Nevertheless, he told Cosimo afterwards that under the grand duchess's frivolous exterior "a quite extraordinary firmness" was to be discerned. The bishop's masculine rationality, however, broke down at last under feminine intransigence. He was reduced to warning the Grand Duchess of Tuscany that remorse for abandoning her children would haunt her for the rest of her life, and that she could expect nothing but hostility from Louis in the future. Then he left the villa, reported to Cosimo the utter failure of his mission, and, in May, took the road back to Versailles.

King Louis was deeply disturbed at his trusted agent's account of the situation. It was impossible for him to press the Church to annul a marriage that he himself had promoted. At the same time, both husband and wife appeared equally determined upon a separation, Cosimo by keeping Marguérite-Louise a prisoner in Tuscany, but not in Florence, and she by her intention of escaping to France.

This last plan seemed about to succeed in 1674, when, on May 15, Marguérite-Louise noted in her diary: "The grand duke having asked whether my vocation to become a nun persisted, and I having answered in the affirmative, he told me that he would beg the King to allow me to enter a convent in France, which His Majesty will select."

The two incompatible partners seemed to have become allies, if only in order that they should see no more of each other. On June 7, Louis agreed to Cosimo's request, subject to certain stipulations about funds, political activities, and etiquette. After much discussion, a Benedictine convent at Montmartre was considered the most suitable for a lady of high rank, orthodox religious convictions, and untarnished virtue. The abbess of that place, however, raised objections, ostensibly on the ground of shortage of accommodation, but really because she did not care for what she had heard of the grand duchess's character.

For Marguérite-Louise, the allaying of such pious scruples was child's play. She wrote an eloquent letter to the abbess, so charmingly submissive in tone that the good mother superior withdrew her opposition. On December 26, the articles of separation were signed. By this document, the grand duchess declared that she would never leave the convent without the King's permission, that she renounced all her privileges as a princess of royal blood, that her attendants would be only such as the abbess approved, that she would bequeath all her possessions to her children, and that her conduct would be in every respect blameless. Cosimo promised to pay for her journey and installation, and to allow her a generous pension.

After prolonged disputes over money for the journey and the quantity of furniture to be taken to Paris, the grand duchess left Poggio a Caiano on June 10, 1675. She had summoned her children to take leave of her, but on their arrival their mother parted from them with little sign of affection. She saw nothing of Cosimo; he merely announced that he would pray regularly for the salvation of her soul. Most Tuscans regretted the departure of their resplendent and lively grand duchess, and they thenceforth regarded her as a martyr to the sour temper of her husband.

The grand duke tried to counteract his unpopularity, and also to give reign to his innate leanings to ostentation, by beginning to live in a much more luxurious style than formerly. His table, in particular, groaned under the inordinate weight of expensive foreign dishes, and he grew enormously fat and unsteady on his legs. Pompous and costly ceremonies multiplied at Florence until the court became a byword for extravagant opulence.

At the same time, Cosimo's obstinate religiosity increased. He began a fierce persecution of Jews and other "heretics." Scientists and philosophers considered themselves fortunate if they were simply sent on embassies abroad rather than being fined, tortured, or imprisoned. In general, the poverty and neglect from which Florentine intellectuals suffered in this reign came to be as notorious elsewhere in Europe as the pretentious vulgarity of the Florentine court.

Meanwhile, the extraordinary situation arose of a possible inheritance by Cosimo's family of the property of his wife's lover, now Duke Charles of Lorraine. Duke Charles, a general of the Holy Roman Empire, had married Eleonora Maria of Austria, sister of the Emperor and widow of the King of Poland. If Charles died childless, his Duchy of Lorraine would revert first to his old love and cousin, Marguérite-Louise, and second to her son Ferdinand. The grand duchess's cupidity was so aroused by this prospect that, when one of the Montmartre convent's nuns told her that Eleonora was pregnant, the rival heiress calmly suggested that it would be easy to bribe the midwife to "stick a pin through the new-born infant's head." She alleged that one of the unwanted deliveries of the present Empress had been disposed of in this way. Eleonora Maria, in fact, bore her new husband more than one son. The eldest, Leopold, duly succeeded to the Duchy of Lorraine in 1690, and Cosimo's attempts to get the Medici rights acknowledged by Vienna caused only laughter.

At this point, Cosimo was actually beginning to miss his wife, and he offered, through a confidential agent, to re-endow her with power, funds, and independence. But she rejected this proposal with scorn. She was apparently beginning to enjoy herself in her old, mad fashion. When the abbess protested her dancing and indoor games with guardsmen and grooms, Marguérite-Louise told the aristocratic old lady that she would set fire to the convent if such objections continued. On June 3, 1680, it appeared that she meant to do so in any case. Her pet dog's basket, placed too near the hearth-fire, suddenly burst into flames. The grand duchess, instead of encouraging her attendants to put out the conflagration, ordered them to run for their lives. The convent did not burn down, but the abbess was alarmed. She requested Cosimo to authorise the installation of a special cistern to guard against future occurrences of this kind. The grand duke complained furiously to Louis—for his wife's rejection of his recent advances had cut him to the quick—and the King forbade the perpetrator of such dangerous antics to frequent his court, as she had lately been doing in defiance of the articles of separation.

Marguérite-Louise was quiet for a while; then, early in 1681, she wrote a letter of many pages to Cosimo, accusing him of deliberately prejudicing Louis against her. "There is not an hour or a day," she scribbled, "when I do not wish someone would hang you . . . we shall both soon go to hell, and I shall have the torment of seeing you there . . . here I shall commit every possible extravagance in order to displease you . . . you will never be able to change me . . . beware if I ever should return, for if I do so you will die by my hand. . . ."

The grand duke was so mortified by this effusion—which had made King Louis roar with laughter—that, to the writer's delight, he fell ill. She at once announced that the moment the invalid perished she would return to Florence and show her beloved citizens what good government, as in the time of Ferdinand II, could mean. "Good taste and philosophy," she exclaimed venomously, "shall then replace hypocrisy!" But, unfortunately for these hopes, Cosimo had the temerity to recover from his bilious attack.

The vegetarian diet ordered by the grand ducal doctors to prevent a recurrence of such illness led the gluttonous convalescent to take up botany as a hobby. He cultivated Indian, American, and Asian plants in his gardens. He also returned, on medical advice, to his former pleasures of hunting on horseback. He took care, on all these expeditions, that a monastery should be close at hand so that he might indulge in a different sort of exercise, that of pious devotion.

The younger set in Florence led an entirely different life from that of its corpulent, gloomy, and ultra-devout ruler. Prince Ferdinand, now a good-looking young man of twenty, fond of horses and music, led the gay and sceptical new generation. He sang and played the harpsichord with considerable talent. His interest in the plastic arts extended to the living human figure, though he liked boys better than girls. Of his elders, he especially adored his Uncle Francesco Maria, the grand duke's own brother, aged twenty-eight.

Young Ferdinand, in the midst of his pleasures, did not express enthusiasm when his father first broached the subject of marriage. He agreed, however, to think over some of the princesses Cosimo suggested, provided that a visit to Venice, then the Mecca of all susceptible European males, preceded serious investigation. The most promising young woman, politically speaking, appeared to be Princess

Violante Beatrice, daughter of the Elector of Bavaria. Ferdinand raised
no objection to her, but he could think of nothing but Venice at this
time, and he rushed off to that city as soon as he had nodded his consent to his father's harangue on matrimony.

Cosimo sent the following phrases after him. "I know," he wrote,
"that I am bound for the peace of my conscience to assure myself
that when the prince finds himself in the freedom of Venice, and
especially during Carnival, he will abstain from diversions that are
damnable to the soul, and neither permitted by divine law nor suited
to the condition of a prince, who should give example to others. And
that he will likewise avoid becoming indecently familiar with musicians
and comedians and will take no part in the conversation, still less the
entertainment, of courtesans. The Duke of Mantua, having forfeited
much of that credit which would otherwise be due to his birth and
rank, and having still various disgusting attachments in Venice, I intend the prince to avoid not only his friendship but also his company."
Ferdinand's response was to take up with a young *castrato* singer
named Cecchino, with whom he soon became as intimate as possible.

The next matrimonial problem was that of Cosimo's daughter, Anna
Maria Luisa, aged eighteen. She was her father's favourite, but suitable
princes fought shy of her, fearing she might have inherited her notorious
mother's disposition. Indeed, the girl showed a great interest in entertainments at this date, and she laughed rather too loudly and too often,
but that was as far as it went, for the moment. As for Gian Gastone,
aged sixteen, and considered by impartial observers to be "comely,
docile, modest, and studious," all the proposals for his matrimonial future fell through either because Cosimo thought the dowries offered too
meagre, or because, in grander spheres, he feared the expense of ensuring that the boy cut a figure worthy of his ancestors.

Ferdinand returned from Venice, with Cecchino, early in 1688, to
find that Cosimo's Florence bored him to death, as it had bored his
mother. He complained that the population consisted almost wholly of a
degraded rabble of monks and nuns, pseudo-repentant whores, renegade
Turks and Jews, and beggars of all descriptions. He could not bear to
look upon this poverty-stricken multitude, forever whining religious
platitudes in and out of season. The Florentines, for their part, could
not bear to look at Cecchino. Even gentle Cosimo disliked the effemi-
nate singer, and he berated the prince's tutor for permitting such a
creature to be brought into the family circle. The grand duke hurried
on with the marriage to Princess Violante, in the hope that it would
cure his son's infatuation with the Venetian, and the contract was
signed at Munich on May 24, 1688. Marguérite-Louise was not consulted about this union, and upon hearing of it, she despatched so
ferocious a letter to Cosimo that the confessor of King Louis, after

perusing a copy, thought it must be the work of a madwoman, "a fury from hell."

Princess Violante, after a proxy marriage, left Munich towards the end of November. Gian Gastone met the fifteen-year-old bride at Bologna, and Ferdinand appeared a few miles outside Florence. The demure little Bavarian fell in love with him instantly, and for the rest of her life. But her bored, haughty husband did not reciprocate these sentiments. Like many homosexuals, he was prepared to act heterosexually when the occasion demanded, but he found Violante too plain for his tastes. The grand duke, however, liked the girl's quiet and gentle manners, the exact opposite of those of Marguérite-Louise at her age. She was also, he gladly discovered, "greatly inclined to piety."

Prince Ferdinand began by treating Violante with the courtesy required, but soon he hardly could bear to look at her. Whether he ever succeeded in performing his conjugal duties is not clear, but it is certain that the couple never had children. Ferdinand immediately became preoccupied with projects for building an opera-house at Pratolino. He supervised personally the painting of the scenery and the construction of the machinery for stage effects, crafts he had learned in Venice, then the most celebrated city in Italy for opera. At the Pratolino theatre, opened on the third floor of the Medici villa there, five musical dramas by Alessandro Scarlatti, then residing in Naples, were produced. They entailed a voluminous correspondence between the composer and the prince. The letters throw an instructive light on Scarlatti's ideas and methods and Ferdinand's appreciation of them, but unfortunately the scores in question have disappeared.

In June 1689, Cosimo received a characteristic letter, through Zipoli, his ambassador in Paris, from his implacable grand duchess:

"I have sold my pearl necklace. Zipoli can testify that I have pawned my diamonds. In short, unless I receive the rest of my due within six weeks, I shall make a violent decision which will astonish the grand duke. My good nature, or rather folly, allows him time for the last payment after which things will go badly for him . . . my patience is exhausted. Tell him that when one has no bread, one's blood boils. Anything may be expected of me when I am driven to extremes. In short, I want my money and I will not be ruined by the grand duke's spending of it. If he had a good conscience, he would not do me the injustice he does. It is theft of my goods and certainly worse than highway robbery, because he does not risk his life in the business. He is all the guiltier because he does it by reason of his hatred of me, and he will have to render account of it on the Day of Judgement. May it please God that all the harm he does me may not cause his damnation. He will never be able to do me as much good as he has done me wrong. He should begin to reflect upon himself and set his conscience in order."

She also appealed to her son Ferdinand, though in terms the very reverse of hectoring. He replied coldly: "I regret that I can do nothing with my august father. I, too, am in such a predicament that I must make a virtue of necessity and can only dispose of my heart."

In fact, father and son were by now, in 1690, at swordspoint about money. This quarrel was actually the consequence of Cosimo's excessive favour to the clergy, for whom he endowed sinecures all over Tuscany, bringing his subjects to the verge of starvation through the taxes he imposed to raise funds for this purpose. Eventually, he realised that he would have to practise economy or be ruined, himself, together with his people. Ferdinand refused to cut down his expenses, and in desperation, his father applied to the hated Cecchino, who graciously arranged a compromise. The prince promised to obey his parent in all things, provided he received a fixed allowance for his private use.

A dispute had arisen in June 1689, about protocol, between Cosimo and the Emperor, who had granted to the Duke of Savoy some of the privileges reserved to kings. The grand duke characteristically protested to Vienna against this promotion of a duke who had not been even a grand duke, over his head. Leopold, to calm the touchy Florentine, offered to arrange a marriage between Anna Maria Luisa de' Medici and the elector palatine, Johann Wilhelm. Anna had already been turned down, for various reasons, by Spanish and Portuguese princes, by the Duke of Savoy himself, and by the heir to the throne of Louis XIV—the last of these plans having been fiercely opposed by the grand duchess on the ground that it might lead to herself being put in the shade at Versailles. In these circumstances Johann Wilhelm, the brother of the Queens of Spain and Portugal, and also of the Empress, did not seem an unhappy choice, especially as, in February 1691, the elector procured for Cosimo the same rank as that so recently accorded to the ruler of Savoy, entitling him to be addressed as "Your Royal Highness" and "Most Serene." Anna was married to Johann Wilhelm by proxy on April 29 of that year. A tall brunette of twenty-two, with black eyes, a clear complexion, and a rather deep voice, the lady at least had a Medicean personal dignity and love of pomp and circumstance. Unfortunately, the bridegroom had just contracted syphilis, but this discovery was not made until later.

Whether or not Cosimo knew about the syphilis, he refused to meet further demands by the Emperor for money, declined a close alliance with Austria on the grounds of his friendship with Louis, and finally, in October, issued a decree against excessive sexual freedom. It began: "Considering that to admit young men into houses to make love to girls and let them dally at doors and windows is a great incentive to rapes, abortions, and infanticides . . . not only youths and maidens, but also their fathers, mothers, and relatives are forbidden to admit love-making in houses with or without permission or at doors or windows by night." Heavy fines and imprisonment were imposed for such offences. Nor did the austere grand duke stop there. One young sodomite was actually beheaded at his orders, and a young man who had contracted a marriage displeasing to Cosimo was imprisoned for life.

Cosimo's religiosity next expressed itself in missionary zeal, and his agents roamed such foreign lands as professed Protestantism. Naturally, he was swindled and duped over and over again, especially by the Londoners of William III. Meanwhile, the ordinary citizens of Florence, plundered and plagued alternately by their fanatical grand duke, resorted to crime. The incidence of serious offences grew by leaps and bounds, followed by correspondingly cruel punishments. The guilty were often tortured to death or castrated.

Yet the intolerant ruler's curiosity about those who had abandoned the Catholic faith remained insatiable. He demanded from his spies full details of the gossip of every court in Europe. He sent for all the latest and best publications, including the Puritan John Milton's *Paradise Lost,* translated into Italian. He collected portraits of the equally heretical mistresses of the late King Charles II of England, whatever the cost. All the same, the general level of culture and civilisation in Florence, which had once led the whole world in that respect, sank to an abysmal level.

Meanwhile, in Paris, the grand duchess was quarrelling violently with the new abbess of her Montmartre convent. After terrorising this comparatively youthful lady with a pistol, for alleged "infamous intrigues" designed to sully the forty-five-year-old princess's chastity, Marguérite-Louise wrote an unusually pathetic letter to Cosimo, in the sanctimonious strain she knew would appeal to him:

"In spite of the many differences which have arisen between us I have always done you the justice to believe that you entertained no rancour against me, knowing the purity of your conscience. . . . I remain here with my holy sisters and what leisure I have I employ in acts of piety and in attendance upon the sick, having never relinquished my original design of devoting myself to their service, not in attendance upon the hospitals in Paris because I do not wish to be in a place where I have friends or relations but a hundred leagues therefrom, where I am seen and known by no one and where I shall have nothing else to engage me but to think of God and the salvation of my soul. There is no danger of my abandoning this resolution. I am tired of the world, with which I am too well acquainted. I therefore pray you, for love not of me, but of that God whom we all adore, that you will contribute to the saving of my soul."

After a long dispute, Cosimo, Louis, and Father La Chaise, the royal confessor, among them forced the grand duchess to retire to the convent of St. Mandé, farther away from the centre of the capital. She was, moreover, to cease going out at night, and to submit to constant supervision by two attendants, one male and one female. Marguérite-Louise soon reported that St. Mandé was a "spiritual brothel," and she persuaded the Archbishop of Paris to give her charge of it. Thereupon, she settled down calmly in the little community with a new lover, Fra Bonaventura, a renegade monk who pretended to be a soldier. For a considerable time, she gave Cosimo no more trouble.

Another matter, the question of the succession, worried the grand duke a great deal. The sophisticated Ferdinand, preoccupied with the production of operas and forever closeted with Cecchino, had nothing in common with his quiet little Bavarian consort. Princess Violante remained barren despite frantic appeals by Cosimo to the Almighty. In her despair, Violante turned to another neglected figure at court, Prince Gian Gastone. He appeared at this date to be of a romantic, melancholy temperament, immersed in the study of antiquities and quite overshadowed by his handsome brother, whom everyone cultivated in the hope of seeing this relatively brilliant man of the world replace his morose parent at the head of affairs. No doubt Gian Gastone and Violante often wept together, for different reasons, but neither seems to have wished to embark on a physically intimate relationship.

The gloom of this period, with the population bitterly resentful of the heedless extravagance and savage bigotry of the grand duke and his clerical policemen, was not lightened by the death of Dowager Grand Duchess Vittoria della Rovere on March 6, 1694. The ponderous old lady had stolidly encouraged her son in all the brutalities and fanaticism that had marked his reign. Her influence remained paramount, even after her mental degeneration and demise. Nothing was changed. Her personal property was left to a frivolous reveller, Cardinal Francesco Maria, Cosimo's younger brother, to be held in trust for Gian Gastone. The universally popular prelate had always been kind to his prematurely weary nephew, whose pallid hypochondria perhaps stimulated the cardinal's own gross gayety.

The matter of Gian Gastone's marriage now became urgent. The elder son obviously was not going to produce an heir, and Cosimo was firmly determined that the Medici line must go on. He consulted his favourite child, the syphilitic but resolutely energetic Anna Maria Luisa, now electress palatine. She proposed a wealthy and highly connected German widow, Anna Maria Francesca of Saxe-Lauenberg, related to herself by marriage and the mother of a small daughter by her late husband, Prince Philip of Neuburg. If Gian Gastone married her he might come to be a prince of the Holy Roman Empire, owing to his wife's claims to the Saxon electorate through her deceased father, who had held that dignity. There were, however, certain difficulties in this plan. The lady in question did not want to marry again, and, in any case, she considered younger sons to be beneath her rank. Her little daughter, too, might prove an embarrassment. Moreover, some people said she was not so rich as had been alleged. Finally, though she was only about Gian Gastone's own age, she had already grown obscenely fat.

Cosimo refused to be balked. He enlisted the support of Johann Wilhelm and bribed the Emperor. He also tried to bribe heaven by taking Gian Gastone on a pilgrimage to the holy house at Loreto in the Marches. The building was supposed to have been the residence of Jesus of Nazareth as a child and to have been afterwards transported to Loreto by angels. Celestial aid in promoting the marriage of Gian Gastone to Anna Maria Francesca was implored at the holy house, the prayers being gilded by the gift of a golden chandelier weighing eighteen pounds.

A pilgrimage of a very different character was undertaken by Prince Ferdinand at about the same time. He felt he needed a change, and he sought it in Venice by transferring his sexual appetites to a female. The patrician beauty he selected happened also to be favoured by the Duke of Mantua. That good-natured nobleman left Ferdinand a free field for the time being, but the lady would not at first surrender. She hinted at a certain impediment, which she refused to specify, to their happiness. "Sir," she told the prince, "my family is infinitely indebted to the House of Medici, so I shall never see you betrayed. Know, then, that I am not in a position to requite you. To do so would condemn you to suffer for it always. Be not dazzled by appearances, which are generally deceptive. And trust one who loves you more than she loves herself."

Ferdinand, blinded by his passion, either could not, or would not, see what she meant by this veiled warning. He persisted in his suit, and, at last, the citadel yielded. A few weeks later, the prince realised both why the Duke of Mantua had withdrawn so suddenly from the siege and why the beleaguered one had notified his successor to "beware of consequences." The symptoms of syphilis appeared. Ferdinand, after medical treatment, transferred his love to a girl singer known as La Bambagia. He brought this amiable creature back with him to Florence, much to Cecchino's vexation.

Prince Ferdinand, on his return, found that the marriage of Gian Gastone to the Saxe-Lauenberg widow had been definitely settled. The younger Medici was on the point of leaving to meet his bride at Düsseldorf, and a farewell interview took place between the brothers. Ferdinand pretended to be unaware of the reason for this meeting. "Whither is Your Highness proceeding?" he enquired. "To Germany, to seek offspring." "Ah. Well, in my own case, as you know, Germany has proved barren ground for our family. I hope you may have better fortune, though I doubt it."

Gian Gastone, after stoically enduring this sneer at his poor little friend, Princess Violante, discovered at Düsseldorf that his worst forebodings were realised. Anna Maria Francesca proved to be both ugly and stupid. She detested urban society. She cared for nothing but horses and rural pursuits. Nevertheless, the ill-matched couple was duly married on July 2, 1697, by the Bishop of Osnabrück. In September they left for the bride's ramshackle castle at Reichstadt, near Prague, where the new Princess of Tuscany spent most of her time in the elaborately equipped stables. The prince found himself far less comfortably accommodated than his wife's livestock. Being the very opposite of a sportsman, he fell into deeper melancholy than ever.

Gian Gastone soon understood why his predecessor had drunk himself to death in three years. The mistress of her castle never stopped talking. She ordered her husband about, cursing and weeping by turns; or else, she perpetrated, merely for the pleasure it gave her, petty frauds. Everything in a typical peasant that seems most objectionable to a townsman characterised the latest bride of the Medici, though she had been born into a ruling family. Her distracted spouse turned to homosexual relations with a lackey, Giuliano Dami, one of his Florentine staff, a young scoundrel as unscrupulous as he was handsome.

Shortly after Gian Gastone's marriage, a treaty was signed at Ryswick, in the Netherlands, between France and the Empire. Most of Italy was then drawn, as Ferdinand and Gian Gastone had been drawn, into the Austrian network of matrimonial links, and Cosimo had to raise an enormous sum to meet the Emperor's increased requirements for funds to administer his enlarged dominions. Since the already grossly overburdened laymen of Tuscany could now barely keep body and soul together, Pope Innocent XII authorised the grand duke to tax, for the first time, his hitherto exempt clergy. This measure, of course, provoked every kind of covert resistance among that extensive and highly privileged section of Cosimo's subjects. Then, like a thunderclap, came the news that Tuscany had been declared by the imperial lawyers to be a fief of the Holy Roman Empire. The grand duke induced Vienna, by the prompt payment of 150,000 crowns, to withdraw this proclamation.

Cosimo was by no means done with trouble. In December, Gian Gastone complained bitterly to his uncle, Francesco Maria, of his horrible existence "among hovels" at Reichstadt. In the spring of 1698, he fled to Aix-la-Chapelle to visit his sister the electress. She was taking the waters there, in the hope of curing her sterility. Anna Maria Luisa had already endured two miscarriages and been reinfected with syphilis by her good-natured but incorrigibly unfaithful consort. Gastone confided that he had long given up all hope of impregnation of his monster of a wife, though she constantly plagued him with her bestial lasciviousness. Then he travelled on to Paris, in secret, disguised under the title of Marquis of Siena. He notified Marguérite-Louise of his arrival, but she kept him waiting five days before asking him to dinner. When they finally met, Gian Gastone's mother behaved as if she hardly knew who he was. The French court, however, was much more polite. His excellent manners—conspicuous in all the Medici, good, bad, and indifferent, for the past three centuries—pleased everyone, especially King Louis.

Cosimo, meanwhile, had been angered by his son's abandonment of the huge huntress whom he had been forced to marry. The grand duke feared that the depressed husband would soon fall under the influence of his half-mad mother, who had recently inherited a fortune from her sister, the Duchess de Guise. Moreover, Anna Maria Francesca had sent her father-in-law a raging diatribe from Reichstadt, swearing that Gian Gastone, apart from his base ingratitude to herself, was impotent. Cosimo frightened Gastone into returning to her, but the young man took his time, going by way of the Netherlands, where the Medici had been popular ever since the reign of Ferdinand II.

After a few days of lukewarm reconciliation at Reichstadt, domestic strife was resumed, more bitterly than ever. The shattered prince made off for the second time, but on this occasion he went only to Prague, taking Giuliano Dami with him. There Gian Gastone, whose sad eyes, slender figure, and delicate complexion had entranced the French court, began to turn into a bloated profligate, a transformation that his always remarkably sensual lips had suggested even in his early youth. Dami converted his master's mind definitely to homosexuality, and wine, dice, and cards, to an inordinate extent, accompanied this diversion. There were street brawls, in the Bohemian fashion, and tobacco, and the chewing of pepper in the form of the long-stemmed herbaceous plant known as *cumin,* which was held in the mouth like a cigar in order to increase one's appetite for alcohol. The formerly fastidious aristocrat was, in fact, gradually adopting the habits of the vilest people of his day.

Gian Gastone's life now alternated between visits to the German cities that had the most repellent reputation for vice, and occasional brief returns to Reichstadt in order to keep his relatives from positively disowning him. Yet the hopelessly soured debauchee could sometimes express himself like a gentleman. To one of Cosimo's scolding letters of 1699, he replied:

"Your Highness must learn that nineteen days after the marriage ring was given, if not earlier, my princess began to give me samples of her capriciousness, peevish faces, and sharp words, because I would not leave Düsseldorf, now and then saying a number of impertinent things about me and my people, and with slight respect to the elector showing that she could no longer remain there. Then there were more grimaces, tears, and tantrums on our journey to Bohemia. She approved of nothing that was done, although the entire journey was made at my expense. She has persisted in this behaviour until now, though I have done all in my power to adapt myself to her sweet disposition, even when contrary to my own convenience, decorum, and interests, even more than I have done for Your Highness and suffered more disgust and affliction for her in these two years than for my own soul. . . .

"She is haughty and vain enough to trample on everyone and govern everyone, believing that she is the greatest lady in the world because she owns these clods of earth in Bohemia. She is irreconcilable in her hatreds and aversions, and all my servants are witnesses to her ill-usage of her own to the point of despair. They only stay here because they cannot find work anywhere else.

"This seems to me the condition on which we can live together henceforth and I can see no other . . . a little in the country with her and a little in town, for I could not continue ten months of the year in the country as she does or ten months running alone with her after all the scenes that have occurred between us . . . because of her miserable character I have just described, which makes those who live with her miserable, it would certainly be impossible to stay with her in the most delicious spot in the world.

"This appears the only way I can live with my wife, not better but not worse, and none can amend it. For, according to her servants, she has always been the same, in widowhood or in wedlock with my predecessor, who was despatched into the other world by excessive drinking to dissipate the rage and disgust he suffered on her account. Let us continue to hope for the best. In time, many things are broken and many patched up. For the present it would be impossible to take her to Florence, first because she cannot leave her possessions, second because she hates Italy and Italians with an extraordinary hatred and before she married me she said that she would never be able to suffer Frenchmen and Italians in her house. But, last, because in Florence I would have to endure her ravings morning, noon, and night, she being unable to betake herself to her possessions, as she had done hitherto, and leave me a little in peace, and I would have to seek a restorative elsewhere, since she is not a diet to be borne for twelve months of the year."

Grand Duke Cosimo, however, was distracted for a time, from the crisis of the succession, by a situation of somewhat greater import for Italy. The feeble-minded and childless King of Spain, Charles II, lay dying, and Louis XIV and Emperor Leopold were both working night and day to assure that the rule of the Spanish dominions would pass into their own respective families. Cosimo, uncertain whom he should support, voyaged to Rome to consult the Pope. Innocent XII was unequivocal in his opinions. He stated bluntly that he had no wish to see the Austrian Habsburgs—Catholic, but allied to that hateful Protestant, William III of England—established in the Spanish territories of Italy. Then, in a gesture of appreciation for the grand duke's priest-like humility and piety, the Pope created Cosimo a canon of the basilica of St. John Lateran.

The advisors of the Spanish King seemed of the same opinion as the Pope, for when Charles II died, on November 1, 1700, it was found that he had bequeathed his throne, and the far-flung Spanish empire, to Philip of Anjou, grandson of the French King. For the remainder of the eighteenth century, as a Spanish observer recorded, Spain was to cry "God bless you!" every time that France sneezed.

Austria, however, was not to acquiesce quietly in this arrangement. Immediately upon King Charles' death, there erupted that conflict known as the War of the Spanish Succession. Early in 1701, Prince Eugène of Savoy crossed into Italy at the head of an Austrian army. He blockaded Mantua, then he invaded Parma and Ferrara. In January 1702, he captured the French general, Villeroi, but overwhelming reinforcements from France, under the Duke of Vendôme, at last drove Eugène out of Mantuan territory. Louis took advantage of this favourable turn in the war to suggest that King Philip V of Spain, his sulky and supercilious young grandson, aged nineteen, should cross the northern Mediterranean to study strategy and tactics under Vendôme. On June 8, Cosimo, Ferdinand, and Violante met the youthful inheritor of the Spanish throne at Leghorn. The two Medici were somewhat disconcerted at their cold reception aboard the royal galley. Only Violante, the King's aunt, was allowed an informal chat with him. It is probable that King Philip behaved so badly because the grand duke still maintained the policy of his great-grandfather, Ferdinand I, in holding Leghorn as a free port, open to Austria as well as to France and Spain.

The war moved away to Hungary and Bavaria, where Eugène met the Duke of Marlborough, commanding Austria's English allies. The two great soldiers contracted a personal friendship. Together they defeated at Blenheim in Bavaria, on August 13, 1704, one of the most efficient armies France had ever sent into Germany.

Cosimo was at this time in his early sixties. He was well described by the French priest and missionary, J. B. Labat, who met him during this period:

"He was tall and plumpish, his expression Austrian, with a protuber-ant lower lip, his upturned moustache white and heavy. Intelligence, nobility, and kindness were in his features. He wore a close-fitting suit of black cloth entirely buttoned, a neckband folded so as to form a kind of cravat, a longish sword, silk stockings, shoes of Morocco leather, and a black cloak. A big skullcap covered his white hair. He had only eight or ten guards or cavalry officers, about the same number of footmen, four little pages, and a pair of two-horse carriages. He sat alone in the first. In the second sat four officers. Twelve Switzers with halberds marched on either side of the carriages, which are driven very slowly. The people in the street do not cheer when he passes, but whoever happens to occupy a carriage in his way gets out and salutes him. He acknowledges their bows with much courtesy."

Such was the impression of a foreigner who knew little of the grand duke's unhappy private life and severe public one. It indicates that Cosimo III, like nearly all the Medici, possessed a native common sense and discretion rendered inoperative in his case only by religious intolerance.

In May 1705, Emperor Leopold died. The plans of his successor, Joseph I, included the annexation of Tuscany. He did not suppose that Cosimo would last much longer, and he had heard that the heir to the Grand Duchy, Prince Ferdinand, spent most of his waking hours in bed, suffering from loss of memory. Moreover, it was obvious that the next son, Gian Gastone, was a moral and physical wreck, quite incapable of administrative work. Joseph anticipated that, with the Medici extinct, their state could be reorganised on business lines, economically governed, and turned into a most profitable province of the Habsburg Empire. At present, clearly enough, the whole territory was falling into ruin.

In 1705, Gian Gastone returned to Florence for a brief visit. He was after money. But so was everyone else. The city was apparently bankrupt. This was probably the real reason why Cosimo had been begging the unresponsive Princess Anna Maria Francesca of Saxe-Lauenberg, for many years now, to take up her residence, with her husband, in the grand ducal capital and to help pay expenses. In 1704, she had remarked that she might consider doing so in another two years, after the settlement of certain negotiations concerning her estates and rank in Bohemia, a matter that would certainly require her presence in her native land during that interval. These promises, however, were revoked after an incident that occurred in the presence of the Arch-bishop of Prague in 1707. This event was the result of a last effort made by Cosimo to persuade the lady to accompany Gian Gastone to Florence, where she could look forward to becoming a crown princess. Pope Clement XI sent the Archbishop of Prague to point out to the sullen Anna Maria her plain Christian duty, but she retorted, in one of her characteristic outbursts of tearful wrath, that her husband was "absolutely impotent" and that she was not going to expose herself to the risk of assassination by his bloodthirsty kindred. This scene was the last straw for Gian Gastone. Shortly afterwards, he left Bohemia for Florence, and he never again saw his wife or attempted to communicate with her personally. The lady, for her part, remained for the next thirty years in Bohemia, a virtual recluse on her estates until released by death in 1741.

Gian Gastone did little in Florence to relieve the gloom of the city. He was seldom seen in public during the daylight hours, and at night, on occasional forays into the taverns, he was always accompanied by his beloved Giuliano Dami. Occasionally, he said or did things that made people believe him to be mad. One day, for example, he had a large bundle of printed ballads deposited at the door of a leading jurist, with a strict order to the great lawyer to read and study them carefully. Another time, he bought up all the stock of a peasant selling brooms, and commanded them to be delivered to the municipal offices "for future use." These sly proceedings indicate more method in the prince's eccentricity than might at first be supposed. If the legal luminary learned how ordinary people talked and what they considered interesting or important, his ideas about justice might well be profitably revised. Nor would a clean-up of the corrupt city administration do much harm, as the purchaser of brooms might well have been insinuating. Such humour resembles that of the sardonic Cosimo the Elder 250 years earlier. The characteristic Medicean wit could never be altogether extinguished by misfortune, or even by despair.

By now, the ambitious Joseph I had begun to be brutally frank with the sexagenarian Cosimo. He advised the grand duke to allow Austrian troops to enter Tuscany, as it seemed certain that, as soon as the popular but now mortally sick Prince Ferdinand expired, the whole population, seeing their last hope gone in his demise, would revolt and dethrone their present austere and priest-ridden tyrant. Driven to desperation by this cynical taunt, and by his ruling passion to preserve the Medici line, the pious but still spirited old autocrat took a step that astounded all Europe. He commanded his brother Cardinal Francesco Maria, then in his fiftieth year and the very image of an ageing bachelor playboy, to obtain papal dispensation from his Holy Orders and take a wife. The prelate objected strongly to this expedient, for as everyone knew, he was more addicted to pederasty than to congress with females. Nonetheless, he felt it his duty, in the end, to give in. He would not have been a Medici if he had not been open to conviction that family considerations must override all others. The chroniclers allege that he was never seen to smile again.

His niece, the electress, whom everyone seems to have liked for her resolute attitude in her misfortunes, encouraged the ex-cardinal playfully. "Take care of yourself," she wrote, "and try to keep your wife content. If you do so, you will soon feel much better. I believe that, after you have changed your ecclesiastical robes for lay dress, there will be rare comedy in your bed-chamber." But she also warned him to avoid casual fornication until after the birth of the "little cousin." He was, furthermore, to keep clear of extremes of heat and cold and to stop taking snuff and tobacco. It appeared that half the Continent was anxiously watching over the unhappy prospective bridegroom's approach to his conjugal duties. The friends of the Medici hoped against hope that he would be equal to the sacrifice, while their enemies gleefully declared that he would never be.

The girl chosen as the cardinal's wife was Eleonora Gonzaga, aged twenty-one, daughter of the last of that famous family that once ruled the dynasty of Mantua. The doctors pronounced her ideal for breeding purposes. Tall and well proportioned, physically attractive, and in perfect health, she gave the impression of a lively disposition and excellent manners. But the ex-cardinal groaned when he saw her. He feared, with some reason, that marriage to this paragon would ruin his already enfeebled constitution. It is possible, though not certain, that he had syphilis. He unquestionably suffered from gout, catarrh, and indigestion in addition to obesity.

Eleonora, too, shuddered when she first beheld her future husband. The waddling gait, bilious eyes, protuberant paunch, and muddy complexion had not been much noticed in the cardinal before his betrothal, when he had been the life and soul of an almost continuous series of gay gatherings. But now his physical shortcomings, accentuated by his openly woebegone expression, appalled his bride. After the ceremony, she refused outright to submit to his embraces. Love philtres were administered to her and priests lectured her, but it was all in vain. She explained eventually, to the scandal of her advisors, that she dreaded infection by "a shameful disease." To his credit, the stout Francesco Maria did not insist. Seeing that he had an intelligent young woman to deal with, he instead pointed out to Eleonora that his illustrious house, which had conferred so many benefits on Italians and had always been friendly to her own dynasty, would be doomed to extinction if she continued to decline to come to the rescue. He spoke with such tact and charm, frankly admitting his own deficiencies and displaying in fact a virtuosity in persuasion worthy of the great Lorenzo himself, that at last Eleonora Gonzaga yielded. She, belonged, too, to an ancient line in danger of extinction. She could appreciate the force of her eminently reasonable, if carnally repulsive, husband's arguments. Many of the male Gonzaga's had fallen on the field of battle to defend their family's inheritance, today so pitifully small. She decided to follow their supreme example, so far as a woman could, by immolating only her natural sensibility, not her life. After all, it was clear that this former satyr would be, like herself, merely performing a disagreeable duty, by no means lusting after an erotic enjoyment he could easily obtain elsewhere.

The marriage, therefore, was finally consummated. But the wife seized every opportunity to avoid repetitions of sexual intimacy. She took to drinking, and she complained of ill health at frequent intervals, and then she danced to the point of exhaustion. No signs of pregnancy appeared. Francesco Maria's mortification, after all he had suffered to meet his elder brother's wishes, killed him in two years. On February 11, 1711, he expired of dropsy in the arms of a Moorish male favourite.

When the news broke, plunging Cosimo into the last depths of miserable frustration, a placard was found affixed to one of the columns supporting the Medici tomb in San Lorenzo. It read:

> *E morto l'idropico,*
> *sta male l'asmatico,*
> *peggio l'etico*
> *e ci rimane l'eretico.*

(Dead is the dropsical one [Francesco Maria].
sick is the asthmatical one [Gian Gastone].
sicker the hectic one [the consumptive syphilitic, Ferdinand].
and we're left with the heretical one [the aggressively orthodox
  Cosimo]).

Cosimo was thus humourously styled a rebel against the Church. The quatrain, a typical specimen of the Florentine wit that had been famous in republican days, really only stabbed hard in the last word; for of these four Medici, Cosimo alone, on account of his religious bigotry, was actually hated in the city.

In May 1711, Joseph I died, and the vigour of the War of the Spanish Succession began to wane. At the peace conference, Cosimo urged that his daughter, Electress Anna Maria Luisa, if she survived both himself and his sons, as seemed likely, should be given sole charge of the Grand Duchy. But the British and Dutch representatives opposed this solution on the ground that kinsmen of the Medici by marriage would be encouraged to put in claims against a mere woman and thus cause unnecessary complications. The conference eventually shelved the question of the Tuscan succession, pending settlement of more important matters.

The lively and ambitious electress herself, whose natural energy was turning to politics as her years advanced, decided to make a bid for the Grand Duchy. The German princes backed her, but the new Austrian Emperor, Charles VI, aged twenty-six, would only allow Anna Maria Luisa, who was forty-three, to succeed her father or brothers on the understanding that he himself would take over when they were all dead. By the Treaty of Utrecht, however, he withdrew this stipulation, and compromised by investing the electress with the rights and duties of a feudatory for Tuscany under the Empire.

On October 30, 1713, Prince Ferdinand died. He had been sick for eighteen of his fifty years, and an epileptic for the last four. Violante nursed him devotedly to the end, which came while she herself lay in bed, exhausted by her labours. He had been by temperament a pessimistic esthete, a homosexual, who was far from pious, considering the majority of priests a set of wily hypocrites. Marguérite-Louise had bequeathed to him her restlessness; Cosimo, his constitutional melancholy. Ferdinand's good taste in all the arts, but especially in music, was remarkable. He bought madonnas by Raphael, Andrea del Sarto, and Parmigianino. He also patronised living painters and, in 1705, organised in Florence the first public exhibition of pictures ever held there. The prince also befriended some fair contemporary poets still read in Italy. But his most serious interest lay in musical composition. He played the harpsichord and certain stringed instruments, probably also the violin, and Scarlatti and Handel were only two of the many notable composers whom he invited to Florence. In opera, he was a perfectionist, employing whole battalions of collaborators and critics. He seems to have preferred refined, flexible comedy to the rigidly patterned tragedy fashionable in the early eighteenth century. He rebuked Scarlatti, in any case, much to that gentleman's indignation, for excessive solemnity.

Anna Maria Francesca, on hearing of Ferdinand's death, indicated verbally and by proxy that she might now be willing to visit Tuscany. Her husband's five years of absence in Florence had evidently caused her to reconsider her position as an abandoned wife, probably less from affection for Gian Gastone than from recognition of his growing political importance as heir-apparent to the Grand Duchy. But that gentleman at once reaffirmed, verbally and by proxy, his unalterable resolution not to have anything more whatever to do with the "impossible" shrew of Reichstadt, saying that he would not dream of receiving her if she ever came to Florence.

On November 26, 1713, Cosimo decreed the electress's succession to himself and Gian Gastone. Charles VI angrily told her husband, the elector, that the grand duke had no right to do such a thing. Louis XIV, on the contrary, congratulated the despot of Tuscany for thus maintaining the age-old authority of his family. Cosimo was also heartened, in 1714, by the betrothal of Philip V of Spain to Elisabeth Farnese, a great-grandniece of the Grand Duke Ferdinand II, father of the present Tuscan ruler. Austria would now think twice, perhaps, the grim old standard-bearer of the last of the Medici must have reflected, before pushing into the Grand Duchy in defiance of a Queen of Spain. All the same, Cosimo did not want a Spanish Tuscany any more than an Austrian one. He was careful, therefore, to remain polite to the Emperor, especially after Louis XIV, a regularly loyal supporter of the Grand Duchy, died in 1715, and, in the following year, a son was born to Philip V.

In June 1716, Johann Wilhelm, elector palatine, died, his health broken by the disease that in those days so often destroyed devoted worshippers of Venus. Anna Maria Luisa, with typical Medicean prudence, stayed on another year at Düsseldorf; but meanwhile she packed up all her portable treasures and despatched them to Florence to await her arrival. The model widow, Princess Violante, and the somewhat bibulous relic of Francesco Maria de' Medici, Eleonora Gonzaga, held separate courts there. The respectable Violante, ironically enough, occupied the Lapeggi villa, where the stout cardinal had formerly revelled.

Gian Gastone continued to keep clear of aristocratic company as much as possible, but he made an exception for his old friend Violante. When she decided to return to her native Munich before Anna Maria Luisa arrived in Florence, in case that socially agreeable but strong-minded lady, some four years her senior, might find fault with her as having once held, as Prince Ferdinand's wife, a more important position in the city than she herself, Gastone objected. He deplored Violante's proposed retirement on the ground that his sister was already sufficiently vain and that she needed the restraint of the princess' presence in the Grand Duchy as a whole, if not in the capital. Cosimo agreed, and Violante was accordingly appointed to govern the city of Siena.

The electress entered Florence on October 22, 1717. Her affectionate father, who had not seen his favourite for twenty-six years, greeted her with an effusiveness he had hardly shown in public before. She at once assumed the behaviour, if not the title, of a grand duchess, disputing the precedence of Princess Violante, as the latter had anticipated, on the inevitable occasions when the two ladies had to meet. Since Prince Ferdinand's death, the little Bavarian was no longer the humble and agreeable servant she had been. Instead, she stood up imperturbably for her rights, and relations between the princess and the elector's widow grew decidedly tense.

Meanwhile, Cosimo and the Emperor continued to argue about who was to rule Tuscany after the death of the childless Anna Maria Luisa. Unfortunately for the grand duke, the Quadruple Alliance of 1718, among Austria, France, the Netherlands, and Britain (joined later by Spain and Savoy), took the view that, whoever might follow the electress, Tuscany was legally a fief of the Empire. Cosimo, weary of the endless and hopeless struggle to render his family, so to speak, immortal, sank once more into the depths of religious fanaticism. He removed all the naked statues from the galleries, streets, and squares of Florence, when his priestly counsellors alleged that these unbreeched figures were exciting the populace to commit the deadly sins of fornication and sodomy.

On September 19, 1721, the hitherto indomitable Marguérite-Louise succumbed at the age of seventy-six. She has recovered from a first paralytic stroke in 1712, and a second in 1713. After these experiences, she still insisted on going out even in the coldest weather. She spent a large part of the years that remained to her in recounting the story of her extraordinary life to anyone who would listen. Narrow-minded to an absurd degree in her uncompromisingly Parisian insularity and xenophobia, she may have hated her husband so much for being her exact opposite in these respects and for being narrow-minded only in his hidebound religious truculence. But this feature in him also infuriated the grand duchess, who had a raging passion for personal freedom. Its persistent frustration until her very last years by the actual circumstances of her marriage drove her to madness at times. Then she would perpetrate the meanest frauds and assume the most degrading masks of hypocrisy. Yet on the few days in her life when all went well, Marguérite-Louise was one of the most stimulating representatives of her epoch full of spirited females.

Marguérite-Louise's last act was, typically, to leave all her property to a distant relative instead of to her children, as she had promised. Cosimo regained it for them after a tedious lawsuit, but his annoyance at this posthumous thrust did not prevent him from according the memory of the deceased a solemn service in San Lorenzo, attended by all the surviving Medici except Anna Maria Luisa and the grand duke himself. Gian Gastone, for his part, went to his mother's commemoration service as he would have gone to any other function proposed to distract him from his empty existence. The two widows, Violante and Eleonora, had never had much to do with the late grand duchess, but they welcomed the opportunity of stressing their importance in the life of the Florentine court.

That year, Spain conceded its feudal rights in Italy to Austria. Only persons acceptable to the Empire, therefore, would in the future govern Tuscany. Cosimo, of course, protested, but without the slightest effect, and he became a sort of political relic, an object merely of vague respect and curiosity. Gian Gastone, on the other hand, appeared actually stimulated by the general decline in his family's fortunes. He began to take over his father's administrative work and to recover some measure of his former wit and good nature. He felt, he said, with the characteristic dry humour of the Medici, like a king in a comedy.

Cosimo III made an edifying end, unctuously demanding forgiveness for his sins against both heaven and his people. Yet one of his last acts was to sign a decree to increase the income tax. He died on October 31, 1723, after a reign of fifty-three years. No other Medici had ever been in power so long or, for that matter, so disastrously. Florence had never been so gloomy or so contemptuously treated by foreigners as under his rule. But to individuals who did not have to obey him, he almost invariably seemed an admirable sovereign, courteous, chaste, and the soul of honour. His relentless ferocity in matters of religion was not then generally recognised to be the obverse of sheer tyranny, but, in fact, this disproportionate obstinacy caused the ruin and misery of his country. The one fatal flaw in his mind, it ran like a widening crack through the fabric of an intelligence Medicean in all respects except for its lack of imaginative gifts.

6. Gian Gastone

Harold Acton, in *The Last of the Medicis,* compared Cosimo III with King George III of Britain and Gian Gastone with George IV of that country. The parallel is indeed quite striking. In each case a dull reactionary with deceptively bluff manners was succeeded by a jaded ruler, whose display of indolence and dissipation concealed both shrewdness and good nature. At any rate, Florence experienced during the fourteen years of Gastone's reign over Tuscany the last bright flare of a candle that had almost been extinguished under Cosimo. To the relief of everyone, a sudden sense of freedom and liveliness replaced the recent regimentation and sullen resignation of the citizens. A sensible economy at the top, instead of Cosimo's incessant improvidence, began to reduce unprofitable expenditure. The sober Princess Violante's cheerful prudence rendered much assistance to her frustrated brother-in-law, who had always been fond of her. Eleonora's taste for strong liquor had less influence on him than might have been expected. He more or less ignored his sister Anna Maria Luisa, whom he still detested for having landed him in the bed of Anna Maria Francesca, the shrew of Saxe-Lauenberg. The electress, her originally quite attractive character soured by the disappointment of her hopes of the succession, retired to the usual consolation of proud women at this date: prayer and the company of the clergy.

As time went on, however, the new grand duke appeared less and less in public. He preferred solitude and a bottle. His contempt for the Church and all its proceedings of outward pomp became notorious. Nonetheless, he lowered the price of corn, reduced taxation, and set beggars to work. A certain modest happiness at last began to brighten the dejection of the population of Tuscany. "There is no town," wrote Montesquieu in 1728, "where men live with less luxury than in Florence . . . with a dark lantern for night and an umbrella for the rain one is completely equipped. It is true that the women are slightly more extravagant, for they keep an old carriage. They are said to spend more in the country, and also at baptisms and weddings. The streets are so well paved with broad flagstones that it is very convenient to go afoot. The grand duke's prime minister, the Marchese di Montemagni, has been seated at his street door swinging his legs. . . . As I went out with my small lantern and umbrella, I thought that the ancient Medici must have left a neighbour's house in this wise. There is a very gentle rule in Florence. Nobody knows, or is conscious of the prince and his court. For that very reason, this little country has the air of a great one."

In the realm of foreign policy, Gian Gastone's temperament made it easy for him to see that his best plan was to allow Austria and Spain to settle their disputes, even those about Tuscany, without him. Montesquieu's final verdict on him, "a good prince, but lazy," seems adequate, though it is hardly possible not to censure an addiction to pederasty that grew so obsessive at last as to keep him in bed with his favourites, first for weeks, then for months, and finally for years. In these circumstances his chief catamite, Giuliano Dami, gradually became the real ruler of Tuscany. In Florence he staged the orgies, dictated the terms of all approaches to the embedded grand duke, pocketed commissions, and arranged public frauds according to a sliding scale of prices. It may be regretted that the Genoese genre painter Alessandro Magnasco (1667–1740), whom Gastone supported in the Pitti Palace for some years, never applied his macabre talent to a delineation of his host. The bulky, somnolent recluse, in the midst of his prancing and grimacing ragamuffins of both sexes, might well have inspired a masterpiece in the vein of deliberate "awfulness," which both men found so amusing.

Yet the last male Medici's mocking humour leavened, from time to time, the twilight of a mind that had never been strong enough, like his mother's or father's, to challenge misfortune. Gastone had simply sunk under it. Nevertheless, his jests, when he did surface for a while, persisted. Sometimes, when his fellow-debauchees had gathered in his bedroom, he would call them, one after another, by the well-known names of grave counsellors and revered matrons. He would order them to adopt pompous attitudes and ceremoniously drink to one another. Then he would exclaim to one of the sturdier beggars: "Well, my Lord Marquess, how does the marchioness yonder appeal to you? You admire her, do you not? To business! Tumble her!" The shameless, extravagantly paid bullies and strumpets needed no second invitation. The grand duke, between roars of laughter, encouraged them with the cries of a huntsman. Such scenes, reported by the participants, became the common gossip of Florence.

Princess Violante tried to put a stop to such entertainments by arranging formal banquets for her brother-in-law, with groups of highborn ladies famous for both wit and beauty. His genuine respect for the princess generally caused him to behave fairly well at these functions, but occasionally, he would roll about in his chair, swear obscenely, belch, and vomit, wiping his slobbering mouth with his periwig. Then Violante and her friends would rise and leave the room so that the grand duke's attendants might carry him out to his coach. It was no wonder that his bedchamber smelled like a dungeon cell and had to be specially perfumed when important foreign visitors were expected.

Middle-class Florentine society, under Cosimo III, had been on the whole somewhat prim, but the French customs introduced by Gian Gastone soon rendered it as licentious as the grand ducal court. The grand duke, however, was not interested in the sophisticated antics of people of rank, or at any rate of fashion. He preferred the violence and uproar of thieves' kitchens, where bottles and wine-glasses flew about, kisses drew blood, and embraces ended in attempts at strangulation. Once or twice in these homicidal affrays Gian Gastone would have been seriously hurt, if not murdered, but for the intervention of his guards, always on the watch for non-amorous outrages upon the person of their master. They knew that if he had died in the midst of some such riot, they would have been the first to be hanged, drawn, and quartered without even the semblance of a trial.

In May 1731, the admirable Princess Violante died. She was the only woman for whom Gastone had ever shown any real affection, but the diarist Settimanni noted:

"While the princess lay dying, she implored him to come and pay her a farewell visit, but no argument would persuade him to do so . . . and when she had passed away and her corpse was ready to be taken to its tomb, a crowd assembled in the Piazza de' Pitti to watch the pomp of her funeral. Some obstacle happened to delay the procession and a clamour arose in consequence. Meanwhile, the grand duke's chamber was filled with youths of venereal rather than martial prowess, detained there by the tumult. The grand duke himself sent repeated messages to speed the corpse upon its last journey. Finally he lost all patience. In a towering rage he sent forth to hurry the procession. It is said that he used infamous invective, unfit for the lowest of harlots, let alone for that gentle, high-born princess."

It might well have been the fact of her death, the hovering, as it were, of the corpse under his windows, that incited Gian Gastone to this apparently callous act. It was perpetrated, perhaps, in a paroxysm of insane grief. A few years previously, he would have been incapable of such an outburst. But now, like all elderly debauchees, he fell into a panic at the very notion of death, as the absolute and eternal end of his pleasure.

In the same year, the long-standing question of the Tuscan succession received what appeared at the time to be its final answer. The son of Philip V of Spain, Don Carlos, still a minor, was to hold the Grand Duchy as a fief under Emperor Charles VI, with Gian Gastone as the Spanish prince's guardian until he came of age. "I am gratified," remarked the grand duke, "by the honour of being appointed tutor to this young man. But I find that at the same time I am under tutelage myself." He was referring to the Spanish garrison that had entered the city in October to familiarise Florentines with their future ruler. "Here I am," Gastone observed, "an old fellow of sixty, and yet the father of such a big boy!" He could not resist the opportunity of joking at even this ultimate degradation of his family, a servitude that would have filled any of his ancestors with horror.

Don Carlos himself arrived at Leghorn on the night of December 27, but instantly collapsed with smallpox. He did not reach Florence until March 9, 1732, when he made a favourable impression with his youthful gayety and eagerness to learn. In fact, he took more after his Italian mother than his French father. There was very little of Spanish grandeur and reserve about him, though there was much of both about his troops. The citizens, so long without a figurehead, since they hardly ever saw Gian Gastone now, gave the lad a tumultuous welcome. The new "tutor," too, the bloated old wreck who lay half dead on his couch hour after hour, day and night, seemed very pleased with Carlos. He gave the boy a velvet-upholstered carriage, drawn by two donkeys, and also a gold-embroidered parasol. "I have just got an heir," the sexagenarian mumbled, as he signed away Tuscany to the son of Elizabeth Farnese, "by this stroke of the pen. And yet I could not get such a thing in thirty-four years of marriage."

He made more pleasantries than ever as his weakening physique allowed his innate mildness of temper, so long befogged by disillusion and ill-fortune, to reappear. Everything amused him now, but most of all the solemn scenes of political and dynastic events. These were certainly proving to be more tedious and futile than they had ever been before in Europe, although they lacked the vigour and dramatic variety that had marked the turbulent history of the Renaissance centuries. The advent of unquestioned autocracy throughout the Continent bestowed upon art and literature a certain baroque splendour, but in politics the impetus of the Counter-Reformation imposed hollow extravagances upon the Catholic determination—which, of course, had its admirable features—to preserve the venerable essence of the Church against the assaults of northern individualists.

The Mediterranean world, its liberty lost and its outstanding personalities helpless under the dictation of a few sovereign families, had been reduced to a cynical acquiescence in theoretically international, but practically domestic, squabbles. These chances and changes, the conferences and the marriage settlements, the treaties and even the wars, though carried on in an atmosphere of portentous ritual, decided nothing. Wearisome as the record may appear, however, such crises of the period have their use as signposts on the roads converging steadily on the path of social revolution that was to alter, towards the end of the eighteenth century, the entire focus of civilisation.

In these circumstances, the satisfaction of Tuscany and of Gian Gastone with Don Carlos, their newly acquired heir, could not endure. The death of Augustus II, King of Poland, in 1733, and his succession by Augustus III, a puppet of Russia, was the occasion for a re-distribution of Italian thrones among representatives of those two great rivals for the domination of Europe, the Bourbons of France and the imperial Habsburgs of Austria. According to the terms of new treaties signed at Turin and at the Escorial in Madrid, Stanislas Leczinski, the father-in-law of King Louis XV, was to replace Augustus III on the Polish throne, while Don Carlos was to exchange Tuscany for Naples and Sicily. The Tuscan grand ducal crown was now to go, after Gian Gastone's death, to Carlos' younger brother, Philip, who was also to have Parma. Milan was to be given to the King of Sardinia, and France was to have Savoy.

Neither party to the treaty, however, was satisfied; war soon broke out, and, as usual, Italy was the battlefield for France and Austria. The two nations fought each other in the North of the peninsula, but with little effect other than mutual slaughter. Peace was arranged in 1735, and according to this new treaty, it was agreed that Francis I, Duke of Lorraine and the son-in-law of Emperor Charles VI, was to rule Tuscany after the death of Gian Gastone. Francis would therefore become both grand duke, as Gastone's heir, and Holy Roman Emperor, as the husband of the future Empress, Maria-Theresa. Emperor Charles died in 1740, and Maria-Theresa did in fact succeed him, but it was not until 1745, after the War of the Austrian Succession, that Francis was able to secure the Empire.

Meanwhile, neither Francis of Lorraine nor Gian Gastone looked forward with much relish to the execution of these plans. Both rulers were politically modest men. Francis had no desire to leave his Duchy of Lorraine, and Gian Gastone, insofar as he cared at all what happened to the Medici inheritance, would have preferred the attractive

Don Carlos, his late ward, to succeed him. Carlos at least would not be likely to put Austrians in charge of Tuscany. The old grand duke growled out another of his bitter jests on the subject of the disposal of his property. "Perhaps either the King of France or the Emperor of Austria will be good enough," he snarled, "to procreate an alternative heir to me, since the prospects of the first two they thought of do not appear satisfactory."

The proposed settlements, in fact, were much disputed in areas they affected. The Spaniards refused to leave Tuscany, and Gian Gastone argued obstinately that no subject of the Emperor had any legal right to the Grand Duchy. No generally acceptable conclusion could be reached. At last, in January 1737, the Spaniards were persuaded to withdraw. They had enough to do elsewhere. An Austrian garrison replaced them, but it dutifully swore allegiance to Gastone. By June, however, Francis' representative in Florence, the Prince de Craon, wrote to his master about the last head of the House of Medici:

"I found this prince in a condition worthy of pity. He could not leave his bed. His beard was long, his sheets and linen very dirty, without ruffles. His sight was dim and enfeebled, his voice low and obstructed. Altogether, he had the air of a man with not a month to live."

Yet Gian Gastone could still be disconcertingly alert at times. He vigourously cursed his sister, the electress, when she tried to enter his bedroom, but later he characteristically relented, sending her word that she could visit him whenever she pleased. She did so, and somewhat tactlessly urged him to adopt a more Christian frame of mind. The dying man was by then too weak to resist her lectures, and he agreed to summon a priest, to whom he duly confessed and from whom he received the sacraments.

This reformation seemed perfectly genuine to the men of religion who surrounded his bed. The invalid of his own accord, they reported, implored the Almighty to forgive his heinous sins, humbly and gratefully accepted the holy oil, and ordered that all the clergy who had helped to save his soul from damnation should be suitably rewarded. He also made, they said, all the proper responses to the ritual prayers. In short, everyone present was reduced to tears by the signs of true contrition and earnest piety that continuously emanated from this notable penitent. These phenomena went on for several days, until death supervened, quite peacefully, in the early afternoon of July 9, 1737.

The Prince de Craon immediately took over Tuscany in the name of Duke Francis of Lorraine. He told the electress that a council, composed of himself and four prominent Florentines, two clerical and two lay, would rule the Grand Duchy for the time being. Francis was just then fighting the Turks in the Balkan peninsula, and he did not enter Florence until January 20, 1739.

The deceased grand duke, in spite of his detestation of administrative detail, had shown a certain amount of responsible common sense in the intervals between his orgies. He had reduced the inordinate power of the clergy pampered by Cosimo III. He had encouraged intellectual activities. He had permitted circulation in Italian of the works of such eminent seventeenth-century scientists as Pierre Gassendi of Provence, and his slightly earlier Italian contemporary Galileo, still anathematised by the average churchman of the day. Gian Gastone had also forbidden, by an edict of 1735, all persecution of his Jewish subjects, so often victimised by his father. The worst of the taxes imposed by the latter, as well as the national debt, had been diminished by his successor. The poor in general, both craftsmen and traders, fared better while Gastone occupied the nominal seat of authority. He was an Italian, after all, and in Florence the Austrians were considered barbarians. There can be no doubt that the end of Medicean government, with all its faults, was regretted. In 1739, the French magistrate and scholar Charles de Brosses wrote: "The Tuscans would give two thirds of their property to have the Medici back, and the other third to get rid of the Lorrainers. They hate them as the Milanese hate the Piedmontese. The Lorrainers ill-use and, what is worse, despise them."

The electress had refused to act as regent, though Francis had offered her the post. She lived on at the Pitti Palace, in austere but splendid isolation. A silent image of taciturn piety and dignity, she occupied herself, when not at church or her private devotions, with completing the family mausoleum begun by Grand Duke Ferdinand I but subsequently neglected for lack of funds. She died rather suddenly in February 1743, the very last of her line. The last will and testament of the old woman, who had begun life as Anna Maria Luisa de' Medici, bequeathed to Florence the greatest collection of works of art then existent in the world. It had been started by Cosimo the Elder and increased right down to the last year of Gian Gastone. Anna Maria directed that none of its items must ever be removed from the city, in order that the collection as a whole might be forevermore enjoyed by all nations.

EPILOGUE

The younger branch of the Medici expired as conclusively with the death of Anna Maria Luisa de' Medici, the electress, as the senior branch had vanished, in 1537, with the murder of Alessandro de' Medici. Then, Florence—and indeed all of Italy—was turned over to the Austrians and to the Spaniards, and the name of Medici was heard no more in the councils of the great. The family had ruled Florence for the greater part of three centuries. For the first half of the period, the city, and the Medici, had flourished. Through the efforts and wisdom of the great Medici of the senior line, the capital of the Tuscan province was raised from the status of a prosperous, but dull, provincial city, to a point where she could claim to rival Periclean Athens in the splendour of her accomplishments and in the glory of her name. It was not the destiny of Florence, however, to grow, but to return to the dead, and, during the last century and a half of Medicean rule, both the city and the family dwindled away in self-indulgence, luxury, and indiscipline. Bernardo Segni, a sixteenth-century Florentine, wrote the conclusion to the tale of Florentine greatness:

> Florence might have been powerful if she had had good laws to direct her, but she never succeeded in this. She never adopted permanently any constitution, either republican or monarchical, that might have made her strong. Always divided within herself, she was condemned to an inferior rank, whereas, if united, she would have been able to maintain and increase her fame and her empire. Thus, there rose up incompetent popular regimes, and even worse regimes of petty potentates, so that the city was not able to nourish and make grow that glory which animates the souls of men of this country.

Yet Clio, the muse of history, is a whimsical creature, and she thrives on the paradoxical in the affairs of men. Long before Florence and the Medici lapsed into obscurity under the ineffectual sway of the six successors of Cosimo I, the revolution that had been wrought in that place and under their egis had spread across Europe. A new life had been infused into peoples that, for a thousand years, had known no change other than that brought about by the petty wars and petty ambitions of restless princes. That revolution was nothing less than an awakening of the European mind, a mind that had slumbered too long already in the warm security provided, and indeed imposed, by the closed circle of an other-worldly theology.

As the ideals of fifteenth-century Florence spread across Italy and crossed the Alps, they left in their wake certain intellectual, spiritual, and material changes that, coming together at certain points in the flow of human events, were to bring down the old world and usher in the new. Learning spread, antique ideals were questioned and then discarded, populations increased, and wealth simultaneously was concentrated in the ruling stratum of society. Inevitably, there was a reaction—one that, appropriately, saw its formal beginnings during the lifetime of the last of the Medici—and a tremendous intellectual, economic, social, and political upheaval swept away, once and for all, the old order in Europe. Then there was a period of reconstruction and consolidation; and the entire cycle began once again, and it has continued into our own time.

To the great men of the House of Medici, and to their city of Florence, we owe at least the form of that revolution. It is, so to speak, the Medicean heritage of the modern world. And one may believe that the end of it is not yet.

BIBLIOGRAPHY

Thousands of volumes relating to Medicean history have been published since the early sixteenth century in Italian, French, English, and German alone. The following books were consulted during the preparation of the present work.

J.C.

La Giostra di Lorenzo de' Medici. L. Pulci. Florentie, 1518.
Dell' Istorie Florentine. S. Ammirato. Firenze, 1600.
Vite di cinque huomini illustri. G. Razzi. Firenze, 1602.
Storia fiorentina. B. Varchi. Augsburg, 1721.
Istoria del Granducato di Toscana. J. R. Galluzzi. Firenze, 1781.
Storia dell' Alessandro de' Medici. M. Rastrelli. Firenze, 1781.
Magni Cosmi Medicei Vita. A. Fabroni. Pisa, 1789.
Histoire des Républiques Italiennes. J. C. L. de Sismondi. Paris, 1809.
Storia d'Italia. F. Guicciardini, ed. Pisa: Rosini, 1822.
Historie Fiorentine. G. Villani, ed. Firenze: Moutier e Dragomanni, 1844.
History of the Commonwealth of Florence. T. A. Trollope. London, 1856.
Croniche di Giovanni. Matteo e Filippo Villani, eds. Trieste: A. Racheli, 1857.
Vite degli Uomini Illustri d'Italia. F. D. Guerrazzi. Milano, 1863–67.
The Life of Lorenzo de' Medici. W. Roscoe. London, 1865.
Storia della Repubblica di Firenze. G. Capponi, ed. Firenze, 1875.
Notizie e Documenti. G. Benedetti. Firenze, 1875.
Geschichte Toscanas. A. von Reumont. Berlin, 1876.
Histoire de Florence. F. T. Perrens. Paris, 1877.
Lorenzo de' Medici. B. Buser. Leipzig, 1879.
Les Médicis. A. Castelnau. Paris, 1879.
Sketches and Studies in Italy. J. A. Symonds. London, 1879.
Florence. C. Yriarte. Paris, 1881.
Cosimo de' Medici Duca di Firenze. L. A. Ferrai. Bologna, 1882.
Diarie fiorentine. C. Landucci, ed. Firenze: I. del Badia, 1883.
Lorenzo de' Medici. A. von Reumont. Leipzig, 1883.
Vita di tre principesse di Casa Medici. L. Ombrosi. Firenze, 1886.
Vita di Ferdinando II Granduca di Toscana. F. Orlando e G. Baccini. Firenze, 1886.
Die politischen Beziehungen Clemens VII zu Karl V. R. Grethen. Hannover, 1887.
Lucrezia Tornabuoni. G. Levantini-Pieroni. Firenze, 1888.
Lorenzino de' Medici. B. Corsini. Siracusa, 1890.
Cosimo I de' Medici. L. Bruni. Torino, 1891.

Vite di uomini illustri del secolo XV. V. da Bisticci, ed. Bologna: Frati, 1892–93.

Leone X. F. S. Nitti. Firenze, 1892.

Cathérine et Marie de' Medici. L. Montal. Limoges, 1892.

Documenti Inediti. G. Conti. Firenze, 1893.

I primi due secole della storia di Firenze. P. Villari. Firenze, 1893–94.

The Monk and the Prince. A. G. Haygood. Atlanta, 1895.

Lorenzo de' Medici. E. Armstrong. London, 1896.

Vita di Niccolò Capponi. B. Segni. Firenze, 1896.

Geschichte von Florenz. R. Davidsohn. Leipzig, 1896.

Tragedie Medicee Domestiche. G. E. Saltini. Firenze, 1898.

Piero di Cosimo. F. Knopp. Halle, 1898.

Cathérine des Médicis. H. Bouchot. Paris, 1899.

Cosimo de' Medici. K. D. Ewart. London, 1899.

Giovanni Bicci de' Medici. B. Dami. Firenze, 1899.

The Medici of the Italian Renaissance. O. Smeaton. Edinburgh, 1901.

Fatti e Anedotti. G. Conti. Firenze, 1902.

Florenz und die Mediceer. E. Heyck. Bielefeld u. Leipzig, 1902.

History of Florence. F. A. Hyett. London, 1903.

L'Italie du XVIe Siecle. P. Gauthiez. Paris, 1904.

The Regency of Marie de' Medici. A. P. Lord. New York and London, 1904.

Donne Medicee avanti il principato. B. Felice. Firenze, 1905.

Glie ultimi anni di Lorenzo Duca di Urbino. A. Verde. Este, 1905.

Gli Ultimi dei Medici a la Successione al granducato di Toscana. E. Robiony. Firenze, 1905.

La Vie de Marie de Médicis. L. Batifol. Paris, 1906.

La vite fiorentina nel seicento. G. Imbert. Firenze, 1906.

La Donna Fiorentina I. del Lungo. Firenze, 1906.

Il Cardinale Ippolito de' Medici. M. d'Ercole. Terlizzi, 1907.

Lorenzo the Magnificent. E. L. S. Horsburgh. London, 1908.

Storia dei Papi dalla fine del Medio Evo. L. Pastor. Roma, 1908.

Firenze dai Medici ai Lorena. G. Conti. Firenze, 1909.

The Medici. F. G. Young. London, 1909.

Mémoires du Duc d'Estrées, ed. Paris: P. Bonnefon, 1910.

Lives of the Early Medici. J. Ross. London, 1910.

Woman in Italy. W. Boulting. London, 1910.

The Romance of a Medici Warrior. C. Hare. London, 1910.

La Vita di Benvenuto Cellini, ed. Milano: A. Butti, 1910.

La Cronica di Dino Compagni. I. del Lungo, ed. Città di Castello, 1913.

La Costituzione politica di Firenze ai Tempi di Lorenzo il Magnifico. V. Ricchioni. Siena, 1913.

Cosimo I Duke of Florence. C. Booth. Cambridge, 1921.

Il Magnifico e la Rinascita. A. Garsia. Firenze, 1923.

The Diary of Samuel Pepys. H. B. Wheatley, ed. London, 1923.

The Golden Age of the Medici. S. Brinton. London, 1925.

La Stirpe de' Medici di Cafaggiuolo. G. Pieraccini. Firenze, 1925.

Lorenzo il Magnifico. E. Rho. Bari, 1926.

Cosimo I granduca. L. Carcereri. Verona, 1926.

Biance Cappello. C. Bax. London, 1927.
The Women of the Medici. Y. Maguire. London, 1927.
The Story of Florence. E. G. Gardner. London, 1928.
La Vita e l'Opera di Lorenzo il Magnifico. L. di San Giusto. Firenze, 1928.
Giovanni delle Bande Nere. E. Allodoli. Firenze, 1929.
L'Ultima Republica Fiorentina. C. Roth. Firenze, 1929.
Lorenzo the Magnificent. D. G. Loth. London, 1930.
The Last Medici. H. Acton. London, 1932.
Trois Médicis. P. Gauthiez. Paris, 1933.
L'Emulo di Bruto. S. A. Nulli. Milano, 1933.
La politica italiana di Lorenzo de' Medici. P. Palmarocchi. Firenze, 1933.
Ferdinando I dei Medici. A. De Rubertis. Venezia, 1933.
Lorenzino de' Medici. L. Lazzarini. Milano, 1935.
The Early Medici. L. C. Morley. London, 1935.
Caterina de' Medici. E. Camillucci. Valdarno: S. Giovanni, 1935.
Memoirs of Sir John Reresby. A. Browning, ed. Glasgow, 1936.
The Private Life of Lorenzo the Magnificent. Y. Maguire. London, 1936.
Florence et les Médicis. G. Truc. Paris, 1936.
Bianca Cappello. C. Giachetti. Firenze, 1936.
Lorenzo il Magnifico. F. G. Fiori. Firenze, 1937.
Laurent le Magnifique. M. Brion. Paris, 1937.
Lorenzo il Magnifico. C. Violini. Milano, 1937.
A Cardinal of the Medici. Hicks Beach. London, 1937.
Cosimo de' Medici. C. S. Gutkind. London, 1938.
Maria de' Medici. G. Datta de Albertis. Milano, 1938.
Tuscan Spring. J. Cleugh. London, 1938.
Galeazzo Maria Sforza. C. Violini. Milano, 1938.
Opere di Niccolò Machiavelli. A. Panella, ed. Milano, 1939.
I Medici. U. Romagnoli. Bologna, 1939.
Saggio di bibliografia medicea. S. Camerani. Firenze, 1940.
Cathérine de Médicis. Princesse H. de Bourbon-Parme. Paris, 1940.
Lorenzo il Magnifico. R. Palmarocchi. Torino, 1941.
La Florence des Médicis. A. Bailly. Paris, 1942.
Lorenzo de' Medici. E. Barfucci. Firenze, 1945.
Caterina de' Medici. I. Luzzatti. Milano, 1946.
I Medici e i lore tempi. U. Dorini. Firenze, 1947.
Lorenzo il Magnifico. U. Dorini. Firenze, 1949.
Storia di Firenze. A. Panella. Firenze, 1949.
The Medici. F. Schevill. London, 1949.
Le Poesie de Lorenzo de' Medici. B. Cicognani. Firenze, 1950.
Bianca Cappello. E. Allodoli. Milano, 1950.
Il Magnifico Lorenzo. E. Bizzarri. Milano, 1950.
Vita di Savonarola. R. Ridolfi. Roma, 1952.
Florence. C. Hutton. London, 1952.
La France de Louis XIII. V. L. Tapié. Paris, 1952.
Henri IV. M. Andrieux. Paris, 1954.
Vita di Niccolò Machiavelli. R. Ridolfi. Roma, 1954.
Lorenzo de' Medici. C. M. Ady. London, 1955.

Histoire de Florence. J. L. Dubreton. Paris, 1957.

L'étrange mort de Henri IV. P. Erlanger. Chambéry, 1957.

Les Médicis. M. Andrieux. Paris, 1958.

The Last of the Medicis. H. Acton. London, 1958.

Lorenzo il Magnifico. L. Ugolini. Torino, 1959.

Lucrezia Tornabuoni. M. Bosanquet. London, 1960.

La Journée des Dupes. G. Mongrédien. Paris, 1961.

History of Florence. F. Schevill. New York and London, 1961.

La Jeunesse de Laurent de Médicis. A. Rochon. Paris, 1963.

Cathérine de Medicis. J. Héritier. Paris, 1963.

The Divine Aretino. J. Cleugh. London, 1965.

The Government of Florence Under the Medici. N. Rubinstein. London, 1966.

The Crisis of the Early Italian Renaissance. H. Baron. London, 1966.

Italian Renaissance Studies. E. F. Jacob, ed. London, 1967.

Florenz. A. Grote. München, 1967.

INDEX

Accademia degli Scossi, 308
Accademia della Crusca, 308–9
Acciaiuoli, Agnolo, 58, 99–100, 104, 109, 190
Acciaiuoli, Donato, 140
Accoramboni, Vittoria, 311, 312
Actium, Battle of, 121
Acton, Harold, 370
"Adam and Eve" (da Vinci), 182
Adimari, Countess degli, 25
Adimari, Antonio, 25
Adimari, Talano, 25
Adimari family, 25, 36
"Adoration of the Magi" (da Vinci), 182
"Adoration of the Magi" (Lippi), 270
Adrian IV, Pope, 250, 251
Adrian VI, Pope, 247
Aeneid, 280
Agrippa, Marcus Vipsanius, 121
Alberti, Leon Battista, 110–11, 114, 178, 180, 185
Alberti family, 36
Albizzi, Atonfrancesco degli, 231
Albizzi, Ginevra degli, 87
Albizzi, Maso degli, 36, 37, 40, 42, 54, 176
Albizzi, Ormanno degli, 48
Albizzi, Rinaldo degli, 40, 54–59, 62, 68, 69, 81; anti-Medicean activities of, 43–51; banished from Florence, 51; death of, 70
Albizzi family, 25, 33, 122
Alchemy, 308
Alcibiades, 277, 278
Aldobrandini family, 25
Alessandri family, 108
Alexander VI, Pope, 89, 197–98, 201, 203, 208, 213, 214, 223, 231; death of, 227; election of, 196–97; Savonarola and, 214–15, 216–17, 218, 219, 221, 222
Alexander VII, Pope, 338–39
Alfonso of Ferrara, 246, 289

Alfonso I, King of Naples, 60, 72–73, 79, 80, 82
Alfonso II, King of Naples, 100, 105, 142, 143, 147, 148, 149, 155, 158, 159, 176, 198, 199, 200, 201, 208
Allori, Angiolo. *See* Bronzino, Il
Altopascio, Battle of (1325), 22
Altoviti, Guglielmo degli, 24
Altoviti family, 25, 36
Ammanati, Bartolommeo, 285, 287
Anacreon, 217
Angelico, Fra, 53, 56, 63, 96, 110, 111, 181, 184, 272
Angevin family, 146
Anghiari, Battle of, 74, 138
Angoulême, Duchess d', 341
Anna Maria Francesca of Saxe-Lauenberg, 357–58, 359, 360, 363–64, 367, 370
Anne of Austria, 323, 326, 328
"Annunciation" (da Vinci), 182
"Annunciation" (Fra Angelico), 53, 181
Antella, Lamberto dell', 213
Antinori, Bernardino, 311
Antoine de Bourbon, King of Navarre, 296–97
Anziani, consuls of, 5
Apatici (society), 309
Apology (Lorenzino de' Medici), 280, 281
Appiani, Camillo degli, 242
Appiani family, 242
Aquinas, St. Thomas, 192
Ardinghelli, Niccolò, 106
Aretino, Pietro, 235–36, 248–49, 255, 271
Arezzo, occupation of (1529), 263
Argyropoulos, Joannes, 115
Ariosto, Emilian Ludovico, 185, 187, 246, 272
Aristogiton, 127
Aristophanes, 192, 217
Aristotle, 64, 174, 185, 337

Arno River, 2, 3, 68, 285, 331; flooding of (1557), 287
Arrabiati party, 210, 260
Arti, consuls of, 5
Astrology, 188
Augustine, St., 174, 177
Augustus, Emperor, 121, 236
Augustus II, King of Poland, 374
Augustus III, King of Poland, 374
Avicenna (physician), 337
Avignon papacy, 21, 28

Baglioni, Commander Malatesta, 262–63, 264, 266
Bagnolo, Treaty of (1484), 155
Bagnone, Stefano da, 133, 134, 135, 137–38
Baldaccio d'Anghiari, 69–70, 71, 74–75, 77; murder of, 74–76, 80, 81, 266
Baldovinetti, Mariotto, 49–50, 110
Bandini, Bernardo, 133, 134–36, 138, 151
Bapponi family, 26
"Baptism of Christ" (Verrocchio), 182, 183
Barbadori, Niccolò, 50
Barbary Coast pirates, 331
Bardi, Contessina de', 40, 47, 70, 87, 94
Bardi, Gemma de', 12
Bardi family, 8, 12, 17, 24, 25, 26, 27, 58
"Bartolommeo Colleoni" (Verrocchio), 185
Bartolommeo, Fra, 268, 270
Basel Council, 43
Battista, Gian, 235
Beaulieu, Peace of (1576), 302, 303
Bella, Gian della, 10–11, 12, 172
Bellay, Joachim du, 298
Belloy, Countess de, 341
Bembo, Pietro, 232, 244, 246, 250, 272
Benci, Donato de', 175
Benedict XI, Pope, 16
Bentivoglio, Ercole, Lord of Bologna, 102
Bernardo, Antonio di, 210
Bertoldo, 178
Bessarion, Patriarch of Constantinople, 63, 64
Bianchi party, 13–18
Bigi party, 210, 222, 226
Biron, Marechal de, 318
"Birth of Venus, The" (Botticelli), 174, 183
Bisticci, Vespasiano da, 64, 97

Black Death, 27
Blenheim, Battle of (1704), 362
Board of National Debt, 118–19
Boboli gardens, 342
Boccaccio, Giovanni, 27, 51, 186, 217, 272, 308
Boiardo, Matteo Maria, 185
Bologna Giovanni da, 308
Bologna (city), 19, 21, 49, 67, 80, 100, 120, 154, 155, 162, 213, 237
Bona of Savoy, 116–17, 120, 127, 144, 154, 198
Bonaventura, Fra, 357
Bonguisi family, 38
Boniface VIII, Pope, 12–13, 14
Bordoni family, 25
Borgia, Cesare, 223, 224–25, 226, 227, 268
Borgia, Lucrezia, 223
Borgia, Rodrigo. *See* Alexander VI, Pope
Borgia family, 229
Borromeo, Beatrice, 138
Borromeo, Carlo, 129, 138
Borso, Duke of Ferrara, 103, 106
Boscoli, Pietro Paolo, 232, 233
Bostichi family, 10
Botticelli, Sandro, 110, 112, 126, 138, 147–48, 156, 174, 175, 178, 182–83, 184, 189, 268, 270, 272
Bourbon, Cardinal Charles de, 306
Bourbon, Duke Charles de, 255
"Boy on a Dolphin" (Verrocchio), 183
Bracciolini, Jacopo, 133, 136, 137
Bracciolini, Poggio, 65, 133
Bramante, 245, 267
Brancacci Chapel, 181
Brandinelli, Volumnio, 338
Brenne (equerry), 326
Brétigny, Treaty of (1360), 30
Brienne, Walter de, Duke of Athens, 22, 24–26
Bronzino, Il, 272, 285
Brosses, Charles de, 376
Brunelleschi, Filippo, 51–52, 96, 110, 111, 179–80, 181, 185, 237, 285
Bruni, Leonardo, 64
Bruto, Michele, 33
Brutus, Marcus Junius, 127, 232, 241, 278, 281
Buonaventuri, Piero, 313
Buondelmonti family, 17
Buon'uomini, consuls of, 5
Burckhardt, Jakob, 96
Burgundy, province of, 254, 348
Buti, Lucrezia, 112

Caesar, Julius, 113, 127, 248
Calabria, Duke of (son of Robert of Naples), 22, 24, 26
Caligula, Emperor, 278
Calixtus III, Pope, 89
"Calling of the Apostles, The" (Ghirlandaio), 184
Cambi (chronicler), 90
Cambio, Arnolfo di, 237
Campaldino, Battle of, 10, 14
Cancellieri family, 13
Capitani del popolo, office of, 32
Cappello, Bianca, 309, 312, 313, 331
Cappello, Carlo, 264–65
Cappello family, 313
Capponi, Agostino, 232, 233
Capponi, Neri, 67, 68, 69–70, 71, 74–76, 77, 83, 84, 88, 96, 172, 203
Capponi, Niccolò, 257, 259–60, 261, 263
Capponi, Piero, 203, 206, 207, 210, 216, 257, 259, 261–62
Cardona, Raimundo de, 230
Carducci, Francesco, 262–63, 264, 265, 266
Carnesecchi (servant), 289, 290
Casalmaggiore, Battle of, 80
Cascina, Battle of, 31
Cassius, Gaius, 127
Castagno, Andrea del, 110, 112, 182
Castelnuovo, fortress of, 106
Castiglione, Baldassare, 174, 232
Castle Sant' Angelo (Rome), 255–56, 259, 267
Castracane, Castruccio, 21–22
Catasto (register of landed properties), 39, 77–78
Câteau-Cambrésis, Treaty of (1559), 287–88
Catherine de' Medici, 241, 248, 252, 258, 281, 285, 287, 289, 292–308, 311, 326, 331; address to Parlement (1557), 294; birth of, 240; death of, 306–8, 314, 315; as Duchess of Anjou, 292–93; Huguenot wars and, 295–304; idealism of, 307; marriage of, 292; peacemaking tour (1578), 304–5; as Queen-Mother, 295–306; regency, 296–98; St. Bartholomew's massacre and, 300–2; unpopularity of, 292, 293, 299
Catholic League, 304–6, 315
Cattaneo, Simonetta, 126–27
Catullus, Gaius Valerius, 159
Cavalcanti, Ginevra, 47
Cavalcanti, Giovanni, 110

Cavalcanti, Guido, 14, 40
Cavalcanti family, 16, 26, 45, 135
Cecchino (singer), 353, 355, 357, 358
Cellini, Benvenuto, 265, 272–73
Cerchi, Vieri de', 13–14, 16
Cerchi family, 25
Charlemagne, 3, 178, 187
Charles of Anjou, 28
Charles of Lorraine, 340, 343, 351
Charles of Valois, 14–15, 16, 18, 28, 176
Charles I, King of England, 327, 330
Charles II, King of England, 356
Charles VII, King of France, 85, 86
Charles VIII, King of France, 158, 199, 200, 214, 257; death of, 221; Italian wars, 201–10, 212, 222, 224, 227, 229; Savonarola and, 204–5, 206, 209, 211–12
Charles IX, King of France, 296, 298, 300, 302
Charles V, Holy Roman Emperor, 243, 247, 251, 253, 256, 261, 262, 263, 274–79, 284–87, 292; abdication of, 286–87; meeting with Clement VII, 64
Charles VI, Holy Roman Emperor, 367, 373, 374
Charles II, King of Spain, 362
Chiaroscuro, technique of, 182, 237, 336
Chigi, Agostino, 235–36
Christina, Queen of Sweden, 338
Christine of France, 319, 326
Christine of Lorraine, 331–32, 333
Chronique de Charles IX (Mérimée), 302
Chrysoloras, Manuel, 55
Cibo, Franceschetto, 160, 161, 196
Cibo, Giambattista. *See* Innocent VIII, Pope
Cibo, Innocenzo, 233
Cicero, 3, 113, 120, 140, 170, 186, 188, 278
Cimabue, Giovanni, 10
Cimento (academy), 337
Città di Castello, 129–30, 133, 142
Clement V, Pope, 17, 18, 19
Clement VI, Pope, 27
Clement VII, Pope (Giulio de' Medici), 156, 225, 231, 232, 250–62, 263, 265, 268–70, 271, 277, 279, 289, 290, 292, 303; Bologna meeting with Charles V, 264; cardinalate, 233, 235, 240, 241, 247–50, 252, 276; death of, 275, 276; foreign affairs, 251; Michel-

angelo and, 267–68; nickname of, 241; papal election of, 250; plots against, 249; popularity of, 241; released from captivity, 261; in tower of Sant' Angelo, 255–56, 259
Clement VIII, Pope, 263
Clement XI, Pope, 363–64
Cola, Antonino da, 242
Cola di Rienzi, 28
Coligny, Admiral Gaspard II de, 297–98; murder of, 300–1, 302
Colleoni, Bartolommeo, 102–3, 105–6, 181
Colonna, Stefano, 263, 264
Colonna, Vittoria, 272
Colonna family, 247
Columbus, Christopher, 208
Comines, Philippe de, 142
Committee of Eight, 150
Committee of Twelve, 150
Common Council, 150
Compagni, Dino, 14
Concini, Marquis d' Ancre, 317, 322–23, 324, 325, 329
Condé, Prince Louis de, 296, 297–98, 299, 302
Condé, Princess de, 302
Condottieri, 30, 38, 60–62, 67, 69, 71, 72, 76, 78, 79, 102, 130, 132, 138, 180, 222, 239, 248, 286, 288; purpose of, 28
Conrad, Count of Lando, 29–30
Constance, Peace of (1183), 5
Constantine the Great, 178, 179
Constantinople, 8, 20, 149, 199
Contarini (ambassador), 293
Contucci, Andrea, 245
Copernicus, Nicolaus, 332
Córdoba, Gonzalo Fernández de, 208, 227, 261
Correr, Giovanni, 299
Cortona, occupation of (1529), 263
Cosimo, Piero di, 268
Cosse, Marshal Charles de, 305
Council of Constance, 37, 65
Council of Eighty, 259
Council of Florence, 63–64
Council of One Hundred, 118, 150
Council of the People, 150
Council of Seventy, 150, 203, 253; abolished (1495), 210
Council of Trent, 284
Council of Twenty, 210
Council of Two Hundred, 275
Counter-Reformation, 373–74
Courtier (Castiglione), 174
Craon, Prince de, 375
Credi, Lorenzo di, 268, 270

Cunha, Admiral Tristan da, 234

D'Albert, Charles, Duke de Luynes, 324
Dami, Giuliano, 359, 360, 364, 371
Dante Alighieri, 14, 15, 19, 20, 170, 174, 187, 188, 272
"David" (Donatello), 52
"David" Verrocchio), 109, 181, 183, 185
Decameron (Boccaccio), 27
De Monarchia (Dante), 187
Descent of the Holy Ghost, 117
Dialogue of the Two Chief Systems of the World (Galileo), 333
Diane de Poitiers, 292, 293, 294, 319
Diaoceto, Jacopo da, 249
"Dies Irae," 192
Divine Comedy (Dante), 20, 26, 184, 189
Dominic, St., 181
Donatello (1386–1466), 52, 96, 110, 178, 179, 180, 181, 184, 185
Donati, Corso, 10, 11, 13–18, 19
Donati, Lisa, 23, 36
Donati, Lucrezia, 106, 126, 186
Donati family, 23, 25, 26, 106
Donato, Agnolo, 140
Don Carlos of Bourbon, 373, 374, 375
Don Quixote, 187
Dori, Leonora, 314–17, 322–24; sorcery trial of, 325
Dovizi, Bernardo, 232
Dower Fund, 154
Dreux, Battle of (1562), 297
Durant, Will, 247

Edict of Amboise (1563), 297, 298
Edict of January (1562), 304
Edward I, King of England, 13, 21
Edward III, King of England, 8, 23, 26, 30
Edward, the Black Prince, 23
Eleonora Maria of Austria, 351
Eleonora di Toledo, 284, 285, 286, 289, 310
Elizabeth of Austria, 300
Elizabeth of Valois, 294, 295
Elizabeth I, Queen of England, 288, 289, 293, 298, 300
Elizabeth, Queen of Spain, 318, 323
Emmanuel Philibert, Duke of Savoy, 294, 295
England, 7, 214, 219, 289, 303, 369; *condottiere,* 30–32; nationalism in, 169

Enlightenment, 337
Entragues, Henriette d', Marquise de Verneuil, 315, 317–18, 319
Épernon, Duke d', 321, 322, 325, 326
Erasmus of Rotterdam, 256, 303
Ercole I Este, Duke of Ferrara, 103, 104, 128, 142, 144
Ercole II Este, Duke of Ferrara, 287
Este family, 114
Estrées, Gabrielle d', 315
Etruria, excavations in, 285
Eugène of Savoy, 362
Eugenius IV, Pope, 42, 50–51, 56, 60–64, 73–74, 76, 78, 79, 80, 81, 86, 111, 112
Euripides, 192
Evelyn, John, 335
"Expulsion of the Sciences from Greece" (Gio da San Gio), 336

Faggiuola, Uguccione della, 17, 19
Farnese, Alessandro. See Paul III, Pope
Farnese, Elizabeth, 368, 373
Farnese, Margherita, 309–10
Farnese, Odoardo, Duke of Parma, 333
Farnese family, 309
Federigo of Aragon, 100, 102, 114, 127
Ferdinand II, King of Aragon, 209, 231, 234
Ferdinand I, Holy Roman Emperor, 286, 288
Ferdinand I, King of Naples, 102, 108, 114, 120, 122, 140, 142, 144–45, 146–48, 149, 154, 158, 161, 165, 168, 176, 191, 195, 196–97, 199–200, 243
Ferrara, 23, 43, 47, 49, 100, 114, 120, 142, 154, 264, 362
Ferrara Council, 63
Ferrucci, Francesco, 265, 266
Feudalism, 10, 11, 28, 169
Ficino, Marsilio, 64, 94, 97, 115, 163, 173, 174, 187, 188, 192, 268, 272
Fiesole, Mino da, 93, 110, 111, 175, 185
Filelfo, Francesco, 70, 110
Filiberta of Savoy, 236, 240
Flagellants (sect), 302
Florence: ancient name of, 2; armorial bearings, 3; ascendancy of Medici family in, 1–41; banking-houses of, 8; city emblem, 2; commercial growth of, 7–8, 9–10, 20; Cosimo the Elder and, 42–98; democracy, 6–7, 12, 35; early

Medici and (1291–1429), 1–42; end of the republic, 262–73, 275; government, 4–7, 9, 10, 11, 25, 35; historical origins of, 2; imperial threat to (1311–13), 19; Lorenzo the Magnificent's rule of, 99–193; political factionalism, 13–18; popolano rule, 11–12; preoccupation with civic independence, 4; sesto supervision, 6; siege of (1529), 263–64; under interdict, 230; union with Fiesole (1000), 3, 4. See also Medici family
Florentine Academy, 309
Florentine History (Villani), 20
Florentine wool, 7–8
Florinus (praetor), 2
Foix, Gaston de, 230
Foix, Odet de, Vicomte de Lautrec, 261
Fortebraccio, Braccio, Lord of Perugia, 130
Fortebraccio, Carlo, 130, 141
Fortebraccio, Niccolò, 61
Fouquet, Nicolas, 342
France, 214, 219, 251, 287–88, 314–30, 334, 362, 369; Florentine bankers in, 158; League of Cambrai, 229; nationalism in, 169; religious wars, 295–306. See also Catherine de Medici; Marie de Medici
Francesca, Piero della, 105
Francezi, Napoleone, 133, 138–39
Francis, St., 181
Francis, Duke of Alençon, 305
Francis I, Duke of Lorraine, 374–75, 376
Francis, Duke of Orléans, 293
Francis I, King of France, 236–37, 240, 251, 253, 254, 260, 261, 262, 270, 284, 287, 291, 292, 294
Francis II, King of France, 293, 294–95, 296
Frateschi party, 262
Frederick III, Duke of Austria, 22
Frederick I Barbarossa, Holy Roman Emperor, 5
Frederick III, Holy Roman Emperor, 85, 155
Frescobaldi, Battista, 151–52
Frescobaldi family, 13, 17, 25, 26, 58
Frundsberg, Georg von, 255

Galastroni, Simone, 11–12
Galigai family, 317
Galileo Galilei, 332–33, 334, 337
Gassendi, Pierre, 376

Gaston, Duke of Orléans, 319, 328, 340, 348
Gavinana, Battle of (1530), 265
Genoa, 5, 8, 72, 80, 106, 121, 143, 212, 263, 264
George III, King of England, 370
George IV, King of England, 370
Germany, 214, 216, 229, 303
Ghianni (dwarf), 336
Ghibelline party, 5, 13, 14, 16, 17, 19, 21, 26, 28, 30, 32, 91; hatred between Guelfs and, 21; meaning of, 4
Ghiberti, Lorenzo, 52, 110, 180
Ghirlandaio, Domenico, 182, 184, 186
Giagiolo (emblem), 2
Ginori, Leonardo, 280
Giordano, Luca, 336
Giostra di Giuliano de' Medici, La, 126
Giostra di Lorenzo de' Medici, La, 106
Giotto de Bondone, 20, 26, 28, 52, 181
Girolami, Raffaello, 265, 266
Gonzaga, Eleonora, 365–66, 368
Gonzaga, Federigo, Marquis of Mantua, 271
Gonzaga, Ferrante, 263, 266
Gonzaga, Francesco, 271
Gonzaga, Vincenzo, 309–10, 312
Gonzaga family, 114, 365–66
Gorini, Fioretta, 156
Goths (tribe), 3
Gozzoli, Benozzo, 63, 110, 111–12, 113, 114, 182, 184
Grand Council of Florence (Consiglio Maggiore), 150, 154, 225, 226, 231, 249, 259
Grandi, 10, 11, 12, 16, 26, 27–28, 40, 41, 43, 50; civic rights of, 9
Great Schism, 37
Gregory I, Pope, 250
Gregory VII, Pope, 250
Gregory XIII, Pope, 309, 310, 312
Guadagni, Bernardo, 45, 46, 48
Guelf party, 5, 10, 11, 13, 18–19, 21, 23, 28, 30, 33, 35, 91, 122; hatred between Ghibellines and, 21; meaning of, 4
Guercheville, Marquise de, 317
Guicciardini, Francesco, 78, 92, 162, 168, 185, 251, 255, 256–57, 259, 262, 268, 269–70, 272, 275, 276–77, 279, 281, 283
Guicciardini, Luigi, 257

Guidi, Francesco, Count of Poppi, 68, 69, 70–71
Guidi, Gualdrada, 68
Guilds, medieval, 9, 33; types of, 7
Guise, Cardinal Charles de, 295, 296, 297
Guise, Duchess de, 360
Guise, Duke de, 322, 340
Guise, Francis, Duke de, 295, 296, 297, 298
Guise, Henri, Duke de, 300, 301, 304, 305–6

Habsburg family, 85, 209, 327, 362, 374
Handel, Georg Friedrich, 367
Hannibal, 144
Hanno (elephant), 234–35, 236
Harmodius, 127
Hawkwood, Sir John, 30–32, 271
Henri II, King of France, 281, 285, 288, 292–95, 319; death of, 295; as duke of Anjou, 292–93; marriage of, 292
Henri III, King of France, 300, 302–6, 323; assassination of, 314–15; homosexuality of, 303–4
Henri IV, King of France, 300, 301, 302, 305, 315–22, 324; assassination of, 321–22; on Catherine de' Medici (quoted), 307–8; marriage of, 315–16; mistresses of, 315, 317, 319
Henri, Duke of Orléans (1607–11), 319
Henri, Prince of Condé (1588–1646), 322, 323, 324, 325–26
Henriette Marie, Queen of England, 319, 327, 330
Henry of Navarre. *See* Henri IV, King of France
Henry VII, King of England, 205
Henry VIII, King of England, 234, 284
Henry VII, Holy Roman Emperor, 18–19
Hipparchus, 127
Hippias, 127
Holy Roman Empire, title to throne of, 5
Homer, 170
Homosexuality, 196, 259, 303–4, 317, 334–35, 338, 339, 354, 367
Hôpital, Michel de l', 296, 302
Horace, 186, 192
Horatius, 243

Huguenots, 315, 327; granted freedom of worship, 296; massacre of, 297, 300–2
Humanism, 169
Hungary, 219
Hutten, Ulrich von, 234–35

Iliad, 187
Innocent VIII, Pope, 157–58, 160, 161, 163, 165, 196, 200
Innocent XII, Pope, 359, 362
Inquisition, 289, 303, 333
Isabella of Aragon, 198, 201
Isabella, Infanta of Spain, 329
Isabella I, Queen of Castile, 208
Italian wars, 42–43, 44, 50, 65–70, 71–73, 75, 82–83, 142–45, 149, 150, 155, 158–59, 215–16, 253–55, 261; end of Florentine Republics, 262–73; French invasion, 201–10, 212, 222; occupation of Florence, 205–7; sack of Rome (1527), 255–56, 303

James IV, King of Scotland, 205
James V, King of Scotland, 295
Jarnac, Battle of (1569), 299
Jerome, St., 177
Jews, 303, 331, 353; persecution of, 351, 376
Joan of Arc, St., 85
Joanna II, Queen of Naples, 38, 60
Johanna of Habsburg, 290, 308, 312, 313, 314
Johann Wilhelm, Elector Palatine, 355–56, 358, 368
John of Bohemia, 23
John XXII, Pope, 22
John XXIII, Pope (Baldassare Cossa), 38
John VII Palaeologus, Emperor, 63, 64, 113
Joseph, Patriarch, 63, 113
Joseph I, Holy Roman Emperor, 363, 364, 366
"Journey of the Magi, The" (Gozzoli), 113
Jubilee Year (1300), 12–13
Julius II, Pope, 229–30, 232–33, 237, 238, 245, 246, 267
Jupiter (planet), satellites of, 332
Justinian, Emperor, 178
Juvenal, 177

Kepler, Johann, 332

La Bambagia (singer), 358
Labat, J. B., 362–63

La Chaise, Father, 356
Lake Trasiemeno, Battle of, 144
La Molinella, Battle of, 105–6
Lampugnani, Gianandrea, 127
Landino, Cristoforo, 188–89, 268
Lando, Michele, 34–35, 176
Landucci (historian), 237
La Renaudie (nobleman), 296
Last of the Medicis, The (Acton), 370
"Last Supper, The" (da Vinci), 182
Last Will and Testament of the Elephant, The, 235
Latin language, 169, 170, 187
League of Cambrai, 229
League of Cognac, 254
League of Malines, 234
Leghorn, port of, 202, 207, 212, 216, 331, 340, 362, 373
Leo X, Pope (Giovanni de' Medici), 118, 139, 157, 185, 195, 197, 200, 203–4, 207, 213, 225, 228, 230, 233–45, 250, 251, 263, 267, 268, 269, 270, 271, 288, 341; academic reputation of, 195; Bologna conference, 237; death of, 244, 246–47, 248; elevation to the cardinalate, 163, 166; fiscal scandals, 245; flight from Florence, 204; foreign policy, 234; Luther and, 243; papal election of, 233; patronage of art and literature, 231–32, 244–46; pet elephant of, 234–35, 236; plots against, 232, 243; return from exile (1512), 231; Urbino campaign, 238–39
Leopold, Duke of Lorraine, 251
Leopold I, Holy Roman Emperor, 355, 362, 363
Libraries, 177–78
Lippi, Filippino, 112, 182, 184, 268, 270
Lippi, Filippo, 110, 112–13
Lippi, Fra Lippo, 96, 119, 175, 184
Livy, 113, 120, 170
Lodi, Treaty of (1454), 86
Loggia dei Lanzi (Lancers Guardroom), 284, 308
Louis IX, King of France, 299
Louis X, King of France, 21
Louis XI, King of France, 109–10, 142, 143–44, 155, 161
Louis XII, King of France, 223–24, 225, 229, 230, 234, 236
Louis XIII, King of France, 318, 321–28, 339
Louis XIV, King of France, 339, 340, 342, 343, 344, 346, 348, 349,

350, 352, 353, 355, 356, 360, 367, 368
Louis XV, King of France, 74
Louis IV, Holy Roman Emperor, 22
Louise of Savoy, 294
Lucca, 15, 20, 21, 22, 23, 24, 25, 42, 63, 143, 154, 212, 263, 285–86; expedition from (1546), 284; Milanese war over, 43
Lucian, 217
Lucretius, 159
Luther, Martin, 260, 284, 303; excommunicated, 243
Lutheran Church, 303
Luynes, Duke de, 326

Machiavelli, Niccolò, 2, 18, 35, 40, 41, 75, 92, 104, 108–9, 114, 153, 168, 185, 188, 226, 227, 228, 229, 230, 232, 241, 246, 251, 261, 268–69, 270, 272, 278, 283
Macinghi-Strozzi, Alessandra, 116
Maddalena (slave), 93
Madeleine de la Tour d'Auvergne, 240
"Madonna and Angels" (Verrocchio), 183
"Madonna and Child" (da Vinci), 182
"Madonna of the Magnificat" (Botticelli), 156
Maffei, Antonio, 134, 135, 137–38
Magdalen of Habsburg, 333, 334–35
Magnasco, Alessandro, 371
Maiano, Benedetto da, 185
Malatesta, Annelena, 76
Malatesta, Galeotto, 31
Malatesta, Pandolfo, 30, 31
Malatesta, Roberto, Lord of Rimini, 144, 176
Malerba, Ser Alberto di, 171
Malvolti, Federigo, 47–48
Mandragola (Machiavelli), 272
Mantua, 23, 90, 110, 114, 142, 144, 155, 273
Maramaldo, Fabrizio, 265–66
Marc Antony, 121
Marciano, Battle of (1554), 286
Margaret of Austria, 262, 274
Marguérite de Valois, 295, 300, 301, 315
Marguérite-Louise d'Orléans, 339–45, 346, 347, 348–57, 360, 367, 369
Maria-Theresa, Empress, 374
Marie de' Medici, 312, 314–30; appointed governor of Anjou, 326; contempt of French nobility toward, 319; death of, 330; in exile, 328–

30; marriage of, 315–16; outlawed from France, 329; as Queen-Regent, 320–21
Marignano, Battle of (1515), 236–37
Marignano, Marquess of, 286
Marlborough, Duke of, 362
Marseilles, Bishop of, 349–50
Martelli, Camilla, 290
Martin V, Pope, 37, 38, 39, 61, 130
Maruffi, Fra Silvestro, 221
Mary Stuart, Queen of Scotland, 293, 294–95
Masaccio (1401–29), 52–53, 112, 181–82, 184
Maximilian I, Holy Roman Emperor, 209, 215–16, 224, 243
Maximilian II, Holy Roman Emperor, 289, 290, 300, 308
Mazarin, Cardinal Jules, 339–40
Medici, Alamanno de', 30
Medici, Alessandro de', 252–53, 256–58, 259, 263, 268, 274–81, 282, 291; appointed *gonfalonier* for life, 267; as duke of Tuscany, 275–81; marriage of, 262, 279; murder of, 280–81, 377
Medici, Andrea de', 30
Medici, Anna Maria Luisa de', 345, 353, 355, 357, 359–60, 366–67, 368, 370, 375, 376, 377; last will and testament of, 376
Medici, Antonio de Bernardino de', 138
Medici, Ardingho de', 9, 12, 15–16, 17, 40
Medici, Averardo de' (fl. 1314), 18, 19, 20, 23
Medici, Averardo "Bicci" de' (fl. 1350), 37–38
Medici, Averardo de' (d. 1434), 42, 43–44, 48, 55, 70
Medici, Bartolommeo de', 30
Medici, Bernardetto de', 69, 71, 73–74
Medici, Bernardino de', 11, 12
Medici, Bernardo de', 17, 20, 21, 24
Medici, Bianca de', 107, 129, 153
Medici, Carlo de' (b. 1430), 93–94
Medici, Cardinal Carlo de' (1595–1666), 344
Medici, Caterina de'. *See* Catherine de' Medici
Medici, Chiarissimo de', 8–9
Medici, Clarice de', 231, 257–58
Medici, Conte di Averardo de', 20, 23
Medici, Cosimino de', 87
Medici, Cosimo de' (1389–1464), 39, 40, 41, 42–98, 99, 101, 104, 108,

109, 110, 111, 114, 115, 119, 120, 122, 126, 129, 140, 145, 150, 151, 172, 173, 177, 180, 181, 184, 185, 189, 200, 203, 221, 249, 268, 273, 285, 288, 291, 307, 337, 364, 376; arrested, 46–48; ascension to power (1434–36), 51–57; Baldaccio murder and, 74–76, 80; cynicism of, 75–76; death of, 95, 113; exiled, 48–49, 50; at Ferrara conference, 43; financial operations, 77–78, 152–53; *gonfalonier*ship of 1435, 55–56; library of, 177; Milanese wars and, 65–70, 71, 72, 73, 75, 82–83; Mugello farm retirement, 44–45; as patron of art and literature, 51–53, 56–57, 64, 65, 79–80, 85–86, 112, 113; political attitudes of, 54, 56, 57–58; recalled from exile, 51, 57, 62, 118; sense of realism, 65–67, 68; Sforza friendship, 80–81
Medici, Cosimo I de' (1519–74), 272, 281–92, 308, 310, 314, 318, 333, 347, 349, 377; character of, 290–92; created Grand Duke of Tuscany, 289–90; death of, 290; Etruria exavations, 285; Lucca battle (1546), 284; Machiavellism of, 283; marriage of, 284, 290; reign of, 281–92; Sienese revolt and, 284–85, 286
Medici, Cosimo II de' (1590–1620), 332–33, 337, 339, 347; character of, 332; death of, 333
Medici, Cosimo III de' (1642–1723), 339, 340–41, 343, 372, 376; birth of, 334; created a canon, 362; death of, 370; education of, 338; in London, 345–46; marriage of, 339–42, 343; protocol dispute, 355; reign of, 347–70; religious intolerance of, 356, 357, 363; unpopularity of, 351
Medici, Eleonora de', 309, 310–11
Medici, Ferdinand de' (1663–1713), 344, 351, 352–55, 357–59, 363, 364, 366; death of, 367, 368; homosexuality of, 354, 367; marriage of, 353–54
Medici, Cardinal Ferdinand I de' (1569–1609), 310, 312, 313–14, 315, 317, 319, 330–32, 337, 347, 362, 376; death of, 319–20; marriage of, 331–32; as patron of the arts, 331; reign of, 330–32; statesmanship, 331
Medici, Ferdinand II de' (1610–70), 329, 333–47, 352, 360, 368; death of, 347; homosexuality of, 334–35, 338, 339; love of money, 335; as patron of arts and sciences, 336–37; reign of, 333–47
Medici, Filigno di Conte de', 35
Medici, Filippo de', 313
Medici, Francesco de' (1541–87), 290, 308–14, 330, 331, 332, 337, 347; death of, 314; patronage of the arts, 308; reign of, 308–14
Medici, Francesco de' (1614–34), 333
Medici, Francesco di Ardingho de', 25
Medici, Francesco di Averardo de', 42
Medici, Cardinal Francesco Maria de', 338, 357, 359, 364–65, 368; death of, 366; marriage of, 364–66; pederasty of, 364
Medici, Garcia de', 289
Medici, Cardinal Giancarlo de', 333, 336, 338–39, 341, 344
Medici, Gian Gastone de', 357, 358–61, 363–64, 366, 367–70; birth of, 348; death of, 376; eccentricity of, 364; edict of 1735, 376; homosexuality of, 359, 360; humour of, 371–72; marriage of, 358–59; reign of, 370–76
Medici, Giovanni de' (d. 1343), 24
Medici, Giovanni di Conte de' (fl. 1356), 27, 28–29
Medici, Giovanni di Averardo "Bicci" (1360–1429), 37–40, 41, 42, 77, 97, 225
Medici, Giovanni de' (1424–63), 70, 72, 79, 94, 97–98; death of, 93, 98, 190; in exile, 47; marriage of, 87
Medici, Giovanni de' (1467–98), 161, 200, 201, 204, 222–23, 248, 270, 281
Medici, Giovanni de' (1475–1521). *See* Leo X, Pope
Medici, Giovanni della Bande Nere (1498–1526), 239–44, 248–49, 251, 253–55, 270, 272, 281, 282, 285, 287, 290, 291; birth of, 223; death of, 255, 256; Urbino campaign, 239–40, 241
Medici, Giovanni Angelo de' (1499–1565). *See* Pius IV, Pope
Medici, Cardinal Giovanni de' (1543–62), 288, 289
Medici, Giuliano de' (1453–78), 94, 106, 126, 129, 130, 156, 163, 195, 228, 267; murder of, 134, 135–37, 138, 141, 145, 151, 153, 231, 238,

241; popularity of, 115; visit to
Milan, 120–21
Medici, Giuliano de' (1479–1516),
195, 225, 228, 230, 267, 268, 271;
death of, 237–38, 252; expelled
from Florence, 213; as *gonfalonier*
of the Church, 233–34, 236, 240;
marriage of, 236, 240
Medici, Giulio de' (1478–1534). *See*
Clement VII, Pope
Medici, Cardinal Ippolito de', 252,
256–58, 259, 262, 263, 272, 274,
275, 277; poisoned, 259, 276, 279
Medici, Isabella de', 309, 311–12
Medici, Cardinal Leopoldo de', 333,
337, 341, 344
Medici, Lorenzino de', 277–79, 280,
281; assassinated, 283
Medici, Lorenzo de' (1394–1440),
41, 47, 48, 49, 200, 285
Medici, Lorenzo de' "the Magnificent"
(1449–92), 18, 37, 47, 63, 90, 91,
94, 99–193, 194, 195, 214, 219, 223,
227, 228, 231, 232, 237, 239, 240–
41, 244, 245, 248, 249, 257, 258,
267, 268, 270, 272, 273, 291, 293,
304, 306, 336, 339; abolishes captain's office, 132; alum contracts,
101, 121, 123; birth of, 87; death of,
166–68, 179, 196, 200, 267; education of, 115, 170; excommunicated,
141; financial operations, 152, 153–
54; honorific title of, 122; idealism
of, 161, 307; legislative government of, 150–51, 152; marriage of,
106–8; Milan visit, 100–1, 104;
Naples visit, 146–48, 150, 159;
Pazzi conspiracy against, 128–40;
physical appearance, 114; Pisa visit,
125–26, 172; political acumen of,
114; Prato rebellion and, 116; religious beliefs of, 142–43; Renaissance society and, 168–93; in Rome,
101, 106; Sarzana campaign, 159;
Savonarola and, 163–68, 191–92,
193, 198, 211; struggle between
papacy and, 128–29, 140–50, 155,
157; transfer of authority to (1469),
115; on unification of Italy, 158–
59; Volterra affair, 123–25, 130
Medici, Lorenzo de' (1463–1507),
281
Medici, Lorenzo de (1492–1519),
118, 231, 232, 234, 238, 241, 252,
267, 268, 281, 291, 292, 307;
created Duke of Urbino, 238; death
of, 240, 241; marriage of, 240

Medici, Lorenzo de' (1599–1648),
339
Medici, Lucrezia de' (1447–82), 107
Medici, Lucrezia de' (b. 1470), 160,
175, 239
Medici, Lucrezia de' (1544–61), 289
Medici, Luisa de', 161, 248
Medici, Maddalena de', 160, 161, 196
Medici, Margherita de', 333, 340
Medici, Maria de' (1445?–70?), 107,
270
Medici, Maria de' (1540–57), 287
Medici, Maria de' (1573–1642). *See*
Marie de' Medici
Medici, Mario de Talento de', 27
Medici, Mattias de', 333, 340, 341
Medici, Ottaviano de', 271
Medici, Pierfrancesco de' (1431–77)
the Elder, 281
Medici, Pierfrancesco de' (d. 1525)
the Younger, 270, 277
Medici, Piero de' (1414–69), 47, 70,
91, 93, 94, 96, 97–114, 120, 122,
140, 145, 156, 184, 185; death of,
109–10, 114, 115; as *gonfalonier*,
99; marriage of, 87; patronage of
art and literature, 110–14; plot
against, 99–100, 102–4; poetry
reading contest, 110–11, 114
Medici, Piero de' (1471–1503), 157,
160, 161, 163, 173, 177, 223, 224,
227–28, 231, 232, 248, 257, 258,
268, 275; character of, 195–96,
213–14; declared an outlaw, 203;
education of, 195; in exile, 203–4,
206, 213–14, 218, 223, 224, 225,
252; French expedition and, 201–3;
homosexuality of, 196, 213, 214;
marriage of, 159, 161; personality
of, 163; at Poggibonsi, 209; quarrel
with cousins, 200
Medici, Piero de' (1554–1604), 309,
311, 312
Medici, Salvestro di Alamanno de',
30–35, 36, 38, 40, 41
Medici, Salvestro di Averardo de', 23–
24, 36, 37–38, 140
Medici, Vieri de', 35, 36, 40
Medici, meaning of, 8
Medici Chapel, 267
Medici family: ascendancy of, 1–41;
coat of arms, 9; decadence (1530–
1743), 274–376; first *gonfalonier*,
12; jealousy between older and
younger branches, 248; return from
exile, 223–50; war-cry of, 203–4
Medici Palace, 36, 63, 79–80, 107,
111–12, 113, 134, 166, 177, 178,

180, 196, 203, 259, 271, 277, 284; sack of, 207, 210
Medici Theatre, 308
Melanchthon, Philipp, 64
Memoirs (Reresby), 346
Mérimée, Prosper, 301-2
Michelangelo, 51, 52, 174, 178-79, 183, 184, 185, 196, 238, 245, 264, 267, 271, 272, 336
Michelet, Jules, 301
Michelozzo di Bartolommeo, 56, 70, 110, 180, 185
Middle Ages, 1, 3, 53, 169, 174, 307
Milan, 1, 20, 21, 23, 42, 50, 59, 60, 61, 72, 78, 84, 88, 100, 105, 114, 120, 122, 126, 127, 141-42, 155, 158, 169, 176, 192, 229, 234, 254, 264, 272. *See also* Italian wars
Milton, John, 356
Modesti, Jacopo, 30
Mohammed II, Sultan of Turkey, 86, 138, 149
Moncontour, Battle of (1569), 299
Monferrato, Marquis of, 30
Monréal, knight of Provence, 28
Montano, Cola, 127
Monte Commune stock, 27
Montefeltro, Federigo da, Duke of Urbino, 105-6, 124, 125, 142, 143
Montefeltro, Guidobaldo da, 227, 238
Montemagni, Marchese di, 371
Montesecco, Giovan Battista, 131, 132-34, 138, 140, 141
Montesquieu, Baron de, 371
Montgomery, Captain, 295
Montluc, General Blaise de, 286
Montmorency, Duc Anne de, 294, 297, 299
Montmorency, Duc Henri II de, 325
Montpensier, Duchess de, 346
Morgante Maggiore (Pulci), 106, 156, 187
Mountbazon, M. de, 324
Murad II, Sultan of Turkey, 64
Museo Nazionale (Florence), 93

Naples, 1, 13, 21, 48, 59, 60, 66, 72, 100, 112, 114, 120, 122, 155, 176, 192, 199, 227, 273
Nardi, Bernardo, 116
Nardi, Jacopo, 276
Nasi, Bartolomea, 175
National Debt Office, 210
Nationalism, 169
National Museum of Florence, 110
Nemours, Duchess of, 317
Neo-Platonism, 174
Neri party, 13-18

Nero, Bernardo del, 218, 219, 222
Neroni, Diotisalvi, 58, 77, 99-100, 104, 105, 190, 204
Netherlands, 251, 289, 303, 320, 329, 345, 346, 360, 369
Niccoli, Niccolò de', 65
Nicholas V, Pope, 81-82, 83, 85, 88, 89
Nori, Francesco, 135, 136
Novara, Battle of, 234

Olgiati, Girolamo, 127
"On the Art of War" (Machiavelli), 269
Oration on the Dignity of Man (Pico della Mirandola), 188
Orcagna (architect), 284
Order of St. Dominic, 56
Ordinamenti della Giustizia (Statutes of Justice), 10, 11, 12, 13, 17, 172
Orlandini, Bartolommeo, 74, 75
Orléans, Duke of, 82
Orme, Philibert de l', 298
Orsini, Alfonsina degli, 159, 161, 194, 196, 238, 240
Orsini, Clarice degli, 106-8, 160-61, 171, 196
Orsini, Jacopo degli, 107
Orsini, Ludovico degli, 312
Orsini, Paolo Giordano degli, Duke of Bracciano, 309, 311-12
Orsini, Virginio degli, 213
Orsini family, 160, 194, 195, 209, 225, 311
Osnabrück, Bishop of, 359
Otto di Guardia (Eight Custodians), 118
Ovid, 217

Palazzo Strozzi, 185
Palazzo Vecchio, 203, 206, 220, 256, 284, 285
Pallaiuolo, Antonio, 181
Palleschi party, 262
Paradise Lost (Milton), 356
Paradiso (Dante), 174
Parlamento, 46-47, 50, 51, 57, 89, 90
Parma, 23, 256, 362; annexation of (to Papal States), 244
Parmigianino, Il (G. F. M. Mazzuoli), 367
Passerini, Cardinal Silvio, 241, 247, 252, 253, 256-58, 259, 269, 274, 275
Paul II, Pope, 101, 114, 121, 128
Paul III, Pope, 275, 278, 284
Paul IV, Pope, 289
Paul V, Pope, 333

Pausanias, 179
Pavia, Battle of (1525), 253–54
Pazzi, Alessandro de', 153
Pazzi, Franceschino de', 129, 130, 134–36, 137, 138
Pazzi, Giovanni de', 129, 138
Pazzi, Guglielmo de', 138, 153
Pazzi, Gugliemo, 129
Pazzi, Jacopo de', 132–33, 136–37, 138, 139
Pazzi, Niccolò, 138
Pazzi, Renato, 138
Pazzi family, 10, 15, 25, 26, 33, 58, 95, 128–40, 148, 160, 175, 204; deprived of coat-of-arms, 138
Pedro of Toledo, Viceroy of Naples, 284, 286
Pepys, Samuel, 345–46
Peretti, Francesco, 311, 312
Pericles, 1
Perugia, 19, 29, 30, 44, 130, 133, 154, 264
Perugino (Pietro Vannucci), 268
Peruzzi, Ridolfo, 50
Peruzzi family, 8, 26, 58
Pervigilium Veneris, 192
Pescia, Domenico Buonvicini da, 220, 221
Petrarch, 28, 51, 133, 170, 186, 188, 217, 272
Petrucci, Alfonso, 243
Petrucci, Cesare, 116, 136, 140
Philibert, Prince of Orange, 263, 264, 265, 266
Philip of Anjou, 362
Philip, Prince of Neuberg, 357
Philip III, King of France, 14
Philip IV, King of France, 13
Philip II, King of Spain, 286, 288, 295, 299, 308
Philip III, King of Spain, 318, 320, 323
Philip IV, King of Spain, 323, 329, 330
Philip V, King of Spain, 362, 368, 373
Piagnoni party, 210
Piccinino (mercenary), 67–75, 79
Piccolomini, Aeneas Sylvius. See Pius II, Pope
Pico della Mirandola, Count Giovanni, 64, 163, 166, 167, 173, 174, 178, 188, 196, 200, 268, 272, 303
Pierleone (physician), 168
Piety Orphanage, 310
Pisa, 8, 13, 20, 24, 25, 30, 37, 125–26, 143, 145, 146, 172, 202, 207, 212, 216, 223, 224, 229–30, 234, 331
Pistoia, siege of (1306), 17

Pitti, Luca, 71, 89, 90, 91, 92–93, 97, 99–100, 102–3, 104, 120, 190, 285
Pitti family, 8, 89, 95, 98, 145
Pitti Gallery, 126
Pitti Palace, 93, 285, 371, 376
Pius II, Pope, 89–90, 91–92, 112, 113
Pius IV, Pope (Giovanni Angelo de' Medici), 288, 289
Pius V, Pope, 289, 290, 300
Plague of 1630, 333
Plagues, 36–37, 43, 333
Plato, 64, 97, 119, 170, 173, 174, 175, 178, 185, 187
Platonic Academy, 64, 156, 173, 179, 196, 339
Platonic love, 174
Pletho, Georgius Gemistus, 64, 173, 174
Plotinus, 187
Podesta (emperor's representative), 5–6, 11, 12, 16, 22, 36, 92, 116, 123, 125, 176; term of office, 9
Poggio Imperiale, Battle of, 144
Politian (poet), 126, 135, 163, 166, 167, 170, 171, 173, 174, 175, 178, 185, 187, 192, 200, 246, 268, 272
Pollaiuolo, Antonio, 110, 112, 184
Pollaiuolo, Piero, 110, 112
Ponte Santa Trinità, 287
Ponte Vecchio, 287
Pontormo, Jacopo da, 271–72
Pontremoli, Nicodemo da, 83
Popolo minuto, 26
Praslin (nobleman), 321
Prato, 116; battle at (1537), 282; Spanish massacre at (1512), 230
Pratolino Theatre, 354
Previchi, Mario de', 235
"Primavera" (Botticelli), 183
Prince, The (Machiavelli), 76, 268–69
Priori, consuls of, 5
Public libraries, beginning of, 79–80
Pucci, Puccio, 42, 54, 71, 77, 96
Puglia, Fra Francesco de, 220
Pulci, Luigi, 106, 156, 187–88, 192, 217, 268, 272

Quadruple Alliance of 1718, 368–69

Radagasius, Chief, 3
Rangoni, Guido, 248
Rapallo, Battle of, 201
"Rape of the Sabines, The" (Bologna), 308

Raphael, 51, 232, 235, 244–45, 246, 267, 268, 270, 271, 272, 336, 367; Vatican frescos of, 244–45
Ravaillac, Jean François, 322
Ravenna, Battle of (1512), 230, 233
Reformation, 64
Renaissance, 1, 6, 52, 90, 108, 111, 166, 267, 268–73, 303, 336, 373; achievements of, 168–69; end of, 291; influences on, 168–69; and Lorenzo the Magnificent, 168–93
René of Anjou, 60, 72, 82, 86, 199
Reparata, St., 3
Reresby, Sir John, 335, 337, 346
"Resurrection, The" (Ghirlandaio), 184
Reuchlin, Johann, 64
Riario, Girolamo, 128–31, 132, 133, 140, 151, 155, 161
Riario, Ottaviano, 223
Riario, Pietro, 128
Riario, Cardinal Raffaello, 133–34, 136, 139, 141
Riccardi Palace, 184
Ricci family, 313
Richelieu, Cardinal Armand Jean du Plessis de, 323–25, 326, 327–30; religious policy of, 326–27
Rinuccini, Ottavio, 217
Robbia, Andrea della, 184
Robbia, Luca della, 52, 110, 114, 175, 180–81, 184
Robert, King of Naples, 18, 19, 22
Rochelle, Peace of (1573), 302
Roman Empire, 2–3
Romano, Giulio, 271, 336
Rome, sack of (1527), 255–56, 303
Rondinelli, Fra Giuliano, 220
Ronsard, Pierre de, 298
Rosa, Salvator, 336, 339
Roscoe, William, 40
Rossellino, Antonio, 185
Rossi, Cardinal Luigi de', 270
Rossi family, 26
"Route of Romano" (Uccello), 52
Rovere, Francesco della. See Sixtus IV, Pope
Rovere, Francesco Maria della, Duke of Urbino, 237, 238–39, 248, 251, 254, 269
Rovere, Cardinal Giuliano della, 157
Rovere, Vittoria della, 334, 338, 341, 343, 344, 347–48, 357
Rubens, Peter Paul, 316, 330
Rucellai family, 25
Rucellai Palace, 180

Sacchetti, Franco, 156–57, 272

Sadoleto, Jacopo, 244
St. Bartholomew's Day massacre, 300–2, 315
St. Denis, Battle of (1567), 298–99
St. Germain-en-Lays, Treaty of (1570), 299
"St. John the Baptist" (da Vinci), 182
St. Peter's, basilica of, 245
St. Quentin, Battle of (1557), 294, 295
St. Simon, Claude de, 327
Sallust, 3
Salviati, Alamanno, 77
Salviati, Bernardo, 282
Salviati, Archbishop Francesco, 129, 130, 131–32, 133, 136, 137, 141
Salviati, Giacomo, 160, 175, 239
Salviati, Jacopo, 129, 133
Salviati, Maria, 239
San Gio, Gio da, 336
San Giorgio, Cardinal, 235
San Giorgio Maggiore, convent of, 56
San Miniato Church, bombardment of, 264
Sansovino, Andrea. See Contucci, Andrea
Sansovino, Jacopo, 237, 267
Santa Maria del Fiore, cathedral of, 2, 52, 180
Santa Maria Novella, 50, 60, 63, 85, 90, 180, 184
Sante Croce, Cardinal, 235
Santi Quattro, Cardinal, 235
Sarto, Andrea del, 237, 270, 271, 367
Sarzana (town), 147, 148, 202, 207, 212; expedition against (1487), 159
Sarzanello, fortress of, 106
Sassetti Chapel, 184
Savonarola, Giorlamo, 163–68, 178, 183, 191–92, 193, 203, 224, 231, 241, 259, 261, 267, 270, 273; arrested, 221; attempted assassination of, 214, 218–19; Charles VIII and, 204–5, 206, 209, 211–12; determination to defend Florence, 205; elected prior of St. Mark's Convent, 165; executed, 222, 223, 228; fame of, 164; Florentine opposition to, 220–22, 226; Lenten spectacle (Shrove Tuesday), 217–18, 219; Lorenzo the Magnificent and, 163–68, 191–92, 193, 198, 211; Piero de' Medici and, 194–223; plan for a Grand Council, 210–11; popularity of, 197; prohibited to preach, 214–15, 219; prophecies of, 165, 200; sermons of, 215, 218, 219; tortured,

221–22; transferred to Bologna (1493), 198; trial of, 222
Scala, Can Grande della, 21
Scarlatti, Alessandro, 354, 367
Scoronconcolo (assassin), 280
Second Punic War, 144
Segni, Bernardo, 377
Sellaio, Jacopo, 112
Senate of Eighty, 210–11
Seneca, 113, 178, 186
Settignano, Desiderio da, 181
Settimanni (diarist), 372
Sforza, Cardinal Ascanio, 197, 199
Sforza, Battista, 105
Sforza, Caterina, 128, 161–62, 222–23, 225, 239, 270
Sforza, Francesco, Duke of Milan, 42, 61–62, 65–68, 71–81, 82, 90, 92, 93, 95, 101, 102, 105, 110; Casalmaggiore battle, 80; friendship with Cosimo the Elder, 80–81; marriage of, 77; papal alliance against, 79; proclaimed Duke of Milan, 83; struggle for Milan, 82–84
Sforza, Francesco Maria, Duke of Milan, 240, 244, 254
Sforza, Galeazzo Maria, Duke of Milan, 90, 102, 103, 105, 106, 113, 116–17, 120–21, 128–30, 154, 161, 198; murder of, 27–28, 130
Sforza, Count Giacomo, 38, 61
Sforza, Gian Galeazzo, Duke of Milan, 127, 154, 198, 201
Sforza, Ippolita, 100, 101, 102, 105
Sforza, Lodovico (Il Moro), Duke of Milan, 144–45, 146, 154, 155, 158, 159, 161, 162, 168, 176, 182, 196–202, 210, 223, 244; in captivity, 224; expelled from Milan, 224; French invasion and, 201–3, 209; proclaims himself Duke of Milan, 201
Sforza family, 101, 128, 154
Shrove Tuesday burning of 1497, 217–18
Siena, 15, 19, 29, 44, 104, 143, 144, 148, 149, 154, 209, 216, 230, 248, 285–86; revolt of 1548, 284–85
Signorelli, Luca, 178
Sismondi, Jean Charles Léonard de, 40
Sistine Chapel, 184, 267
Sixtus IV, Pope, 121, 128–33, 140–50, 155, 157, 161, 229
Sixtus V, Pope, 312
Slave trade, 8
Socrates, 174, 192

Soderini, Cardinal Francesco, 247
Soderini, Lorenzo, 266
Soderini, Maria, 277, 280
Soderini, Niccolò, 99–100, 102–4, 105, 115, 116, 190
Soderini, Piero, 226–30, 231, 233
Soderini, Tommaso, 77, 115–17, 120–22, 123, 145, 263, 277
Song of Bacchus, 186
Sophocles, 159
Spain, 7, 214, 219, 229, 251, 288, 289, 329, 334, 369, 371; nationalism in, 169
Spini family, 38
Staatliches Museum (Berlin), 156
"Stabat Mater," 192
Stanislas I Leczinski, King of Poland, 374
Statute of 1357 (Florence), 32
Strozzi, Carlo, 32
Strozzi, Filippo, 145, 231, 257, 258, 259, 279, 282–83, 287
Strozzi, Matteo, 263
Strozzi, Palla, 55–56, 81
Strozzi, Piero, 279, 282, 284, 286, 287
Strozzi family, 8, 26, 27, 33, 36, 45, 55, 58, 95
Strozzi Palace, 282
Sulla, General, 2
Sully, Duc de, 321, 322
Syphilis (spirocheta pallida), 208–9, 221, 240, 355, 358

Tacitus, 3, 177
Tasso, Torquato, 185
Tavannes, Gaspard de Sauix, Seigneur de, 293–94
Tebaldeo (poet), 248
Ten of War Committee, 44, 228, 259
Theologica Platonica (Ficino), 187
Thucydides, 27
Tiberius, Emperor, 3
Titian, 278, 287
"Tobias and the Angel" (Verrocchio), 183
Tornabuoni, Giovanni, 101, 157
Tornabuoni, Lorenzo, 219
Tornabuoni, Lucrezia Maria, 87, 101, 107, 114, 119, 155–57, 188, 190, 240–41
Tornabuoni Chapel, 184
Tornabuoni family, 45, 58
Tosinghi family, 15
Tossa, Rosso della, 17
Tranchedini, Nicodemo, 90–91, 101
"Tribute Money, The" (Masaccio), 52

Ubaldini family, 30
Uccello, Paolo, 52, 110, 112, 182
Uffizi gallery, 105, 272, 308
University of Padua, 332
University of Pisa, 133, 172, 178, 291
University of Rome, 244
Urban VIII, Pope, 333
Utrecht, Treaty of, 367
Uzés, Duchess d', 305
Uzzano, Niccolò da, 38–39, 41, 42, 43

Valentinois, Duchess of. *See* Diane de
    Poitiers
Valori, Baccio, 266, 275, 282
Valori, Filippo, 197
Valori, Francesco, 210, 216–17, 221
Valori, Niccolò, 103
Vasari, Giorgio, 10, 112, 182, 217,
    237, 285, 308
Vassy, massacre of Huguenots at, 297
Vatican Library, 82
Vaudemont, Louise de, 302, 305
Vendetta, rules of, 21
Vendôme, Duke of, 362
Venetian Constitution, 210
Veneziano, Domenicao, 182
Veneziano, Domenico, 110
Venice, 1, 8, 21, 47, 48, 49, 56, 58,
    59, 61, 63, 65, 66, 72, 78, 80, 82,
    84, 88, 100, 105, 114, 122, 126,
    141, 142, 155, 158, 169, 176, 192,
    224, 226, 264, 272, 280, 299, 312,
    354; annexation of (to Papal
    States), 244; League of Cambrai,
    229
Verrocchio, Andrea del, 106, 109,
    178, 181, 182, 183–84, 185, 267
Vespucci, Amerigo, 126, 138
Vespucci, Marco, 126
Vespucci, Piero, 138–39
Vespucci Chapel, 184
Vettori, Francesco, 275

Villa Medici (Rome), 331
Villani, Giovanni, 2, 16, 20, 22, 25,
    26, 27
Villeroi, General François de
    Neufville, 362
Vinci, Leonardo da, 178, 182, 183,
    184, 224, 246, 268, 272
Violante Beatrice, Princess, 352–53,
    354, 357, 359, 362, 367, 368, 370,
    371, 372–73
Virgil, 119, 170, 185, 186, 187, 236
Visconti, Bianca, Duchess of Milan,
    67, 72, 77, 82, 90
Visconti, Carlo, 127
Visconti, Filippo Maria, Duke of
    Milan, 39, 42, 51, 59–62, 65, 66,
    69, 70, 72–73, 77, 79, 80, 82, 83
Visconti, Galeazzo, 22, 27, 30–31
Visconti, Gian Galeazzo, 37
Visconti, Matteo, 65
Visconti, Matteo, Duke of Milan, 20,
    21, 22
Visconti family, 62, 66, 191, 223
Vitelli, Alessandro, 282
Vitelli, Niccolò, 129
Vitelli, Paolo, 224
Vitelli, Vitellozzo, 225
Viterbo alum mines, 121
Vitruvius, Marcus, 179
Vitry, Marquis de, 326
Vocabulario della Crusca, 308
Volterra, alum mines of, 123
Volterra, Cardinal, 235

War of the Austrian Succession, 374
War of the Spanish Succession, 362
War of the Three Henrys, 305–6
Werner (mercenary commander), 28
White Company, 30–31
William III, King of England, 356,
    362

Zipoli (ambassador), 354

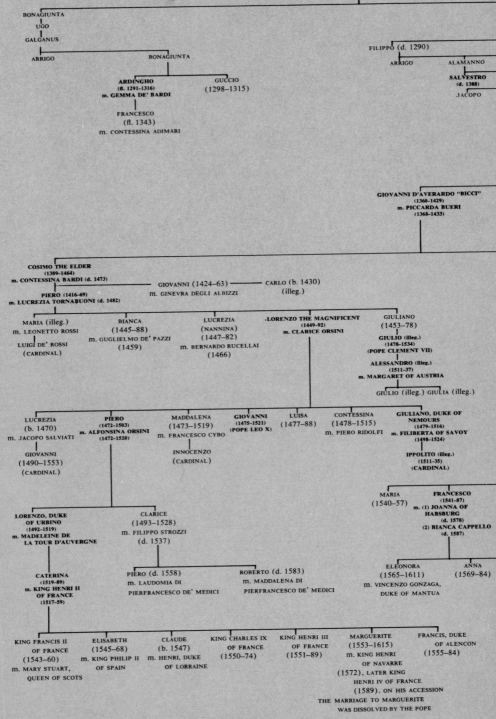

THE HOUSE OF MEDICI

(Names of special importance in bold face; names of unknown pedigree omitted.)

GIAMBUONI (fl. 1200)

BONAGIUNTA

UGO

GALGANUS

ARRIGO

BONAGIUNTA

ARDINGHO (fl. 1291–1316) m. GEMMA DE' BARDI

GUCCIO (1298–1315)

FRANCESCO (fl. 1343) m. CONTESSINA ADIMARI

FILIPPO (d. 1290)

ARRIGO

ALAMANNO

SALVESTRO (d. 1388)

JACOPO

GIOVANNI D'AVERARDO "BICCI" (1360–1429) m. PICCARDA BUERI (1368–1433)

COSIMO THE ELDER (1389–1464) m. CONTESSINA BARDI (d. 1473)

GIOVANNI (1424–63) m. GINEVRA DEGLI ALBIZZI

CARLO (b. 1430) (illeg.)

PIERO (1416–69) m. LUCREZIA TORNABUONI (d. 1482)

MARIA (illeg.) m. LEONETTO ROSSI

LUIGI DE' ROSSI (CARDINAL)

BIANCA (1445–88) m. GUGLIELMO DE' PAZZI (1459)

LUCREZIA (NANNINA) (1447–82) m. BERNARDO RUCELLAI (1466)

LORENZO THE MAGNIFICENT (1449–92) m. CLARICE ORSINI

GIULIANO (1453–78)

GIULIO (illeg.) (1478–1534) (POPE CLEMENT VII)

ALESSANDRO (illeg.) (1511–37) m. MARGARET OF AUSTRIA

GIULIO (illeg.) GIULIA (illeg.)

LUCREZIA (b. 1470) m. JACOPO SALVIATI

GIOVANNI (1490–1553) (CARDINAL)

PIERO (1472–1503) m. ALFONSINA ORSINI (1472–1520)

MADDALENA (1473–1519) m. FRANCESCO CYBO

INNOCENZO (CARDINAL)

GIOVANNI (1475–1521) (POPE LEO X)

LUISA (1477–88)

CONTESSINA (1478–1515) m. PIERO RIDOLFI

GIULIANO, DUKE OF NEMOURS (1479–1516) m. FILIBERTA OF SAVOY (1498–1524)

IPPOLITO (illeg.) (1511–35) (CARDINAL)

LORENZO, DUKE OF URBINO (1492–1519) m. MADELEINE DE LA TOUR D'AUVERGNE

CLARICE (1493–1528) m. FILIPPO STROZZI (d. 1537)

PIERO (d. 1558) m. LAUDOMIA DI PIERFRANCESCO DE' MEDICI

ROBERTO (d. 1583) m. MADDALENA DI PIERFRANCESCO DE' MEDICI

CATERINA (1519–89) m. KING HENRI II OF FRANCE (1517–59)

MARIA (1540–57)

FRANCESCO (1541–87) m. (1) JOANNA OF HABSBURG (d. 1578) (2) BIANCA CAPPELLO (d. 1587)

ELEONORA (1565–1611) m. VINCENZO GONZAGA, DUKE OF MANTUA

ANNA (1569–84)

KING FRANCIS II OF FRANCE (1543–60) m. MARY STUART, QUEEN OF SCOTS

ELISABETH (1545–68) m. KING PHILIP II OF SPAIN

CLAUDE (b. 1547) m. HENRI, DUKE OF LORRAINE

KING CHARLES IX OF FRANCE (1550–74)

KING HENRI III OF FRANCE (1551–89)

MARGUERITE (1553–1615) m. KING HENRI OF NAVARRE (1572), LATER KING HENRI IV OF FRANCE (1589). ON HIS ACCESSION THE MARRIAGE TO MARGUERITE WAS DISSOLVED BY THE POPE

FRANCIS, DUKE OF ALENCON (1555–84)

KING LOUIS XIII OF FRANCE (1601–43)